THE
New World
Reader

Thinking and Writing
About the Global Community

Third Edition

Gilbert H. Muller

The City University of New York
LaGuardia College

WADSWORTH
CENGAGE Learning™

Australia • Brazil • Japan • Korea • Mexico • Singapore • Spain • United Kingdom • United States

WADSWORTH
CENGAGE Learning™

The New World Reader: Thinking and Writing About the Global Community, Third Edition
Gilbert H. Muller

Senior Publisher: Lyn Uhl
Acquisitions Editor: Kate Derrick
Development Editor: Kathy Sands-Boehmer
Senior Assistant Editor: Kelli Strieby
Editorial Assistant: Jake Zucker
Media Editor: Cara Douglass-Graff
Marketing Manager: Jennifer Zourdos
Marketing Coordinator: Ryan Ahern
Marketing Communications Manager: Stacey Purviance
Project Manager, Editorial Production: Georgia Young
Art Director: Jill Ort
Print Buyer: Marcia Locke
Permissions Editor: Katie Huha
Production Service: Cadmus
Photo Manager: John Hill
Cover Designer: Walter Kopec
Cover Image: Getty Images/Bruno Morandi/Robert Harding
Compositor: Cadmus

Text Credits: "Andalusia's Journey" by Edward Said, originally published in *Travel & Leisure*. Copyright © 2002 by Edward Said, reprinted with permission of The Wylie Agency LLC.
"The I'm-Not-Ugly American" by Ann Hulbert, originally published in *The New York Times Magazine*. Copyright © 2006 by Anne Hulbert, reprinted with permission of The Wylie Agency LLC.

Library of Congress Control Number: 2009933928

ISBN-13: 978-1-4390-8338-3

ISBN-10: 1-4390-8338-X

Wadsworth
20 Channel Center Street
Boston, MA 02210
USA

Cengage Learning is a leading provider of customized learning solutions with office locations around the globe, including Singapore, the United Kingdom, Australia, Mexico, Brazil and Japan. Locate your local office at **international.cengage.com/region**

Cengage Learning products are represented in Canada by Nelson Education, Ltd.

For your course and learning solutions, visit
www.cengage.com.

Purchase any of our products at your local college store or at our preferred online store
www.ichapters.com

Printed in the United States of America
2 3 4 5 6 7 13 12 11 10

For Sadie Rain and Vivian Dalia
Global Girls

Brief Contents

RHETORICAL CONTENTS   xiii

PREFACE   xxiii

1. Thinking, Reading, and Writing About the New Global Era   1

2. New American Mosaic: Are We Becoming a Universal Nation?   29

3. America and the World: How Do Others Perceive Us?   69

4. Speaking in Tongues: Does Language Unify or Divide Us?   110

5. Global Relationships: Are Sex and Gender Roles Changing?   149

6. The Challenge of Globalization: What Are the Consequences?   185

7. Culture Wars: Whose Culture Is It, Anyway?   231

8. The Clash of Civilizations: Is Conflict Avoidable?   271

9. The Age of Terror: What Is the Just Response?   315

10. Global Aid: Can We Reduce Disease and Poverty?   350

11. The Fate of the Earth: Can We Preserve the Global Environment?   399

APPENDIX A. Conducting Research in the Global Era   437

APPENDIX B. Glossary of Rhetorical Terms   461

APPENDIX C. Glossary of Globalization Terms   467

INDEX   473

iv

Contents

RHETORICAL CONTENTS   xiii

PREFACE   xxiii

1 | Thinking, Reading, and Writing About the New Global Era   1

Critical Thinking   3
    Narration and Description   4
    Exposition   5
    Argument and Persuasion   8
Thinking About an Essay: Nicholas D. Kristof, "China: The Educated Giant"   10

"One reason China is likely to overcome the U.S. as the world's most important country in this century is that China puts more effort into building human capital than we do."

Reading Critically   13
    Steps to Reading Critically   15
    Reading Visual Texts   16
Reading an Essay Critically: Susan Bordo, "The Globalization of Eating Disorders"   17

"If eating disorders were biochemical, as some claim, how can we account for their gradual 'spread' across race, gender, and nationality?"

Writing in Response to Reading   22
    Prewriting   23
    Drafting   24
    Revision   25
Writing in Response to an Essay: Lorraine Ali, "Not Ignorant, Not Helpless"   26

"Still, Muslim women are feeling like pawns in a political game: jihadists portray them as ignorant lambs who need to be protected from outside forces, while the United States considers them helpless victims of a backward society. . . ."

2 | New American Mosaic: Are We Becoming a Universal Nation?   29

Lee C. Bollinger, "Why Diversity Matters"   31

v

"The reality is that as much as we may want to believe that racial prejudice is a relic of history, conscience and experience tell us better."

Andrew Lam, "All Things Asian Are Becoming Us"　36

"If the world is experiencing globalization, the union between East and West, where a new hybrid culture is thriving, is just part of that process."

Ishmael Reed, "America: The Multinational Society"　40

"The United States is unique in the world: The world is here."

Dwight N. Hopkins, "Beyond Black and White: The Hawaiian President"　45

"What race is Obama?"

Bharati Mukherjee, "American Dreamer"　49

"We must be alert to the dangers of a 'us' vs. 'them' mentality."

Arthur M. Schlesinger Jr., "The Cult of Ethnicity"　56

"The growing diversity of the American population makes the quest for unifying ideals and a common culture all the more urgent."

Charles Bowden, "Our Wall"　60

"Borders everywhere attract violence, violence prompts fences, and eventually fences can mutate into walls."

3 | America and the World: How Do Others Perceive Us?　69

Ann Hulbert, "The I'm-Not-Ugly American"　72

"In essence, the mission of the American as World Citizen is to try and fit in better, or at any rate to stick out less."

Fouad Ajami, "The Resilience of American Power"　76

"For all the talk about the rise of China and India these societies. . . are in no position to inherit the American place in the order of nations."

Alkman Granitsas, "Americans Are Tuning Out the World"　80

"With the whole world apparently trying to get to America, the average American can only ask: Why look to the rest of the world?"

Moises Naim, "Hungry for America"　84

"The world wants America back."

Dominic Hilton, "Fashionable Anti-Americanism"　87

"Anti-Americanism, when not perpetrated by true haters, is often a stale mockery of America, born of our own fascination."

Paul Johnson, "America's New Empire for Liberty"　97

"From the Evil Empire to an Empire for Liberty is a giant step, a contrast as great as the appalling images of the wasted twentieth century and the brightening dawn of the twenty-first."

Sasha Abramsky, "Waking Up from the American Dream"   102
"The questions largely boil down to the following: Where has the world's faith in America gone? Where is the American Dream headed?"

4 Speaking in Tongues: Does Language Unify or Divide Us?   110

Manuel Munoz, "Leave Your Name at the Border"   112
"I was born in 1972, part of a generation that learned both English and Spanish."

Amy Tan, "Mother Tongue"   118
"Lately, I've been giving more thought to the kind of English my mother speaks."

Chang-rae Lee, "Mute in an English-Only World"   125
". . . having been raised in a Korean immigrant family, I saw every day the exacting price and power of language, especially with my mother, who was an outsider in an English-only world."

Robin Tolmach Lakoff, "The Power of Words in Wartime"   129
"Bullets and bombs are not the only tools of war. Words, too, play their part."

Charles Foran, "Lingua Franchise"   132
"English isn't just exploding across the universe; it is being exploded on contact with other societies and languages."

William H. Frey, "Multilingual America"   136
"The number of individuals who speak a language other than English at home is on the rise."

Isabel Allende, "Reading the History of the World"   144
"To me, not reading is like having the spirit imprisoned."

5 Global Relationships: Are Sex and Gender Roles Changing?   149

Anna Quindlen, "The End of Swagger"   151
"A simple primer on the state of the world: women do most of the good stuff and get most of the bad."

Lizette Alvarez, "Arranged Marriages Get a Little Reshuffling"   155
"They are young, hip, South Asians in their twenties who glide seamlessly between two cultures, carefully cherry picking from the West to modernize the East."

Kofi A. Annan, "In Africa, AIDS Has a Woman's Face"   159
"If we want to save Africa from two catastrophes, we would do well to focus on saving Africa's women."

Jose Contreras, "Legal in Unlikely Places" 164

"The growing maturity of the gay-rights movement in the West is having a marked effect on the developing world."

Mike Ceaser, "A Dark Window on Human Trafficking" 170

"Police-car lights flashed and prostitutes, pimps, reporters, and police officers milled about."

Barbara Ehrenreich and Annette Fuentes, "Life on the Global Assembly Line" 175

"This is the world's new industrial proletariat: young, female, Third World."

6 | The Challenge of Globalization: What Are the Consequences? 185

Thomas L. Friedman, "Prologue: The Super-Story" 187

"I define globalization as the inexorable integration of markets, transportation systems, and communication systems to a degree never witnessed before."

Pico Iyer, "The Global Village Finally Arrives" 193

"I wake up to the sound of my Japanese clock radio, put on a T-shirt sent me by an uncle in Nigeria and walk out into the street, past German cars, to my office."

Fareed Zakaria, "The Rise of the Rest" 198

"The post-American world is naturally an unsettling prospect for Americans, but it shouldn't be."

Johan Norberg, "The Noble Feat of Nike" 204

"If you want to be trendy these days, you don't wear Nikes; you boycott them."

Joseph S. Nye Jr., "Fear Not Globalization" 208

"Contrary to conventional wisdom . . . globalization is neither homogenizing nor Americanizing the cultures of the world."

Robert Koehler, "Slumdog Millionaire" 211

"Boyle's film has been celebrated as an expression of globalization, and it's certainly true that the story itself couldn't exist in a world before globalization took effect in once-protectionist India."

Benjamin R. Barber, "The Educated Student: Global Citizen or Global Consumer?" 220

"The citizen is the person who acknowledges and recognizes his or her interdependence in a neighborhood, a town, a state, in a nation—and today, in the world."

7 | Culture Wars: Whose Culture Is It, Anyway?   231

Barbara Ehrenreich, "Cultural Baggage"   233
"I watched one group after another . . . stand up and proudly proclaim their roots while I just sank back ever deeper into my seat."

Mac Margolis, "It's a Mall World After All"   237
"For residents of the developing world, malls increasingly serve as surrogate civic centers, encouraging social values that go beyond conspicuous spending."

Henry Louis Gates Jr., "Whose Culture Is It, Anyway?"   243
"A curriculum that reflects the achievement of the world's great cultures, not merely the West's, is not 'politicized.'"

Richard Pells, "Does the World Still Care About American Culture?"   246
"For most of the 20th century, the dominant culture in the world was American. That is no longer true."

Octavio Paz, "Hygiene and Repression"   251
"In our countries food is communion, not only between those together at table but between ingredients; Yankee food, impregnated with Puritanism, is based on exclusions."

Heather Havrilesky, "Besieged by 'Friends'"   256
"Still, at a time when the 'patriotic' view often simply means pervasive xenophobia, it's valuable to witness the resentment and anger welling up from those who feel their cultural identity has been taken hostage by Hollywood."

Jamaica Kincaid, "On Seeing England for the First Time"   260
"When I saw England for the first time, I was a child in school sitting at a desk."

8 | The Clash of Civilizations: Is Conflict Avoidable?   271

K. Oanh Ha, "American Dream Boat'"   273
"I wanted so badly to be a full-fledged American, whatever that meant. At home, though, my parents pushed traditional Vietnamese values."

Margaret Atwood, "When Afghanistan Was at Peace"   278
"'Don't go to Afghanistan,' my father said when told of our plans. 'There's going to be a war there.'"

Mikal Gilmore, "'Battlestar' Apocalypse"   282
"What has set Battlestar Galactica apart is its insistence on rising to the occasion, its willingness to unflinchingly face the complex horrors of our past several years."

Karen Armstrong, "Fundamentalism Is Here to Stay"   286

"Thus fundamentalism does not represent a clash between civilizations, but a clash within civilizations."

Samuel P. Huntington, "The West and the Rest: Intercivilizational Issues"   293

"Western peoples have far more in common with each other than they have with Asian, Middle Eastern, or African people."

Amartya Sen, "A World Not Neatly Divided"   297

"When people talk about clashing civilizations, as so many politicians and academics do now, they can sometimes miss the central issue."

Edward Said, "Andalusia's Journey"   300

"For an Arab, such as myself, to enter Granada's 13th-century Alhambra palace is to leave behind a modern world of disillusionment, strife, and uncertainty."

9 The Age of Terror: What Is the Just Response?   315

Naomi Shihab Nye, "To Any Would-Be Terrorists"   317

"Because I feel a little closer to you than many Americans could possibly feel, or ever want to feel, I insist that you listen to me.

Reza Aslan, "Losing the 'War'"   323

"The truth is that the phrase 'war on terror' has always been problematic. . . ."

Thane Rosenbaum, "The War on Terror Has Not Gone Away"   326

"Lapsing into the complacency that might expose America to the repeat performance of mass murder is not a sound trade-off for economic health."

Bill Powell, "Generation Jihad"   329

"A common sentiment among members of Generation Jihad is frustration with a perceived scarcity of opportunity and disappointment at public policies that they believe target Muslims unfairly."

Jeffrey Rosen, "Bad Luck: Why Americans Exaggerate the Terrorist Threat"   336

"The terrorist threat is all too real, but newspapers and TV stations around the globe are still managing to exaggerate it."

Philip Bobbitt, "'Terror' Is the Enemy"   340

"In a war against terror, the aim is not the conquest of territory or the advancement of ideology, but the protections of civilians."

Arundhati Roy, "The Algebra of Infinite Justice"   344

"The American people ought to know that it is not them, but their government's policies, that are so hated."

10 Global Aid: Can We Reduce Disease and Poverty? 350

Jeffrey Sachs, "What I Did on My Summer Vacation" 352
"We're not merely leaving these people to their fate but actually driving them into greater poverty without any sense of responsibility because we're not even compensating in other ways."

Peter Singer, "The Singer Solution to World Poverty" 361
"I can see no escape from the conclusion that each one of us with wealth surplus to his or her essential needs should be giving most of it to help people suffering from poverty so dire as to be life-threatening."

Bill Gates, "Saving the World Is Within Our Grasp" 368
"I believe we stand at a moment of unequaled opportunity."

Sara Corbett, "Can the Cellphone Help End Global Poverty?" 371
"Even as sales continue to grow, it is yet to be seen whether the mobile phone will play a significant, sustained role in alleviating poverty in the developing world."

Anuradha Mittal, "Technology Won't Feed the World's Hungry" 386
"More than 60 million tons of excess, unsold food grain rotted in India last year because the hungry were too poor to buy it."

Kenneth Rogoff, "A Development Nightmare" 389
"Is it possible that, deep down, the world's wealthy fear what will happen if the developing countries really did catch up, and if the advantages their own children enjoy were shared by all?"

Vivienne Walt and Amanda Bower, "Follow the Money" 393
"Some migrants are now using their economic clout to perform work usually done by big aid organizations."

11 The Fate of the Earth: Can We Preserve the Global Environment? 399

Rachel Carson, "The Obligation to Endure" 401
"Can anyone believe it is possible to lay down such a barrage of poisons on the surface of the earth without making it unfit for life?"

Al Gore, "The Climate for Change" 408
"The inspiring and transformative choice by the American people to elect Barack Obama as our 44th president lays the foundation for another fateful choice that he—and we—must make. . . to protect its primary endowment: the integrity and livability of the planet."

Andy Rooney, "Talking Trash" 413
"The Earth could end up as one huge, uninhabitable dump."

Jared Diamond, "Lessons from Lost Worlds" 416

"People often ask if I am an optimist or a pessimist about our future. I answer that I'm cautiously optimistic."

Bill McKibben, "A Place that Makes Sense"   420

"How we thirst for places that make sense."

Jane Goodall, "To Save Chimps"   426

"It became clear that, to protect chimpanzees and their forest habitat, it would be necessary to help human populations around Gombe."

Jonathan Schell, "A Hole in the World"   431

"The emptiness of the sky can spread. We have been warned."

APPENDIX A. Conducting Research in the Global Era   437

Introduction   437

The Research Process   438

The Writing Process   450

Documentation   452

APPENDIX B. Glossary of Rhetorical Terms   461

APPENDIX C. Glossary of Globalization Terms   467

INDEX   473

Rhetorical Contents

Narration

Bharati Mukherjee	"American Dreamer"	49
Charles Bowden	"Our Wall"	60
Ann Hulbert	"The I'm-Not-Ugly American"	72
Dominic Hilton	"Fashionable Anti-Americanism"	87
Manuel Munoz	"Leave Your Name at the Border"	112
Amy Tan	"Mother Tongue"	118
Chang-rae Lee	"Mute in an English-Only World"	125
Charles Foran	"Lingua Franchise"	132
Isabel Allende	"Reading the History of the World"	144
Barbara Ehrenreich	"Cultural Baggage"	233
Jamaica Kincaid	"On Seeing England for the First Time"	260
K. Oanh Ha	"American Dream Boat"	273
Margaret Atwood	"When Afghanistan Was at Peace"	278
Edward Said	"Andalusia's Journey"	300
Jeffrey Sachs	"What I Did on My Summer Vacation"	352
Sara Corbett	"Can the Cellphone Help End Global Poverty?"	371
Andrew Rooney	"Talking Trash"	413

Description

Susan Bordo	"The Globalization of Eating Disorders"	17
Andrew Lam	"All Things Asian Are Becoming Us"	36
Charles Bowden	"Our Wall"	60
Ann Hulbert	"The I'm-Not-Ugly American"	72
Dominic Hilton	"Fashionable Anti-Americanism"	87
Manuel Munoz	"Leave Your Name at the Border"	112
Amy Tan	"Mother Tongue"	118
Chang-rae Lee	"Mute in an English-Only World"	125
Isabel Allende	"Reading the History of the World"	144
Joseph Contreras	"Legal in Unlikely Places"	164

Mac Margolis   "It's A Mall World After All"   237

Jamaica Kincaid   "On Seeing England for the First Time"   260

K. Oanh Ha   "American Dream Boat"   273

Edward Said   "Andalusia's Journey"   300

Bill Powell   "Generation Jihad"   329

Sara Corbett   "Can the Cellphone Help End Global Poverty?"   371

Kenneth Rogoff   "A Development Nightmare"   389

Vivienne Walt and Amanda Bower   "Follow the Money"   393

Bill McKibben   "A Place that Makes Sense"   420

Illustration

Nicholas D. Kristof   "China: The Educated Giant"   10

Susan Bordo   "The Globalization of Eating Disorders"   17

Lee C. Bollinger   "Why Diversity Matters"   31

Ishmael Reed   "America: The Multinational Society"   40

Arthur M. Schlesinger Jr.   "The Cult of Ethnicity"   56

Charles Bowden   "Our Wall"   60

Fouad Ajami   "The Resilience of American Power"   76

Moises Naim   "Hungry for America"   84

Robin Tolmach Lakoff   "The Power of Words in Wartime"   129

William H. Frey   "Multilingual America"   136

Anna Quindlen   "The End of Swagger"   151

Lizette Alvarez   "Arranged Marriages Get a Little Reshuffling"   155

Joseph Contreras   "Legal in Unlikely Places"   164

Barbara Ehrenreich and Annette Fuentes   "Life on the Global Assembly Line"   175

Thomas L. Friedman   "Prologue: The Super-Story"   188

Pico Iyer   "The Global Village Finally Arrives"   193

Fareed Zakaria   "The Rise of the Rest"   198

Johan Norberg   "The Noble Feat of Nike"   204

Joseph S. Nye Jr.   "Fear Not Globalization"   208

Robert Koehler   "Slumdog Millionaire"   211

Barbara Ehrenreich   "Cultural Baggage"   233

Mac Margolis   "It's a Mall World After All"   237

Richard Pells   "Does the World Still Care About American Culture?"   246

Octavio Paz   "Hygiene and Repression"   251

Mikal Gilmore   "'Battlestar' Apocalypse"   282

Samuel P. Huntington   "The West and the Rest: Intercivilizational Issues"   293

Reza Aslan   "Losing the 'War'"   323

Amartya Sen   "A World Not Neatly Divided"   297

Edward Said   "Andalusia's Journey"   300

Naomi Shihab Nye   "To Any Would-Be Terrorists"   317

Thane Rosenbaum   "The War on Terror Has Not Gone Away"   326

Jeffrey Rosen   "Bad Luck: Why Americans Exaggerate the Terrorist Threat"   336

Philip Bobbitt   "'Terror' Is the Enemy"   340

Jeffrey Sachs   "What I Did on My Summer Vacation"   352

Peter Singer   "The Singer Solution to World Poverty"   361

Bill Gates   "Saving the World Is Within Our Grasp"   368

Sara Corbett   "Can the Cellphone Help End Global Poverty?"   371

Vivienne Walt and Amanda Bower   "Follow the Money"   393

Rachel Carson   "The Obligation to Endure"   401

Al Gore   "The Climate for Change"   408

Jared Diamond   "Lesson from Lost Worlds"   416

Bill McKibben   "A Place that Makes Sense"   420

Jane Goodall   "To Save Chimps"   426

Comparison and Contrast

Nicholas D. Kristof   "China: The Educated Giant"   10

Susan Bordo   "The Globalization of Eating Disorders"   17

Bharati Mukherjee   "American Dreamer"   49

Charles Bowden   "Our Wall"   60

Fouad Ajami "The Resilience of American Power" 76

Manuel Munoz "Leave Your Name at the Border" 112

Amy Tan "Mother Tongue" 118

Kofi A. Annan "In Africa, AIDS Has a Woman's Face" 159

Barbara Ehrenreich and
Annette Fuentes "Life on the Global Assembly Line" 175

Thomas L. Friedman "Prologue: The Super-Story" 188

Fareed Zakaria "The Rise of the Rest" 198

Joseph S. Nye Jr. "Fear Not Globalization" 208

Henry Louis Gates Jr. "Whose Culture Is It, Anyway?" 243

Richard Pells "Does the World Still Care About American Culture?" 246

Octavio Paz "Hygiene and Repression" 251

Heather Havrilesky "Besieged by 'Friends'" 256

Jamaica Kincaid "On Seeing England for the First Time" 260

Arundhati Roy "The Algebra of Infinite Justice" 344

Rachel Carson "The Obligation to Endure" 401

Bill McKibben "A Place that Makes Sense" 420

Definition

Lee C. Bollinger "Why Diversity Matters" 31

Dwight N. Hopkins "Beyond Black and White: The Hawaiian President" 45

Bharati Mukherjee "American Dreamer" 49

Charles Bowden "Our Wall" 60

Dominic Hilton "Fashionable Anti-Americanism" 87

Paul Johnson "America's New Empire for Liberty" 97

Sasha Abramsky "Waking Up from the American Dream" 102

Manuel Munoz "Leave Your Name at the Border" 112

Lizette Alvarez "Arranged Marriages Get a Little Reshuffling" 155

Thomas L. Friedman "Prologue: The Super-Story" 188

Pico Iyer "The Global Village Finally Arrives" 193

Benjamin R. Barber "The Educated Student: Global Citizen or Global Consumer?" 220

Richard Pells "Does the World Still Care About American Culture?" 246

Karen Armstrong "Fundamentalism Is Here to Stay" 286
Edward Said "Andalusia's Journey" 300
Philip Bobbitt "'Terror' is the Enemy" 340

Classification

Lorraine Ali "Not Ignorant, Not Helpless" 26
Andrew Lam "All Things Asian Are Becoming Us" 36
Dwight N. Hopkins "Beyond Black and White: The Hawaiian President" 45
Fouad Ajami "The Resilience of American Power" 76
Alkman Granitsas "Americans Are Tuning Out the World" 80
Sasha Abramsky "Waking Up from the American Dream" 102
Amy Tan "Mother Tongue" 118
Robin Tolmach Lakoff "The Power of Words in Wartime" 129
William H. Frey "Multilingual America" 136
Thomas L. Friedman "Prologue: The Super-Story" 188
Benjamin R. Barber "The Educated Student: Global Citizen or Global Consumer?" 220
Samuel P. Huntington "The West and the Rest: Intercivilizational Issues" 293
Amartya Sen "A World Not Neatly Divided" 297
Philip Bobbitt "'Terror' is the Enemy" 340

Process Analysis

Nicholas D. Kristof "China: The Educated Giant" 10
Arthur M. Schlesinger Jr. "The Cult of Ethnicity" 56
Dominic Hilton "Fashionable Anti-Americanism" 87
Lizette Alvarez "Arranged Marriages Get a Little Reshuffling" 155
Joseph Contreras "Legal in Unlikely Places" 164
Arundhati Roy "The Algebra of Infinite Justice" 344
Peter Singer "The Singer Solution to World Poverty" 361
Vivienne Walt and Amanda Bower "Follow the Money" 393
Rachel Carson "The Obligation to Endure" 401

Al Gore   "The Climate for Change"   408

Jane Goodall   "To Save Chimps"   426

Causal Analysis

Nicholas D. Kristof   "China: The Educated Giant"   10

Lee C. Bollinger   "Why Diversity Matters"   31

Ishmael Reed   "America: The Multinational Society"   40

Ann Hulbert   "The I'm-Not-Ugly American"   72

Fouad Ajami   "The Resilience of American Power"   76

Moises Naim   "Hungry for America"   84

Dominic Hilton   "Fashionable Anti-Americanism"   87

Paul Johnson   "America's New Empire for Liberty"   97

Charles Foran   "Lingua Franchise"   132

Isabel Allende   "Reading the History of the World"   144

Anna Quindlen   "The End of Swagger"   151

Lizette Alvarez   "Arranged Marriages Get a Little Reshuffling"   155

Kofi A. Annan   "In Africa, AIDS Has a Woman's Face"   159

Joseph Contreras   "Legal in Unlikely Places"   164

Barbara Ehrenreich and Annette Fuentes   "Life on the Global Assembly Line"   175

Fareed Zakaria   "The Rise of the Rest"   198

Joseph S. Nye Jr.   "Fear Not Globalization"   208

Benjamin R. Barber   "The Educated Student: Global Citizen or Global Consumer?"   220

Barbara Ehrenreich   "Cultural Baggage"   233

Henry Louis Gates Jr.   "Whose Culture Is It, Anyway?"   243

Octavio Paz   "Hygiene and Repression"   251

Karen Armstrong   "Fundamentalism Is Here to Stay"   286

Edward Said   "Andalusia's Journey"   300

Reza Aslan   "Losing the 'War'"   323

Thane Rosenbaum   "The War on Terror Has Not Gone Away"   326

Bill Powell   "Generation Jihad"   329

Jeffrey Rosen   "Bad Luck: Why Americans Exaggerate the Terrorist Threat"   336

Arundhati Roy   "The Algebra of Infinite Justice"   344

Jeffrey Sachs   "What I Did on My Summer Vacation"   352

Bill Gates   "Saving the World Is Within Our Grasp"   368

Sara Corbett   "Can the Cellphone Help End Global Poverty?"   371

Rachel Carson   "The Obligation to Endure"   401

Al Gore   "The Climate for Change"   408

Jared Diamond   "Lesson from Lost Worlds"   416

Jane Goodall   "To Save Chimps"   426

Argument and Persuasion

Nicholas D. Kristof   "China: The Educated Giant"   10

Susan Bordo   "The Globalization of Eating Disorders"   17

Lee C. Bollinger   "Why Diversity Matters"   31

Ishmael Reed   "America: The Multinational Society"   40

Arthur M. Schlesinger Jr.   "The Cult of Ethnicity"   56

Dwight N. Hopkins   "Beyond Black and White: The Hawaiian President" 45

Fouad Ajami   "The Resilience of American Power"   76

Moises Naim   "Hungry for America"   84

Sasha Abramsky   "Waking Up from the American Dream" 102

Robin Tolmach Lakoff   "The Power of Words in Wartime"   129

Anna Quindlen   "The End of Swagger"   151

Kofi A. Annan   "In Africa, AIDS Has a Woman's Face" 159

Barbara Ehrenreich and Annette Fuentes   "Life on the Global Assembly Line"   175

Fareed Zakaria   "The Rise of the Rest"   198

Johan Norberg   "The Noble Feat of Nike"   204

Joseph S. Nye Jr.   "Fear Not Globalization"   208

Robert Kohler   "Slumdog Millionaire"   211

Henry Louis Gates Jr.   "Whose Culture Is It, Anyway?"   243

Octavio Paz   "Hygiene and Repression"   251

Samuel P. Huntington   "The West and the Rest: Intercivilizational Issues"   293

Amartya Sen "A World Not Neatly Divided" 297

Naomi Shihab Nye "To Any Would-Be Terrorists" 317

Thane Rosenbaum "The War on Terror Has Not Gone Away" 326

Jeffrey Rosen "Bad Luck: Why Americans Exaggerate the Terrorist Threat" 336

Arundhati Roy "The Algebra of Infinite Justice" 344

Peter Singer "The Singer Solution to World Poverty" 361

Bill Gates "Saving the World Is Within Our Grasp" 368

Anuradha Mittal "Technology Won't Feed the World's Hungry" 386

Kenneth Rogoff "A Development Nightmare" 389

Rachel Carson "The Obligation to Endure" 401

Al Gore "The Climate for Change" 408

Andy Rooney "Talking Trash" 413

Bill McKibben "A Place that Makes Sense" 420

Jane Goodall "To Save Chimps" 426

Jonathan Schell "A Hole in the World" 431

Culture or Conflict?
Images of Globalization

Introduction   1

Coca-Cola in Egypt   2

Big Bird in Shanghai   3

Ecotourists   4

Sophisticated Ladies   5

Globalization Protest   6

Modern Conveniences   7

Mixing Cultures   8

Is Beauty Universal? Global Body Images

Introduction   1

Tattoo Man   2

Kindergarten Kids   3

Dubai Britney   4

Persian Beauty   5

Barbie at 50   6

Equal Marriage   7

Obese Girl Band   8

PREFACE

We live in a world of transformations, affecting almost every aspect of what we do. For better or worse, we are being propelled into a global order that no one fully understands, but which is making its effects felt upon all of us.

—Anthony Giddens

Now in its third edition, *The New World Reader* presents provocative essays about contemporary global issues and challenges. The book provides students with the resources needed to think and write in ways that foster varieties of global understanding and citizenship. In a time marked by terrorist attacks on many continents and ongoing interventions in Iraq and Afghanistan, students have been challenged to reconsider and reflect upon the relationship between America and its place in the world. Salman Rushdie observes that the West has met the "rest," and the writers in this text deal with this reality as well as those global forces that increasingly shape our lives. These writers from a variety of backgrounds and perspectives reveal that globalization is *the* big story, the most pressing issue of our times.

Students using *The New World Reader* will find interconnected chapters and selections dealing with such strategic global questions as the changing demographics of the United States, the impact of terrorism on individuals as well as entire populations, the nature of globalization, the clash of cultures and civilizations, the changing roles of women and men in the global arena, the ways in which first-world nations can successfully address global poverty and disease, and the state of the global environment. Challenged by such well-known contemporary thinkers and writers as Anna Quindlen, Peter Singer, Amy Tan, Bharati Mukherjee, Kofi Annan, and Edward Said, today's students will be encouraged to come to grips with a world that, in Anthony Giddens's words, is now subject to complex and often mystifying transformations.

This book demonstrates that critical thinking about our new global century begins when students consider unfamiliar perspectives and arguments, when they are open to new global ideas and perceptions. Put differently, this text combines and encourages intercultural and transnational inquiry. As such, the design of the anthology encourages students to ask not only who they are in this society but also who they are in the world. Many of the diversity themes that teachers of college writing find especially productive and stimulating—gender and sexuality, race and ethnicity, class and cultural orientation—lend themselves to these issues of local and global perception. The selections in the text present a tapestry of diversity in both a local and a global light, moving from personalized encounters with cultures to analytical and argumentative treatment of topics. Students are provided the opportunity to move across cultures and continents, interrogating and assessing authors' insights into our evolving transnational society.

The writers in *The New World Reader* present keen emotional and intellectual insights into our new global era. Most of the essays are relatively brief and provocative and serve as models for the types of personal, analytical, and argumentative papers that college composition teachers ask their students to write. Many of the essays were written after September 11, 2001, and most since 1990. Drawn from a wide variety of authorial backgrounds and sources, and offering diverse angles of opinion and perspectives, the readings in this text lend themselves to thoughtful responses, class debate, small-group discussion, and online research. Some of the longer essays—for example, Jamaica Kincaid on the nature of colonialism and Edward Said on the cross-cultural glories of Andalusia's history—orient students to those forms of discourse that they will encounter in humanities and social science courses. With introductions to chapters and writers, previewing questions, a three-part apparatus following each essay, two four-color photo essays, three appendices offering guidelines on conducting research in the global era and defining rhetorical and global terms, and extensive web resources, *The New World Reader* can serve as the core text in composition courses.

Features

Lively Selections in Chapters that Challenge Our Understanding of Ourselves and Others

The New World Reader presents seventy-two essays in eleven interrelated chapters. The first chapter introduces students to the challenges of thinking, reading, and writing about their place in the new global era. Ten subsequent chapters, each consisting of essays that move from personal and op-ed pieces to more complex selections, focus on key aspects of our increasingly globalized culture, presenting ideas and themes that radiate through the text.

- **Chapter 1. Thinking, Reading, and Writing About the New Global Era.** This concise introductory chapter offers guidelines for students as they think, read, and write about key issues in post–September 11 America and the world. Clear thinking about the "new world order" involves knowledge of both what has gone before and what lies ahead, as well as mastery of the analytical and cognitive skills at the heart of the reading and writing processes. Three brief essays permit students to practice their critical thinking, reading, and writing skills: Nicholas D. Kristof on contrasting approaches to education in the United States and China, Susan Bordo on the globalization of eating disorders, and Lorraine Ali on how neither jihadists nor most Americans accurately see or portray Muslim women.

- **Chapter 2. New American Mosaic: Are We Becoming a Universal Nation?** Presenting compelling insights into the new American demographics Bharati Mukherjee, Arthur M. Schlesinger Jr., and others examine the ways in which both native and "fourth wave" patterns of acculturation are changing the face of the American nation while fostering a greater appreciation of other cultures. The chapter introduces students to the idea that globalization is not only "out there" but also "here"—a phenomenon that might very well be embodied (as Dwight N. Hopkins suggests in his essay) in President Barack Obama.

- **Chapter 3. America and the World: How Do Others Perceive Us?** Suggested by teachers who used earlier editions of *The New World Reader*, this chapter explores the implications (and reverberations) of America's increasingly interventionist position on the global stage. Ann Hulbert, Fouad Ajami, and Moises Naim are among the multinational writers exploring global attitudes toward the idea of America.

- **Chapter 4. Speaking in Tongues: Does Language Unify or Divide?** Presenting essays by Amy Tan, Isabel Allende, and other provocative writers, this chapter explores the varied ways in which language forms identity and cultural relationships in our increasingly polyglot world.

- **Chapter 5. Global Relationships: Are Sex and Gender Roles Changing?** Across the globe, the perception of gender and the larger struggle for human rights vary in the amount of change they are undergoing. Anna Quindlen argues for justice for women, Joseph Contreras offers a revealing appreciation of his sexual orientation and changing family values in Latin America and elsewhere, and Mike Ceaser opens a "dark window" on human trafficking. The last essay, by Barbara Ehrenreich and Annette Fuentes, "Life on the Global Assembly Line," is a contemporary classic, detailing the exploitation of women in factories overseas.

- **Chapter 6. The Challenge of Globalization: What Are the Consequences?** The debate over globalization, whether framed in economic, political, environmental, or cultural terms, serves increasingly to define our lives in the twenty-first century. Essays by Thomas L. Friedman, Fareed Zakaria, Pico Iyer, and others argue the benefits and dangers of globalization.

- **Chapter 7. Culture Wars: Whose Culture Is It, Anyway?** This chapter examines the impact of popular American culture on the nation and on the world. From American-style shopping malls in developing nations to the broadcast of American sitcoms in Islamic nations, the new American landscape has had a global impact. Among writers offering critical appraisals of the contemporary culture wars are Henry Louis Gates Jr., Octavio Paz, and Jamaica Kincaid.

- **Chapter 8. The Clash of Civilizations: Is Conflict Avoidable?** Building on the issues raised in the first seven chapters, this unit offers a critical examination of the clash-of-civilizations debate. Essays by such prominent global analysts as Amartya Sen and Samuel P. Huntington alert students to the fact that today's global conflicts do not spring spontaneously from September 11, 2001, but rather have deep historical and political antecedents.

- **Chapter 9. The Age of Terror: What Is the Just Response?** In the third edition of *The New World Reader*, this chapter has been revised to take at once a broader and deeper view of the causes and consequences of international terror. Bill Powell explores the social and cultural frustrations that impel some young men toward jihadist movements, while Thane Rosenbaum argues that the "war on terror" has not gone away.

- **Chapter 10. Global Aid: Can We Reduce Disease and Poverty?** Suggested by reviewers and inspired by recent hopeful developments in the global struggle for economic justice, this chapter describes the many ways in which people worldwide are working to raise the living standards of their fellow citizens. Frontline reporting by Sara Corbett in Africa and Anuradha Mittal in India, among other perspectives, describes the monumental undertakings of often ordinary citizens and workers.

- **Chapter 11. The Fate of the Earth: Can We Preserve the Global Environment?** From global warming to weapons of mass destruction, the Earth's ecology faces major challenges. Essays by Rachel Carson, Al Gore, Jane Goodall, Bill McKibben, and others offer insights into how we might save the environment—and the world—for future generations.

Three Distinctive Appendices

- **Appendix A.** Conducting Research in the New Global Era. This unit provides students with cutting-edge, practical information on the kinds of research skills they are expected to acquire during their college careers. The appendix stresses the new world of information technology that increasingly guides research and offers extensive guidelines on locating and evaluating print and online sources.

- **Appendix B.** Glossary of Rhetorical Terms. Concise definitions of dozens of key rhetorical terms provide a handy reference for students.

- **Appendix C.** Glossary of Globalization Terms. This appendix makes the vocabulary of globalization, drawn from political science, history, economics, and other disciplines, accessible to students.

A Second Table of Contents by Rhetorical Mode

This rhetorical table of contents adds flexibility for teachers who prefer to organize their syllabus around such traditional forms as narration and description, comparison and contrast, process and causal analysis, and argumentation and persuasion.

Consistent Editorial Apparatus with a Sequenced Approach to Exercises

The New World Reader provides brief introductions to all chapters, highlighting the central issues raised by the writers in each section. All readings contain substantial author headnotes followed by a prereading question. Following each essay, three carefully sequenced sets totaling ten questions provide students with the opportunity to respond to the form and content of the text in ways that promote reading, writing, discussion, group work, and Internet exploration.

- **Before Reading.** One question asks students to think about their current understanding or interpretation of an event or a condition.

- **Thinking About the Essay.** Five questions build on the student's ability to comprehend how the writer's ideas develop through essential rhetorical and stylistic techniques.

- **Responding in Writing.** Three writing activities reflect and expand the questions in the first section, offering opportunities for students to write personal, analytical, and argumentative responses to the text.

- **Networking.** Two questions encourage small-group and Internet work. One question promotes collaborative learning. The other question provides practice in the use of Internet and library sources to conduct deeper exploration and research into issues raised by the author.

Exciting Visual Materials

Students today need to read and analyze visual as well as written texts. *The New World Reader* integrates photographs, artwork, cartoons, graphs, and maps into the chapters. The third edition includes a popular four-color insert devoted to examining the question of "Culture or Conflict?" as well as a four-color insert on standards of global beauty. These illustrations add a visual dimension to aid students' comprehension of the issues raised by written texts. All visual materials offer questions for informed response and analysis.

Instructor's Resource Manual

The New World Reader 3E Online Instructor's Resource Manual provides an abundance of materials to give instructors maximum flexibility in planning and customizing their courses. This manual helps instructors prepare for class more quickly and effectively with such resources as discussion suggestions and suggested answers for questions on the text readings. The IRM can be found on the password-protected instructor's Companion Website.

Companion Website

This complimentary-access Companion Website contains an extensive library of interactive exercises and animations that cover grammar, mechanics, and punctuation. It also includes a complete library of student papers and a section on avoiding plagiarism.

NEW to this Edition

For the third edition of *The New World Reader*, we have strengthened the emphasis on contemporary global issues by offering essays on very recent topics and trends. Students and teachers will be able to ponder the emergence of Barack Obama as a new type of American president; consider the prospects for "saving the world" (as Bill Gates puts in his essay); and interrogate the causes underlying the surge in worldwide human trafficking. Such current issues, integrated into the book's well-received and flexible pattern of organization, enhance the book's appeal.

- **Twenty-five New Selections.** Provocative and compelling essays include work by such well-known authors, commentators, and public advocates and intellectuals as Nicholas D. Kristof, Anna Quindlen, Al Gore, Jane Goodall, and Peter Singer.

- **Exciting New Authors.** To introduce students to emerging writers with fresh ideas and perspectives—and also to established professionals who might not be well-known as writers—we present Manuel Munoz on the complexities raised by one's name; Lee C. Bollinger (president of Columbia University) on the need for diversity in college admissions; Jose Contreras on the globalization of gay rights; Sara Corbett on the penetration of cellular technology into even the poorest parts of the world—and more.

- **Fresh Visuals for Critical Thinking and Response.** Drawn from a wide range of modes including photographs, advertisements, and cartoons, these new images (including two color inserts) offer students and teachers the opportunity to investigate stylistic and thematic links across print and visual dimensions.

Acknowledgments

This book is the result of very special relationships—and considerable serendipity—among friends, collaborators, reviewers, and supporters. I was first alerted to the possibility of developing a global reader by my good friend and former colleague John Chaffee, an acclaimed author and specialist in critical thinking and philosophy. To John I offer my gratitude for his faith in an old friend.

I learned long ago that any college text is only as good as the editorial staff developing it, and here there are several special people who saved me much grief, improved the book, and prevented me from sounding at times like a turgid academician. First and foremost, I want to especially acknowledge Kathy Sands-Boehmer, the senior development editor for this book, who juggled countless electronic transmissions, assembled the text with amazing intelligence and unfailing good humor, and kept the train running on time. To Lyn Uhl, my publisher, and Kate Derrick, my sponsoring editor, I want to extend my thanks for their support. I am grateful to Matt Baker, the project manager, and Georgia Young, my content project manager, for their careful attention to detail. I am also grateful to Mary Dalton-Hoffman for her fine work in tracking down permissions.

I would like to thank my friend and agent, John Wright, who negotiated the contract for this book. Finally, I express love and gratitude to my wife, Laleh Mostafavi-Muller, a specialist in international relations and the Middle East, who offered support and advice as the design for this book evolved.

Several reviewers wrote detailed appraisals of the manuscript, recommendations for changes and improvements, and praise and cautionary advice, and their collective wisdom informs this book. Thanks go to the following reviewers for the third edition:

Maryam Barrie, Washtenaw Community College
James Borton, University of South Carolina, Sumter
William K. Lawrence, George Mason University
Anna Maheshwari, Schoolcraft College
Steven Mayers, City College of San Francisco
Avantika Rohatgi, San Jose State University
Karl Shaddox, University of Alabama, Huntsville

We continue to be grateful for the insights of reviewers whose suggestions helped in the development of the first and second editions of *The New World Reader:*

Cathryn Amdahl, Harrisburg Area Community College
Sandra L. Clark, University of Wyoming
Debra L. Cumberland, Winona State University
John Dailey, New Jersey City University
Stephen F. Evans, University of Kansas
Eileen Ferretti, Kingsborough Community College

Len Gougeon, University of Scranton
Tim Gustafson, University of Minnesota
Jeff Henderson, Kalamazoo Valley Community College
Dr. Nancy Nanney, Chair, Humanities Division, West Virginia University
   at Parkersburg
Pearlie Peters, Rider University
Gail Samis, Salisbury University English Department
Renee Schlueter, Kirkwood Community College
Henry Schwarz, Georgetown University
Micheline M. Soong, Hawaii Pacific University
Anne Meade Stockdell-Giesler, Ph.D., University of Tampa
Randall J. VanderMey, Westmont College
William Vaughn, Central Missouri State University
Mark Wiley, California State University, Long Beach
Rosemary Winslow, Catholic University
Julie Yen, California State University, Sacramento

~Gilbert H. Muller

Thinking, Reading, and Writing About the New Global Era

Global forces are shaping societies, nations, and international systems as never before. Evolving trends—among them the spread of worldwide communications networks, the "clash of civilizations," **terrorism** in many regions and most continents, environmental challenges, and transnational population shifts—suggest that the last century, the "American century" as *Time* magazine's Henry Luce called it, is over and we have entered a new era. In a world where much seems increasingly interconnected, it is no longer sufficient to think locally. Instead, we need to reflect critically on new global realities, assessing the ways in which other peoples, belief systems, traditions, and cultures impact our lives. In the twenty-first century, our well-being and arguably our very survival will depend on our ability to harness the forces unleashed by the dynamics of the new global era.

Regardless of what we choose to call this emerging era—the post-9/11 world, the new world order, the post–cold war period, the age of **globalization,** the information age—we exist today in a global landscape characterized by rapid transformations. To comprehend these transformations, we should not confuse, as the historian Francis Fukuyama reminds us, our national needs with our universal ones. We must also consider what writer and *New York Times* syndicated columnist Thomas Friedman terms the "super-story." For Friedman (who asserts in one of his books that the world is "flat"), the super-story involves all the trends of globalization including world trade, the formation of transnational economic and political alignments, the spread of **information technology,** even new dating and marriage patterns, that affect national and transnational behavior. Writers like Fukuyama and Friedman offer insights into global challenges and the arguments surrounding them. To meet these

An Azad University student uses an Internet café in Tehran, Iran. Access to the Internet is still highly restricted in some countries and by some cultures.

Thinking About the Image

1. Closely examine all of the details of this photograph. (For example, what is on the table next to this woman's elbow?) In what ways does this photograph reinforce standard images in the American media of Muslim women? In what ways is the photograph surprising?

2. Do you agree that access to the Internet provides a kind of empowerment? Why or why not?

3. In her essay "When Afghanistan Was at Peace," Margaret Atwood notes of her book *The Handmaid's Tale* (partly inspired by her travels in Afghanistan) that "there is freedom to and freedom from. But how much of the first should you have to give up in order to assure the second?" How might the woman in this photograph respond?

4. Do a search for Islamic Azad University. Visit this website and compare it to that of your own college. What are the similarities between your schools and how they present themselves? How are they different?

challenges, we must recognize that we are connected to one another both in the United States and to people around the world. No longer isolated by two oceans and seemingly immune to the world's turmoil, we suddenly have to reexamine and re-argue our complex fate.

In order to comprehend our complex fate and prepare for life in the twenty-first century, we will explore in this book some of the key ways we perceive and interact with our new world. In our flattened world, as Thomas Friedman terms it, where everything seems close and immediate—where cell phones, cable, and the Internet connect us instantaneously to a polyglot universe of people and events—we will try to establish parameters for what it means to exist in this global era. Family, community, state, and nation no longer suffice in the construction of our new identity, for today we are citizens of the world. As such, we have to find ways to manage change, negotiate transnational borders, understand diverse viewpoints, and defuse major conflicts if we are to survive and prosper in the new global era.

Critical Thinking

Are you ready for the brave new world of the twenty-first century, the new global era? Do you know enough about *globalization*—the interplay of cultures, societies, economies, and political systems—that is changing your world? Assuredly, you will study this new era in various courses, prepare for careers in it, sit next to people from around the world in your classes, and perhaps even marry into it. The three thousand people from around the world who died in the World Trade Center disaster were working, collaborating, and living in this new world. Among the dead were civilians and citizens from sixty-two countries, including 250 Indians, 200 Pakistanis, 200 Britons, and 23 Japanese. Sadly, there were other individuals—those who perpetrated this event—who felt threatened by the new international order represented by the 9/11 victims.

Your success in college hinges in part on your ability to make choices based on knowledge, experience, and careful reflection about the new world order. You will have to think critically about the global contexts that influence you and your nation. *Critical thinking* is clear thinking: it is a type of mental practice in which you respond to issues logically and, for the purposes of this course, deal with texts and the meanings they generate among class members. Often you will have to *rethink* your opinions, beliefs, and attitudes, and this too is a hallmark of critical thinking—the willingness to discard weak ideas or biased opinions for more mature or simply more logical intellectual opinions. For example, how do you define a *terrorist?* Why would Americans define a terrorist as anyone who takes the lives of innocent civilians, while others around the world view such individuals not as terrorists but as freedom fighters or defenders of the faith? Such questions do not admit easy or facile responses. They require deep and complex thought, for we live in a complex world.

To work effectively with the readings in this text, which deal with varieties of global experience, you need to develop a repertoire of critical thinking skills. In all likelihood, you have come to college possessing many of these skills. But it is important to refine, strengthen, and expand these skills to achieve a degree of authority over any given body of knowledge. How then do you think critically—in other words study and interpret—any given text? How do you look closely at the ideas of writers and evaluate them? How do you respond critically in writing? Having a repertoire of critical thinking skills creates the foundation for being a critical reader and writer.

Every writer in this textbook had a project much like the projects that you will develop: to articulate clearly and convincingly a key idea or nucleus of related ideas about an aspect of human experience—whether in the United States or elsewhere. They developed their ideas by using the repertoire of critical thinking skills—which for our purposes we can associate with key rhetorical strategies. **Rhetoric** is the art of writing or speaking, often to convince an audience about a particular issue. **Rhetorical strategies** are the key patterns that writers employ in this effort to clarify ideas and opinions. We divide these patterns into three major groups: *narration* and *description; exposition* (consisting of definition, comparison and contrast, illustration, process analysis, causal analysis, and classification); and *argument* and *persuasion*. These are not just the classic patterns of rhetoric but also powerful ways of thinking about and understanding our world.

Research demonstrates that different people think most effectively in different ways, or **cognitive styles.** You might like to argue—hopefully not in the style of *Crossfire* or *Hardball*—where viewpoints often are reduced simplistically to positions on the political "right" or "left"—but rather with reasonableness and respect. Or you might be great at telling a story to make a point. Or perhaps you have a talent for analyzing global events. All writing reflects one or more of those cognitive styles that we see reflected in narration and description, exposition, and argumentation. You can gain control over your reading and writing practices by selecting from among these major rhetorical strategies or thinking styles.

Narration and Description

Narration can be briefly described as telling a story, and **description** as the use of vivid **sensory detail**—sight, sound, smell, taste, touch—to convey either a specific or an overall impression. Although narration and description are not always treated in studies of reasoning, the truth of the matter is that it is foolish not to consider these strategies as aspects of the thinking process. The study of narration and description reveals that this type of thinking can produce authority in college writing.

Some composition theorists actually believe that narration and description, relying as they do on the creation of a personal **voice**—your personal response—is the gateway to successful student writing. For example, where were you during a recent national or global crisis? How did you feel? What was your response? How did you get through the day and the aftermath? If you were answering these questions in an essay, you would need to employ a special kind of thinking and reflection, one in which you get in touch with your feelings and find vivid ways to express and make sense of them. It would be useless to say that you are not engaged in reasoning because you would employ narration and description—perhaps even insert **visual texts** downloaded from the Web—to arrive at your personal form of truth about the event. In all likelihood, you would also state or imply a **thesis** (a main idea) and even other generalizations about the event that go beyond pure narration or description; in fact, the vast majority of essays, while they might reflect one or two dominant rhetorical patterns or styles of organizational thought, tend to reveal mixed patterns or approaches to the writing process.

Exposition

Exposition is a relatively broad term that defines a type of writing in which you explain or convey information about a subject. Expository writing is the form of writing that in all likelihood you will be required to produce in college courses. In an expository essay, you set forth facts and ideas—in other words, detailed explanations—to support a thesis, or main idea. As a form of critical thinking, expository writing provides a way of clarifying many of the cultural, political, and economic forces that mold global events today.

To produce effective expository essays, you need to develop skill and fluency in the use of several key rhetorical strategies, among them *definition, comparison* and *contrast, illustration, causal analysis, process analysis,* and *classification.* The use of any one or several of the patterns will dictate your approach to a given topic or problem, and the effective application of these strategies will help to create an authoritative voice, for the readers of your expository essay will see that you are using these rhetorical patterns to think consistently about a body of information and present it coherently. Once again, you employ specific reasoning abilities to make sense of your world.

When you consider the international events that increasingly shape both local and personal life—indeed, that are shaping your identity—it is clear that you must think critically about the best way to approach these events. The way you are able to reason about events, the perspectives you may develop on a particular problem, will inform your understanding of the subject and your ability to convey this understanding in writing.

Think about a term that already has been introduced and that you will encounter in numerous essays in this collection—*globalization*. This is one of the many terms that you will have to look at closely as you come to an understanding of the global forces shaping lives, identities, **cultures,** and civilizations in the twenty-first century. How might you unravel the significance of this word, gain authority over it, explore its relevance to various texts that you will read, and ultimately express your understanding of it in writing?

To start, *definition* of a complex term like *globalization* might be in order. (Definitions for many of the key terms relating to globalization appear in Appendix C.) As a way of thinking about a subject, **definition** is a statement about what a word or phrase means. It is always useful to be able to state this meaning in one or two sentences, as we have already done earlier in this chapter—"the interplay of cultures, societies, economies, and political systems" in the world today. But entire books have been and are being written about globalization, for it is a complex and controversial subject. We call these longer explanations **extended definitions,** which typically rely on other rhetorical strategies to expand the field of understanding. Finally, you might very well have a highly personal understanding of a term like *globalization.* Perhaps you have witnessed or read about workers in overseas factories producing Nikes for a few cents a day and consequently have mixed feelings about the Nikes you are wearing today. In this instance, *globalization* has a special meaning for you, and we term this special meaning a **stipulative definition** because it is colored highly by your experience. Remember, as with all discussions of rhetorical strategies, you are developing and polishing critical thinking skills. With definition, you are taking abstract ideas and making them comprehensible and concrete.

A second way to approach *globalization* would be through comparative thinking. **Comparison** and **contrast** is a cognitive process wherein you consider the similarities and differences of things. Imagine that your instructor asks you to write an essay entitled "Two Ways of Looking at Globalization." The title itself suggests that you have to employ a comparative method to explain and analyze this phenomenon. You would need a thesis to unify this comparative approach, and three or four key points of comparison and/or contrast to support it. The purpose of comparison and contrast is usually to state a preference for one thing over the other or to judge which one is superior. For example, if you maintain that globalization is about inclusion, while those opposing globalization define it as a new form of colonialism or exploitation, you are evaluating and judging two positions.

Any approach to a subject requires a thoughtful and accurate use of **illustration**—that is, the use of examples to support an idea. Illustration, which we also call **exemplification,** enables you to make abstract ideas concrete. Normally, several examples or one key extended example serves to illustrate your main and minor ideas about a subject. If, for example, you want to demonstrate that globalization is a trend that will foster understanding among nations and peoples, you would have to provide facts, statistics, examples, details drawn from personal experience, testimonials, and expert opinions to support your position. Illustration is the bedrock of virtually all ways of thinking, reading, and writing about a topic. Whether telling a story, explaining a topic, or arguing a point (which we deal with in the next section), illustration provides the evidence required to produce a powerful text. Illustration teaches the value of using the information of others—typically the texts of others—in order to build a structure for your own paper.

Causal and *process analysis* are two other forms of intellectual practice that can shape your critical approaches to topics. **Causal analysis,** sometimes called **cause-and-effect analysis,** answers the basic human question *Why?* It deals with a chain of happenings and the predictable consequences of these happenings. Like all the forms of thinking presented in this introductory section, causal analysis parallels our everyday thinking patterns. When we ask why terrorists attacked some city or tourist destination, why so many people in the **Third World** oppose globalization, or why the Internet can foster international cooperation, we are looking for causes or conditions and examining consequences and results (or effects). **Process analysis,** on the other hand, answers the question *How?* It takes things apart in order to understand how they operate or function. Many varieties of process analysis deal with "how-to" subjects involving steps in a correct sequence—for example, how to prepare fajitas. But process analysis is also central to the treatment of broad global trends. How did globalization come about? How do we combat overpopulation of the planet? How do we prevent global warming? Process analysis can help explain the subtle and complex nature of relationships existing within a chain of events.

The last major form of exposition is **classification,** in which information is divided into categories or groups for the purpose of clarifying relationships among them. Some experts would term classification a "higher-order" reasoning skill. In actuality, classification again resembles a great deal of everyday thinking: we classify friends, teachers, types of music, types of cuisine, and so forth. Classification is a way of taking a large body of information and breaking it down (dividing it) into categories for better understanding. It relies on analytical ability—critical thinking that explores parts within a whole. For example, if you were to write an essay entitled "Approaches to Globalization," you could establish three categories— political, economic, and cultural—to divide your subject into coherent parts. The secret to using classification effectively is to avoid the temptation to have your categories overlap excessively. (Did you notice that classification was used to organize this section on exposition?)

Writers skilled in exposition are smart and credible. They write with authority because they can think clearly in a variety of modes. With exposition you make critical thinking choices, selecting those rhetorical strategies that provide the best degree of understanding for your readers, your audience.

Argument and Persuasion

Argument is a special type of reasoning. It appears in texts—written, spoken, or visual—that express a debatable point of view. Stated more rigorously, argument is a process of reasoning in which the truth of some main proposition (or claim) is shown to be true (that is, based on the truth of other minor propositions or premises). Closely allied to argument is **persuasion,** in which you invite an audience through rational, emotional, and ethical appeals to adopt your viewpoint or embark on a course of action. Aristotle in his *Rhetoric* spoke of the appeals as *logos, ethos,* and *pathos*—reason, beliefs, and emotion working together to guide an audience to a proper understanding or judgment of an issue. Argument—the rational component in persuasion—enables you to think responsibly about global issues and present your viewpoints about them in convincing fashion.

The dividing line between various forms of exposition and argumentation is a fine one. Where does a *thesis* leave off and a *claim* (the main argumentative point) begin? Some experts would say that "everything's an argument," and in the arena of global affairs this seems to be true. Issues of religion, race, class, gender, and culture are woven into the very fabric of both our local and global lives, and all of these issues trigger vigorous positions and responses. And the international environment is such that conflict and change seemingly provoke argumentative viewpoints and positions.

The distinctive feature of argumentative thinking is that you give reasons in support of a **claim** or **major proposition**. The claim is what you are trying to prove in an argument. The **reasons,** also called **minor propositions,** offer proof for the major claim. And you support each minor proposition with **evidence**—those various types of illustration mentioned in the previous section as well as logical explanations or abstract thinking used to buttress your basic reasons. If you don't "have the facts"—let's say about global inequality, the Kyoto Protocol on Climate Change, or the worldwide reach of McDonald's—you will not be able to stake a claim and defend it vigorously.

The British philosopher Steven Toulmin emphasizes that underpinning any argument or claim is a **warrant,** which he defines as an assumption, belief, or principle that is taken for granted. The warrant validates the link between the claim and the support. It might be stated or unstated. Many practices of nations, beliefs of citizens, and policies of political groups rest on such warrants. For example, if you assume that the United States is now the world's only **superpower**—a warrant—you can use this principle to claim that the United States should use its power to intervene in rogue states. Or if you believe that people have the right to free themselves from oppression—a warrant at the heart of the Declaration of Independence—you might use this warrant to claim that oppressed citizens have the right to start revolutions to break their chains.

Consider the warrants concerning the war on terrorism embedded in the following paragraph, written by Harold Hongju Koh, a former assistant secretary of state in the Clinton administration and a professor of international law at Yale University:

> Our enemies in this war are out to destroy our society precisely because it is open, tolerant, pluralistic and democratic. In its place, they seek to promote one that is closed, vengeful, repressive and absolutist. To secure genuine victory, we must make sure that they fail, not just in their assault on our safety but also in their challenge to our most fundamental values.
>
> —"Preserving American Values"

Here the writer predicates his claim about the need to achieve victory over our "enemies" on an entire catalog of "fundamental values" that in essence are warrants—that is, principles and beliefs. Also notice the way in which he employs the comparative method to structure his argument in this brief but revealing paragraph.

By their explosive or contentious nature, many global subjects and international issues call for argumentative responses. Your topic might be global warming, the Patriot Act, immigration along the United States–Mexico border, outsourcing of jobs, or the possibility of peace between Israel and the Palestinians. In such instances, your opinions and beliefs will require you to recognize that other people, nations, and cultures might approach the argument from entirely different perspectives. Thus one unique challenge when developing arguments on international topics requires you to cross cultural boundaries, understand the attitudes and assumptions held by people outside your country, and contend with diverting opinions in a global context.

Stated differently, arguments on global topics require you to recognize competing global perspectives. In all likelihood, your argumentative paper will be grounded in a Western tradition based in part on rationalism, Judeo-Christian values, and various systems of freedom and individual rights. (It will be based as well on classic Greek and Roman principles of argument.) But warrants inherent in the Western tradition do not necessarily make your claim universal. Consider that newspapers around the world use almost two dozen euphemisms for *terrorist,* including *attacker, bomber, commando, criminal, extremist, fighter, guerrilla, hostage-taker, insurgent, militant, radical, rebel,* and *separatist.* (On the website www.newssafety.com, Reuters' Nidal alMughrabi offers advice on this matter to fellow reporters in Gaza: "Never use the word terrorist or terrorism describing Palestinian gunmen and militants; people consider them heroes of the conflict.") How you define and interpret a word can determine the method and purpose of an argument.

Not everyone experiences the world or argues global issues from your system of opinions and beliefs. Fortunately, the Internet and the World Wide Web, various translation engines that open international newspaper sites to research, broadcast and visual clips, and even international discussion groups offer you ways to interact globally with other writers, their text, and their arguments. By searching globally for non-U.S. viewpoints and contending with them, you will be able to write distinctive argumentative papers that go beyond mainstream propositions.

Before launching arguments over "homeland security," the pros and cons of globalization, the Arab-Israeli conflict, the rise of interracial and intercultural dating, or any other global or transnational subject, you once again have an obligation to think clearly and critically about these matters. Argumentation provides a logical way to present a viewpoint, deal fairly with opposing viewpoints, and hopefully arrive at a consensus. The psychologist Carl Rogers offers a new way of looking at argumentation when he suggests that both the communicator presenting an argument and the audience are participants in a dialogue—much like psychotherapy—in which they try to arrive at knowledge, understanding, and truth. At its best, argument results in intelligent discourse, a meeting of the minds, and even a strengthening of civic values.

Thinking About an Essay

China: The Educated Giant

NICHOLAS D. KRISTOF

Nicholas D. Kristof is a reporter and columnist for the *New York Times*. He was born in Chicago, Illinois, in 1959 and received a B.A. degree from Harvard University (1981) and a law degree from Oxford University (1983). He also has a diploma in Arabic language from the American University in Cairo. He writes: "Since my student days, when I began to travel with a backpack around Africa and Asia, I have had a fascination with foreign lands, cultures, and languages." Kristof and his wife, Sheryl WuDunn, who is also a *New York Times* reporter, won the Pulitzer Prize for their coverage of the Tiananmen Square massacre in 1989. Based in Asia for many years, Kristof and WuDunn have used their experiences there to write *China Awakes* (1994), *The Japanese Economy at the Millennium* (1999), and *Thunder from the East: Portrait of a Rising Asia* (2000). In the following essay, which appeared in the *Saturday Evening Post* in 2007, Kristof makes a provocative claim about the relative merits of the Chinese and American educational systems.

With China's trade surplus with the United States soaring, the tendency   1
in the U.S. will be to react with tariffs and other barriers. But instead
we should take a page from the Chinese book and respond by boosting
education.

One reason China is likely to overcome the U.S. as the world's most   2
important country in this century is that China puts more effort into building human capital than we do.

The area in south Guangdong Province is my wife's ancestral home-   3
town. Sheryl's grandparents left villages here because they thought they
could find better opportunities for their children in "Meiguo"—"Beautiful
Country," as the U.S. is called in Chinese. And they did. At Sheryl's family
reunions, you feel inadequate without a doctorate.

But that educational gap between China and America is shrinking   4
rapidly. I visited several elementary and middle schools accompanied
by two of my children. And in general, the level of math taught even in
peasant schools is similar to that in my kids' own excellent schools in the
New York area.

My kids' school system doesn't offer foreign languages until the seventh   5
grade. These Chinese peasants begin English studies in either first grade or
third grade, depending on the school.

Frankly, my daughter got tired of being dragged around schools and   6
having teachers look patronizingly at her schoolbooks and say, "Oh, we
do that two grades younger."

There are, I think, four reasons why Chinese students do so well.   7

First, Chinese students are hungry for education and advancement and   8
work harder. In contrast, U.S. children average 900 hours a year in class
and 1,023 in front of a television.

Here in Sheryl's ancestral village, the students show up at school at   9
about 6:30 a.m. to get extra tutoring before classes start at 7:30. They
go home for a lunch break at 11:20 and then are back at school from
2:00 p.m. until 5:00. They do homework every night and weekend, and
an hour or two of homework each day during their eight-week summer
vacation.

The second reason is the China has an enormous cultural respect for   10
education, part of its Confucian legacy, so governments and families alike
pour resources into education. Teachers are respected and compensated
far better, financially and emotionally, in China than in America.

Recently, I wrote about the boomtown of Dongguan, which had no 11
colleges when I first visited it 20 years ago. The town devotes 21 percent
of its budget to education, and it now has four universities. An astonishing 58 percent of the residents age 18 to 22 are enrolled in a university.

A third reason is that Chinese believe that those who get the best grades 12
are the hardest workers. In contrast, Americans say in polls that the best
students are the ones who are innately the smartest. The upshot is that
Chinese kids never have an excuse for mediocrity.

Chinese education has its own problems, including bribes and fees to 13
get into good schools, huge classes of 50 or 60 students, second-rate equipment and lousy universities. But the progress in the last quarter-century is
breathtaking.

It's also encouraging that so many Chinese will shake their heads over 14
this column and say it really isn't so. They will complain that Chinese
schools teach rote memorization but not creativity or love of learning. That
kind of debate is good for the schools and has already led to improvements
in English instruction, so that urban Chinese students can communicate
better in English that Japanese or South Koreans.

After I visited Sheryl's ancestral village, I posted a video of it on the 15
Web. Soon I was astonished to see an exciting posting on my blog from a
woman who used to live in that village.

Litao Mai, probably one of my distant in-laws, grew up in a house she 16
could see on my video. Her parents had only a third-grade education, but
she became the first person in the village to go to college. She now works
for Merrill Lynch in New York and describes herself as "a little peasant
girl" transformed into "a capitalist on Wall Street."

That is the magic of education, and there are 1.3 billion more behind 17
Ms. Mai.

So let's not respond to China's surpluses by putting up trade barriers. 18
Rather, let's do as we did after the Soviet Union's launch of Sputnik in
1957: raise our own education standards to meet the competition.

Questions for Critical Thinking

1. What is *your* opinion of China as an emerging world power? What
   assumptions and attitudes do you bring to the subject? How open are you
   to an essay entitled "China: The Educated Giant"? Why would such a topic
   invite—almost demand—careful critical thinking? What assumptions do you
   think Kristof makes about his readers?

2. Why does Kristof refer to his family in this essay? Do you agree or disagree
   with the effectiveness of this strategy? Answer these questions in groups
   of three or four class members.

3. Where does Kristof use narration and description to organize part of the essay? What is the effect?

4. Kristof employs numerous expository strategies in this essay. Locate and identify them, explaining what they contribute to the substance and the organization of the essay.

5. Does Kristof construct an argument in this essay or is he simply reporting an educational or cultural development? How do you know?

Reading Critically

Most of the essays in this book were written within the last ten years, but the ideas in them run through the history of cultures and civilizations. Consequently, we have to "read" the contemporary ideas contained in these selections through lenses that scan centuries and continents. We have to read critically—analyzing, interpreting, and reassessing new and old ideas in the light of our own experience. When, for example, a writer accuses the United States of **imperialism**, we need to understand the history of this phenomenon as well as interrogate its relevance to the American experience. Is the United States the new imperial power? Are we facing the same conflicts and contradictions that imperial powers through the ages have confronted? To read actively is to be able to think critically about ideas in texts that have deep roots in world history.

As you read the selections in this book, you will discover that careful, critical reading about global issues can complement the talent you already have as a member of the generation that has grown up during the **information age**. Some say that college students have so much trouble with written texts because their culture privileges new forms of technology—call it visual or computer literacy—over older forms of print like the essays you find in this collection. But just as you probably think critically about information acquired through electronic and visual media, you can readily acquire an ability to read written texts critically and to respond to them in discussion and writing. One of the paradoxes of our era is that although we are spending more and more time in front of our computers, we also are buying more books and magazines.

Our most respected thinkers still use the written word to convey their ideas about the issues of our day. They might post these texts on the Web in various forms ranging from online magazines to blogs, but the reality is that these texts appear before us as products of the print universe. Only print can fully convey the intricacy of ideas writers have about our contemporary lives. Speech cannot rival the power of the printed word, as our propensity for tuning out the "talking heads" on television demonstrates. Moreover, with speech we rarely have the opportunity to go back and evaluate what has been said; with written texts, we can assess the presentation of ideas. As a reader, therefore, you have an obligation to deal seriously with the ideas presented by the writers (many of them famous) in this book and to respond critically and coherently to them. You need to learn strategies that will permit you to read texts in this manner.

There are various ways in which readers can respond to any given text. You, a reader, bring varieties of personal experience—and indeed your personality—to a written text. Your social and cultural background also affects your response to texts. In short, there are several ways to respond critically to both written and visual communication.

You bring numerous personal experiences to the reading of any given text. After all, you have attitudes and opinions, likes and dislikes—a unique range of experience. You construct meaning through these personal experiences, which are rooted in your cultural background and community. If, for example, you read an essay on Islam (there are several in this book) and are Muslim yourself, you probably have personal experience of the text that might or might not be shared by other members of the class.

Along with personal experience, you also *think* about a text in special ways. Cognitive psychologists assert that when you were very young, you probably could not always distinguish fantasy from reality (which is why young children respond so powerfully to fairy tales and cartoons). When you were older—say in junior high school—you were able to seek one true meaning in a text. Then, as in your high school years, you developed an ability to consider multiple meanings and interpretations. The critical intelligence that you bring to a college environment is one that must reason, hypothesize, argue, classify, define, and predict as you contend with any given text that deals with complex global issues.

Of course, the text itself is also important: you cannot center all of its meaning on your personal experience. In fact, some teachers will tell you to eliminate personal experience, moralizing, and impressionistic opinion from your writing and focus on the intrinsic meaning of the text. Thus you become a hunter of the "truth" of a text, which reveals itself in the language, style, and structure of the work. Fortunately, there are rhetorical strategies and **conventions** that govern texts (many introduced in this book) that will help you to discover these formal truths.

The college classroom—especially the English classroom—is the place where you wrestle with the truths of a text. In this environment, you are not an isolated reader but part of a community of readers. This community or society of readers reflects the diverse features of gender, race, and ethnicity, class, education, religion, politics, region, and nation. As a member of this group, you want to share insights with others for the purpose of understanding or consensus (if there is an argument framing the text and discussion). You do not surrender your personal impressions of a text as much as you become a member of what the critic Stanley Fish calls the "interpretive community." In this book, every essay contains an exercise designed to strengthen your reading and writing skills within smaller interpretative or collaborative communities.

Finally, the act of reading critically leads you into the deepest regions of culture and the forces that reveal and inform our experience of the world. Cultural theorists contend that deeply held worldviews and ideologies—for instance, **capitalism** and **socialism,** or Islam and Christianity—are the bedrock of any social configuration. Various institutions, power structures, cultural conventions, gender roles, and "fields of discourse" like medicine and law dictate the ways we respond to a text. As you read the essays in the next chapter, "New American Mosaic," from a cultural perspective, you will have to assess the way your viewpoint on **immigration** has been formed by these deep structures of culture. Through such analysis, you can avoid biased, nationalistic, and religiously intolerant ways of thinking about a text, engaging instead in critical thought and sound, and reflective argument.

When reading argumentative essays in a global context, you should consider these critical questions:

- What is the purpose of the text? What claim or main idea does the writer want to develop?
- What is the writer's background? Was the writer born in the United States or overseas?
- Who is the writer's audience? Does the writer demonstrate an awareness that U.S. and non-U.S. readers might respond differently to the content and method of the text?
- Does the writer consider the values, assumptions, and experiences of readers from other cultures?
- Does the writer treat opposing viewpoints or perspectives, especially if they come from non-U.S. sources, accurately and fairly?
- What reasons or minor propositions support the writer's claim?
- How accurate and representative is the writer's supporting evidence? Does the writer rely solely on evidence from U.S. sources, or does credible evidence from reliable global sources also appear?
- Is the shape of the writer's argument logically convincing?

Steps to Reading Critically

With a basic understanding of how ways of reading influence your approach to a text, you can now follow steps that will enable you to read critically. You should treat any "system" for critical reading flexibly, but with the conviction that it is important to extract and evaluate the meanings that we professional writers want to convey to their audience. Here are guidelines for effective critical reading.

1. *Start with the conviction that critical reading, like critical thinking, requires active reading.* It is not like passively watching television. Instead, critical reading involves intellectual engagement with the text. Consequently, read with a pen or pencil in hand, underlining or circling key

words, phrases, and sentences, asking questions in the margins, making observations—a process called **annotation**. These annotations will serve as guidelines for a second reading and additional responses in writing.

2. *Pause from time to time to reflect on what you are reading.* What is the writer's main idea? What are his or her basic methods (recall the rhetorical strategies) for developing ideas? What tone, or voice, does the writer convey, and why? What is the writer's **purpose?** Is it to argue an issue, explain, analyze, or what? What varieties of illustration or evidence does the writer provide?

3. *Employ your critical thinking skills to interrogate the text.* Use some of the reader response theories to explore its deepest meanings. For example, test the text against your personal experience or against certain cultural preconceptions. Think critically about the writer's argument, if there is one, and whether it withstands the test of logic and the conventions of argumentation.

4. *Consider the implied **audience** for the text.* How does the writer address you as part of this audience? Do you actually feel that you are part of this primary audience, a secondary reader, or largely forgotten or excluded? If you feel excluded, what features of the essay have caused you to be removed from this community of readers? How might you make yourself a part of this "universe of discourse" nevertheless?

5. Write a *précis, or summary of the essay.* These "shorthand" techniques will help you to focus your thoughts and prepare for class discussions and subsequent writing assignments.

These five steps for critical reading should suggest that critical reading, much like critical thinking and critical writing, involves re-reading. If you follow these guidelines, you will be able to enter the classroom community of readers with knowledge and authority and be prepared for productive class discussion.

Reading Visual Texts

You have to read **visual texts**—advertisements, tables and graphs, cartoons, artwork, photographs and illustrations—with the same care you bring to the critical reading of written texts. Indeed, "visuals" seem like the new mother of our information age, for we are bombarded with images that invite, sometimes demand, our response. Whether dealing with spam on our computers, contending with that ubiquitous beer commercial on television, responding to a photograph of the latest disaster in a newspaper account, or trying to decipher what a graph on the federal deficit *really* means, we know that visual texts are constructions designed to influence us in carefully contrived ways.

We must, therefore, attempt to be critical readers of visual texts so that the powerful images of our culture and civilization do not seduce or overwhelm us without proper evaluation. Visual texts, after all, tend to be instruments of persuasion. A symbol like the American eagle, the Islamic crescent, or the red star of China can trigger powerful personal and collective responses. Similarly, political advertisements and commercials often manipulate visual texts to persuade voters to act for a candidate or against (as with negative ads) an opposing candidate. To bring this discussion to the local level, log on to your campus website. What forms of visual text do you encounter that enhance the written text? Look especially for images that suggest that your campus is culturally and globally diverse.

To read visual texts with the same critical authority you bring to scrutinizing written texts, you should consider the following questions:

- In what culture or context did the image originate? Who is the author? What is the source?
- What implicit messages are conveyed by the images and symbols?
- How is the visual designed or organized, and what is the effect of this arrangement?
- What is the purpose of the visual? What does the visual want the viewer to believe?
- What evidence is provided, and how can it be verified?
- What is the relationship of the visual to the printed text?

Visual images complement and at times overwhelm print or even make printed text unnecessary. Whether appearing on T-shirts, in ads in the glossiest fashion magazines, or marching across a computer screen, visual images usher us into a world of meaning. And we need to apply the same critical perspective to this visual universe that we do to its print counterpart.

Reading an Essay Critically

The Globalization of Eating Disorders

Susan Bordo

Susan Bordo was born in 1947 in Newark, New Jersey. She attended Carleton University (B.A., 1972) and the State University of New York at Stony Brook (Ph.D., 1982). A well-known feminist scholar, Bordo is the Singletary Chair in the Humanities and a professor of English and Women's Studies at the University of Kentucky. In this selection, written as a preface to the tenth anniversary edition of her Pulitzer Prize–nominated book *Unbearable Weight: Feminism, Western Culture, and the Body* (2003), Bordo offers an overview of a new kind of epidemic, fueled by Western media images, that is affecting cultures around the world.

Susan Bordo, "The Globalization of Eating Disorders" from UNBEARABLE WEIGHT: Feminism, Western Culture, and the Body, 2003. Reprinted by permission of the author.

The young girl stands in front of the mirror. Never fat to begin with, 1
she's been on a no-fat diet for a couple of weeks and has reached
her goal weight: 115 lb., at 5'4"—exactly what she should weigh, according to her doctor's chart. But in her eyes she still looks dumpy. She
can't shake her mind free of the "Lady Marmelade" video from Moulin
Rouge. Christina Aguilera, Pink, L'il Kim, and Mya, each one perfect in
her own way: every curve smooth and sleek, lean-sexy, nothing to spare.
Self-hatred and shame start to burn in the girl, and envy tears at her stomach, enough to make her sick. She'll never look like them, no matter how
much weight she loses. Look at that stomach of hers, see how it sticks
out? Those thighs—they actually jiggle. Her butt is monstrous. She's fat,
gross, a dough girl.

As you read the imaginary scenario above, whom did you picture 2
standing in front of the mirror? If your images of girls with eating and
body image problems have been shaped by *People* magazine and Lifetime
movies, she's probably white, North American, and economically secure.
A child whose parents have never had to worry about putting food on the
family table. A girl with money to spare for fashion magazines and trendy
clothing, probably college-bound. If you're familiar with the classic psychological literature on eating disorders, you may also have read that she's
an extreme "perfectionist" with a hyper-demanding mother, and that she
suffers from "body-image distortion syndrome" and other severe perceptual and cognitive problems that "normal" girls don't share. You probably
don't picture her as black, Asian, or Latina.

Read the description again, but this time imagine twenty-something 3
Tenisha Williamson standing in front of the mirror. Tenisha is black, suffers
from anorexia, and feels like a traitor to her race. "From an African-
American standpoint," she writes, "we as a people are encouraged to
embrace our big, voluptuous bodies. This makes me feel terrible because I
don't want a big, voluptuous body! I don't ever want to be fat—ever, and
I don't ever want to gain weight. I would rather die from starvation than
gain a single pound."[1] Tenisha is no longer an anomaly. Eating and body
image problems are now not only crossing racial and class lines, but gender
lines. They have also become a global phenomenon.

Fiji is a striking example. Because of their remote location, the Fiji 4
islands did not have access to television until 1995, when a single station
was introduced. It broadcasts programs from the United States, Great Britain,
and Australia. Until that time, Fiji had no reported cases of eating disorders,

1. From the Colours of Ana website (http://coloursofana.com//ss8.asp). [This and subsequent
notes in the selection are the author's.]

and a study conducted by anthropologist Anne Becker showed that most Fijian girls and women, no matter how large, were comfortable with their bodies. In 1998, just three years after the station began broadcasting, 11 percent of girls reported vomiting to control weight, and 62 percent of the girls surveyed reported dieting during the previous months.[2]

Becker was surprised by the change; she had thought that Fijian 5 cultural traditions, which celebrate eating and favor voluptuous bodies, would "withstand" the influence of media images. Becker hadn't yet understood that we live in an empire of images, and that there are no protective borders.

In Central Africa, for example, traditional cultures still celebrate volup- 6 tuous women. In some regions, brides are sent to fattening farms, to be plumped and massaged into shape for their wedding night. In a country plagued by AIDS, the skinny body has meant—as it used to among Italian, Jewish, and black Americans—poverty, sickness, death. "An African girl must have hips," says dress designer Frank Osodi. "We have hips. We have bums. We like flesh in Africa." For years, Nigeria sent its local version of beautiful to the Miss World competition. The contestants did very poorly. Then a savvy entrepreneur went against local ideals and entered Agbani Darego, a light-skinned, hyper-skinny beauty. (He got his inspiration from M-Net, the South African network seen across Africa on satellite television, which broadcasts mostly American movies and television shows.) Agbani Darego won the Miss World Pageant, the first Black African to do so. Now, Nigerian teenagers fast and exercise, trying to become "lepa"—a popular slang phrase for the thin "it" girls that are all the rage. Said one: "People have realized that slim is beautiful."[3]

How can mere images be so powerful? For one thing, they are never 7 "just pictures," as the fashion magazines continually maintain (disingenuously) in their own defense. They speak to young people not just about how to be beautiful but also about how to become what the dominant culture admires, values, rewards. They tell them how to be cool, "get it together," overcome their shame. To girls who have been abused they may offer a fantasy of control and invulnerability, immunity from pain and hurt. For racial and ethnic groups whose bodies have been deemed "foreign," earthy, and primitive, and considered unattractive by Anglo-Saxon norms, they may cast the lure of being accepted as "normal" by the dominant culture.

2. Reported in Nancy Snyderma, *The Girl in the Mirror* (New York: Hyperion, 2002), p. 84.
3. Norimitsu Onishi, "Globalization of Beauty Makes Slimness Trendy," *The New York Times,* Oct. 3, 2002.

In today's world, it is through images—much more than parents, teachers, 8
or clergy—that we are taught how to be. And it is images, too, that teach us
how to see, that educate our vision in what's a defect and what is normal,
that give us the models against which our own bodies and the bodies of
others are measured. Perceptual pedagogy: "How to Interpret Your Body
101." It's become a global requirement.

I was intrigued, for example, when my articles on eating disorders 9
began to be translated, over the past few years, into Japanese and Chinese. Among the members of audiences at my talks, Asian women had
been among the most insistent that eating and body image weren't problems for their people, and indeed, my initial research showed that eating
disorders were virtually unknown in Asia. But when, this year, a Korean
translation of *Unbearable Weight* was published, I felt I needed to revisit
the situation. I discovered multiple reports on dramatic increases in eating
disorders in China, South Korea, and Japan. "As many Asian countries
become Westernized and infused with the Western aesthetic of a tall,
thin, lean body, a virtual tsunami of eating disorders has swamped Asian
countries," writes Eunice Park in *Asian Week* magazine. Older people can
still remember when it was very different. In China, for example, where
revolutionary ideals once condemned any focus on appearance and there
have been several disastrous famines, "little fatty" was a term of endearment for children. Now, with fast food on every corner, childhood obesity
is on the rise and the cultural meaning of fat and thin has changed. "When
I was young," says Li Xiaojing, who manages a fitness center in Beijing,
"people admired and were even jealous of fat people since they thought
they had a better life. ... But now, most of us see a fat person and think
'He looks awful.'"[4]

Clearly, body insecurity can be exported, imported, and marketed— 10
just like any other profitable commodity. In this respect, what's happened
with men and boys is illustrative. Ten years ago men tended, if anything,
to see themselves as better looking than they (perhaps) actually were. And
then (as I chronicle in detail in my book *The Male Body*) the menswear
manufacturers, the diet industries, and the plastic surgeons "discovered"
the male body. And now, young guys are looking in their mirrors, finding
themselves soft and ill defined, no matter how muscular they are. Now
they are developing the eating and body image disorders that we once
thought only girls had. Now they are abusing steroids, measuring their
own muscularity against the oiled and perfected images of professional

4. Reported in Elizabeth Rosenthal, "Beijing Journal: China's Chic Waistline: Convex to
Concave," *The New York Times*, Dec. 9, 1999.

athletes, body-builders, and *Men's Health* models. Now the industries in body-enhancement—cosmetic surgeons, manufacturers of anti-aging creams, spas and salons—are making huge bucks off men, too.

What is to be done? I have no easy answers. But I do know that we   11 need to acknowledge, finally and decisively, that we are dealing here with a cultural problem. If eating disorders were biochemical, as some claim, how can we account for their gradual "spread" across race, gender, and nationality? And with mass media culture increasingly providing the dominant "public education" in our children's lives—and those of children around the globe—how can we blame families? Families matter, of course, and so do racial and ethnic traditions. But families exist in cultural time and space—and so do racial groups. In the empire of images, no one lives in a bubble of self-generated "dysfunction" or permanent immunity. The sooner we recognize that—and start paying attention to the culture around us and what it is teaching our children—the sooner we can begin developing some strategies for change.

Reading and Responding to an Essay

1. After reading Bordo's essay, reread and annotate it. Underline or circle key words, phrases, and sentences. Ask questions and make observations in the margins. Next to the title, write a phrase or sentence explaining what you think the title means.

2. In class groups of three or four, discuss your personal responses to this essay. Share with group members your experience of the text and why you respond to it the way you do. Would you say that your ideal image of physical beauty is based on personal or shared values? Do you know people whose ideas of beauty contrast with your own? Do you think of this difference as a matter of opinion, cultural difference, or simply personal taste?

3. Bordo claims, "In today's world, it is through images—much more than parents, teachers, or clergy—that we are taught to be." How essential is this premise to the writer's claim? What kinds of evidence does she use to support the claim?

4. Examine the language, style, and structure of the essay. Do you find the writer's style to be engaging or accessible? Why or why not? Why does she repeat words and phrases (termed *anaphora* in rhetoric)? Where does she employ description, illustration, comparison, and the basis of case studies followed by general diagnosis—basically a problem-solution method of essay development?

5. Explain the ways in which you could interpret this essay from psychological, cultural, and social perspectives.

Writing in Response to Reading

The distinguished writers in this book, many of them recipients of major awards such as the Nobel and Pulitzer Prizes, are professionals. When dealing typically with local and world events—especially with the relationship of a liberal and open society like the United States to the world community—they employ a broad range of stylistic and rhetorical skills to construct meaning. They write for numerous reasons or purposes, although an argumentative edge appears in many of the essays. All engage in strategic thinking and rethinking as they tackle the promises and prospects of our new global era.

It is useful at the outset of a course in college writing to think like a professional writer or at least a professional writer in the making. With each essay you write, imagine that you are trying to produce "publishable prose." Indeed, you will have the opportunity to write letters to the editor, post papers on the Web, pool and present research findings with other classmates, and engage in many tasks that assume the character of the professional writer who composes for a specific audience and for a specific purpose. At the least, by treating yourself as a writer capable of producing publishable prose, you will impress your instructor with your seriousness and aspirations.

Many of the issues and momentous events treated by the writers in this book demand no less than a "professional" response based on your ability to deal critically in writing with the strategic questions the essays raise. Indeed, critical thinking and writing about our common global condition is one measure of a pluralistic and tolerant society. By thinking and rethinking, writing and rewriting about your world, you contribute to the creation of open democratic discourse.

How, then, do you write about the new global era and its many challenges, or about any other topic for that matter? Globalization has changed the way people think about themselves and their relation to the world. Even ideas have become global; communication of these ideas now can span the world in milliseconds. As a writer in this brave new world of globalization, you need to apply in writing that repertoire of critical thinking skills mentioned at the outset of this chapter to make sense of contemporary life on this planet.

To start, you must have a basic understanding of the world of global interrelationships that characterizes life in the twenty-first century. The noted historian Paul Kennedy, who has an essay in this book, defines globalization as "the ever-growing integration of economies and societies because of new communications, newer trade and investment patterns, the transmissions of cultural images and messages, and the erosion of local and traditional ways of life in the face of powerful economic forces from abroad." Kennedy, as we might expect from a historian, is quick to note that this new world of globalization did not spring immediately from the ashes of 9/11 but can be detected in different guises in the rise and fall of great civilizations. For example, what the British Empire once termed "progress," we now call globalization. Today, the United States is the Great Power—its financial, cultural, military, and hi-tech capacities unrivaled by other nations. Whether its Great Power status—its overarching control of the forces of globalization—will create new forms of "progress" for peoples and nations around the world is the central debate underlying the chapters in this book.

Writers like Paul Kennedy are "professional" in the sense that they know their subject. They are informed. But their informed essays do not result from some divinely inspired moment of creativity. When professional writers sit down to tackle an issue of importance, they know that beyond the knowledge they bring to the subject, they will have to consider various perspectives on the subject and even experiment with various methods of composition. Everyone composes differently, but it is fair to say that a good essay is the result of planning, writing, and revision, and such an essay reflects some of the key thinking strategies outlined in the first part of this chapter. There is a common consensus among professionals, including teachers of writing, that a **composing process**, consisting of *prewriting, drafting*, and *revision*, is the best way to approach the creation of a successful essay.

Prewriting

Prewriting is that preliminary stage in the composing process in which you map out mentally and in writing your overall approach to the subject. Prewriting in the context of this book begins when you read critically and respond to an essay. Perhaps you annotate the essay, summarize it mentally, or take notes on paper or the computer. Or maybe you take notes during class discussion. Next, you size up the nature of the writing project appearing in the exercises at the end of the essay or provided by the instructor. At this early stage, it is clear that already you are thinking, responding, and writing critically about the project at hand.

Composing processes are unique to each writer, but there are certain areas of the prewriting process that are necessary for you to consider:

- *Who is your audience?* A college writing assignment means that your primary audience will be your professor, who knows the "print code" and anticipates well-organized and grammatically correct prose. But there are secondary audiences to consider as well, and you might have to adjust your level of discourse to them. If you are working collaboratively, you have members of the group to satisfy. If you exchange papers with an-other class member for evaluation, this also creates a new audience. Or perhaps you will need to create an electronic portfolio of your best work as a graduation requirement; here the people who assess the quality of the portfolio become judges of your work.

- *What is your purpose?* Is your purpose to tell a story, describe, inform, argue, evaluate, or combine any number of these basic goals? Knowing your purpose in advance of actually drafting the essay will permit you to control the scope, method, and tone of the composition.
- *What is your thesis or claim?* Every paper requires a controlling idea or assertion. Think about and write down, either in shorthand or as a complete sentence, the main idea or claim that you plan to center your paper on.
- *How will you design your essay?* Planning or outlining your paper in advance of actually writing it can facilitate the writing process. Complete outlines, sketch outlines, sequenced notes, visual diagrams can all serve as aids once the actual drafting begins.
- *How can you generate preliminary content?* Notes can be valuable. **Brainstorming,** in which you write without stop for a certain amount of time, can also activate the creative process. Joining online discussion groups or working collaboratively in the classroom also can result in raw content and ideas for development.

Prewriting provides both content and a plan of operation before moving to the next stage in the composing process.

Drafting

Once you have attended to the preliminary, or prewriting, stage in the composing process, you can move to the second stage, which is the actual **drafting** of the paper. Applying an Aristotelian formula, be certain to have a beginning, middle, and end. Your introduction—ideally one opening paragraph—should center the topic, be sufficiently compelling to engage your reader, and contain a thesis or claim. The body of the essay should offer a series of paragraphs supporting your main idea or central assertion. The conclusion should wrap things up in an emphatic or convincing way.

Here is a checklist for drafting an essay:

- Does your title illuminate the topic and capture the reader's interest?
- Does your opening paragraph "hook" the reader? Does it establish and limit the topic? Does it contain a thesis or claim?
- Do all body paragraphs support the thesis? Is there a main idea (called a **topic sentence**) controlling each paragraph? Are all paragraphs well developed? Do they contain sufficient examples or evidence?
- Does the body hold together? Is there a logical sequence to the paragraphs? In other words, is the body of the essay **unified** and **coherent,** with **transitions** flowing from sentence to sentence and paragraph to paragraph?

- Have you selected the best critical thinking strategies to develop the paper and meet the expectations set out in your introduction?
- Is your conclusion strong and effective?

Think of drafting as the creation of a well-constructed plot. This plot does not begin, develop, and end haphazardly, but rather in a carefully considered sequence. Your draft should reveal those strategies and elements of the composing process that produce an interesting and logically constructed plot.

Revision

There are professional writers who rarely, if ever, revise their work, and there are others who spend forever getting every word and sentence just right. Yet most professional writers do some amount of **revision,** either on their own initiative or in response to other experts, normally editors and reviewers. As the American poet Archibald MacLeish observed, the composing process consists of the "endless discipline of writing and rewriting and rewriting."

Think of the essay that in all likelihood you have put up on your computer screen not as a polished or final product but as a rough draft. Use the grammar and spell checker features of your software program to clean up this draft, remembering that this software is not infallible and sometimes is even misleading. Then revise your essay, creating a second draft, with the following questions serving as guidelines:

- Is the essay long enough to satisfy the demands of the assignment?
- Is the topic suitable for the assignment?
- Is there a clear thesis or claim?
- Is the purpose or intention of the essay clear?
- Is the essay organized sensibly? Are the best rhetorical patterns used to facilitate reader interest and comprehension?
- Are all sentences grammatically correct and sufficiently varied in structure?
- Is there sufficient evidence, and is all information derived from other sources properly attributed?
- Does the manuscript conform to acceptable guidelines for submitting written work?

Successful writing blends form and content to communicate effectively with an audience. The guidelines offered in this section tap your ability to think and write critically about the global issues raised in this book. To be a global citizen, you must become aware of others, make sense of the world, and evaluate varieties of experience. To be a global writer, you have to translate your understanding of these global relationships into well-ordered and perceptive prose.

Writing in Response to an Essay

Not Ignorant, Not Helpless

Lorraine Ali | Lorraine Ali writes about music and popular culture. Currently a staff writer for *Newsweek,* Ali was formerly a senior critic for *Rolling Stone* and has also written for *The New York Times, The Village Voice,* and *Harper's Bazaar.* She was voted Music Journalist of the Year in 1997 and won a 2002 Excellence in Journalism Award from the National Arab Journalist Association. In this selection, which appeared in the December 12, 2005, issue of *Newsweek,* Ali considers how the image of the oppressed woman of Islamic culture—a stereotype born of Western moral indignation—can become as oppressive as the oppression that is denounced.

If I'd never known a Muslim woman, I'd probably pity any female 1
born into Islam. In America we've come to see these women as timid creatures, covered from head to toe, who scurry rather than walk. They have no voices, no rights and no place outside the home. But I grew up around secular Muslims (my father was an Iraqi Shiite) in Los Angeles, stayed with ultrareligious relatives in Baghdad and met dozens more Muslim women on travels through the Middle East. I've watched them argue politics with men at the dinner table in Baghdad, slap husbands on the back of the head for telling off-color jokes in Egypt and, at a recent Arab Women's Media Conference in Amman, fiercely debate their notions of democracy from under hijabs and J. Lo–inspired hairdos. The West's exposure to Muslim women is largely based on Islam's most extreme cases of oppression: Taliban-dominated Afghanistan, Wahhabi-ruled Saudi Arabia, and postrevolutionary Iran. Under those regimes, women were and are ordered to cover. Many Afghan women are forbidden to attend school, and no Saudi woman is allowed to drive. Yet despite the spread of ultraconservative versions of Islam over the past few decades, these societies are not the norm in the Muslim world. In Egypt, female cops patrol the streets. In Jordan, women account for the majority of students in medical school. And in Syria, courtrooms are filled with female lawyers. "Women are out working, in every profession, and even expect equal pay," says Leila Ahmed, Harvard Divinity School

professor and author of *Women and Gender in Islam*. "Though the atmosphere in Muslim countries is becoming more restrictive, no matter how conservative things get they can't put the genie back in the bottle."

Still, Muslim women are feeling like pawns in a political game: jihadists 2 portray them as ignorant lambs who need to be protected from outside forces, while the United States considers them helpless victims of a backward society to be saved through military intervention. "Our empowerment is being exploited by men," says Palestinian Muslim Rima Barakat. "It's a policy of hiding behind the skirts of women. It's dishonorable no matter who's doing it." Scholars such as Khaled Abou El Fadl, an expert on Islamic law and author of *The Great Theft: Wrestling Islam From the Extremists*, says this is an age-old problem. "Historically the West has used the women's issue as a spear against Islam," he says. "It was raised in the time of the Crusades, used consistently in colonialism and is being used now. Muslim women have grown very, very sensitive about how they're depicted on either side."

Surely the late feminist Doria Shafik felt the scorn of men—Arab and 3 British—while fighting for the right to vote in 1940s Egypt. Yet Shafik persevered and cast her first ballot in Cairo in 1956. "I render thanks unto God to have been born in the land of mysteries," she later wrote. "To have grown up in the shadow of the palms, to have lived within the arms of the desert, guardian of secrets ... to have seen the brilliance of the solar disk and to have drunk as a child from the Nile sacred river." Millions of Muslim Arab women still love the societies they're born into, regardless of jihadist manipulation or American intervention. If reform is to come, they will surely be the ones who push it forward.

Responding in Writing

1. As a prewriting strategy, brainstorm about this article for five minutes. Try to capture your impressions of the essay as you respond to the elements in it.

2. In class groups of three or four, list aspects of life in the United States that are (or may be) viewed as "backward" from another culture's point of view (the existence of capital punishment in the United States, for example. Write a brief essay in which you seek to qualify or overturn one of these national stereotypes.

3. Write an analysis of this essay. What evidence in the essay suggests that Ali had a specific audience in mind? Describe her intended audience as it may be inferred from the text. Do you feel included in this group of targeted readers? Why or why not? What is her thesis or claim? How does she develop the introduction, body, and conclusion? What is the nature of her evidence? What ideas about America and world culture does she want the audience to gain from a critical reading of the text?

4. "Professional" writing is partly the result of an author's mastery of the subject. A writer's *ethos* may consist of a wide range of tonal qualities: moral authority, sincerity, good humor, humility, seriousness of purpose. Consider your response to the voice you hear in this essay. Do you feel that Ali's personal disclosure in the opening paragraph contributes to her moral authority? Write a personal disclosure of your own that you feel would establish your authority to speak on a certain subject relating to religion, gender, or American or world culture.

5. Go online and find out more about the roles of Muslim women in a specific country. Write a report on your findings and summarize it in an oral presentation to the class.

New American Mosaic: Are We Becoming a Universal Nation?

Martin Luther King Jr. believed in the need for what he termed a "world house," a commitment to a society of global inclusion. "We are all caught up in an inescapable web of mutuality, tied in a single garment of destiny," he declared. Indeed, there are interconnected forces governing our world, and American demographic trends reflect the transnational movement of peoples on today's planet. Accelerating this transformation has been the recent arrival of tens of millions of immigrants to the United States. Instead of repeating earlier immigration patterns in which peoples arrived from Europe, these new immigrants travel here from all parts of the globe: Asia, Africa, the Caribbean, Central and South America. Today, new immigrants are changing the traditional notion of what it means to be "American." Arguably, because of the strikingly diverse nature of its citizenry, America is in the process of becoming a universal nation.

The writers in this chapter reflect in their own ethnic and racial origins the broad mosaic—some prefer to call it a kaleidoscope—that characterizes life in the United States today. Consider the historical magnitude of this national transformation. True, North America once belonged to native tribes; and the legacy of slavery, which began in 1621 when a Dutch man-of-war ship brought the first Africans to the Jamestown colony, also served to diversify the nation in ways that we continue to grapple with today. But from colonial times to 1965, the United States drew its population largely from Europe. First came the English, Scots-Irish, Germans, and French. The second great wave that began in the 1870s and continued up to World War I brought tens of millions of immigrants from southern and eastern Europe. For centuries, immigrants from non-European parts of the world were systematically excluded, with restrictive quotas

29

© Steve Kelley/The Times-Picayune

Thinking About the Image

1. Are the people portrayed in this cartoon stereotypes? How can you tell? Do you find the stereotypes offensive, or do they help the cartoon make sense? Can you think of any comedians or hip-hop artists who use stereotypes in a way that points out an uncomfortable truth?
2. This cartoon uses irony to make its point. What specifically is ironic about this cartoon?
3. What political situation or issue is Steve Kelley, the cartoonist, responding to in this cartoon? What is his opinion? Does he make his point effectively?

preserving certain assumptions about the racial and ethnic character of the nation. For example, in her haunting memoir *China Men*, the acclaimed writer Maxine Hong Kingston devotes an entire chapter to listing the dozens of immigration statutes designed to exclude people from China from America's shores.

The Immigration Act of 1965 abolished all such quotas and opened the United States—for the first time in the nation's history—to the world's population. Now everyone presumably had a fair opportunity to achieve the

American Dream, whatever this ambiguous term might mean. And arrive they did—from Mexico, Vietnam, India, Nigeria, Cuba, the Philippines, Iran, and China—all seeking a place in the new global nation. Of course, this contemporary collision and intersection of peoples, races, and cultures is not only an American phenomenon; many countries in Europe are dealing with similar patterns. But nowhere is this new global reality more apparent than in the United States. In certain states—California, for example—and in many major American cities, "minorities" have become majorities. According to the most recent census data, by 2056 the "average" American will be as likely to trace his or her origins to the Hispanic world, Asia, or the Pacific islands as to Europe. These demographic changes are often reflected on college campuses, with students from scores of national backgrounds speaking dozens of languages sharing classes together.

The story of American civilization is still unfinished, but the authors in this chapter suggest certain directions it will take. They write about conflicts and challenges posed by the new American Dream, which is ostensibly open to, if not necessarily desired by, all the peoples of the world. They wrestle with America's complex fate. They ask collectively: How can America continue to be a beacon for peoples from around the planet seeking work, safety, security, freedom, the right to freely practice and preserve their own customs and beliefs? They ask: Can America be—should it be—the model for a universal nation?

Why Diversity Matters

LEE C. BOLLINGER

Lee C. Bollinger is an acclaimed First Amendment scholar and university administrator. Born in Santa Rosa, California in 1946 and raised there and in Bend, Oregon, Bollinger attended the University of Oregon (BS, 1968) and subsequently received his law degree from Columbia University Law School (1971). As president of two distinguished universities—Michigan and then Columbia—Bollinger has been in the front lines in the debate over college diversity and affirmative action. Bollinger's support for an open, pluralistic educational culture and society is inherent in his scholarship, notably *The Tolerant Society: Freedom of Speech and Extremist Speech in America* (1968) and *Images of a Free Press* (1991). In the following essay from the June 1, 2007, issue of *The Chronicle of Higher Education*, Bollinger claims that we cannot understand America—or the world—without being exposed to a full spectrum of peoples and beliefs.

Before Reading

Do you think that affirmative action is still relevant to college life today, or have we moved into what some call a "post-racial" environment that makes affirmative action unnecessary? Explain.

During this frantic admissions season, it is easy for our applicants to think that the most important moment in their college career is when they rip open the mail to find out where they got in and where they didn't. But we in higher education understand that the admissions process has less to do with rewarding each student's past performance—although high performance is clearly essential—than it does with building a community of diverse learners who will thrive together and teach one another. 1

When it comes to creating the kinds of diversity we sorely need in this country, however, disturbing trends and setbacks are making it difficult for many public schools and universities to succeed. The reality is that as much as we may want to believe that racial prejudice is a relic of history, conscience and experience tell us better. 2

Even now, the Supreme Court is considering two public-school cases out of Washington and Kentucky that would subvert the resounding principle that *Brown v. Board of Education* established 53 years ago on May 17, 1954, that "separate is inherently unequal." If successful, both cases would ban local districts from developing voluntary desegregation programs that seek to maintain racial balance in our schools and counteract the worst resegregation crisis we have faced since the early days of the civil-rights movement. 3

According to the 2000 census, only 14 percent of white students attend multiracial schools, while nearly 40 percent of both black and Latino students attend intensely segregated schools where 90 percent to 100 percent are from minority groups. Further, almost half of all black and Latino students attend schools where three-quarters or more students are poor, compared with only 5 percent of white students; in extremely poor schools, 80 percent of the students are black and Latino. 4

Beyond elementary and secondary schools, higher education continues to face its own challenges, including statewide bans on affirmative action. Recent news reports have noted how hard some of our leading public universities are working to revise recruitment and admissions policies to comply with those bans without jeopardizing the diversity of the students who attend their campuses. What's important, however, is why those universities are trying so hard to maximize diversity—even though no law requires it, and in several states affirmative action is explicitly forbidden. 5

Lee C. Bollinger "Why Diversity Matters" *The Chronicle of Higher Education* Washington: June 1, 2007, Vol. 53, Iss. 39, pg. B20. Reprinted by permission of the author.

I have been deeply involved in two U.S. Supreme Court cases—*Gratz* 6
v. Bollinger and *Grutter v. Bollinger* (2003)—that ultimately upheld the
constitutionality of affirmative-action policies at public universities. Let
me suggest why, having vindicated the legality of affirmative action, higher
education must not lose the practical and political battles to maintain
racially, ethnically, and socioeconomically diverse student bodies.

Universities understand that to remain competitive, their most important 7
obligation is to determine—and then deliver—what future graduates will
need to know about their world and how to gain that knowledge. While
the last century witnessed a new demand for specialized research, prizing
the expert's vertical mastery of a single field, the emerging global reality
calls for new specialists who can synthesize a diversity of fields and draw
quick connections among them. In reordering our sense of the earth's interdependence, that global reality also cries out for a new age of exploration,
with students displaying the daring, curiosity, and mettle to discover and
learn entirely new areas of knowledge.

The experience of arriving on a campus to live and study with class- 8
mates from a diverse range of backgrounds is essential to students'
training for this new world, nurturing in them an instinct to reach out
instead of clinging to the comforts of what seems natural or familiar.
We know that connecting with people very—or even slightly—different
from ourselves stimulates the imagination; and when we learn to see
the world through a multiplicity of eyes, we only make ourselves more
nimble in mastering—and integrating—the diverse fields of knowledge
awaiting us.

Affirmative-action programs help achieve that larger goal. And the uni- 9
versities that create and carry them out do so not only because overcoming
longstanding obstacles to people of color and women in higher education
is the right thing to do, but also because policies that encourage a comprehensive diversity help universities achieve their mission. Specifically,
they are indispensable in training future leaders how to lead all of society,
and by attracting a diverse cadre of students and faculty, they increase our
universities' chances of filling in gaps in our knowledge with research and
teaching on a wider—and often uncovered—array of subjects.

At the same time, such policies foster a greater spirit of community on 10
campuses as well as between universities and the cities and town they call
home. The days of the gated university are past, and affirmative action is
crucial to making our universities welcoming places for community members
to visit, take classes, and inspire their children to dream.

Opponents of affirmative action forget that broader purpose in their 11
demand for what they see as a "pure" admissions meritocracy based on how

students perform in high school and on standardized tests. But it is far less important to reward past performance—and impossible to isolate a candidate's objective talent from the contextual realities shaping that performance—than to make the best judgment about which applicants can contribute to help form the strongest class that will study and live together. For graduate schools and employment recruiters, that potential is the only "merit" that matters because in an increasingly global world, it is impossible to compete without already knowing how to imagine, understand, and collaborate with a diverse and fluid set of colleagues, partners, customers, and government leaders.

By abolishing all public affirmative-action programs, voters in   12 California and Michigan (and other states if affirmative-action opponents are successful) have not only toppled a ladder of equal opportunity in higher education that so many of us fought to build and the Supreme Court upheld in 2003. They will almost assuredly make their great public universities less diverse—and have, in fact, done so in California, where the impact has become clear—and therefore less attractive options to potential students and, ultimately, less valuable contributors to our globalized society.

As the president of a private university, I am glad that independent   13 institutions retain the autonomy to support diversity efforts that make our graduates more competitive candidates for employers and graduate schools, as well as better informed citizens in our democracy and the world. But as an alumnus of one public university and a former president of another, I worry about a future in which one of America's great success stories slides backward from the mission of providing generations of young Americans with access to an affordable higher education.

From the establishment of the land-grant colleges in the 1860s to the   14 GI Bill after World War II to the Higher Education Act of 1965, our public universities have advanced the notion that in educating college students for the world they will inhabit, it is necessary to bring people together from diverse parts of society and to educate them in that context. Far from being optional or merely enriching, it is the very essence of what we mean by a liberal or humanistic education.

It is also vital for establishing a cohesive, truly national society—one   15 in which rising generations learn to overcome the biases they absorb as children while also appreciating the unique talents their colleagues bring to any equation. Only education can get us there.

As Thurgood Marshall knew so well: "The legal system can open doors   16 and sometimes even knock down walls. But it cannot build bridges. . . . We will only attain freedom if we learn to appreciate what is different and muster the courage to discover what is fundamentally the same." Cutting affirmative action short now only betrays that history of social progress.

And, in the process, it threatens the core value of academically renowned public universities at a time when many Americans list rising tuition costs as one of their gravest economic concerns.

All of this leads to the conclusion that diversity—one of the great 17 strengths of American education—is under siege today. At the elementary- and secondary-school levels, resegregation is making it exceedingly difficult for minority students to get the resources that inspire rising generations to apply to and then attend college. At the same time, the elimination of affirmative action programs at our public universities is keeping admissions officials from lifting those same students up to offset the structural inequalities they had to face in getting there.

As we honor the parents, students, lawyers, and nine justices who spoke 18 with one voice in *Brown* on that May day 53 years ago, we would all do well to remember that when it comes to responsible diversity programs— those that help our public schools and our great public universities fulfill their historic roles as avenues of economic and cultural mobility—what is wise is also what is just.

Thinking About the Essay

1. What is Bollinger's **claim** and where does he state it? On what **warrant** does Bollinger base his claim? Discuss why you agree or disagree with his claim and the warrant underpinning it.

2. Where and why does Bollinger use emotional and ethical appeals in his approach to his primary audience? At what points does he stress his authority in addressing this audience?

3. What minor propositions does Bollinger use to buttress his claim?

4. What forms of evidence does Bollinger use to support his argument?

5. How does Bollinger refute the arguments of those opposed to affirmative action? Do you find his strategy to be effective? Justify your response.

Responding in Writing

6. Summarize the main points of reasoning that inform Bollinger's claim, and then discuss the extent to which you find his argument reasonable and convincing.

7. Bollinger asserts that students must be educated for twenty-first century realities. Write an essay in which you explore the relevance of diversity and affirmative action to this challenge.

8. Write a response to Bollinger explaining why (or why not) you agree with his premise, and how his essay reflects life and conditions on your college campus.

Networking

9. Form small groups and debate the merits of diversity and affirmative action in higher education. Select one member of the group to join a class forum presenting the results of your debate.

10. Go online and read about the decision of the Supreme Court in the two public-school cases that Bollinger alludes to in paragraph 3. How do these decisions relate to Bollinger's conclusion that diversity is under siege today?

All Things Asian Are Becoming Us

ANDREW LAM

Andrew Lam is known as both a prolific journalist and a widely anthologized short story writer. Many listeners also know his voice, as a regular commentator on National Public Radio's *All Things Considered*. Lam's awards include the Society of Professional Journalists' Outstanding Young Journalist Award (1993), The Media Alliance Meritorious award (1994), The World Affairs Council's Excellence in International Journalism Award (1992), the Rockefeller Fellowship at UCLA (1992), and the Asian American Journalists Association National Award (1993; 1995). He co-founded New California Media, an association of 400 ethnic media organizations in California. Lam was born in Vietnam and came to the United States in 1975 when he was eleven years old. His story was featured in the PBS documentary *My Journey Home*, in which a film crew followed him back to his home in Vietnam. In the following selection, Lam reflects on how elements of traditional and popular Asian culture have, within his lifetime, radically altered the cultural identity of Americans and the way they experience the world.

Before Reading

What products of Asian culture attract you the most? When you experience another culture as an imported commodity, do you feel that (in some sense) you become *part* of that culture? Do you have proprietary feelings toward certain aspects of your native culture? Explain your response.

Rudyard Kipling's famous line "East is East and West is West, and never   1
the twain shall meet" no longer applies. Today, East and West are commingled, and in this country, the East is on the rise.

Andrew Lam, "All Things Asian Are Becoming Us." Andrew Lam is an editor with New America Media and the author of "Perfume Dreams: Reflection on the Vietnamese Diaspora." Reprinted by permission.

Take movies. American audiences are growing more familiar with movies from China, Japan and South Korea. Quentin Tarantino is planning a kung fu movie entirely in Mandarin, and Zhang Yimou's stylized martial arts films like *Hero* and *House of Flying Daggers* are popular across the country. Hollywood is remaking Japanese blockbusters like *The Ring* and *Shall We Dance?* 2

What many Asian Americans once considered proprietary culture— kung fu, acupuncture, ginseng, incense, Confucian dramas, beef noodle soup and so on—has spilled irrevocably into the mainstream. 3

Three decades ago, who would have thought that sushi would become an indelible part of American cuisine? Or that Vietnamese fish sauce would be found on aisle 3 of Safeway? Or that acupuncture would be accepted by some HMOs? That feng shui would become a household word? Or that Asian writers, especially Indian, would play a large and important role in the pantheon of American letters? 4

American pundits tend to look at the world through a very old prism— they associate globalization as synonymous with Americanization: i.e., how the United States influences the world. What many tend to overlook, in the age of porous borders, is how much the world has changed the United States. 5

Evidence of the Easternization of America is piling up. 6

Japanese animation is a good example. There are more than 20 anime shows on cable channels, ranging from *Sailor Moon* to *Pokemon* to the latest teenage craze, *Kagemusha*, a series about a half-human, halfdemon warrior on a quest. *Spirited Away* beat out Disney movies to win the Oscar for best animation in 2003. 7

Sales of Japanese comic books, DVDs and videocassettes reached $500 million in the United States last year. 8

Mandarin-language films like *Crouching Tiger, Hidden Dragon*, by Ang Lee, and *Hero*, by Zhang Yimou, were top draws across the United States. Asian Americans have been featured as stars as in *Harold and Kumar Go to White Castle* and *Better Luck Tomorrow*. 9

Asian stars in Hollywood include Ang Lee, Joan Chen, Justin Lin, John Woo, Jackie Chan, Jet Li, Chow Yun Fat, Michelle Yeow. 10

Sandip Roy, host of a San Francisco radio show called "Up Front" and a film critic, points to the "Bollywoodization" of the United States. 11

"Deepak Chopra has long been managing the spiritual fortunes of Hollywood's golden people," he says. "Britney Spears' new album has a Bhangra remix of one of her singles. Images from old Indian matchbooks and posters now retail as birthday cards. The vinyl seat covers of Indian rickshaws are turning into tote bags for Manhattan's chic. And yoga is now the new aerobics." 12

That this country is falling under Asia's spell shouldn't be surprising. 13
If the world is experiencing globalization, the union between East
and West, where a new hybrid culture is thriving, is just part of that
process.

Suddenly, Beijing, Bombay, Bangkok and Tokyo are much closer to 14
the United States than we thought. And in as much as we feel reassured in
seeing the Thai teenager in Bangkok wearing his baseball cap backward
under the golden arches of McDonald's, Americans have learned to savor
the taste of lemongrass in our soup and that tangy burnt chili on our fried
fish.

Writer Richard Rodriguez once observed that "Each new wave of 15
immigrants brings changes as radical as Christopher Columbus did to the
Indians."

Eastern religions represent one of those changes. In Los Angeles, 16
there are more than 300 Buddhist temples. Buddhism, writes Diana Eck,
professor of comparative religions at Harvard University, "challenges
many Americans at the very core of their thinking about religion—at
least, those of us for whom religion has something to do with one we
call God."

One cannot accept that acupuncture works on one's arthritis with- 17
out considering the essence that lies behind such an art, the flow of the
chi—the energy that flows through all things—and its manipulation with
needles.

One must eventually contemplate what ancient Taoist priests saw, the 18
invisible flow of energy, which involves a radically different way of experiencing the world.

One cannot diligently practice meditation without considering one's 19
psychological transformation and the possibility of enlightenment, of spiritual revelation, waiting at the edge of one's breath.

A century ago, Carl Jung, a great interpreter of the psychic dif- 20
ferences between East and West, described the Westerner as basically
extroverted, driven by desire to conquer, and the Easterner as a classic
introvert, driven by desire to escape suffering. The introvert tends to
dismiss the "I," Jung wrote, because in the East, it is identified with
selfishness and libidinous delusions. To reach spiritual maturity, the I
must be dissolved.

All that has been turned on its head. Many a Westerner, tired of mate- 21
rialism, turns slowly inward in search of spiritual uplift, while introversion
and ego-dissolving are no longer consuming Asian quests.

On my wall, I keep two pictures to remind me of the extraordinary 22
ways East and West have changed.

One is from a *Time* magazine issue on Buddhism in the United States. 23
On it, a group of American Buddhists sits serenely in lotus position on a
wooden veranda in Malibu contemplating the Pacific Ocean. The other is
of the Vietnamese American astronaut Eugene Trinh, who flew on a NASA
space shuttle.

Tu Weiming, the Confucian scholar at Harvard, said this is a new 24
"era where various traditions exist side by side for the first time for the
picking."

American artists and writers have often looked to the East. What is new 25
in the age of globalization is that Asia is the active agent in the interaction,
projecting its vision westward with confidence.

Thinking About the Essay

1. Why do you think Lam chose not to title his essay, "We Are Becoming All
   Things Asian"?

2. How does Lam develop the meaning of the term *globalization*? What
   alternate terms (or plays on the term *globalization*) appear in the course of
   the essay?

3. What is new, according to Lam, about the influence of Asian culture in
   both the transformation of American culture and the current process of
   globalization?

4. Why does Lam devote so much attention to Buddhism as an example of a
   "cultural import" affecting the United States?

5. Does the final paragraph follow logically from preceding paragraphs, or is it
   simply a restatement of earlier ideas? Does Lam conflate "American" with
   "Western"? Justify your response.

Responding in Writing

6. Reread the statement by Richard Rodriguez quoted in paragraph 15. List
   three or four examples of radical changes brought about by past waves of
   immigration.

7. Do you agree with Lam's statements in paragraphs 17–19 that one must
   adopt, or at least entertain, the ideologies and values underlying a cultural
   practice like acupuncture or meditation? Write a brief essay in which you
   attack or defend this assumption.

8. According to Lam, theories about fundamental differences between Eastern
   and Western sensibilities (Carl Jung's, for example) have been "turned on
   [their] head" (paragraph 21). Lam offers a brief illustration, but no other
   evidence. Write a brief essay in which you present evidence in support of
   Lam's claim.

Networking

9. List the names of Asian films that you and your classmates have seen. Is there variety among the films on this list, or do they tend to belong to a narrow range of genres or to a single genre (such as the martial arts epic)?

10. Choose one recent Asian film that was also released and marketed in the United States. Visit the United States and Asian online promotional sites that advertise the film to these two different audiences. Is the film promoted in different ways? If you cannot find a version with translated text, then compare the images that appear on each site.

America: The Multinational Society

ISHMAEL REED | Ishmael Reed was born in 1938 in Chattanooga, Tennessee, and is a well-known novelist, poet, and essayist who lives in Oakland and teaches at the University of California at Berkeley. An activist who advocates the rights of people of color, and notably African Americans, he has been at the forefront of major literary and political movements for decades. Reed's extensive literary production includes such works of fiction as *Mumbo Jumbo* (1972) and *Japanese by Spring* (1993), volumes of verse such as *Secretary to the Spirits* (1975), and several collections of essays, among them *Airing Dirty Laundry* (1993). Reed also has been an editor, playwright, songwriter, television producer, and publisher. In the following essay, which first appeared in *Writin' Is Fightin'* (1988) and has become a contemporary classic, Reed argues for a new definition of American culture.

Before Reading

Do you think that the United States is becoming a universal nation, composed of peoples and cultural styles from around the world? Why or why not?

> At the annual Lower East Side Jewish Festival yesterday, a Chinese woman ate a pizza slice in front of Ty Thuan Duc's Vietnamese grocery store. Beside her a Spanish-speaking family patronized a cart with two signs: "Italian Ices" and "Kosher by Rabbi Alper." And after the pastrami ran out, everybody ate knishes.
>
> —*The New York Times*, June 23, 1983

On the day before Memorial Day, 1983, a poet called me to describe   1
a city he had just visited. He said that one section included mosques,
built by the Islamic people who dwelled there. Attending his reading, he
said, were large numbers of Hispanic people, forty thousand of whom lived
in the same city. He was not talking about a fabled city located in some
mysterious region of the world. The city he'd visited was Detroit.

A few months before, as I was leaving Houston, Texas, I heard it   2
announced on the radio that Texas's largest minority was Mexican
American, and though a foundation recently issued a report critical of
bilingual education, the taped voice used to guide the passengers on the air
trams connecting terminals in Dallas Airport is in both Spanish and English. If the trend continues, a day will come when it will be difficult to travel
through some sections of the country without hearing commands in both
English and Spanish; after all, for some western states, Spanish was the first
written language and the Spanish style lives on in the western way of life.

Shortly after my Texas trip, I sat in an auditorium located on the   3
campus of the University of Wisconsin at Milwaukee as a Yale professor—
whose original work on the influence of African cultures upon those of
the Americas has led to his ostracism from some monocultural intellectual
circles—walked up and down the aisle, like an old-time southern evange-
list, dancing and drumming the top of the lectern, illustrating his points
before some serious Afro-American intellectuals and artists who cheered
and applauded his performance and his mastery of information. The
professor was "white." After his lecture, he joined a group of Milwaukeeans
in a conversation. All of the participants spoke Yoruba, though only the
professor had ever traveled to Africa.

One of the artists told me that his paintings, which included African   4
and Afro-American mythological symbols and imagery, were hanging in
the local McDonald's restaurant. The next day I went to McDonald's and
snapped pictures of smiling youngsters eating hamburgers below paintings
that could grace the walls of any of the country's leading museums. The
manager of the local McDonald's said, "I don't know what you boys are
doing, but I like it," as he commissioned the local painters to exhibit in his
restaurant.

Such blurring of cultural styles occurs in everyday life in the United   5
States to a greater extent than anyone can imagine and is probably
more prevalent than the sensational conflict between people of different
backgrounds that is played up and often encouraged by the media. The
result is what the Yale professor, Robert Thompson, referred to as a
cultural bouillabaisse, yet members of the nation's present educational
and cultural Elect still cling to the notion that the United States belongs

to some vaguely defined entity they refer to as "Western civilization," by which they mean, presumably, a civilization created by the people of Europe, as if Europe can be viewed in monolithic terms. Is Beethoven's Ninth Symphony, which includes Turkish marches, a part of Western civilization, or the late nineteenth- and twentieth-century French paintings, whose creators were influenced by Japanese art? And what of the cubists, through whom the influence of African art changed modern painting, or the surrealists, who were so impressed with the art of the Pacific Northwest Indians that, in their map of North America, Alaska dwarfs the lower forty-eight in size?

Are the Russians, who are often criticized for their adoption of "Western"   6
ways by Tsarist dissidents in exile, members of Western civilization? And what of the millions of Europeans who have black African and Asian ancestry, black Africans having occupied several countries for hundreds of years? Are these "Europeans" members of Western civilization, or the Hungarians, who originated across the Urals in a place called Greater Hungary, or the Irish, who came from the Iberian Peninsula?

Even the notion that North America is part of Western civilization   7
because our "system of government" is derived from Europe is being challenged by Native American historians who say that the founding fathers, Benjamin Franklin especially, were actually influenced by the system of government that had been adopted by the Iroquois hundreds of years prior to the arrival of large numbers of Europeans.

Western civilization, then, becomes another confusing category like   8
Third World, or Judeo-Christian culture, as man attempts to impose his small-screen view of political and cultural reality upon a complex world. Our most publicized novelist recently said that Western civilization was the greatest achievement of mankind, an attitude that flourishes on the street level as scribbles in public restrooms: "White Power," "Niggers and Spics Suck," or "Hitler was a prophet," the latter being the most telling, for wasn't Adolf Hitler the archetypal monoculturalist who, in his pigheaded arrogance, believed that one way and one blood was so pure that it had to be protected from alien strains at all costs? Where did such an attitude, which has caused so much misery and depression in our national life, which has tainted even our noblest achievements, begin? An attitude that caused the incarceration of Japanese-American citizens during World War II, the persecution of Chicanos and Chinese Americans, the near-extermination of the Indians, and the murder and lynchings of thousands of Afro-Americans.

Virtuous, hardworking, pious, even though they occasionally would   9
wander off after some fancy clothes, or rendezvous in the woods with the

town prostitute, the Puritans are idealized in our schoolbooks as "a hardy band" of no-nonsense patriarchs whose discipline razed the forest and brought order to the New World (a term that annoys Native American historians). Industrious, responsible, it was their "Yankee ingenuity" and practicality that created the work ethic. They were simple folk who produced a number of good poets, and they set the tone for the American writing style, of lean and spare lines, long before Hemingway. They worshiped in churches whose colors blended in with the New England snow, churches with simple structures and ornate lecterns.

The Puritans were a daring lot, but they had a mean streak. They 10 hated the theater and banned Christmas. They punished people in a cruel and inhuman manner. They killed children who disobeyed their parents. When they came in contact with those whom they considered heathens or aliens, they behaved in such a bizarre and irrational manner that this chapter in the American history comes down to us as a late-movie horror film. They exterminated the Indians, who taught them how to survive in a world unknown to them, and their encounter with the calypso culture of Barbados resulted in what the tourist guide in Salem's Witches' House refers to as the Witchcraft Hysteria.

The Puritan legacy of hard work and meticulous accounting led to the 11 establishment of a great industrial society; it is no wonder that the American industrial revolution began in Lowell, Massachusetts, but there was the other side, the strange and paranoid attitudes toward those different from the Elect.

The cultural attitudes of that early Elect continue to be voiced in 12 everyday life in the United States: the president of a distinguished university, writing a letter to the *Times*, belittling the study of African civilizations; the television network that promoted its show on the Vatican art with the boast that this art represented "the finest achievements of the human spirit." A modern up-tempo state of complex rhythms that depends upon contacts with an international community can no longer behave as if it dwelled in a "Zion Wilderness" surrounded by beasts and pagans.

When I heard a schoolteacher warn the other night about the invasion 13 of the American educational system by foreign curriculums, I wanted to yell at the television set, "Lady, they're already here." It has already begun because the world is here. The world has been arriving at these shores for at least ten thousand years from Europe, Africa, and Asia. In the late nineteenth and early twentieth centuries, large numbers of Europeans arrived, adding their cultures to those of the European, African, and Asian settlers who were already here, and recently millions have been entering the country from South America and the Caribbean, making Yale Professor Bob Thompson's bouillabaisse richer and thicker.

One of our most visionary politicians said that he envisioned a time   14 when the United States could become the brain of the world, by which he meant the repository of all of the latest advanced information systems. I thought of that remark when an enterprising poet friend of mine called to say that he had just sold a poem to a computer magazine and that the editors were delighted to get it because they didn't carry fiction or poetry. Is that the kind of world we desire? A humdrum homogeneous world of all brains but no heart, no fiction, no poetry; a world of robots with human attendants bereft of imagination, of culture? Or does North America deserve a more exciting destiny? To become a place where the cultures of the world crisscross. This is possible because the United States is unique in the world: The world is here.

Thinking About the Essay

1. How does the author's introductory paragraph set the stage for the development of his main claim or argument? Explain his argument in your own words. Does Reed develop his argument through **induction** or **deduction?** How do you know?

2. Reed begins in a personal mode of discourse, frequently using an "I" **point of view.** He then shifts to a more objective analytical and argumentative style before returning to the first-person point of view at the end of the essay. What is his purpose here? Do you find this strategy to be effective or confusing, and why?

3. What types of details and examples does the author employ? Why does Reed use so many examples in a relatively brief essay?

4. Identify and analyze the various rhetorical strategies—especially definition and comparison and contrast—that appear in this essay.

5. Why does Reed develop a series of questions in his closing paragraph?

Responding in Writing

6. Demonstrate in a personal essay the ways in which you come into contact with various races, ethnicities, and cultures on a daily basis. Be certain that you establish a clear thesis and develop several examples.

7. Write an argumentative essay in which you state your position on Reed's key assertion that the idea of Western or European civilization is wrong-headed.

8. In an analytical essay, explain some of the ways in which America's perception of itself as a **monoculturalist** or **Eurocentric** nation has caused problems in its relationship with the rest of the world.

Networking

9. In small groups, discuss your response to Reed's key assertion that "the United States is unique in the world: The world is here."

10. Select a partner and search the Internet together for information on American Puritanism. Present a brief oral report on your findings, explaining how the Puritan legacy continues to operate—as Reed suggests—in American society.

Beyond Black and White: The Hawaiian President

Dwight N. Hopkins

Dwight N. Hopkins, who was born in Richmond, Virginia, in 1953, is a professor of theology at the University of Chicago. He holds degrees from Harvard University (B.A., 1976), Union Theological Seminary (M.Div., 1984), and the University of Cape Town (Ph.D., 2000). Much of Hopkins's work deals with the intersection of race and religion in the modern world. Among his books are *Shoes that Fit Our Feet: Sources for a Constructive Black Theology* (1993), *Heart and Head: Black Theology—Past, Present, and Future* (2002), and *Being Human: Race, Culture, and Religion* (2005). In this essay, which appeared in the February 10, 2009, issue of *Christian Century*, Hopkins offers a provocative assessment of Barack Obama as a new type of American.

Before Reading

Do you think that Americans will ever transcend their preoccupation with race? Why or why not?

Since the November presidential election, friends, colleagues and casual   1
acquaintances throughout the United States and across the world have written me and claimed Barack Obama as the son of their state, race, country or region. Of course, countless black Americans have celebrated the fact that "in our lifetime, one of us is in the White House."

How is it possible that Hawaii claims Obama as its own; Indonesia and   2
parts of Asia perceive him as reflective of their experiences; Kenya cries in

ecstasy to have a blood relative on 1600 Pennsylvania Avenue; all of Africa embraces him as a close kin of that continent; Kansans believe his roots sink deep within their soil; and black Americans, without much critical self-reflection, relish the idea that the 44th president is black like them?

The fact that Obama is perceived as belonging in a variety of ways to 3
such disparate groups points up at least one persistent and absurd concept in race relations in America: the one-drop rule.

Coming out of slavery and segregation, the one-drop rule was one of 4
the most egregious dimensions of white supremacy. When Africans arrived in the New World in chains, all of their children were called black and thus were en slaved, even if one biological parent was white. If it was deter-mined that a person who looked white had any African or black ancestors, that white person was reclassified as black. A drop of black blood in one's genealogy could instantly transform a white citizen into a black slave.

Long after slavery the one-drop rule persisted in racial classification, 5
and oddly enough, was eventually accepted by black Americans. This led to all manner of absurdities. Walter White, a pioneering leader of the NAACP, was so white-looking that he once attended a high-society function where some of the whites present wondered why he had brought his "black" wife. The irony was that White was, according to the one-drop rule, black, and his so-called black wife was actually white.

The one-drop-of-black-blood rule is unique to the U.S. It presupposes 6
a black-white paradigm. On one extreme are "white" people, on the other, "black" people. Lost in these absolutes is the kaleidoscope of Asian Americans, Caribbean Americans, African Americans, Pacific Islander Americans, Latino-Hispanic Americans, Middle Eastern Americans, European Americans, American Indians and all the complexities of identity that make us unique human beings.

What race is Obama? Shortly after the election, the venerable John 7
Lewis, a member of Congress from Georgia, stated that no black person who had come out of segregation and the civil rights movement could have been elected the first black president. And in fact Obama did not. Obama redefines what it means to be black. His ancestors did not come from the glorious West African empires of centuries ago. To my knowledge, he has no biological connection to those empires' encounter with the European slave trade. His family history does not flow from de jure and de facto segregation. During the civil rights struggle, the black power movement and reparation efforts, he was living in Asia and the Pacific Islands. He has never lived in the (segregated or nonsegregated) southern U.S. In his major speeches, he has not mentioned two heroic icons of black manhood—Martin Luther King Jr. and Malcolm X. He was not born into nor did he grow

up in a black church. He did not assemble black preachers and civil rights stalwarts together and from that base launch his presidential campaign.

Obama is Hawaiian. He is familiar with flip-flops, surfing, snorkeling, 8 Aloha Spirit and 'Ohana family values. Before he lived in Chicago's segregated black community, his social reality was Asia and the Pacific more than the southern U.S. Born in Hawaii in 1961, he grew up alongside Japanese Hawaiians, Chinese Hawaiians, Filipino Hawaiians, Pacific Island Hawaiians, Native Hawaiians and white Hawaiians. The black-white paradigm of the mainland did not dominate his reality. In fact, whites were and still ate a minority in Hawaii, and except for the occasional vacationer and military personnel, blacks were and are a rarity.

Obama spent ages six to ten in Indonesia, going to school and speaking 9 Indonesian. His Indonesian stepfather gave him an ape as a pet. This pet was not caged but lived in their backyard.

Obama was nurtured in a white environment. His Kansan white mother 10 (not from the South) reared him with the help of his white grandparents. (All accounts indicate that no black men or women, boys or girls ever lived in his home until he married and had his own children.) To illustrate how different his upbringing was from that of most black Americans, who call their grandmothers Big Mama, Ma Dear or Grandma, Obama's intimate name for his white grandmother was Toot--the Hawaiian endearment for grandmother.

Obama has never identified himself as an Afrocentric person of a 11 pan-Africanist. Yet he is more African than the overwhelming majority of black Americans. There need be no genetic test to find out what West African "tribe" his ancestors came from centuries ago. His ancestry is from Kenya, a country in East Africa from which the enslaved rarely came. His father voluntarily came to the U.S. as a student in 1959. Before that, he was a goat herder in Kenya. President Obama has visited the exact location where his father and other ancestors were born. He understands the "tribal" language, politics, economics, religions, foods, songs, indigenous names, folktales, clothing, dances, illnesses, personalities and gravesites. When he pours libations (spilling liquids on the ground in memory of the dead), he is not talking about unknown Africans lost in the slave trade. Like Africans born on the continent, he can pour libations to his specific blood family members and directly on family gravesites. Some of those burial grounds ate still next to family compounds in Kenya. Obama doesn't have to change his English "slave master's" name to an African one; his name is already African.

Growing up, Obama was certainly aware of the mainland's obsession 12 with race. Witness the Afro hairstyle he adopted at Punahou, one of the most elite private schools in the U.S., and his idolizing of NBA star Julius "Dr. J" Erving. But it wasn't until he was 22 and came to the heavily segregated South Side of Chicago that, for the first time in a sustained manner, he engaged the particularities (and some might say the peculiarities) of traditional black-white race relations, including the one-drop rule.

Segregated Chicago offered Obama three things: a black family through 13 marriage, a black community through grass roots organizing and a black church through baptism.

While black Americans may not be quite right in their declaration that 14 Obama is only "one of us," the 44th president does symbolize a change in the U.S. If not going so far as to redefine race in America, Obama might expand what race means. Perhaps he will help the millions of Americans with black and white parents, black and Asian parents and black and Latino/Hispanic parents integrate the various tuggings of their identities—identities that have been too often forced into narrow racial options.

Like all American citizens, this Hawaiian, Polynesian, Indonesian, 15 Asian, white, Kenyan and black human being is caught up in the narrative of the black-white paradigm, a structure still rooted in the absurdity of the one-drop-of-black-blood rule. Yes, he is black. But no one can understand him deeply who does not appreciate the rainbow racial mixtures of his Hawaiian origins.

Thinking About the Essay

1. How does Hopkins's title reveal his purpose? What is his claim, and where does he state it?

2. Why does Hopkins begin in a personal mode? Which paragraphs constitute his introduction, and how does he use this introduction to structure the body of the essay?

3. Hopkins is writing for a specialized group of readers? Why would these readers be especially interested in his essay? Would a more general audience be equally absorbed by this article? Why or why not?

4. How successful do you think Hopkins is in explaining the paradox of race in America and how Barack Obama transcends conventional notions of black and white? Justify your assessment by referring to specific passages and motifs in the essay.

5. In part, this essay is about the limitations of racial categorization, but Hopkins is also interested in the causal connections that have perpetuated such classification throughout American history. Where in the essay does Hopkins analyze the reasons why Americans are so preoccupied with race and the effects of this obsession?

Responding in Writing

6. Hopkins argues that the election of Barack Obama to the presidency in 2008 is a watershed in the history of America's history of racial classification. In an argumentative essay, agree or disagree with the writer's claim.

7. In an analytical essay, explore the reasons why you think Americans have been so preoccupied with race. Do you think that today's younger Americans are moving beyond racial classification? Justify your response with compelling reasons.

8. Hopkins claims that Barack Obama is a "Hawaiian President." Explain why you agree or disagree with this notion.

Networking

9. Form two groups and debate the proposition that the election of Barack Obama to the presidency means that Americans have finally transcended the politics of race.

10. Go online and find out more about Barack Obama's life in Hawaii. Then construct your own profile of Obama based on this information.

American Dreamer

BHARATI MUKHERJEE

Bharati Mukherjee was born in Calcutta, India, in 1940. She attended the universities of Calcutta and Baroda, where she received a master's degree in English and ancient English culture. In 1961 she came to the United States to attend the Writer's Workshop at the University of Iowa, receiving a Ph.D. degree in English and comparative literature. Mukherjee became an American citizen in 1988; she is married to the writer Clark Blaise, with whom she has published two books, *Days and Nights in Calcutta* and *The Sorrow of the Terror*. Mukherjee's books of fiction include *The Middleman and Other Stories*, which won the 1988 National Book Critics Circle Award for fiction; *Jasmine* (1989); *The Holder of the World* (1993); and *The Tree Bride* (2004). She is currently professor of English at the University of California at Berkeley. In the following essay, which was published in 1993 in *Mother Jones*, Mukherjee displays both narrative power and keen analytical strength in rejecting any hyphenated status as an American.

Before Reading

Mukherjee, writing in 1993, hyphenates such words as African-American and Asian-American. As a matter of style, why don't we use hyphenated race compounds today? Why do these terms even exist?

The United States exists as a sovereign nation. "America," in contrast, exists as a myth of democracy and equal opportunity to live by, or as an ideal goal to reach.   1

I am a naturalized U.S. citizen, which means that, unlike native-born citizens, I had to prove to the U.S. government that I merited citizenship. What I didn't have to disclose was that I desired "America," which to me is the stage for the drama of self-transformation.   2

I was born in Calcutta and first came to the United States—to Iowa City, to be precise—on a summer evening in 1961. I flew into a small airport surrounded by cornfields and pastures, ready to carry out the two commands my father had written out for me the night before I left Calcutta: Spend two years studying creative writing at the Iowa Writers' Workshop, then come back home and marry the bridegroom he selected for me from our caste and class.   3

In traditional Hindu families like ours, men provided and women were provided for. My father was a patriarch and I a pliant daughter. The neighborhood I'd grown up in was homogeneously Hindu, Bengali-speaking, and middle-class. I didn't expect myself to ever disobey or disappoint my father by setting my own goals and taking charge of my future.   4

When I landed in Iowa 35 years ago, I found myself in a society in which almost everyone was Christian, white, and moderately well-off. In the women's dormitory I lived in my first year, apart from six international graduate students (all of us were from Asia and considered "exotic"), the only non-Christian was Jewish, and the only nonwhite an African-American from Georgia. I didn't anticipate then, that over the next 35 years, the Iowa population would become so diverse that it would have 6,931 children from non-English-speaking homes registered as students in its schools, nor that Iowans would be in the grip of a cultural crisis in which resentment against immigrants, particularly refugees from Vietnam, Sudan, and Bosnia, as well as unskilled Spanish-speaking workers, would become politicized enough to cause the Immigration and Naturalization Service to open an "enforcement" office in Cedar Rapids in October for the tracking and deporting of undocumented aliens.   5

In Calcutta in the '50s, I heard no talk of "identity crisis"—communal 6 or individual. The concept itself—of a person not knowing who he or she is—was unimaginable in our hierarchical, classification-obsessed society. One's identity was fixed, derived from religion, caste, patrimony, and mother tongue. A Hindu Indian's last name announced his or her forefathers' caste and place of origin. A Mukherjee could *only* be a Brahmin from Bengal. Hindu tradition forbade intercaste, interlanguage, interethnic marriages. Bengali tradition even discouraged emigration: To remove oneself from Bengal was to dilute true culture.

Until the age of 8, I lived in a house crowded with 40 or 50 relatives. 7 My identity was viscerally connected with ancestral soil and genealogy. I was who I was because I was Dr. Sudhir Lal Mukherjee's daughter, because I was a Hindu Brahmin, because I was Bengali-speaking, and because my *desh* —the Bengali word for homeland—was an East Bengal village called Faridpur.

The University of Iowa classroom was my first experience of coeduca- 8 tion. And after not too long, I fell in love with a fellow student named Clark Blaise, an American of Canadian origin, and impulsively married him during a lunch break in a lawyer's office above a coffee shop.

That act cut me off forever from the rules and ways of upper-middle-class 9 life in Bengal, and hurled me into a New World life of scary improvisations and heady explorations. Until my lunch-break wedding, I had seen myself as an Indian foreign student who intended to return to India to live. The five-minute ceremony in the lawyer's office suddenly changed me into a transient with conflicting loyalties to two very different cultures.

The first 10 years into marriage, years spent mostly in my husband's 10 native Canada, I thought of myself as an expatriate Bengali permanently stranded in North America because of destiny or desire. My first novel, *The Tiger's Daughter*, embodies the loneliness I felt but could not acknowledge, even to myself, as I negotiated the no man's land between the country of my past and the continent of my present. Shaped by memory, textured with nostalgia for class and culture I had abandoned, this novel quite naturally became an expression of the expatriate consciousness.

It took me a decade of painful introspection to put nostalgia in per- 11 spective and to make the transition from expatriate to immigrant. After a 14-year stay in Canada, I forced my husband and our two sons to relocate to the United States. But the transition from foreign student to U.S. citizen, from detached onlooker to committed immigrant, has not been easy.

The years in Canada were particularly harsh. Canada is a country that 12 officially, and proudly, resists cultural fusion. For all its rhetoric about a cultural "mosaic," Canada refuses to renovate its national self-image to include its changing complexion. It is a New World country with Old World concepts of a fixed, exclusivist national identity. Canadian official rhetoric designated me as one of the "visible minority" who, even though I spoke the Canadian languages of English and French, was straining "the absorptive capacity" of Canada. Canadians of color were routinely treated as "not real" Canadians. One example: In 1985 a terrorist bomb, planted in an Air-India jet on Canadian soil, blew up after leaving Montreal, killing 329 passengers, most of whom were Canadians of Indian origin. The prime minister of Canada at the time, Brian Mulroney, phoned the prime minister of India to offer Canada's condolences for India's loss.

Those years of race-related harassments in Canada politicized me 13 and deepened my love of the ideals embedded in the American Bill of Rights. I don't forget that the architects of the Constitution and the Bill of Rights were white males and slaveholders. But through their declaration, they provided us with the enthusiasm for human rights, and the initial framework from which other empowerments could be conceived and enfranchised communities expanded.

I am a naturalized U.S. citizen and I take my American citizenship very 14 seriously. I am not an economic refugee, nor am I a seeker of political asylum. I am a voluntary immigrant. I became a citizen by choice, not by simple accident of birth.

Yet these days, questions such as who is an American and what is 15 American culture are being posed with belligerence, and being answered with violence. Scapegoating of immigrants has once again become the politicians' easy remedy for all that ails the nation. Hate speeches fill audi-toriums for demagogues willing to profit from stirring up racial animosity. An April Gallup poll indicated that half of Americans would like to bar almost all legal immigration for the next five years.

The United States, like every sovereign nation, has a right to formulate 16 its immigration policies. But in this decade of continual, large-scale diaspo-ras, it is imperative that we come to some agreement about who "we" are, and what our goals are for the nation, now that our community includes people of many races, ethnicities, languages, and religions.

The debate about American culture and American identity has to date 17 been monopolized largely by Eurocentrists and ethnocentrists whose rhetoric has been flamboyantly divisive, pitting a phantom "us" against a demonized "them." All countries view themselves by their ideals. Indians idealize the cul-tural continuum, the inherent value system of India, and are properly incensed when foreigners see nothing but poverty, intolerance, strife, and injustice.

Americans see themselves as the embodiments of liberty, openness, and 18 individualism, even as the world judges them for drugs, crime, violence, bigotry, militarism, and homelessness. I was in Singapore in 1994 when the American teenager Michael Fay was sentenced to caning for having spray-painted some cars. While I saw Fay's actions as those of an individual, and his sentence as too harsh, the overwhelming local sentiment was that vandalism was an "American" crime, and that flogging Fay would deter Singapore youths from becoming "Americanized." Conversely, in 1994, in Tavares, Florida, the Lake County School Board announced its policy (since overturned) requiring middle school teachers to instruct their students that American culture, by which the board meant European-American culture, is inherently "superior to other foreign or historic cultures." The policy's misguided implication was that culture in the United States has not been affected by the American Indian, African-American, Latin-American, and Asian-American segments of the population. The sinister implication was that our national identity is so fragile that it can absorb diverse and immigrant cultures only by recontextualizing them as deficient.

Our nation is unique in human history in that the founding idea of   19
"America" was in opposition to the tenet that a nation is a collection of like-looking, like-speaking, like-worshipping people. The primary criterion for nationhood in Europe is homogeneity of culture, race, and religion—which has contributed to blood-soaked balkanization in the former Yugoslavia and the former Soviet Union.

America's pioneering European ancestors gave up the easy homogeneity   20
of their native countries for a new version of Utopia. Now, in the 1990s, we have the exciting chance to follow that tradition and assist in the making of a new American culture that differs from both the enforced assimilation of a "melting pot" and the Canadian model of a multicultural "mosaic."

The multicultural mosaic implies a contiguity of fixed, self-sufficient,   21
utterly distinct cultures. Multiculturalism, as it has been practiced in the United States in the past 10 years, implies the existence of a central culture, ringed by peripheral cultures. The fallout of official multiculturalism is the establishment of one culture as the norm and the rest as aberrations. At the same time, the multiculturalist emphasis on race- and ethnicity-based group identity leads to a lack of respect for individual differences within each group, and to vilification of those individuals who place the good of the nation above the interests of their particular racial or ethnic communities.

We must be alert to the dangers of an "us" vs. "them" mentality. In   22
California, this mentality is manifesting itself as increased violence between minority, ethnic communities. The attack on Korean-American merchants in South Central Los Angeles in the wake of the Rodney King beating trial is only one recent example of the tragic side effects of this mentality. On the national level, the politicization of ethnic identities has encouraged the

scapegoating of legal immigrants, who are blamed for economic and social problems brought about by flawed domestic and foreign policies.

We need to discourage the retention of cultural memory if the aim of   23
that retention is cultural balkanization. We must think of American culture and nationhood as a constantly reforming, transmogrifying "we."

In this age of diasporas, one's biological identity may not be one's   24
only identity. Erosions and accretions come with the act of emigration. The experience of cutting myself off from a biological homeland and settling in an adopted homeland that is not always welcoming to its dark-complexioned citizens has tested me as a person, and made me the writer I am today.

I choose to describe myself on my own terms as an American, rather   25
than as an Asian-American. Why is it that hyphenation is imposed only on non-white Americans? Rejecting hyphenation is my refusal to categorize the cultural landscape into a center and its peripheries; it is to demand that the American nation deliver the promises of its dream and its Constitution to all its citizens equally.

My rejection of hyphenation has been misrepresented as race treach-   26
ery by some India-born academics on U.S. campuses who have appointed themselves guardians of the "purity" of ethnic cultures. Many of them, though they reside permanently in the United States and participate in its economy, consistently denounce American ideals and institutions. They direct their rage at me because, by becoming a U.S. citizen and exercising my voting rights, I have invested in the present and not the past; because I have committed myself to help shape the future of my adopted homeland; and because I celebrate racial and cultural mongrelization.

What excites me is that as a nation we have not only the chance to   27
retain those values we treasure from our original cultures but also the chance to acknowledge that the outer forms of those values are likely to change. Among Indian immigrants, I see a great deal of guilt about the inability to hang on to what they commonly term "pure culture." Parents express rage or despair at their U.S.-born children's forgetting of, or indif-ference to, some aspects of Indian culture. Of those parents I would ask: What is it we have lost if our children are acculturating into the culture in which we are living? Is it so terrible that our children are discovering or are inventing homelands for themselves?

Some first-generation Indo-Americans, embittered by racism and by   28
unofficial "glass ceilings," construct a phantom identity, more-Indian-than-Indians-in-India, as a defense against marginalization. I ask: Why don't you get actively involved in fighting discrimination? Make your voice heard. Choose the forum most appropriate for you. If you are a citizen, let your

vote count. Reinvest your energy and resources into revitalizing your city's disadvantaged residents and neighborhoods. Know your constitutional rights, and when they are violated, use the agencies of redress the Constitution makes available to you. Expect change, and when it comes, deal with it!

As a writer, my literary agenda begins by acknowledging that America 29 has transformed me. It does not end until I show that I (along with the hundreds of thousands of immigrants like me) am minute-by-minute transforming America. The transformation is a two-way process: It affects both the individual and the national-cultural identity.

Others who write stories of migration often talk of arrival at a new 30 place as a loss, the loss of communal memory and the erosion of an original culture. I want to talk of arrival as a gain.

Thinking About the Essay

1. What is the significance of the title? How is Mukherjee a dreamer? Why does the idea of America inspire dreams? What impact does the American Dream have on one's identity? For example, Mukherjee says in paragraph 7 that she had a clear sense of identity when she was in India. How has this sense of identity changed now that she is an American?

2. What is Mukherjee's purpose in writing this essay? Does she want to tell a story, analyze an issue, argue a position? Remember that this article appeared in *Mother Jones*, a progressive or left-of-center magazine. What does her primary audience tell you about her intentions?

3. Why does Mukherjee divide her essay into four parts? What are the relationships among these sections? Why has she used this pattern of organization? Where does she employ comparison and contrast and definition to achieve coherence among these parts?

4. Mukherjee refers to Eurocentrics and ethnocentrics. What do these terms mean to you? Discuss your understanding of these terms with other members of the class.

Responding in Writing

5. Write a summary of Mukherjee's essay, capturing as many of her major ideas as possible in no more than 300 words.

6. Write your own essay titled "American Dreamer," referring specifically to the dreams that immigrants—perhaps even you or members of your family—have had about coming to this country.

7. Mukherjee asserts, "We must be alert to the dangers of an 'us' vs. 'them' mentality (paragraph 23)." Write an argumentative essay responding to this statement, referring to other assertions by Mukherjee to amplify your own position.

Networking

8. In small groups, develop a summary of Mukherjee's essay. Next, compose a list of outstanding questions you still might have about her essay. For example, has she overlooked or diminished the importance of a specific topic, or has she personalized the subject too much? Finally, collaborate on a letter to the author in which you lay out your concerns.

9. Download from a search engine all the information that you can find about Bharati Mukherjee. Then compose a brief analytical profile of the author in which you highlight her career and the impact that living in several cultures has had on her work. Use "American Dreamer" as a foundation for this presentation, and be certain to provide citations for your web research. (For information on citing online sources, see Appendix A: Conducting Research in the New Global Era.)

The Cult of Ethnicity

ARTHUR M. SCHLESINGER JR.

Arthur Meine Schlesinger Jr. was born in Columbus, Ohio, in 1917. Graduating from Harvard University in 1938, he embarked on a multifaceted career as historian, popular writer, university professor, political activist, and advisor to presidents. Among other positions he has held, he served as President Kennedy's special assistant for Latin American affairs. Schlesinger published dozens of books, most notably *The Age of Jackson*, which received the 1946 Pulitzer Prize for history, and *A Thousand Days*, which won the Pulitzer for biography in 1966. Although he never received an advanced degree, Schlesinger was awarded numerous honorary doctorates and for years was distinguished professor at the Graduate Center of the City University of New York. He died in 2007. In the essay that follows, which was published in *Time* magazine in 1991, Schlesinger offers a critique of multiculturalism and an endorsement of those values and attitudes that frame our commonality.

Before Reading

Do you support various ethnic studies programs and departments on your campus? Would you major in such a discipline? Why or why not?

The history of the world has been in great part the history of the mixing   1
of peoples. Modern communication and transport accelerate mass
migrations from one continent to another. Ethnic and racial diversity is
more than ever a salient fact of the age.

But what happens when people of different origins, speaking dif-   2
ferent languages and professing different religions, inhabit the same
locality and live under the same political sovereignty? Ethnic and racial
conflict—far more than ideological conflict—is the explosive problem
of our times.

On every side today ethnicity is breaking up nations. The Soviet Union,   3
India, Yugoslavia, Ethiopia, are all in crisis. Ethnic tensions disturb and
divide Sri Lanka, Burma, Indonesia, Iraq, Cyprus, Nigeria, Angola, Lebanon,
Guyana, Trinidad—you name it. Even nations as stable and civilized as
Britain and France, Belgium and Spain, face growing ethnic troubles. Is
there any large multiethnic state that can be made to work?

The answer to that question has been, until recently, the United States.   4
"No other nation," Margaret Thatcher has said, "has so successfully
combined people of different races and nations within a single culture."
How have Americans succeeded in pulling off this almost unprecedented
trick?

We have always been a multiethnic country. Hector St. John de   5
Crevecoeur, who came from France in the 18th century, marveled at the
astonishing diversity of the settlers—"a mixture of English, Scotch, Irish,
French, Dutch, Germans and Swedes ... this promiscuous breed." He
propounded a famous question: "What then is the American, this new
man?" And he gave a famous answer: "Here individuals of all nations are
melted into a new race of men." *E pluribus unum.*

The U.S. escaped the divisiveness of a multiethnic society by a brilliant   6
solution: the creation of a brand-new national identity. The point of
America was not to preserve old cultures but to forge a new, American
culture. "By an intermixture with our people," President George Washington
told Vice President John Adams, immigrants will "get assimilated to our
customs, measures and laws: in a word, soon become one people." This
was the ideal that a century later Israel Zangwill crystallized in the title
of his popular 1908 play, *The Melting Pot*. And no institution was more
potent in molding Crevecoeur's "promiscuous breed" into Washington's
"one people" than the American public school.

The new American nationality was inescapably English in language,   7
ideas and institutions. The pot did not melt everybody, not even all the white
immigrants; deeply bred racism put black Americans, yellow Americans,
red Americans and brown Americans well outside the pale. Still, the infusion

of other stocks, even of nonwhite stocks, and the experience of the New World reconfigured the British legacy and made the U.S., as we all know, a very different country from Britain.

In the 20th century, new immigration laws altered the composition of the American people, and a cult of ethnicity erupted both among non-Anglo whites and among nonwhite minorities. This had many healthy consequences. The American culture at last began to give shamefully overdue recognition to the achievements of groups subordinated and spurned during the high noon of Anglo dominance, and it began to acknowledge the great swirling world beyond Europe. Americans acquired a more complex and invigorating sense of their world—and of themselves.   8

But, pressed too far, the cult of ethnicity has unhealthy consequences. It gives rise, for example, to the conception of the U.S. as a nation composed not of individuals making their own choices but of inviolable ethnic and racial groups. It rejects the historic American goals of assimilation and integration.   9

And, in an excess of zeal, well-intentioned people seek to transform our system of education from a means of creating "one people" into a means of promoting, celebrating and perpetuating separate ethnic origins and identities. The balance is shifting from *unum* to *pluribus*.   10

That is the issue that lies behind the hullabaloo over "multiculturalism" and "political correctness," the attack on the "Eurocentric" curriculum and the rise of the notion that history and literature should be taught not as disciplines but as therapies whose function is to raise minority self-esteem. Group separatism crystallizes the differences, magnifies tensions, intensifies hostilities. Europe—the unique source of the liberating ideas of democracy, civil liberties and human rights—is portrayed as the root of all evil, and non-European cultures, their own many crimes deleted, are presented as the means of redemption.   11

I don't want to sound apocalyptic about these developments. Education is always in ferment, and a good thing too. The situation in our universities, I am confident, will soon right itself. But the impact of separatist pressures on our public schools is more troubling. If a Kleagle of the Ku Klux Klan wanted to use the schools to disable and handicap black Americans, he could hardly come up with anything more effective than the "Afrocentric" curriculum. And if separatist tendencies go unchecked, the result can only be the fragmentation, resegregation and tribalization of American life.   12

I remain optimistic. My impression is that the historic forces driving toward "one people" have not lost their power. The eruption of ethnicity   13 is, I believe, a rather superficial enthusiasm stirred by romantic ideologues on the one hand and by unscrupulous con men on the other: self-appointed spokesmen whose claim to represent their minority groups is carelessly accepted by the media. Most American-born members of minority groups, white or nonwhite, see themselves primarily as Americans rather than primarily as members of one or another ethnic group. A notable indicator today is the rate of intermarriage across ethnic lines, across religious lines, even (increasingly) across racial lines. "We Americans," said Theodore Roosevelt, "are children of the crucible."

The growing diversity of the American population makes the quest 14 for unifying ideals and a common culture all the more urgent. In a world savagely rent by ethnic and racial antagonisms, the U.S. must continue as an example of how a highly differentiated society holds itself together.

Thinking About the Essay

1. Why does the writer employ the word *cult* in the title? What connotations does this word have? How does it affect the tone of the essay?

2. Consider the first two paragraphs of this essay, which constitute the writer's introduction. What thesis or claim does the writer advance? Why does he present his main idea in two brief paragraphs instead of one?

3. Summarize Schlesinger's argument. How does he state the problem and then proceed to offer a solution?

4. Note the many references to historical figures that the writer presents. Why has he employed this technique?

5. Examine paragraph 11, which consists of two very long sentences and one shorter one. How does the writer achieve coherence? Why does he place certain words within quotation marks? What assumptions does he make about his audience in presenting relatively complex sentence structures?

Responding in Writing

6. Schlesinger writes, "The balance is shifting from *unum* to *pluribus*" (paragraph 10). Write an essay in which you agree or disagree with this statement, offering your own reasons and support for the position you take.

7. Write an essay with the title "The Cult of _____." You might want to select sports, celebrity, thinness, or any other subject that appeals to you.

8. Do you think that our commonality as Americans and citizens of the world outweighs our uniqueness? How can the two be reconciled? Write an essay that explores this issue.

Networking

9. In small groups talk about whether Schlesinger's portrait of America rings true, whether it describes you and your classmates as college students. What would you add to the writer's remarks? What, if anything, do you consider misleading or exaggerated? On the basis of your collective views, write notes for a letter to Schlesinger about his essay.

10. Using any search engine, download information on multiculturalism. Use the material you have assembled to write an essay in which you offer your own extended definition of this term. Be certain to cite at least three sources that you have discovered. (For information on citing online sources, see Appendix A.)

Our Wall

CHARLES BOWDEN

Charles Bowden is a reporter, journalist, autobiographer, and editor whose writing focuses on environmental, cultural, and political issues. Born in 1945 and a longtime resident of Arizona, Bowden writes typically of the American Southwest—its landscape, peoples, and mixed cultures. Among his works are *Killing the Hidden Waters* (1977), *Blue Desert* (1986), *The Sonoran Desert* (1992), and *Down by the River: Drugs, Money, Murder, and Family* (2002). Bowden is also a frequent contributor to major American magazines. In this article from the May 2007 issue of *National Geographic*, Bowden offers an incisive account of the conflicts provoked by the expanding wall along the U.S–Mexican border.

Before Reading

The U.S.–Mexico border is almost 2,000 miles long. Can fences and walls prevent the passage of peoples back and forth across this border? Should they? Justify your response.

In the spring of 1929, a man named Patrick Murphy left a bar in Bisbee, Arizona, to bomb the Mexican border town of Naco, a bunny hop of about ten miles. He stuffed dynamite, scrap iron, nails, and bolts into suitcases and dropped the weapons off the side of his crop duster as part of a deal with Mexican rebels battling for control of Naco, Sonora. When his flight ended, it turned out he'd hit the wrong Naco, managing to destroy   1 property mainly on the U.S. side, including a garage and a local mining company. Some say he was drunk, some say he was sober, but everyone agrees he was one of the first people to bomb the United States from the air.

Borders everywhere attract violence, violence prompts fences, and eventually fences can mutate into walls. Then everyone pays attention because a wall turns a legal distinction into a visual slap in the face. We seem to love walls, but are embarrassed by them because they say something unpleasant about the neighbors—and us. They flow from two sources: fear and a desire for control. Just as our houses have doors and locks, so do borders call forth garrisons, customs officials, and, now and then, big walls. They give us divided feelings because we do not like to admit we need them.   2

Now as the United States debates, fortifying its border with Mexico, walls have a new vogue. At various spots along the dusty, 1,952-mile boundary, fences, walls, and vehicle barriers have been constructed since the 1990s to slow the surge in illegal immigration. In San Diego, nine miles of a double-layered fence have been erected. In Arizona, the state most overrun with illegal crossings, 65 miles of barriers have been constructed already. Depending on the direction of the ongoing immigration debate, there may soon be hundreds more miles of walls.   3

The 800 or so residents of Naco, Arizona, where Patrick Murphy is part of local lore, have been living in the shadow of a 14-foot-high steel   4

© Diane Cook and Len Jenshel

United States–Mexico border wall.

wall for the past decade, National Guard units are helping to extend the 4.6-mile barrier 25 miles deeper into the desert. The Border Patrol station is the biggest building in the tiny town; the copper roof glistens under the blistering sun. In 2005, a pioneering bit of guerilla theater took place here when the Minutemen, a citizen group devoted to securing the border, staked out 20 miles of the line and patrolled it. Today about 8,000 people live in Naco, Sonora, on the Mexican side of the metal wall that slashes the two communities.

Only a dirt parking lot separates the Gay 90s bar from the Naco wall.   5
Inside, the patrons are largely bilingual and have family ties on both sides of the line. Janet Warner, one of the bartenders, has lived here for years and is one of those fortunate souls who has found her place in the sun. But thanks to the racks of stadium lights along the wall, she has lost her nights, and laments the erasure of the brilliant stars that once hung over her life. She notes that sometimes Mexicans jump the new steel wall, come in for a beer, then jump back into Mexico. The bar began in the late 1920s as a casino and with the end of Prohibition added alcohol. The gambling continued until 1961, when a new county sheriff decided to clean up things. On the back wall are photographs of Ronald and Nancy Reagan when they'd stop by on their way to a nearby Mexican ranch.

The bar is one of only a handful of businesses left. The commercial   6
street leading to the border is lined with defunct establishments, all dead because the U.S government sealed the entry to Mexico after 9/11 and rerouted it to the east. Leonel Urcadez, 54, a handsome man who has owned the bar for decades, has mixed feelings about the wall. "You get used to it" he says. "When they first built it, it was not a bad idea—cars were crossing illegally from Mexico and the Border Patrol would chase them. But it's so ugly."

The two Nacos came into being in 1897 around a border crossing   7
that connected copper mines in both nations. By 1901 a railroad linked the mines. A big miners' strike in 1906, one cherished by Mexicans as foreshadowing the revolution in 1910, saw troops from both nations facing each other down at the line. The town of Naco on the Mexican side changed hands many times during the actual revolution—at first the prize was revenue from the customs house. Later, when Arizona voted itself dry in 1915, the income came from the saloons. Almost every old house in Naco, Arizona, has holes from the gun battles. The Naco Hotel, with its three-foot mud walls, advertised its bulletproof rooms.

The boundary between Mexico and the United States has always been   8
zealously insisted upon by both countries. But initially Mexicans moved north at will. The U.S. patrols of the border that began in 1904 were

mainly to keep out illegal Asian immigrants. Almost 900,000 Mexicans legally entered the United States to free the violence of the revolution. Low population in both nations and the need for labor in the American Southwest made this migration a non-event for decades. The flow of illegal immigrants exploded after the passage of the North American Free Trade Agreement in the early 1990s, a pact that was supposed to end illegal immigration but wound up dislocating millions of Mexican peasant farmers and may small industrial workers.

The result: Naco was overrun by immigrants on their way north. At night, 9
dozens, sometimes hundreds, of immigrants would crowd into motel rooms and storage rental sheds along the highway. The local desert was stomped into a powder of dust. Naco residents found their homes broken into by desperate migrants. Then came the wall in 1996, and the flow of people spread into the high desert outside the town.

The Border Patrol credits the wall, along with better surveillance 10
technology, with cutting the number of illegal immigrants captured near Naco's 33-mile border by half in the past year. Before this new heightening of enforcement, the number caught each week, hiding in arroyos thick with mesquite and yucca, often exceeded the town's population. At the moment, the area is relatively quiet as "coyotes," or people smugglers, pause to feel out the new reality, and the National Guard has been sent in to assist the Border Patrol. At the nearby abandoned U.S. Army camp, the roofs are collapsing and the adobe bricks dribble mud onto the floor. Scattered about are Mexican water bottles—illegals still hole up here after climbing the wall.

Residents register a hodgepodge of feelings about the wall. Even those 11
who have let passing illegal immigrants use their phones or given them a ride say the exodus has to stop. And even those sick of finding trash in their yards understand why the immigrants keep coming.

"Sometimes I feel sorry for the Mexicans," says Bryan Tomlinson, 45, 12
a custodial engineer for the Bisbee school district. His brother Don chimes in, "But the wall's a good thing."

A border wall seems to violate a deep sense of identity most Americans 13
cherish. We see ourselves as a nation if immigrants with our own goddess, the Statue of Liberty, a symbol so potent that dissident Chinese students fabricated a version of it in 1989 in Tiananmen Square as the visual representation of their yearning for freedom.

Walls are curious statements of human needs. Sometimes they are built 14
to keep restive populations from fleeing. The Berlin Wall was designed to keep citizens from escaping from communist East Germany. But most walls are for keeping people out. They all work for a while, until human

appetites or sheer numbers overwhelm them. The Great Wall of China, built mostly after the mid-14th century, kept northern tribes at bay until the Manchu conquered China in the 17th century. Hadrian's Wall, standing about 15 feet high, 9 feet wide, and 73 miles long, kept the crazed tribes of what is now Scotland from running amok in Roman Britain—from A.D. 122 until it was overrun in 367. Then you have the Maginot Line, a series of connected forts built by France after World War I to keep the German army from invading. It was a success, except for one flaw: The troops of the Third Reich simply went around its northwestern end and invaded France through the Netherlands and Belgium. Now tourists visit its labyrinth of tunnels and underground barracks.

In 1859 a rancher named Thomas Austin released 24 rabbits in   15 Australia because, he noted, "the introduction of a few rabbits could do little harm and might provide a touch of home, in addition to a spot of hunting." By that simple act, he launched one of the most extensive barriers ever erected by human beings: the rabbit fences of Australia, which eventually reached 2,023 miles. Within 35 years, the rabbits had overrun the continent, a place lacking sufficient and dedicated rabbit predators. For a century and a half, the Australian government has tried various solutions: imported fleas, poisons, trappers. Nothing has denied the new immigrants. The fences themselves failed almost instantly—rabbits expanded faster than barriers could be built, careless people left gates open, holes appeared, and, of course, the rabbits simply dug under them.

In Naco all the walls of the world are present in one compact bundle.   16 You have Hadrian's Wall or the Great Wall of China because the barrier is intended to keep people out. You have the Maginot Line because a 15-minute walk takes you to the end of the existing steel wall. You have the rabbit fences of Australia because people still come north illegally, as do the drugs.

Perhaps the closest thing to the wall going up on the U.S.–Mexico   17 border is the separation wall being built by Israel in the West Bank. Like the new American wall, it is designed to control the movement of people, but it faces the problem of all walls—rockets can go over it, tunnels can go under it. It offends people, it comforts people, it fails to deliver security. And it keeps expanding.

Rodolfo Santos Esquer puts out *El Mirador*, a weekly newspaper in   18 Naco, Sonora, and he finds the wall hateful. He stands in his cramped office—a space he shares with a small shop peddling underwear—and says, "It looks like the Berlin Wall. It is horrible. It is ugly. You feel more racism now. It is a racist wall. If people get close to the wall, the Border Patrol calls the Mexican police, and they go and question people."

And then he lightens up because he is a sunny man, and he says it actually 19
hasn't changed his life or the lives of most people in town. Except that the
coyotes now drive to the end of the wall before crossing. And as the wall
grows in length, the coyotes raise their rates. Santos figures half the town
is living off migrants going north—either feeding them and housing them
or guiding them into the U.S. Passage to Phoenix, about 200 miles away,
is now $1,500 and rising. He notes that after the wall went up in 1996,
the migration mushroomed. He wonders if there is a connection, if the
wall magically beckons migrants. Besides, he says, people just climb over
it with ropes.

Santos fires up his computer and shows an image he snapped in the 20
cemetery of a nearby town. There, there, he points as he enlarges a section
of the photo. Slowly a skull-shaped blur floats into view against the black
of the night—a ghost, he believes. The border is haunted by ghosts—the
hundreds who die each year from heat and cold, the ones killed in car wrecks
as the packed vans of migrants flee the Border Patrol, and the increasing
violence erupting between smugglers and the agents of Homeland Security.
Whenever heat is applied to one part of the border, the migration simply
moves to another part. The walls in southern California drove immigrants
into the Arizona desert and, in some cases, to their deaths. We think of
walls as statements of foreign policy, and we forget the intricate lives of the
people we wall in and out.

Emanuel Castillo Erunez, 23, takes crime and car wreck photos for *El* 21
Mirador. He went north illegally when he was 17, walked a few days, then
was picked up and returned to Mexico. He sits on a bench in the plaza,
shielded by a New York Yankees cap, and sums up the local feeling about
the wall simply: "Some are fine with it, some are not." He thinks of going
north again, but then he thinks of getting caught again. And so he waits.

There is a small-town languor about Naco, Sonora, and the wall 22
becomes unnoticeable in this calm. The Minutemen and National Guard
terrify people. At the Hospedaje Santa Maria, four people wait for a chance
to go over the wall and illegally enter the wealth of the United States. It is a
run-down, two-story building, one of many boarding houses for migrants
in Naco. Salvador Rivera, a solid man in his early 30s, has been here about
a year. He worked in Washington State, but, when his mother fell ill, he
returned home to Nayarit, Mexico, and is now having trouble getting past
the increased security. He left behind an American girlfriend he can no
longer reach.

"For so many years, we Mexicans have gone to the U.S. to work. I don't 23
understand why they put up a wall to turn us away. It's not like we're
robbing anybody over there, and they don't pay us very much."

United States–Mexico border wall.

But talk of the wall almost has to be prompted. Except for those engaged   24
in smuggling drugs or people, border crossers in Naco, Sonora, continue
to enter through the main gate, as they always have. They visit relatives on
the other side, as they always have. What has changed is this physical statement, a big wall lined with bright lights that says, yes, we are two nations.

Jesus Gastelum Ramirez lives next door to the wall, makes neon signs,   25
and looks like Willie Nelson. He watches people climb the wall and he
understands a reality forgotten by most U.S. lawmakers—that simply to
go through the wire instantly raises a person's income tenfold. Gastelum
knows many of his neighbors smuggle people, and he understands.

Until recently, a volleyball team from the Mexican Naco and a team   26
from the U.S. Naco used to meet once a year at the point where the wall
ends on the west side of town, put up a net on the line, bring kegs of beer,
and play a volleyball game. People from both Nacos would stream out to
the site and watch. And then the wall would no longer exist for a spell. But
it always confronts the eye.

Dan Duley, 50, operates heavy equipment and is a native of the Naco area.   27
He was living in Germany after serving in the Air Force when the Berlin Wall
came down, and he thought that was a fine thing. But here he figures something has to be done. "We need help," he says. "We're being invaded. They've
taken away our jobs, our security. I'm just a blue-collar man living in a small
town. And I just wish the government cared about a man who was blue."

Culture or Conflict?
Images of Globalization

This portfolio of images from around the world presents a visual paradox: Is global culture a happy consumer wonderland where the fries are always crisp and the music always loud? Or has globalization simply packaged and marketed a bland, simplified version of the basics of culture, such as food and fashion, to an increasingly busy and distracted global population?

For millennia, trade between nation-states has introduced and shared aspects of culture, but the electronic telecommunication that is available now between countries has enabled instant blending of customs and has caused regional cultures and languages to fight to keep their own traditions vibrant. French-speaking Quebecois agitate for independence from the rest of English-speaking Canada. The ecotourism movement struggles to maintain the integrity of fragile cultures and environments, even as it imports Western tourists with their cash, cameras, and expectations for plumbing. The slow-food movement, which originated in Italy, calls on communities to nurture biodiversity and sustainable agriculture through renewed appreciation of their culinary heritage.

As you examine the following images, be especially attentive to the irony that lies in the details. *Irony* is a quality of being unexpected, incongruous, or out of place, juxtapositions that make something as common as a bottle of soda seem suddenly, entirely strange. That strangeness leads to a realization that there is more to the image than meets the eye; the nomad's tent topped by a satellite dish or the camel carrying an expensive mountain bicycle can be perceived either as a widening of opportunities and experiences or a flattening out of cultural vitality.

Many readings in this book describe the clashing of cultures and civilizations. Can consumer culture, based on these images, foster cooperation rather than clashes? After all, in a 1996 *New York Times* op-ed piece, foreign correspondent Thomas Friedman argued that no two countries that both have a McDonald's have ever fought a war against each other. What do you think?

1

© AP Enric Marti

Coca-Cola in Egypt. An Egyptian girl drinks from a bottle of Coca-Cola in a shop in downtown Cairo, Egypt. After an Internet rumor that the Coca-Cola logo, if looked at upside-down or in a mirror, reads "No Mohammed, No Mecca" in Arabic, a top religious authority in Egypt studied the label and finally declared that "there is no defamation to the religion of Islam from near or far."

Considering the Image

1. Why would Coca-Cola be a target for such a rumor? Can you think of other examples in which consumer goods were boycotted as the symbols of a larger culture, value system, or belief?

2. What, to your eye, is particularly revealing or compelling about this image? What does the photographer want you to see? Does this image support or contradict images that you see in the media about women in the Middle East?

© Joe McNally

Big Bird in Shanghai.   More than 90 percent of the households in the twelve major cities of the People's Republic of China have television sets. One of the favorite programs, reaching 120 million Chinese viewers, is *Sesame Street*. Here, Big Bird, known as *Zhima Jie,* appears on Shanghai television.

Considering the Image

1. How did the photographer capture a specific mood in this picture? What is the expression on the children's faces? Why does Big Bird loom over them? Do you think that there are universal values that make *Sesame Street* popular not just in China but throughout the world? Justify and explain your response.

2. Do you think the photographer wants to make a statement about "cultural imperialism" or the impact of globalization on national cultures, or simply capture a specific moment and scene? Explain your response. Why might globalization, which involves in part the transnational movement of media across cultures, be a force for democracy in China and elsewhere?

© Bob Krist

Ecotourists. Tourists photograph a Huli Wigman, a representative of the Huli people of Papua New Guinea. The Huli are an indigenous people whose subsistence-based way of life has changed little for centuries. They have a particular reverence for birds; the Wigmen (certain men in this intricate clan-based society) wear elaborate headdresses woven of human hair and decorated with flowers and feathers to perform ritual dances that suggest the behavior of local birds.

Considering the Image

1. This photograph was used to illustrate a report on the rights and responsibilities of ecotourists and the groups that sponsor and profit from ecotourism. Why would that group, which advocates for the well-being of indigenous peoples and the preservation of endangered environments, consider this photograph a compelling example of the need for rights to be respected and responsibilities to be upheld?

2. Whose perspective do you assume as you look at this photograph: the native person's, the tourists', or the photographer's taking in the entire scene?

Sophisticated Ladies. Nakshatra Reddy is a biochemist who is married to a prosperous businessman in Mumbai (formerly Bombay). Her daughter, Meghana, dressed in a PVC suit of her own design, is a model and former host on a local music channel.

Considering the Image

1. How does the photographer stage or set up this scene? How does the photographer emphasize certain cultural contrasts between mother and daughter, and what is the purpose? Why is it important for viewers to know that mother and daughter represent a wealthy Indian family rather than a middle-class or poor one?

2. The daughter in this family represents a familiar Western type. How would you describe her? What are her sources of imitation? Do you think that the daughter has succumbed to the lure of Western popular culture, or might she be making a statement about her global identity? Explain your response.

5

Globalization Protest. A man dressed as death partakes in a protest against globalization in Tegucigalpa, Honduras, on Saturday, October 12, 2002. The banner behind him reads, "Out of Respect for the People's Sovereignty, Not for Free Trade Treaties."

Considering the Image

1. What details stand out in this photograph? What is the dominant impression? Does the photographer want to make a statement or simply capture a moment in time? Explain your response.

2. Were you surprised to discover from this photograph that not all nations and regions of the world approve of globalization? Why or why not? Why would Hondurans protest globalization? Conduct research with two other class members to find out more about the impact of globalization on Honduras or another Central American or South American nation.

Modern Conveniences. The *ger* is the traditional, portable home of the nomadic people of Mongolia. A cone-shaped structure of felt stretched over a timber frame, with an opening in the top or a pipe to vent smoke from the stove, the *ger* is a symbol both of freedom and of hospitality. Many residents of Mongolia's capital, Ulaan Baatar, still live in traditional *gers,* and in keeping with their nomadic routes, any visitor is warmly greeted and offered shelter and food, as well as many modern conveniences. Here, a *ger* is outfitted with a satellite dish.

Considering the Image

1. This photo suggests not so much a clash of cultures as a fusion of ancient ways and modern technology. Why might a nomadic culture, like that of rural Mongolia, value the latest in communications technology?

2. Many writers define the so-called electronic gap or digital divide as one of the great challenges—and opportunities—for the twenty-first century. What does this image suggest to you about the digital divide? Granted, we do not know from this photograph if that satellite dish is being used to watch CNN or MTV; should that even matter? Why or why not?

© Angelo Cavalli/The Image Bank/Getty Images

Mixing Cultures.   Sadhu (Hindu ascetic) using a mobile phone. Pashupatinath (Hindu temple), Kathmandu, Nepal, 2005.

Considering the Image

1. What impression do you think this photograph conveys? What sensory images and elements, such as sight and colors, stand out? How do these elements highlight the impact of Western popular culture on traditional Indian culture? How is the photograph composed so as to illustrate the blending (or conflict) of cultures?

2. What point do you think the photographer is attempting to make? Does the photographer advance a thesis or claim about the clash of civilizations, or the viability of old cultural practices in an age of globalization? Justify your response.

But then, as in many conversations on the border, the rhetoric calms 28
down. Duley, along with many other Naco residents, believes the real solution has to be economic, that jobs must be created in Mexico. There is an
iron law on this border: The closer one gets to the line, the more rational the
talk becomes because everyone has personal ties to people on the other side.
Everyone realizes the wall is a police solution to an economic problem. The
Mexicans will go over it, under it, or try to tear holes in it, Or, as is often the
case, enter legally with temporary visiting papers and then melt into American communities. Of the millions of illegal immigrants living in the United
States, few would have come if there wasn't a job waiting for them.

Over in Naco, Sonora, the final night of a fiesta is in full roar. Men 29
drinking beer move by on horseback, groups of girls in high heels prance
past. Nearby, folks play bingo, and in the band shell a group does a sound
check for the big dance. Looming over the whole party is a giant statue of
Father Hidalgo with his bald head and wild eyes. He launched the Mexican Wars of Independence in 1810. Two blocks away, the steel wall glows
under a battery of lights.

In the Gay 90s bar in Naco, Arizona, a quinceanera, the 15th-birthday 30
celebration that introduces a young girl to the world, is firing up. There are
200 people in the saloon's back room, half from Mexico and half from the
U.S. The boys wear rented tuxedo vests, the girls are dressed like goddesses.
One man walks in with a baby in a black polka-dot dress with pink trim.

The birthday girl, Alyssa, stands with her family for an official portrait. 31

Walls come and go, but quinceaneras are forever, I say to the man with 32
the baby. He nods his head and smiles.

The steel barrier is maybe a hundred feet away. Outside in the darkness, 33
Mexicans are moving north, and Border Patrol agents are hunting them down.
Tomorrow, work will continue on the construction of the wall as it slowly
creeps east and west from the town. Tourists already come to look at it.

I have no doubt someday archaeologists will do excavations here and 34
write learned treatises about the Great Wall of the United States. Perhaps
one of them will be the descendant of a Mexican stealing north at this
moment in the midnight hour.

Thinking About the Essay

1. Toward what type of audience does Bowden aim his essay? How does he
   address the expectations of this audience?

2. What is Bowden's thesis (or claim), and where does he state it? Is his
   purpose to inform, argue, persuade, express emotions, or entertain—or
   a combination of some of these? Justify your response by citing specific
   passages and techniques.

3. According to Bowden, what does a wall **symbolize**? Might there be multiple meanings?

4. Cite instances where Bowden uses narration and description. Why does he employ these strategies? What is the effect?

5. Bowden employs many **allusions** to walls in this essay. List some of them. What is his purpose? In this connection, explain your response to Bowden's concluding paragraph.

Responding in Writing

6. Bowden writes in paragraph 2, "Borders everywhere attract violence, violence prompts fences, and eventually fences can mutate into walls." On the other hand, poet Robert Frost observes that good fences make good neighbors. Where do you stand? Write an essay in response to this question.

7. Argue for or against the proposition that erecting fences and walls along the U.S–Mexican border is a threat to American democracy.

8. Compose a position paper in which you offer a list of recommendation designed to solve the problem of undocumented immigrants in the United States.

Networking

9. With the class divided into two groups, debate the proposition that fences and walls need to be expanded along the U.S.–Mexico border.

10. Conduct online research on one of the walls that Bowden mentions in his essay. Use this source material to explain the relevance of your subject to the American experience today. Utilize at least three sources, and be sure to document the information that you borrow.

America and the World: How Do Others Perceive Us?

One of the key elements supporting the idea of America is a belief in freedom, democracy, and human rights—what we often term American exceptionalism. This ideal, as we saw in the previous chapter, has been a motivating impulse in all waves of immigration, especially for the flood of peoples from around the world who have found their way to the United States since 1965, transforming the nation into a global village. But does the rest of the world believe that the United States is truly a "city upon a hill" as President Ronald Reagan (borrowing a phrase from one of the nation's first immigrants, Governor John Winthrop of Massachusetts Bay Colony) declared? Are we truly a beacon of democratic promise for other nations? Do we promote democracy and human rights everywhere? Or are we the "ugly Americans" discussed by Ann Hulbert in the first essay in this chapter? What ideals and values—especially when projected by American foreign policy or even American tourists abroad—do we actually represent?

Today the conflicts inherent in the "war on terror" and "clash of civilizations"—framed by a suspicion of American-style capitalism, democracy, and imperialism—fuel a widespread belief that the world's reigning superpower acts out of self-interest rather than altruism. For many, the United States is not a bastion of democracy but a destructive element—a Great Satan in the minds of some. That we led the wars of the last century against the totalitarian forces of Nazism, fascism, and communism apparently has become a historic footnote. That we provide international aid today to developing Nations and victims of natural disasters, that we share information and technology openly, that we promote democracy at great human and material cost

© Kevin Lee/Newsmakers/Getty Images

Chinese customers buy snacks from a store decorated with ads for an American soft drink company in Beijing, China.

Thinking About the Image

1. What is your response to this image? Is it positive or negative? Explain your response.

2. Identify and analyze the elements in this photograph that contribute to the dominant impression or overall effect. What point of view, if any, does the photographer want to convey?

3. Why is this image divided into three parts? What relationships do you detect among the units? What is the dominant impression?

4. Research the Pepsi Cola Corporation in China and its impact on local culture. Write a summary of your findings.

all seem lost in a maelstrom of anti-Americanism. In a world of predators, the United States appears to many as the most insatiable enemy. Yet with the election of Barack Obama to the presidency in 2008, there is hope that there will be a revival of American exceptionalism around the world.

The truth, of course, is that the image America projects to the world has always been a function of what others have projected onto it. As the world's superpower, the United States faces today the option of not only inspiring ideals of democracy and freedom in the rest of the world but of trying to remake nations and regions—as in the case of Iraq and the broader Middle East—according to those ideals. The problem is that the very *idea* of America is symbolically saturated with conflicting aspirations and associations. The ideals that America would transmit to the world will inevitably clash with rival ideals that have been projected from afar. If, for example, we are guardians of the free world, then what forces are we guarding the world *against*? How can the United States unilaterally pursue debatable policies and still maintain moral authority on the world stage? What ideals, beyond self-interest, would justify intervention in the affairs of other nations? For instance, the current administration promotes secular democracy in the Middle East; but many in the area view American actions as an amoral attempt to control the region, destroy traditional societies, and guarantee access to oil.

Of course, not everyone hates the United States or is cynical about its role in the world. The Islamic Republic of Iran might denounce America as the Great Satan (and England as the Lesser Satan), but Iranians love Americans in particular and the West in general. Again, the truth lies in the beholder and the ways in which we construct national mythologies for ourselves. Some might engage in a frenzy of anti-Americanism and even want to harm the United States for what they perceive America does to the rest of the world; but many others around the world, especially in moments of crisis, are thankful for American food during famine, tents and medical supplies after earthquakes and tsunamis, the promotion of human rights, and even military intervention (as in Bosnia) to prevent genocide. The global village does admire America's political and economic freedoms, along with its wealth, culture, and technology, even as it might be appalled by certain foreign policy doctrines and behavior on the world stage.

The essays in this chapter deal with America's complex relationship with the rest of the world and with the psychological factors behind both current anti-American and pro-American attitudes. The invasion of Iraq in 2003, an attempt to transmit ideals to another part of the world, has changed the image of America in ways that we are only beginning to understand. ("As the savagery of the images coming out of Iraq demonstrate all too well," writes Sasha Abramsky in an essay appearing in this chapter, "we live in a world where image is if not everything, at least crucial.") The famous film footage of the cavalry charge up San Juan Hill that made Theodore Roosevelt's reputation during the Spanish-American War was, as we now know, a staged reenactment filmed after the real charge took place. Today, more than a hundred years after Roosevelt's charge, it is no easy task to alter the perception of America as an aggressive imperialist power; but it is still possible, after the fact, to examine and learn from the images, actions, and mythologies that are at its source.

The I'm-Not-Ugly American

ANN HULBERT

Ann Hulbert is a writer and editor who contributes frequently to such major publications as *New Republic*, *New York Review of Books*, and *New York Times Book Review*. She also has published *The Interior Castle: The Art and Life of Jean Stafford* (1992) and *Raising America: Experts, Parents, and a Century of Advice about Children* (2003). Born in 1956, Hulbert earned a B.A. and M.A. at Harvard University (1977). In this selection from the September 3, 2006, issue of *New York Times Magazine*, Hulbert offers a whimsical personal account of the "the mission of the American as World Tourist."

Before Reading

Refer to the chart included in this selection. What does it tell you about international responses to Americans? Why do you think that the phrase "ugly American" has entered the global conversation? Try to find out where this phrase originated.

Going through passport control on our return from a recent two-week   1
trip to Istanbul and the Turkish coast, my family and I faced the routine question, "And what was the purpose of your travels?" Asked at the start, I might well have answered "personal diplomacy" instead of "vacation." In an era plagued by anti-Americanism—and by terrorism alerts and battles in the Middle East, not to mention bird flu—summer travel abroad, especially to a Muslim country, has acquired an aura of more than mere tourism. Sun and fun were in store, of course, yet as we packed, we weren't feeling like carefree sightseers exactly.

Anxious cultural emissaries was more like it, and high on our list of   2
goals—along with seeing the Hagia Sophia—was not being mistaken for ugly Americans. I went so far as to veto one of my teenage son's T-shirt choices, an item from his array of Quaker-school stuff, of all things. The text printed on it wasn't very likely to offend (or, for that matter, be understood). "The Fighting Quakers" it said, followed by the joke, "Beat them 'til they reach consensus." What worried me was the accompanying caricature of a Ben Franklin look-alike, with his teeth bared and his dukes up. The pilgrim as pugilist: we didn't need to be walking billboard for belligerence.

Manners of the Republic

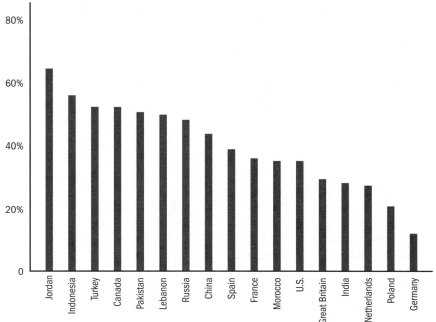

Percent of respondents who think Americans are rude.
Source: Spring 2005 Survey, Pew Global Attitudes Project, a project of the Pew Research Center.
Reprinted by permission.

I was, I have since discovered, proceeding in just the hypersensitive fash- 3
ion recommended to U.S. travelers by the "World Citizens Guide," a pamphlet published by a nonprofit organization called Business for Diplomatic
Action, founded two years ago to help burnish America's image abroad.
B.D.A.'s president, a renowned advertising executive named Keith Reinhard
(the wizard behind the McDonald's account, with its award-winning "You
deserve a break today" jingle), decided that the beleaguered national brand
couldn't be rescued by the likes of the State Department's Karen Hughes
alone. Public diplomacy needed a boost from the private sector.

Give America a break today is the B.D.A. booklet's basic message to citi- 4
zens and businesses: don't behave with the rude arrogance that has become
the national trademark. Be humble and patient and steer clear of politics.
Strive for sartorial modesty and cultural awareness—read a book (I chose
Orhan Pamuk) and learn a phrase (my husband inspired awe by discovering
the unusual Turkish word for an especially delicious variety of watercress
and then ordering it wherever we went). Adopt dulcet tones and always be
ready to listen, not lecture, and to flash a smile. "It's a universal equalizer."

The advice is all very practical. But it's also a little pat and, as that   5
salute to smiles as a social leveler suggests, naively patronizing in a way
that's worth examining. Critics of public diplomacy have been quick to
disparage the American belief that international tensions can be eased by
dispatching an official to proclaim that deep down we are all united by
our love for, say, children—a Hughes staple—when the animus, in fact,
arises from real policy differences with the U.S. government. The pursuit
of private diplomacy rests on the opposite innocent illusion: just tone down
crass Americans' noisy cultural differences from others, and political and
economic harmony can follow. But what if Americans have no monopoly
on brashness and don't really rate any longer as the overweening, cultural
trendsetters our demonizers, and we, reflexively assume.

In essence, the mission of the American as World Citizen is to try and   6
fit in better, or at any rate to stick out less: just what the U.S. as a nation
is resented for making no attempt to do. But it's hard to know which
of our features cry out for modulation. Does Turkey, a proudly secular
and deeply devout society, distrust us for our wild popular culture or
for our moralizing piety? Whatever might be the case, a mere 17 percent
of respondents registered a positive image of Americans, according to
a recent Pew survey, and only 3 percent expressed confidence in Bush,
putting Turkey at the top of the list of U.S. detractors. Meanwhile, two
recent pop-culture sensations—a pulp thriller called *Metal Storm* and a
film called *Valley of the Wolves*—feature the U.S. military as marauding invaders. Paradoxically enough, the Turkish forces who take brutal
revenge resemble nothing so much as their nemesis. There isn't much
difference, it seems, between the Hollywood invasion thriller and the
anti-Hollywood invasion thriller.

What may be the most confusing of all is the warm welcome U.S.   7
visitors actually receive in a country that is as culturally cacophonous as
America and labors under no inhibitions when it comes to boasting and
bullying. The demurely dressed American tourist (shoulders and knees
covered, often in khaki) can't walk a block in Istanbul without seeing Turks
wearing hijabs and jiljabs (those modest coatdress coverings) side by side
with tank tops and tight jeans—and without getting lectured about where
the true cradle of cultural diversity lies. Here's a collision of secularism
and Islamism, the Turks are right, that owes more to Ataturk and centuries
of entanglement with Europe than to the corrosive allure of New World
exports.

Busily monitoring our well-known tendency to strident self-importance,   8
earnest American practitioners of personal diplomacy can risk missing
the genuinely humbling lesson of being abroad: an awareness of how

bewildering another country's *own* blend of boorishness and fervent belief, of openness and defiance, of backwardness and progress and of internal dissentions can be. In the end, it's as narcissistic to assume we're the overbearing cause of everybody else's national identity crisis in a dizzying world as it is to imagine that we can orchestrate the solutions to them. The sobering, and liberating, truth is that our britches are not that big.

Thinking About the Essay

1. What **tone** or personal voice does Hulbert establish in her introductory paragraph? Does she sustain this tone throughout the essay? Justify your response.

2. What is Hulbert's thesis? Does she state this thesis or imply it? Explain.

3. Hulbert refers to the pamphlet "World Citizen's Guide". What does she think of it and its author? Why does she allude to Karen Hughes in the same paragraph? (Find out about Karen Hughes.)

4. Is Hulbert's purpose to contrast American and Turkish culture or is her intention more nuanced? Explain.

5. What, ultimately, is Hulbert's perception of "ugly Americans"? What conclusions does she draw in her final paragraph? Do you agree or disagree with her assessment, and why?

Responding in Writing

6. How does a label like "ugly American" both reflect or define a certain cultural or global attitude and at the same time simplify or distort it? Write an essay that critiques this global perception.

7. Write a personal essay describing a time when you found yourself serving as a representative or symbol of your nation or, if you have not traveled abroad, of your family, town, or ethnic background.

8. Write a letter to the editor of you college newspaper outlining ways in which students on spring vacation can avoid being stereotyped as "ugly Americans" or "spoiled college kids."

Networking

9. In small groups, discuss Hulbert's essay and write a collaborative critique of it in 100 words or less. Select one member to join a panel presenting your critique to the class.

10. Conduct online research to locate the origin of the phrase "ugly American." Summarize your findings in a brief essay.

The Resilience of American Power

FOUAD AJAMI

Fouad Ajami was born in Lebanon in 1946 and emigrated to the United States in 1964. He was raised as a Shiite Muslim. A political scientist with a doctorate from the University of Washington, Ajami has taught at Princeton University and, since 1980, at Johns Hopkins University, where today he is Majid Khadduri Professor of Islamic studies and director of Middle Eastern studies. He is also a contributing editor to *U.S. News & World Report* and a consultant to *CBS News*. Ajami received a prestigious MacArthur Fellowship in 1982 for his work on Middle Eastern politics and culture. His work includes *The Vanished Imam: Musa al Sadr and the Shia of Lebanon* (1986), *Beirut: City of Regrets* (1988), *The Arab Predicament* (1981, revised edition 1992), and *The Dream Palace of the Arabs* (1998). In the following essay, published in *The U.S. News & World Report* on November 3, 2008, Ajami argues that obituaries of the American imperial republic are premature.

Before Reading

Do you see the United States as a generally positive or benevolent force in world affairs? What, in your view, is the primary cause of anti-American sentiment around the world?

So this great imperial democracy of ours has been financing its deficits, and its consumer society, with the savings of the sovereign wealth funds of China, Singapore, the United Arab Emirates, and Saudi Arabia. Great powers throughout history, we know, were creditor nations, whereas ours is the quintessential indebted society. We could hear the gloating of America's critics and enemies as soon as the subprime loan crisis descended upon us. From Malaysia to Venezuela, and from Europeans we had badgered about their brand of a capitalism more regulated than ours, there were unsparing critics who savored this moment. For them, we had gotten our comeuppance. Our Masters of the Universe, with their financial "derivatives" and new "instruments," were only pretenders.

There can be no doubt that we were due for our moment of reckoning. But Edward Gibbon wannabes should proceed with caution. It is not yet

1

2

A public display of anti-American sentiment in Tehran.

time to pen *The Decline and Fall of the American Empire*. Rome was long dead and buried when Gibbon, working in London, published his first volume of *The History of the Decline and Fall of the Roman Empire* in 1776. The destiny of the American empire is still unfolding. The bailout package, a staggering $700 billion, is only 5 percent of our national output; the country could afford it. While some may seek to write the obituaries of the American imperial republic, a survey of universities placing in the top 500 globally, conducted by Shanghai University, gave the United States a huge lead in such institutions: 159 versus 31 in Japan, 30 in China (the data include Hong Kong and Taiwan), and 2 in India.

For all the talk about the rise of China and India, these societies, long mired in poverty and squalor and handicapped by dominant traditions

3

of inequality and caste, are in no position to inherit the American place in the order of nations. They lack the openness of the United States, its sense of obligation to other lands, its willingness to defend the global order.

After the partisanship in our country subsides, Americans know   4
that the alternative to the American order in the world is not the hegemony of China or Russia or India but rather outright anarchy. The Chinese, shrewd about the ways of the world, acknowledge this. They are content to work and prosper, and move large numbers of their people out of poverty, under American primacy and tutelage. The Chinese hold well over a trillion dollars in American treasury securities. They are not about to bring the house down. The Chinese know Asia's bloody history. American hegemony has been benign, and the alternatives to it are infinitely worse. Likewise in the volatile Persian Gulf: The commerce of that vital region and the traffic of its oil depend upon the American Navy. No one in that tinderbox wants a *Pax Iranica*, and the Indians and the Europeans are not contenders to assume what has been America's role.

Backlash. Critics of American primacy in the world often bemoan   5
America's ways abroad. A "torture narrative" dwells on the transgressions committed at Abu Ghraib by some of our soldiers; books filled with outrage tell about the war fought in the shadows against al Qaeda and its affiliates. Pollsters return from Karachi and Cairo with numbers that demonstrate our alienation from public opinion in these places. A writer or two has stepped forth to tell us that America's borders have closed in the face of would-be immigrants and students seeking higher education in our midst.

But I read those indictments as an adopted son of this country, and   6
I view this narrative with a jaundiced eye. Our borders are still open—ask the Somalis now living in Nebraska and Maine and Minnesota. We may not fight every "war of liberation" in every corner of the Earth, but from the Balkans to Afghanistan and Iraq, history bears witness not to America's heavy hand but to its willingness to mount wars of rescue. America's embassies are besieged by those who dream of a new life on American soil. It is the fate of great, universal powers to be both loved and derided.

America may no longer be able to afford the indulgence of the period   7
now behind us. We no doubt will have to persuade nations in Europe and Asia to pay for the order afforded them by an American security umbrella. The price of our primacy has risen.

But no prettier or more merciful and benevolent alternative to America's leadership is anywhere over the horizon. Save for the most virulent of America's enemies and critics, the world fully knows its need of America's protection. 8

Thinking About the Essay

1. Ajami wrote this essay for a weekly news magazine. How would you describe the audience he addresses based on his opinions, style, paragraph organization, and conclusion?

2. Why does Ajami develop an introductory paragraph that does not contain a claim or thesis? Where does he state his main idea? Explain whether or not you find this placement effective.

3. What is the relevance of Ajami's allusion to Edward Gibbon in paragraph 2?

4. Rather than providing supporting information for his claim, Ajami relies on his own opinions, assertions, and generalizations as well as personal or anecdotal evidence. Do you think this strategy is sufficient to support his claim? Justify your response.

5. Throughout the essay Ajami makes comparative statements about other nations. List all the countries he contrasts with the United States. What is his purpose here? How effective is this strategy in organizing the essay and framing the writer's ideas? Explain.

Responding in Writing

6. Write an argumentative essay on why or why not you think the world still requires the application of American power.

7. Write a comparative essay in which you contrast "hard" and "soft" American power, the first relying on unilateralism and military might and the second on diplomacy and global cooperation.

8. Ajami writes that he is an "adopted son of this country." Write an essay explaining how Ajami's background might influence his argument.

Networking

9. In small groups, discuss Ajami's opinions about America's "torture narrative." Broaden the discussion to include such topics as Guantanamo, "black holes," and rendition. Summarize your discussion for class members.

10. Conduct online research to find out more about Edward Gibbon's *The History of the Decline and Fall of the Roman Empire.* Then write an essay explaining this work to the modern American experience.

Americans Are Tuning Out the World

ALKMAN GRANITSAS

> Alkman Granitsas is an American-born journalist who has reported on global issues in Asia and Europe for more than ten years. He has been a staff writer for the *Asian Wall Street Journal* and has contributed articles to *Business Week,* the *Far Eastern Economic Review,* and numerous other journals. Granitsas is currently based in Athens, where he is writing a book on the Balkans. In the following essay, from the November 24, 2005, issue of the online journal *Yale Global,* Granitsas warns against the consequences of a trend toward cultural and political isolationism in the United States.

Before Reading

Do you believe that America is "a shining city on the hill"? Why or why not?

For all the talk about a global village, there are actually two communities in the world today: Americans and everyone else. The average Frenchman, Brazilian, or Pakistani is becoming more attuned to the American way of life, but Americans themselves are increasingly tuning out the rest of the globe. At a time when U.S. power, benefiting from globalization, is unchallenged in the world, a disinterested electorate could be a recipe for trouble. 1

Foreigners have long bemoaned the "isolationist" attitude of Americans—safely protected by two oceans and their tabula rasa history. But over the last several decades, that isolation has deepened. Americans now pay less attention to international affairs, and read less foreign news than at any time in the last two generations. Relative to the global boom in international travel, tourism, and business, fewer Americans go overseas or study a foreign language at university. The truth is that Americans are becoming relatively less—not more—engaged with the world in general. 2

A few facts. Since the early 1970s, the American public has paid less and less attention to foreign affairs. According to Gallup polls from presidential election years 1948 through 1972, Americans used to rank foreign 3 affairs as the most important issue facing the nation. Since then, however, with the single exception of the 2004 elections, the economy has been ranked first.

Over the same period, the percentage of American university students 4 studying a foreign language has steadily declined. According to a report funded by the U.S. Department of Education, in 1965, more than 16 percent of all American university students studied a foreign language. Now only 8.6 percent do.

It has long been known that fewer Americans have passports, and 5 travel less, than their counterparts in other developed economies. And while a record 21 percent of all Americans now have passports and are traveling more, the number going overseas in the past 20 years—not just to neighboring Canada and Mexico—has grown at a slower rate than the number of overseas visitors to America or the growth in international tourism in general. And indeed, during the late 1980s and early 1990s, the number of Americans even applying for a passport declined in several years.

American media coverage of foreign affairs has also been diminishing. 6 For example, according to a 2004 Columbia University survey, the presence of foreign news stories in American newspapers has been dropping since the late 1980s. In 1987, overseas news accounted for about 27 percent of front page stories in American newspapers—about the same as a decade earlier. By 2003, foreign news accounted for just 21 percent of front page stories, while coverage of domestic affairs more than doubled over the same period. On television, both the number of American network news bureaus overseas and the amount of air-time spent on foreign news fell by half in the 1990s.

Why are Americans progressively tuning out the rest of the world? The 7 reason is twofold. But both confirm the cherished belief of most Americans: that their country is a "shining city on the hill." And the rest of the world has relatively little to offer.

Consider first, that for the past 45 years, Americans have witnessed a 8 massive immigration boom. Since 1960, more than 20 million immigrants have come to the United States—the greatest influx of newcomers in the last hundred years, surpassing even the wave of immigrants that arrived in the first three decades of the 20th century. Two-thirds of these newcomers—more than 15 million—have come in just the past 25 years.

That they should come bears out the myth that America is a melting 9 pot of peoples. Indeed, the iconic images of the first Plymouth Rock Pilgrims and the Ellis Island immigrants of the early 1900s are at the very center of American popular mythology. More recently, news footage of Mexican-Americans rushing the fences on the southern borders shows that America attracts all comers. And every single American—from the mid-western blue collar worker to the pedigreed New England blueblood—knows their forebears came from someplace else. Chances are they've met or know someone—the Bangladeshi working at the 7-Eleven, the Chinese scientist on TV, the Somali cab driver at the airport—who has come even more recently.

With the whole world apparently trying to get to America, the average   10 American can only ask: why look to the rest of the world? After all, why would everyone try to come here if there was anything worthwhile over there? It is telling that according to a 2002 National Geographic survey, 30 percent of Americans believed the population of America to be between 1 and 2 billion people. For most Americans, it must seem like everyone is rushing the fences these days.

The second reason is that for much of the last two decades most (but   11 not all) Americans have seen their economic well-being grow relative to the rest of the world. Through much of the 1990s, American consumer confidence and real disposable income have risen at their fastest levels since the relatively golden age of U.S. economic growth of the 1960s. These have been matched by perceptions of increased wealth from a stock market rally that, with interruptions, lasted from the early 1980s until three years ago.

Why should that matter? Because since the days of ancient Rome, it is   12 an axiom of political science that economic well-being dulls the appetite of citizens to participate in civil affairs. It is something that de Tocqueville observed more than a hundred years ago.

"There is, indeed, a most dangerous passage in the history of a demo-   13 cratic people," de Tocqueville observed. "When the taste for physical gratifications among them has grown more rapidly than their education and their experience of free institutions ... the discharge of political duties appears to them to be a troublesome impediment which diverts them from their occupations and business."

Long before 9/11, the Asian tsunami, SARS, the bird flu, and the   14 relatively weaker dollar, Americans were already growing less interested in the rest of the world. Since then, they have found even more reasons to tune out.

The implications, however, are disturbing. Because of America's preem-   15 inent position in world affairs—and its role in "globalization," its foreign policy matters more than any other country on earth. But can America shape a responsible foreign policy with such an uninformed electorate? The world may be turning into a "global village," but the average American has moved to the suburbs.

Thinking About the Essay

1. What is Granitsas's claim and where does he state it? Do you detect any warrant underpinning his claim? Explain.

2. How does Granitsas connect perceptions about immigration to the United States to the isolationist attitude of the average American?

3. Where does the essay shift from factual support of a claim to the causal analysis and attribution of psychological motives?

4. Why does Granitsas quote Alexis de Tocqueville at length (paragraph 13)? Who was de Tocqueville, and what does quoting him add to the argument of the essay?

5. Where in the essay does the author provide answers immediately following the question he has posed? Are there rhetorical questions anywhere in the essay? Why are these questions left unanswered, and what function do they serve in the essay?

Responding in Writing

6. In a brief essay, critique the "axiom" that economic well-being dulls the appetite of citizens to participate in civil affairs. Can you think of exceptions to this rule?

7. Write down your response to the popular view that Americans have a "*tabula rasa* history." Why would non-Americans view American history in this way?

8. Make a list of the factual indicators Granitsas mentions in the essay as measures of the engagement of the American public. What are the diagnostic limitations of each indicator? Analyze these indicators in an essay.

Networking

9. Do you rank foreign affairs as the most important issue facing the United States? Poll members of your class and, in a class discussion, attempt to explain the majority opinion.

10. Compare the coverage of one foreign affairs issue over the course of a week in two online journals, one published in the United States and one published in a foreign country (the French *Le Monde,* for example, or the British *Guardian*).

Hungry for America

MOISES NAIM

Moises Naim is currently editor and publisher of *Foreign Policy* magazine. He received a Ph.D. from Massachusetts Institute of Technology and returned to his native Venezuela to serve as professor and dean at Instituto de Estudios Superiores de Administracion, in Caracas. As Venezuela's minister of trade and industry in the 1990s, Naim helped to engineer major economic reforms. He was also the director of projects on economic reforms in Latin America at the Carnegie Endowment for International Peace, and worked for the World Bank as executive director and senior advisor to the president. Naim is the author or editor of eight books and numerous essays dealing with a wide variety of subjects, with the political economy of international trade and investment, multilateral organizations, economic reform, and globalization among them. In this selection, which was published in *Foreign Policy's* January/February 2008 issue, Naim argues that the world is ready—and waiting—for the return of the United States.

Before Reading

Can the election of a new U.S. president actually improve global perceptions of America, or is anti-Americanism so strong in certain parts of the world that no new president can alter it? What is your opinion?

The world wants America back. For the next several years, world politics 1
will be reshaped by a strong yearning for American leadership. This trend will be as unexpected as it is inevitable: unexpected given the powerful anti-American sentiments sweeping the world, and inevitable given the vacuums that only the United States can fill and that others will increasingly demand that it fills.

This renewed international appetite for U.S. leadership will not merely 2
result from the election of a new president in 2008, though having a new occupant in the White House will certainly help. But other, more compelling factors are fueling the world's hunger for America. Almost a decade of U.S. disengagement and distraction have allowed international and regional problems to swell to the point where a growing number of foreign leaders are feeling that "someone had better do something, fast." And very often, the only nation that has the will and means to "do something" is the United States.

Moises Naim, "Hungry for America," from FOREIGN POLICY, Jan/Feb 2008, pp. 111–112. www.foreignpolicy.com. Reprinted by permission of the Copyright Clearance Center.

Not that anti-Americanism will suddenly disappear; it never will. Nor will   3
America's enemies go away. But strong anti-American currents will increasingly coexist with equally strong international demands for the United States
to play a larger role in world affairs. This trend, whereby American influence
is welcomed and even sought, will become, in a manner not seen since 9/11,
one of the defining features of the international political landscape.

Of course, the America that the world wants back is not the one that   4
preemptively invades potential enemies, bullies allies, or disdains international law. The demand is for an America that rallies other nations prone
to sitting on the fence while international crises are boiling out of control;
for a superpower that comes up with innovative international initiatives
to tackle the great global challenges of the day, such as climate change,
nuclear proliferation, and violent Islamic fundamentalism. The demand
is for an America that enforces the rules that facilitate international commerce and works and works effectively to stabilize an accident-prone
global economy. Naturally, the world also wants a superpower willing to
foot the bill with a largesse that no other nation can match.

These are not just naïve expectations. Foreign leaders know that, even   5
in the best circumstances, the next U.S. president will not be able to deliver
on all these things. They also understand that American leadership always
comes at a price. And the price can be hefty. Appearing too closely allied
with the United States is a risky political position for elected politicians
everywhere. Still, some have shown a surprising readiness to do so. Last
March, President George W. Bush traveled to Latin America, a region he
has largely ignored. The trip was bound to be inconsequential as the U.S.
president had nothing concrete to offer.

Yet, all the Latin American presidents who were asked to host this lame   6
duck, empty-handed, and politically radioactive guest readily agreed to do
so; some even lobbied not to be left off his itinerary. What was in it for
them? The hope of getting the superpower to do something for them. The
leftist Brazilian President Luiz Inácio "Lula" da Silva, who is a personal
friend and staunch supporter of Bush's nemesis Hugo Chávez, wanted help
with his country's ethanol industry. In Turkey, like Brazil, the population
is deeply critical of the United States. Yet, like his Brazilian counterpart,
Prime Minister Recep Tayyip Erdogan has openly courted the Bush administration. The Turkish president knows that the United States is his country's best ally in the effort to get Turkey into the European Union.

Lula and Erdogan are not unique. They are just two in a long list of world   7
leaders who understand that, though the United States may sometimes use a
heavy hand, the alternatives are much worse. Few want to see the world's stage
led by autocratic regimes like Russia or China. An ineffectual Europe does

not offer much in the way of leadership. And, short of these options, there are few possibilities besides living in an anarchic vacuum. Many of these foreign leaders will therefore be willing to pay the price that comes with American leadership. They only ask that it not require subservience to the whims of a giant with more power than brains and whose legitimacy is undermined by regular displays of incompetence, recklessness, and ignorance.

Opinion polls in multiple countries show that the legitimacy and pres-   8
tige of the United States has deteriorated. Yet, the same populations that say they don't want the United States to be the world's leader also say that they don't want America to withdraw from world affairs. For example, 93 percent in South Korea, 78 percent in France, and 71 percent in Mexico say that the United States should play a role in solving international problems. Moreover, despite the overall negative perceptions of the United States, most people surveyed believe that bilateral relations between the United States and *their* country are improving. In no country surveyed does the population think that their nation's relations with the United States are getting worse.

And they are right. Not just because the world wants it to be the case,   9
but because Americans are likewise yearning for the United States to be more respected abroad. Sixty-nine percent of Americans say they believe it is best for the United States to take an active part in world affairs. This popular demand is also shared by part of the policymaking elite. One of its most senior members recently called for a new direction in the way the United States thinks about world affairs. "Success," he said, "will be less a matter of imposing ones's will and more a function of shaping the behavior of friends, adversaries, and, most importantly, the people in between." And later: "[T]here is a need for a dramatic increase in spending on the civilian instruments of national security—diplomacy, strategic communications, foreign assistance, civic action, and economic reconstruction and development." The American making this appeal for a drastic departure from the Bush administration's overly militarized foreign policy is none other than Robert Gates, the current secretary of defense.

The demand abroad for change in the way America behaves is obvious. The United States is once again ready to supply the leadership.

Thinking About the Essay

1. The title of this essay reveals the writer's position. Why or why not was this choice a good idea?

2. This essay was written at the start of the 2008 presidential year in the United States. As such, do you think that Naim is a fair judge of the Bush presidency and the presidency that would succeed it, or is he biased in his assessment? Justify your response.

3. In part, Naim structures his essay by using causal analysis. Identify both the necessary and sufficient reasons why the world continues to be "hungry for America."

4. Explain the ways in which Naim uses comparative analysis to organize his essay.

5. How convincing or reasonable do you find Naim's conclusion? Does it flow logically from the introduction and body, or do you think Naim overstates his case? Explain.

Responding in Writing

6. Write your own essay entitled "Hungry for America," using the outcome of the 2008 presidential contest as a sequel to Naim's article.

7. Write a comparative analysis of the essays by Naim and Ajami in this chapter.

8. Write a letter to the editor, Naim himself, explaining why you agree or disagree with the assumptions he makes in "Hungry for America."

Networking

9. Exchange your essay "Hungry for America" and peer critique it, focusing on the writer's thesis or claim, the main points in the argument, and the use of supporting evidence.

10. Naim refers to global opinion polls on American leadership. Conduct online research and try to locate a recent poll, and then summarize and evaluate these data in a brief essay.

Fashionable Anti-Americanism

DOMINIC HILTON

A self-described satirist, Dominic Hilton is a commissioning editor and regular columnist for openDemocracy.net, which is where the following selection first appeared in January 2005. In the column, Hilton explores some of the causes of anti-American sentiment at home and abroad and argues that "most of the time, it's not America's fault the world so condemns it."

Before Reading

Do you associate certain attitudes toward the United States with specific regions or with "types" of Americans? What would be your definition of "anti-American" criticism?

Dominic Hilton, "Fashionable Anti-Americanism." This article was originally published on the independent online magazine www.opendemocracy.net. Reprinted by permission of open/Democracy.

The United States of America is on a *hiding to nothing*.   1
        In the conspiratorial alleys of the "Arab Street," Uncle Sam is flogged   2
like a habitual adulterer. In the bars and cafés of Europe, Yankee Doodle
is lashed like a mutinous sailor. Even in the privacy of his own backyard,
Brother Jonathan is grilled like a jumbo dog.

Ritual condemnation of the USA has been *la tendance du jour* since   3
the *Mayflower* hauled anchor at Plymouth in 1620. But mankind has
advanced some over the past four centuries: nowadays, taking pot-shots
at the United States is a booming multi-billion-dollar industry, and one my
bank manager is keen I invest in.

Regrettably, however, I can't indulge in the unceasing chorus of   4
Yank-bashing. My financial balance suffers for it, but I'm what's known
in intellectual circles as an "Americaphile." I told this to an American pal
who'd taken shore leave on a recent trip past Europe. "Oh, so you're the
one," he grinned.

His story is important. A pleasant chap—polite, open-minded, affable   5
and adorably moral—he'd nevertheless found it hard to ignore the clear
anti-American sentiment swilling around the old continent like the contents
of an open sewer. In Paris, he explained, waiters had served him swiftly and
attentively—a sure sign they'd identified him as an American pig and been
keen to see the back of him.

I listened to his sad tale, then told him to quit worrying. While unde-   6
niably profuse these days, I said, anti-Americanism is not as alarming as
many Americans are making out. Much of it is not serious. In fact, I qualified, most America-thumping is pathetically hypocritical, embarrassingly
imbecilic, perilously ruinous and, worst of all, as derisorily fashionable
as those ludicrous woolly boots everyone's presently sporting. "But the
world hates me and my nation!" he cried in response. "Fahgedaboudit,"
I shrugged, in a hopeless attempt at a New York accent that nobody was
buying.

Still, despite the best efforts of myself, most of Washington, and the   7
entire populace of the Midwestern states, the fact remains it's difficult for
Americans not to notice how they're the subject of global derision. Most
of us would find that kind of thing hard to handle. We'd start to worry
about ourselves and feel painfully conscious of our shortcomings. We'd
look in the mirror, analysing, criticising, assessing and judging. We might
consider therapy, confessional. We'd be reborn and either guest on *Oprah*
or volunteer on Karl Rove's staff.

Since 9/11, America has been aware of and concerned about the   8
amount of anti-Americanism inside and outside its borders. Some of this
has been caricatured, some of it earnestly analysed. Interest goes right to

the top. "Why do they hate us?" President George W. Bush asked Congress two weeks after 9/11. His administration splashes out $68 million per annum on "Al-hurra," an Arabic satellite station which aims to tell "the truth about the values of the policies of the United States" to Middle Eastern couch potatoes. It was Bush who hired the legendary Madison Avenue advertising guru Charlotte Beers to market his nation to the Muslim world. She quit after eighteen months.

Some of this is understandable. It's also understandable that "Why do they hate us?" has limits. In a recent *Newsweek* article, Fareed Zakaria expressed concern that with his lofty second inaugural address, Bush had ripened the opportunity for America's critics to charge his nation with hypocrisy for the cavernous gap between its high ideals and its not-so-pure actions. But when Bush declared "America's vital interests and our deepest beliefs are now one," he was also telling the world how (with some noteworthy exceptions) the charge of American hypocrisy might lose legitimacy. The speech combined time-honoured American idealism with a smidgen of "put up or shut up." Two birds with one stone. "Will you give us a break?" the president was saying. "We're doing our best here. Cut us some slack, why don't you?"

Quite right. It would be futile for America to respond in a soul-searching manner to the trash talk of its detractors. Why? Because most of the time, it's not America's fault the world so condemns it. It's not that America does everything right. America is imperfect, thank God. Its commitment to (and achievement of) imperfection is arguably its greatest feat. For this, we should love it. Criticism remains entirely valid. If America makes a bonehead move—something it does as well as most of us—we should jeer and blow raspberries. Though this is not what we do. The industry of anti-American sentiment is just that—an industry. It should not be mistaken for legitimate and considered concern. "I hate America" is the world's default position. Knocking America is a form of displacement. It helps non-Americans avoid focusing on their own big problems. In fact, strip it of its lacy hosiery and the world's relationship with America is disgustingly Freudian.

Threats and Fads

First, let's distinguish between different types of anti-Americanism. Thomas Friedman put it well in a recent column: "for Europeans, anti-Americanism is a hobby. For too many in the Muslim world it has become a career." In other words, anti-Americanism that breeds terrorism and tyranny is a big, big problem. But anti-Americanism that falls into the category of "indulgent fad" is generally immaterial. Except this is not quite true, is it?

Friedman missed something. For more and more Europeans, and more and more Americans, anti-Americanism is an ever more profitable career path. It is very material.

So let's rework this: anti-Americanism that breeds terrorism and tyranny   12 is a major problem for us all and one the United States of America must fully address; anti-Americanism that doesn't result in suicide missions is not America's problem, it's the problem of its moron perpetrators—though it benefits nobody good. Non-Americans that find comfort in blaming America for all the world's ills—poverty, war, environmental destruction, the death of high culture, their own pitiful inadequacies—suffer for such fatuous bunkum. Their own houses rot as they drone on at dinner parties and terrorist camps about American "crimes against humanity." The rhetoric of Osama bin Laden is curiously similar to that of Harold Pinter (though notably less profane). Pinter, I hazard a guess, is less dangerous.

They are all morons, but the difference is that America can and should   13 ignore the dinner guests. They pose no threat. Especially not an intellectual one. The philosophy of "damn you if you do, damn you if you don't" is not worthy of serious contemplation. Insularly isolationist or intensely imperial, America is castigated for both, often by the same people. This is what's technically known as a no-win situation. "The illogicality at base consists in reproaching the United States for some shortcoming, and then for its opposite," writes Jean-Francois Revel in his aptly-titled *Anti-Americanism*. "Here is a convincing sign that we are in the presence, not of rational analysis, but of obsession."

Many of those who say America does not live up to its own ideals and   14 rhetoric would surely be the first to protest if it did. If America invades and "liberates" Iraq, they say, it should also invade and liberate North Korea, Burma, China, Zimbabwe, etc. I'd love to see their reaction if America took up the challenge. Yes, America talks a good game—but this should be celebrated, and, yes, held to account. As it stands, though, whether the "indispensable nation," the "universal country," the "last, best hope," the "shining city upon a hill," the "global policeman," the "lone super duper-power," the "empire in denial" or Jefferson's "empire of liberty," the US plays the traditional lead role of the world's whipping-boy. We might suppose this is inevitable. *C'est le prix du pouvoir* (as Jacques Chirac might put it).

American Booty

America does not want to be charged with hypocrisy by hypocrites. By   15 definition, however, it always will be. In all its guises, anti-Americanism is an infatuation and an excuse. Anti-Americanism is "the dog ate my homework" of international relations.

"Power is fascinating. ... But being fascinating is also power," says 16
Timothy Garton Ash in his new book *Free World*. Fair point. But
fascination quickly spills into fixation. "At least part of the Western
left—or rather the Western far left—is now so anti-American, or so anti-
Bush, that it actually prefers authoritarian or totalitarian leaders to *any*
government that would be friendly to the United States," writes Anne
Applebaum in *The Washington Post*. "Many of the same people who
would refuse to condemn a dictator who is anti-American cannot bring
themselves to admire democrats who admire, or at least don't hate, the
United States."

Applebaum is on to something. This goes beyond Saddam apologia. It's 17
getting into the realm of anti-democracy. To some, democratic movements
are only legitimate if also anti-American. Ukrainians in Independence
Square were pro-American, not pro-Castro. Must've been a CIA plot.

In a recent sweeping commentary for *Commentary* magazine entitled 18
"Americanism—and Its Enemies," David Gelernter suggested "Americanism" is a religion and that "anti-Americanism is closely associated with
anti-Christianism *and* anti-Semitism. ... America has *remained* an object
of hatred within nations that have themselves gone over to American-style
democracy; has been hated by people who had nothing whatsoever to fear
from American power."

Actually, it's worse than that. America has *remained* an object of hatred 19
from those who directly gain from American generosity. Some of America's
most sour critics preach their gospels in America's palatial universities.
A highly desirable standard of living is endowed on those who make their
living attacking America's highly desirable standard of living. Ditto its
liberty.

"Since the end of the cold war, anti-Americanism has overtaken soccer 20
as the world's most popular sport," Tom Friedman writes in *Longitudes
and Attitudes*. "And there is this general assumption in intellectual circles
that America is to be blamed first for whatever happens, and a given that
American intellectuals will play along and accept this role as the world's
punching bag. And when you refuse to do this in mixed company, it's as
if you unleashed a huge fart at a cocktail party—people look at you funny
and just start to back away."

American Cool

But it's not just the left-leaning intellectual class that's guilty of rank hypoc- 21
risy in its attitude towards Uncle Sam. It'd be comforting to think so, but
you don't have to wear elbow pads on your corduroy jacket to participate
in this orgy of anti-American infantilism. The kids are at it too.

As 2004 faded into history, the *Financial Times* ran a feature under 22
the headline "Tarnished image: is the world falling out of love with U.S.
brands?" "Poll after poll has shown that allegations of human rights
abuses and the failure to find weapons of mass destruction in Iraq have
tarnished the international reputation of the U.S.," the article reckoned,
worrying aloud about a "subtle tarnishing of brands in the minds of millions of ordinary consumers." Joseph Nye, of Harvard and "soft power"
fame, offered his wisdom: "U.S. brands have benefited from a sense that it
is fashionable, chic and modern to be American. The other side of that coin
is when U.S. policies become unpopular, there is a cost."

A net incline in Abu Ghraib scandals. A net decline in Pepsi sales? 23
Impossible to measure, even with the advent of Mecca Cola. Besides,
"It is more a subject of debate between intellectuals than something
that is hampering the development of these brands with consumers,"
says Maurice Levy, chief executive of the marketing group Publicis.
But subheads like "Cool would come from Tokyo rather than LA" are
not entirely bullshit. Cool is important. The most popular is never the
coolest. America has become like a manufactured pop band. Kids go for
thrash metal.

Though hang on, where did thrash metal originate? America's diversity, 24
its sheer vastness, makes life hard for its opponents. The land of Disney is
the land of *Easy Rider*. The home of televangelists is the home of hip-hop.
America *is* "cool"—even in its failings. The bad trip that was the Vietnam War was replayed in a succession of überhip purple haze movies like
Apocalypse Now!, *The Deerhunter*, *Rambo*, *Platoon*, *Full Metal Jacket*,
Born on the Fourth of July, and TV shows like *Tour of Duty* with its Rolling Stones soundtrack.

My generation grew up with these movies, the Sheen-Duvall-Hopper- 25
Brando-DeNiro-Walken-Stallone-Sheen-Defoe-Berenger-Cruise out-of-
control American soldier with a bandanna, an ironic peace tattoo on their
helmet—wild-eyed boys in the fug of drugs. We pretended these were
negative images of an out-of-control America. Nonsense. To my generation,
these movies were an updated confirmation of American cool. How cool to
burn villages, to collect skulls, to play Russian roulette, to rape and pillage
your way across the jungle to the psychedelic strains of Jim Morrison, then
return home and be messed-up about what you done out in 'Nam—or what,
ahem, you were *made* to do. These movies were so very, very *American*.

In essence, what we are witnessing is a pseudo-rejection of the USA. All 26
this "I hate America as much as you hate America!" baloney is a cultural
phenomenon, little to do with any meaningful or cultivated sense of "politics."
Across Europe, gigantic music stores stuffed to the gunwales with American

pop, rock and urban do a sideline in hipster books. Virtually without exception these dazzling paperback digests are rabidly anti-American (*Why Do We Hate America?*), anti-Bush/anti-American (*The Bush-Haters' Handbook*), anti-globalisation/anti-American (*American Dream/Global Nightmare*), anti-American culture/anti-American (*Fat Land: How Americans Became the Fattest People in the World*).

For the most part adorned with colourful depictions of the universally   27 attractive symbols of Americana, the covers tell a story of their own: as beacon or pariah, America sells. Here lies the reading choice of today's youth, of societies most cool, and these cash-in volumes are horribly high in the sales charts. It's not just the dreadlocked, nose-ringed student-acolytes who pack the theatres to hear the nasal drone of the world's Noam Chomskys, it's the kids who lap up American culture, obese and spotty from a diet of McDonald's and Coca-Cola, baggily clad in Nike, Gap and Levi's, plugged into their iPods digitally replete with Eminem or 50 Cent. *These* are the kids whose street cred relies on their miserable detestation of the shallow, candied, military behemoth that is the USA.

Unlike back in '68, "I hate America" is now "organised." Not organised   28 in the leftist sense, I mean organised in the Ben and Jerry's sense. Attractively packaged, nice tasting, creamy, chocolaty, cookie-dough anti-Americanism that clogs the arteries and numbs the brain.

Fashion trumps sophistication. America's insignia are ubiquitous—   29 from Ralph Lauren jumpers to Primal Scream album covers to the end of a flaming match in the Arab Street, looking modish even when being burned. I've seen kids on TV in Osama bin Laden t-shirts and New York Yankees' baseball caps (Hello? You don't see the irony?). I've watched young British men in the nondescript north-of-London town of Luton clad in "New York" sweatshirts holding up banners of the extremist Islamic group al-Muhajiroun.

Our rebels are American. So are our anti-Americans. Michael Moore is   30 one of America's biggest exports. America makes anti-Americanism profitable for America. What a country!

Ideals and Piggybacks

Now, even I admit there's something a little fishy at times about America's   31 claim to moral exceptionality. When Gelenter writes about Americans being "positive that their nation is superior to all others—*morally* superior, closer to God," I can only think of Hegel's conviction that 1830s Prussia was the perfect and ultimate achievement of mankind, and how this apple-sauce led to Marxism.

Nevertheless, there's something too easy about knocking the believer.   32
America is going to say and think big things about it self. Look at its history, and then understand that the United States is a nation, and acts as
such—in its own interests and with a powerful identity. In his response
to Bush's second inaugural, the American commentator David Brooks
identified "this weird intermingling of high ideals with gross materialism"
which so defines his country. In the spirit of Washington and Kennedy, the
president waxed lyrical on mankind's highest ideals. Later that evening,
"drunken, loud and privileged twenty somethings" carried each other pig-
gyback down K Street.

"The people who detest America take a look at this odd conjunction   33
and assume the materialistic America is the real America; the ideals are a
sham," Brooks wrote. "The real America, they insist, is the money-grub-
bing, resource-wasting, TV-drenched, unreflective bimbo of the earth. The
high-toned language, the anti-Americans say, is just a cover for the quest
for oil, or the desire for riches, dominion and war. But of course they've
got it exactly backward. It's the ideals that are real."

The ideals *are* real. Not because they are America's, but because they   34
are ideals and they are the right ideals. Those who don't revel in extremism, dictatorship and political stagnation have to decide whose camp they
want to be in. Does Europe really feel more allied to communist China
than conservative America? The European Union and China share "a
convergence of views about the United States, its foreign policy and its
global behaviour," says David Shambaugh of George Washington University. This should send a shudder down the spine of democrats. Who truly
wants to believe the late Susan Sontag and her assertion that America is
"a doomed country ... founded on a genocide"? Get over yourself. I'm
sticking with my stateside compadre John Hulsman, who believes "there
is little doubt we have all benefited from the 'naïve' optimism that has
enabled America to do amazing things not just for itself, but also for all
mankind."

Into the Mirror

Anti-Americanism, when not perpetrated by *true* haters, is often a stale   35
mockery of America, born of our own fascination. This is our (the world's)
problem, not America's. Jean-Francois Revel suggests that we "project our
faults onto America so as to absolve ourselves." As he says of his native
France, and Barry Rubin and Judith Colp Rubin say of the last four hundred years, some of this "Hating America" is born of fear, some of plain
old weakness, some of outright jealousy. The left, in particular, is green

with envy. Twentieth-century Communism only served to augment belief in the American Dream. "The success of America was thus a devastating blow to the Left," writes Michael Ledeen. "It wasn't supposed to happen. And American success was particularly galling because it came at the expense of Europe itself, and of the embodiment of the Left's most utopian dream: the Soviet Union."

But some leftists are getting tired of it. The narrative of left-wing anti-   36
Americanism "has ceased to be critical, but become predestinarian," says John Lloyd. Such stasis serves nobody except the tyrants, the terrorists, and the unoriginal, knee-jerk loudmouths who cash in on the fashion-ability of the flaming Spangled Banner (categorised by Barry Rubin as "self-interest").

Even Americans are caught up in this silly love-hate relationship. "How   37
can you have patience for people who claim they love America but clearly can't stand Americans?," Annette Bening's flag-burning power-woman asks the eponymous Michael Douglas in Aaron Sorkin and Rob Reiner's eco-friendly, anti-gun liberal dream *The American President*. Same ques-tion, the other way round, from right-wing firebrand Ann Coulter: a recent explosion was hilariously titled "Liberals love America like O.J. loved Nicole."

This is all a little daft. After the fascistic and communistic horrors of   38
the 20th century, we are bloody lucky to live in a world led by the United States in which the central geopolitical questions are "Should we spread liberty and democracy? And if so, how far?" We should ride our luck a little, before we run it out. "[America's] interaction with the rest of the world must be a conversation, not a monologue," says the new U.S. secretary of state, Condoleezza Rice. That goes both ways. In Asia, "consumers are increasingly indifferent to U.S. brands and are paying great attention to Asian trends and products," reports the *Financial Times*. The rest of the world should swallow a spoonful of this medicine. When President Bush declares how, "In a world moving towards liberty, we are determined to show the meaning and promise of liberty," we should let him get on with it, and try dusting off our own promises.

America is not the panacea, nor is it the devil. Our problems are   39
generally *our* problems. The world would do well to be a little more like America, a tad more insular, self-involved.

Non-Americans love to quote John Kennedy's famous call, "And so,   40
my fellow Americans, ask not what your country can do for you; ask what you can do for your country." Why? It is the second part of Kennedy's couplet we should heed and let roll off our tongues: "My fellow citizens of

the world, ask not what America will do for you, but what together we can do for the freedom of man." This still stands. And freedom, like charity, discipline and intelligence, begins at home.

Thinking About the Essay

1. What is your reaction to the abrasive irony of the opening paragraph? Does the paragraph establish a tone that remains consistent throughout the essay? Are you offended by the author's poking fun at Islamic laws and customs? Why or why not?

2. Highlight instances of caricature, hyperbole, and synechdoche (using a part or individual for a whole or class) in the essay. How do these strategies function to establish tone? Look up some definitions of *satire*. Does this essay qualify as satire, or is it best described by another term? Explain your response.

3. What function do the quotations serve in this essay? Does Hilton quote other writers in order to critique their ideas, as corroboration for his own views, or as a way of challenging and complicating the argument of the essay?

4. In the final paragraphs of the essay, Hilton seems to defend the Bush administration's interventionist policies at the same time he argues for an isolationist attitude. How do these two aspects of the argument complement or contradict each other?

5. Paraphrase the psychological explanation for anti-American feelings Hilton offers in the final section of the essay. Where does this appear as a theme earlier in the essay?

Responding in Writing

6. In a brief essay, explain what it means for an attitude to become a commodity. Are there any popular attitudes that you would characterize in terms of a self-sustaining "industry"? What makes them so?

7. Use Hilton's statement in the fifth section of the essay (his response to David Brooks) to compose an argumentative essay: "The ideals *are* real. Not because they are America's, but because they are ideals and they are the right ideals." What do you consider to be genuinely American ideals? Why are they "right"? Do you feel comfortable speaking of them as universal ideals?

8. In a comparative essay, analyze what you see as important differences between anti-American attitudes and the global attitudes spawned by the foreign policies of the Bush administration. Explain whether or not you think the foreign policy of the new Obama administration can alter anti-American sentiment.

Networking

9. In groups of three or four, discuss one example of an anti-American attitude mentioned in the essay and explain to the class why it should or should not be considered a species of anti-Americanism.

10. This article was published in an online journal and generated a considerable amount of online discussion. Find a blog or discussion group in which the article is referenced and post a response of your own.

America's New Empire for Liberty

PAUL JOHNSON | Paul Johnson, a British historian and author, is also known as a conservative spokesperson and a widely read journalist who appears frequently in *The New York Times, The Wall Street Journal, The Spectator,* and *The Daily Telegraph*. In the early 1980s, he served as speechwriter and adviser to British Prime Minister Margaret Thatcher. Johnson was educated at Magdalen College, Oxford, and first came to prominence in the 1950s as a writer for the *New Statesman* (which he would later edit). Johnson is currently a distinguished visiting fellow at the Hoover Institution. In the following selection, published in *The Hoover Digest* of July 16, 2003, Johnson defines and defends his concept of "defensive imperialism" and envisions a future role for the United States as an imperial power.

Before Reading

Can you think of any terms (e.g., "final solution") so loaded with meaning that they resist any possible attempt at redefinition?

For America, September 11 was a new Great Awakening. It realized, for the first time, that it was itself a globalized entity. It no longer had frontiers. Its boundaries were the world, for from whatever part of the world harbored its enemies, it could be attacked and, if such enemies possessed weapons of mass destruction, mortally attacked. For this reason America was obliged to construct a new strategic doctrine, replacing totally that of National Security Council Paper 68 of 1949, which laid down the doctrine of containment. In a globalized world the United States now has to anticipate its enemies, search out and destroy their bases, and disarm states

Paul Johnson, "America's New Empire for Liberty," THE HOOVER DIGEST, 2003, no. 4. Reprinted by permission of The Hoover Institution.

likely to aid them. I call this "defensive imperialism." It is a novel kind but embraces elements of all the old. NSC-68 of 1949, significantly, specifically repudiates imperialism. Its replacement will necessarily embrace it in its new form. There are compelling reasons why the United States is uniquely endowed to exercise this kind of global authority.

First, America has the language of the twenty-first century. English is   2 already the premier world language in many respects, and this century will see its rapid extension and consolidation. As first the Greeks, then the Romans, discovered, possession of a common language is the first vital and energizing step toward embracing common norms of law, behavior, and culture. A more secure world will be legislated for, policed, and adjudicated in English. Second, America has, and will continue to acquire, the pioneering technology of the twenty-first century, its lead being widened by its success in providing a clear climate of freedom in which inventors and entrepreneurs of all kinds can operate.

In the nineteenth century, the great age of the formal empires, the   3 imperialist thrust was backed by the Industrial Revolution, producing manufactured goods much cheaper and in far greater quantity than ever before. In 1800 it was Asia that produced the majority (57 percent) of world manufactured output, the West only 29 percent; by 1900 the West was producing 86 percent, Asia only 10 percent. Today, America's production of world wealth, both absolutely and relatively, is accelerating. In the last quarter of the twentieth century, it added $5 trillion to its annual GDP. By 2050 the U.S. share of global output will constitute more than a quarter of the world total and will be as much as three times as big, for instance, as that of the European Union.

Traditionally, successful imperialism has reflected high birthrates and   4 the ability to export large surplus populations. The climax of European imperialism in the nineteenth century coincided with the European population explosion. America has never exported people overseas. On the contrary, its growing power and wealth have reflected its ability to attract and absorb immigrants. That continues. America now accepts more immigrants than the rest of the world put together. The amazing ability of groups such as the Cubans, the Hong Kong Chinese, the Vietnamese, and other new arrivals to grow roots and create wealth is a key part of America's continuing success story. But America also has a high birthrate. Its population is now coming up to the 300 million mark. By 2050 it will be more than 400 million. By contrast, Europe's population will shrink and the percentage of working age will fall rapidly. The ability of America to sustain a global role is demonstrated by the demographic figures, especially those on the working population. By 2050, the Japanese working population will have shrunk by 38 percent; that of Russia, Ukraine, and Belarus, by 46 percent; and the 15 EU nations, by various totals—8 percent in France, 41 percent in Italy, 35 percent in Spain, 21 percent in Germany. In the EU countries as a whole—both members and candidate members—only Great Britain and Ireland will have increased their working population by 2050. All the rest (except Luxembourg) will decline by an average of 19 percent in existing members, 38 percent in the rest.

Meanwhile America's working population will have increased by more than 54 million (31 percent), an increase greater than the present working population of Germany. This does not take into account either working hours or productivity, both of which hugely increase the productive power of America over Europe. 5

Population forecasts are notoriously unreliable, and some predictions of what is likely to happen in Europe (and Japan) in this century are so alarming as to be discounted. But clearly there is a marked and growing contrast between old Europe and young America. And the combination of accelerating technology and an expanding workforce will be irresistible in terms of economic and military power. America is able to shoulder its burdens with courage and determination. But it is not alone. Britain, with much smaller resources but with long and varied experience, has a resolve equal to America's to do its fair share. When I was a boy in the 1930s, a quarter of the world on the map was colored red—that is, part of the British Empire and Commonwealth of Nations. It was a liberal empire and a democratic commonwealth, and its aim, as with America in the Philippines, was to prepare its components for self-government. There have been some outstanding successes: Canada, Newfoundland, New Zealand, Australia, Singapore, Hong Kong, and, most of all, India; with a billion inhabitants it has become the world's largest democracy. There have been tragic failures too, notably in Africa. But we have learned from the failures too. The knowledge we gained is at America's disposal, particularly in the training of military and civilian administrators who must take on the kind of work now being done in Iraq and Afghanistan. One idea I would like to see explored—with all deliberate speed—is the creation of an Anglo-American staff college for training men and women, both from the armed forces and from government, in the skills to rescue failed or fragile nations and to take former tyrannies and dictatorships into the magic circle of justice and democracy. We have a vast project ahead of us, and we need to be educated for it. 6

In this project, what part is there for continental Europe? The answer is as large a one as the Europeans wish to play, are capable of playing, and are anxious to play in good faith. But I am bound to say recent events have not 7 shown Europeans in a good light. It will be some time before the expanded European Union shows whether it is viable, economically and politically, and whether it can generate the resources and display the will to make a worthwhile contribution in military or any other terms. My guess is that the United States of Europe, a ramshackle structure already, is heading for disaster: economic bankruptcy and political implosion. Looking at it from Britain's viewpoint, we should keep well clear of the mess. In emotional and cerebral terms, the English Channel is wider than the Atlantic, and I would prefer to see the expansion of the North Atlantic free trade area rather than that of a bureaucratic, antidemocratic, and illiberal Europe.

The Bush administration is only beginning to grasp the implications 8 of the course on which it has embarked. It still, albeit with growing difficulty, speaks the language of anti-imperialism. But that is the jargon of the twentieth century or at least its second half. Who says it will be the prevailing discourse of the twenty-first? As it happens, imperialism became a derogatory term in America only during the Civil War, when the South accused the North of behaving like a European empire. It then became politically correct to speak only of "American exceptionalism." Internationally *imperialism* became a dirty word early in the twentieth century, and it was the Communists who were chiefly responsible for turning it into a hate word. And it is worth recalling too that up to 1860 empire was not a term of abuse in the United States. George Washington himself spoke of "the rising American Empire." Thomas Jefferson, aware of the dilemma, claimed that America was "an empire for liberty." That is what America is becoming again, in fact if not in name. America's search for security against terrorism and rogue states goes hand in hand with liberating their oppressed peoples. From the Evil Empire to an Empire for Liberty is a giant step, a contrast as great as the appalling images of the wasted twentieth century and the brightening dawn of the twenty-first. But America has the musculature and the will to take giant steps, as it has shown in the past.

Another factor has received too little attention. It may be that humanity is 9 on the eve of an entirely new age of exploration and settlement—in space. In 1450 no one in old Europe imagined that the discovery and colonization of the New World was just over the historical horizon. Yet the technology of oceanic ships and navigation was already in place and within 50 years in use, and an entire new hemisphere was brought into our grasp. No forethought had been given to who might own it. Today imperialism is a technical possibility and may become a reality much sooner than we think. And when it happens it will develop as with the age of Columbus, with dramatic speed, the adventurous moving much faster than the international lawyers and statesmen. We ought to be thinking about it now. One thing is certain. The United States will be in the forefront of this new imperialism. Indeed it has already taken the first steps by imposing a unilateral ban on rival weapons systems in space. The role of first space imperialist is likely to be imposed on America simply by its wealth, power, and technology.

One thing is clear: America is unlikely to cease to be an empire in the 10 fundamental sense. It will not share its sovereignty with anyone. It will continue to promote international efforts of proven worth, such as the General Agreement on Tariffs and Trade, and to support military alliances such as NATO where appropriate. But it will not allow the United Nations or any other organization to infringe on its natural right to defend itself as it sees fit. The new globalization of security will proceed with the United Nations if possible, without it if necessary. The empire for liberty is the dynamic of change.

Thinking About the Essay

1. What is the significance of Johnson's allusion, in the opening paragraph, to a new "Great Awakening"? Where do you find related metaphors in the essay?

2. According to Johnson, what distinguishes America as a unique imperialist power?

3. How does Johnson employ illustration in this essay? Are the illustrations essential to his argument? Do they seem arbitrarily chosen? Why or why not?

4. Why does Johnson switch abruptly to a digression on the exploration and settlement of space (paragraph 9)? Does this paragraph fit logically within the larger argument of the essay?

5. How would you describe the tone of the final paragraph? Why does Johnson wait until the end of the essay to address the future role of the United Nations?

Responding in Writing

6. Johnson coins the term "defensive imperialism" in his opening paragraph. Write a two-or three-sentence definition that might serve as a dictionary entry.

7. In paragraph 6, Johnson notes that some imperialist exploits of the past have resulted in "tragic failures." In an essay, speculate on some unintended consequences that may arise (or have arisen) from imperialist projects of the kind Johnson envisions.

8. Some scholars assert that the cold war was a period of imperialist expansion. In an essay of your own, consider how the example of cold war *geopolitical* imperialism changes the connotations of a term that Johnson seems to associate more with the example of the British Commonwealth. What is the difference between imperialism and colonialism?

Networking

9. In groups of three or four, write down a cluster of connotations you associate with the term *imperialism*. Share your findings with the class.

10. Go online and look up the text of National Security Council Paper 68 of 1949. What "twentieth-century" concept of imperialism is contained in the language of its repudiation?

Waking Up from the American Dream

SASHA ABRAMSKY

Sasha Abramsky is a freelance journalist and author who writes on politics and culture. He was born in England and studied politics, philosophy, and economics at Balliol College, Oxford, and moved to New York in 1993 to study journalism at Columbia University. His first book, *Hard Time Blues: How Politics Built a Prison Nation* (2002), examines the American prison system. Abramsky is currently a Senior Fellow at the New York City–based Demos Foundation. In the following essay, published in the July 23, 2004, issue of *The Chronicle of Higher Education*, Abramsky asks why foreign sympathy for America, inspired by faith in the American Dream, has dissipated at the turn of the new century.

Before Reading

Do you feel that the recent crisis of confidence in the United States among other nations also reflects a global loss of confidence in the ideal of the American Dream?

Last year I visited London and stumbled upon an essay in a Sunday 1 paper written by Margaret Drabble, one of Britain's pre-eminent ladies of letters. "My anti-Americanism has become almost uncontrollable," she wrote. "It has possessed me, like a disease. It rises up in my throat like acid reflux, that fashionable American sickness. I now loathe the United States and what it has done to Iraq and the rest of the helpless world."

The essay continued in the same rather bilious vein for about a thousand 2 words, and as I read it, two things struck me: The first was how appalled

Sasha Abramsky, "Waking Up from the American Dream," from THE CHRONICLE OF HIGHER EDUCATION, 7/23/04. Sasha Abramsky is a Senior Fellow at the Demos Institute and author of *Conned: How Millions Went to Prison, Lost the Vote, and Helped Send George W. Bush to the White House* (The New Press, 2006). Reprinted by permission.

I was by Drabble's crassly oversimplistic analysis of what America was all about, of who its people were, and of what its culture valued; the second was a sense somewhat akin to fear as I thought through the implications of the venom attached to the words of this gentle scribe of the English bourgeoisie. After all, if someone whose country and class have so clearly benefited economically from the protections provided by American military and political ties reacts so passionately to the omnipresence of the United States, what must an angry, impoverished young man in a failing third world state feel?

I grew up in London in the 1970s and 1980s, in a country that was   3
struggling to craft a postcolonial identity for itself, a country that was, in many ways, still reeling from the collapse of power it suffered in the post–World War II years. Not surprisingly, there was a strong anti-American flavor to much of the politics, the humor, the cultural chitchat of the period; after all, America had dramatically usurped Britannia on the world stage, and who among us doesn't harbor some resentments at being shunted onto the sidelines by a new superstar?

Today, however, when I talk with friends and relatives in London, when   4
I visit Europe, the anti-Americanism is more than just sardonic asides, rueful Monty Python–style jibes, and haughty intimations of superiority. Today something much more visceral is in the air. I go to my old home and I get the distinct impression that, as Drabble put it, people really *loathe* America somewhere deep, deep in their gut.

A Pew Research Center Global Attitudes Project survey recently found   5
that even in Britain, America's staunchest ally, more than 6 out of 10 people polled believed the United States paid little or no attention to that country's interests. About 80 percent of French and German respondents stated that, because of the war in Iraq, they had less confidence in the trustworthiness of America. In the Muslim countries surveyed, large majorities believed the war on terror to be about establishing U.S. world domination.

Indeed, in many countries—in the Arab world and in regions, such   6
as Western Europe, closely tied into American economic and military structures—popular opinion about both America the country and Americans as individuals has taken a serious hit. Just weeks ago, 27 of America's top retired diplomats and military commanders warned in a public statement, "Never in the 2¼ centuries of our history has the United States been so isolated among the nations, so broadly feared and distrusted."

If true, that suggests that, while to all appearances America's allies   7
continue to craft policies in line with the wishes of Washington, underneath the surface a new dynamic may well be emerging, one not too dissimilar to the Soviet Union's relations with its reluctant satellite states in Eastern Europe during the cold war. America's friends may be quiescent in public,

deeply reluctant to toe the line in private. Drabble mentioned the Iraq war as her primary *casus belli* with the United States. The statement from the bipartisan group calling itself Diplomats and Military Commanders for Change focused on the Bush administration's recent foreign policy. But to me it seems that something else is also going on.

In many ways, the Iraq war is merely a pretext for a deeper discontent   8
with how America has seemed to fashion a new global society, a new economic, military, and political order in the decade and a half since the end of the cold war. America may only be riding the crest of a wave of modernization that, in all likelihood, would have emerged without its guiding hand. But add to the mix a discontent with the vast wealth and power that America has amassed in the past century and a deep sense of unease with the ways in which a secular, market-driven world divvies up wealth and influence among people and nations, and you have all the ingredients for a nasty backlash against America.

I'm not talking merely about the anti-globalism of dispossessed Third   9
World peasants, the fears of the loss of cultural sovereignty experienced by societies older and more traditional than the United States, the anger at a perceived American arrogance that we've recently been reading so much about. I'm talking about something that is rooted deeper in the psyches of other nations. I guess I mean a feeling of being marginalized by history; of being peripheral to the human saga; of being footnotes for tomorrow's historians rather than main characters. In short, a growing anxiety brought on by having another country and culture dictating one's place in the society of nations.

In the years since I stood on my rooftop in Brooklyn watching the   10
World Trade Center towers burn so apocalyptically, I have spent at least a part of every day wrestling with a host of existential questions. I can't help it—almost obsessively I churn thoughts over and over in my head, trying to understand the psychological contours of this cruel new world. The questions largely boil down to the following: Where has the world's faith in America gone? Where is the American Dream headed?

What is happening to that intangible force that helped shape our   11
modern world, that invisible symbiotic relationship between the good will of foreigners and the successful functioning of the American "way of life," that willingness by strangers to let us serve as the repository for their dreams, their hopes, their visions of a better future? In the same way that the scale of our national debt is made possible only because other countries are willing to buy treasury bonds and, in effect, lend us their savings, so it seems to me the American Dream has been largely facilitated by the willingness of other peoples to lend us their expectations for the future.

Without that willingness, the Dream is a bubble primed to burst. It hasn't burst yet—witness the huge numbers who still migrate to America in search of the good life—but I worry that it is leaking seriously.

Few countries and cultures have risen to global prominence as quickly 12 as America did in the years after the Civil War. Perhaps the last time there was such an extraordinary accumulation of geopolitical, military, and economic influence in so few decades was 800 years ago, with the rise of the Mongol khanates. Fewer still have so definitively laid claim to an era, while that era was still unfolding, as we did—and as the world acknowledged—during the 20th century, "the American Century."

While the old powers of Europe tore themselves apart during World 13 War I, the United States entered the war late and fought the fight on other people's home terrain. While whole societies were destroyed during World War II, America's political and economic system flourished, its cities thrived, and its entertainment industries soared. In other words, as America rose to global pre-eminence during the bloody first half of the 20th century, it projected outward an aura of invulnerability, a vision of "normalcy" redolent with consumer temptations and glamorous cultural spectacles. In an exhibit at the museum on Ellis Island a few years back, I remember seeing a copy of a letter written by a young Polish migrant in New York to his family back home. Urging them to join him, he wrote that the ordinary person on the streets of America lived a life far more comfortable than aristocrats in Poland could possibly dream of.

In a way America, during the American Century, thus served as a safety 14 valve, allowing the world's poor to dream of a better place somewhere else; to visualize a place neither bound by the constraints of old nor held hostage to the messianic visions of revolutionary Marxist or Fascist movements so powerful in so many other parts of the globe.

Throughout the cold war, even as America spent unprecedented amounts 15 on military hardware, enough was left over to nurture the mass-consumption culture, to build up an infrastructure of vast proportions. And despite the war in Vietnam, despite the dirty wars that ravaged Latin America in the 1980s, despite America's nefarious role in promoting coups and dictatorships in a slew of countries-cum-cold-war-pawns around the globe, somehow much of the world preserved a rosy-hued vision of America that could have been culled straight from the marketing rooms of Madison Avenue.

Now something is changing. Having dealt with history largely on its 16 own terms, largely with the ability to deflect the worst of the chaos to arenas outside our borders (as imperial Britain did in the century following the defeat of Napoleon in 1815, through to the disastrous events leading up to World War I in 1914), America has attracted a concentrated fury and vengeful ire of disastrous proportions. The willingness to forgive, embodied in so much of the world's embrace of the American Dream, is being replaced by a rather vicious craving to see America—which, under the Bush administration, has increasingly defined its greatness by way of military triumphs—humbled. Moreover, no great power has served as a magnet for such a maelstrom of hate in an era as saturated with media images, as susceptible to instantaneous opinion-shaping coverage of events occurring anywhere in the world.

I guess the question that gnaws at my consciousness could be rephrased   17 as: How does one give an encore to a bravura performance? It's either an anticlimax or, worse, a dismal failure—with the audience heading out the doors halfway through, talking not of the brilliance of the earlier music, but of the tawdriness of the last few bars. If the 20th century was the American Century, its best hopes largely embodied by something akin to the American Dream, what kind of follow-up can the 21st century bring?

In the immediate aftermath of September 11, an outpouring of genuine, if   18 temporary, solidarity from countries and peoples across the globe swathed America in an aura of magnificent victimhood. We, the most powerful country on earth, had been blindsided by a ruthless, ingenious, and barbaric enemy, two of our greatest cities violated. We demanded the world's tears, and, overwhelmingly, we received them. They were, we felt, no less than our due, no more than our merit. In the days after the trade center collapsed, even the Parisian daily *Le Monde*, not known for its pro-Yankee sentimentality, informed its readers, in an echo of John F. Kennedy's famous "Ich bin ein Berliner" speech, that "we are all Americans now."

Perhaps inevitably, however, that sympathy has now largely dissipated.   19 Powerful countries under attack fight back—ruthlessly, brutally, with all the economic, political, diplomatic, and military resources at their disposal. They always have; like as not, they always will. In so doing, perhaps they cannot but step on the sensibilities of smaller, less powerful dare I say it, less *imperial* nations and peoples. And as Britain, the country in which I grew up, discovered so painfully during the early years of World War II, sometimes the mighty end up standing largely alone, bulwarks against history's periodic tidal waves. In that fight, even if they emerge successful, they ultimately emerge also tarnished and somewhat humbled, their power and drive and confidence at least partly evaporated on the battlefield.

In the post–September 11 world, even leaving aside Iraq and all the   20 distortions, half-truths, and lies used to justify the invasion, even leaving aside the cataclysmic impact of the Abu Ghraib prison photographs, I believe America would have attracted significant wrath simply in doing what had to be done in routing out the Taliban in Afghanistan, in reorienting its foreign policy to try and tackle international terror networks and breeding grounds. That is why I come back time and again in my mind to the tactical brilliance of Al Qaeda's September 11 attacks: If America hadn't responded, a green light would have been turned on, one that signaled that the country was too decadent to defend its vital interests. Yet in responding, the response itself was almost guaranteed to spotlight an empire bullying allies and enemies alike into cooperation and subordination and, thus, to focus an inchoate rage against the world's lone standing super-power. Damned if we did, damned if we didn't.

Which brings me back to the American Dream. In the past even as our   21
power grew, much of the world saw us, rightly or wrongly, as a moral beacon, as a country somehow largely outside the bloody, gory, oft-tyrannical history that carved its swath across so much of the world during the American Century. Indeed, in many ways, even as cultural elites in once-glorious Old World nations sneered at upstart, crass, consumerist America, the masses in those nations idealized America as some sort of Promised Land, as a place of freedoms and economic possibilities simply unheard of in many parts of the globe. In many ways, the American Dream of the last 100-some years has been more something dreamed by foreigners from afar, especially those who experienced fascism or Stalinism, than lived as a universal reality on the ground in the United States.

Things look simpler from a distance than they do on the ground. In   22
the past foreigners might have idealized America as a place whose streets were paved if not with gold, at least with alloys seeded with rare and precious metals, even while those who lived here knew it was a gigantic, complicated, multifaceted, continental country with a vast patchwork of cultures and creeds coexisting side by messy side. Today, I fear, foreigners slumber with dreamy American smiles on their sleeping faces no more; that intangible faith in the pastel-colored hue and soft contours of the Dream risks being shattered, replaced instead by an equally simplistic dislike of all things and peoples American.

Paradoxically these days it is the political elites—the leaders and policy   23
analysts and defense experts—who try to hold in place alliances built up in the post–World War II years as the *pax Americana* spread its wings, while the populaces shy away from an America perceived to be dominated by corporations, military musclemen, and empire-builders-in-the-name-of-democracy; increasingly they sympathize with the unnuanced critiques of the Margaret Drabbles of the world. The Pew survey, for example, found that sizable majorities in countries such as Jordan, Morocco, Turkey, Germany, and France believed the war on terror to be largely about the United States wanting to control Middle Eastern oil supplies.

In other words, the *perception*—never universally held, but held by   24
enough people to help shape our global image—is changing. Once our image
abroad was of an exceptional country accruing all the power of empire
without the psychology of empire; now it is being replaced by something
more historically normal—that of a great power determined to preserve and
expand its might, for its own selfish interests and not much else. An exhibit
in New York's Whitney Museum last year, titled "The American Effect,"
presented the works of 50 artists from around the world who portrayed
an America intent on world dominance through military adventurism and
gross consumption habits. In the run-up to the war in Iraq, Mikhail Gor-
bachev lambasted an America he now viewed as operating in a manner "far
from real world leadership." Nelson Mandela talked of the United States as
a country that "has committed unspeakable atrocities in the world."

Maybe the American Dream always was little more than marketing   25
hype (the author Jeffrey Decker writes in *Made in America* that the term
itself was conjured up in 1931 by a populist historian named James Truslow Adams, perhaps as an antidote to the harsh realities of Depression-era
America). But as the savagery of the images coming out of Iraq demonstrate all too well, we live in a world where image is if not everything, at
least crucial. Perhaps I'm wrong and the American Dream will continue to
sweeten the sleep of those living overseas for another century. I certainly
hope, very much, that I'm wrong—for a world denuded of the Dream,
however far from complex reality that Dream might have been, would
be impoverished indeed. But I worry that that encore I mentioned earlier
won't be nearly as breathtaking or as splendid as the original performance
that shaped the first American century.

Thinking About the Essay

1. Why does Abramsky wait until paragraph 3 to inform the reader that
   he grew up in London? What effect does this strategic withholding of
   information have upon you as a reader?

2. List some of the illustrations that Abramsky invokes as "barometers" of
   public sentiment.

3. According to Abramsky, why is it important for the future of America that
   foreigners continue to idealize the country and believe in some concept of
   an American Dream?

4. How does Abramsky characterize American power as being the result of a
   symbiotic relationship or exchange with the rest of the world?

5. The concluding sentence picks up an extended metaphor (or conceit) that
   was introduced earlier in the essay. How effective is this metaphor as a
   structuring device?

Responding in Writing

6. Do you feel that the Iraq war is merely a pretext for a deeper discontent with America? In a brief essay, speculate on the nature of the discontent underlying one critique of the Iraq war that you have heard expressed.

7. Reread the no-win scenario outlined in paragraph 20. Do you agree with Abramksy's statement that America "would have attracted significant wrath simply in doing what had to be done"? Defend your opinion in an argumentative essay.

8. Have you ever felt "marginalized by history," as a result of your place of birth, time of birth, or other factors beyond your control? Write an essay explaining some of the factors that would contribute to that feeling.

Networking

9. In groups of three or four, list some key features of the American Dream, and share these lists with the class. Is there a concept of the American Dream common to everyone in the class?

10. Go online and view (or read about) some of the works that were on display in The American Effect exhibit at New York's Whitney Museum. Do you detect a "party line" in the way these artists view America? Are there perceptions of America that Abramsky might consider "nuanced"?

CHAPTER 4

Speaking in Tongues: Does Language Unify or Divide Us?

The diverse voices in the previous chapters reflect some of the numerous ethnic and racial aspects of the new American mosaic—as well as global perceptions of American exceptionalism. Part of this mosaic is the variety of languages we hear on American streets and college campuses. Of course, you have been taught to speak and write the same language—that standard variety of English that places you in the college classroom today. Knowing the standard English "code" provides you with a powerful tool, offering pragmatic and liberating ways to gain control over your world.

However, other languages might compete for your attention at home or in your community. Powerful constituencies—politicians and advertisers among them—exploit this fact. For example, some Anglo politicians try to speak Spanish to Latino crowds (often to the amusement of native Spanish speakers). Other constituencies, threatened by our multilingual world, try to enact "English-only" laws in various states. Moreover, governments often use language—for example, words like "patriotism" or "Islamic fascism"—to advance political goals. Language can unify or divide a community or nation, but basically it remains a mark of your identity. To know a language or languages permits you to navigate your community, culture, and even global society.

Imagine, for example, what it would be like if you were illiterate. For one thing, you wouldn't be in college. You might not be able to read a menu or fill out a job application. You might not be interested in voting because you cannot read the names of the candidates. Illiteracy in reality is common around the world—and far more common in the United States than you might think.

We have vivid reminders of both the cost of illiteracy and also the power of literacy in film and literature. In the film *Driving Miss Daisy*, the character played by Morgan Freeman goes through most of his life pretending to read the daily newspaper. When Daisy (played by

The neighborhood of Elmhurst, Queens, in New York City, is one of the most ethnically and linguistically diverse places in the world. At Elmhurst's Newtown High School alone, students come from more than 100 countries and at least 39 languages are spoken. In this photograph, local schoolchildren take part in the neighborhood's annual International Day Festival on May 27, 1999.

Thinking About the Image

1. Recall a class photograph from your childhood. Was your school as diverse as this group of schoolchildren, or not? What are the advantages of being exposed to so many nationalities and languages at such a young age? What are the disadvantages?
2. News photographers often shoot many images of the same event, sometimes even multiple rolls of film, and then decide with their editors which unique image best captures the spirit of the event. Why do you think this photo was selected?
3. Are there parades for various ethnic or social groups in your community? How are those events covered in the local news media?
4. Would this parade have achieved its purpose, or appealed to its audience, as effectively if the marchers were adults instead of children? Why or why not? Would the message (or purpose) have been different? In what way?

Jessica Tandy) teaches him to read, his world—and his comprehension of it—expands. Or consider one of the memorable sequences in *The Autobiography of Malcolm X*. Malcolm teaches himself to read and write when he is in prison. He starts at the beginning of the dictionary and works his way to the end. Going into prison as Richard Little, he comes out as Malcolm X, his identity reconstructed not only by the acquisition of a new system of belief—Islam—but also by a newly acquired literacy. In his writing and in his recovered life, Malcolm X harnessed the power of language to transform himself and his understanding of the world.

Think of language, then, as a radical weapon. Language permits you to share experiences and emotions, process information, analyze situations and events, defend a position, advocate a cause, and make decisions. Language contributes to the growth of the self. Language is the bedrock of our academic, social, and professional lives. Language is a liberating force—but some writers in this chapter remind us that language can also be culturally and politically divisive.

The idea that language is the key to our identity and our perception of the world is not new. Early Greek and Roman philosophers believed that you could not be a good thinker or writer unless you were a good person. Assuming that you are a good person, you possess a repertoire of mental skills that you can bring to bear on various situations and dimensions of your life. You can draw inferences, interpret conditions, understand causal relationships, develop arguments, make intelligent choices, and so forth. But have you ever found yourself in a situation where you know what you mean but not how to say it? Or think of how difficult it must be for people acquiring a second language; they know what they mean in their primary language but cannot express it in their new one. The essays in this chapter deal with precisely this situation.

The writers in this chapter illuminate the power and paradox of language. They link language, culture, politics, and identity. They use language with skill intelligence, and emotion. They work with the problems and contradictions of language, seeking answers to the question, Who am I, and where do my words—my languages—fit into the American as well as the world mosaic?

Leave Your Name at the Border

Manuel Munoz

Manuel Munoz, who was born in 1972 in Dinuba, California, has written two well-received collections of short fiction, *Zigzagger* (2003) and *The Faith Healer of Olive Avenue* (2007), inspired by his childhood in the San Joaquin Valley. The son of farmworkers in California's Central Valley, Munoz was the first person in his family to go to college, receiving a B.A. from Harvard University and an M.F.A. from Cornell University. The recipient of a National Endowment for the Arts fellowship in fiction and the Whiting Writers' Award, Munoz contributes stories and essays to periodicals including the *Boston Review*, *Edinburgh Review*, and *The New York Times*. In this article from the August 1, 2007, issue of *The New York Times*, Munoz discusses the problems and power of code-switching as he ponders the ways in which various constituencies perceive him—and his name.

Before Reading

Do you have an immigrant name, a mainstream or assimilated name, or something in between? Is your name "white" or "not white"? What do you think your name—first or last—tells others about who you are and where you are from?

At the Fresno airport, as I made my way to the gate, I heard a name over the intercom. The way the name was pronounced by the gate agent made me want to see what she looked like. That is, I wanted to see whether she was Mexican. Around Fresno, identity politics rarely deepen into exacting terms, so to say "Mexican" means, essentially, "not white." The slivered self-identifications Chicano, Hispanic, Mexican-American and Latino are not part of everyday life in the Valley. You're either Mexican or you're not. If someone wants to know if you were born in Mexico, they'll ask. Then you're From Over There—de allá. And leave it at that.

The gate agent, it turned out, was Mexican. Well-coiffed, in her 30s, she wore foundation that was several shades lighter than the rest of her skin. It was the kind of makeup job I've learned to silently identify at the mall when I'm with my mother, who will say nothing about it until we're back in the car. Then she'll point to the darkness of her own skin, wondering aloud why women try to camouflage who they are.

I watched the Mexican gate agent busy herself at the counter, professional and studied. Once again, she picked up the microphone and, with authority, announced the name of the missing customer: "Eugenio Reyes, please come to the front desk."

You can probably guess how she said it. Her Anglicized pronunciation wouldn't be unusual in a place like California's Central Valley. I didn't have a Mexican name there either: I was an instruction guide.

When people ask me where I'm from, I say Fresno because I don't expect them to know little Dinuba. Fresno is a booming city of nearly 500,000 these days, with a diversity—white, Mexican, African-American,

Armenian, Hmong and Middle Eastern people are all well represented—that shouldn't surprise anyone. It's in the small towns like Dinuba that surround Fresno that the awareness of cultural difference is stripped down to the interactions between the only two groups that tend to live there: whites and Mexicans. When you hear a Mexican name spoken in these towns, regardless of the speaker's background, it's no wonder that there's an "English way of pronouncing it."

I was born in 1972, part of a generation that learned both English and   6
Spanish. Many of my cousins and siblings are bilingual, serving as translators for those in the family whose English is barely functional. Others have no way of following the Spanish banter at family gatherings. You can tell who falls into which group: Estella, Eric, Delia, Dubina, Melanie. It's intriguing to watch "American" names begin to dominate among my nieces and nephews and second cousins, as well as with the children of my hometown friends. I am not surprised to meet 5-year-old Brandon or Kaitlyn. Hardly anyone questions the incongruity of matching these names with last names like Trujillo or Zepeda. The English-only way of life partly explains the quiet erasure of cultural difference that assimilation has attempted to accomplish. A name like Kaitlyn Zepeda doesn't completely obscure her ethnicity, but the half-step of her name, as a gesture, is almost understandable.

Spanish was and still is viewed with suspicion: Always the language of   7
the vilified illegal immigrant, it segregated schoolchildren into English-only and bilingual programs; it defined you, above all else, as part of a lower class. Learning English, though, brought its own complications. It was simultaneously the language of the white population and a path toward the richer, expansive identity of "American." But it took getting out of the Valley for me to understand that "white" and "American" were two very different things.

Something as simple as saying our names "in English" was our   8
unwittingly complicit gesture of trying to blend in. Pronouncing Mexican names correctly was never encouraged. Names like Daniel, Olivia and Marco slipped right into the mutability of the English language. I remember a school ceremony at which the mathematics teacher, a white man, announced the names of Mexican students correctly and caused some confusion, if not embarrassment. Years later we recognized that he spoke in deference to our Spanish-speaking parents in the audience, caring teacher that he was.

These were difficult names for a non-Spanish speaker: Araceli,   9
Nadira, Luis (a beautiful name when you glide the u and the i as you're supposed to). We had been accustomed to having our birth names altered for convenience. Concepción was Connie. Ramón was Raymond. My cousin Esperanza was Hope—but her name was pronounced "Hopie"

because any Spanish speaker would automatically pronounce the e at the end.

Ours, then, were names that stood as barriers to a complete embrace 10 of an American identity, simply because their pronunciations required a slip into Spanish, the otherness that assimilation was supposed to erase. What to do with names like Amado, Lucio or Élida? There are no English "equivalents," no answer when white teachers asked, "What does your name mean?" when what they really wanted to know was "What's the English one?" So what you heard was a name butchered beyond recognition, a pronunciation that pointed the finger at the Spanish language as the source of clunky sound and ugly rhythm.

My stepfather, from Ojos de Agua, Mexico, jokes when I ask him 11 about the names of Mexicans born here. He deliberately stumbles over pronunciations, imitating our elders who have difficulty with Bradley and Madelyn. "Ashley Sánchez. ¿Tú crees?" He wonders aloud what has happened to the "nombres del rancho"—traditional Mexican names that are hardly given anymore to children born in the States: Heraclio, Madaleno, Otilia, Dominga. My stepfather's experience with the Anglicization of his name—Antonio to Tony—ties into something bigger than learning English. For him, the erasure of his name was about deference and subservience. Becoming Tony gave him a measure of access as he struggled to learn English and get more fieldwork.

This isn't to say that my stepfather welcomed the change, only that 12 he could not put up much resistance. Not changing put him at risk of being passed over for work. English was a world of power and decisions, of smooth, uninterrupted negotiation. Clear communication meant you could go unsupervised. Every gesture made toward convincing an employer that English was on its way to being mastered had the potential to make a season of fieldwork profitable. It's curious that many of us growing up in Dinuba adhered to the same rules. Although as children of farm workers we worked in the fields at an early age, we'd also had the opportunity to stay in one town long enough to finish school. Most of us had learned English early and splintered off into a dual existence of English at school, Spanish at home. But instead of recognizing the need for fluency in both languages, we turned it into a peculiar kind of battle. English was for public display. Spanish was for privacy—and privacy quickly turned to shame. The corrosive effect of assimilation is the displacement of one culture over another, the inability to sustain more than one way of being. It isn't a code word for racial and ethnic acculturation only. It applies to needing to belong, of seeing from the outside and wondering how to get in and then, once inside, realizing there are always those still on the fringe.

When I went to college on the East Coast, I was confronted for the   13
first time by people who said my name correctly without prompting; if
they stumbled, there was a quick apology and an honest plea to help
with the pronunciation. But introducing myself was painful: already
shy, I avoided meeting people because I didn't want to say my name, felt
burdened by my own history. I knew that my small-town upbringing and
its limitations on Spanish would not have been tolerated by any of the
students of color who had grown up in large cities, in places where the
sheer force of their native languages made them dominant in their neighborhoods. It didn't take long for me to assert the power of code-switching
in public, the transferring of words from one language to another, regardless of who might be listening. I was learning that the English language
composed new meanings when its constrictions were ignored, crossed
over or crossed out. Language is all about manipulation, or not listening
to the rules.

When I come back to Dinuba, I have a hard time hearing my name said   14
incorrectly, but I have an even harder time beginning a conversation with
others about why the pronunciation of our names matters. Leaving a small
town requires an embrace of a larger point of view, but a town like Dinuba
remains forever embedded in an either/or way of life. My stepfather still
answers to Tony and, as the United States–born children grow older, their
Anglicized names begin to signify who does and who does not "belong"—
who was born here and who is de allá.

My name is Manuel. To this day, most people cannot say it correctly,
the way it was intended to be said. But I can live with that because I love
the alliteration of my full name. It wasn't the name my mother, Esmeralda,   15
was going to give me. At the last minute, my father named me after an
uncle I would never meet. My name was to have been Ricardo. Growing
up in Dinuba, I'm certain I would have become Ricky or even Richard, and
the journey toward the discovery of the English language's extraordinary
power in even the most ordinary of circumstances would probably have
gone unlearned.

I count on a collective sense of cultural loss to once again swing the   16
names back to our native language. The Mexican gate agent announced
Eugenio Reyes, but I never got a chance to see who appeared. I pictured an
older man, cowboy hat in hand, but I made the assumption on his name
alone, the clash of privileges I imagined between someone de allá and a
Mexican woman with a good job in the United States. Would she speak to
him in Spanish? Or would she raise her voice to him as if he were hard of
hearing?

But who was I to imagine this man being from anywhere, based on his 17
name alone? At a place of arrivals and departures, it sank into me that the
currency of our names is a stroke of luck: because mine was not an easy
name, it forced me to consider how language would rule me if I allowed it.
Yet I discovered that only by leaving. My stepfather must live in the Valley,
a place that does not allow that choice, every day. And Eugenio Reyes—
I do not know if he was coming or going.

Thinking About the Essay

1. Why do you think that Munoz begins his essay—and ends it as well—at
   the Fresno, California, airport? On what and whom does he focus, and how
   does this focus serve to illuminate his broader analysis?

2. What is Munoz's thesis, and where does he state it? How does the
   "corrosive effect of assimilation" inform this thesis?

3. Munoz organizes this essay around a series of contrasts. What is
   the primary contrast? What are additional contrasts that inform this
   comparative structure?

4. Why does Munoz introduce so many names in this essay—sometimes
   lists of names as in paragraphs 6 and 9? Do you find these names to be a
   distraction or do they reinforce the writer's thesis? Explain.

5. Explain the ways in which Munoz merges narrative, personal experience,
   analysis, and perhaps even argument in this essay. What does his strategy
   tell you about mixing modes or patterns when writing an essay?

Responding in Writing

6. Write a personal essay about your own name, combining narrative,
   descriptive, and expository techniques.

7. Write an analytical paper on what Munoz terms "the power of code-
   switching in public" (paragraph 13).

8. Argue for or against the proposition that assimilation can have a corrosive
   effect.

Networking

9. In groups of three or four, develop a list of all the names—and variants
   of names—that Munoz introduces in his essay. Discuss the relevance of
   these names to Munoz's argument. Appoint one member of the group to
   present your evaluation.

10. Go online and find out more about "code-switching." Provide a critique of
    your research in a brief paper.

Mother Tongue

AMY TAN

Amy Tan was born in San Francisco, California, in 1952, only two and a half years after her parents emigrated from China to the United States. She was educated at San Jose State University and the University of California at Berkeley and then worked as a reporter and technical writer. Tan is best known as a novelist whose fiction focuses on the conflict in culture between Chinese parents and their Americanized children. Her first novel, *The Joy Luck Club* (1989), was highly popular and adapted by Hollywood as a feature film. Tan's other novels are *The Kitchen God's Wife* (1991), *The Hundred Secret Senses* (1995), *The Bonesetter's Daughter* (2001), and *Saving the Fish from Drowning* (2006). Tan published a nonfiction work, *The Opposite of Fate: A Book of Musings*, in 2003. Tan's complicated relationship with her mother, Daisy, who died of Alzheimer's disease in 1999 at the age of eighty-three, is central to much of her fiction. In this essay, published in 1990 in *The Threepenny Review*, Tan, who has a master's degree in linguistics, invokes her mother in exploring the "Englishes" that immigrants employ as they navigate American culture.

Before Reading

How many "Englishes" do you speak, and what types of English do you speak in various situations? Is the English you speak in the classroom the same as you speak in your home or dormitory?

I am not a scholar of English or literature. I cannot give you much more   1
than personal opinions on the English language and its variations in this country or others.

I am a writer. And by that definition, I am someone who has always   2
loved language. I am fascinated by language in daily life. I spend a great deal of my time thinking about the power of language—the way it can evoke an emotion, a visual image, a complex idea, or a simple truth. Language is the tool of my trade. And I use them all—all the Englishes I grew up with.

Recently, I was made keenly aware of the different Englishes I do   3
use. I was giving a talk to a large group of people, the same talk I had

already given to half a dozen other groups. The nature of the talk was about my writing, my life, and my book, *The Joy Luck Club*. The talk was going along well enough, until I remembered one major difference that made the whole talk sound wrong. My mother was in the room. And it was perhaps the first time she had heard me give a lengthy speech, using the kind of English I have never used with her. I was saying things like, "The intersection of memory upon imagination" and "There is an aspect of my fiction that relates to thus-and-thus"—a speech filled with carefully wrought grammatical phrases, burdened, it suddenly seemed to me, with nominalized forms, past perfect tenses, conditional phrases, all the forms of standard English that I had learned in school and through books, the forms of English I did not use at home with my mother.

Just last week, I was walking down the street with my mother, and I again found myself conscious of the English I was using, the English I do use with her. We were talking about the price of new and used furniture and I heard myself saying this: "Not waste money that way." My husband was with us as well, and he didn't notice any switch in my English. And then I realized why. It's because over the twenty years we've been together I've often used that same kind of English with him, and sometimes he even uses it with me. It has become our language of intimacy, a different sort of English that relates to family talk, the language I grew up with.

So you'll have some idea of what this family talk I heard sounds like, I'll quote what my mother said during a recent conversation which I videotaped and then transcribed. During this conversation, my mother was talking about a political gangster in Shanghai who had the same last name as her family's, Du, and how the gangster in his early years wanted to be adopted by her family, which was rich by comparison. Later, the gangster became more powerful, far richer than my mother's family, and one day showed up at my mother's wedding to pay his respects. Here's what she said in part:

"Du Yusong having business like fruit stand. Like off the street kind. He is Du like Du Zong—but not Tsung-ming Island people. The local people call putong, the river east side, he belong to that side local people. That man want to ask Du Zong father take him in like become own family. Du Zong father wasn't look down on him, but didn't take seriously, until that man big like become a mafia. Now important person, very hard to inviting him. Chinese way, came only to show respect, don't stay for dinner. Respect for making big celebration, he shows up. Mean gives lots of respect. Chinese custom. Chinese social life that way. If too important won't have to stay too long. He come to my wedding. I didn't see, I heard it. I gone to boy's side, they have YMCA dinner. Chinese age I was nineteen."

You should know that my mother's expressive command of English belies how much she actually understands. She reads the *Forbes* report, listens to *Wall Street Week*, converses daily with her stockbroker, and reads all of Shirley MacLaine's books with ease—all kinds of things I can't begin to understand. Yet some of my friends tell me they understand 50 percent of what my mother says. Some say they understand 80 to 90 percent. Some say they understand none of it, as if she were speaking pure Chinese. But to me, my mother's English is perfectly clear, perfectly natural. It's my mother tongue. Her language, as I hear it, is vivid, direct, full of observation and imagery. That was the language that helped shape the way I saw things, expressed things, made sense of the world.

Lately, I've been giving more thought to the kind of English my mother speaks. Like others, I have described it to people as "broken" or "fractured" English. But I wince when I say that. It has always bothered me that I can think of no way to describe it other than "broken," as if it were damaged and needed to be fixed, as if it lacked a certain wholeness and soundness. I've heard other terms used, "limited English," for example. But they seem just as bad, as if everything is limited, including people's perceptions of the limited English speaker.

I know this for a fact, because when I was growing up, my mother's "limited" English limited *my* perception of her. I was ashamed of her English. I believed that her English reflected the quality of what she had to say. That is, because she expressed them imperfectly her thoughts were imperfect. And I had plenty of empirical evidence to support me: the fact that people in department stores, at banks, and at restaurants did not take her seriously, did not give her good service, pretended not to understand her, or even acted as if they did not hear her.

My mother has long realized the limitations of her English as well. When I was fifteen, she used to have me call people on the phone to pretend I was she. In this guise, I was forced to ask for information or even to complain and yell at people who had been rude to her. One time it was a call to her stockbroker in New York. She had cashed out her small portfolio and it just so happened we were going to go to New York the next week, our very first trip outside California. I had to get on the phone and say in an adolescent voice that was not very convincing, "This is Mrs. Tan."

And my mother was standing in the back whispering loudly, "Why he 11 don't send me check, already two weeks late. So mad he lie to me, losing me money."

And then I said in perfect English, "Yes, I'm getting rather con- 12 cerned. You had agreed to send the check two weeks ago, but it hasn't arrived."

Then she began to talk more loudly. "What he want, I come to New 13 York tell him front of his boss, you cheating me?" And I was trying to calm her down, make her be quiet, while telling the stockbroker, "I can't tolerate any more excuses. If I don't receive the check immediately, I am going to have to speak to your manager when I'm in New York next week." And sure enough, the following week there we were in front of this astonished stockbroker, and I was sitting there red-faced and quiet, and my mother, the real Mrs. Tan, was shouting at his boss in her impeccable broken English.

We used a similar routine just five days ago, for a situation that was 14 far less humorous. My mother had gone to the hospital for an appointment, to find out about a benign brain tumor a CAT scan had revealed a month ago. She said she had spoken very good English, her best English, no mistakes. Still, she said, the hospital did not apologize when they said they had lost the CAT scan and she had come for nothing. She said they did not seem to have any sympathy when she told them she was anxious to know the exact diagnosis, since her husband and son had both died of brain tumors. She said they would not give her any more information until the next time and she would have to make another appointment for that. So she said she would not leave until the doctor called her daughter. She wouldn't budge. And when the doctor finally called her daughter, me, who spoke in perfect English—lo and behold—we had assurances the CAT scan would be found, promises that a conference call on Monday would be held, and apologies for any suffering my mother had gone through for a most regrettable mistake.

I think my mother's English almost had an effect on limiting my 15 possibilities in life as well. Sociologists and linguists probably will tell you that a person's developing language skills are more influenced by peers. But I do think that the language spoken in the family, especially in immigrant families which are more insular, plays a large role in shaping the language of the child. And I believe that it affected my results on achievement tests, IQ tests, and the SAT. While my English skills were never judged as poor, compared to math, English could not be considered my strong suit. In grade school I did moderately well, getting perhaps B's, sometimes B-pluses, in English and scoring perhaps in the sixtieth or seventieth percentile on achievement tests. But those scores were not good enough to override the opinion that my true abilities lay in math and science, because in those areas I achieved A's and scored in the ninetieth percentile or higher.

This was understandable. Math is precise; there is only one correct   16
answer. Whereas, for me at least, the answers on English tests were always a judgment call, a matter of opinion and personal experience. Those tests were constructed around items like fill-in-the-blank sentence completion, such as, "Even though Tom was, Mary thought he was." And the correct answer always seemed to be the most bland combinations of thoughts, for example, "Even though Tom was shy, Mary thought he was charming," with the grammatical structure "even though" limiting the correct answer to some sort of semantic opposites, so you wouldn't get answers like, "Even though Tom was foolish, Mary thought he was ridiculous." Well, according to my mother, there were very few limitations as to what Tom could have been and what Mary might have thought of him. So I never did well on tests like that.

The same was true with word analogies, pairs of words in which   17
you were supposed to find some sort of logical, semantic relationship— for example, "*Sunset* is to *nightfall* as _____ is to _____." And here you would be presented with a list of four possible pairs, one of which showed the same kind of relationship: *red* is to *stoplight, bus* is to *arrival, chills* is to *fever, yawn* is to *boring*. Well, I could never think that way. I knew what the tests were asking, but I could not block out of my mind the images already created by the first pair," *sunset* is to *nightfall*"—and I would see a burst of colors against a darkening sky, the moon rising, the lowering of a curtain of stars. And all the other pairs of words—red, bus, stoplight, boring—just threw up a mass of confusing images, making it impossible for me to sort out something as logical as saying: "A sunset precedes nightfall" is the same as "a chill precedes a fever." The only way I would have gotten that answer right would have been to imagine an associative situation, for example, my being disobedient and staying out past sunset, catching a chill at night, which turns into feverish pneumonia as punishment, which indeed did happen to me.

I have been thinking about all this lately, about my mother's English,   18
about achievement tests. Because lately I've been asked, as a writer, why there are not more Asian Americans represented in American literature. Why are there few Asian Americans enrolled in creative writing programs?

Why do so many Chinese students go into engineering? Well, these are broad sociological questions I can't begin to answer. But I have noticed in surveys—in fact, just last week—that Asian students, as a whole, always do significantly better on math achievement tests than in English. And this makes me think that there are other Asian-American students whose English spoken in the home might also be described as "broken" or "limited." And perhaps they also have teachers who are steering them away from writing and into math and science, which is what happened to me.

Fortunately, I happen to be rebellious in nature and enjoy the challenge 19 of disproving assumptions made about me. I became an English major my first year in college, after being enrolled as pre-med. I started writing non-fiction as a freelancer the week after I was told by my former boss that writing was my worst skill and I should hone my talents toward account management.

But it wasn't until 1985 that I finally began to write fiction. And 20 at first I wrote using what I thought to be wittily crafted sentences, sentences that would finally prove I had mastery over the English language. Here's an example from the first draft of a story that later made its way into *The Joy Luck Club,* but without this line: "That was my mental quandary in its nascent state." A terrible line, which I can barely pronounce.

Fortunately, for reasons I won't get into today, I later decided 21 I should envision a reader for the stories I would write. And the reader I decided upon was my mother, because these were stories about mothers. So with this reader in mind—and in fact she did read my early drafts—I began to write stories using all the Englishes I grew up with: the English I spoke to my mother, which for lack of a better term might be described as "simple"; the English she used with me, which for lack of a better term might be described as "broken"; my translation of her Chinese, which could certainly be described as "watered down"; and what I imagined to be her translation of her Chinese if she could speak in perfect English, her internal language, and for that I sought to preserve the essence, but neither an English nor a Chinese structure. I wanted to capture what language ability tests can never reveal: her intent, her passion, her imagery, the rhythms of her speech and the nature of her thoughts.

Apart from what any critic had to say about my writing, I knew I had 22 succeeded where it counted when my mother finished reading my book and gave me her verdict: "So easy to read."

Thinking About the Essay

1. Explain the multiple meanings of Tan's title and how they illuminate the essay. What are the four ways Tan says language can work?

2. What is Tan's thesis, and where does it appear? How do we know her point of view about other "Englishes"? Does she state it directly or indirectly, and where?

3. How do narration and description interact in this essay? How does Tan describe her mother? What is the importance of dialogue?

4. What is Tan's viewpoint about language? Does she state that language should always be "simple"? Why or why not? To the extent that Tan's mother is an intended audience for her essay, is her language simple? Explain your answer by specific reference to her words and sentences. Finally, why does Tan's mother find her daughter's writing easy to understand?

5. How and where does Tan use humor in this essay? Where does Tan employ amusing anecdotes? What is her purpose in presenting these anecdotes, and how do they influence the essay's overall tone?

Responding in Writing

6. Tan suggests that the way we use language reflects the way we see the world. Write an essay based on this observation. Feel free to present an analytical paper or a narrative and descriptive essay, or to blend these patterns as does Tan.

7. Should all Americans speak and write the same language? Answer this question in an argumentative essay.

8. Tan writes about the "shame" she once experienced because of her mother's speech (paragraph 9). Write an essay about the dangers of linking personality or behavior to language. Can this linkage be used to promote racist, sexist, or other discriminatory ideas?

Networking

9. With two other class members, draw up a list of all the "Englishes" you have encountered. For example, how do your parents speak? What about relatives? Friends? Classmates? Personalities on television? Share your list with the class.

10. Conduct Internet or library research on the role of stereotyping by language in American radio and/or film. You might want to look into the popularity of the Charlie Chan series or Amos and Andy, or focus on a particular film that stereotypes a group. Present your information in an analytical and evaluative essay.

Mute in an English-Only World

CHANG-RAE LEE

Chang-rae Lee was born in 1965 in Seoul, South Korea. He and his family emigrated to the United States in 1968. Lee attended public schools in New Rochelle, New York; graduated from Yale University (B.A., 1987); and received an M.F.A. degree from the University of Oregon (1993). His first novel, *Native Speaker* (1995), won several prizes, including the Ernest Hemingway Foundation/PEN Award for First Fiction. He has also written *A Gesture Life* (1999) and *Aloft* (2004), and he has published fiction and nonfiction in many magazines, including *The New Yorker* and *Time*. Lee has taught in the creative writing programs at the University of Oregon and Hunter College; today he is part of the Humanities Council and creative writing program at Princeton University. In the following essay, which appeared on the op-ed page of *The New York Times* in 1996, Lee remembers his mother's efforts to learn English, using literary memoir to comment on recent laws passed by certain towns in New Jersey requiring English on all commercial signs.

Before Reading

Should all commercial signs have English written on them, in addition to any other language? What about menus in ethnic restaurants?

When I read of the troubles in Palisades Park, N.J., over the proliferation 1 of Korean-language signs along its main commercial strip, I unexpectedly sympathized with the frustrations, resentments and fears of the longtime residents. They clearly felt alienated and even unwelcome in a vital part of their community. The town, like seven others in New Jersey, has passed laws requiring that half of any commercial sign in a foreign language be in English.

Now I certainly would never tolerate any exclusionary ideas about who 2 could rightfully settle and belong in the town. But having been raised in a Korean immigrant family, I saw every day the exacting price and power of language, especially with my mother, who was an outsider in an English-only world.

In the first years we lived in America, my mother could speak only the 3 most basic English, and she often encountered great difficulty whenever she went out.

We lived in New Rochelle, N.Y., in the early '70s, and most of the local   4
businesses were run by the descendants of immigrants who, generations
ago, had come to the suburbs from New York City. Proudly dotting Main
Street and North Avenue were Italian pastry and cheese shops, Jewish
tailors and cleaners and Polish and German butchers and bakers. If my
mother's marketing couldn't wait until the weekend, when my father had
free time, she would often hold off until I came home from school to buy
the groceries.

Though I was only 6 or 7 years old, she insisted that I go out shopping   5
with her and my younger sister. I mostly loathed the task, partly because
it meant I couldn't spend the afternoon playing catch with my friends but
also because I knew our errands would inevitably lead to an awkward
scene, and that I would have to speak up to help my mother.

I was just learning the language myself, but I was a quick study, as children   6
are with new tongues. I had spent kindergarten in almost complete silence,
hearing only the high nasality of my teacher and comprehending little but the
cranky wails and cries of my classmates. But soon, seemingly mere months
later, I had already become a terrible ham and mimic, and I would crack up
my father with impressions of teachers, his friends and even himself. My
mother scolded me for aping his speech, and the one time I attempted to
make light of hers I rated a roundhouse smack on my bottom.

For her, the English language was not very funny. It usually meant   7
trouble and a good dose of shame, and sometimes real hurt. Although she
had a good reading knowledge of the language from university classes in
South Korea, she had never practiced actual conversation. So in America,
she used English flashcards and phrase books and watched television with
us kids. And she faithfully carried a pocket workbook illustrated with
stick-figure people and compound sentences to be filled in.

But none of it seemed to do her much good. Staying mostly at home   8
to care for us, she didn't have many chances to try out sundry words and
phrases. When she did, say, at the window of the post office, her readied
speech would stall, freeze, sometimes altogether collapse.

One day was unusually harrowing. We ventured downtown in the   9
new Ford Country Squire my father had bought her, an enormous station
wagon that seemed as long—and deft—as an ocean liner. We were shopping for a special meal for guests visiting that weekend, and my mother had
heard that a particular butcher carried fresh oxtails—which she needed for
a traditional soup.

We'd never been inside the shop, but my mother would pause before   10
its window, which was always lined with whole hams, crown roasts and

ropes of plump handmade sausages. She greatly esteemed the bounty with her eyes, and my sister and I did also, but despite our desirous cries she'd turn us away and instead buy the packaged links at the Finast supermarket, where she felt comfortable looking them over and could easily spot the price. And, of course, not have to talk.

But that day she was resolved. The butcher store was crowded, and as we stepped inside the door jingled a welcome. No one seemed to notice. We waited for some time, and people who entered after us were now being served. Finally, an old woman nudged my mother and waved a little ticket, which we hadn't taken. We patiently waited again, until one of the beefy men behind the glass display hollered our number. 11

My mother pulled us forward and began searching the cases, but the oxtails were nowhere to be found. The man, his big arms crossed, sharply said, "Come on, lady, whaddya want?" This unnerved her, and she somehow blurted the Korean word for oxtail, soggori. 12

The butcher looked as if my mother had put something sour in his mouth, and he glanced back at the lighted board and called the next number. 13

Before I knew it, she had rushed us outside and back in the wagon, which she had double-parked because of the crowd. She was furious, almost vibrating with fear and grief, and I could see she was about to cry. 14

She wanted to go back inside, but now the driver of the car we were blocking wanted to pull out. She was shooing us away. My mother, who had just earned her driver's license, started furiously working the pedals. But in her haste she must have flooded the engine, for it wouldn't turn over. The driver started honking and then another car began honking as well, and soon it seemed the entire street was shrieking at us. 15

In the following years, my mother grew steadily more comfortable with English. In Korean, she could be fiery, stern, deeply funny and ironic; in English, just slightly less so. If she was never quite fluent, she gained enough confidence to make herself clearly known to anyone, and particularly to me. 16

Five years ago, she died of cancer, and some months after we buried her I found myself in the driveway of my father's house, washing her sedan. I liked taking care of her things; it made me feel close to her. While I was cleaning out the glove compartment, I found her pocket English workbook, the one with the silly illustrations. I hadn't seen it in nearly 20 years. The yellowed pages were brittle and dog-eared. She had fashioned a plain-paper wrapping for it, and I wondered whether she meant to protect the book or hide it. 17

I don't doubt that she would have appreciated doing the family 18
shopping on the new Broad Avenue of Palisades Park. But I like to think,
too, that she would have understood those who now complain about the
Korean-only signs.

I wonder what these same people would have done if they had seen my 19
mother studying her English workbook—or lost in a store. Would they
have nodded gently at her? Would they have lent a kind word?

Thinking About the Essay

1. What is the author's purpose? Is he trying to paint a picture of his mother, describe an aspect of the immigrant experience, convey a thesis, argue a point, or what? Explain your response.

2. What is unusual about Lee's introduction? How does his position on the issue raised defy your expectations?

3. Lee offers stories within stories. How are they ordered? Which tale receives greatest development, and why?

4. Lee uses **colloquial language** in this essay. Identify some examples. What is the effect?

5. What is the dominant impression that you have of Lee's mother? How does he bring her to life?

Responding in Writing

6. Construct a profile of the writer. What do we learn about Lee? What are his values? What is his attitude toward English? How does this son of immigrant parents establish himself as an authority? How does he surprise us with his perspective on language?

7. In a personal essay, tell of a time when you were embarrassed either by the language of someone close to you or by your own use of language in a social or business situation.

8. Both Amy Tan and Chang-rae Lee focus on their mothers' handling of their second language—English. Write a comparative essay in which you explain the similarities and differences in the authors' approaches to their subject.

Networking

9. With two other class members, discuss the emotional appeal of Lee's essay. Look especially at his conclusion. Share your responses with the class.

10. Write an e-mail to your instructor, suggesting two additional questions you would ask about Lee's essay if you were teaching it.

The Power of Words in Wartime

ROBIN TOLMACH LAKOFF

Robin Tolmach Lakoff was born in Brooklyn, New York, in 1942 and educated at Radcliffe College (B.A., 1964), Indiana University (M.A., 1965), and Harvard University (Ph.D., 1967). An influential linguist who serves on the faculty at the University of California at Berkeley, Lakoff has written several studies focusing on the influence of language on social attitudes—especially attitudes toward women and "others." Among her most important works are *Language and Women's Place* (1975), *Talking Power: The Politics of Language in Our Lives* (1990), and *The Language of War* (2000). The following essay appeared in the *The New York Times* on May 18, 2004.

Before Reading

What does "stereotyping" mean? What is the relationship between stereotyping and such words in wartime as "terrorist," "jihadist," "invader," "infidel"?

An American soldier refers to an Iraqi prisoner as "it." A general speaks not of "Iraqi fighters" but of "the enemy." A weapons manufacturer doesn't talk about people but about "targets."

Bullets and bombs are not the only tools of war. Words, too, play their part.

Human beings are social animals, genetically hard-wired to feel compassion toward others. Under normal conditions, most people find it very difficult to kill.

But in war, military recruits must be persuaded that killing other people is not only acceptable but even honorable.

The language of war is intended to bring about that change, and not only for soldiers in the field. In wartime, language must be created to enable combatants and noncombatants alike to see the other side as killable, to overcome the innate queasiness over the taking of human life. Soldiers, and those who remain at home, learn to call their enemies by names that make them seem not quite human—inferior, contemptible and not like "us."

The specific words change from culture to culture and war to war. The names need not be obviously demeaning. Just the fact that we can name them gives us a sense of superiority and control. If, in addition, we give them nicknames, we can see them as smaller, weaker and childlike—not worth taking seriously as fully human.

The Greeks and Romans referred to everyone else as "barbarians"— etymologically those who only babble, only go "bar-bar." During the American Revolution, the British called the colonists "Yankees," a term with a history that is still in dispute. While the British intended it disparagingly, the Americans, in perhaps the first historical instance of reclamation, made the word their own and gave it a positive spin, turning the derisive song "Yankee Doodle" into our first, if unofficial, national anthem. 7

In World War I, the British gave the Germans the nickname "Jerries," from the first syllable of German. In World War II, Americans referred to the Japanese as "Japs." 8

The names may refer to real or imagined cultural and physical differences that emphasize the ridiculous or the repugnant. So in various wars, the British called the French "Frogs." Germans have been called "Krauts," a reference to weird and smelly food. The Vietnamese were called "slopes" and "slants." The Koreans were referred to simply as "gooks." 9

The war in Iraq has added new examples. Some American soldiers refer to the Iraqis as "hadjis," used in a derogatory way, apparently unaware that the word, which comes from the Arabic term for a pilgrimage to Mecca, is used as a term of respect for older Muslim men. 10

The Austrian ethologist Konrad Lorenz suggested that the more clearly we see other members of our own species as individuals, the harder we find it to kill them. 11

So some terms of war are collective nouns, encouraging us to see the enemy as an undifferentiated mass, rather than as individuals capable of suffering. Crusaders called their enemy "the Saracen," and in World War I, the British called Germans "the Hun." 12

American soldiers are trained to call those they are fighting against "the enemy." It is easier to kill an enemy than an Iraqi. 13

The word "enemy" itself provides the facelessness of a collective noun. Its non-specificity also has a fear-inducing connotation; enemy means simply "those we are fighting," without reference to their identity. 14

The terrors and uncertainties of war make learning this kind of language especially compelling for soldiers on the front. But civilians back home also need to believe that what their country is doing is just and necessary, and that the killing they are supporting is in some way different from the killing in civilian life that is rightly punished by the criminal 15 justice system. The use of the language developed for military purposes by civilians reassures them that war is not murder.

The linguistic habits that soldiers must absorb in order to fight make   16
atrocities like those at Abu Ghraib virtually inevitable. The same language that creates a psychological chasm between ''us'' and ''them'' and enables American troops to kill in battle, makes enemy soldiers fit subjects for torture and humiliation. The reasoning is: They are not really human, so they will not feel the pain.

Once language draws that line, all kinds of mistreatment become imag-   17
inable, and then justifiable. To make the abuses at Abu Ghraib unthinkable, we would have to abolish war itself.

Thinking About the Essay

1. Lakoff wrote this essay as an op-ed article for a newspaper. What aspects of style, thesis placement, paragraph organization, length, and tone does she employ to satisfy the demands of an op-ed contribution?

2. What is Lakoff's purpose in this essay? Does she want to inform readers about language, analyze words in wartime, argue about the Iraq war, or what?

3. Lakoff organizes her essay around causes and effects, using a series of examples to support her causal analysis. Trace this strategy through the essay, trying to determine where language is a cause, an effect, or both.

4. How logical do you find Lakoff's article, and why? Do you think that she succumbs to any logical fallacies or exaggerates in order to make a point? Justify your response.

5. How effective do you find Lakoff's attempt to link the language stemming from the war in Iraq with that of the language used to invoke the "enemy" in wars stretching back in history to ancient Greece? Is this sufficient support for her thesis or claim? Explain.

Responding in Writing

6. Select one word that appears prominently in discussions of the war in Iraq (or Afghanistan, or both), and demonstrate the ways in which government and the press invoke this word to influence public attitudes.

7. Write a cause-and-effect essay in which you demonstrate the ways in which language can stereotype certain types of people—for example, immigrants, Muslims, gays, Africans.

8. Argue for or against the proposition that Lakoff presents a convincing argument in "The Power of Words in Wartime." Refer to specific strategies she employs to support your position.

Networking

9. Lakoff refers to Konrad Lorenz in paragraph 11. With one other class member, go online and find out more about this person. Then explain in class discussion why you think Lakoff refers to him in her essay.

10. Go online to find out more about Abu Ghraib, a topic that Lakoff injects into her essay. Download at least three images of this episode, and then write a brief essay, with illustrations, highlighting Lakoff's claim about the "psychological chasm between 'us' and 'them.'"

Lingua Franchise

CHARLES FORAN

Charles Foran is from Toronto and holds degrees from the University of Toronto and University College, Dublin. He has taught at universities in China, Hong Kong, and Canada. Foran is the author of eight books, including four novels, and writes regularly for Canadian journals. He has also produced radio documentaries for the Canadian Broadcasting Company's *Ideas* program on subjects ranging from Hong Kong Cinema to contemporary Indian writing. In the following piece, which first appeared in *The Walrus Magazine* in November 2004, Foran looks at how English has been adopted and adapted in the global marketplace.

Before Reading

What elements of a slang dialect make an appearance in your casual speech? How many people do you know who practice this dialect?

In a restaurant in Singapore's Little India district I chatted recently with a man doling out bowls of fish-head curry. He called me a "*mat saleh,*" Malay for 'white foreigner.' He also dubbed a woman who walked past us an "S.P.G."—a 'Sarong Party Girl.' According to him, upper-crust Singaporians who put on posh accents were "chiak kantang." "Chiak" is Hokkien for 'eating,' "kantang" a mangling of the Malay for 'potatoes.' 'Eating potatoes': affecting Western mannerisms.

Singapore has four official languages: Mandarin, English, Malay, and Tamil. At street level, however, there is no mother tongue. Except for among older Chinese, who still speak the Hokkien dialect, the city-state's lingua franca is actually Singlish, a much-loved, much-frowned-upon hodge-podge of languages and slang. When the man in the restaurant asked if I could pay with a smaller bill, he expressed it this way: "Got, lah?" I recognized that bit of cobbling. In Hong Kong, where I was then living, Cantonese speakers sprinkle their English with similar punctuation. 'Lah' often denotes a question, like 'eh' for Canadians. 'Wah' infers astonishment. Once, when I was walking through that city's nightclub district with a Chinese friend, we nearly knocked into a Canto-pop star, a young man of smoldering Elvis looks. "Wah, now can die!" my friend said, only half-jokingly.

3   If English is the region's compromise tongue, default neutral terrain for doing deals and making friends, loan words and hybrid street dialects serve to advance its utility. It is the same across most of Asia. In the Philippines, Tagalog speakers refer to a look-alike as a "Xerox" and an out-dated fad as a "chapter." "Golets," they say, meaning 'Let's go.' Anything first-rate in Bombay gets called "cheese," from 'chiz,' the Hindi word for 'object.' In Japan, students on a Friday night announce "Let's beer!" and salarymen quit smoking because of a "dokuto-sutoppu" a 'doctor-stop,' or orders from their physician. The majority of these word constructions would be no more comprehensible to a North American than the latest slang out of England or Australia. They belong to the places that formed them.

4   All this activity marks an interesting point from which to examine the latest evidence surrounding the explosion of English, which now boasts 1.9 billion competent speakers worldwide. In the view of Montreal writer Mark Abley, author of *Spoken Here: Travels Among Threatened Languages*, "no other language has ever enjoyed the political, economic, cultural, and military power that now accompanies English." English, he says, acts like a "brand name" and serves as a "repository of global ambition." Describing a quiz given to young Malaysians that contained references to American culture, Abley reports: "The obvious theme is the United States. But the subtler theme, I think, is power."

5   "Language annihilation," he writes, may just be one battle in the "wider war"—"the fight to sustain diversity on a planet where globalizing, assimilating, and eradicating occur on a massive scale." Mark Abley is far from alone in linking the spread of English with fears of a bland consumerist empire—i.e. with a certain vision of American might. Geoffrey Hull, an Australian linguist quoted in *Spoken Here,* advises the banning of unsubtitled English programming on TV in East Timor. "English," Hull warns, "is a killer language."

6   Such unease isn't hard to understand. Of the 6,000 living languages, some 90 percent are at risk of vanishing before the end of this century. These are tongues spoken by fewer than 100, 000 people, and rarely as the only means of communication. For some linguists, the death of each marks

the disappearance of a world view. Without a language to call one's own, original stories stop being told and unique conversations with God diminish. English triumphs just one set of stories and one conversation.

But is the link between the "tidal wave" of English, as Abley describes 7 it, and the threat to variety so direct? History isn't without precedents for this kind of upheaval. With a few centuries of the empire in Ancient Greece, for instance, languages spoken by Trojans, Sumerians, Lydians, Etruscans and Scythians, to name a few, had been rendered extinct. Each of those societies contributed to the first great renaissance in western civilization. Classical Greek itself went on to serve as a foundation for a few other languages, including this one.

Cries of English the cultural barbarian aren't new, either. In the 19th 8 century, France's *civilisatrice* and Germany's *kultur* programs granted the colonial aggressions of those nations a patina of benevolence. England's ambitions, in contrast, were given no similar benefit of the doubt, being equated from the start with an unbridled lust for power. Over the past fifty years, as the U.S. has come to supplant Cruel Britannia as the primary 'exporter' of the tongue, it has come to bear most of the criticisms. When a Muslim group recently denounced the Arabic version of the *Idol* TV series because it "facilitates the culture of globalization led by America," it didn't matter that the program had originated in England. In certain minds, English can only ever be the language of McDonald's and Nike, Madonna and Cruise.

By this reasoning, English couldn't form a natural part of Singaporian 9 street life or Filipino cross-language talk. It couldn't be the rightful possession of the millions of Indians who now call it their mother tongue. But the truth is, English isn't just exploding across the universe; it is being exploded on contact with other societies and languages. No single political power or region, it could be argued, can fairly claim it as its exclusive spokesperson.

In Asia, at least, English certainly feels this protean. The Hong Kong 10 author Nury Vittachi has been charting the emergence of a pan-Southeast-Asian argot. He calls the argot 'Englasian,' the wonky dialect of international business types and youthful hipsters. Vittachi even penned a short play in Englasian called *Don't Stupid Lah, Brudder.* The setting is a bar in a Jakarta hotel and the characters are a Malaysian investor, an Indian accountant, and an Australian entrepreneur. The Malay says things like "No nid-lah, sit-sit, don't shy." The Auzzie counters with "Don't do yer lolly, mate. Let's have a squiz." Of the three, the Indian is the most readily intelligible. She speaks of how she might be able to "facilitate my cousin-brother, a revered Sydneysider."

Spend any time in the region and two things become obvious. First,   11
English still makes only a minor noise, and only in the major cities. Its
consumer blandishments pale against home-grown magazines, movies, and
pop singers. No major Asian language, be it Mandarin, Malay, Japanese,
or any of the fourteen principal Indian tongues, is at risk of vanishing.
Interestingly, those languages are themselves killing off their own sub-
dialects and non-standard variants. The world is everywhere too connected
for the health of the linguistically vulnerable.

The second observation relates to the playfulness of inventions like   12
Singlish. If Asians are threatened by the growing presence of English, they
are expressing their fear in the strangest manner—by inviting the danger
into their homes. Linguists praise a language for its capacity to acquire and
assimilate expressions from elsewhere. Such openness is taken as a sign of
confidence and growth. The principal languages of nearly half of humanity
are, by this measure, prospering. English isn't storming these cultures to
wage war on them. The locals, at least, aren't under that impression. They
view the language mostly as a tool, one they can manipulate, and even
make their own.

Thinking About the Essay

1. What is the pun in the title? Is this, in your opinion, an appropriate title for
   the essay?

2. What is the effect of the rapid translations of phrases and terms given in
   the first two paragraphs? How important is the narrator's identity or point
   of view?

3. According to the author, how do languages work at the "street level," in
   contrast to the "official" level? In what sense do loan words and hybrid
   street dialects "advance [the] utility" of English (paragraph 3)?

4. What is the author's attitude toward the critic Geoffrey Hull and his
   conclusion that English is a "killer language" (paragraph 5)?

5. What does Foran mean when he writes (in paragraph 11) that the "world is
   everywhere too connected for the health of the linguistically vulnerable"?

Responding in Writing

6. Is it true that the death of a language "marks the disappearance of a world
   view" (paragraph 6)? In a brief essay, consider the relationship between
   language and thought. How can language *give birth* to a worldview?

7. Do you agree with Foran's claim that "no single political power or region …
   can fairly claim [English] as its exclusive spokesperson" (paragraph 9)?
   Respond to this statement in an argumentative essay.

8. Compare Foran's critique of those who view language as an instrument of commercial exploitation with Robin Lakoff's argument in "The Power of Words in Wartime." Where do these writers' positions converge and where do they diverge?

Networking

9. As a class, make a list of words or phrases that have been recently acquired and assimilated in American English. Is it accurate to say of any of these new acquisitions that they also introduce a new set of *concepts*?

10. Go online and perform a Google search of one of the terms or phrases Foran heard in the Singapore restaurant (paragraphs 1–2). How does this language appear in print, online, in contrast to the spoken context Foran describes?

Multilingual America

WILLIAM H. FREY

William H. Frey is a senior fellow of demographic studies at the Metropolitan Policy Program at the Brookings Institution in Washington, DC. He is also on the faculty of the Population Studies Center at the University of Michigan. In the following essay, which appeared in the July/August 2002 issue of *American Demographics,* Frey analyzes the rise in American households where the inhabitants speak a language other than English. The writer offers data drawn from the 2000 United States Census to trace recent population shifts, the rise of ethnic communities in urban and nonurban areas, and the impact on the American "melting pot" of people who speak a language other than English at home.

Before Reading

How can English be taught to new immigrants who stay in their own ethnic communities and prefer to speak their own language at home? If you were involved in policymaking, what programs would you design for these individuals?

America's identity as a melting pot now extends beyond multiple races   1
and cultures to also include numerous languages. Ours is an increasingly multilingual nation, due to a new wave of immigration.

The number of individuals who speak a language other than English at   2
home is on the rise. This population is also on the move: No longer restricted to traditional port-of-entry cities, such as New York and Los Angeles,

foreign-language speakers are now sprouting up in certain Southeastern and Western states.

For the first time, thanks to Census 2000 long-form data, we are able to identify these new locations where residents who speak a foreign language are making their presence felt. Although relatively small, this population is beginning to constitute a critical mass in many communities—reason alone for businesses seeking new markets to take note. 3

Nationally, Americans age 5 and older who speak a language other than English at home grew 47 percent in the past decade. According to Census 2000, this group now accounts for slightly less than 1 in 5 Americans (17.9 percent). About three-fifths of this group speak Spanish at home (59.9 percent), another fifth speaks another Indo-European language (21.3 percent) and almost 15 percent speak an Asian language. 4

Overall, foreign-language speakers grew by about 15 million during the 1990s, with new Spanish speakers contributing about 11 million people and new Asian speakers almost 2.5 million. Continued immigration from Latin America and Asia has increased the number of people who speak languages native to those regions. 5

Foreign-Language Havens

These foreign-language speakers are concentrated in 10 states, each where 20 percent or more of the residents speak a language other than English at home. Led by California (40 percent), this group includes several other Western states as well as New York, New Jersey, Florida and Rhode Island. The concentration is even more evident when one looks at individual metropolitan areas. (See Table 4.1.) 6

In six metros, including Miami and Laredo, Texas, those who speak only English at home are in the minority. In five Mexican border towns in this category, Spanish accounts for more than 96 percent of non-English languages spoken. 7

Other areas where more than one-third of the population speaks a language other than English at home include Los Angeles, San Antonio, San Francisco, New York and San Diego. 8

By far, the two largest metros that house the most foreign-language-speakers are Los Angeles and New York, with more than 7 million and 6 million foreign-language speakers, respectively. Together, these two gateways increased their foreign-language-speaking populations by 3.5 million between 1990 and 2000, accounting for 24 percent of the country's total gain. (See Figure 4.1.) 9

Eight metropolitan areas with the largest populations that speak a foreign language accounted for almost half (46 percent) of the nation's total gain. 10

Others include Phoenix, Atlanta, Las Vegas, Seattle and Denver—cities that became secondary magnets for new immigrant groups during the 1990s.

Multilingual Expansion

Although many immigrant gateway metros still hold the lion's share [11] of inhabitants who speak a foreign language, the 1990s was a decade of extensive redistribution of foreign-born residents and hence, of

TABLE 4.1   Spanish and Asian Language Magnets
There is some overlap between the lists of communities forming new, fast-growing enclaves of speakers of Spanish and Asian languages. The areas below all have at least 5,000 Spanish-speaking or Asian-speaking residents.

Persons speaking Spanish at home: Metro areas with greatest growth, 1990–2000	% Increase 1990–2000
Fayetteville-Springdale-Rogers, AR MSA*	609%
Elkhart-Goshen, IN MSA	403%
Raleigh-Durham–Chapel Hill, NC MSA	381%
Charlotte-Gastonia–Rock Hill, NC-SC MSA	376%
Greensboro-Winston-Salem–High Point, NC MSA	367%
Green Bay, WI MSA	354%
Hickory-Morganton-Lenoir, NC MSA	338%
Atlanta, GA MSA	314%
Fort Smith, AR-OK MSA	310%
Sioux City, IA-NE MSA	306%

Persons speaking Asian language at home: Metro areas with greatest growth, 1990–2000	
Hickory-Morganton-Lenoir, NC MSA	467%
Las Vegas, NV-AZ MSA	220%
Charlotte-Gastonia–Rock Hill, NC-SC MSA	182%
Lincoln, NE MSA	172%
Greenville-Spartanburg-Anderson, SC MSA	170%
Atlanta, GA MSA	157%
Greensboro-Winston-Salem–High Point, NC MSA	156%
Austin-San Marcos, TX MSA	156%
Raleigh-Durham–Chapel Hill, NC MSA	128%
Grand Rapids-Muskegon-Holland, MI MSA	127%

Source: William H. Frey analysis, 1990 and 2000 U.S. Census.
*MSA = Metropolitan Statistical Area as defined by the Office of Management and Budget.

FIGURE 4.1   Native Tongues

Ten states have the largest shares of foreign-language speakers (more than one in five speaks a foreign language at home). These include several Western states, New York, New Jersey, Florida, and Rhode Island.

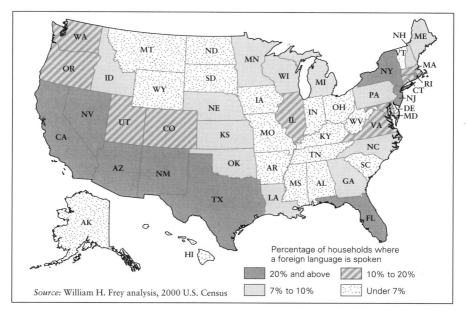

Percentage of households where a foreign language is spoken

- 20% and above
- 10% to 20%
- 7% to 10%
- Under 7%

Source: William H. Frey analysis, 2000 U.S. Census

foreign-language speakers. Areas that had little prior familiarity with Spanish-speaking residents or those who speak an Asian language gained exposure to cultural as well as linguistic differences in their communities.

States that now have the fastest growing non-English-speaking popula-   12 tions are not typically those with the highest percentages of such people. (See Figure 4.2.) Most are Southeastern and Western states that began to attract new immigrants, often in response to an increased demand for services due to an influx of migrants from other states.

In the Southeast, this includes Georgia, North Carolina, Arkansas,   13 Tennessee and Virginia; in the West, Arizona, Nevada, Utah, Oregon, Washington, Idaho and Colorado. Several interior states with small foreign-born populations, such as Nebraska, are also attracting new non-English-speaking residents to take a variety of service jobs.

Similar geographic patterns are evident in metropolitan areas with the   14 fastest growth of foreign-language speakers. For example, Fayetteville, Ark., increased its non-English-speaking population by a whopping 368

FIGURE 4.2 Foreign-Language Growth, 1990–2000

The states with the fastest-growing non-English-speaking populations are not typically those with the highest percentages of foreign-language speakers. Such states include Georgia and North Carolina as well as Nebraska and Washington.

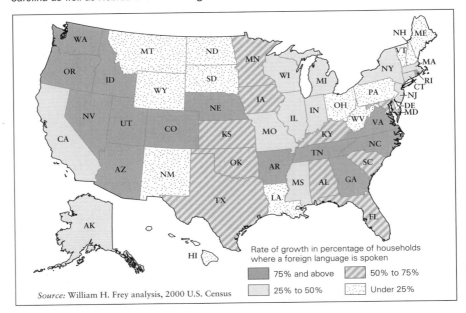

Rate of growth in percentage of households where a foreign language is spoken

- 75% and above
- 50% to 75%
- 25% to 50%
- Under 25%

Source: William H. Frey analysis, 2000 U.S. Census

percent during the 1990s. Six of the seven fastest-growing areas (Las Vegas being the exception) are in the South, including the North Carolina metros of Hickory, Raleigh-Durham–Chapel Hill, Charlotte and Greensboro.

Although in many of these enclaves foreign-language speakers account ¹⁵ for only a small percentage of the area's total population, this is not the case for all. Las Vegas, for example, increased its share of residents who speak a foreign language to 24 percent, from 13 percent, between 1990 and 2000. Similar increases can be seen for Orlando and Naples, Fla.; Phoenix and Dallas. Significant gains also occurred in small Iowa cities, such as Sioux City, Waterloo and Des Moines.

Spanish and Asian Language Magnets

While Spanish dominates the foreign languages spoken at home on the ¹⁶ national level, this is not true for all parts of the United States. For example, fewer than half the foreign-language speakers in San Francisco and New York City speak Spanish. In the former, nearly as many speak Asian languages; in the latter, a large number of residents continue to speak other European languages at home.

Spanish represents more than half the foreign languages spoken at 17 home in only nine states. These are located mostly on the Mexican border and in the West. Metro areas with the largest Spanish-speaking shares of their populations reflect the same geographic pattern.

In contrast, metropolitan areas that house large shares of Asian popula- 18 tions are fewer and farther between. Honolulu tops the group, with Asian languages spoken by almost 9 out of 10 people who speak a non-English language at home, followed by San Francisco, Los Angeles, San Diego and Stockton, Calif.

Considerable overlap exists between communities forming new, fast- 19 growing enclaves for Spanish speakers and those who speak an Asian language. (See Tables 4.2 and 4.3.) Of the 15 metro areas with the fastest-growing

TABLE 4.2   Metros with Highest Shares of Foreign-Language Speakers, 2000
Six metros, including Laredo and Miami, have populations where the minority speak only English at home. In five Mexican border towns in this category, Spanish is the non-English language spoken in more than 96 percent of homes.

Name	*Percent speaking non-English languages at home*	*Percent who speak these languages at home*			
		Spanish	*Asian language*	*European language*	*Other*
Laredo, TX MSA	91.9%	99.4%	0.3%	0.3%	0.0%
McAllen-Edinburg-Mission, TX MSA	83.1%	99.0%	0.5%	0.4%	0.0%
Brownsville-Harlingen–San Benito, TX MSA	79.0%	99.1%	0.4%	0.4%	0.1%
El Paso, TX MSA	73.3%	97.1%	1.0%	1.6%	0.3%
Las Cruces, NM MSA	54.4%	96.7%	0.7%	1.9%	0.7%
Miami–Fort Lauderdale, FL CMSA	51.5%	80.0%	1.9%	16.7%	1.4%
Salinas, CA MSA	47.3%	83.5%	9.1%	6.5%	0.9%
Los Angeles–Riverside–Orange County, CA CMSA	46.8%	70.7%	18.2%	9.1%	1.9%
Yuma, AZ MSA	45.5%	95.6%	1.5%	1.9%	0.9%
Merced, CA MSA	45.2%	77.7%	11.6%	10.4%	0.4%

Source: William H. Frey analysis, 2000 U.S. Census.

TABLE 4.3   Metros with Largest Number of Foreign-Language Speakers, 2000
The two largest metros with foreign-language speakers are Los Angeles and New York. Together they increased their foreign-language-speaking population by 3.5 million during the 1990s—about 24 percent of the nation's total gain.

Largest number of foreign-language speakers, 2000	Number of people
Los Angeles–Riverside–Orange County, CA CMSA	7, 080.474
New York–Northern New Jersey–Long Island, NY-NJ-CT-PA CMSA	6, 614.354
San Francisco–Oakland–San Jose, CA CMSA	2, 368.377
Chicago-Gary-Kenosha, IL-IN-WI CMSA	2, 116.043
Miami–Fort Lauderdale, FL CMSA	1, 869.966
Houston-Galveston-Brazoria, TX CMSA	1, 372.010
Dallas–Fort Worth, TX CMSA	1, 163.502
Washington-Baltimore, DC-MD-VA-WV CMSA	1, 158.677
Boston-Worcester-Lawrence, MA-NH-ME-CT CMSA	1, 042.727

Source: William H. Frey analysis, 1990 and 2000 U.S. Census.

Spanish-speaking populations, six are on the list of fast-growing, Asian-language-speaking areas. These include Atlanta and Las Vegas, as well as North Carolina metros Raleigh-Durham, Charlotte, Greensboro and Hickory.

These areas are attracting new residents as a result of local universities 20 or the labor market pulls associated with general population growth and the fast-growing economies of the "New Sun Belt."

English Proficiency

One issue raised when people who speak a foreign language become new 21 residents of a community is how well they can conduct their lives in English. While it's no surprise that immigrants who have lived in the U.S. for a long time become fluent in English, Census 2000 reveals that this may not be the case with new arrivals.

The Census Bureau asked people who speak a language other than 22 English at home this question: How well does this person speak English? (The choices were: very well, well, not well or not at all.) Between 1990 and 2000, there was a larger increase of Spanish speakers who could not speak English very well than of those who could. However, for Asian language speakers, there was a larger increase between 1990 and 2000 of those who could speak English very well.

To a great extent, Spanish speakers arriving in non-gateway areas are 23 less likely to speak English very well. Among the metros with the lowest percentages of Spanish speakers speaking English very well are Greensboro, Raleigh-Durham, Charlotte and Hickory in North Carolina; Atlanta and other newer destinations for Spanish-speaking residents.

Among areas where Spanish speakers have high levels of English pro- 24 ficiency are university towns like Gainesville, Fla., and Lubbock, Texas, as well as locales with long-standing Spanish-speaking residents, such as Albuquerque, N.M.

The same pattern occurs among residents who speak an Asian language, 25 with lower levels of proficiency where such settlers are relatively new (e.g., Lincoln, Neb.; Grand Rapids, Mich.; Minneapolis–St. Paul, Minn.; Greensboro, N.C. and Atlanta). High levels of proficiency tend to be in university communities such as Gainesville, Fla.; Raleigh-Durham and Chapel Hill, N.C.; Champagne-Urbana, Ill. and Colorado Springs, Colo.

These patterns of English proficiency mirror the national picture. 26 States with the lowest levels of English proficiency tend to be those that had the fastest growth of foreign-language residents during the 1990s. Nebraska, Nevada, Oregon, North Carolina and Georgia are part of this group of states, which also includes some longer-term havens for foreign-born and foreign-language-speaking residents. For example, less than half (49 percent) of California's foreign-born residents speak English very well.

The new census data provides insights into this fast growing group of 27 Americans who speak a language other than English at home. It also highlights the fact that if the U.S. is to continue to live up to its reputation as a melting pot, this influx of foreign-language speakers will require special efforts on the parts of schools, local organizations and grassroots groups to enable these new residents to become fully integrated members of their communities.

Thinking About the Essay

1. How would you describe the writer's audience for this essay? What assumptions does he make about this audience? How does he mold his style to the expectations of the audience?

2. Explain the significance of the writer's title. What approach does he take to his subject? In other words, what is his purpose? How does his purpose govern his thesis?

3. Where is the thesis stated? How does the conclusion reinforce the thesis or color it with a mildly argumentative edge?

4. Frey employs a considerable amount of data in this essay. How relevant are these data? What aspects of the data do you find interesting? What aspects, if any, do you find weak or irrelevant? There are several visual illustrations in this essay. What types of data do they present? How do you "read" them in terms of their significance? What do they contribute to the article?

5. The author divides his essay into sections. Summarize each section. How does each section flow from the previous unit? Is the author able to achieve unity and coherence? Justify your response.

Responding in Writing

6. Use the data provided by Frey to write your own essay entitled "Our Shrinking Language Tapestry." Make your essay more argumentative than Frey's. Take a stand on the demographics Frey provides, and back up your claim with at least three good reasons or minor propositions.

7. If you belong to a family in which members normally speak a language other than English, tell about their attitude toward the use of English. Or imagine that you are part of such a household. What would your perception of your native language and this second language—English—be?

8. In the last paragraphs, Frey implies that it is important to learn English to become "fully integrated" into one's community. In an argumentative essay, agree or disagree with his statement.

Networking

9. In groups of four, obtain a copy of the 2000 United States Census, and focus on the data about immigration patterns and language use that this document provides. Then construct a group report of approximately 1,000 words highlighting and interpreting this data.

10. Go to one or more search engines and type in "English only" or "English Only Movement." Try other combinations if necessary. Download relevant information, and then participate in a class discussion of this controversy.

Reading the History of the World

ISABEL ALLENDE | Isabel Allende, the daughter of a Chilean diplomat, was born in 1942 in Lima, Peru. Isabel moved from Peru to Chile, where she was living and working at the time her uncle, Salvador Allende, the president of Chile, was assassinated during an army coup, assisted by the CIA, in 1973. "In that moment," she says, "I realized that everything was possible—that violence was a dimension that was always around you." The Allende family did not think that the new regime would last, and Isabel Allende continued to work as a noted journalist. However, when it became too dangerous to remain in Chile, the family went into exile in Venezuela. Allende's first novel, *The House of the Spirits* (1985), established her as a significant writer in the tradition of "magic realism" associated with the Nobel Prize winner Gabriel García Márquez. Other novels include *Of Love and Shadows* (1987), *Eva Luna* (1988), *Daughter of Fortune* (1999), and *Zorro* (2005). Allende has also written two memoirs, *Paula* (1995) and *The Sum of Our Days* (2007) as well as stories for children. Allende has spoken of the "wind of exile" that makes it necessary to recover memories of one's native land. In this essay, which appears in a collection of essays on reading by well-known writers, *Speaking of Reading* (1995), she invokes the act of reading as one way to salvage these memories.

Before Reading

Allende declares that only through reading can we fully become aware of "injustice and misery and violence." Would you agree or disagree, and why?

Reading is like looking through several windows which open to an 1 infinite landscape. I abandon myself to the pleasure of the journey. How could I know about other people, how could I know about the history of the world, how could my mind expand and grow if I could not read? I began to read when I was very small; I learned to read and write practically when I was a baby. For me, life without reading would be like being in prison, it would be as if my spirit were in a straitjacket; life would be a very dark and narrow place.

I was brought up in a house full of books. It was a big, strange, somber 2 house, the house of my grandparents. My uncle, who lived in the house, had a lot of books—he collected them like holy relics. His room held a ton of books. Few newspapers were allowed in that house because my grandfather was a very patriarchal, conservative man who thought that newspapers, as well as the radio, were full of vulgar ideas (at that time we didn't have TV), so the only contact I had with the world, really, was through my uncle's books. No one censored or guided my reading; I read anything I wanted.

I began reading Shakespeare when I was nine, not because of the language or the beauty, but because of the plot and the great characters. I have always been interested in adventure, plot, strong characters, history, animals. As a child, I read children's books, most of the Russian literature, many French authors, and later, Latin American writers. I think I belong to the first generation of writers in Latin America who were brought up reading Latin American literature; earlier generations read European and North American literature. Our books were very badly distributed. 3

Books allow me to see my feelings put into words. After I read the feminist authors from North America, I could finally find words for the anger that I had all my life. I was brought up in a male chauvinist society and I had accumulated much anger, yet I couldn't express it. I could only be angry and do crazy things, but I couldn't put my anger into words and use it in a rational, articulate way. After I read those books, things became clearer to me, I could talk about that anger and express it in a more positive way. 4

The same thing happened with politics. I was aware of injustice and misery and political violence, but I couldn't express my feelings until I read about those issues and realized that other people had been dealing with them for centuries, and had already invented the words to express what I was feeling. 5

I have often been separated from my mother, whom I love very much. She now lives in Chile and we write a letter to each other every day. We talk about what we've read or what we are writing. I do it the first thing every morning of my life, even when I'm traveling. It's as if I were writing a journal. It's like having a long conversation with her; we are connected with a strong bond. This same bond also connects me with my daughter, who is living in Spain, because when I write the letter to my mother, I make a copy that goes to my daughter, and they do the same. This is becoming a very strange network of letters. 6

My mother is a much better reader than I. My reading is very fast, hectic, disorganized, and impatient. If I'm not caught in the first pages I abandon the book. My mother, however, is very patient and goes very slowly. She is the only person who reads my manuscripts, helping me to edit, revise, and correct them. She has a strong sense of poetry and such good taste. She's very well informed, very cultivated, very sensitive, and loves reading. 7

I have tried to give my children the love of books. My daughter is a good reader. She's a psychologist and has to read a lot of professional books, but she loves novels, short stories, poetry. My son, however, doesn't read any fiction. He's a scientific person with a mathematical mentality. I've tried to imagine how his mind and heart work, without nourishment from books, but I can't. He's a great boy, but how can he do it? I don't know. 8

My uncle, Salvador Allende, who was President of Chile before he was   9
assassinated during the military coup, hardly affected my life. I liked him
and loved him, but only as I do other relatives. He was the best man at
my wedding. I was never involved in politics, and never participated in his
government. (I became interested in politics only after the coup.) He was
not a very strong reader of fiction, actually. He was always reading reports,
essays, books about politics, sociology, economy, etc. He was a very well-
informed person and he read very fast, his eyes practically skimming across
the page to get the necessary information, but when he wanted to relax, he
would rather watch a movie than read.

During the three years of Allende's government, any Chilean could buy   10
books of "Quimantu," the state publishing house, for very little money, the
equivalent of two newspapers. In this way he hoped to promote culture.
His goal was that every single Chilean could read and write and be able to
buy as many books as he or she wanted by the end of his term.

My own experience of life, my biography, my feelings, my self as a per-   11
son, affect my reading. The writer puts out half of the book, but then I read
the book in my own unique manner. This is why reading is so interesting;
we as readers don't have passive roles, but very active ones. We must integrate into the text our own experiences of life and our own feelings. While
reading a book, we are constantly applying our own knowledge.

Our backgrounds determine our strengths and interests as readers. Many   12
themes that are extremely popular in North America are impossible for me to
read because they aren't part of my culture—I just don't care about them. For
example, I can't relate to those books by daughters who write against their
mothers. But if I read a book by Toni Morrison or Louise Erdrich that deals
with being a woman and part of an ethnic minority, I can relate to its content. Also, I like Latin American authors very much, especially Jorge Amado,
García Márquez, Mario Vargas Llosa, Juan Rulfo, Jorge Luis Borges, and
many others. There are a few Latin American women writers that I enjoy as
well, but they have been badly distributed and poorly reviewed. Latin American literature has been an exclusively male club, to say the least.

I have met many people, including well-informed, educated people,   13
who actually take pride in the fact that they haven't read anything by a
woman. Recently, I received a clipping from a newspaper in Chile. It was
a public letter to me from a Chilean entertainer apologizing that he had
never before read any of my books because I am a woman. He wrote that
he never read literature written by women. After he made a special effort
to read my books, he felt he must apologize to me and say that I could
actually write.

I will always be interested in programs of illiteracy because it is such a   14
common problem in my continent: 50 percent of the population of Latin
America cannot read or write, and of those who can, only a few can afford
books or have the habit of reading. To me, not reading is like having the
spirit imprisoned.

Thinking About the Essay

1. List the images, metaphors, and **similes** that Allende presents in her
   introductory paragraph. What is her purpose? What is the effect?

2. State Allende's thesis. Is it stated or implied? Explain.

3. What strategies does Allende employ to blend personal experience and
   analysis? What, specifically, is she analyzing, and how does she develop
   her topics?

4. Allende devotes two paragraphs to her uncle, Salvador Allende (paragraphs
   9 and 10). Why? How do these paragraphs influence the tone of the entire
   essay?

5. What causal connections does Allende establish between the acts of
   reading and writing and the state of society in Latin America?

Responding in Writing

6. Write an essay in which you describe your reading habits as a child and as
   an adult. Did you live in a house filled with books? Did you enjoy reading?
   What were your favorite books? Who were the readers and nonreaders in
   your family? Answer these questions in a personal essay.

7. Allende refers to the fact that half of the population in Latin America is
   illiterate. Write an analytical essay that examines the impact of illiteracy on
   a society or nation.

8. Imagine a reading plan for your children, and write about it. Will you leave
   reading development exclusively to teachers? How will you regulate your
   child's reading and television viewing habits? Do you agree with Allende
   that reading can open children to "an infinite landscape" (paragraph 1)?

Networking

9. Discuss in small groups the nature of your reading habits during various
   stages in your life. Report to the class on your discoveries.

10. Find out more about Salvador Allende and the Allende family. Search the
    Internet or conduct an advanced search with the assistance of a college
    librarian. Try to find specific information on Allende's literacy crusade.

Global Relationships: Are Sex and Gender Roles Changing?

CHAPTER 5

As we move into the twenty-first century, the roles of men and women in the United States and around the world are in flux. In the United States, there are increasing numbers of American women in many professional fields—medicine, law, education, politics, and corporate life. And, with more men—"Mr. Moms"—staying home and caring for their children, either by preference or necessity, there is greater equality in domestic responsibilities. At the same time, a woman's right to choose or even obtain social services is under attack. And it was only in the summer of 2003 that the United States Supreme Court struck down a Texas law that had made sex between consenting adult males in the privacy of their homes a crime.

This national opposition in certain quarters to equality of rights in human relations is reflected in reactionary global attitudes and practices. Issues of race, sexual orientation, and ethnicity complicate the roles of women and men on a global scale. In certain nations, women can still be stoned to death for sexual "crimes"; in others, homosexuality can be punished by incarceration and even execution. Slave trafficking in women and children fuels a vibrant sex industry here and around the world. And children—stolen, bought, or extorted from poor parents from South America to Southeast Asia—can wind up in the United States as "adopted" boys and girls.

American women do seem to have advantages over many of their global counterparts, for when we consider the situation of women globally, the issue of equal rights and human rights becomes acute. From increasing AIDS rates among global women, to their exploitation as cheap labor or sex workers, to female infanticide, to the continuing resistance of men in traditional societies to any thought of gender equality, the lives of women in many parts of the world are perilous. Gendered value systems in traditional societies change glacially, and often under

149

Hindu women take part in a speed-dating event at a London nightclub. Daters meet for a few minutes before moving on to the next date. Traditionally, relationships and marriages in this community were arranged by the families of the potential bride and groom.

Thinking About the Image

1. You probably know how awkward it can be to meet someone new. How do you think this photographer captured such an intimate, difficult moment between these two people?

2. What key characteristics do you see that distinguish groups of people or ethnicities in this photograph?

3. This photograph originally accompanied "Arranged Marriages Get a Little Reshuffling" by Lizette Alvarez (p. 155). How accurately does the photograph illustrate the article? Newspaper editors have a limited amount of space to fill each day—why do you think this newspaper's editors wanted to include a photograph with this story?

4. If you could take a snapshot of dating culture in your own social group, what would you need to include in order to best capture its essence? Describe the image using very specific language.

only the most extreme conditions. For example, before the massacre of more than 800,000 Tutsi by their Hutu neighbors in Rwanda in 1993, women could not work or appear alone in the market; with the killing of so many of the men, Rwandan women suddenly had to assume responsibility for tasks they formerly had been excluded from. Women are the ones who are displaced disproportionately by wars, ethnic conflicts, famine, and environmental crises.

In this new global era, the destinies of women and men around the world are intertwined. Global forces have brought them together. The role of democracy in promoting human rights, the challenge to spread wealth from North to South and West to East, the need to prevent wars, even the degradation of the environment—have notable implications for men and women. Some argue that global forces—which we will detect in some essays in this chapter and study in detail in the next chapter—are notably hostile to women. Others argue that to the extent that nations can promote peace and democracy, produce prosperity, improve health and the environment, and reduce racism and ethnocentrism, both women and men will be the beneficiaries.

The essays in this chapter present insights into the roles of men and women around the world. The writers inquire into the impact of economics, politics, race, gender and sexual orientation, and culture on the lives of women and men. They invite us to reconsider the meaning of human rights, self-determination, and equality from a gendered perspective. In the twenty-first century, new ideas have emerged about the roles and rights of women and men. The essays that follow reveal some of the challenges that must be overcome before the concept of equal rights and opportunities for women and men can be realized.

The End of Swagger

Anna Quindlen

Anna Quindlen is the author of several best-selling novels including *Object Lessons* (1991), *Black and Blue* (1998), and *Blessings* (2002). She is also an influential journalist whose syndicated columns have appeared in *The New York Times* and *Newsweek*. She won the Pulitzer Prize for Commentary in 1992. Quindlen acknowledges that she frequently focuses in her fiction and nonfiction on the lives of women: "I tend to write about what we have come, unfortunately, to call women's issues. Those are issues that directly affect my life and those are issues that are historically underreported." Quindlen wrote the following article for her "Last Word" column in the February 2, 2009, issue of *Newsweek*. In it, she greets the new Obama administration with observations about the welfare of women and American foreign policy.

Before Reading

What do you think of Hillary Clinton? In her capacity as Secretary of State, can she—should she—promote the interests and welfare of American and global women?

As Barack Obama and Hillary Rodham Clinton begin to use their uncom-   1
mon authority and intelligence to implement a new American international agenda, it might behoove them to read a speech given some years ago
in Beijing. It read in part: "If there is one message that echoes forth from
this conference, let it be that human rights are women's rights, and women's
rights are human rights for one and for all. Let us not forget that among
those rights are the right to speak freely—and the right to be heard. Women
must enjoy the rights to participate fully in the social and political lives of
their countries if we want freedom and democracy to thrive and endure."

Secretary Clinton was first lady when she spoke those words at a United   2
Nations conference on women in 1995. Some of the participants wept to
hear an influential American commit to a view of the world so many of
them shared: that the way for nations to prosper was to pay attention to
women's rights, women's welfare and women's concerns.

President Obama has chosen a secretary of state who can make that   3
course of action an integral part of the American strategy around the
world. Their partnership promises a new paradigm. Obama is the first
post-macho president, a man raised by the kind of struggling single mother
who is the canary in the mine of health and welfare everywhere. Clinton
is a female leader with proven mettle; there is not a country on earth that
does not know of her power and her ability. Together they can free the
United States to finally pursue policies that emphasize collaboration and
connection instead of confrontation.

A simple primer on the state of the world: women do most of the good   4
stuff and get most of the bad. No whine, just fact. They harvest food and
raise children, tend to the aged and the ill. Yet according to the Global
Fund for Women, two thirds of the world's uneducated children are girls,
and, naturally, two thirds of the world's poorest people are female. Not
coincidentally, women make up only about 16 percent of parliament members worldwide. Simple mathematics dictates that if we are interested in
promoting prosperity, education and good government, the United States
must focus on the welfare of women. One study shows that the key to
reducing childhood malnutrition is maternal education. Another shows a

Anna Quindlen "The End of Swagger" from *Newsweek*. New York: Feb 2, 2009. Reprinted
by permission of International Creative Management, Inc. Copyright © 2009 by Anna
Quindlen for NEWSWEEK.

connection between more women in political leadership and less corruption and incompetence.

For those who prefer stories to statistics, there is the moving new documentary *Pray the Devil Back to Hell*. It follows a group of Liberian women weary of the murders, maiming and rapes that accompanied civil war in the African nation. They put on white T-shirts and parked themselves conspicuously, day after day, on the road leading to the president's house, embarrassing and infuriating him in the process. When male power brokers gathered for peace talks in Ghana, posturing and dithering for days, then weeks, the women blockaded the meeting hall with their bodies, making it impossible for the men to leave.

A woman is now the president of Liberia.

Those are the kinds of conclusions that put people's backs up, particularly if those people happen to be male. Isn't it just another form of sexism, they argue, to suggest that women are better, or different? Hasn't Secretary Clinton shown herself to possess a killer instinct as finally honed as that of any male counterpart? Yes, she has, and perhaps now that everyone knows she can be the toughest person in the room, she is uniquely positioned to go the other way. "Soft diplomacy could be her greatest strength," says Kavita Ramdas, president of the Global Fund for Women. "This is the time to get rid of militarism as a dominant theme, not only because it's wrong, but because it doesn't work."

That was another theme in the president's inaugural speech, that effectiveness, not ideology, is key. That should be the ethos that guides foreign policy as well. The notion of winning, illusory in our age, should be replaced with what works to cement alliances and raise the standard of living worldwide. The best rear-guard action in the war on terror, for example, is a war on poverty and ignorance. You could argue that the clearest suggestion that our values will prevail in Afghanistan are the girls who returned to school even after acid was thrown in their faces to keep them in the old condition of subjugation. Their scars are a flag of freedom.

To reread the Clinton speech in Beijing is to see a woman preparing to cast aside the schisms created by overweening American exceptionalism. She spoke from her heart when she told women from around the world that the universal experience of being female overrides the bright lines of division created by religion, class, place. "When families flourish, communities and nations do as well," she said.

It's worth noting that there were some in her husband's administration who didn't want her to make that speech. If she led a department that saw engaging and enriching women as a linchpin of its work, she might well be accused of feminizing foreign policy. Both she and the president could respond: so what? An American foreign policy informed by swagger and arrogance has been a conspicuous failure, making the United States not respected but reviled. It is no wonder that President Obama ended his inaugural remarks about international friendship with the promise "We are ready to lead once more." The world's women are ready for that, too.

Thinking About the Essay

1. What is Quindlen's claim, and where does she state it? What are her minor propositions or supporting points? How does she deal with the opposition?

2. Why does Quindlen begin her essay by quoting from a 1995 speech? Do you find this opening strategy effective? Why or why not?

3. According to Quindlen, Barack Obama is "the first post-macho president" (paragraph 3). What is her purpose here?

4. Would you say that Quindlen's tone is confrontational, angry, imploring, hopeful, despairing, or something else? Explain.

5. Throughout the essay, Quindlen provides several types of evidence. Identify these types, and evaluate their effectiveness. Do you find her evidence sufficient to make her case? Justify your response.

Responding in Writing

6. In a sense, Quindlen composes this essay as an invocation for the Obama administration that began on January 20, 2009, and a plea for a certain type of action. Write your own greeting, focusing on women's issues and foreign policy.

7. Based on your own observations, how important are women's issues in American foreign policy? Write an argumentative essay responding to this question.

8. Women have led—and are leading—modern nations, among them England, Israel, Germany, India, Liberia. Do you think a woman will ever be president of the United States? Answer this question in a speculative essay.

Networking

9. In small groups, debate the proposition that sexism no longer is a major factor in American politics and that men and women now occupy a level playing field in seeking public office. Summarize your debate for the class.

10. Conduct online research to find out more about the Global Fund for Women, which Quindlen mentions in paragraph 4. Access the fund's website and summarize your findings.

Arranged Marriages Get a Little Reshuffling

LIZETTE ALVAREZ

> In the following article, which appeared in *The New York Times* in 2003, Lizette Alvarez, a journalist for the newspaper, examines the changing attitudes and rituals concerning the traditional practice of arranged marriages. Writing from London, she focuses on "young, hip, South Asians." These young people do not reject traditions governing relations between the sexes. Instead, they "reshuffle" these conventions so that they may work successfully for them in the twenty-first century.

Before Reading

What is your attitude toward arranged marriage? In many Western nations, divorce rates approach 50 percent. Why not try arranged marriage if choosing your own mate is so frustrating and perilous?

They are young, hip, South Asians in their 20s who glide seamlessly 1 between two cultures, carefully cherry picking from the West to modernize the East.

They can just as easily listen to Justin Timberlake, the pop star, as Rishi 2 Rich, the Hindu musical dynamo. They eat halal meat but wear jeans and T-shirts to cafes.

Now these young Indians and Pakistanis are pushing the cultural 3 boundaries created by their parents and grandparents one step further: they are reshaping the tradition of arranged marriages in Britain.

While couples were once introduced exclusively by relatives and friends, 4 the Aunt Bijis, as Muslims call their matchmakers, are now being slowly nudged out by a boom in Asian marriage Web sites, chat rooms and personal advertisements. South Asian speed dating—Hindus one night, Muslims the next—is the latest phenomenon to hit London, with men and women meeting each other for just three minutes at restaurants and bars before moving on to the next potential mate.

Arranged marriages are still the norm within these clannish, tight-knit 5 communities in Britain, but, with the urging of second-and third-generation children, the nature of the arrangement has evolved, mostly by necessity.

What the young Indians and Pakistanis of Britain have done, in effect, 6 is to modernize practices that had evolved among the urban middle class in India in recent decades, allowing the prospective bride and groom a little more than one fleeting meeting to make up their minds.

The relaxation that had crept in since the 1960s allowed the couple, 7 after an initial meeting before their exte1nded families, to meet alone several times, either with family members in another room or at a restaurant, before delivering a verdict. Now, the meetings take place in public venues without the family encounter first.

"The term we use now is 'assisted' arranged marriage," said Maha 8 Khan, a 23-year-old London Muslim woman. "The whole concept has changed a lot. Parents have become more open and more liberal in their concept of marriage and courtship."

Gitangeli Sapra, a trendy, willowy British Sindhu who at 25 jokes that 9 she is on her way to spinsterhood, is an avid speed dater with no qualms about advertising her love of modern arranged marriages. She even wrote a column about it for *The Sunday Times*.

"It's not based on love," she said, "which can fizzle out." 10

Ms. Sapra had attended 10 of the more formal arranged meetings— 11 awkward, drawn-out affairs in which the young man, his mother and several other relatives came over to meet the young woman and her family. She wore her best Indian outfit, a sari or elegant Indian pants and top. She sat quietly, which is almost impossible to fathom, considering her chattiness. When called upon, she poured tea, and then talked briefly to her potential mate in a side room.

"The matriarchs do the talking," she said over a glass of wine at an 12 Italian restaurant. "You sit there looking cute and like the ideal housewife."

"To be honest, it's an easy way to get a rich man, with my mother's 13 blessing," she added, with a laugh.

None of them worked out, though, and Ms. Sapra has moved on to 14 speed dating with the blessings of her mother.

The very concept raises the hackles of some more old-fashioned par- 15 ents, but many are coming around, in part out of desperation. If Ms. Sapra finds someone on a speed date, she will quickly bring him home to her mother.

The abiding principles behind an arranged marriage still remain 16 strong—lust does not a lasting marriage make and family knows best. But parents and elders, eager to avoid alienating their children, making them miserable or seeing them go unmarried, have shown considerable flexibility. This is especially pronounced among the middle class, whose members tend to have integrated more into British life.

"The notion of arrangement has become more fluid," said Yunas   17
Samad, a sociology professor at Bradford University, who has studied
marriage in the Muslim community. "What is happening is that the
arranged marriage is becoming a bit more open and children are getting a
bit more say in this so it becomes a nice compromise. There is the comfort
of family support and a choice in what they are doing."

"It's a halfway house, not completely traditional and not completely the   18
same as what is happening in British society," he added.

To the surprise of parents and elders, this new hybrid between East and   19
West has actually stoked enthusiasm for an age-old tradition that many
young people privately viewed as crusty and hopelessly unhip.

Now they see it as an important way to preserve religion and identity,   20
not to mention a low-maintenance way of finding a mate. "It's like your
parents giving you a black book of girls," said Ronak Mashru, 24, a London
comedian whose parents are from India.

The young people also recognize that arranged marriages—in which   21
similar education and income levels, religious beliefs and character outweigh
the importance of physical attraction—can well outlast love marriages.

"The falling-in-love system has failed," said Rehna Azim, a Pakistani   22
family lawyer who founded an Asian magazine, *Memsahib*.

South Asian unions are viewed as marriages between families, not   23
individuals. Divorce is anathema, while respect and standing within a
community are paramount. A lot of people have much invested in making
a match work.

Similarly, several customs have survived dating: decisions have to be   24
made relatively quickly, often after the second or third meeting, and,
Ms. Sapra said, "once you've said yes, there is no turning back."

Dowries remain common and background still matters, too.   25

"Our mums look at the C.V.'s," said Vani Gupta, 30, a speed dater.   26
"They figure out whether we're compatible on paper—right job, right
background, right caste. It's nice to know your parents have done the work
for you. You feel more secure."

These middle-class women, most of them educated professionals or   27
university students, are looking for more modern men, who accept working wives and help around the house. But a "mechanic won't try for a
lawyer and a lawyer would not look for a mechanic," she said.

Ms. Sapra, for example, is looking for a fellow Sindhu, and a Gujarati   28
Indian typically seeks another Gujarati.

Muslims still keep it mostly within the family and the same region   29
of Pakistan. Cousins still frequently marry cousins, or at least second or
third cousins, and many British Pakistanis still find their brides back

in Pakistan. But now more men are marrying white British women who convert to Islam, and others insist on finding a Muslim bride there who speaks English, eats fish and chips and watches *East Enders*, a popular soap opera.

Parents and elders have had to adapt, in large part because the number   30
of potential partners is much smaller here than in their home countries. Rather than see an educated daughter go unwed, parents and elders have accepted these more modern approaches, "Women are not going to be put back in some kind of bottle," Professor Samad said.

Ms. Azim said, "Parents can say my child had an arranged marriage,   31
and he can say, 'Yeah, it's arranged. But I like her.'"

Thinking About the Essay

1. Writing for *The New York Times*, Alvarez knows her primary audience. What assumptions does she make about this audience? What secondary audiences would be interested in her topic, and why?

2. Does this article have a thesis? If so, where is it? If not, why not?

3. How does this essay reflect journalistic practice? Point to aspects of style, paragraph organization, article length, and other journalistic features. Is the tone of the article strictly neutral and objective (one aspect of journalistic method), or does it shade toward commentary or perhaps even contain an implicit argument? Explain.

4. How many people were interviewed for this article? Who are they, and what are their backgrounds? Taken together, how do they embody some of the main points that Alvarez wants to make about courtship practices among some Asians today?

5. What rhetorical practices—for example, definition, comparison and contrast, process and causal analysis—can you locate in this essay? Toward what purpose does the writer use them?

Responding in Writing

6. What is the difference between people who use Internet dating sites to make their own contacts and establish their own relationships and people from traditional societies who use the Internet to "cherry pick" prospective mates, whom they then present to their parents for appraisal. Which method strikes you as safer or potentially more successful, and why?

7. What is so great about "modern" dating and courtship practices if they often end in frustration and failure? Why not try something old, tried, and tested—like arranged marriage? Imagine that your parents insist on an

arranged marriage for you. Write a personal response to this situation. Do not write that you would try to subvert the entire ritual. Instead, explain how you might "manage" this process to make the outcome acceptable.

8. Alvarez, presenting one principle behind the need for arranged marriages, writes that "lust does not a lasting marriage make" (paragraph 16). Do you agree or disagree with this claim? Provide at least three reasons to justify your response.

Networking

9. In class discussion, design a questionnaire about attitudes toward arranged marriage. Aim for at least five questions that can be answered briefly. Then have each class member obtain several responses to the questionnaire from other students. Compile the results, discuss them, and arrive at conclusions.

10. Investigate an Internet dating site. Sign up for it if you feel comfortable, or simply monitor the site for information. Report your findings to the class.

In Africa, AIDS Has a Woman's Face

KOFI A. ANNAN | Kofi A. Annan was born in the Gold Coast, as Ghana was known under British rule, in 1938. The son of a Fonte nobleman, he graduated in1957 from Mfantsipim, a prestigious boarding school for boys that had been founded by the Methodist Church; Ghana won its independence from Great Britain that same year. After studies at the University of Science and Technology in Kumasi, Annan came to the United States on a Ford Foundation fellowship in 1959, completing his degree in economics at Macalester College in St. Paul, Minnesota. He also has a master's degree in management from the Massachusetts Institute of Technology (1972). Annan has worked for the United Nations in various capacities for four decades and was secretary-general of the United Nations from 1997 to 2006. In the following essay, which appeared in *The New York Times* in 2003, he writes about one of the many "problems without borders" that he believes we must deal with from an international perspective.

Before Reading

Consider the impact that AIDS has on a developing nation or an entire region. What are the economic consequences of the AIDS epidemic in these countries? What happens to the condition of women in such societies?

A combination of famine and AIDS is threatening the backbone of   1
Africa—the women who keep African societies going and whose work makes up the economic foundation of rural communities. For decades, we have known that the best way for Africa to thrive is to ensure that its women have the freedom, power and knowledge to make decisions affecting their own lives and those of their families and communities. At the United Nations, we have always understood that our work for development depends on building a successful partnership with the African farmer and her husband.

Study after study has shown that there is no effective development   2
strategy in which women do not play a central role. When women are fully involved, the benefits can be seen immediately: families are healthier; they are better fed; their income, savings and reinvestment go up. And, what is true of families is true of communities and, eventually, of whole countries.

But today, millions of African women are threatened by two simulta-   3
neous catastrophes: famine and AIDS. More than 30 million people are now at risk of starvation in southern Africa and the Horn of Africa. All of these predominantly agricultural societies are also battling serious AIDS epidemics. This is no coincidence: AIDS and famine are directly linked.

Because of AIDS, farming skills are being lost, agricultural development   4
efforts are declining, rural livelihoods are disintegrating, productive capacity to work the land is dropping and household earnings are shrinking—all while the cost of caring for the ill is rising exponentially. At the same time, H.I.V. infection and AIDS are spreading dramatically and dispropor-tionately among women. A United Nations report released last month shows that women now make up 50 percent of those infected with H.I.V. worldwide—and in Africa that figure is now 58 percent. Today, AIDS has a woman's face.

AIDS has already caused immense suffering by killing almost 2.5 million   5
Africans this year alone. It has left 11 million African children orphaned since the epidemic began. Now it is attacking the capacity of these coun-tries to resist famine by eroding those mechanisms that enable populations to fight back—the coping abilities provided by women.

Kofi A. Annan, "In Africa, AIDS Has a Woman's Face," THE NEW YORK TIMES, December 29, 2002. © 2002, The New York Times. Reprinted by permission.

In famines before the AIDS crisis, women proved more resilient than 6 men. Their survival rate was higher, and their coping skills were stronger. Women were the ones who found alternative foods that could sustain their children in times of drought. Because droughts happened once a decade or so, women who had experienced previous droughts were able to pass on survival techniques to younger women. Women are the ones who nurture social networks that can help spread the burden in times of famine.

But today, as AIDS is eroding the health of Africa's women, it is 7 eroding the skills, experience and networks that keep their families and communities going. Even before falling ill, a woman will often have to care for a sick husband, thereby reducing the time she can devote to planting, harvesting and marketing crops. When her husband dies, she is often deprived of credit, distribution networks or land rights. When she dies, the household will risk collapsing completely, leaving children to fend for themselves. The older ones, especially girls, will be taken out of school to work in the home or the farm. These girls, deprived of education and opportunities, will be even less able to protect themselves against AIDS.

Because this crisis is different from past famines, we must look beyond 8 relief measures of the past. Merely shipping in food is not enough. Our effort will have to combine food assistance and new approaches to farming with treatment and prevention of H.I.V. and AIDS. It will require creating early-warning and analysis systems that monitor both H.I.V. infection rates and famine indicators. It will require new agricultural techniques, appropriate to a depleted work force. It will require a renewed effort to wipe out H.I.V.-related stigma and silence.

It will require innovative, large-scale ways to care for orphans, with 9 specific measures that enable children in AIDS-affected communities to stay in school. Education and prevention are still the most powerful weapons against the spread of H.I.V. Above all, this new international effort must put women at the center of our strategy to fight AIDS.

Experience suggests that there is reason to hope. The recent United 10 Nations report shows that H.I.V. infection rates in Uganda continue to decline. In South Africa, infection rates for women under 20 have started to decrease. In Zambia, H.I.V. rates show signs of dropping among women in urban areas and younger women in rural areas. In Ethiopia, infection levels have fallen among young women in the center of Addis Ababa.

We can and must build on those successes and replicate them elsewhere. 11 For that, we need leadership, partnership and imagination from the international community and African governments. If we want to save Africa from two catastrophes, we would do well to focus on saving Africa's women.

Thinking About the Image

1. Although the map on the facing page did not appear with Kofi Annan's editorial, it was produced by a United Nations group formed to educate people about, and actively combat, H.I.V./AIDS. In what ways does this map visually represent the trends Annan describes? How does the map make the urgency of his argument more immediate?

2. Is there any information on the map that surprises you?

3. If you were a delegate to the United Nations from an African or Asian nation, what questions or responses would you have for Secretary-General Kofi Annan?

4. Use the information in this map to support your answer to any of the "Responding in Writing" questions.

Thinking About the Essay

1. What is the tone of Annan's introductory paragraph and the entire essay? What is his purpose? Point to specific passages to support your answer.

2. Annan employs causal analysis to develop this essay. Trace the causes and effects that he presents. What are some of the primary causes and effects? What secondary causes and effects does he mention?

3. This essay is rich in the use of examples. What types of illustration does Annan present to support his thesis?

4. Locate other rhetorical strategies—for example, comparison and contrast—that appear as structuring devices in this essay.

5. This essay presents a problem and offers a solution. Explain this strategy, paying careful attention to how the pattern evolves.

Responding in Writing

6. In a brief essay, explain what you have learned about AIDS in Africa from Annan's essay. Do you share his sense of optimism about the ability of the nations involved and the international community to solve the problem? Why or why not?

7. Explain your personal viewpoint on the increase of AIDS among the women of the world—not just in Africa but in Asia, Russia, Europe, and elsewhere.

8. Write an essay on another threat to women—either in a particular country or region, or around the world.

FIGURE 5.1   Regional Estimates of H.I.V./AIDS Infection as of December 2002

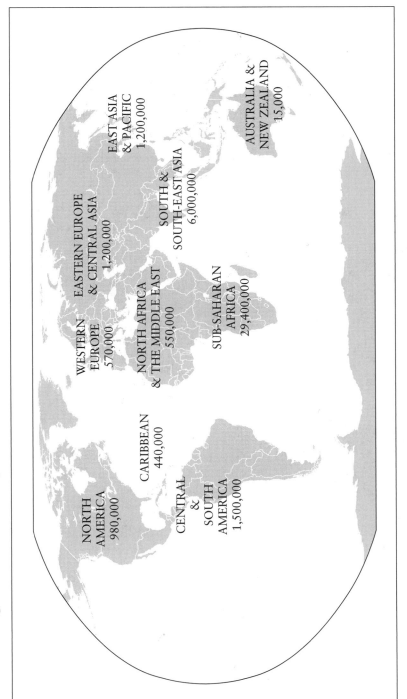

NORTH AMERICA
980,000

CENTRAL & SOUTH AMERICA
1,500,000

CARIBBEAN
440,000

WESTERN EUROPE
570,000

NORTH AFRICA & THE MIDDLE EAST
550,000

EASTERN EUROPE & CENTRAL ASIA
1,200,000

SUB-SAHARAN AFRICA
29,400,000

EAST ASIA & PACIFIC
1,200,000

SOUTH & SOUTH-EAST ASIA
6,000,000

AUSTRALIA & NEW ZEALAND
15,000

Source: Estimated number of adults and children living with H.I.V./AIDS during 2002, from "UNAIDS/WHO H.I.V./AIDS Regional Estimates as of the end of 2002" (United Nations/World Health Organization), October 2003.

Networking

9. Form working groups of four or five class members, and draw up an action plan to solicit funds on your campus for United Nations AIDS relief efforts in sub-Saharan Africa. Then create a master plan based on the work of other class groups. Decide if you want to present this plan to the campus administration for approval.

10. Search the Internet for information on the United Nations programs to alleviate the AIDS epidemic around the world. Then write a letter to your congressional representative explaining why (or why not) Congress should support these efforts.

Legal in Unlikely Places

JOSEPH CONTRERAS

Joseph Contreras, a native Californian, joined the staff of *Newsweek* in 1980 as a correspondent in the magazine's Los Angeles bureau. His reporting on world issues is truly global in scope: Contreras has served as *Newsweek* bureau chief in Miami, Mexico City, Buenos Aires, Johannesburg, and Jerusalem. Contreras, who is known for his expertise on Latin American issues, established his early reputation with a series on the Colombian drug wars of the 1980s and the revolution in Peru. As Jerusalem bureau chief, Contreras reported on the political rise of Benjamin Netanyahu in the 1990s and the deterioration of the Middle East peace process in the years following Israel's 1996 election. As Miami bureau chief, he covered the Elián Gonzalez custody battle and the controversy over the 2000 U.S. presidential election. He was appointed *Newsweek's* Latin America regional editor in 2002, and he is currently stationed in southern Sudan where he serves as a pubic information officer for a UN peacekeeping mission. In the following selection from the September 17, 2007, issue of *Newsweek International*, Contreras examines gay power in global—and especially Latin American—perspective.

Before Reading

What does "machismo" mean? How might one think that machismo might likely clash with gay rights?

After eight years together, Gilberto Aranda and Mauricio List walked into   1
a wedding chapel in the Mexico City neighborhood of Coyoacan last
April and tied the knot in front of 30 friends and relatives. Aranda's disap-
proving father was not invited to the springtime nuptials. For the newlyweds,
the ceremony marked the fruit of the gay-rights movement's long struggle to
gain recognition in Mexico. The capital city had legalized gay civil unions
only the month before. "After all the years of marches and protests," says
Aranda, 50, a state-government official, "a sea change was coming."

The sea change spreads beyond Mexico City, a cosmopolitan capital   2
that is home to a thriving community of artists and intellectuals.

The growing maturity of the gay-rights movement in the West is having a   3
marked effect on the developing world. In the United States, the Republican
Party is in trouble in part because it has made a fetish of its opposition to gay
marriage. At least some gays in big cities like New York question why they
are still holding "pride" parades, as if they were still a closeted minority and
not part of the Manhattan mainstream. Since 2001, Western European countries like Belgium, the Netherlands and Spain have gone even farther than the
United States, placing gay and lesbian partners on the same legal footing as
their heterosexual counterparts. And now, the major developing powers of
Asia, Latin America and Africa are following the liberal road—sometimes
imitating Western models, sometimes not—but in all cases setting precedents
that could spread to the remaining outposts of official homophobia.

In Mexico, the declining clout and prestige of the Roman Catholic   4
Church have emboldened gay-rights activists and their allies in state legis-
latures and city councils to pass new laws legalizing same-sex civil unions,
starting with Mexico City in November. The rising influence of tolerant
Western pop culture has encouraged gay men and lesbians to proclaim
their sexuality in gay-pride marches like the one in the Brazilian city of Sao
Paulo in June, which drew 3 million participants, according to the event's
organizers. It was the largest ever in Brazil.

Western models also helped inspire South Africa to legalize civil unions   5
in November 2006, thus becoming the first country in the developing
world to do so. In China, the trend goes back to the climate of economic
reform that tool hold in the 1980s, ending the persecution of the era of
Mao Zedong, who considered homosexuals products of the "moldering
lifestyle of capitalism."

Among left-wing movements in many developing countries, globaliza-   6
tion is a favorite scapegoat for all of the planet's assorted ills. But even those
who resist the West's basically conservative free-market economic orthodoxy

are quick to acknowledge the social liberalism—including respect for the rights of women and minorities of all kinds—that is the West's main cultural and legal export. "I think it helped that Spain and other parts of Europe had passed similar laws," says longtime Mexican gay-rights activist Alejandro Brito. "These types of laws are becoming more about human rights than gay issues."

Key people have hastened the trend in some countries. Some activists   7
single out a few political celebrities for de-stigmatizing their cause, including Nelson Mandela, who readily embraced British actor Sir Ian McKellen's suggestion that he support a ban on discrimination on the basis of sexual preference in South Africa's first post-apartheid constitution, and former prime minister Tony Blair, whose government was the first to recognize civil partnerships between same-sex couples. They also point to activist judges in Brazil, South Africa, and the European Court of Human Rights, who have handed down landmark rulings that unilaterally granted gay, lesbian and transgender communities new rights. These include a judicial order that gays be admitted into the armed forces of European Union member states.

The biggest and perhaps most surprising change is in Latin America,   8
the original home of machismo. In 2002, the Buenos Aires City Council approved Latin America's first-ever gay-civil-union ordinance, and same-gender unions are the law of the land in four Brazilian states today. Last year and openly homosexual fashion designer was elected to Brazil's National Congress with nearly half a million votes. In August a federal-court judge in the Brazilian state of Rio Grande do Sul broke new legal ground when he ordered the national-health-care system to subsidize the cost of sex-change operations in public hospitals, thereby putting sexual "reassignment" on par with heart surgery, organ transplants and AIDS treatment as medical procedures worthy of taxpayer support.

By the year-end, Colombia could become the first country in Latin   9
America to grant gay and lesbian couples full rights to health insurance, inheritance and social-security benefits. A bill containing those reforms is working its way through the National Congress at present. And even Cuba has turned a corner. In the 1960s and early 1970s homosexuals in Cuba were blacklisted or even banished to forced-labor camps along with Jehovah's Witnesses, Catholic priests and other so-called social misfits. HIV patients were locked away in sanitariums as recently as 1993. Several Cuban cities now host gay and lesbian film festivals. The hit TV program on the island's state-run airwaves last year was *The Hidden Side of the*

Moon, a soap opera about a married man who falls in love with a man and later tests positive for HIV.

The push for "more modern ways of thinking" about minorities, 10 feminists and homosexuals has roots that go back to the political ferment that shook the region in the late 1960s and 1970s, says Braulio Peralta, author of the 2006 book on gay rights in Mexico, *The Names of the Rainbow.* But it has gained in recent years, due in part to troubles in the Roman Catholic Church, which includes eight out of 10 Mexicans and long stood opposed to any attempt to redefine marriage laws. Last November, the Mexico City Legislature took up the civil-union law just as the country's top cardinal, Norberto Rivera Carrera, was facing charges that he had sheltered a Mexican priest accused of sexually abusing children in California. The prelate chose to stay under the radar as the vote loomed. "The Catholic Church was facing a credibility crisis," says longtime Mexico City–based gay-rights activist Brito. "So many of its leaders including Rivera knew that if they fiercely opposed the gay-union law, the news media would eat them alive."

The change in attitudes is most vivid in the sparsely populated 11 border state of Coahuila, an unlikely setting for blazing trails on gay rights. The left-wing political party that rules the national capital has made few inroads here. Yet soon after the state's young governor, Humberto Moreira Valdes, was elected in 2006, he backed a civil-union bill modeled on France's pacts of civil solidarity, and in the state capital of Saltillo the progressive Catholic bishop added his support. The 62-year-old prelate, Raul Vera, says he was comfortable doing so in part because the bill stopped short of calling for same-sex marriage. "As the church I said we could not assume the position of homophobes," he says. "We cannot marginalize gays and lesbians. We cannot leave them unprotected."

That seems to be the prevailing consensus in South Africa's ruling 12 party. The constitution adopted by South Africa after the African National Congress (ANC) took power in 1994 was the world's first political charter to outlaw discrimination on the basis of sexual orientation. In November 2006, the national Parliament overwhelmingly approved a civil-union bill after the country's constitutional court called for amendments to a 44-year-old marriage law that denied gay and lesbian couples the legal right to wed. In pushing for approval of the Civil Union Act, the ruling ANC shrugged off both conservative opposition parties and religious leaders, some of whom accused the government of imposing the morality of a "radical homosexual minority" on

South Africans. President Thabo Mbeki had been blasted by gay rights activists in the past for trying to downplay his country's raging HIV/AIDS epidemic, but on the issue of same-sex civil unions his government stood firm.

The sweeping terms of the 2006 Civil Union Act placed South Africa   13
in a select club of nations that have enacted similar laws and that, until last year, included only Canada, Belgium, Spain and the Netherlands. But there are glimmers of change in other nations. China decriminalized sodomy a decade ago and removed homosexuality from its list of mental disorders in 2001. Police broke up a gay and lesbian festival in Beijing in 2005 but took no action last February against an unauthorized rally in support of legalizing gay marriage. The Chinese Communist Party has established gay task forces in all provincial capitals to promote HIV/AIDS awareness and prevention. An in April a Web site launched a weekly hour-long online program called Connecting Homosexuals with an openly gay host. It is the first show in China to focus entirely on gay issues.

Tolerance, however, by no means spans the globe. Homosexuality   14
remains taboo throughout the greater Middle East. In most of the Far East, laws permitting gay and lesbian civil unions are many years if not decades away. In Latin America, universal acceptance of homosexuality is a long way off. Jamaica is a hotbed of homophobia. Even in Mexico, the first couple to take advantage of Coahuila's new civil-union statute were fired from their jobs as sales clerks after their boss realized they were lesbians. The new Mexico City law grants same-gender civil unions property and inheritance rights, but not the right to adopt children.

Even Mexican gays who still struggle against daily bias see signs of   15
improvement, however. In 2003 Jose Luis Ramirez landed work as a buyer at the Mexico City headquarters of a leading department-store chain, and things were going swimmingly until he brought his boyfriend to a company-hosted dinner with clients. "My boss's face just dropped," recalls Ramirez. Ramirez was subsequently denied promotions and left the company last year. But sexuality "isn't an issue" with his current employer, a new household-furnishings retailer.

Tolerance is now the majority, at least among the young. A 2005 poll by   16
the Mitofsky market-research firm found that 50 percent of all Mexicans between the ages of 18 and 29 supported proposals to allow gay marriage. Karla Lopez met Karina Almaguer on the assembly line of a Matamoros auto-stereo factory. The two became the first Mexican couple to marry under the civil-union bill; Lopez, now 30, is a mother of three. She urges

more gays and lesbians to follow her example and come out publicly. "I felt strange at first because people would judge us and look at us from head to toe," she says. "But I now feel more secure and at ease." If more political leaders, clergymen and judges act to legitimize folks like Karla Lopez, the new mood of tolerance will surely proliferate across the planet in her lifetime.

Thinking About the Essay

1. What is Contreras's purpose in this essay? Does he want to inform, shock, persuade, or argue, or a combination of these? Point to words and phrases that support your position.

2. In your own words, state the thesis that emerges from Contreras's essay. Does the thesis emerge from the title? Why or why not? How does the title reflect the writer's overall purpose?

3. Explain the use of exemplification or illustration to structure and unify the essay. Is there a pattern to this use of illustration, or does Contreras simply hop from one example to the next?

4. What comparative and causal patterns of development can you detect in this essay? Why are they effective—or do you think they are not?

5. How are the introductory and concluding paragraphs linked? Why does Contreras frame his essay in this manner?

Responding in Writing

6. Are you convinced that acceptance of gay rights is growing globally? Answer this question in a brief argumentative essay, referring to Contreras's essay if you wish.

7. Write a personal essay explaining your own attitude toward gay rights.

8. Write an essay of causal analysis in which you explain why global gay rights is part of the larger effort to promote universal human rights.

Networking

9. Working in small groups, collaborate in finding out more about the position of the Catholic Church—a subject that Contreras alludes to in his essay—on homosexuality and gay rights. Appoint one member of your group to join a class panel discussing this topic.

10. If your class has a virtual whiteboard, participate in listing all the examples that Contreras introduces in his essay. Contribute to a general discussion of the use of examples in essay writing.

A Dark Window on Human Trafficking

MIKE CEASER

Mike Ceaser is a journalist who writes frequently for *The Chronicle of Higher Education*. He specializes in Latin American affairs. Ceaser also has written for *Americas*, *The Lancet*, *National Catholic Reporter*, and other publications. In the following essay, published in the *Chronicle* on July 25, 2008, Ceaser investigates the unsavory world of human trafficking in young girls across South American and North American borders.

Before Reading

How would you define "human trafficking"? Why has this phenomenon become such a recent problem worldwide?

Police-car lights flashed and prostitutes, pimps, reporters, and police 1 officers milled about. One by one, the neon signs displaying scantily clad women went dark. Finally, the police sealed the gates beneath the billboard of two naked women amid the moon and stars.

While the police closed the La Luna nightclub for employing underage 2 girls as prostitutes, a pair of graduate students from Dominican University, near Chicago, stood by urging them on. For the students, the shuttering of the club was a personal victory.

"I don't think that prostitution can be a choice that you make," said 3 Tracy O'Dowd, who, along with Sergio Velarde, had assisted in winning the court battle against the owners of the nightclub. "I think you're brought there one way or another."

Ms. O'Dowd and Mr. Velarde, both master's-degree students in social 4 work, had come here three months earlier, in late January, to work as interns at the Our Youth Foundation, which is based in Ecuador and battles the exploitation of children. Concerned about human trafficking and interested in Latin America, both had studied the issue of trafficking at Dominican. Before leaving home, they learned that the sexual exploitation of minors was common in Ecuador, and that the country's corrupt and inefficient legal system rarely took action against those responsible.

Only in 2005 did Ecuador pass its first major law against human traf- 5 ficking; in 2007 the United States' "Trafficking in Persons Report" said that Ecuador "does not fully comply with the minimum standards for the elimination of trafficking," though the report also noted improvements in prosecutions, public education, and support for victims.

Mr. Velarde, whose parents and grandparents emigrated from Mexico 6 to the United States, speaks passionately about the challenges faced by migrants, who are often exploited even when they are not the victims of traffickers. Once, while visiting relatives in the Mexican state of Chihuahua, his family encountered immigrants from Central America who had been abandoned there and told they were in the United States. The many fast-food restaurants made the locale resemble a U.S. city.

Mr. Velarde believes that in "individualistic" American society, people 7 are leery of supporting and assisting immigrants—even those who were brought to the United States against their will.

"Once the stigma is placed on immigrants, it doesn't matter how you 8 got there," Mr. Velarde says. "If you got there on your free will or against your free will, you're always going to have that stigma."

But he and Ms. O'Dowd found that human trafficking in Ecuador differs 9 fundamentally from what they'd read about in other nations, and soon found themselves swept up in a landmark legal battle against traffickers. Human trafficking generally refers to the carrying of people across borders deceitfully or against their will, for prostitution or forced labor. While that happens to Ecuadoreans, here the crime most commonly consists of forcing young girls into brothels, through coercion or outright kidnapping. Sometimes young men seek out girls from poor, troubled families and pretend to fall in love with them—and then "sell" them to brothel owners.

"Here, they do this whole fantasy couple, fantasy relationship, and 10 then all of a sudden, 'I don't have any more money, so you have to work,'" says Mr. Velarde. "But the girl still believes they're a couple, and he still kind of treats them as a couple."

It's an often-invisible crime. 11

Mr. Velarde says that in his visits to poor communities, he discovered 12 that people often don't know that such cases involve human trafficking, or are so poor that they assume their absent daughters must be better off.

Most families never imagine that their daughters have ended up at a 13 place like La Luna, a complex of three huge nightclub-brothels, which had come to represent both the crime and the legal invulnerability often enjoyed by the perpetrators. Adult prostitution is legal in Ecuador, but La Luna was notorious for employing underage girls. In January 2006, pressured by the Our Youth Foundation and others, the police finally raided the club and rescued 11 girls ages 13 through 17, who were taken to a safe house operated by the foundation.

The trial of the club's five owners, repeatedly postponed, dragged 14
on until this March. Ms. O'Dowd and Mr. Velarde met three of the
victims, now ages 15 through 17, when the girls prepared to testify for
the prosecution. Then the two demonstrated in front of the courthouse in
support of the victims—and faced off against a group backing the brothel
owners.

"We stood outside the courtroom for three hours," Ms. O'Dowd wrote 15
in the blog she posted as part of her course work. "There were about 50
people there to support these girls, and there were about 20 supporting
the traffickers. We waited with posters saying 'No to sexual exploitation,'
'Justice that comes late isn't justice.'"

In the first days of April, the court issued its verdict: All the men were 16
guilty.

"The five men on trial were sentenced to 16 years," Mr. Velarde blogged 17
on April 4, "and it was a huge win."

Children's-rights advocates called the club's shuttering in April a land- 18
mark because of its size and wealth. And officials present at the closing vowed that it was the start of a crackdown on brothels employing
minors.

But while La Luna became the face of exploitation here, the crime's 19
roots lie in the city's poor and socially troubled barrios. And it was there
that the Dominican interns did the nitty-gritty and often frustrating work
intended to prevent the children of vulnerable families from ever being
misled into prostitution.

The interns did this in places like a nondescript neighborhood of brick 20
and concrete houses that Ms. O'Dowd visited one overcast day.

She knocked on the door of a home where the father had been 21
imprisoned for sexually abusing one of his daughters. Then, surrounded
by children, Ms. O'Dowd sat on a couch with the mother in the tidy
living room and asked about the family's situation and needs: How
were they doing financially? Did the children need notebooks for
school? Would they like counseling? But the woman seemed resigned
and hopeless. Between sobs, she described how the absence of her
husband, an auto mechanic, had left the family financially devastated.
She was even hostile to the Our Youth Foundation, which she blamed
for taking him away.

"What I want is for you to help me, to get my husband out of jail," 22
she pleaded. Ms. O'Dowd left feeling frustrated by the mother's attitude
and lack of appreciation for the danger to her daughters.

Even united families face the threat of trafficking because of the poverty 23
and social dislocation caused by Ecuador's heavy migration from the country
side to the wealthier cities.

Another morning, Mr. Velarde rode a series of buses and then a pickup 24
truck up a dirt road to a neighborhood of crude homes scattered among
bushes on a mountainside high above Quito, the capital. In a house
of uninsulated brick and concrete lived an indigenous family who had
migrated from the coast in search of work. The mother cleans houses when
pain from a kidney stone permits, while the children's stepfather earns
about $30 per month as a security guard.

Inside the home, Mr. Velarde and an intern from an Ecuadorean univer- 25
sity interviewed the family and left satisfied that they were making do with
their limited resources. But while the group waited for a bus back down the
mountainside, the mother unexpectedly mentioned that two years earlier
her daughter, now 14 years old, was kidnapped by a family acquaintance,
who raped her and held her captive for eight days while trying to "sell"
her to a brothel.

Although the family succeeded in rescuing the girl, she is still afraid to 26
leave the house. Then the mother described how the local schoolteacher
accosts female students, forcing the family to send their daughters to a more
distant school—which means a perilous walk back home every evening.

"Sometimes I think about the other girls who are getting bigger," their 27
mother worried, "that the same thing could happen to them."

The interns reported the family's situation to the foundation, for 28
follow-up assistance. "That her daughter was kidnapped—that just
changes the whole situation," Mr. Velarde observed afterward. "Research
says that if they've had such a thing with a sister, a cousin, . . . then they're
vulnerable."

Ms. O'Dowd and Mr. Velarde returned to Chicago this spring feeling 29
hopeful that Ecuador was taking real steps against trafficking, through
both police actions and new laws. But the court case against the club fell
short of being a complete victory: The owners' sentences were slashed from
16 years to six.

Their Ecuadorean experience left the Dominican students with hopes 30
of continuing to fight human trafficking, either in the United States,
where they feel the problem has received too little attention, or back in
Latin America. But the visit to Ecuador also changed them both, making
them more interested in preventing the circumstances that make people
vulnerable to trafficking. Although thousands of people are believed

to be victims of human trafficking into the United States each year, the United States does not include itself in its own annual trafficking report.

"As a country, I think we've focused more on everyone else," says   31
Mr. Velarde, "and when you have eyes on everybody else, you don't have eyes on your own situation."

Thinking About the Essay

1. How does Ceaser devise his introduction? What techniques does he use to create a dramatic situation throughout the essay? Are these strategies effective? Why or why not?

2. Ceaser profiles two students. Who are they, and what do we learn about them? What is the writer's attitude toward them? Justify your response.

3. Does Ceaser have a thesis or claim in this essay? Explain.

4. Ceaser wrote this article for a specialized audience—college teachers and administrators. Why would this readership be interested in the subject? Why might the essay appeal to a broader audience?

5. In analyzing the trafficking of young South American girls to the United States for the purpose of prostitution, Ceaser relies on causal analysis. Examine the causes and effects—both primary and secondary—that the writer traces.

Responding in Writing

6. In an investigative essay, analyze the causes behind the increase in the trafficking of women across international borders.

7. Argue for or against the proposition that American society is too tolerant of human trafficking for the purpose of prostitution, especially if the victims are undocumented immigrants.

8. Do you believe that we are responsible collectively for such realities as human trafficking? Write a persuasive essay in which you respond to this question.

Networking

9. In small groups, discuss Ceaser's assertion that "individualistic" American society creates the conditions that foster a tolerance for human trafficking.

10. Go online and find out more about human trafficking in girls and young women from South America to the United States. Write an investigative report based on your findings.

Life on the Global Assembly Line

Barbara Ehrenreich and Annette Fuentes

Barbara Ehrenreich was born in 1941 in Butte, Montana. She attended Reed College (B.A., 1963) and Rockefeller University (Ph.D. in biology, 1968). A self-described socialist and feminist, Ehrenreich uses her scientific training to investigate a broad range of social issues: health care, the plight of the poor, the condition of women around the world. Her scathing critiques of American health care in such books as *The American Health Empire* (with John Ehrenreich, 1970), *Complaints and Disorders: The Sexual Politics of Sickness* (with Deirdre English, 1973), and *For Her Own Good* (with English, 1978) established her as an authority in the field. In her provocative *The Hearts of Men: American Dreams and the Flight from Commitment* (1983), Ehrenreich surveys the decline of male investment in the family from the 1950s to the 1980s. A prolific writer during the 1980s and 1990s, Ehrenreich most recently published the award-winning book *Nickel and Dimed: On (Not) Getting By in America* (2001). She is also a frequent contributor to magazines, including *The Nation, Esquire, Radical America, The New Republic*, and *The New York Times*, while serving as a contributing editor to *Ms.* and *Mother Jones*. The classic essay that appears here, written for *Ms.* in 1981 with Annette Fuentes, a New York–based journalist and adjunct professor at Columbia University, was among the first articles to expose the plight of working women around the world.

Before Reading

What experiences or expectations do you bring to a new job? What happens if you discover you are being exploited?

Ms.; 1981 January   1

flash forward   2

Globalization has changed the rules of the game. The nation-state   3
as we understand it is a state that is bargaining, struggling, being
swallowed up by the forces of globalization. In 1985, on the eve of
the Nairobi conference, our message about development was really
new, that you can't just talk about gender equality without considering

equality of what. Do you want equal shares of a poisoned pie? It was a message that had a galvanizing effect on people, because by Beijing, globalization issues had become part of everyone's vocabulary. No longer was it a situation where the North worries about gender equality and the South about development.

—Economist Gita Sen, *Ford Foundation Report*, Winter 2000

Every morning, between four and seven, thousands of women head out for the day shift. In Ciudad Juarez, they crowd into *ruteras* (run-down vans) for the trip from the slum neighborhoods to the industrial parks on the outskirts of the city. In Penang they squeeze, 60 or more at a time, into buses for the trip to the low, modern factory buildings of the Bayan Lepas free trade zone. In Taiwan, they walk from the dormitories—where the night shift is already asleep in the still-warm beds—through the checkpoints in the high fence surrounding the factory zone.   4

This is the world's new industrial proletariat: young, female, Third World. Viewed from the "first world," they are still faceless, genderless "cheap labor," signaling their existence only through a label or tiny imprint "made in Hong Kong," or Taiwan, Korea, the Dominican Republic, Mexico, the Philippines. But they may be one of the most strategic blocs of womanpower in the world. Conservatively, there are 2 million Third World female industrial workers employed now, millions more looking for work, and their numbers are rising every year.   5

It doesn't take more than second-grade arithmetic to understand what's happening. In the U.S., an assembly-line worker is likely to earn, depending on her length of employment, between $3.10 and $5 an hour. In many Third World countries, a woman doing the same work will earn $3 to $5 a day.   6

And so, almost everything that can be packed up is being moved out to the Third World: garment manufacture, textiles, toys, footwear, pharmaceuticals, wigs, appliance parts, tape decks, computer components, plastic goods. In some industries, like garment and textile, American jobs are lost in the process, and the biggest losers are women, often black and Hispanic. But what's going on is much more than a matter of runaway shops. Economists are talking about a "new international division of labor," in which the process of production is broken down and the fragments are dispersed to different parts of the world, while control over the overall process and technology remains safely at company headquarters in "first world" countries.   7

The American electronics industry provides a classic example: circuits are printed on silicon wafers and tested in California; then the wafers are shipped to Asia for the labor-intensive process by which they are cut into tiny chips and bonded to circuit boards; final assembly into products such as calculators or military equipment usually takes place in the United States.   8

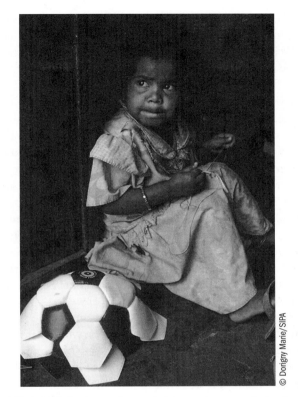

This three-year-old in India helps her mother and sisters make soccer balls—for 75 cents a day.

Garment manufacture too is often broken into geographically separated steps, with the most repetitive, labor-intensive jobs going to the poor countries of the southern hemisphere.

So much any economist could tell you. What is less often noted is the gender breakdown of the emerging international division of labor. Eighty to 90 percent of the low-skilled assembly jobs that go to the Third World are performed by women in a remarkable switch from earlier patterns of foreign-dominated industrialization. Until now, "development" under the aegis of foreign corporations has usually meant more jobs for men and—compared to traditional agricultural society—a diminished economic status for women. But multinational corporations and Third World governments alike consider assembly-line work—whether the product is Barbie dolls or missile parts—to be "women's" work.

It's an article of faith with management that only women can do, or will do, the monotonous, painstaking work that American business is exporting to the Third World. The personnel manager of a light assembly plant in Taiwan told anthropologist Linda Gail Arrigo, "Young male workers are too restless and impatient to do monotonous work with no career value. If displeased, they sabotage the machines and even threaten the foreman. But girls? At most, they cry a little."

A top-level management consultant who specializes in advising 11 American companies on where to relocate, gave us this global generalization: "The [factory] girls genuinely enjoy themselves. They're away from their families. They have spending money. Of course it's a regulated experience too—with dormitories to live in—so it's a healthful experience."

What is the real experience of the women in the emerging Third World 12 industrial work force? Rachael Grossman, a researcher with the Southeast Asia Resource Center, found women employees of U.S. multinational firms in Malaysia and the Philippines living four to eight in a room in boarding-houses, or squeezing into tiny extensions built onto squatter huts near the factory. Where companies do provide dormitories, they are not of the "healthful," collegiate variety. The American Friends Service Committee reports that dormitory space is "likely to be crowded—while one shift works, another sleeps, as many as twenty to a room."

Living conditions are only part of the story. The work that multinational 13 corporations export to the Third World is not only the most tedious, but often the most hazardous part of the production process. The countries they go to are, for the most part, those that will guarantee no interference from health and safety inspectors, trade unions, or even freelance reformers.

Consider the electronics industry, which is generally thought to be the 14 safest and cleanest of the exported industries. The factory buildings are low and modern, like those one might find in a suburban American industrial park. Inside, rows of young women, neatly dressed in the company uniform or T-shirt, work quietly at their stations. There is air conditioning (not for the women's comfort, but to protect the delicate semiconductor parts they work with), and high-volume piped-in Bee Gees hits (not so much for entertainment, as to prevent talking).

For many Third World women, electronics is a prestige occupation, at 15 least compared to other kinds of factory work. They are unlikely to know that in the United States the National Institute on Occupational Safety and Health (NIOSH) has placed electronics on its select list of "high health-risk industries using the greatest number of toxic substances." If electronics assembly work is risky here, it is doubly so in countries where there is no equivalent of NIOSH to even issue warnings. In many plants toxic chemicals and solvents sit in open containers, filling the work area with fumes that can literally knock you out. "We have been told of cases where ten to twelve women passed out at once," an AFSC field worker in northern Mexico told us, "and the newspapers report this as 'mass hysteria.'"

Some of the worst conditions have been documented in South Korea, where the garment and textile industries have helped spark that country's "economic miracle." Workers are packed into poorly lit rooms, where summer temperatures rise above 100 degrees. Textile dust, which can cause permanent lung damage, fills the air. Management may require forced overtime of as much as 48 hours at a stretch, and if that seems to go beyond the limits of human endurance, pep pills and amphetamine injections are thoughtfully provided. In her diary (originally published in a magazine now banned by the South Korean government), Min Chong Suk, 30, a sewing-machine operator, wrote of working from 7 A.M. to 11:30 P.M. in a garment factory: "When [the apprentices] shake the waste threads from the clothes, the whole room fills with dust, and it is hard to breathe. Since we've been working in such dusty air, there have been increasing numbers of people getting tuberculosis, bronchitis, and eye diseases. Since we are women, it makes us so sad when we have pale, unhealthy, wrinkled faces like dried-up spinach. It seems to me that no one knows our blood dissolves into the threads and seams, with sighs and sorrow."

In all the exported industries, the most invidious, inescapable health hazard is stress. Lunch breaks may be barely long enough for a woman to stand in line at the canteen or hawkers' stalls. Visits to the bathroom are treated as privileges. Rotating shifts—the day shift one week, the night shift the next—wreak havoc with sleep patterns. Because inaccuracies or failure to meet production quotas can mean substantial pay losses, the pressures are quickly internalized; stomach ailments and nervous problems are not unusual.

As if poor health and the stress of factory life weren't enough to drive women into early retirement, management actually encourages a high turnover in many industries. "As you know, when seniority rises, wages rise," the management consultant to U.S. multinationals told us. He explained that it's cheaper to train a fresh supply of teenagers than to pay experienced women higher wages. "Older" women, aged 23 or 24, are likely to be laid off and not rehired.

The lucky ones find husbands. The unlucky ones find themselves at the margins of society—as bar girls, "hostesses," or prostitutes.

There has been no international protest about the exploitation of Third World women by multinational corporations—no thundering denunciations from the floor of the United Nations' General Assembly, no angry resolutions from the Conference of the Non-Aligned Countries. Sociologist Robert Snow, who has been tracing the multinationals on their way south and eastward for years, explained why. "The Third World governments want the multinationals to move in. There's cutthroat competition to attract the corporations."

The governments themselves gain little revenue from this kind of investment—especially since most offer tax holidays and freedom from export duties in order to attract the multinationals in the first place. Nor do the people as a whole benefit, according to a highly placed Third World woman within the U.N. "The multinationals like to say they're contributing to development," she told us, "but they come into our countries for one thing—cheap labor. If the labor stops being so cheap, they can move on. So how can you call that development? It depends on the people being poor and staying poor." But there are important groups that do stand to gain when the multinationals set up shop in their countries: local entrepreneurs who subcontract to the multinationals; "technocrats" who become local management; and government officials who specialize in cutting red tape for an "agent's fee" or an outright bribe. 21

In the competition for multinational investment, local governments advertise their women shamelessly. An investment brochure issued by the Malaysian government informs multinational executives that: "the manual dexterity of the Oriental female is famous the world over. Her hands are small, and she works fast with extreme care. . . . Who, therefore, could be better qualified by nature and inheritance, to contribute to the efficiency of a bench-assembly production line than the Oriental girl?" 22

Many "host" governments are willing to back up their advertising with whatever brutality it takes to keep "their girls" just as docile as they look in the brochures. Even the most polite and orderly attempts to organize are likely to bring down overkill doses of police repression: 23

In Guatemala in 1975 women workers in a North American–owned garment factory drew up a list of complaints that included insults by management, piecework wages that turned out to be less than the legal minimum, no overtime pay, and "threats of death." In response, the American boss called the local authorities to report that he was being harassed by "Communists." When the women reported for work the next day they found the factory surrounded by two fully armed contingents of military police. The "Communist" ringleaders were picked out and fired. 24

In the Dominican Republic in 1978, workers who attempted to organize at La Romana industrial zone were first fired, then obligingly arrested by the local police. Officials from the AFL-CIO have described the zone as a "modern slave-labor camp," where workers who do not meet their production quotas during their regular shift must stay and put in unpaid overtime until they do meet them, and many women workers are routinely 25 strip-searched at the end of the day. During the 1978 organizing attempt, the government sent in national police in full combat gear armed with automatic weapons. Gulf & Western supplements the local law with its own company-sponsored motorcycle club, which specializes in terrorizing suspected union sympathizers.

In Inchon, South Korea, women at the Dong-II Textile Company 26 (which produces fabrics and yarn for export to the United States) had succeeded in gaining leadership in their union in 1972. But in 1978 the government-controlled, male-dominated Federation of Korean Trade Unions sent special "action squads" to destroy the women's union. Armed with steel bars and buckets of human excrement, the goons broke into the union office, smashed the office equipment, and smeared the excrement over the women's bodies and in their hair, ears, eyes, and mouths.

Crudely put (and incidents like this do not inspire verbal delicacy), 27 the relationship between many Third World governments and the multinational corporations is not very different from the relationship between a pimp and his customers. The governments advertise their women, sell them, and keep them in line for the multinational "johns." But there are other parties to the growing international traffic in women—such as the United Nations' Industrial Development Organization (UNIDO), the World Bank, and the United States government itself.

UNIDO has been a major promoter of "free trade zones." These are 28 enclaves within nations that offer multinationals a range of creature comforts, including: freedom from paying taxes and export duties; low-cost water, power, and buildings; exemption from whatever labor laws may apply in the country as a whole; and, in some cases, such security features as barbed-wire, guarded checkpoints, and government-paid police.

Then there is the World Bank, which over the past decade has lent 29 several billion dollars to finance the roads, airports, power plants, and even the first-class hotels that multinational corporations need in order to set up business in Third World countries.

But the most powerful promoter of exploitative conditions for Third 30 World women workers is the United States government itself. For example, the notoriously repressive Korean textile industry was developed with the help of $400 million in aid from the U.S. State Department. Malaysia became a low-wage haven for the electronics industry thanks to technical assistance financed by AID and to U.S. money (funneled through the Asian Development Bank) to set up free trade zones.

But the most obvious form of United States involvement, according 31 to Lenny Siegel, the director of the Pacific Studies Center, is through "our consistent record of military aid to Third World governments that are capitalist, politically repressive, and are not striving for economic independence."

What does our government have to say for itself? According to AID 32
staffer Emmy Simmons, "we can get hung up in the idea that it's exploitation without really looking at the alternatives for women. These people have to go somewhere."

Anna, for one, has nowhere to go but the maquiladora. Her family left 33
the farm when she was only six, and the land has long since been bought up by a large commercial agribusiness company. After her father left to find work north of the border, money was scarce for years. So when the factory where she now works opened, Anna felt it was "the best thing that had ever happened" to her. As a wage-earner, her status rose compared to her brothers with their on-again, off-again jobs. Partly out of her new sense of confidence she agreed to meet with a few other women one day after work to talk about wages and health conditions. That was the way she became what management called a "labor agitator" when, six months later, 90 percent of the day shift walked out in the company's first south-of-the-border strike.

Women like Anna need their jobs desperately. They know the risks of 34
organizing. Beyond that—if they do succeed in organizing—the company can always move on in search of a still-docile, job-hungry work force. Yet thousands of women in the Third World's industrial work force have chosen to fight for better wages and working conditions.

One particularly dramatic instance took place in South Korea in 1979. 35
Two hundred young women employees of the YH textile-and-wig factory staged a peaceful vigil and fast to protest the company's threatened closing of the plant. On the fifth day of the vigil, more than 1,000 riot police, armed with clubs and steel shields, broke into the building where the women were staying and forcibly dragged them out. Twenty-one-year-old Kim Kyong-suk was killed during the melee. It was her death that touched off widespread rioting throughout Korea that many thought led to the overthrow of President Park Chung Hee.

So far, feminism, first-world style, has barely begun to acknowledge 36
the Third World's new industrial womanpower. Jeb Mays and Kathleen Connell, cofounders of the San Francisco–based Women's Network on Global Corporations, are two women who would like to change that: "There's still this idea of the Third World woman as 'the other'—someone exotic and totally unlike us," Mays and Connell told us. "But now we're talking about women who wear the same styles in clothes, listen to the same music, and may even work for the same corporation. That's

an irony the multinationals have created. In a way, they're drawing us together as women."

Saralee Hamilton, an AFSC staff organizer says: "The multinational 37 corporations have deliberately targeted women for exploitation. If feminism is going to mean anything to women all over the world, it's going to have to find new ways to resist corporate power internationally." She envisions a global network of grass-roots women capable of sharing experiences, transmitting information, and—eventually—providing direct support for each other's struggles. It's a long way off; few women anywhere have the money for intercontinental plane flights or even long-distance calls, but at least we are beginning to see the way. "We all have the same hard life," wrote Korean garment worker Min Chong Suk. "We are bound together with one string."

Thinking About the Essay

1. Describe the writers' argumentative purpose in this essay. Is it to convince or persuade—or both? Explain.

2. Who is the intended audience for this essay? What is the level of diction? How are the two connected?

3. Examine the writers' use of illustration in this essay. How do they use these illustrations to support a series of generalizations? Ehrenreich and Fuentes cite various studies and authorities. Identify these instances and explain the cumulative effect.

4. Ehrenreich and Fuentes draw on a number of rhetorical strategies to advance their argument. Explain their use of comparison and cause-and-effect analysis.

5. Evaluate the writers' conclusion. Does it effectively reinforce their argument? Why or why not?

Responding in Writing

6. Ehrenreich and Fuentes wrote this article originally for *Ms.* magazine. Why would the essay appeal to the *Ms.* audience? What elements would also appeal to a general audience? Write a brief essay that answers these questions, providing specific examples from the text.

7. Write a personal essay in which you describe a job that you had (or have) in which you were exploited. Provide sufficient illustrations to support your thesis.

8. The writers imply that workforce women around the world are exploited more than men. Write an essay in which you agree or disagree with their claim.

Networking

9. Form small groups, and read the drafts of each other's essays. After general comments about how to improve the first draft, concentrate on ways to provide even greater illustration to support each writer's thesis or claim.

10. With another class member, do a Web search for new examples of the global exploitation of working women. Limit your focus to one of the countries mentioned by Ehrenreich and Fuentes. Think about whether the conditions that the two writers exposed more than twenty years ago are better or worse today. Share your conclusions with the rest of the class.

The Challenge of Globalization: What Are the Consequences?

Quick! Where was your cell phone manufactured? What is the origin of the clothes you are wearing today—and how much do you think the workers were paid to produce it? What will your lunch or dinner consist of: pizza, fried rice, tacos, a California roll? The ordinary features of our daily lives capture the forces of globalization that characterize our new century and our changed world. *New York Times* columnist Thomas Friedman, who writes persuasively on the subject—and who has an essay in this chapter— terms globalization the "super-story," the one all-embracing subject that dominates national and transnational developments today. As we see from the essays in this chapter, the concept of globalization already influences many major trends in economic, social, cultural, and political life in the twenty-first century.

It could be argued, of course, that globalization is nothing new: after all, Greece "globalized" much of the known world as far as India. Then Rome created its global dominion from England to Persia. More recently, for almost three centuries—from the seventeenth to the twentith— England ruled the waves and a majority of the world's nations. And from the twentieth century to the present, the United States has assumed the mantle of the world's major globalizing power. (Some critics claim that globalization might simply be a mask for "Americanization.") With antiglobalization demonstrations and riots now commonplace in the United States, Europe, and the Third World, we have to acknowledge that there *is* something about contemporary globalization that prompts debate and demands critical analysis. Lawyer, consumer advocate, writer, and three-time presidential candidate Ralph Nader states the case against globalization boldly: "The essence of globalization is a subordination of human rights, of labor rights, consumer rights, environmental rights, democracy rights, to the imperatives of global trade and investment."

A multiethnic group of protesters representing a wide range of causes marches in Richmond, California, to protest globalization.

Thinking About the Image

1. How many different ideas or causes do you see represented in this photograph? What does that suggest about this particular protest? About the antiglobalization movement in general?

2. What is the photographer's perspective on this event? Is anyone looking directly at the lens? Would your response to the photograph—or the story it tells—be different if there was a focus on just one or two people? If the photographer was farther away and captured a larger crowd in the frame?

3. What other kinds of images do you associate with street protests? Based on the fact that this one photograph was chosen to represent an entire day of protest, what can you infer about the tone of the protest and the response of the community?

4. Street protest is a kind of rhetoric, in that the demonstrators have a purpose and an audience. How clear is the purpose of these protesters? Who is their audience? Do you think such protests will make any difference to people like the child on p. 177?

But is Nader correct? Robert Rubin, who was secretary of the treasury during the Clinton administration and a prominent figure in the financial community, objects: "I think a healthy economy is the best environment in which to pursue human rights." The oppositional viewpoints of Nader and Rubin suggest that discussion of globalization often produces diverse opinions and that consequently we must think carefully and openly about the globalizing trends molding our lives today.

One trend that is clear today, as the twenty-first century begins, is that capitalism has triumphed over all its main rivals: communism, fascism, and socialism. Thus capitalism is the dominant if not the sole model of development for the nations of the world. Where capitalism collides with alternative visions of development—for example, Islamic economics in Iran—the result proves disastrous. The question that many people—especially young people on college and university campuses around the world—ask is whether or not capitalism can meaningfully address the numerous questions of social justice raised by globalization. If, for example, the environmental policy of the United States aids the interests of its energy companies, can this policy benefit others in the developing world? Or does the policy exclude almost everyone in a developing nation? Such questions can be asked about virtually every key issue raised by Ralph Nader and others who are skeptical of globalization as an overpowering economic force around the world.

The writers in this chapter and the next offer a variety of perspectives and critical insights into the nature and effects of globalization trends. Because of developments in information technology, people in the most distant parts of the world now are as close to us as someone in the dorm room next door—and perhaps more compelling. We certainly see poverty, famine, the degradation of the environment, and civil wars close-up. But is all this suffering the result of predatory multinational corporations and runaway capitalism? After all, both globalization *and* civil society are increasing worldwide, and the connections between the two require subtle critical analysis. The writers in this chapter bring such critical ability to their treatment of the social implications of current globalization trends.

Prologue: The Super-Story

Thomas L. Friedman

A noted author, journalist, and television commentator, and currently an op-ed contributor to *The New York Times*, Thomas L. Friedman writes and speaks knowledgeably about contemporary trends in politics and global development. He was born in Minneapolis, Minnesota, in 1953, and was educated at Brandeis University (B.A., 1975) and St. Anthony's College (M.A., 1978). Friedman covered the Middle East for *The New York Times* for ten years, and for five years he was bureau chief in Beirut, writing about both the Lebanese civil war and the Israel-Palestine conflict. He recorded these experiences in *From Beirut to Jerusalem* (1989), for which he won the National Book Award for nonfiction. A strong proponent of American intervention to solve seemingly intractable problems like the Arab-Israeli conflict, Friedman writes at the end of *From Beirut to Jerusalem,* "Only a real friend tells you the truth about yourself. An American friend has to help jar these people out of their fantasies by constantly holding up before their eyes the mirror of reality." In 2002, Friedman received the Pulitzer Prize for Commentary for his reports on terrorism for *The New York Times*. His other books include *The Lexus and the Olive Tree: Understanding Globalization* (2000), *The World Is Flat* (2005), *Hot, Flat, and Crowded* (2008), and a collection of articles and essays, *Longitudes and Attitudes: Exploring the World After September 11* (2002), in which the following selection serves as the book's prologue.

Before Reading

How would you define the word *globalization*? Is it simply a trend in which nations interrelate economically, or are other forces involved? Do you think that globalization is good or bad? Justify your response.

Iam a big believer in the idea of the super-story, the notion that we all   1
carry around with us a big lens, a big framework, through which we look at the world, order events, and decide what is important and what is not. The events of 9/11 did not happen in a vacuum. They happened in the context of a new international system—a system that cannot explain everything but *can* explain and connect more things in more places on more days than anything else. That new international system is called globalization. It came together in the late 1980s and replaced the previous international system, the cold war system, which had reigned since the

end of World War II. This new system is the lens, the super-story, through which I viewed the events of 9/11.

I define globalization as the inexorable integration of markets, transportation systems, and communication systems to a degree never witnessed before—in a way that is enabling corporations, countries, and individuals to reach around the world farther, faster, deeper, and cheaper than ever before, and in a way that is enabling the world to reach into corporations, countries, and individuals farther, faster, deeper, and cheaper than ever before.

Several important features of this globalization system differ from those of the cold war system in ways that are quite relevant for understanding the events of 9/11. I examined them in detail in my previous book, *The Lexus and the Olive Tree,* and want to simply highlight them here.

The cold war system was characterized by one overarching feature— and that was *division.* That world was a divided-up, chopped-up place, and whether you were a country or a company, your threats and opportunities in the cold war system tended to grow out of who you were divided from. Appropriately, this cold war system was symbolized by a single word— *wall,* the Berlin Wall.

The globalization system is different. It also has one overarching feature—and that is *integration.* The world has become an increasingly interwoven place, and today, whether you are a company or a country, your threats and opportunities increasingly derive from who you are connected to. This globalization system is also characterized by a single word—*web,* the World Wide Web. So in the broadest sense we have gone from an international system built around division and walls to a system increasingly built around integration and webs. In the cold war we reached for the hotline, which was a symbol that we were all divided but at least two people were in charge—the leaders of the United States and the Soviet Union. In the globalization system we reach for the Internet, which is a symbol that we are all connected and nobody is quite in charge.

Everyone in the world is directly or indirectly affected by this new system, but not everyone benefits from it, not by a long shot, which is why the more it becomes diffused, the more it also produces a backlash by people who feel overwhelmed by it, homogenized by it, or unable to keep pace with its demands.

The other key difference between the cold war system and the globalization system is how power is structured within them. The cold war system was built primarily around nation-states. You acted on the world in that system through your state. The cold war was a drama of states confronting states, balancing states, and aligning with states. And, as a system, the cold war was balanced at the center by two superstates, two superpowers: the United States and the Soviet Union.

The globalization system, by contrast, is built around three balances, which overlap and affect one another. The first is the traditional balance of power between nation-states. In the globalization system, the United States is now the sole and dominant superpower and all other nations are subordinate to it to one degree or another. The shifting balance of power between the United States and other states, or simply between other states, still very much matters for the stability of this system. And it can still explain a lot of the news you read on the front page of the paper, whether it is the news of China balancing Russia, Iran balancing Iraq, or India confronting Pakistan.   8

The second important power balance in the globalization system is between nation-states and global markets. These global markets are made up of millions of investors moving money around the world with the click of a mouse. I call them the Electronic Herd, and this herd gathers in key global financial centers—such as Wall Street, Hong Kong, London, and Frankfurt—which I call the Supermarkets. The attitudes and actions of the Electronic Herd and the Supermarkets can have a huge impact on nation-states today, even to the point of triggering the downfall of governments. Who ousted Suharto in Indonesia in 1998? It wasn't another state, it was the Supermarkets, by withdrawing their support for, and confidence in, the Indonesian economy. You also will not understand the front page of the newspaper today unless you bring the Supermarkets into your analysis. Because the United States can destroy you by dropping bombs, but the Supermarkets can destroy you by downgrading your bonds. In other words, the United States is the dominant player in maintaining the globalization game board, but it is hardly alone in influencing the moves on that game board.   9

The third balance that you have to pay attention to—the one that is really the newest of all and the most relevant to the events of 9/11—is the balance between individuals and nation-states. Because globalization has brought down many of the walls that limited the movement and reach of people, and because it has simultaneously wired the world into networks, it gives more power to *individuals* to influence both markets and nation-states than at any other time in history. Whether by enabling people to use the Internet to communicate instantly at almost no cost over vast   10 distances, or by enabling them to use the Web to transfer money or obtain weapons designs that normally would have been controlled by states, or by enabling them to go into a hardware store now and buy a five-hundred-dollar global positioning device, connected to a satellite, that can direct a hijacked airplane—globalization can be an incredible force-multiplier for individuals. Individuals can increasingly act on the world stage directly, unmediated by a state.

So you have today not only a superpower, not only Supermarkets, but 11
also what I call "super-empowered individuals." Some of these super-empowered individuals are quite angry, some of them quite wonderful—but all of them are now able to act much more directly and much more powerfully on the world stage.

Osama bin Laden declared war on the United States in the late 1990s. 12
After he organized the bombing of two American embassies in Africa, the U.S. Air Force retaliated with a cruise missile attack on his bases in Afghanistan as though he were another nation-state. Think about that: on one day in 1998, the United States fired 75 cruise missiles at bin Laden. The United States fired 75 cruise missiles, at $1 million apiece, at a person! That was the first battle in history between a superpower and a super-empowered angry man. September 11 was just the second such battle.

Jody Williams won the Nobel Peace Prize in 1997 for helping to build 13
an international coalition to bring about a treaty outlawing land mines. Although nearly 120 governments endorsed the treaty, it was opposed by Russia, China, and the United States. When Jody Williams was asked, "How did you do that? How did you organize one thousand different citizens' groups and nongovernmental organizations on five continents to forge a treaty that was opposed by the major powers?" she had a very brief answer: "E-mail." Jody Williams used e-mail and the networked world to super-empower herself.

Nation-states, and the American superpower in particular, are still 14
hugely important today, but so too now are Supermarkets and super-empowered individuals. You will never understand the globalization system, or the front page of the morning paper—or 9/11—unless you see each as a complex interaction between all three of these actors: states bumping up against states, states bumping up against Supermarkets, and Supermarkets and states bumping up against super-empowered individuals—many of whom, unfortunately, are super-empowered angry men.

Thinking About the Essay

1. Friedman constructs this essay and entitles it a "prologue." What is the purpose of a prologue? What subject matter does the writer provide in his prologue?

2. The writer is not afraid to inject the personal "I" into his analysis—a strategy that many composition teachers will warn you against. Why does Friedman start with his personal voice? Why can he get away with it? What does the personal voice contribute to the effect of the essay?

3. In addition to his personal voice, what other stylistic features make Friedman's essay, despite its complicated subject matter, accessible to ordinary readers? How does he establish a colloquial style?

4. This essay offers a series of definitions, comparisons, and classifications as structuring devices. Locate instances of these three rhetorical strategies and explain how they complement each other.

5. Friedman uses September 11 as a touchstone for his essay. Why does he do this? What is the effect?

Responding in Writing

6. Write a 250-word summary of Friedman's essay, capturing all the important topics that he presents.

7. Take one major point that Friedman makes in this essay and write a paper on it. For example, you might want to discuss why September 11 represents a key transition point in our understanding of globalization. Or you might focus on the concept of the Supermarket or the Electronic Herd.

8. Think about the world today, and write your own "super-story" in which you define and classify its primary features.

Networking

9. Divide into two roughly equal groups, and conduct a debate on whether or not globalization is a good or bad phenomenon. Use Friedman's essay as a reference point. Your instructor should serve as the moderator for this debate.

10. Join the Electronic Herd and develop a list of links to sites thatdeal with globalization. Contribute your list to the others generatedby class members in order to create a superlist for possible future use.

The Global Village Finally Arrives

PICO IYER

Pico Iyer was born in 1957, in Oxford, England, to Indian parents, both of them university professors. Educated at Oxford University and Harvard University, Iyer has been a writer for *Time* magazine since 1982 and a prolific author of travel books, essays, and fiction. His first full-length travel book is the acclaimed *Video Night in Kathmandu: And Other Reports from the Not-so-Far East* (1988). He followed the success of this book with *The Lady and the Monk: Four Seasons in Kyoto* (1991), *Tropical Classical: Essays from Several Directions* (1997), *The Global Soul: Jet Lag, Shopping Malls, and the Search for Home* (2000), *Sun after Dark: Flights into the Foreign* (2004), and *The Open Road: The Global Journey of the Fourteenth Dalai Lama* (2008), among others. Iyer also has published a novel, *Cuba and the Night* (1995). Iyer calls writing "an intimate letter to a stranger." In this essay, published in *Time* magazine on December 2, 1993, he invites us to view his world in southern California—and the world in general—in polyglot terms.

Before Reading

Look around you or think about your college—its students, courses, clubs, cultural programs, and so forth. Would you say that your campus reflects what Iyer terms a "diversified world"? Why or why not?

This is the typical day of a relatively typical soul in today's diversified world. I wake up to the sound of my Japanese clock radio, put on a T-shirt sent me by an uncle in Nigeria and walk out into the street, past German cars, to my office. Around me are English-language students from Korea, Switzerland and Argentina—all on this Spanish-named road in this Mediterranean-style town. On TV, I find, the news is in Mandarin; today's baseball game is being broadcast in Korean. For lunch I can walk to a sushi bar, a tandoori palace, a Thai cafe or the newest burrito joint (run by an old Japanese lady). Who am I, I sometimes wonder, the son of Indian parents and a British citizen who spends much of his time in Japan (and is therefore—what else?—an American permanent resident)? And where am I?

I am, as it happens, in Southern California, in a quiet, relatively   2
uninternational town, but I could as easily be in Vancouver or Sydney
or London or Hong Kong. All the world's a rainbow coalition, more and
more; the whole planet, you might say, is going global. When I fly to
Toronto, or Paris, or Singapore, I disembark in a world as hyphenated
as the one I left. More and more of the globe looks like America, but an
America that is itself looking more and more like the rest of the globe.
Los Angeles famously teaches 82 different languages in its schools. In
this respect, the city seems only to bear out the old adage that what is
in California today is in America tomorrow, and next week around the
globe.

In ways that were hardly conceivable even a generation ago, the new   3
world order is a version of the New World writ large: a wide-open frontier
of polyglot terms and postnational trends. A common multiculturalism
links us all—call it Planet Hollywood, Planet Reebok or the United Colors
of Benetton. Taxi and hotel and disco are universal terms now, but so too
are karaoke and yoga and pizza. For the gourmet alone, there is tiramisu
at the Burger King in Kyoto, echt angel-hair pasta in Saigon and enchiladas
on every menu in Nepal.

But deeper than mere goods, it is souls that are mingling. In Brussels, a   4
center of the new "unified Europe," 1 new baby in every 4 is Arab. Whole
parts of the Paraguayan capital of Asunción are largely Korean. And when
the prostitutes of Melbourne distributed some pro-condom pamphlets,
one of the languages they used was Macedonian. Even Japan, which
prides itself on its centuries-old socially engineered uniculture, swarms
with Iranian illegals, Western executives, Pakistani laborers and Filipina
hostesses.

The global village is defined, as we know, by an international youth   5
culture that takes its cues from American pop culture. Kids in Perth and
Prague and New Delhi are all tuning in to *Santa Barbara* on TV, and wrig-
gling into 501 jeans, while singing along to Madonna's latest in English.
CNN (which has grown 70-fold in 13 years) now reaches more than 140
countries; an American football championship pits London against Barcelona. As fast as the world comes to America, America goes round the
world—but it is an America that is itself multi-tongued and many hued,
an America of Amy Tan and Janet Jackson and movies with dialogue in
Lakota.

For far more than goods and artifacts, the one great influence being   6
broadcast around the world in greater numbers and at greater speed
than ever before is people. What were once clear divisions are now

tangles of crossed lines: there are 40,000 "Canadians" resident in Hong Kong, many of whose first language is Cantonese. And with people come customs: while new immigrants from Taiwan and Vietnam and India—some of the so-called Asian Calvinists—import all-American values of hard work and family closeness and entrepreneurial energy to America, America is sending its values of upward mobility and individualism and melting-pot hopefulness to Taipei and Saigon and Bombay.

Values, in fact, travel at the speed of fax; by now, almost half the   7
world's Mormons live outside the U.S. A diversity of one culture quickly becomes a diversity of many: the "typical American" who goes to Japan today may be a third-generation Japanese American, or the son of a Japanese woman married to a California serviceman, or the offspring of a Salvadoran father and an Italian mother from San Francisco. When he goes out with a Japanese woman, more than two cultures are brought into play.

None of this, of course, is new: Chinese silks were all the rage in   8
Rome centuries ago, and Alexandria before the time of Christ was a paradigm of the modern universal city. Not even American eclecticism is new: many a small town has long known Chinese restaurants, Indian doctors and Lebanese grocers. But now all these cultures are crossing at the speed of light. And the rising diversity of the planet is something more than mere cosmopolitanism: it is a fundamental recoloring of the very complexion of societies. Cities like Paris, or Hong Kong, have always had a soigné, international air and served as magnets for exiles and émigrés, but now smaller places are multinational too. Marseilles speaks French with a distinctly North African twang. Islamic fundamentalism has one of its strongholds in Bradford, England. It is the sleepy coastal towns of Queensland, Australia, that print their menus in Japanese.

The dangers this internationalism presents are evident: not for nothing   9
did the Tower of Babel collapse. As national borders fall, tribal alliances, and new manmade divisions, rise up, and the world learns every day terrible new meanings of the word Balkanization. And while some places are wired for international transmission, others (think of Iran or North Korea or Burma) remain as isolated as ever, widening the gap between the haves and the have-nots, or what Alvin Toffler has called the "fast" and the "slow" worlds. Tokyo has more telephones than the whole continent of Africa.

Nonetheless, whether we like it or not, the "transnational" future is   10
upon us: as Kenichi Ohmae, the international economist, suggests with

his talk of a "borderless economy," capitalism's allegiances are to products, not places. "Capital is now global," Robert Reich, the Secretary of Labor, has said, pointing out that when an Iowan buys a Pontiac from General Motors, 60% of his money goes to South Korea, Japan, West Germany, Taiwan, Singapore, Britain and Barbados. Culturally we are being reformed daily by the cadences of world music and world fiction: where the great Canadian writers of an older generation had names like Frye and Davies and Laurence, now they are called Ondaatje and Mistry and Skvorecky.

As space shrinks, moreover, time accelerates. This hip-hop mishmash 11
is spreading overnight. When my parents were in college, there were all of seven foreigners living in Tibet, a country the size of Western Europe, and in its entire history the country had seen fewer than 2,000 Westerners. Now a Danish student in Lhasa is scarcely more surprising than a Tibetan in Copenhagen. Already a city like Miami is beyond the wildest dreams of 1968; how much more so will its face in 2018 defy our predictions of today?

It would be easy, seeing all this, to say that the world is moving toward 12
the Raza Cosmica (Cosmic Race), predicted by the Mexican thinker José Vasconcelos in the '20s—a glorious blend of mongrels and mestizos. It may be more relevant to suppose that more and more of the world may come to resemble Hong Kong, a stateless special economic zone full of expats and exiles linked by the lingua franca of English and the global marketplace. Some urbanists already see the world as a grid of 30 or so highly advanced city-regions, or technopoles, all plugged into the same international circuit.

The world will not become America. Anyone who has been to a base- 13
ball game in Osaka, or a Pizza Hut in Moscow, knows instantly that she is not in Kansas. But America may still, if only symbolically, be a model for the world. E Pluribus Unum, after all, is on the dollar bill. As Federico Mayor Zaragoza, the director-general of UNESCO, has said, "America's main role in the new world order is not as a military superpower, but as a multicultural superpower."

The traditional metaphor for this is that of a mosaic. But Richard 14
Rodriguez, the Mexican-American essayist who is a psalmist for our new hybrid forms, points out that the interaction is more fluid than that, more human, subject to daily revision. "I am Chinese," he says, "because I live in San Francisco, a Chinese city. I became Irish in America. I became Portuguese in America." And even as he announces this new truth, Portuguese women are becoming American, and Irishmen are becoming

Portuguese, and Sydney (or is it Toronto?) is thinking to compare itself with the "Chinese city" we know as San Francisco.

Thinking About the Essay

1. How does Iyer's introductory paragraph set the stage for the rest of the essay? What is the setting? Why does he use a personal voice? What is his reason for writing? Is his thesis stated or implied? Explain.

2. Iyer presents us with an interesting example of an illustrative essay. Draw up a list of all the examples, references, authorities, and allusions that he presents. Why—from start to finish and in every paragraph—does he offer so many illustrations? What is the overall effect?

3. Does the writer have an argument or claim that he develops in this essay, or does he merely want to make a major point? Explain your response.

4. What is the tone of this essay? Put differently, do you think that Iyer embraces his new "transnational" world, likes it, dislikes it, is worried about it, or what? Locate passages that confirm your response.

5. How does Iyer use definitions in constructing his analysis of the global village? Cite examples of his approach.

Responding in Writing

6. Narrate—as Iyer does at the start of his essay—a typical day in your life. Turn this day into an exploration of how you fit into the "Global Village." Provide examples throughout the essay to support your thesis.

7. "The world," writes Iyer, "will not become America" (paragraph 13). Write an essay arguing for or against his view.

8. Write an extended definition of globalization. Refer to Iyer's essay for ideas as you develop this paper.

Networking

9. Discuss Iyer's essay with class members, and then write a collective letter telling him of the group's response to the issues he raises. Ask about his interest in travel and globalization, and pose one or two questions for his response.

10. As a travel writer, Iyer has visited some of the more remote and exotic parts of the planet. What exotic or romantic part of the world interests you? Go online and find information about this place. Plan travel arrangements and a budget. Prepare an outline or itinerary for a two-week trip to your dream destination.

The Rise of the Rest

FAREED ZAKARIA

Fareed Zakaria, author, political scientist, and magazine and television news commentator, was born and raised in Bombay, India, the son of politically progressive parents who were also practicing Muslims. (His father was a leading politician and his mother edited the *Times of India*.) Zakaria emigrated to the United States to attend Yale University, and received a Ph.D. in political science at Harvard University, where he studied under the influential international relations expert Samuel P. Huntington. At the age of twenty-eight, Zakaria accepted an offer to edit *Foreign Affairs* magazine. One of the first articles Zakaria accepted for publication was Huntington's controversial essay on the clash of civilizations (which Huntington later expanded into a book). Zakaria is the author of *From Wealth to Power: The Unusual Origins of America's World Role* (1998), *The Future of Freedom: Illiberal Democracy at Home and Abroad* (2004), and *The Post-American World* (2008). He writes a regular column for *Newsweek* and appears frequently on television news shows as a foreign affairs analyst. In the following essay, published in the December 1–December 15, 2008, issue of *New York Times Upfront (upfrontmagazine.com)*, Zakaria makes a provocative claim about the relationship of the United States to other emerging world powers in the new era of globalization.

Before Reading

Could the rise of such nations as China, Brazil, and India as surperpowers actually be beneficial for the future of the United States? Explain your position on this issue.

The world's tallest building is now in Dubai. The largest publicly traded company is in China. The largest passenger airplane is built in Europe. The biggest movie industry is India's Bollywood, not Hollywood. And in the most recent *Forbes* rankings, only two of the world's 10 richest people are American. 1

Just 10 years ago, the United States—which for the last century has been used to leading the world—would have topped all these lists. Of course, some of these lists are a bit silly, but they actually do reflect a seismic shift in power and attitudes. 2

For the last 20 years, America's superpower status has been largely unchallenged—something that hasn't happened since the Roman Empire dominated the known world 2,000 years ago. 3

But at the same time, the global economy has accelerated dramatically. Many nations outside the industrialized West have been growing at rates that were once unthinkable. In fact, this is something much broader than the much-talked-about rise of China, or even Asia. It is the rise of the rest—the rest of the world. 4

Why is this happening? It's because globalization has truly taken hold: More countries are making goods, and communications technology is leveling the playing field. Together, this has created huge opportunities for growth in many nations. 5

At the military and political level, the U.S. still remains supreme. But in every other way—industrial, financial, social, cultural—the distribution of power is moving away from American dominance. 6

America's Perception

The post-American world is naturally an unsettling prospect for Americans, but it shouldn't be. These changes are not about the decline of America, but rather about the rise of everyone else. It is the result of a series of positive trends that have created an international climate of unprecedented peace and prosperity—which in the long run will only benefit America. 7

But that's not the world that Americans perceive. We are told that we live in dark, dangerous times. Terrorism, rogue states, nuclear pro- liferation, financial panics, outsourcing, and illegal immigrants all loom large in the national discourse. But just how dangerous is today's world, really? 8

Researchers at the University of Maryland have found that global violence is actually at its lowest levels since the 1950s. Harvard professor Steven Pinker concludes that we are probably living "in the most peaceful time of our species' existence." 9

Then why do we think we live in scary times? Part of the reason is that as violence has been ebbing, information has been exploding. The last 20 years have produced an information revolution—24-hour news channels, cell phones, the Internet—that brings us news and, most crucially, images from around the world all the time. 10

Of course, the threats we face are real. Islamic jihadists, for example, really do want to attack civilians everywhere. But it is increasingly clear that militants and suicide bombers make up a tiny portion of the world's 1.3 billion Muslims. They can do real damage, but the combined efforts of the world's governments have effectively put them on the run. 11

Since 9/11, the main branch of Al Qaeda (the gang run by Osama bin   12
Laden) has not been able to launch a single major terror attack in the West
or any Arab country. Of course, one day they will manage to strike again,
but the fact that they have been stymied for seven years indicates we need
not despair.

We do need to figure out how to deal with rogue states like Iran, which   13
pose real threats. But look at them in context. The American economy is 68
times the size of Iran's. The U.S. military budget is 110 times bigger. None
of the problems we face compare with the dangers posed by Nazi Germany
in the first half of the 20th century or the Soviet Union in the second half.
Those were great global powers bent on world domination.

Meanwhile, compare Russia and China with where they were 35 years   14
ago. Both (particularly Russia) were great threats, actively conspiring
against the United States, arming guerrilla movements across the globe,
funding insurgencies and civil wars. Now they are more integrated into the
global economy and society than at any point in at least 100 years. They
are neither friends nor foes, cooperating with the United States and the
West on some issues, obstructing on others.

Trade & Technology

The Iraq War has produced deep, lasting chaos and dysfunction in that   15
country, and sent more than 2 million refugees into neighboring countries.
But I've been struck by how little Iraq's troubles have destabilized the region.
Everywhere you go, people angrily denounce American foreign policy, but
most Middle Eastern countries are booming. Iraq's neighbors—Turkey, Jordan, and Saudi Arabia—are enjoying unprecedented prosperity.

Across the globe there is enormous vitality. For the first time ever, most   16
countries around the world are practicing sensible economics—opening up
their markets and embracing trade and technology. The results are stunning. The share of people living on $1 a day has plummeted from 40 per-
cent in 1981 to 18 percent in 2004 and is projected to drop to 12 percent
by 2015 (see graph on next page).

There remains real poverty in the world—most worryingly in 50   17
basket-case countries with a total of 1 billion people—but the overall trend
has never been more encouraging.

The most immediate effect of global growth is the appearance of new   18
economic powerhouses on the scene like China, India, and Brazil. If these
countries all feel that they have a stake in the existing global order, there
will be less danger of war, depression, panics, and breakdowns.

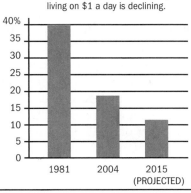

LESS GLOBAL POVERTY
The percentage of the world's people living on $1 a day is declining.

SOURCE: THE POST-AMERICAN WORLD BY FAREED ZAKARIA

So America's chief priority should be to bring these rising nations into 19 the global system. To do that, the U.S. needs to make its own commitment to the system clear. Until now, the United States was so dominant that it was able to be the global rule-maker but not always play by the rules.

As economic fortunes rise, so does nationalism. Imagine that your 20 country has been poor and marginal for centuries. Finally, things turn around and it becomes a symbol of economic progress and success. You would be proud, and anxious that your people win respect throughout the world.

The United States, accustomed to leading the world, isn't used to deal- 21 ing with so many rising nations with strong, nationalistic viewpoints. It will take some getting used to. Our challenge is this: Whether the problem is a trade dispute or a human-rights tragedy like Darfur or climate change, the only solutions that will work are those involving many nations.

With the current global financial crisis and its origins in the U.S. 22 housing market, some may conclude that the U.S. has had its day. But the U.S. will not only weather the current financial storm; it's likely to come out on the other side more stable and secure. The American economy remains extremely dynamic and flexible. And the rise of developing economies like China, India, and Brazil—which are also feeling the heat of the global crisis—will continue to fuel global growth in the long run.

Over the last 20 years, America has benefited massively from unusually 23 robust growth, low unemployment and inflation, and received hundreds of billions of dollars in investment—much of it from rising powers like China. These are not signs of fundamental economic collapse.

The United States is currently ranked as the globe's most competitive 24 economy by the World Economic Forum. It remains dominant in many industries of the future like nanotechnology, biotechnology, and dozens of smaller high-tech fields. Its universities are the finest in the world.

There's been a lot of discussion about a recent statistic that in 2004, 25 950,000 engineers graduated in China and India, while only 70,000 graduated in the U.S. But those numbers are wildly off the mark. If you exclude the car mechanics and repairmen—who are all counted as engineers in Chinese and Indian statistics—it turns out, the United States trains more engineers per capita than either of the Asian giants.

The real issue is that most of these American engineers are immigrants. 26 Foreign students and immigrants account for almost 50 percent of all science researchers in the United States. In 2006, they received 40 percent of all Ph.D.'s.

When these graduates settle in the U.S., they create economic oppor- 27 tunity. Half of all Silicon Valley start-ups have one founder who is an immigrant or first-generation American (see box, below). The potential for a new burst of American productivity depends not on our education system or R&D spending, but on our immigration policies. If these people are allowed to come to the U.S. and then encouraged to stay, then innovation will happen here. If they leave, they'll take it with them.

America's Great Strength

This openness is America's great strength. The U.S. remains the most open, 28 flexible society in the world, able to absorb other people, cultures, ideas, goods, and services.

The rise of the rest of the world is one of the most thrilling stories in 29 history. Billions of people are escaping from poverty. The world will be enriched as they become consumers, producers, inventors, thinkers, dreamers, and doers.

This is all happening because of American ideas and actions. For 60 30 years, the United States has pushed countries to open their markets, free up their politics, and embrace trade and technology. American diplomats, business people, and intellectuals have urged people in distant lands to be unafraid of change, to join the advanced world, to learn the secrets of our success.

Yet just as they are beginning to do so, Americans are becoming suspi- 31 cious of trade, openness, immigration, and investment—because now it's not Americans going abroad, but foreigners coming to America.

Generations from now, when historians write about these times, they 32 might note that by the turn of the 21st century, the United States had succeeded in its great, historical mission—globalizing the world. We don't want them to write that along the way, we forgot to globalize ourselves.

Thinking About the Essay

1. What is Zakaria's purpose in writing this essay? For example, does he want to argue a position, educate readers, persuade his audience to accept a basic premise or assumption, or some combination of these? Does the title provide any clue to the writer's purpose? Explain.

2. Why does Zakaria withhold his thesis or claim until the last paragraph in the first section of his essay? What effect does he achieve?

3. How does the organization of Zakaria's essay contribute to the force of his writing? Cite at least two examples to support your response.

4. What types of evidence and comparative information does Zakaria provide to support his major points?

5. Explain the overall tone that Zakaria establishes in this essay, pointing to specific words, phrases, and sentences that illuminate the writer's position.

Responding in Writing

6. Using Zakaria's essay as a springboard, write your own essay titled "The Rise of the Rest" in which you address the issue of America's role in the age of globalization.

7. Write a comparative essay focusing on the relationship between the United States and one other nation in this globalized world.

8. In an argumentative essay, respond to the proposition that the United States is destined to find its power reduced because of the forces of globalization.

Networking

9. In groups of three or four, discuss the meaning and implication of Zakaria's phrase, the "post-American world." What additional features can you add to the content of Zakaria's essay? Provide a summary of your discussion to class members.

10. Conduct online research to locate two articles on globalization that offer optimistic assessments of this phenomenon and two other essays that offer antiglobalization critiques. Provide a synopsis of your findings for class members.

The Noble Feat of Nike

JOHAN NORBERG

Johan Norberg contributed this article to London's *The Spectator* in June 2003. In the essay, he takes issue with those who think that globalization is the invention of "ruthless international capitalists." In arguing his case, Norberg centers his discussion on one symbol of globalization—Nike—suggesting that we simply have to look at our "feet" to understand Nike's "feat" in advancing a benign form of globalization. Norberg is the author of *In Defense of Global Capitalism,* and writer and presenter of the recent documentary *Globalization Is Good.* Since 2007, Norberg has been associated with the Cato Institute, a conservative Washington-based think tank.

Before Reading

Check your sneakers. Where were they made? What do you think the workers earned to manufacture them? Do you think they were exploited? Explain your response.

Nike. It means victory. It also means a type of expensive gym shoe. In the minds of the anti-globalisation movement, it stands for both at once. Nike stands for the victory of a Western footwear company over the poor and dispossessed. Spongy, smelly, hungered after by kids across the world, Nike is the symbol of the unacceptable triumph of global capital. 1

A Nike is a shoe that simultaneously kicks people out of jobs in the West, and tramples on the poor in the Third World. Sold for 100 times more than the wages of the peons who make them, Nike shoes are hate-objects more potent, in the eyes of the protesters at this week's G8 riots, than McDonald's hamburgers. If you want to be trendy these days, you don't wear Nikes; you boycott them. 2

So I was interested to hear someone not only praising Nike sweatshops, but also claiming that Nike is an example of a good and responsible business. That someone was the ruling Communist party of Vietnam. 3

Today Nike has almost four times more workers in Vietnam than in the United States. I travelled to Ho Chi Minh to examine the effects of multinational corporations on poor countries. Nike being the most notorious multinational villain, and Vietnam being a dictatorship with a 4 documented lack of free speech, the operation is supposed to be a classic of conscience-free capitalist oppression.

In truth the work does look tough, and the conditions grim, if we 5 compare Vietnamese factories with what we have back home. But that's not the comparison these workers make. They compare the work at Nike with the way they lived before, or the way their parents or neighbours still work. And the facts are revealing. The average pay at a Nike factory close to Ho Chi Minh is $54 a month, almost three times the minimum wage for a state-owned enterprise.

Ten years ago, when Nike was established in Vietnam, the workers had 6 to walk to the factories, often for many miles. After three years on Nike wages, they could afford bicycles. Another three years later, they could afford scooters, so they all take the scooters to work (and if you go there, beware; they haven't really decided on which side of the road to drive). Today, the first workers can afford to buy a car.

But when I talk to a young Vietnamese woman, Tsi-Chi, at the factory, 7 it is not the wages she is most happy about. Sure, she makes five times more than she did, she earns more than her husband, and she can now afford to build an extension to her house. But the most important thing, she says, is that she doesn't have to work outdoors on a farm any more. For me, a Swede with only three months of summer, this sounds bizarre. Surely working conditions under the blue sky must be superior to those in a sweatshop? But then I am naively Eurocentric. Farming means 10 to 14 hours a day in the burning sun or the intensive rain, in rice fields with water up to your ankles and insects in your face. Even a Swede would prefer working nine to five in a clean, air-conditioned factory.

Furthermore, the Nike job comes with a regular wage, with free or sub- 8 sidised meals, free medical services and training and education. The most persistent demand Nike hears from the workers is for an expansion of the factories so that their relatives can be offered a job as well.

These facts make Nike sound more like Santa Claus than Scrooge. 9 But corporations such as Nike don't bring these benefits and wages because they are generous. It is not altruism that is at work here; it is globalisation. With their investments in poor countries, multinationals bring new machinery, better technology, new management skills and production ideas, a larger market and the education of their workers. That is exactly what raises productivity. And if you increase produc- tivity—the amount a worker can produce—you can also increase his wage.

Nike is not the accidental good guy. On average, multinationals in the 10 least developed countries pay twice as much as domestic companies in the same line of business. If you get to work for an American multinational in a low-income country, you get eight times the average income. If this is exploitation, then the problem in our world is that the poor countries aren't sufficiently exploited.

The effect on local business is profound: "Before I visit some foreign factory, especially like Nike, we have a question. Why do the foreign factories here work well and produce much more?" That was what Mr. Kiet, the owner of a local shoe factory who visited Nike to learn how he could be just as successful at attracting workers, told me: "And I recognise that productivity does not only come from machinery but also from satisfaction of the worker. So for the future factory we should concentrate on our working conditions."   11

If I was an antiglobalist, I would stop complaining about Nike's bad wages. If there is a problem, it is that the wages are too high, so that they are almost luring doctors and teachers away from their important jobs.   12

But—happily—I don't think even that is a realistic threat. With growing productivity it will also be possible to invest in education and healthcare for Vietnam. Since 1990, when the Vietnamese communists began to liberalise the economy, exports of coffee, rice, clothes and footwear have surged, the economy has doubled, and poverty has been halved. Nike and Coca-Cola triumphed where American bombs failed. They have made Vietnam capitalist.   13

I asked the young Nike worker Tsi-Chi what her hopes were for her son's future. A generation ago, she would have had to put him to work on the farm from an early age. But Tsi-Chi told me she wants to give him a good education, so that he can become a doctor. That's one of the most impressive developments since Vietnam's economy was opened up. In ten years 2.2 million children have gone from child labour to education. It would be extremely interesting to hear an antiglobalist explain to Tsi-Chi why it is important for Westerners to boycott Nike, so that she loses her job, and has to go back into farming, and has to send her son to work.   14

The European Left used to listen to the Vietnamese communists when they brought only misery and starvation to their population. Shouldn't they listen to the Vietnamese now, when they have found a way to improve people's lives? The party officials have been convinced by Nike that ruthless multinational capitalists are better than the state at providing workers with high wages and a good and healthy   15 workplace. How long will it take for our own anticapitalists to learn that lesson?

Thinking About the Essay

1. Examine the writer's introduction. Why is it distinctive? How does Norberg "hook" us and also set the terms of his argument? Why is Nike an especially potent symbol around which to organize an essay on globalization?

2. Explain the writer's claim and how he defends it. Identify those instances in which he deals with the opposition. How effective do you think his argument is? Justify your answer.

3. What is the writer's tone in this essay? Why is the tone especially effective in conveying the substance of Norberg's argument?

4. Analyze the writer's style and how it contributes to his argument. Identify specific stylistic elements that you consider especially effective.

5. To a large extent, the writer bases his argument on direct observation. How can you tell that he is open-minded and truthful in the presentation of facts? What is the role of a newspaper or journal in claiming responsibility for the accuracy of this information?

Responding in Writing

6. Select a symbol of globalization and write an essay about it. You may use Nike if you wish, or Coca-Cola, McDonald's, or any other company that has a global reach.

7. Write a rebuttal to Norberg's essay. Try to answer him point by point.

8. Why have clothing manufacturing and other forms of manufacturing fled from the United States and other industrialized nations to less developed parts of the world? Write a causal analysis of this trend, being certain to state a thesis or present a claim that illustrates your viewpoint on the issue.

Networking

9. In groups of four, examine your clothes. List the countries where they were manufactured. Share the list with the class, drawing a global map of the countries where the various items were produced.

10. Check various Internet sites for information on Nike and its role in globalization. On the basis of your findings, determine whether or not this company is sensitive to globalization issues. Participate in a class discussion of this topic.

Fear Not Globalization

JOSEPH S. NYE JR.

Joseph Samuel Nye Jr. was born in South Orange, New Jersey, in 1937; his father was a stockbroker and his mother an art gallery owner. He received undergraduate degrees from Princeton University (1958) and Oxford University (1960) and a Ph.D. degree from Harvard University (1964) in political science. Currently, he is dean of Harvard's Kennedy School of Government. A prolific writer and well-known authority in international relations, Nye has served in the U.S. Department of State and on the committees of such prominent organizations as the Ford Foundation and the Carnegie Endowment for International Peace. A frequent guest on television programs, including *Nightline* and the *The NewsHour with Jim Lehrer,* Nye also writes frequently for *The New York Times, The Christian Science Monitor, Atlantic Monthly,* and *The New Republic.* His most recent book is *Soft Power: The Means to Success in World Politics* (2004). The title of the following essay, which appeared in *Newsday* on October 8, 2002, captures Nye's essential thesis about the forces of globalization in today's world.

Before Reading

Is globalization a force for good or bad? Will it turn all nations, cultures, and peoples into reflections of each other?

When anti-globalization protesters took to the streets of Washington   1
recently, they blamed globalization for everything from hunger to the destruction of indigenous cultures. And globalization meant the United States.

The critics call it Coca-Colonization, and French sheep farmer Jose   2
Bove has become a cult figure since destroying a McDonald's restaurant in 1999.

Contrary to conventional wisdom, however, globalization is neither   3
homogenizing nor Americanizing the cultures of the world.

To understand why not, we have to step back and put the current   4
period in a larger historical perspective. Although they are related, the long-term historical trends of globalization and modernization are not the same. While modernization has produced some common traits, such as

large cities, factories and mass communications, local cultures have by no means been erased. The appearance of similar institutions in response to similar problems is not surprising, but it does not lead to homogeneity.

In the first half of the 20th century, for example, there were some similarities among the industrial societies of Britain, Germany, America and Japan, but there were even more important differences. When China, India and Brazil complete their current processes of industrialization and modernization, we should not expect them to be replicas of Japan, Germany or the United States. 5

Take the current information revolution. The United States is at the forefront of this great movement of change, so the uniform social and cultural habits produced by television viewing or Internet use, for instance, are often attributed to Americanization. But correlation is not causation. Imagine if another country had introduced computers and communications at a rapid rate in a world in which the United States did not exist. Major social and cultural changes still would have followed. Of course, since the United States does exist and is at the leading edge of the information revolution, there is a degree of Americanization at present, but it is likely to diminish over the course of the 21st century as technology spreads and local cultures modernize in their own ways. 6

The lesson that Japan has to teach the rest of the world is that even a century and a half of openness to global trends does not necessarily assure destruction of a country's separate cultural identity. Of course, there are American influences in contemporary Japan (and Japanese influences such as Sony and Pokémon in the United States). Thousands of Japanese youths are co-opting the music, dress and style of urban black America. But some of the groups they listen to dress up like samurai warriors on stage. One can applaud or deplore such cultural transfers, but one should not doubt the persistence of Japan's cultural uniqueness. 7

The protesters' image of America homogenizing the world also reflects a mistakenly static view of culture. Efforts to portray cultures as unchanging more often reflect reactionary political strategies than descriptions of reality. The Peruvian writer Mario Vargas Llosa put it well when he said that arguments in favor of cultural identity and against globalization "betray a stagnant attitude toward culture that is not borne out by historical fact. Do we know of any cultures that have remained unchanged through time? To find any of them one has to travel to the small, primitive, magico-religious communities made up of people ... who, due to their primitive condition, become progressively more vulnerable to exploitation and extermination." 8

Vibrant cultures are constantly changing and borrowing from other cultures. And the borrowing is not always from the United States. For example, 9 many more countries turned to Canada than to the United States as a model for constitution-building in the aftermath of the Cold War. Canadian views of how to deal with hate crimes were more congenial to countries such as South Africa and the post-Communist states of Eastern Europe than America's First Amendment practices.

Globalization is also a two-edged sword. In some areas, there has been 10 not only a backlash against American cultural imports, but also an effort to change American culture itself. American policies on capital punishment may have majority support inside the United States, but they are regarded as egregious violations of human rights in much of Europe and have been the focus of transnational human rights campaigns. American attitudes toward climate change or genetic modification of food draw similar criticism. More subtly, the openness of the United States to the world's diasporas both enriches and changes American culture.

Transnational corporations are changing poor countries but not homog- 11 enizing them. In the early stages of investment, a multinational company with access to the global resources of finance, technology and markets holds the high cards and often gets the best of the bargain with the poor country. But over time, as the poor country develops a skilled workforce, learns new technologies, and opens its own channels to global finance and markets, it is often able to renegotiate the bargain and capture more of the benefits.

As technical capabilities spread and more and more people hook up to 12 global communications systems, the U.S. economic and cultural preponderance may diminish. This in turn has mixed implications for American "soft" power, our ability to get others to do what we want by attraction rather than coercion. Less dominance may mean less anxiety about Americanization, fewer complaints about American arrogance and a little less intensity in the anti-American backlash. We may have less control in the future, but we may find ourselves living in a world somewhat more congenial to our basic values of democracy, free markets and human rights.

Thinking About the Essay

1. What is Nye's purpose in writing this article? How can you tell? What type of audience does Nye have in mind for his essay? Why does he produce such an affirmative tone in dealing with his subject?

2. Which paragraphs constitute Nye's introduction? Where does he place his thesis, and how does he state it?

3. Break down the essay into its main topics. How does Nye develop these topics? What strategies does he employ—for example, causal analysis, comparison and contrast, illustration—and where?

4. Analyze Nye's topic sentences for his paragraphs. How do they serve as clear guides for the development of his paragraphs? How do they serve to unify the essay?

5. How does Nye's concluding paragraph serve as an answer both to the issue raised in his introduction and to other concerns expressed in the body of the essay?

Responding in Writing

6. From your own personal experience of globalization, write an essay in which you agree or disagree with Nye's assertion that there is little to fear from globalization.

7. Try writing a rebuttal to Nye's argument, explaining why there is much to fear about globalization. Deal point by point with Nye's main assertions. Be certain to provide your own evidence in support of your key reasons.

8. Write an essay that responds to the following topic sentence in Nye's essay: "Vibrant cultures are constantly changing and borrowing from other cultures" (paragraph 9). Base your paper on personal experience, your reading, and your knowledge of current events.

Networking

9. With four other classmates, imagine that you have to teach Nye's essay to a class of high school seniors. How would you proceed? Develop a lesson plan that you think would appeal to your audience.

10. With the entire class, arrange a time when you can have an online chat about Nye's essay. As a focal point for your discussion, argue for or against the idea that he does not take the dangers of globalization seriously enough.

Slumdog Millionaire

ROBERT KOEHLER

Robert Koehler is a film and culture critic who writes for *Variety, Cinema Scope, The Christian Science Monitor*, and other publications. He also blogs on *filmjourney.org*. In his film criticism, as the following essay demonstrates, Koehler typically ranges beyond the specific film under discussion to place it in broader cultural, literary, and historical contexts. His approach to *Slumdog Millionaire*, the "feel-good" movie of 2008 that won the Academy Award for Best Picture, reflects this in-depth analytical approach. Koehler's provocative essay appeared in *CINEASTE*'s Spring 2009 issue.

Before Reading

How does film reflect the forces of globalization today? Can films made in India or elsewhere ever be as popular as American films that appear overseas? Why or why not?

Danny Boyle's *Slumdog Millionaire* is the film of the moment for 1 the "new middlebrow"—that audience able to perceive momentous changes in the world and culture when they're reported in, say, *The New York Times*, but one, at the same time, that wouldn't have the slightest clue that the most thrilling new rushes of creative filmmaking since the nouvelle vague originate in the apartments and editing rooms of Manila, Kuala Lumpur, Barcelona, and Buenos Aires. This new middlebrow has a fresh object of adoration in Boyle's entertainment, since it quite conveniently summarizes and expresses so many wishes, hopes, and romantic yearnings of the West toward what is perceived as the troubled East—with today's West resembling nothing so much as the West of the Sixties and its taste for turning Indian style into various forms of Hippie Chic. (*Slumdog* is paisley cinema, pure and simple.) Boyle's feverish, woozy, drunken, and thoroughly contrived picaresque film also conveniently packages misperceptions about India (and the East) that continue to support the dominant Western view of the Subcontinent, making the film a potent object to examine not only what is cockeyed about an outsider's view (particularly, an Englishman's view) of India, but even more, what is misperceived by a middlebrow critical establishment and audience about what comprises world cinema.

Suitably then, the creative godfather of *Slumdog*, more than Bollywood 2 musical fantasies, is Charles Dickens. Certain Bollywood tropes are obediently followed, such as the innocent hero rising above terrible circumstances, the determined pursuit of a love against all odds and that stock Bollywood type, the snarling (often mustachioed) nemesis. But, including the much discussed group-dance finale, these are tropes included almost by necessity and play onscreen in a notably rote fashion. They are alien to Boyle, which is why the Dickens model is more culturally and even cinematically germane when addressing the issues inside *Slumdog*. Dickens's picaresque novels about young underdog heroes struggling and managing to eventually thrive in social settings weighed heavily against them were grist for, first, Vikas Swarup's novel, *Q & A*, and then, Simon Beaufoy's loosely adapted screenplay, which greatly compresses the novel's episodes and sections, renames characters and—for as outlandish as the final film is—actually tones down the adventure's more incredible events and coincidences.

If Dickens's milieu was the early years of the Industrial Revolution, the   3
film's setting is the new era of globalism, in which India is undergoing its own
revolution. Jamal (Dev Patel) is Pip, Nicholas Nickleby, and Oliver Twist
rolled into one, a lad who by sheer gumption has managed to land a spot
as a contestant on the hugely popular *Who Wants to Be a Millionaire?* even
though he's a humble (but oh so smart) chai wallah (or tea servant) at a cellphone sales center. When he's first seen on screen, though, Jamal is in trouble:
A fat cop is abusing him in a police station, though that's nothing next to the
electrocution he receives from the chief inspector (veteran Indian actor Irrfan
Khan), who's convinced that Jamal has cheated on the show. How, his caste-
based logic goes, could a "slumdog" like Jamal have won ten million rupees
(and only one question away from winning 100 million) without cheating?
Even the most scurrilous and bigoted of Mumbai cops likely wouldn't go all
Abu Ghraib on a poor teen boy for cheating on TV, and it's just the start of
the film's endless supply of stunning exaggeration-for-effect gambits that are
more like a two-by-four upside the head than anything that might be termed
in polite company as "dramatic touches." Boyle appears to have absorbed
this exaggeration into his directorial bloodstream, since, in at least the film's
first half and lingering long into the second, he indulges in a rush of shots
filmed with an obsessively canted camera, the technique lovingly nurtured
by Orson Welles to convey states of eruption and dislocation, but grievously
abused by Boyle through repetitive excess until it reeks of desperation.

© FILM 4/CELADOR FILMS/Pathe International/The Kobal Collection/Picture-Desk

Publicity shot from *Slumdog Millionaire*.

So, we get it: Jamal has everything stacked against him as he must 4
convince these thugs with badges how he knew the questions thrown to him
by the show's supercilious and remarkably condescending host, Prem (Anil
Kapoor), and that he will—it is written—prevail. From here, the rest of the
movie comprises Jamal's case, which begins with the wildly implausible
notion that Jamal remembers more or less everything in his life inside the
framework of a Dickens novel, and ends with his endless and, um, dogged
pursuit of his only true love, the beautiful (can she be anything else?) Latika
(Frieda Pinto). Of course, wild implausibility has been Boyle's general stock-
in-trade for some time, beginning with his *Clockwork Orange* pastiche,
Trainspotting (which followed his Hammer pastiche, *Shallow Grave*, and
preceded his Roland Emmerich pastiche, *The Beach*, a film so awful that it
would have killed many lesser mortals' directing careers on the spot, and
nearly killed Boyle's). *28 Days Later* was intrinsically implausible—about
zombies apparently ready to race Usain Bolt in the Olympics—but so burly,
aggressive, and spectacularly rude that it didn't allow a moment's pause for
reflection. Is Boyle's last movie, *Sunshine*, about a space crew on a mission
straight for the sun, any more ridiculous than *Slumdog Millionaire*, which
suggests that a little Muslim boy raised in Mumbai's worst hellholes can
become rich and famous? (Well, maybe a little more.)

Because *Slumdog* isn't conceived as a genre piece with its own built-in 5
conventions (horror, sci-fi) but is rather a self-consciously contrived picaresque situated in the real world of Indian class structure, Muslim/ Hindu
religious conflicts, underworld crime rings, and pop media, the sheer
impulse to push the story into a frothy romance functions as a betrayal of
its fundamental material. In the end, when Jamal has won (because, as the
viewer is reminded more times than is worth counting, his victory is destined to happen), he becomes India's new superstar, its latest populist hero,
a seeming sensation, a bolt out of the blue. So where is he? Squatting ever
so quietly, alone, unmolested, unnoticed by anyone in Mumbai's central
train station, where he spots Latika, also alone, and where they then run
to each other and break into a Bollywood-style number. The effect of this
scene turned the first audience at Telluride, based on eyewitness accounts,
all goofy in the head. ("I wanted to run outside and scream and holler at
the mountains," one starry-eyed survivor told me.)

It's hard to argue against such sentiment or reaction: for sure, early 6
viewers of Julie Andrews running down that Austrian meadow in *The
Sound of Music* were similarly nutty. Some are just mad for *Slumdog
Millionaire*—including far, far too many critics—and they won't hear a
discouraging word. As the cultlike object of many in the new middlebrow,
no argument is heard, and some express outright shock when their beloved

new movie is broken apart, knocked, or outright dismissed as what it is—a really, really minor movie, with really, really big problems. Just as the score by composer A.R. Rahman, a crafty and fairly cynical Bollywood hand, is bogus "Indian" music from top to bottom, with an excess of quasi-hip-hop stylings, electronic beat patterns and vocalese gumming up the works and sounding like the kind of backgrounds one might hear in a TV travel advert, so the closing number is bogus Bollywood following on the heels of bogus social drama.

The problem, for the fresh-scrubbed middlebrow and for the rest of us, is that if the real thing isn't known—that is, genuinely Indian cinema—how to judge the Fox Searchlight facsimile? 7

Really, though, *Slumdog* is fun, so let your quibbles just drift away, sit back, relax and let it spill all over you like a nice mango lassi. That's certainly the refrain of too many of the post-Telluride reviews, which recognized Boyle's brazen manipulations and absurd storytelling jumps of even marginal logic for what they were but still joined in the cheering (a word that I counted in at least ten reviews). And they're right; it is fun—fun as a cultural fabrication to question. Consider this overlooked yet central aspect of the film's many conceits: *Slumdog* uses TV as a national arena, and precisely as the medium wherein Jamal not only escapes his class, but (when the show is reviewed on tape during the police station interrogation) uses it as a tool to justify his existence. The film at once reinforces the myths of reality game show TV as actual rather than manufactured suspense and as a machine for getting rich quick, while—in total contradiction—suggests that TV can also be a partner with the police in torture. As at so many other points, Boyle and Beaufoy try to have it both ways: Jamal proves his mettle by deploying his life experiences in order to be the ideal game show star, while the show itself (via Prem, who says that he "owns" the show and reveals that he's also from the slums) collaborates with police to persecute and torture Jamal, even though Prem also knows—an important point—that Jamal isn't cheating. The basis for arranging for Jamal's arrest is a collapsing house of cards on close inspection, since the arrest is not only a surprise to the show's producer, but couldn't have possibly been managed by Prem, who has after all been on the show during airtime. 8

Perhaps Prem is jealous of his fellow slumdog? An interesting, even profound, character point—one that's right there, hanging like ripe narrative fruit, and which would have been even more interesting had Beaufoy and Boyle bothered to pluck it. The Dickensian sensibility, with its ironies and coincidences, is imposed here but never truly developed and only selectively applied—Dickens's picaresque tales, laden with social criticism and narrative athleticism, never fail to point a harsh finger at unjust authority 9 (something Boyle is clearly uncomfortable doing) through a romance of the hero's ultimately improbable triumph over odds (something Boyle bases his whole movie on, culminating with the ersatz Bollywood finale). As a result, the exchanges of colonialism in *Slumdog Millionaire* are too delicious not to notice. In a single film, we have: the celebration of the export of a British gameshow to the Indian viewing public; a narrative structured on the show itself and the (British) Dickens picaresque; a disastrously tone-deaf and colorblind depiction of the world experienced by Muslim lower classes as decorated in gloriously erotic and lush colors as perhaps only a European-based director (Boyle) and cinematographer (the usually brilliant and ingenious Anthony Dod Mantle) could manage; a British-themed call center as the opening of opportunity and upward mobility for Jamal.

In its expressly liberal intentions to depict an India in which a single 10 Muslim boy can win a nation's heart, *Slumdog Millionaire* massages the Western viewer's gaze on a country and culture they barely know, save for a vague sense of cultural exports like the occasional Bollywood movie or song. Perhaps especially now, after the fearsome attacks by Islamist extremists on Mumbai's most cherished institutions and on Western tourists, Boyle's film is just the soft pillow for concerned Western viewers

Publicity shot from *Slumdog Millionaire*.

to plump their heads; surely, there's hope, when even a Muslim lad who is abused, scorned, and rejected can recover his dignity, win the girl and thrive in a world free of terror. It's precisely the India of which Westerners, starting with its former British masters, heartily dream, an India where everything is possible.

The Indian reality, of course, is far more complex, and it has taken 11 filmmakers of sublime artistry and a subtle grasp of the huge Indian spectrum like Mani Ratnam, Shonali Bose, Buddhadeb Dasgupta, Girish Kasaravalli, and Murali Nair to express that complexity on screen. Opportunities for lower classes to free themselves from the old constraints are indeed greater now in India than ever before, largely through the jobs created by the nation's exploding high-tech and manufacturing sectors, which have literally created a middle class where one barely existed before. That new middle class is full of Jamals, using the new social streams fostered by computers and the Web to find types of work that simply never existed before in the Indian economy. The now infamous call centers—an aspect Boyle's film hardly glances at— are mere slivers of this new economy. But it is new, and therefore has only just begun to make its presence felt in a nation of such vast stretches and distances of geography, culture, religious traditions, and economic status.

It's here that Boyle's vision of India goes truly south, since it rein- 12 forces his target audience's general ignorance of reference points in Indian cinema. An affectionate nod in an early sequence to the Bollywood spectacles starring Amitabh Bachchan is typical: His enduring superstar status aside, the particular Amitabh movies visually cited in *Slumdog Millionaire* are actually too old for Jamal—a lower-class boy born in the late Eighties—to have seen (except, perhaps, on videotape). The brief Amitabh film reel in *Slumdog* is more properly seen as reflective of Boyle's own personal memory bank of the Bollywood movies seen in his youth, and therefore useful for Boyle's purposes, since Amitabh remains the one Bollywood superstar widely known in the West. (He's also something of an insider's joke here, since he was the original host of the Indian *Millionaire* show titled, *Kaun Banega Crorepati? (Who Will Become a Crorepati?)*.

Slumdog Millionaire may be minor, but in one way it's important: It 13 serves as the ideal vehicle for the new middlebrow's perception of what makes up world cinema. For starters, as a non-Indian movie with Indian actors (pros based in the U.K. and India, plus newcomers and nonpros), dialog, settings and music, it provides a comfortable substitute for a genuine Indian film (say, by the above-mentioned, neglected and under-seen Ratnam, Dasgupta, or Nair). The new middlebrow can thus say they've covered their current Indian cinema; after all, they've seen—and enjoyed—*Slumdog Millionaire*.

Boyle's film has been celebrated as an expression of globalization, and   14
it's certainly true that the story itself couldn't exist in a world before glo-balization took effect in once-protectionist India, and that Jamal's progress is globalization incarnate. But a truer manifestation of globalization is the explosion of world cinema itself, and how the past decade and a half has seen the spread of national cinemas to an unmatched degree in the art form's history. This has been possible only through the combined forces of globalization and the absorption of previous experimentation in film grammar and theory; the ways in which local filmmakers in their local conditions have responded to the challenges of making cinema on their own terms has made the current period probably the most exciting ever from a global perspective.

India is an interesting example in this regard, since its many languages and   15
regions have produced a wide range of filmmaking styles and voices, most of which continue to struggle (like Ratnam, who himself dances between more genres and forms than Steven Soderbergh) to be seen abroad. We're living in the midst of a paradoxical climate, however: Just as world cinema and its locally-based voices (and not glib fly-by-night tourists like Boyle) are more aggressively active than ever, and more exciting in their expressions, the outlets in the U.S. for this work are shrinking. Distributors, burned by too many subtitled films that bomb at the box office, have narrowed their shopping lists at festivals and markets. Alternative outlets, from festivals to pay-per-view, can contain only so many titles. Video is the last refuge, mean-ing that cinema made by artists ends up being seen (if at all) on TV.

Boyle is obviously keenly aware of this condition in his own film about   16
characters raised speaking Hindu: He manages to compress the Hindu dialogue into about fifteen minutes' total running time (a fraction of the full running time of 116 minutes), and then offer up subtitles for the Hindu in distractingly snazzy lines of text that dance all over the screen like a hyperkinetic TV ad—apparently the perfect solution for otherwise worldly minded folks who hate reading subtitles. In the future, *Slumdog Millionaire* might be seen as a talisman of a potentially degraded film culture, in which audiences were sufficiently dumbed-down to accept the fake rather than the real thing, and in a new middlebrow haze, weren't able to perceive the difference.

Thinking About the Essay

1. What are Koehler's major complaints against *Slumdog Millionaire*? What is his purpose in using such sharp language to register his complaints? Cite examples of his biting, ironic (even sarcastic) style and tone, and explain why or why not you think style and tone reinforce his purpose and claim.

2. Koehler introduces his essay by describing the "new middlebrow." How does he describe or define this audience? Where else in the essay does he allude to it? What is his intention? Do you find his statements about "new middlebrow" to be potentially offensive? Why or why not?

3. Explain the ways in which Koehler places *Slumdog Millionaire* within the context of globalization. What does he have to say about this interrelationship? How does he lay out his case?

4. Where does Koehler allude to Charles Dickens, and why does he establish this analogy between the nineteenth-century British novelist and a twenty-first-century film?

5. Does Koehler make any concessions about *Slumdog Millionaire*? Why or why not? Would further concessions—or a more temperate style and tone—have strengthened his argument? Explain.

Responding in Writing

6. Do you think Koehler makes a strong case against *Slumdog Millionaire*? Respond to this question in an argumentative essay.

7. Write your own extended definition of "new middlebrow," relating it to types of films that have global or international settings and themes.

8. Rent *Slumdog Millionaire*. After viewing it, write a review for your college newspaper that focuses on the ways the film touches of issues of globalization.

Networking

9. Help to organize a forum of four or five class members who will present their responses to Koehler's essay, concentrating on the provocative ways in which he attacks *Slumdog Millionaire* (and its "new middlebrow" audience).

10. Go online and find five reviews of *Slumdog Millionaire*. Write a critique in which you identify the reasons why some critics liked the film, others disliked it, and still others had mixed responses.

© David Horsey / Tribune Media Services

Thinking About the Image

1. What is ironic about the narrative in this cartoon?

2. What do the visual images contribute to this man's story?

3. Cartoons are also a kind of rhetoric, in that they have a purpose and an audience. A cartoonist uses visuals as well as language to move or persuade that audience. How effective is Horsey's rhetoric in serving his purpose? Who is his audience, and how effectively does he address them?

The Educated Student: Global Citizen or Global Consumer?

BENJAMIN R. BARBER

Born in New York City in 1939, Benjamin R. Barber attended school in Switzerland and London before receiving a B.A. degree from Grinnell College in 1960 and a Ph.D. degree from Harvard University in 1966. Barber is Walt Whitman Professor Emeritus, Rutgers

University; Distinguished Senior Fellow, Demos; Director, CivWorld; and the author of many books including the classic *Strong Democracy* (1984); international bestseller *Jihad vs. McWorld* (Times Books, 1995), and the most recent, *Consumed: How Markets Corrupt Children, Infantilize Adults and Swallow Citizens Whole*. He is also a playwright and author, with Patrick Watson, of *The Struggle for Democracy* television series. In the essay that appears next, which appeared in the magazine *Liberal Education* (a publication of the Association of Colleges and Universities) in 2002, Barber raises important questions about the status of civic education in the contemporary global era.

Before Reading

Should today's college students be educated in global affairs? If so, how should such programs be handled by schools and colleges? If not, why not? What connections do you see between education and citizenship?

I want to trace a quick trajectory from July 4, 1776 to Sept. 11, 2001. 1
It takes us from the Declaration of Independence to the declaration of interdependence—not one that is actually yet proclaimed but one that we educators need to begin to proclaim from the pulpits of our classrooms and administrative suites across America.

In 1776 it was all pretty simple for people who cared about both edu- 2
cation and democracy. There was nobody among the extraordinary group of men who founded this nation who did not know that democracy—then an inventive, challenging, experimental new system of government—was dependent for its success not just on constitutions, laws, and institutions, but dependent for its success on the quality of citizens who would constitute the new republic. Because democracy depends on citizenship, the emphasis then was to think about what and how to constitute a competent and virtuous citizen body. That led directly, in almost every one of the founders' minds, to the connection between citizenship and education.

Whether you look at Thomas Jefferson in Virginia or John Adams in 3
Massachusetts, there was widespread agreement that the new republic, for all of the cunning of its inventive and experimental new Constitution, could not succeed unless the citizenry was well educated. That meant that in the period after the Revolution but before the ratification of the Constitution, John Adams argued hard for schools for every young man in Massachusetts

Benjamin Barber "The Educated Student: Global Citizen or Global Consumer?" Published originally in Association of American Colleges and Universities. Reprinted by permission of Benjamin Barber.

(it being the case, of course, that only men could be citizens). And in Virginia, Thomas Jefferson made the same argument for public schooling for every potential citizen in America, founding the first great public university there. Those were arguments that were uncontested.

By the beginning of the nineteenth century this logic was clear in the   4
common school movement and later, in the land grant colleges. It was clear in the founding documents of every religious, private, and public higher education institution in this country. Colleges and universities had to be committed above all to the constituting of citizens. That's what education was about. The other aspects of it—literacy, knowledge, and research—were in themselves important. Equally important as dimensions of education and citizenship was education that would make the Bill of Rights real, education that would make democracy succeed.

It was no accident that in subsequent years, African Americans and   5
then women struggled for a place and a voice in this system, and the key was always seen as education. If women were to be citizens, then women's education would have to become central to suffragism. After the Civil War, African Americans were given technical liberty but remained in many ways in economic servitude. Education again was seen as the key. The struggle over education went on, through *Plessy vs. Ferguson* in 1896—separate, but equal—right down to the 1954 *Brown vs. Board of Education,* which declared separate but equal unconstitutional.

In a way our first 200 years were a clear lesson in the relationship   6
between democracy, citizenship, and education, the triangle on which the freedom of America depended. But sometime after the Civil War with the emergence of great corporations and of an economic system organized around private capital, private labor, and private markets, and with the import from Europe of models of higher education devoted to scientific research, we began to see a gradual change in the character of American education generally and particularly the character of higher education in America's colleges and universities. From the founding of Johns Hopkins at the end of the nineteenth century through today we have witnessed the professionalization, the bureaucratization, the privatization, the commercialization, and the individualization of education. Civics stopped being the envelope in which education was put and became instead a footnote on the letter that went inside and nothing more than that.

With the rise of industry, capitalism, and a market society, it came to pass   7
that young people were exposed more and more to tutors other than teachers in their classrooms or even those who were in their churches, their synagogues—and today, their mosques as well. They were increasingly exposed

to the informal education of popular opinion, of advertising, of merchandising, of the entertainment industry. Today it is a world whose messages come at our young people from those ubiquitous screens that define modern society and have little to do with anything that you teach. The large screens of the multiplex promote content determined not just by Hollywood but by multinational corporations that control information, technology, communication, sports, and entertainment. About ten of those corporations control over 60 to 70 percent of what appears on those screens.

Then, too, there are those medium-sized screens, the television sets   8
that peek from every room of our homes. That's where our children receive not the twenty-eight to thirty hours a week of instruction they might receive in primary and secondary school, or the six or nine hours a week of classroom instruction they might get in college, but where they get anywhere from forty to seventy hours a week of ongoing "information," "knowledge," and above all, entertainment. The barriers between these very categories of information and entertainment are themselves largely vanished.

Then, there are those little screens, our computer screens, hooked up to   9
the Internet. Just fifteen years ago they were thought to be a potential new electronic frontier for democracy. But today very clearly they are one more mirror of a commercialized, privatized society where everything is for sale. The Internet which our children use is now a steady stream of advertising, mass marketing, a virtual mall, a place where the violence, the values—for better or worse—of these same universal corporations reappear in video games and sales messages. Ninety-five to 97 percent of the hits on the Internet are commercial. Of those, 25 to 30 percent are hits on pornographic sites. Most of our political leaders are deeply proud that they have hooked up American schools to the Internet, and that we are a "wired nation." We have, however, in effect hooked up our schools to what in many ways is a national sewer.

In the nineteenth century, Alexis de Tocqueville talked about the "immense   10
tutelary power" of that other source of learning, not education, but public opinion. Now public opinion has come under the control of corporate conglomerates whose primary interest is profit. They are willing to put anything out there that will sell and make a profit.

We have watched this commercialization and privatization, a distor-   11
tion of the education mission and its content, going to the heart of our schools themselves. Most American colleges and universities now are participants—and in some ways beneficiaries—but ultimately victims of the cola wars. Is your college a Pepsi college or a Coke college? Which do you have a contract with? And which monopoly do your kids have to drink

the goods of? While you are busy teaching them the importance of critical choices, they can only drink one cola beverage on this campus. Choice ends at the cafeteria door.

Go to what used to be the food services cafeteria of your local college or 12 university and in many cases you will now find a food court indistinguishable from the local mall featuring Taco Bell, Starbucks, McDonald's, and Burger King. Yes, they are feeding students, but more importantly, they are creating a venue in the middle of campus for what is not education, but an acquisition-of-brands learning. Brand learning means getting young people on board: any merchandiser will tell you, "If we can get the kids when they are in high school and college to buy into our brand, we've got them for life."

Consequences of De-funding

Part of privatization means the de-funding of public institutions, of culture 13 and education, and the de-funding of universities, and so these institutions make a pact with the devil. A real mischief of the modern world (one that colleges haven't yet encountered) is Channel One, which goes into our nation's junior high schools and high schools—particularly the poor ones, those in the inner-city that can't afford their own technology or their own equipment. It makes this promise: "We're not going to give it to you, but we'll lease you some equipment: television sets, maybe a satellite dish, some modems, maybe even a few computers, if you do one thing. Once a day make sure that every student in this school sits in the classroom and watches a very nice little twelve-minute program. Only three minutes of it will be advertising. Let us feed advertising to your kids during a history or a social studies class, and we will lend you some technology."

Most states—New York state is the only one that has held out—in 14 America have accepted Channel One, which is now in over twelve or thirteen thousand high schools around the nation. Our students sit during class time, possibly a social studies or history class, and watch advertising. I dare say, if somebody said they were going to give you some equipment as long as you watch the message of Christ or the church of Christ for three minutes a day, or said they were going to give you some equipment as long as you listen to the message of the Communist Party or the Democratic party during class for three out of twelve minutes, there would be an outcry and an uproar. Totalitarianism! State propaganda! Theocracy! But because they have been so degradingly de-funded, we have allowed our schools to be left without the resources to resist this deal with the devil.

Tell me why it is in the modern world that when a political party or 15
a state takes over the schools and spews its propaganda into them and
takes over every sector of society, we call that political totalitarianism and
oppose it as the denial of liberty. And when a church or a religion takes
over every sector of society and spews its propaganda forth in its schools,
we call it theocratic and totalitarian and go to war against it. But when the
market comes in with its brands and advertising and takes over every sector
of society and spews its propaganda in our schools, we call it an excellent
bargain on the road to liberty. I don't understand that, and I don't think
we should put up with it, and I don't think America should put up with it.
I know the people who sell it would not sit still for a minute if their own
children, sitting in private schools somewhere, were exposed to that commercial advertising. They're not paying $25,000 a year to have their kids
watch advertising in the classroom. But, of course, it's not their children's
schools that are at risk; it's mostly the schools of children of families who
don't have much of a say about these things.

Imagine how far Channel One has come from Jefferson's dream, from 16
John Adams's dream, the dream of the common school. And how low we
have sunk as a society where we turn our heads and say, "Well, it's not so
bad, it's not really, it's just advertising." Advertisers know how valuable
the legitimizing venue of the classroom is and pay double the rates of prime
time to advertise on Channel One, not because the audience is so broad but
because it is the perfect target audience and because it gets that extraordinary legitimization of the American classroom where what kids believe you
"learn" in your classroom has to be true.

Commercialization and privatization go right across the board. You see 17
them in every part of our society. You see cultural institutions increasingly
dependent on corporate handouts. Because we will not fund the arts, the
arts, too, like education have to make a profit. In our universities and colleges, scientists are now selling patents and making deals that the research
they do will benefit not humanity and their students, but the shareholders
of corporations, and so their research will otherwise be kept private. Again,
most administrators welcome that because they don't have to raise faculty
research budgets. The corporate world will take care of that.

These practices change the nature of knowledge and information. They 18
privatize, making research a part of commercial enterprise. That's the kind
of bargain we have made with our colleges and universities. We hope that
somehow the faculty will remain insulated from it. We hope the students
won't notice, but then when they're cynical about politics and about the
administration, and cynical about their own education, and when they

look to their own education as a passport to a hot job and big money—and nothing else—we wonder what's going on with them.

But of course students see everything; they have noses for hypocrisy. 19 Students see the hypocrisy of a society that talks about the importance of education and knowledge and information while its very educational institutions are selling their own souls for a buck, and they're doing it because the society otherwise won't support them adequately, is unwilling to tax itself, is unwilling to ask itself for sufficient funds to support quality education. That's where we are. That's where we were on September 10.

What We've Learned

On September 11 a dreadful, pathological act occurred, which nonethe- 20 less may act in a brutal way as a kind of tutorial for America and for its educators. On that day, it suddenly became apparent to many people who'd forgotten it that America was no longer a land of independence or sovereignty, a land that could "go it alone." America was no longer capable of surviving as a free democracy unless it began to deal in different terms with a world that for 200 years it had largely ignored and in the last fifty or seventy-five years had treated in terms of that sad phrase "collateral damage." Foreign policy was about dealing with the collateral damage of America being America, America being commercialized, America being prosperous, America "doing well" in the economic sense—if necessary, at everybody else's expense.

September 11 was a brutal and perverse lesson in the inevitability of 21 interdependence in the modern world—and of the end of independence, where America could simply go it alone. It was the end of the time in which making a buck for individuals would, for those that were doing all right, be enough; somehow the fact that the rest of the world was in trouble and that much of America was in trouble—particularly its children (one out of five in poverty)—was incidental. After thirty years of privatization and commercialization, the growing strength of the ideology that said the era not just of government, but of big government was over; that said, this was to be the era of markets, and markets will solve every problem: education, culture, you name it, the markets can do it.

On September 11 it became clear that there were areas in which the 22 market could do nothing: terrorism, poverty, injustice, war. The tragedy pointed to issues of democracy and equality and culture, and revealed a foreign policy that had been paying no attention. In the early morning of September 12, nobody called Bill Gates at Microsoft or Michael Eisner at

Disney and said "Help us, would you? You market guys have good solutions. Help us get the terrorists." Indeed, the heroes of September 11 were public officials, public safety officers: policemen, firemen, administrators, even a mayor who found his soul during that period. Those were the ones we turned to and suddenly understood that they played a public role representing all of us.

Suddenly, Americans recognized that its citizens were the heroes. Not 23 the pop singers, fastball pitchers, and the guys who make all the money in the NBA; not those who've figured out how to make a fast buck by the time they're thirty, the Internet entrepreneurs. In the aftermath of 9/11, it was particularly those public-official-citizens. All citizens because in what they do, they are committed to the welfare of their neighbors, their children, to future generations. That's what citizens are supposed to do: think about the communities to which they belong and pledge themselves to the public good of those communities.

Hence the importance of the civic professions like teaching. In most 24 countries, in fact, teachers and professors are public officials. They are seen, like firemen and policemen, as guardians of the public good, of the res publica, those things of the public that we all care about. On September 11 and the days afterwards, it became clear how important those folks were. As a consequence, a kind of closing of a door occasioned by the fall of the towers became an opening of a window of new opportunities, new possibilities, new citizenship: an opportunity to explore interdependence. Interdependence is another word for citizenship.

Citizenship in the World

The citizen is the person who acknowledges and recognizes his or her 25 interdependence in a neighborhood, a town, a state, in a nation—and today, in the world. Anyone with eyes wide open during the last thirty to forty years has known that the world has become interdependent in ineluctable and significant ways. AIDS and the West Nile Virus don't carry passports. They go where they will. The Internet doesn't stop at national boundaries; it's a worldwide phenomenon. Today's telecommunications technologies define communications and entertainment all over the world without regard to borders. Global warming recognizes no sovereignty, and nobody can say he or she won't have to suffer the consequences of polluted air. Ecology, technology, and of course economics and markets are global in character, and no nation can pretend that its own destiny is any longer in its own hands in the manner of eighteenth- and nineteenth-century nations.

In particular, this nation was the special land where independence   26
had been declared, and our two oceans would protect us from the world.
We went for several hundred years thinking America was immune to the
problems and tumult and prejudices of the wars of the world beyond the
oceans. And then 9/11—and suddenly it became clear that no American
could ever rest comfortably in bed at night if somewhere, someone else in
the world was starving or someone's children were at risk. With 9/11 it
became apparent that whatever boundaries once protected us and whatever new borders we were trying to build including the missile shield (a new
technological "virtual ocean" that would protect us from the world) were
irrelevant.

Multilateralism becomes a new mandate of national security, a neces-   27
sity. There are no oceans wide enough, there are no walls high enough
to protect America from the rest of our world. What does that say about
education? It means that for the first time a lot of people who didn't care
about civic education—the education of citizens, the soundness of our own
democracy, the ability of our children to understand the world—now suddenly recognize this is key, that education counts. Multicultural education
counts because we have to understand the cultures of other worlds. Language
education counts because language is a window on other cultures and
histories.

Citizenship is now the crucial identity. We need to think about what   28
an adequate civic education means today, and what it means to be a
citizen. We need education-based community service programs. We
need experiential learning, not just talking about citizenship but exercises in doing it. We need to strongly support the programs around the
country that over the '80s and '90s sprang up but have recently been
in decline.

But we also need new programs in media literacy. I talked about the   29
way in which a handful of global corporations control the information
channels of television, the Internet, and Hollywood. We need young people
who are sophisticated in media, who understand how media work, how
media affect them, how to resist, how to control, how to become immune
to media. Media literacy and media studies from my point of view become
a key part of how we create a new civic education. Of course history, the
arts, sociology, and anthropology, and all of those fields that make young
people aware of the rest of the world in a comparative fashion are more
important than ever before.

We are a strange place because we are one of the most multicultural   30
nations on Earth with people in our schools from all over the world, and
yet we know less than most nations about the world from which those

people come. At one and the same time, we are truly multicultural, we represent the globe, and yet we know little about it.

Coming Full Circle

In coming full circle, the trajectory from the Declaration of Independence 31
200 years ago to the declaration of interdependence that was sounded on September 11 opens an opportunity for us as educators to seize the initiative to make civic education central again. The opportunity to free education from the commercializers and privatizers, to take it back for civic education and for our children, and to make the schools of America and the world the engines of democracy and liberty and freedom that they were supposed to be. And that's not just an abstraction. That starts with addressing commercialization directly: confronting Channel One and the food court at your local college, the malling of your cafeterias, and the sellout of corporate research.

There are things that every one of us can do inside our own colleges 32
and universities. If we do, our students will notice. And if we really make our colleges and universities democratic, civic, independent, autonomous, international, and multilateral again, we will no longer even need civics classes. Our students will take one look at what we've done in the university and understand the relationship between education and democracy. That must be our mission. I hope that as individual citizens, teachers, administrators, you will take this mission seriously. I certainly do, and I know that as before, the future of liberty, the future of democracy in both America and around the world, depends most of all on its educational institutions and on the teachers and administrators who control them. Which means we really are in a position to determine what our future will be.

Thinking About the Essay

1. This essay reflects Barber's deep historical and political knowledge and his passionate concern for the role of education in civic and global life. What assumptions does he make about his primary audience—who, we can infer from the place of publication—are educators? What "message" does he want to convey to his primary audience? What secondary audiences might he have in mind, and how does he manage to appeal to them?

2. State Barber's thesis in your own words. Does he ever present a thesis statement or does he imply it? Explain.

3. In part, this essay reflects a rhetorical strategy known as process analysis. How does Barber take us through a step-by-step historical process? Point to specific stages in this process. How does the process come full circle? In other words, how does he tie September 11, 2001, to July 4, 1776?

4. Barber divides his essay into five parts. Summarize each part. What logical relationships do you see between and among them? How do these sections progress logically from one stage of Barber's argument to the next?

5. What definitions does Barber offer for such key terms as *democracy, education, civic responsibility, globalization,* and *multilateralism*? What is his purpose? Why does he introduce such abstract terms? What other broad abstractions does he discuss, and where?

Responding in Writing

6. In a personal essay, discuss the quality of your own education. To what extent do you feel your education has provided you with a sense of what it takes to create or sustain a democracy or a sense of civic responsibility? To what extent have you been encouraged to think of yourself as a citizen of the world? To what extent have you been affected by the forces of consumerism? Explore these issues—and any others raised by Barber—in your paper.

7. Barber writes that "students see everything; they have noses for hypocrisy" (paragraph 19). Clearly, you agree with this notion. But what precisely are you hypocritical about when you think about education, democracy, terrorism, consumerism, and some of the other "big" words that Barber discusses? In fact, do you have a nose for hypocrisy or might you actually be hypocritical? (For example, if you believe in democracy as a necessary civic institution, do you vote in elections?) Write an essay exploring the subject of hypocrisy.

8. Are you a global citizen or a global consumer? Must you be one or the other, or can you be both and still be a good citizen—of your country and of the world? Examine this subject in a reflective essay.

Networking

9. In small groups, look over the syllabi for the various courses that you are taking this term. Which ones explicitly address some of the main issues raised by Barber? Does the English course in which you're presently enrolled reflect these issues? Present your findings to the class.

10. Locate websites for the Walt Whitman Center for the Culture and Politics of Democracy or the Democracy Collaborative. Take notes on these organizations, and then prepare a paper on their missions and programs.

Culture Wars: Whose Culture Is It, Anyway?

As we have seen in earlier chapters, the power and influence of the United States radiate outward to the rest of the world in many ways. Nowhere is this more visible than in the impact of various American cultural manifestations—ranging from food, to clothing, to music, to television, and film—on other countries. When a French farmer burns down a McDonald's, terrorists destroy a disco in Bali, or clerics in Iran attempt to ban Barbie dolls from stores, we sense the opposition to American cultural hegemony. Conversely, when Iranians do find ways to buy Barbies and also turn on their banned satellite systems to catch the latest *CSI* episode, or when street merchants in Kenya sell University of Michigan T-shirts, we detect the flip side of the culture wars—the mesmerizing power of American culture throughout the world. Sometimes it seems that American culture, wittingly or unwittingly, is in a battle for the world's soul.

We also have to acknowledge that the culture wars color American life as well. At home, current debates over immigration, affirmative action, gay marriage, and much more impinge on our daily lives and dominate media presentations. It might be fashionable to say that we all trace our DNA to Africa and that ideally we are all citizens of the world, but the issue of what sort of culture we represent individually or collectively is much more complicated. Tiger Woods might be the icon for the New American, or for the new Universal Person, but his slightest actions and words can prompt cultural controversy. American culture cuts many ways; it is powerful, but also strange and contradictory.

The culture wars take us to the borders of contradiction both at home and abroad. It is too facile to say that we are moving "beyond" monoculturalism at home or that the rest of the world doesn't have to

Muslim tourists eat in a McDonald's restaurant in the Egyptian Red Sea resort of Sharm el-Sheikh. After several years of low tourism, Egypt is once again a popular tourist destination.

Thinking About the Image

1. If McDonald's is stereotypically American, what is stereotypically Egyptian about this image? Why do you think the photographer is emphasizing those stereotypes?
2. Think about other images of globalization you have seen in this book. How effective is the "rhetoric" of globalization here?
3. Why is something so seemingly basic as food such a potent symbol of cultural meaning and pride? Does this photograph capture this symbolism effectively? Why or why not?

embrace American culture if it doesn't want to. What is clear is that the very *idea* of American culture, in all its diversity, is so pervasive that it spawns numerous viewpoints and possibilities for resolution. After all, culture is a big subject: it embraces one's ethnic, racial, class, religious, sexual, and national identity. We can't be uncritical about culture. We have to understand how culture both molds and reflects our lives.

The writers in this chapter offer perspectives—all of them provocative and engaging—on national and transnational culture. They deal with the ironies of culture at home and the paradoxes of American cultural influence abroad. Some of the writers engage in self-reflection, others in rigorous analysis. All refuse to view culture in simplistic terms. In reading them, you might discover that whether you grew up in the United States or another country, culture is at the heart of who you are.

Cultural Baggage

Barbara Ehrenreich

Barbara Ehrenreich was born in 1941 in Butte, Montana. She attended Reed College (B.A., 1963) and Rockefeller University (Ph.D. in biology, 1968). A self-described socialist and feminist, Ehrenreich uses her scientific training to investigate a broad range of social issues: health care, the plight of the poor, the condition of women around the world. Her scathing critiques of American health care in such books as *The American Health Empire* (with John Ehrenreich, 1970), *Complaints and Disorders: The Sexual Politics of Sickness* (with Deirdre English, 1973), and *For Her Own Good* (with English, 1978) established her as an authority in the field. In her provocative *The Hearts of Men: American Dreams and the Flight from Commitment* (1983), Ehrenreich surveys the decline of male investment in the family from the 1950s to the 1980s. A prolific writer during the 1980s and 1990s, Ehrenreich most recently published the award-winning book, *Nickel and Dimed: On (Not) Getting By in America* (2001). She is also a frequent contributor to magazines, including *The Nation, Esquire, Radical America, The New Republic,* and *The New York Times,* while serving as a contributing editor to *Ms.* and *Mother Jones.* Her fresh insights into the complex contours of American society can be seen in "Cultural Baggage," published in *The New York Times Magazine* in 1992, where Ehrenreich offers a new slant on the idea of "heritage."

Before Reading

What is your ethnic or religious heritage? Do you feel comfortable explaining or defending it? Why or why not?

An acquaintance was telling me about the joys of rediscovering her ethnic and religious heritage. "I know exactly what my ancestors were doing 2,000 years ago," she said, eyes gleaming with enthusiasm, "and I can do the same things now." Then she leaned forward and inquired politely, "And what is your ethnic background, if I may ask?"

"None," I said, that being the first word in line to get out of my mouth. Well, not "none," I backtracked. Scottish, English, Irish—that was something, I supposed. Too much Irish to qualify as a WASP; too much of the hated English to warrant a "Kiss Me, I'm Irish" button; plus there are a number of dead ends in the family tree due to adoptions, missing records, failing memories and the like. I was blushing by this time. Did "none" mean I was rejecting my heritage out of Anglo-Celtic self-hate? Or was I revealing a hidden ethnic chauvinism in which the Britannically derived serve as a kind of neutral standard compared with the ethnic "others"?

Throughout the 1960s and '70s I watched one group after another— African Americans, Latinos, Native Americans—stand up and proudly reclaim their roots while I just sank back ever deeper into my seat. All this excitement over ethnicity stemmed, I uneasily sensed, from a past in which their ancestors had been trampled upon by my ancestors, or at least by people who looked very much like them. In addition, it had begun to seem almost un-American not to have some sort of hyphen at hand, linking one to more venerable times and locales.

But the truth is, I was raised with none. We'd eaten ethnic foods in my childhood home, but these were all borrowed, like the pasties, or Cornish meat pies, my father had picked up from his fellow miners in Butte, Montana. If my mother had one rule, it was militant ecumenism in all matters of food and experience. "Try new things," she would say, meaning anything from sweet-breads to clams, with an emphasis on the "new."

As a child, I briefly nourished a craving for tradition and roots. I immersed myself in the works of Sir Walter Scott. I pretended to believe that the bagpipe was a musical instrument. I was fascinated to learn from a grandmother that we were descended from certain Highland clans and longed for a pleated skirt in one of their distinctive tartans.

But in *Ivanhoe*, it was the dark-eyed "Jewess" Rebecca I identified with, not the flaxen-haired bimbo Rowena. As for clans: Why not call them tribes—those bands of half-clad peasants and warriors whose idea of cuisine was stuffed sheep gut washed down with whisky? And then there was the sting of Disraeli's remark—which I came across in my early teens—to the effect that his ancestors had been leading orderly, literate lives when my

ancestors were still rampaging through the Highlands daubing themselves   7
with blue paint.

Motherhood put the screws on me, ethnicity-wise. I had hoped that by   8
marrying a man of Eastern European Jewish ancestry I would acquire for
my descendants the ethnic genes that my own forebears so sadly lacked. At
one point I even subjected the children to a seder of my own design, including a little talk about the flight from Egypt and its relevance to modern
social issues. But the kids insisted on buttering their matzos and snickering
through my talk. "Give me a break, Mom," the older one said. "You don't
even believe in God."

After the tiny pagans had been put to bed, I sat down to brood over   9
Elijah's wine. What had I been thinking? The kids knew that their Jewish
grandparents were secular folks who didn't hold seders themselves. And if
ethnicity eluded me, how could I expect it to take root in my children, who
are not only Scottish English Irish, but Hungarian Polish Russian to boot?

But, then, on the fumes of Manischewitz, a great insight took form in
my mind. It was true, as the kids said, that I didn't "believe in God." But
this could be taken as something very different from an accusation—a
reminder of a genuine heritage. My parents had not believed in God either,
nor had my grandparents or any other progenitors going back to the great-
great level. They had become disillusioned with Christianity generations
ago—just as, on the in-law side, my children's other ancestors had shaken
off their Orthodox Judaism. This insight did not exactly furnish me with an
"identity," but it was at least something to work with: We are the kind of
people, I realized—whatever our distant ancestors' religions—who do not
believe, who do not carry on traditions, who do not do things just because
someone has done them before.

The epiphany went on: I recalled that my mother never introduced   10
a procedure for cooking or cleaning by telling me, "Grandma did it this
way." What did Grandma know, living in the days before vacuum cleaners
and disposable toilet mops? In my parents' general view, new things were
better than old and the very fact that some ritual had been performed in
the past was a good reason for abandoning it now. Because what was the
past, as our forebears knew it? Nothing but poverty, superstition and grief.
"Think for yourself," Dad used to say. "Always ask why."

In fact, this may have been the ideal cultural heritage for my particular   11
ethnic strain—bounced as it was from the Highlands of Scotland across the
sea, out to the Rockies, down into the mines and finally spewed out into
high-tech, suburban America. What better philosophy, for a race of migrants,
than "think for yourself"? What better maxim, for a people whose whole
world was rudely inverted every 30 years or so, than "try new things"?

The more tradition-minded, the newly enthusiastic celebrants of Purim 12 and Kwanzaa and Solstice, may see little point to survival if the survivors carry no cultural freight—religion, for example, or ethnic tradition. To which I would say that skepticism, curiosity and wide-eyed ecumenical tolerance are also worthy elements of the human tradition and are at least as old as such notions as "Serbian" or "Croatian," "Scottish" or "Jewish." I make no claims for my personal line of progenitors except that they remained loyal to the values that may have induced all of our ancestors, long, long ago, to climb down from the trees and make their way into the open plains.

A few weeks ago I cleared my throat and asked the children, now mostly 13 grown and fearsomely smart, whether they felt any stirrings of ethnic or religious identity, which might have been, ahem, insufficiently nourished at home. "None," they said, adding firmly, "and the world would be a better place if nobody else did, either." My chest swelled with pride, as would my mother's, to know that the race of "none" marches on.

Thinking About the Essay

1. Why is Ehrenreich's title perfect for this essay? How does the title reflect her thesis?

2. What is Ehrenreich's purpose in asking so many questions in this essay? Is the strategy effective? Why or why not?

3. How would you describe the tone of this essay—the writer's attitude or approach to her subject? Locate phrases, sentences, and passages that support your response.

4. Ehrenreich traces a pattern of causality in this essay as she describes not only her own experience of ethnic and religious heritage but that of others as well. Trace this pattern of cause and effect throughout the article. Where do other rhetorical strategies—for example, illustration, comparison, or definition—come into play?

5. Examine paragraphs 10–13. How do they serve as an extended conclusion to the argument Ehrenreich presents?

Responding in Writing

6. Write your own personal essay with the title "Cultural Baggage." Like Ehrenreich, use the personal, or "I," point of view and focus on your own experience of your ethnic and religious heritage. Be certain to have a clear thesis that helps to guide your approach to the subject.

7. As an exercise, argue against Ehrenreich's claim that it is best to have "no cultural freight—religion, for example, or ethnic tradition" (paragraph 12).

8. Write a comparative paper in which you analyze the concepts of cultural pride and cultural baggage. Establish a controlling thesis, and develop at least three major comparative topics for this essay.

Networking

9. Form two equal groups of class members. One group should develop an argument in favor of cultural heritage, the other opposing it. Select one spokesperson from each group and have them debate the issue in front of the class.

10. Ehrenreich says she is a socialist. Go online and locate information on this term, as well as additional information on Ehrenreich herself. Then use this information to write a paper describing how "Cultural Baggage" reflects Ehrenreich's socialist views.

It's a Mall World After All

MAC MARGOLIS | In the following piece, which appeared in the December 5, 2005, *Newsweek International*, columnist Mac Margolis defends a much maligned and distinctively American export to the world by looking at the variety of its manifestations around the world and its almost inadvertent role as a social and political institution. Margolis is a recipient of the Maria Moors Cabot Prize for outstanding reporting on Latin America—the oldest international awards in journalism.

Before Reading

In what sense do you regard malls as an institution? Do you associate malls with democratic or other values?

When the Los Angeles firm Altoon + Porter Architects set out to design   1
a shopping arcade in Riyadh, Saudi Arabia, a few years ago, it faced a delicate mission: to raise a glitzy pleasure dome full of Western temptations in the maw of fundamentalist Islam. Not that the Saudis were consumer innocents; King Khalid airport in Riyadh fairly hums with wealthy Arabs bound for the lavish shops of Paris and London. But the trick was to lure women buyers—the royalty of retail—who are not allowed to shed their veils in public. "Women can't be expected to buy anything if they can't try

it on," says architect Ronald Altoon, managing partner of the firm. So Altoon + Porter came up with an ecumenical solution: the Kingdom Centre, a three-story glass-and-steel Xanadu of retail with an entire floor—Women's Kingdom—devoted exclusively to female customers. "We took the veil off the women and put it on the building," says Altoon.

The modest proposal paid off. In Women's Kingdom, Saudi women can   2
shop, schmooze, dine or even loll about at the spa without upsetting the sheiks or subverting Sharia, the country's strict Islamic laws. Normally the third level of any mall is a dud, but it's become the most profitable floor in the whole arcade. The Kingdom Centre may not be revolutionary; no one is burning veils at the food court. Still, it represents a small but meaningful freedom for Saudi women. And its success points to the irrepressible global appetite for consumer culture, as well as to the growing role that the right to shop plays in fostering democratization and development.

It's been more than two decades since John B. Hightower, the director   3
of New York City's South Street Seaport Museum, a combination cultural center and shopping arcade, brazenly declared that "shopping is the chief cultural activity of the United States." Since then, it has also become one of America's chief exports: shopping malls, once a peculiarly American symbol of convenience and excess, now dot the global landscape from Santiago to St. Petersburg and Manila to Mumbai. In 1999, India boasted only three malls. Now there are 45, and the number is expected to rise to 300 by 2010. The pint-size Arab Emirate of Dubai, sometimes known as the Oz of malls, clocked 88.5 million mall visitors last year; nearly 180 million Brazilians mob shopping arcades every month—almost as many as in the United States. Where elephants and giraffes once gamboled along the Mombasa road leading into Nairobi, the African mall rat is now a far more common sight, with four gleaming new malls to scavenge in at the Kenyan capital and three more in the works. And no one can keep pace with China, where foreign investors are scrambling to get a piece of a real-estate boom driven in part by mall mania. "The same energy and dynamism that the shopping industry brought to North America 30, 40 years ago is now reaching overseas," says Michael Kercheval, head of the International Council of Shopping Centers, an industry trade association and advisory group. "Now it's reached the global masses."

Indeed, the planet appears deep in the grip of the retail version of   4
an arms race. For years, the West Edmonton Mall in Alberta, Canada, with 20,000 parking spaces, an ice-skating rink, a miniature-golf course and four submarines (more than in the Canadian Navy) on display, had reigned as the grandest in the world. Last October it was overtaken by the $1.3 billion Golden Resources Shopping Center in northwest Beijing,

with 20,000 employees and nearly twice the floor space of the Pentagon. Developers in Dubai are breaking ground on not one but two malls they claim will be even bigger, one of which boasts a man-made, five-run ski slope. Yet all these have been eclipsed by the behemoth South China Mall, which opened its doors in the factory city of Dongguan this year. By the end of the decade, China is likely to have at least seven of the world's 10 largest malls—many of them equipped with hotels, on the theory that no one can possibly see everything in a single day.

To those who malign malls as the epitome of all that is wrong with   5
American culture, their spread is like a pestilence upon the land. Dissident scholars churn out one dystopian tract—"One Nation Under Goods," "The Call of the Mall"—after another. Critics despair of whole nations willing to cash in their once vibrant downtowns and street markets for a wasteland of jerry-built nowhere, epic traffic jams and marquees ablaze with fatuous English names (Phoenix High Street, Palm Springs Life Plaza and Bairong World Trade Center Phase II). To some, this is an assault on democracy itself. "Shopping malls are great for dictatorships," says Emil Pocock, a professor of American studies at Eastern Connecticut State University, who takes students on field trips to malls to study consumer society. "What better way to control folks than to put them under a dome and in enclosed doors?" The "malling of America," in the words of author and famous mall-basher William Kowinski, has become the malling of the world.

As it turns out, that may not be such a bad thing. Rather than presage   6
or hasten the decline of the traditional downtown, as many critics fear, the rise of the mall is actually serving as a catalyst for growth, especially in developing nations. In China, the booming retail sector has sucked in a fortune in venture capital and spawned dozens of joint ventures with international investors looking to snap up Chinese urban properties. In late July, the Simon Property Group, a major U.S. developer, teamed up with Morgan Stanley and a government-owned Chinese company to launch up to a dozen major retail centers throughout China over the next few years. Malls are a leading force in driving India's $330 billion retailing industry, which already accounts for a third of national GDP and recently overtook Russia's. Similarly, a burst of consumer spending in the Philippines— thanks to overseas nationals who send between $6 billion and $7 billion back every year—has fueled a real-estate boom, led by megamalls.

Most developing-world malls are integrated in the heart of the inner   7
cities instead of strewn like beached whales along arid superhighways. "In China, 80 percent of shoppers walk to the mall," says Kercheval of the ICSC. In some megacities, including New Delhi, Nairobi and Rio, urban sprawl has flung customers into outlying neighborhoods, many of

which spring up around brand-new shopping centers. That means malls are no longer catering just to the elite. "We used to talk exclusively about A-class shoppers," says Kercheval. "Now we are seeing the arrival of B-, C- and D-class customers. The developing-world mall is becoming more democratic."

In many places, malls are welcome havens of safety and security. In Rio,   8
where teenagers (especially young men) are the main victims of street crime, parents breathe easier when they know their kids are at play in the mall, some of which deploy 100 or more private police. "Safety is one of our biggest selling points," says Paulo Malzoni Filho, president of the Brazilian Association of Shopping Centers. "When I enter into one of these malls, it feels like I have landed in a foreign country," says Parag Mehta, a regular at the Inorbit mall in the busy northern Mumbai suburb of Malad.

And as malls break new ground around the world, the one-size-fits-all   9
business model created in North American suburbia is giving way to region-alized versions. Malls may conjure up the specter of a flood of U.S. brands and burgers, but in reality, local palates and preferences often prevail. On a recent evening in Beijing's Golden Resources Shopping Center, Kentucky Fried Chicken and Papa John's were nearly deserted, while the Korean restaurant just around the corner was packed. Chile has long welcomed foreign investors, yet the leading retailers at malls in Santiago are two local chains, Falabella and Almacenes Paris. In San Salvador, capital of El Salva-dor, the Gallerias shopping arcade houses a Roman Catholic church that holds mass twice a day—an intriguing metaphysical twist on the concept of the anchor store. In many developing countries, malls have attracted banks, art galleries, museums, car-rental agencies and even government services such as passport offices and motor-vehicle departments, becoming de facto villages instead of just shopping centers.

For residents of the developing world, malls increasingly serve as   10
surrogate civic centers, encouraging social values that go beyond conspicuous spending. China is home to some 168 million smokers, but they are not allowed to partake at the smoke-free malls. That's not the only environmental plus; many Chinese malls are equipped with a soft-switching system that stabilizes the electrical current and conserves energy. In the Middle East, arcades such as Riyadh's Kingdom Centre are among the few public spaces where women can gather, gab or just walk about alone in public. "Malls are not just places to shop, they are places to imagine," says Xia Yeliang, a professor at Beijing University's School of Economics. "They bring communities together that might not otherwise encounter one another and create new communities."

For some societies, malls even offer a communal respite from the past.   11
In Warsaw, where World War II demolished most of the historic shopping
district—and dreary chockablock communist-era architecture finished the
job—one of the most revered public spaces around is the local mall. "For
decades Poles dressed up for Sunday mass," says Grzegorz Makowski, a
sociologist at Warsaw University and expert on consumer culture. "Now
they dress for a visit to the shopping mall."

Still, for some critics, no amount of social or economic development   12
can hide the fact that all modern malls are at heart temples of rampant consumerism. Jan Gehl, a leading Danish champion of urban renaissance and
a professor of architecture at the Royal Academy of Fine Arts in Copenhagen, likes to show his students pictures of malls around the world and
ask them where each one is located. Many look so indistinguishable that
they can't tell. (Only now are some clues beginning to appear.) Even Victor
Gruen, the Viennese Jewish émigré who fled Hitler's Europe and created
the first indoor-shopping arcade in the Minneapolis suburbs in the 1950s,
eventually grew disgusted by the soulless concrete-box-with-parking mon-
strosities rendered in his name. "I refuse to pay alimony to these bastards
of development," he growled during a 1978 speech in London, fleeing back
to Europe. By then there was no escape; malls were already marching on
the Old World.

Half a century on, some of the resistance to malls speaks more to nos-   13
talgia for an illusory past than a rejection of the present. Ancient Turkey
certainly had its bazaar rats. And what is the contemporary shopping
center if not a souk with a Cineplex? "Maybe the mall is just a modern
and more comfortable version of what has always been," says Stephen
Marshall of the Young Foundation, a London think tank. "It's quite possible the ancients would have seen our malls with all that technology as
terrific places."

Certainly mall developers seem to have learned from their early   14
excesses. Instead of garish bunkers with blind walls and plastic rain forests, newer malls boast sculpture gardens, murals, belvederes and gentle
lighting. Lush creepers, great ferns, cacti and feathery palms tumble down
the interior of the Fashion Mall, a boutique arcade, in Rio de Janeiro.
The Kingdom Centre in Riyadh won an international design award in
2003. And while "big" may still be beautiful in mallworld, more and
more developers are launching arcades built to modest scale, deliberately
emulating yesterday's main streets or the Old World piazzas they replaced.
This may not be the much-vaunted consumer's arcadia the mallmeisters
had always hoped for, but global malls seem oddly to come closer to the

bold democratic ideal than the originals ever did. And when it rains, everybody stays dry.

Thinking About the Essay

1. Highlight three passing allusions that occur in the essay (the allusion to Xanadu in the opening paragraph, for example). Is there a chain of association between the series of allusions you see in the essay?

2. Why does Margolis focus on the "ecumenical solution" devised by the architectural firm Altoon Porter in his beginning paragraph? How does this illustration serve to set up the other examples in the essay?

3. Where in the essay does Margolis address critics of malls as a cultural phenomenon? What is his response to these critics?

4. How does Margolis connect the "right to consumer culture" with democratic rights and values? Do you feel he is successful in making this connection? Why or why not?

5. Margolis concludes the piece by asserting that "global malls seem oddly to come closer to the bold democratic ideal than the originals ever did." Where in the essay has Margolis considered those precedents? Do you feel he has offered enough historical evidence to support his conclusion?

Responding in Writing

6. Do you see evidence in your own community that mall developers "have learned from their early excesses"? Write a brief critique of the architectural style and layout of your local mall.

7. Respond to Margolis's observation in paragraph 11 that malls "offer a communal respite from the past." Do you see this as a stereotypically American attitude toward the past? Would you characterize what malls offer as a "respite from the past" or as an "*escape* from the past"?

8. In a brief essay, reflect on the reasons for your own resistance to or enthusiasm for malls. Would you describe your feelings in terms of nostalgia for a past model in the process of being replaced, or in terms of progress? What is the nature of this progress? What is lost or gained in the move to a new model of commerce?

Networking

9. In groups of three or four, list at least three "social values" (i.e., not consumer values) that are promoted or made possible by your local mall.

10. Go online and look up images of at least five different malls located in five different countries. What signs of individual character do you see?

Whose Culture Is It, Anyway?

Henry Louis Gates Jr.

Henry Louis Gates Jr. is one of the most respected figures in the field of African American studies. Born in 1950 in Keyser, West Virginia, he received a B.A. degree (summa cum laude) from Harvard University (1973) and M.A. (1974) and Ph.D. degrees (1979) from Clare College, Cambridge University. A recipient of numerous major grants, including the prestigious MacArthur Prize Fellowship, and a professor at Harvard University, Gates in numerous essays and books argues for a greater diversity in arts, literature, and life. In one of his best-known works, *Loose Canons: Notes on the Culture Wars* (1992), Gates states, "The society we have made simply won't survive without the values of tolerance. And cultural tolerance comes to nothing without cultural understanding." Among his many publications are *The Signifying Monkey: Toward a Theory of Afro-American Literary Criticism* (1988), which won both a National Book Award and an American Book Award; *Colored People, A Memoir* (1994); *The Future of the Race* (with Cornel West, 1996); *Wonders of the African World* (1999) and *In Search of Our Roots* (2009). In the following essay, which appeared originally in *The New York Times* on May 4, 1991, Gates analyzes the cultural diversity movement in American colleges and universities.

Before Reading

Gates argues elsewhere that we must reject "ethnic absolutism" of all kinds. What do you think he means by this phrase? Exactly how does a college or university—perhaps your institution—transcend this problem?

I recently asked the dean of a prestigious liberal arts college if his school would ever have, as Berkeley has, a 70 percent non-white enrollment. "Never," he replied. "That would completely alter our identity as a center of the liberal arts." 1

The assumption that there is a deep connection between the shape of a college's curriculum and the ethnic composition of its students reflects a disquieting trend in education. Political representation has been confused with the "representation" of various ethnic identities in the curriculum. 2

The cultural right wing, threatened by demographic changes and the   3
ensuing demands for curricular change, has retreated to intellectual protectionism, arguing for a great and inviolable "Western tradition," which
contains the seeds, fruit and flowers of the very best thought or uttered in
history. (Typically, Mortimer Adler has ventured that blacks "wrote no
good books.") Meanwhile, the cultural left demands changes to accord
with population shifts in gender and ethnicity. Both are wrongheaded.

I am just as concerned that so many of my colleagues feel that the ratio-   4
nale for a diverse curriculum depends on the latest Census Bureau report
as I am that those opposed see pluralism as forestalling the possibility of a
communal "American" identity. To them, the study of our diverse cultures
must lead to "tribalism" and "fragmentation."

The cultural diversity movement arose partly because of the fragmen-   5
tation of society by ethnicity, class and gender. To make it the culprit for
this fragmentation is to mistake effect for cause. A curriculum that reflects
the achievement of the world's great cultures, not merely the West's, is not
"politicized"; rather it situates the West as one of a community of civilizations. After all, culture is always a conversation among different voices.

To insist that we "master our own culture" before learning others—as   6
Arthur Schlesinger Jr. has proposed—only defers the vexed question: What
gets to count as "our" culture? What has passed as "common culture"
has been an Anglo-American regional culture, masking itself as universal.
Significantly different cultures sought refuge underground.

Writing in 1903, W. E. B. Du Bois expressed his dream of a high culture   7
that would transcend the color line: "I sit with Shakespeare and he winces
not." But the dream was not open to all. "Is this the life you grudge us," he
concluded, "O knightly America?" For him, the humanities were a conduit
into a republic of letters enabling escape from racism and ethnic chauvinism. Yet no one played a more crucial role than he in excavating the long
buried heritage of Africans and African-Americans.

The fact of one's ethnicity, for any American of color, is never neutral: 8
One's public treatment, and public behavior, are shaped in large part by
one's perceived ethnic identity, just as by one's gender. To demand that
Americans shuck their cultural heritages and homogenize themselves into
a "universal" WASP culture is to dream of an America in cultural white
face, and that just won't do.

So it's only when we're free to explore the complexities of our hyphen-   9
ated culture that we can discover what a genuinely common American
culture might actually look like.

Is multiculturalism un-American? Herman Melville didn't think so.   10
As he wrote: "We are not a narrow tribe, no. . . . We are not a nation, so

much as a world." We're all ethnics; the challenge of transcending ethnic chauvinism is one we all face.

We've entrusted our schools with the fashioning and refashioning of 11 a democratic polity. That's why schooling has always been a matter of political judgment. But in a nation that has theorized itself as plural from its inception, schools have a very special task.

Our society won't survive without the values of tolerance, and cultural 12 tolerance comes to nothing without cultural understanding. The challenge facing America will be the shaping of a truly common public culture, one responsive to the long-silenced cultures of color. If we relinquish the ideal of America as a plural nation, we've abandoned the very experiment America represents. And that is too great a price to pay.

Thinking About the Essay

1. Gates poses a question in his title. How does he answer it? Where does he state his thesis?

2. The essay begins with an anecdote. How does it illuminate a key aspect of the problem Gates analyzes?

3. Gates makes several references to other writers—Mortimer Adler, Arthur Schlesinger Jr. (who appears in an earlier chapter), W. E. B. Du Bois, and Herman Melville. Who are these figures, and how do they provide a frame or context for Gates's argument?

4. How does the writer use comparison and contrast and causal analysis to advance his argument?

5. How does the concluding paragraph serve as a fitting end to the writer's argument?

Responding in Writing

6. Write a comparative essay in which you analyze the respective approaches to multiculturalism by Arthur Schlesinger Jr. (see chapter 2) and Gates.

7. Gates speaks of "our hyphenated culture" (paragraph 9). Write a paper examining this phrase and applying it to your own campus.

8. Are you on "the cultural left" or "the cultural right" (to use Gates's words in paragraph 3), or somewhere in the middle? Write a personal essay responding to this question.

Networking

9. Form four working groups of classmates. Each group should investigate the ethnic composition of your campus, courses, and programs designed to foster pluralism and multiculturalism, and the institution's policy on

affirmative action. Draft a document in which you present your findings and conclusions concerning the state of the cultural diversity movement on your campus.

10. Search the World Wide Web for sites that promote what Gates terms "'universal' WASP culture" (paragraph 8). What sort of ideology do they promote? Where do they stand in terms of the culture wars? What impact do you think they have on the course of contemporary life in the United States?

Does the World Still Care About American Culture?

RICHARD PELLS | Richard Pells, who was born in Kansas City, Missouri, in 1941, studied at Rutgers University (BA, 1963) and Harvard University (M.A.,1964; Ph.D., 1969). He is a professor of history at the University of Texas at Austin. His books include *Radical Visions and American Dreams* (1973) and *Not Like Us: How Europeans Have Loved, Hated, and Transformed American Culture Since World War II* (1997). Pells currently is working on a new study titled *Modernist America: Art, Music, Movies, and the Globalization of American Culture* (Yale University Press, forthcoming). In the following article from the March 8, 2009, issue of *The Chronicle of Higher Education*, Pells examines the causes behind the decline of global interest in American culture.

Before Reading

Do you accept the premise that the rest of the world is less interested in American culture today than it was during most of the twentieth century?

For most of the 20th century, the dominant culture in the world was   1 American. Now that is no longer true. What is most striking about attitudes toward the United States in other countries is not the anti-Americanism they reflect, or the disdain for former President George W. Bush, or the opposition to American foreign policies. Rather, people abroad are increasingly indifferent to America's culture.

American culture used to be the elephant in everyone's living room.   2 Whether people felt uncomfortable with the omnipresence of America's

Richard Pells "Does the World Still Care About American Culture?" Originally appeared in *The Chronicle of Higher Education*, Mar 6, 2009, Vol. 55, Iss 26; pg B4. Reprinted by permission of the author.

high or popular culture in their countries, they could not ignore its power or its appeal. American writers and artists were superstars—the objects of curiosity, admiration and envy. Today they are for the most part unnoticed or regarded as ordinary mortals, participants in a global rather than a distinctively American culture.

America's elections still matter to people overseas. As someone who 3 has taught American studies in Europe, Latin America and Asia, I received e-mail messages from friends abroad asking me who I thought would win the presidency in November. But I rarely get queries about what I think of the latest American movie. Nor does anyone ask me about American novelists, playwrights, composers or painters.

Imagine any of these events or episodes in the past happening now: 4 In 1928, fresh from having written "Rhapsody in Blue" and the "Piano Concerto in F Major," George Gershwin traveled to Paris and Vienna. He was treated like an idol. As America's most famous composer, he met with many of the leading European modernists: Schoenberg, Stravinsky, Prokofiev, Ravel. At one point, Gershwin asked Stravinsky if he could take lessons from the great Russian. Stravinsky responded by asking Gershwin how much money he made in a year. Told the answer was in six figures, Stravinsky quipped, "In that case . . . I should study with you."

In the 1930s, Louis Armstrong and Duke Ellington toured throughout 5 Europe, giving concerts to thousands of adoring fans, including members of the British royal family. In the 1940s and '50s, Dave Brubeck, Miles Davis, Dizzy Gillespie, Benny Goodman and Charlie Parker often gave concerts in Western and Eastern Europe, the Soviet Union, the Middle East, Africa, Asia and Latin America. The Voice of America's most popular program in the 1960s was a show called Music USA, specializing in jazz, with an estimated 100 million listeners around the world. In the 1940s and '50s as well, Leonard Bernstein was invited to conduct symphony orchestras in London, Moscow, Paris, Prague, Tel Aviv and Milan.

If you were a professor of modern literature at a foreign university, 6 your reading list had to include Bellow, Dos Passos, Faulkner, Hemingway and Steinbeck. If you taught courses on the theater, it was obligatory to discuss *Death of a Salesman, The Iceman Cometh, Long Day's Journey Into Night* and *A Streetcar Named Desire.*

If you wanted to study modern art, you did not—like Gene Kelly in 7 *An American in Paris*—journey to the City of Light (all the while singing and dancing to the music of Gershwin) to learn how to become a painter. Instead you came to New York, to sit at the feet of Willem de Kooning and Jackson Pollock. Or later you hung out at Andy Warhol's "factory," surrounded by celebrities from the arts and the entertainment world.

If dance was your specialty, where else could you find more creative   8
choreographers than Bob Fosse or Jerome Robbins? If you were an aspiring
filmmaker in the 1970s, the movies worth seeing and studying all originated in America. What other country could boast of such cinematic talent
as Woody Allen, Robert Altman, Francis Ford Coppola, George Lucas,
Martin Scorsese and Steven Spielberg?

Of course, there are still American cultural icons who mesmerize a   9
global audience or whose photos are pervasive in the pages of the world's
tabloid newspapers. Bruce Springsteen can always pack an arena wherever
he performs. The Broadway musical *Rent* has been translated into more
than 20 languages. Hollywood's blockbusters still make millions of dollars
abroad. America's movie stars remain major celebrities at international
film festivals.

But there is a sense overseas today that America's cultural exports   10
are not as important, or as alluring, as they once were. When I lecture
abroad on contemporary American culture, I find that few of America's current artists and intellectuals are household names, luminaries
from whom foreigners feel they need to learn. The cultural action is
elsewhere—not so much in Manhattan or San Francisco but in Berlin
(the site of a major film festival) and Mumbai (the home of Indian filmmakers and media entrepreneurs who are now investing in the movies
of Spielberg and other American directors). The importance of Mumbai
was reinforced, spectacularly, when *Slumdog Millionaire* won the Oscar
for best picture.

What accounts for the decline of interest in American art, literature and   11
music? Why has American culture become just another item on the shelves
of the global supermarket?

The main answer is that globalization has subverted America's influence. During the 1990s, many people assumed that the emergence of what
they called a global culture was just another mechanism for the "Americanization" of the world. Be it Microsoft or McDonald's, Disney theme parks
or shopping malls, the movies or the Internet, the artifacts of American
culture seemed ubiquitous and inescapable.

Yet far from reinforcing the impact of American culture, globalization   12
has strengthened the cultures of other nations, regions and continents.
Instead of defining what foreigners want, America's cultural producers find
themselves competing with their counterparts abroad in shaping people's
values and tastes. What we have in the 21st century is not a hegemonic
American culture but multiple forms of art and entertainment—voices,
images and ideas that can spring up anywhere and be disseminated all over
the planet.

American television programs like *Dallas* and *Dynasty* were once the 13
most popular shows on the airwaves, from Norway to New Zealand. Now
many people prefer programs that are locally produced. Meanwhile, cable
and satellite facilities permit stations like Al-Jazeera to define and interpret
the news from a Middle Eastern perspective for people throughout the
world.

Since 2000, moreover, American movies have steadily lost market share
in Europe and Asia. In 1998, the year *Titanic* was released abroad, American films commanded 64 percent of the ticket sales in France. Ten years
later, Hollywood's share of the French market has fallen to 50 percent.
Similarly, in 1998, American films accounted for 70 percent of the tickets
sold in South Korea. Today that figure has fallen to less than 50 percent.

As in the case of television programs, audiences increasingly prefer 14
movies made in and about their own countries or regions. Indian films are
now more popular in India than are imports from Hollywood. At the same
time, American moviegoers are increasingly willing to sample films from
abroad (and not just in art houses), which has led to the popularity in the
United States of Japanese cartoons and animated films as well as recent
German movies like *The Lives of Others*.

After World War II, professors and students from abroad were eager to 15
study in the United States. America was, after all, the center of the world's
intellectual and cultural life. Now, with the rise of continental exchange
programs and the difficulties that foreign academics face obtaining U.S.
visas, it is often easier for a Dutch student to study in Germany or France
or for a Middle Eastern student to study in India, than for either of them
to travel to an American university. That further diminishes the impact of
American culture abroad.

Crowds, especially of young people, still flock to McDonald's—whether 16
in Beijing, Moscow or Paris. But every country has always had its own
version of equally popular fast food. There are wurst stands in Germany
and Austria, fish-and-chips shops in England, noodle restaurants in South
Korea and Singapore, kabob outlets on street corners in almost any city
(including in America), all of which remain popular and compete effectively with the Big Mac.

Finally, cellphones and the Internet make information and culture 17
instantly available to anyone, without having to depend any longer on
American definitions of what it is important to know. Indeed, globalization has led not to greater intellectual and political uniformity but to the
decentralization of knowledge and culture. We live today in a universe full
of cultural options, and we are therefore free to choose what to embrace
and what to ignore.

I am not suggesting that America's culture is irrelevant. It remains 18 one—but only one—of the cultural alternatives available to people abroad and at home. Moreover, it is certainly conceivable that President Barack Obama will improve America's currently dreadful image in the world, encouraging people to pay more attention not only to American policies but also to American culture—which the Bush administration, despite its efforts at cultural diplomacy, was never able to do.

But it is doubtful that America will ever again be the world's pre-eminent 19 culture, as it was in the 20th century. That is not a cause for regret. Perhaps we are all better off in a world of cultural pluralism than in a world made in America.

Thinking About the Essay

1. What claim does Pells establish in his introductory paragraph? What minor propositions does he provide to support his claim?

2. Where does Pells inject information about himself into this essay? What is his purpose? Do you think his strategy is effective? Justify your response.

3. Does Pells ever establish a clear definition of American culture or does he force us to induce it? Explain. Could there be alternative definitions of American culture that compete with Pells's understanding of the word? Why or why not?

4. Trace the pattern of cause-and-effect that Pells establishes. According to Pells, what are the primary and secondary causes for the decline of global interest in American culture?

5. Pells alludes to numerous cultural figures and artistic works in this essay. What expectations does he have of his audience here? Would readers be less likely to relate to his essay—or accept his argument—if they were not familiar with Gene Kelly or had not read or seen *The Iceman Cometh*? Explain.

Responding in Writing

6. Write an argumentative essay in which you attempt to refute Pells's claim that the world is losing interest in American culture. Provide supporting points and examples to buttress your argument.

7. Write a causal analysis of the impact of globalization on the dissemination of American culture around the world.

8. Reverse Pells's claim and write an essay contending or explaining why Americans are far more interested in the cultures of other nations and regions than they were in the past.

Networking

9. Working in small groups, develop a list of all the references and allusions in Pells's essay and then identify as many as possible. Based on this list, establish what your group thinks that Pells means by American culture.

10. Conduct online research on one American musician, writer, artist, filmmaker, or actor mentioned in the essay—for example, Louis Armstrong, Ernest Hemingway, or Woody Allen—and explore the reception of this individual overseas. What conclusions can you draw from your research?

Hygiene and Repression

OCTAVIO PAZ | Octavio Paz was born in 1914 near Mexico City, into a family that was influential in the political and cultural life of the nation. Paz published poetry and short stories as a teenager and came to the attention of the famous Chilean poet Pablo Neruda, who encouraged him to attend a congress of leftist writers in Spain. Subsequently, Paz was drawn into the Spanish Civil War, fighting against the Fascist forces of Francisco Franco. Paz moved continuously for decades—Los Angeles, New York, Mexico City, and France—and served in his country's diplomatic corps for twenty years. During this time he published one of his most famous works, *The Labyrinth of Solitude* (1950), a study of Mexican culture and identity. A prolific writer of both poetry and prose, the author of more than four dozen books, Paz was awarded the Nobel Prize for Literature in 1990. He died in April 1998. Paz was a professor of comparative literature at Harvard University from 1973 to 1980, and during this period he wrote the following essay, which appears in *Convergences Essays on Art and Literature* (1997). In this essay, Paz offers a fine comparative investigation of rival cultural cuisines.

Before Reading

How would you describe "American" food? How does it reflect American culture? And how would you describe Spanish or French or Indian cuisine and the ways it captures its respective culture?

Traditional American cooking is a cuisine without mystery: simple, 1
nourishing, scantily seasoned foods. No tricks: a carrot is a homely,

honest carrot, a potato is not ashamed of its humble condition, and a steak is a big, bloody hunk of meat. This is a transubstantiation of the democratic virtues of the Founding Fathers: a plain meal, one dish following another like the sensible, unaffected sentences of a virtuous discourse. Like the conversation among those at table, the relation between substances and flavors is direct: sauces that mask tastes, garnishes that entice the eye, condiments that confuse the taste buds are taboo. The separation of one food from another is analogous to the reserve that characterizes the relations between sexes, races, and classes. In our countries food is communion, not only between those together at table but between ingredients; Yankee food, impregnated with Puritanism, is based on exclusions. The maniacal preoccupation with the purity and origin of food products has its counterpart in racism and exclusivism. The American contradiction—a democratic universalism based on ethnic, cultural, religious, and sexual exclusions—is reflected in its cuisine. In this culinary tradition our fondness for dark, passionate stews such as moles, for thick and sumptuous red, green, and yellow sauces, would be scandalous, as would be the choice place at our table of *huitlacoche*, which not only is made from diseased young maize but is black in color. Likewise our love for hot peppers, ranging from parakeet green to ecclesiastical purple, and for ears of Indian corn, their grains varying from golden yellow to midnight blue. Colors as violent as their tastes. Americans adore fresh, delicate colors and flavors. Their cuisine is like watercolor painting or pastels.

American cooking shuns spices as it shuns the devil, but it wallows in slews of cream and butter. Orgies of sugar. Complementary opposites: the almost apostolic simplicity and soberness of lunch, in stark contrast to the suspiciously innocent, pregenital pleasures of ice cream and milkshakes. Two poles: the glass of milk and the glass of whiskey. The first affirms the primacy of home and mother. The virtues of the glass of milk are twofold: it is a wholesome food and it takes us back to childhood. Fourier detested the family repast, the image of the family in civilized society, a tedious daily ceremony presided over by a tyrannical father and a phallic mother. What would he have said of the cult of the glass of milk? As for whiskey and gin, they are drinks for loners and introverts. For Fourier, Gastrosophy was the science of combining not only foods but guests at table: matching the variety of dishes is the variety of persons sharing the meal. Wines, spirits, and liqueurs are the complement of a meal, hence their object is to stimulate the relations and unions consolidated round a table. Unlike wine, pulque, champagne, beer, and vodka, neither whiskey nor gin accompanies meals. Nor are they apéritifs or digestifs. They are drinks that accentuate uncommunicativeness and unsociability. In a gastrosophic age they would not enjoy much of a reputation. The universal favor accorded them reveals the situation of our societies, ever wavering between promiscuous association and solitude.

Ambiguity and ambivalence are resources unknown to American   3
cooking. Here, as in so many other things, it is the diametrical opposite of the extremely delicate French cuisine, based on nuances, variations, and modulations—transitions from one substance to another, from one flavor to another. In a sort of profane Eucharist, even a glass of water is transfigured into an erotic chalice:

> *Ta lèvre contre le cristal*
> *Gorgée à gorgée y compose*
> *Le souvenir pourpre et vital*
> *De la moins éphémère rose.**

It is the contrary as well of Mexican and Hindu cuisine, whose secret is the shock of tastes: cool and piquant, salt and sweet, hot and tart, pungent and delicate. Desire is the active agent, the secret producer of changes, whether it be the transition from one flavor to another or the contrast between several. In gastronomy as in the erotic, it's desire that sets substances, bodies, and sensations in motion; this is the power that rules their conjunction, commingling, and transmutation. A reasonable cuisine, in which each substance is what it is and in which both variations and contrasts are avoided, is a cuisine that has excluded desire.

Pleasure is a notion (a sensation) absent from traditional Yankee cuisine.   4
Not pleasure but health, not correspondence between savors but the satisfaction of a need—these are its two values. One is physical and the other moral; both are associated with the idea of the body as work. Work in turn is a concept at once economic and spiritual: production and redemption. We are condemned to labor, and food restores the body after the pain and punishment of work. It is a real *reparation,* in both the physical and the moral sense. Through work the body pays its debt; by earning its physical sustenance, it also earns its spiritual recompense. Work redeems us and the sign of this redemption is food. An active sign in the spiritual economy of humanity, food restores the health of body and soul. If what we eat gives us physical and spiritual health, the exclusion of spices for moral and hygienic reasons is justified: they are the signs of desire, and they are difficult to digest.

Health is the condition of two activities of the body, work and sports.   5
In the first, the body is an agent that produces and at the same time

*Your lip against the crystal/Sip by sip forms therein/The vital deep crimson memory/Of the least ephemeral rose.—Stéphane Mallarmé,"Verre d' eau."

redeems; in the second, the sign changes: sports are a wasteful expenditure of energy. This is a contradiction in appearance only, since what we have here in reality is a system of communicating vessels. Sports are a physical expenditure that is precisely the contrary of what happens in sexual pleasure, since sports in the end become productive—an expenditure that produces health. Work in turn is an expenditure of energy that produces goods and thereby transforms biological life into social, economic, and moral life. There is, moreover, another connection between work and sports: both take place within a context of rivalry; both are competition and emulation. The two of them are forms of Fourier's "Cabalist" passion. In this sense, sports possess the rigor and gravity of work, and work possesses the gratuity and levity of sports. The play element of work is one of the few features of American society that might have earned Fourier's praise, though doubtless he would have been horrified at the commercialization of sports. The preeminence of work and sports, activities necessarily excluding sexual pleasure, has the same significance as the exclusion of spices in cuisine. If gastronomy and eroticism are unions and conjunctions of substances and tastes or of bodies and sensations, it is evident that neither has been a central preoccupation of American society—as ideas and social values, I repeat, not as more or less secret realities. In the American tradition the body is not a source of pleasure but of health and work, in the material and the moral sense.

The cult of health manifests itself as an "ethic of hygiene." I use the word ethic because its prescriptions are at once physiological and moral. A despotic ethic: sexuality, work, sports, and even cuisine are its domains. Again, there is a dual concept: hygiene governs both the corporeal and the moral life. Following the precepts of hygiene means obeying not only rules concerning physiology but also ethical principles: temperance, moderation, reserve. The morality of separation gives rise to the rules of hygiene, just as the aesthetics of fusion inspires the combinations of gastronomy and erotica. In India I frequently witnessed the obsession of Americans with hygiene. Their dread of contagion seemed to know no bounds; anything and everything might be laden with germs: food, drink, objects, people, the very air. These preoccupations are the precise counterpart of the ritual preoccupations of Brahmans fearing contact with certain foods and impure things, not to mention people belonging to a caste different from their own. Many will say that the concerns of the American are justified, whereas those of the Brahman are superstitions. Everything depends on the point of view: for the Brahman the bacteria that the American fears are illusory, while the moral stains produced by contact with alien people are real. These stains are stigmas that isolate him: no member of his caste would dare touch him until he had performed long and complicated rites of purification. The fear of social isolation is no less intense than that of illness. The hygienic taboo of the American and the ritual taboo of the Brahman have a common basis: the concern for purity. This basis is religious even though, in the case of hygiene, it is masked by the authority of science.

In the last analysis, the cult of hygiene is merely another expression of the   7
principle underlying attitudes toward sports, work, cuisine, sex, and races. The other name of purity is separation. Although hygiene is a social morality based explicitly on science, its unconscious root is religious. Nonetheless, the form in which it expresses itself, and the justifications for it, are rational. In American society, unlike in ours, science from the very beginning has occupied a privileged place in the system of beliefs and values. The quarrel between faith and reason never took on the intensity that it assumed among Hispanic peoples. Ever since their birth as a nation, Americans have been modern; for them it is natural to believe in science, whereas for us this belief implies a negation of our past. The prestige of science in American public opinion is such that even political disputes frequently take on the form of scientific polemics, just as in the Soviet Union they assume the guise of quarrels about Marxist orthodoxy. Two recent examples are the racial question and the feminist movement: are intellectual differences between races and sexes genetic in origin or a historico-cultural phenomenon?

The universality of science (or what passes for science) justifies the   8
development and imposition of collective patterns of normality. Obviating the necessity for direct coercion, the overlapping of science and Puritan morality permits the imposition of rules that condemn peculiarities, exceptions, and deviations in a manner no less categorical and implacable than religious anathemas. Against the excommunications of science, the individual has neither the religious recourse of abjuration nor the legal one of *habeas corpus*. Although they masquerade as hygiene and science, these patterns of normality have the same function in the realm of eroticism as "healthful" cuisine in the sphere of gastronomy: the extirpation or the separation of what is alien, different, ambiguous, impure. One and the same condemnation applies to blacks, Chicanos, sodomites, and spices.

Thinking About the Essay

1. Paz's title is intriguing—as challenging perhaps as the essay. How does the title capture the substance of the essay?

2. Explain Paz's argument. What is his claim? What are his warrants? What support does he present, and how is it organized?

3. The writer composes dense, relatively long paragraphs, filled with figurative language, various allusions (notably to Fourier), difficult words, and complex

sentences. Take one paragraph and analyze it as completely as possible. Would you say that Paz is writing for a Harvard audience? What exactly is a Harvard audience?

4. Sexuality is a theme, or motif, that runs through this essay. Trace its development in the essay and explain its contribution to the selection.

5. Paz uses a variety of rhetorical strategies—notably comparison and contrast—to organize his essay. Identify these strategies and explain how they function.

Responding in Writing

6. Select your favorite cuisine, and in an analytical essay explain why you prefer it to all other cuisines.

7. Write an essay comparing any two cuisines. Be certain to link these two cuisines to the nations or cultures they illuminate.

8. Paz makes an implicit criticism of American food in his essay. Write an argumentative essay in which you agree or disagree with his thoughts on the subject.

Networking

9. In small groups, select just one dish—for example, pizza or tacos or hamburger—and discuss ways in which this food reflects its culture. Draw up a list of these cultural attributes, and present it to the class.

10. Go to Google or another search engine and find out more about Octavio Paz. Focus on his thoughts about politics and then, in class discussion, show how his political views are reflected in the tone of "Hygiene and Repression."

Besieged by "Friends"

HEATHER HAVRILESKY

Heather Havrilesky is TV and entertainment correspondent for *Salon.com*. She attended Duke University before becoming an online journalist. With illustrator Terry Colon, she created the popular weekly cartoon *Filler* for *Suck.com*. Her writing has appeared in *New York* magazine, *Spin*, *The Washington Post*, and National Public Radio's *All Things Considered*. In the following essay, which appeared in *Salon.com* in September 2005, Havrilesky reviews a new documentary that investigates the reaction in the Middle East to Hollywood's depictions of the Arab world.

Before Reading

How do you respond to depictions of Americans and American culture that you see in foreign films and television?

It must be tough living in the Middle East, what with all the dust and the 1
camels and the angry terrorists running around, looking for stuff to blow up. I bet it's hard to get your coffee in the morning, with all those terrorists shouting that the line is too long, or threatening to level the joint because they specifically said "soy" or "no foam" and the little drummer boy behind the counter didn't hear them right the first time.

Despite the fact that most Arabs on the big screen have several sticks of 2
dynamite packed into their BVDs, most of us aren't stupid enough to think that the Muslim world is filled with Wile E. Coyotes in robes. Still, when kids grow up watching *True Lies*, *The Siege* and *Rules of Engagement*, in which even a one-legged Yemeni girl totes a machine gun, it's not too hard to see how their perspectives get twisted beyond recognition. In his documentary *Hollywood in the Muslim World* Charles C. Stuart discovers a well of anger and frustration in the Middle East over American depictions of Arabs, anger that some believe stokes the flames of extremism.

As Stuart points out at the start of his film, by the year 2000, Arab 3
television had grown into a half-billion dollar a year industry. With 100 satellite channels, Arab governments can no longer control the content of every broadcast. These days, people in Cairo, Egypt; Beirut, Lebanon; and Qatar are familiar with shows like *Friends*, *Sex and the City* and *Will & Grace*, as well as countless American movies. Two months before the war with Iraq began, Stuart visited the Middle East and talked with citizens in Egypt, Iraq, Lebanon and Qatar about the influence of Hollywood and American pop culture in the Middle East.

Many of those interviewed resented the pervasive influence of Holly- 4
wood, claiming that such "cultural pollution" is a threat to Muslim identity. One filmmaker in Beirut expressed regret at the way kids in Lebanon grow up with so many American influences. "I feel that Lebanon has lost part of its identity by imitating or having all the American things here. This winter I didn't go to any Starbucks café, I don't like Dunkin Donuts . . . But the marketing of all these things is done in such a way that it reaches the children. I mean, who goes to McDonald's here? The children. Because at the same time, you have a McDonald's, a ticket to see a Disney film and you have a gadget. It's a market."

Heather Havrilesky, "Besieged by 'Friends'" from Salon.com, July 14, 2003. This article first appeared in Salon.com at http://www.Salon.com. An online version remains in the Salon archives. Reprinted with permission.

When Stuart interviewed a bunch of kids about their favorite American   5
movies, a 19-year-old man interrupted them, fearing that the filmmaker
was exploiting the children. When Stuart asked for the young man's point
of view, he angrily railed off a list of Hollywood's stereotypes. "Do you see
any camels around here?" he asked.

Others Stuart interviewed saw the influx of American culture as part of   6
a U.S. campaign to stereotype Arabs. "We know that there is a war, a war
of propaganda, and a media war against the Arabs and the Muslims," said
one network representative.

Whether or not they agreed with the assertion that American stereo-   7
types are intentionally denigrating, many subjects feel certain that Americanization in the Muslim world is pushing some Arabs to embrace more
extremist beliefs. Or, as professor Abdullah Schleifer of the American
University in Cairo put it, "Radical fundamentalism is a reaction to radical
Westernization or modernization."

As paranoid, oversensitive or wildly professorial as such remarks   8
might seem, consider how American stereotypes conveniently mirror our
government's foreign policy at any given time. While mid-century movies
about World War II seem laughably dated in their depiction of psychoti-
cally evil Japanese soldiers, the trauma of Pearl Harbor stoked paranoia
and hatred toward Japan in such a way that prejudices were absolutely
taken for granted as holding some grain of truth. Meanwhile, in early
Hollywood movies like *The Sheik* and *Lawrence of Arabia*, Arabs were
depicted as exotic, wildly sexual beings. By the early '80s, with the Iran
hostage crisis and rising turmoil in the Middle East, Hollywood's depictions of Arabs and Muslims became darker and more foreboding. Today,
the trauma of Sept. 11 enables many to cast a blind eye on the way Hollywood perpetuates extreme prejudice against Arabs in America and in
the Middle East.

Unfortunately, Stuart doesn't explore such points. As fascinating   9
as it is to meet the writers of the Arab sitcom *Shabab Online*, which
appears to be a badly blocked *Friends* with perpetually grinning actors,
or to visit "The Friends Cafe," a coffee joint in Beirut modeled after
"Central Perk," most of Stuart's interviews don't move past surface
observations and he seems to touch on a wide range of subjects without delving too deep or pulling the threads together into a cohesive
narrative.

Still, at a time when the "patriotic" view often simply means per-   10
vasive xenophobia, it's valuable to witness the resentment and anger
welling up from those who feel their cultural identity has been taken
hostage by Hollywood. And we can hardly blame them—if we were

forced to watch reruns of *Shabab Online* on every channel, we'd be angry, too.

Thinking About the Essay

1. What is the purpose of Havrilesky's ironic opening? Does she avoid sounding flippant? How does she control (or fail to control) her use of irony?

2. According to the writer, how have American stereotypes of foreign cultures changed in response to wars and other events in American history?

3. Why do you think the 19-year-old man interrupted the interview of the children (paragraph 5)? Why does Havrilesky mention this incident?

4. What is Havrilesky's major criticism of the documentary? Is the documentary itself the primary focus of the review, or is it more of a stimulus for the reviewer's own meditations on the issue?

5. How effective is Havrilesky's conclusion? In what ways does it relate to the thematic concerns of the opening paragraph?

Responding in Writing

6. In paragraph 8, Havrilesky characterizes theories about the Americanization of the Muslim world as "paranoid, oversensitive, or wildly professorial...." Other authors included in this chapter have characterized reservations about cultural hegemony as "academic" or merely theoretical. Evaluate this stereotype in an essay. Do you think it is a fair characterization? What are the limitations and dangers of appealing to this stereotype?

7. Respond to the views expressed by the Beirut filmmaker and quoted in paragraph 4. Do you believe those who market American products target children, or is there another explanation for the way Middle Eastern youth respond to American culture?

8. Charles C. Stuart conducted his interviews two months before the war with Iraq began in 2003. How do you think those interviewed in the Middle East would respond differently to Stuart's questions if they were asked today? Speculate on their likely responses in a brief essay, and offer some explanation for the change of attitude.

Networking

9. In groups of three or four, make a list of popular stereotypes currently associated with America and Americans that have been transmitted by Hollywood to other parts of the world. Then discuss how these stereotypes have complicated your relations with people from other cultures. Share your stories with the rest of the class.

10. Go online and locate the program schedule for a Middle Eastern television satellite network. How much of the programming is American in origin? What programs (like *Shabab Online*) appear to be a repackaging of an American program?

On Seeing England for the First Time

JAMAICA KINCAID

Jamaica Kincaid was born Elaine Potter Richardson in 1949 in St. John's, Antigua, in the West Indies. After emigrating to the United States, she became a staff writer for *The New Yorker,* with her short stories also appearing in *Rolling Stone,* the *Paris Review,* and elsewhere. She has taught at Harvard University and other colleges while compiling a distinguished body of fiction and nonfiction, notably *Annie John* (1958), *A Small Place* (1988), *Lucy* (1991), *The Autobiography of My Mother* (1996), and *Among Flowers: A Walk in the Himalaya* (2005). The stories collected in *At the Bottom of the River* (1984) won the Morton Dauwen Zabel Award from the American Academy and Institute of Arts and Letters. Although Kincaid has turned recently in her writing to the relatively peaceful world of gardening, the typical tone of her fiction and essays is severely critical of the social, cultural, and political consequences of colonialism and immigration. In "On Seeing England for the First Time," published in *Transition* in 1991, Kincaid thinks about the time when Great Britain was associated with the forces of globalization throughout the world.

Before Reading

It was once said that the sun never sets on the British Empire. What does this statement mean? Could the same be said of the United States today?

When I saw England for the first time, I was a child in school sitting at 1 a desk. The England I was looking at was laid out on a map gently, beautifully, delicately, a very special jewel; it lay on a bed of sky blue—the background of the map—its yellow form mysterious, because though it

looked like a leg of mutton, it could not really look like anything so familiar as a leg of mutton because it was England—with shadings of pink and
green, unlike any shadings of pink and green I had seen before, squiggly
veins of red running in every direction. England was a special jewel all right,
and only special people got to wear it. The people who got to wear England
were English people. They wore it well and they wore it everywhere: in
jungles, in deserts, on plains, on top of the highest mountains, on all the
oceans, on all the seas, in places where they were not welcome, in places
they should not have been. When my teacher had pinned this map up on
the blackboard, she said, "This is England"—and she said it with authority,
seriousness, and adoration, and we all sat up. It was as if she had said, "This
is Jerusalem, the place you will go to when you die but only if you have been
good." We understood then—we were meant to understand then—that
England was to be our source of myth and the source from which we got
our sense of reality, our sense of what was meaningful, our sense of what
was meaningless—and much about our own lives and much about the very
idea of us headed that last list.

    At the time I was a child sitting at my desk seeing England for the first   2
time, I was already very familiar with the greatness of it. Each morning
before I left for school, I ate a breakfast of half a grapefruit, an egg, bread
and butter and a slice of cheese, and a cup of cocoa; or half a grapefruit,
a bowl of oat porridge, bread and butter and a slice of cheese, and a cup
of cocoa. The can of cocoa was often left on the table in front of me. It
had written on it the name of the company, the year the company was
established, and the words "Made in England." Those words," Made in
England," were written on the box the oats came in too. They would also
have been written on the box the shoes I was wearing came in; a bolt of
gray linen cloth lying on the shelf of a store from which my mother had
bought three yards to make the uniform that I was wearing had written
along its edge those three words. The shoes I wore were made in England;
so were my socks and cotton undergarments and the satin ribbons I wore
tied at the end of two plaits of my hair. My father, who might have sat
next to me at breakfast, was a carpenter and cabinet maker. The shoes he wore
to work would have been made in England, as were his khaki shirt and
trousers, his underpants and undershirt, his socks and brown felt hat. Felt
was not the proper material from which a hat that was expected to provide
shade from the hot sun should be made, but my father must have seen and
admired a picture of an Englishman wearing such a hat in England, and
this picture that he saw must have been so compelling that it caused him to
wear the wrong hat for a hot climate most of his long life. And this hat—a
brown felt hat—became so central to his character that it was the first thing

he put on in the morning as he stepped out of bed and the last thing he took off before he stepped back into bed at night. As we sat at breakfast a car might go by. The car, a Hillman or a Zephyr, was made in England. The very idea of the meal itself, breakfast, and its substantial quality and quantity was an idea from England; we somehow knew that in England they began the day with this meal called breakfast and a proper breakfast was a big breakfast. No one I knew liked eating so much food so early in the day; it made us feel sleepy, tired. But this breakfast business was Made in England like almost everything else that surrounded us, the exceptions being the sea, the sky, and the air we breathed.

At the time I saw this map—seeing England for the first time—I did   3
not say to myself, "Ah, so that's what it looks like," because there was no longing in me to put a shape to those three words that ran through every part of my life, no matter how small; for me to have had such a longing would have meant that I lived in a certain atmosphere, an atmosphere in which those three words were felt as a burden. But I did not live in such an atmosphere. My father's brown felt hat would develop a hole in its crown, the lining would separate from the hat itself, and six weeks before he thought that he could not be seen wearing it—he was a very vain man—he would order another hat from England. And my mother taught me to eat my food in the English way: the knife in the right hand, the fork in the left, my elbows held still close to my side, the food carefully balanced on my fork and then brought up to my mouth. When I had finally mastered it, I overheard her saying to a friend, "Did you see how nicely she can eat?" But I knew then that I enjoyed my food more when I ate it with my bare hands, and I continued to do so when she wasn't looking. And when my teacher showed us the map, she asked us to study it carefully, because no test we would ever take would be complete without this statement: "Draw a map of England."

I did not know then that the statement "Draw a map of England" was   4
something far worse than a declaration of war, for in fact a flat-out decla-ration of war would have put me on alert, and again in fact, there was no need for war—I had long ago been conquered. I did not know then that this statement was part of a process that would result in my erasure, not my physical erasure, but my erasure all the same. I did not know then that this statement was meant to make me feel in awe and small whenever I heard the word "England": awe at its existence, small because I was not from it. I did not know very much of anything then—certainly not what a blessing it was that I was unable to draw a map of England correctly.

After that there were many times of seeing England for the first time.   5
I saw England in history. I knew the names of all the kings of England. I

knew the names of their children, their wives, their disappointments, their triumphs, the names of people who betrayed them; I knew the dates on which they were born and the dates they died. I knew their conquests and was made to feel glad if I figured in them; I knew their defeats. I knew the details of the year 1066 (the Battle of Hastings, the end of the reign of the Anglo-Saxon kings) before I knew the details of the year 1832 (the year slavery was abolished). It wasn't as bad as I make it sound now; it was worse. I did like so much hearing again and again how Alfred the Great, traveling in disguise, had been left to watch cakes, and because he wasn't used to this the cakes got burned, and Alfred burned his hands pulling them out of the fire, and the woman who had left him to watch the cakes screamed at him. I loved King Alfred. My grandfather was named after him; his son, my uncle, was named after King Alfred; my brother is named after King Alfred. And so there are three people in my family named after a man they have never met, a man who died over ten centuries ago. The first view I got of England then was not unlike the first view received by the person who named my grandfather.

This view, though—the naming of the kings, their deeds, their disappointments—was the vivid view, the forceful view. There were other views, subtler ones, softer, almost not there—but these were the ones that made the most lasting impression on me, these were the ones that made me really feel like nothing. "When morning touched the sky" was one phrase, for no morning touched the sky where I lived. The mornings where I lived came on abruptly, with a shock of heat and loud noises. "Evening approaches" was another, but the evenings where I lived did not approach; in fact, I had no evening—I had night and I had day and they came and went in a mechanical way: on, off; on, off. And then there were gentle mountains and low blue skies and moors over which people took walks for nothing but pleasure, when where I lived a walk was an act of labor, a burden, something only death or the automobile could relieve. And there were things that a small turn of a head could convey—entire worlds, whole lives would depend on this thing, a certain turn of a head. Everyday life could be quite tiring, more tiring than anything I was told not to do. I was told not to gossip, but they did that all the time. And they ate so much food, violating another of those rules they taught me: do not indulge in gluttony. And the foods they ate actually: if only sometime I could eat cold cuts after theater, cold cuts of lamb and mint sauce, and Yorkshire pudding and scones, and clotted cream, and sausages that came from up-country (imagine, "up-country"). And having troubling thoughts at twilight, a good time to have troubling thoughts, apparently; and servants who stole and left in the middle of a crisis, who were born with a limp or some other

6

kind of deformity, not nourished properly in their mother's womb (that last part I figured out for myself; the point was, oh to have an untrustworthy servant); and wonderful cobbled streets onto which solid front doors opened; and people whose eyes were blue and who had fair skins and who smelled only of lavender, or sometimes sweet pea or primrose. And those flowers with those names: delphiniums, foxgloves, tulips, daffodils, floribunda, peonies; in bloom, a striking display, being cut and placed in large glass bowls, crystal, decorating rooms so large twenty families the size of mine could fit in comfortably but used only for passing through. And the weather was so remarkable because the rain fell gently always, only occasionally in deep gusts, and it colored the air various shades of gray, each an appealing shade for a dress to be worn when a portrait was being painted; and when it rained at twilight, wonderful things happened: people bumped into each other unexpectedly and that would lead to all sorts of turns of events—a plot, the mere weather caused plots. I saw that people rushed: they rushed to catch trains, they rushed toward each other and away from each other; they rushed and rushed and rushed. That word: rushed! I did not know what it was to do that. It was too hot to do that, and so I came to envy people who would rush, even though it had no meaning to me to do such a thing. But there they are again. They loved their children; their children were sent to their own rooms as a punishment, rooms larger than my entire house. They were special, everything about them said so, even their clothes; their clothes rustled, swished, soothed. The world was theirs, not mine; everything told me so.

If now as I speak of all this I give the impression of someone on the outside looking in, nose pressed up against a glass window, that is wrong. My nose was pressed up against a glass window all right, but there was an iron vise at the back of my neck forcing my head to stay in place. To avert my gaze was to fall back into something from which I had been rescued, a hole filled with nothing, and that was the word for everything about me, nothing. The reality of my life was conquests, subjugation, humiliation, enforced amnesia. I was forced to forget. Just for instance, this: I lived in a part of St. John's, Antigua, called Ovals. Ovals was made up of five streets, each of them named after a famous English seaman—to be quite frank, an officially sanctioned criminal: Rodney Street (after George Rodney), Nelson Street (after Horatio Nelson), Drake Street (after Francis Drake), Hood Street, and Hawkins Street (after John Hawkins). But John Hawkins was knighted after a trip he made to Africa, opening up a new trade, the slave trade. He was then entitled to wear as his crest a Negro bound with a cord. Every single person living on Hawkins Street was descended from a slave. John Hawkins's ship, the one in which he transported the people

7

he had bought and kidnapped, was called *The Jesus*. He later became the treasurer of the Royal Navy and rear admiral.

Again, the reality of my life, the life I led at the time I was being shown 8
these views of England for the first time, for the second time, for the one-hundred-millionth time, was this: the sun shone with what sometimes seemed to be a deliberate cruelty; we must have done something to deserve that. My dresses did not rustle in the evening air as I strolled to the theater (I had no evening, I had no theater; my dresses were made of a cheap cotton, the weave of which would give way after not too many washings). I got up in the morning, I did my chores (fetched water from the public pipe for my mother, swept the yard), I washed myself, I went to a woman to have my hair combed freshly every day (because before we were allowed into our classroom our teachers would inspect us, and children who had not bathed that day, or had dirt under their fingernails, or whose hair had not been combed anew that day, might not be allowed to attend class). I ate that breakfast. I walked to school. At school we gathered in an auditorium and sang a hymn, "All Things Bright and Beautiful," and looking down on us as we sang were portraits of the Queen of England and her husband; they wore jewels and medals and they smiled. I was a Brownie. At each meeting we would form a little group around a flagpole, and after raising the Union Jack, we would say, "I promise to do my best, to do my duty to God and the Queen, to help other people every day and obey the scouts' law."

Who were these people and why had I never seen them, I mean really 9
seen them, in the place where they lived? I had never been to England. No one I knew had ever been to England, or I should say, no one I knew had ever been and returned to tell me about it. All the people I knew who had gone to England had stayed there. Sometimes they left behind them their small children, never to see them again. England! I had seen England's representatives. I had seen the governor general at the public grounds at a ceremony celebrating the Queen's birthday. I had seen an old princess and I had seen a young princess. They had both been extremely not beautiful, but who of us would have told them that? I had never seen England, really seen it, I had only met a representative, seen a picture, read books, memorized its history. I had never set foot, my own foot, in it.

The space between the idea of something and its reality is always 10
wide and deep and dark. The longer they are kept apart—idea of thing, reality of thing—the wider the width, the deeper the depth, the thicker and darker the darkness. This space starts out empty, there is nothing in it, but it rapidly becomes filled up with obsession or desire or hatred or love—sometimes all of these things, sometimes some of these things,

sometimes only one of these things. The existence of the world as I came to know it was a result of this: idea of thing over here, reality of thing way, way over there. There was Christopher Columbus, an unlikable man, an unpleasant man, a liar (and so, of course, a thief) surrounded by maps and schemes and plans, and there was the reality on the other side of that width, that depth, that darkness. He became obsessed, he became filled with desire, the hatred came later, love was never a part of it. Eventually, his idea met the longed-for reality. That the idea of something and its reality are often two completely different things is something no one ever remembers; and so when they meet and find that they are not compatible, the weaker of the two, idea or reality, dies. That idea Christopher Columbus had was more powerful than the reality he met, and so the reality he met died.

And so finally, when I was a grown-up woman, the mother of two chil-   11
dren, the wife of someone, a person who resides in a powerful country that takes up more than its fair share of a continent, the owner of a house with many rooms in it and of two automobiles, with the desire and will (which I very much act upon) to take from the world more than I give back to it, more than I deserve, more than I need, finally then, I saw England, the real England, not a picture, not a painting, not through a story in a book, but England, for the first time. In me, the space between the idea of it and its reality had become filled with hatred, and so when at last I saw it I wanted to take it into my hands and tear it into little pieces and then crumble it up as if it were clay, child's clay. That was impossible, and so I could only indulge in not-favorable opinions.

There were monuments everywhere; they commemorated victories,   12
battles fought between them and the people who lived across the sea from them, all vile people, fought over which of them would have dominion over the people who looked like me. The monuments were useless to them now, people sat on them and ate their lunch. They were like markers on an old useless trail, like a piece of old string tied to a finger to jog the memory, like old decoration in an old house, dirty, useless, in the way. Their skins were so pale, it made them look so fragile, so weak, so ugly. What if I had the power to simply banish them from their land, send boat after boatload of them on a voyage that in fact had no destination, force them to live in a place where the sun's presence was a constant? This would rid them of their pale complexion and make them look more like me, make them look more like the people I love and treasure and hold dear, and more like the people who occupy the near and far reaches of my imagination, my history, my geography, and reduce them and everything they have ever known to

figurines as evidence that I was in divine favor, what if all this was in my power? Could I resist it? No one ever has.

And they were rude, they were rude to each other. They didn't like each 13 other very much. They didn't like each other in the way they didn't like me, and it occurred to me that their dislike for me was one of the few things they agreed on.

I was on a train in England with a friend, an English woman. Before 14 we were in England she liked me very much. In England she didn't like me at all. She didn't like the claim I said I had on England, she didn't like the views I had of England. I didn't like England, she didn't like England, but she didn't like me not liking it too. She said, "I want to show you my England, I want to show you the England that I know and love." I had told her many times before that I knew England and I didn't want to love it anyway. She no longer lived in England; it was her own country, but it had not been kind to her, so she left. On the train, the conductor was rude to her; she asked something, and he responded in a rude way. She became ashamed. She was ashamed at the way he treated her; she was ashamed at the way he behaved. "This is the new England," she said. But I liked the conductor being rude; his behavior seemed quite appropriate. Earlier this had happened: we had gone to a store to buy a shirt for my husband; it was meant to be a special present, a special shirt to wear on special occasions. This was a store where the Prince of Wales has his shirts made, but the shirts sold in this store are beautiful all the same. I found a shirt I thought my husband would like and I wanted to buy him a tie to go with it. When I couldn't decide which one to choose, the salesman showed me a new set. He was very pleased with these, he said, because they bore the crest of the Prince of Wales, and the Prince of Wales had never allowed his crest to decorate an article of clothing before. There was something in the way he said it; his tone was slavish, reverential, awed. It made me feel angry; I wanted to hit him. I didn't do that. I said, my husband and I hate princes, my husband would never wear anything that had a prince's anything on it. My friend stiffened. The salesman stiffened. They both drew themselves in, away from me. My friend told me that the prince was a symbol of her Englishness, and I could see that I had caused offense. I looked at her. She was an English person, the sort of English person I used to know at home, the sort who was nobody in England but somebody when they came to live among the people like me. There were many people I could have seen England with; that I was seeing it with this particular person, a person who reminded me of the people who showed me England long ago as I sat in church or at my desk, made me feel silent and afraid, for I wondered if, all these years of our friendship, I had had a friend or had been in the thrall of a racial memory.

I went to Bath—we, my friend and I, did this, but though we were 15 together, I was no longer with her. The landscape was almost as familiar as my own hand, but I had never been in this place before, so how could that be again? And the streets of Bath were familiar, too, but I had never walked on them before. It was all those years of reading, starting with Roman Britain. Why did I have to know about Roman Britain? It was of no real use to me, a person living on a hot, drought-ridden island, and it is of no use to me now, and yet my head is filled with this nonsense, Roman Britain. In Bath, I drank tea in a room I had read about in a novel written in the eighteenth century. In this very same room, young women wearing those dresses that rustled and so on danced and flirted and sometimes disgraced themselves with young men, soldiers, sailors, who were on their way to Bristol or someplace like that, so many places like that where so many adventures, the outcome of which was not good for me, began. Bristol, England. A sentence that began "That night the ship sailed from Bristol, England" would end not so good for me. And then I was driving through the countryside in an English motorcar, on narrow winding roads, and they were so familiar, though I had never been on them before; and through little villages the names of which I somehow knew so well though I had never been there before. And the countryside did have all those hedges and hedges, fields hedged in. I was marveling at all the toil of it, the planting of the hedges to begin with and then the care of it, all that clipping, year after year of clipping, and I wondered at the lives of the people who would have to do this, because wherever I see and feel the hands that hold up the world, I see and feel myself and all the people who look like me. And I said, "Those hedges" and my friend said that someone, a woman named Mrs. Rothchild, worried that the hedges weren't being taken care of properly; the farmers couldn't afford or find the help to keep up the hedges, and often they replaced them with wire fencing. I might have said to that, well if Mrs. Rothchild doesn't like the wire fencing, why doesn't she take care of the hedges herself, but I didn't. And then in those fields that were now hemmed in by wire fencing that a privileged woman didn't like was planted a vile yellow flowering bush that produced an oil, and my friend said that Mrs. Rothchild didn't like this either; it ruined the English countryside, it ruined the traditional look of the English countryside.

It was not at that moment that I wished every sentence, everything I 16 knew, that began with England would end with "and then it all died; we don't know how, it just all died." At that moment, I was thinking, who are these people who forced me to think of them all the time, who forced me to think that the world I knew was incomplete, or without substance, or did not measure up because it was not England; that I was incomplete, or without substance, and did not measure up because I was not English. Who were these people? The person sitting next to me couldn't give me a clue; no one person could. In any case, if I had said to her, I find England ugly, I hate England; the weather is like a jail sentence, the English are a very ugly people, the food in England is like a jail sentence, the hair of English people is so straight, so dead looking, the English have an unbearable smell so different from the smell of people I know, real people of course, she would have said that I was a person full of prejudice. Apart from the fact that it is I—that is, the people who look like me—who made her aware of the unpleasantness of such a thing, the idea of such a thing, prejudice, she would have been only partly right, sort of right: I may be capable of prejudice, but my prejudices have no weight to them, my prejudices have no force behind them, my prejudices remain opinions, my prejudices remain my personal opinion. And a great feeling of rage and disappointment came over me as I looked at England, my head full of personal opinions that could not have public, my public, approval. The people I come from are powerless to do evil on grand scale.

The moment I wished every sentence, everything I knew, that began 17 with England would end with "and then it all died, we don't know how, it just all died" was when I saw the white cliffs of Dover. I had sung hymns and recited poems that were about a longing to see the white cliffs of Dover again. At the time I sang the hymns and recited the poems, I could really long to see them again because I had never seen them at all, nor had anyone around me at the time. But there we were, groups of people longing for something we had never seen. And so there they were, the white cliffs, but they were not that pearly majestic thing I used to sing about, that thing that created such a feeling in these people that when they died in the place where I lived they had themselves buried facing a direction that would allow them to see the white cliffs of Dover when they were resurrected, as surely they would be. The white cliffs of Dover, when finally I saw them, were cliffs, but they were not white; you would only call them that if the word "white" meant something special to you; they were dirty and they were steep; they were so steep, the correct height from which all my views of England, starting with the map before me in my classroom and ending with the trip I had just taken, should jump and die and disappear forever.

Thinking About the Essay

1. Based on your careful reading of this essay, summarize Kincaid's understanding of cultural imperialism. Does the fact that she writes

about England and not the United States diminish the importance of her argument? Explain.

2. Kincaid divides her essay into two major parts. What is her intention? What is the effect?

3. Kincaid establishes several contrasts between England and Antigua. What are they? How does this comparative method serve to organize the essay?

4. The writer's paragraphs tend to be quite long. Analyze the way she develops her introductory and concluding paragraphs. Also examine the longest paragraph in the essay (paragraph 6) and explain how she achieves coherence in the presentation of her ideas.

5. How does Kincaid's use of the personal voice—the "I" point of view—affect the tone and purpose of her essay? By adopting this personal perspective, what does Kincaid want the audience to infer about her and her experience of cultural imperialism?

Responding in Writing

6. Write an account of your early education. What did you learn about the country where you were born and its relationship to the rest of the world? How did your early education influence or mold your global understanding today?

7. Write an essay analyzing Kincaid's various views on England and what they ultimately mean to her. Has she convinced you about her perspective on the subject? Why or why not? Be certain to deal with her concluding paragraph and her reference to the "white cliffs of Dover."

8. Imagine that you live in a country that has a history of colonization. (Perhaps you or your family has actually experienced this condition.) What would your attitude toward the colonizing or globalizing power be? Write a paper exploring this real or imaginary situation.

Networking

9. With three other class members, draw up a complete list of the contrasts that Kincaid establishes between Antigua and England. Arrive at a consensus about why she is so preoccupied with England—not just as a child but also as an adult writing about the experience. Select one member of your group as a representative in a class panel discussion that talks about these contrasts.

10. Go online and find information about Antigua. Evaluate Kincaid's impressions of her native island with what you have learned about it.

The Clash of Civilizations: Is Conflict Avoidable?

8

CHAPTER

The spread of Coca-Cola, Hollywood films, and rock and roll around the world—all the trappings of American popular culture—combined with the broader economic and political forces generated by America's superpower status, has helped fuel what we call the "clash of civilizations." The phrase, coined by the American political scientist Samuel Huntington, who has an essay in this chapter, suggests that we are in a new era in which the forces of globalization have brought entire civilizations, rather than separate nations, into conflict with each other. The nature of this conflict goes to the heart of what we mean by cultural identity—who am I, and where do I belong?—and how we see ourselves in relation to our civilization and other civilizations we come into contact with.

According to Huntington, whose long article appeared in the summer 1993 issue of *Foreign Affairs* and subsequently in an expanded book, *The Clash of Civilizations and the Remaking of World Order* (1996), the world can be divided into seven or perhaps eight contemporary civilizations: Western, Latin American, Islamic, Sinic or Chinese (which includes China, Taiwan, Korea, and Vietnam), Japanese, Hindu, Orthodox (Russia, Serbia, Greece), and African. "Human history," writes Huntington, "is the history of civilizations. It is impossible to think of the development of humanity in any other terms." Historically there have been numerous conflicts between and among these civilizations. However, Huntington's thesis is that with the rise of the West since 1500, other civilizations—notably the Islamic and Chinese—have resented this "rise" and reacted against it. Furthermore, in the inevitable cycles of history, other civilizations will rise in reaction to the dominance of the Western world and become dominant themselves, thus leading to a new clash with global consequences.

Palestinian schoolgirls walk past Israeli soldiers in Hebron, one of the most contested and violent cities of the West Bank—a region jointly controlled by Israel and the Palestinian Authority. The tomb of Abraham, considered the patriarch of both Judaism and Islam, is located in Hebron; rivalries here extend for millennia.

Thinking About the Image

1. What elements make this photograph especially compelling? Consider the expressions on the faces of the schoolgirls, the size and positioning of the soldiers, and the details of the setting.
2. Do you think that the photographer reinforces conventional depictions of the Arab-Israeli conflict in the American media, or is the photographer trying to present a different perspective? Explain your response.
3. Do you believe that the photographer advances an argument concerning Israel's occupation of the West Bank? Why or why not?

Huntington's broad thesis has come under scrutiny and attack on all sides, and some of his critics appear in this chapter. Yet it could be argued that what we see most clearly in the world today—the conflict between the Western and Islamic worlds or the gradual ascendancy of China as the next major world power—confirms Huntington's basic claim. Conversely, if you think that reality actually contradicts Huntington's thesis, then you could argue that Western forms of culture, democracy, and modernization actually are cutting across all civilizations and triumphing over them. Benjamin Barber (whose essay appears in chapter 6) maintains that there will be raging conflicts among civilizations in the future, but that "McWorld," as he terms the West, will triumph over "Jihad." Thus Western civilization will not decline but will defeat the forces of fundamentalism and totalitarianism.

The essays in this chapter deal with the clash of civilizations from a variety of perspectives. We can't deny that conflicts among civilizations exist; some are religious, others ethnic, still others cultural. The writers invite us to consider our own loyalties, and whether we associate with one culture, nation, or civilization or with many. Are there commonalities among civilizations, or must we be forever in conflict? Must we always deal with threats to our gods, our ancestors, our civilization? Or, in a world of 6 billion people, are there tangible signs that we needn't think of "inferior" and "superior" civilizations but rather of a world showing signs of heightened tolerance, integration, and harmony? The way we answer these questions will determine the fabric of future civilizations.

American Dream Boat

K. OANH HA | K. Oanh Ha was born in Vietnam in 1973. As she relates in the following essay, she left Vietnam with her family in July 1979, journeying with other "boat people" to the United States. Raised in California, she covers globalization for KQED Radio in San Francisco. Her stories explore the business of globalization as well as its social and cultural impact. Prior to working in radio, she was a staff writer for the *San Jose Mercury News*. She is working on a novel that is based loosely on her family's escape from Vietnam. In this personal narrative that she published in *Modern Maturity* in 2002, Ha provides a gentle affirmation of how—when it comes to love—civilizations need not clash.

Before Reading

Have you dated someone whose background represents a culture or civilization entirely different from yours? If not, do you know of a couple who signify this coming together of civilizations? How do you—or they—work out any "clashes"?

The wedding day was only two weeks away when my parents called with yet another request. In accordance with Vietnamese custom, they fully expected Scott Harris, my fiancé, and his family to visit our family on the   1 morning of the wedding, bearing dowry gifts of fruit, candies, jewelry, and a pig, in an elaborate procession.

"But it's not going to mean anything to Scott or his family. They're not   2
Vietnamese!" I protested. My parents were adamant: "Scott is marrying a Vietnamese. If he wants to marry you, he'll honor our traditions."

Maybe there's no such thing as a stress-free wedding. Small or large,   3
there's bound to be pressure. But our February 12 wedding was a large do-it-yourselfer that required a fusion of Vietnamese and American traditions—a wedding that forced me and my parents to wrestle with questions about our identities, culture, and place in America. After nearly 20 years here, my family, and my parents in particular, were determined to have a traditional Vietnamese wedding of sorts, even if their son-in-law and Vietnam-born, California-raised daughter are as American as they can be.

And so I grudgingly called Scott that night to describe the wedding pro-   4
cession and explain the significance of the ritual. It's a good thing that he is a patient, easygoing man. "I'll bring the pig," he said, "but I'm worried it'll make a mess in the car."

"Oh! It's a *roasted* pig," I told him, laughing.   5

I was six years old when my family fled Vietnam in July 1979, just one   6
family among the thousands who collectively became known as the "boat people," families who decided it was better to risk the very real possibility of death at sea than to live under Communist rule. But, of course, I never understood the politics then. I was just a child following my parents.

My memories are sketchy. There was the time that Thai pirates wielding   7
saber-like machetes raided our boat. Two years ago, I told my mother, Kim Hanh Nguyen, how I remembered a woman dropping a handful of jewelry into my rice porridge during the raid with the instructions to keep eating. "That was no woman," my mother said. "That was me!" When we reached the refugee camp in Kuala Lumpur, my mother used the wedding ring and necklace to buy our shelter.

In September 1980, we arrived in Santa Ana, California, in Orange   8
County, now home to the largest Vietnamese community outside of Vietnam. Those who had left in 1975, right after the end of the war and the American withdrawal, had been well-educated, wealthy, and connected with the military. My family was part of the wave of boat people—mostly middle-class and with little education—who sought refuge in America.

For nearly a year after we arrived, we crowded into the same three-   9
bedroom apartment, all 13 of us: brothers, sisters, cousins, uncles, aunts, sisters-in-law, and my father's mother. There were only four of us children in my immediate family then, three born in Vietnam and one born shortly after our resettlement in the U.S.

We started school and watched Mr. Rogers on PBS in the afternoons, 10
grew to love hamburgers and ketchup and longed to lose our accents.
We older kids did lose our accents—and those who came later never had
accents to begin with because they were born here. When we first came,
I was the oldest of three children, all born in Vietnam. Now I have seven
siblings, 22 years separating me from my youngest brother, who will start
kindergarten in the fall.

In some ways, I was the stereotypical Asian nerd. I took honors classes, 11
received good grades, and played the violin and cello. But there was a part
of me that also yearned to be as American as my blond-haired neighbors
across the street. I joined the school's swim and tennis teams, participated
in speech competitions (which were attended by mostly white students)
and worshipped Esprit and Guess. My first serious boyfriend was white
but most of my friends were Asians who were either born in the U.S. or
immigrated when they were very young. None of us had accents and we
rarely spoke our native languages around one another. The last thing we
wanted to be mistaken for was FOBs—fresh off the boat. I even changed
my name to Kyrstin, unaware of its Nordic roots.

I wanted so badly to be a full-fledged American, whatever that meant. 12
At home though, my parents pushed traditional Vietnamese values. I spent
most of my teenage years baby-sitting and had to plead with my then
overly strict parents to let me out of the house. "Please, please. I just want
to be like any other American kid."

My parents didn't understand. "You'll always be Vietnamese. No one's 13
going to look at you and say you're an American," was my mother's often-
heard refrain.

I saw college as my escape, the beginning of the trip I would undertake 14
on my own. We had come to America as a family but it was time I navi-
gated alone. College was my flight from the house that always smelled of
fish sauce and jasmine tea.

At UCLA, I dated the man who would become my husband. Though 15
he's 17 years older than I am, my parents seemed to be more concerned
with the cultural barriers than our age difference. "White Americans are
fickle. They don't understand commitment and family responsibility like
we Asians do," I was told.

Soon after I announced my engagement, my father, Minh Phu Ha, and 16
I had a rare and intimate conversation. "I'm just worried for you," he said.
"All the Vietnamese women I know who have married whites are divorced
from them. Our cultures are too far apart."

My father, I think, is worried that none of his kids will marry Vietnamese. 17
My sisters are dating non-Vietnamese Asians while my brother is dating a

white American. "It's just that with a Vietnamese son-in-law, I can talk to him," my father explained to me one day. "A Vietnamese son-in-law would call me '*Ba*' and not by my first name."

Although my parents have come to terms with having Scott as their son   18
in-law and to the prospect of grandchildren who will be racially mixed, there are still times when Scott comes to visit that there are awkward silences. There are still many cultural barriers.

I still think of what it all means to marry a white American. I worry   19
that my children won't be able to speak Vietnamese and won't appreciate that part of their heritage. I also wonder if somehow this is the ultimate fulfillment of a latent desire to be "American."

Vietnamese-Americans, like Chinese-Americans, Indian-Americans,   20
and other assimilated immigrants, often speak of leading hyphenated lives, of feet that straddle both cultures. I've always been proud of being Vietnamese. As my family and I discussed and heatedly debated what the wedding event was going to look like, I began to realize just how "American" I had become.

And yet there was no denying the pull of my Vietnamese roots. Four   21
months before the wedding, I traveled back to Vietnam for the second time since our family's escape. It was a trip I had planned for more than a year. I was in Saigon, the city of my birth, to research and write a novel that loosely mirrors the story of my own family and our journey from Vietnam. The novel is my tribute to my family and our past. I'm writing it for myself as much as for my younger siblings, so they'll know what our family's been through.

I returned to Vietnam to connect with something I can't really name but   22
know I lost when we left 20 years ago. I was about to start a new journey with the marriage ahead, but I needed to come back to the place where my family's journey began.

Scott came along for the first two weeks and met my extended family.   23
They all seemed to approve, especially when he showed he could eat pungent fish and shrimp sauce like any other Vietnamese.

During my time there I visited often with family members and talked   24
about the past. I saw the hospital where I was born, took a walk through our old house, chatted with my father's old friends. The gaps in the circle of my hyphenated life came closer together with every new Vietnamese word that I learned, with every Vietnamese friend that I made.

I also chose the fabric for the tailoring of the *ao dai*, the traditional   25
Vietnamese dress of a long tunic over flowing pants, which I would change into at the reception. I had my sisters' bridesmaid gowns made. And I had a velvet ao dai made for my 88-year-old maternal grandmother, *Bâ Ngoai*,

to wear to the wedding of her oldest grandchild. "My dream is to see you on your wedding day and eat at your wedding feast," she had told me several times.

Bâ Ngoai came to the U.S. in 1983, three years after my family landed in Orange County as war refugees. As soon as we got to the United States, my mother filed immigration papers for her. Bâ Ngoai made that journey at age 73, leaving the only home she had known to be with my mother, her only child. Bâ Ngoai nurtured and helped raise us grandchildren. 26

I had extended my stay in Vietnam. Several days after my original departure date, I received a phone call. Bâ Ngoai had died. I flew home carrying her ao dai. We buried her in it. 27

In Vietnamese tradition, one is in mourning for three years after the loss of a parent or grandparent. Out of respect and love for the deceased, or *hieu,* decorum dictates that close family members can't get married until after the mourning period is over. But my wedding was only a month and a half away. 28

On the day we buried my grandmother, my family advised me to burn the white cloth headband that symbolized my grief. By burning it, I ended my official mourning. 29

Through my tears I watched the white cloth become wispy ashes. My family was supportive. "It's your duty to remember and honor her," my father told me. "But you also need to move forward with your life." 30

On the morning of our wedding, Scott's family stood outside our house in a line bearing dowry gifts. Inside the house, Scott and I lighted incense in front of the family altar. Holding the incense between our palms, we bowed to my ancestors and asked for their blessings. I looked at the photo of Bâ Ngoai and knew she had to be smiling. 31

Thinking About the Essay

1. How do you interpret the title? What aspects of the essay does it capture?

2. There are several characters in this essay. Who are they? How are they described? What sort of persona does Ha create for herself as the "I" narrator?

3. Why does Ha begin the essay in the present and then shift to the past? Trace the narrative pattern throughout her essay.

4. Often when you write a personal essay, it is valuable to create a central conflict. What is the conflict (or conflicts) in this selection? How does Ha develop and resolve it? Does this conflict lead to a thesis? Why or why not?

5. Explain the various moods and tones that Ha imbues her narrative with. Do they "clash" or not? Are they finally reconciled? Justify your response.

Responding in Writing

6. In a brief essay, explain why Ha's essay tells us about the clash of civilizations and how we might resolve it.

7. Write a narrative essay in which you tell of a relationship in which the people come from different civilizations. You can base this essay on personal experience, the experience of family or friends, or a situation drawn from television or film.

8. Do you think that the narrator and her husband will have a happy marriage? Why or why not? Cite what you have learned about them in the essay as support for your response.

Networking

9. In a group of four, discuss the relationship between Scott and "Kyrstin" Oanh. Do you think it is healthy and viable, or do you sense potential problems? Summarize your decision for the rest of the class.

10. Search the Internet for more information on the Vietnamese boat people. Where have they settled in the United States? How do they preserve their culture and civilization? How often do they intermarry with Americans outside their background? Discuss your findings with the class.

When Afghanistan Was at Peace

MARGARET ATWOOD

Margaret Atwood, born in 1939, is a Canadian novelist, poet, short story writer, and literary critic whose work explores the troubled contours of the modern world. Atwood's second collection of poetry, *The Circle Game* (1966), was published to critical acclaim. Equally impressive is a distinguished series of novels, including *Life Before Man* (1979), *The Handmaid's Tale* (1986), *Cat's Eye* (1988), *The Blind Assassin* (2000), and *The Penelopiad* (2005). Atwood's writing often blends the intensely personal experience with global realities. In "When Afghanistan Was at Peace," published in October 2001 in *The New York Times Magazine*, Atwood describes a world ruined by clashing civilizations.

Before Reading

Reflect on what you know about Afghanistan. How many "civilizations" have attempted to conquer and control it? Why is the United States fighting in Afghanistan today? What problems do you foresee for Afghanistan's future?

In February 1978, almost 23 years ago, I visited Afghanistan with my   1
spouse, Graeme Gibson, and our 18-month-old daughter. We went
there almost by chance: we were on our way to the Adelaide literary
festival in Australia. Pausing at intervals, we felt, would surely be easier
on a child's time clock. (Wrong, as it turned out.) We thought Afghanistan would make a fascinating two-week stopover. Its military history
impressed us—neither Alexander the Great nor the British in the 19th
century had stayed in the country long because of the ferocity of its
warriors.

"Don't go to Afghanistan," my father said when told of our plans.   2
"There's going to be a war there." He was fond of reading history books.
"As Alexander the Great said, Afghanistan is easy to march into but hard
to march out of." But we hadn't heard any other rumors of war, so off we
went.

We were among the last to see Afghanistan in its days of relative   3
peace—relative, because even then there were tribal disputes and
super-powers in play. The three biggest buildings in Kabul were the
Chinese Embassy, the Soviet Embassy and the American Embassy,
and the head of the country was reportedly playing the three against
one another.

The houses of Kabul were carved wood, and the streets were like a   4
living "Book of Hours": people in flowing robes, camels, donkeys, carts
with huge wooden wheels being pushed and pulled by men at either end.
There were few motorized vehicles. Among them were buses covered with
ornate Arabic script, with eyes painted on the front so the buses could see
where they were going.

We managed to hire a car in order to see the terrain of the famous   5
and disastrous British retreat from Kabul to Jalalabad. The scenery was
breathtaking: jagged mountains and the "Arabian Nights" dwellings
in the valleys—part houses, part fortresses—reflected in the enchanted
blue-green of the rivers. Our driver took the switchback road at
breakneck speed since we had to be back before sundown because of
bandits.

The men we encountered were friendly and fond of children: our curly-   6
headed, fair-haired child got a lot of attention. The winter coat I wore
had a large hood so that I was sufficiently covered and did not attract
undue notice. Many wanted to talk; some knew English, while others spoke
through our driver. But they all addressed Graeme exclusively. To have
spoken to me would have been impolite. And yet when our interpreter
negotiated our entry into an all-male teahouse, I received nothing worse
than uneasy glances. The law of hospitality toward visitors ranked higher

than the no-women-in-the-teahouse custom. In the hotel, those who served meals and cleaned rooms were men, tall men with scars either from dueling or from the national sport, played on horseback, in which gaining possession of a headless calf is the aim.

Girls and women we glimpsed on the street wore the chador, the   7
long, pleated garment with a crocheted grill for the eyes that is more comprehensive than any other Muslim cover-up. At that time, you often saw chic boots and shoes peeking out from the hem. The chador wasn't obligatory back then; Hindu women didn't wear it. It was a cultural custom, and since I had grown up hearing that you weren't decently dressed without a girdle and white gloves, I thought I could understand such a thing. I also knew that clothing is a symbol, that all symbols are ambiguous and that this one might signify a fear of women or a desire to protect them from the gaze of strangers. But it could also mean more negative things, just as the color red can mean love, blood, life, royalty, good luck—or sin.

I bought a chador in the market. A jovial crowd of men gathered   8
around, amused by the spectacle of a Western woman picking out such a non-Western item. They offered advice about color and quality. Purple was better than light green or the blue, they said. (I bought the purple.) Every writer wants the Cloak of Invisibility—the power to see without being seen—or so I was thinking as I donned the chador. But once I had put it on, I had an odd sense of having been turned into negative space, a blank in the visual field, a sort of antimatter—both there and not there. Such a space has power of a sort, but it is a passive power, the power of taboo.

Several weeks after we left Afghanistan, the war broke out. My father   9
was right, after all. Over the next years, we often remembered the people we met and their courtesy and curiosity. How many of them are now dead, through no fault of their own?

Six years after our trip, I wrote *The Handmaid's Tale*, a speculative fic-   10
tion about an American theocracy. The women in that book wear outfits derived in part from nuns' costumes, partly from girls' schools' hemlines and partly—I must admit—from the faceless woman on the Old Dutch Cleanser box, but also partly from the chador I acquired in Afghanistan and its conflicting associations. As one character says, there is freedom to and freedom from. But how much of the first should you have to give up in order assuring the second? All cultures have had to grapple with that and our own—as we are now seeing—is no exception. Would I have written

the book if I never had visited Afghanistan? Possibly. Would it have been the same? Unlikely.

Thinking About the Essay

1. Does Atwood provide a thesis sentence in this essay? Why or why not? How does her title imply a thesis? If you were writing a thesis sentence of your own for this essay, what would it be?

2. What is Atwood's purpose in writing this narrative essay? Consider that this essay was published shortly after the events of 9/11. Is narration an appropriate strategy for her purpose? Why or why not?

3. Narrative essays typically use description to flesh out the story. Find descriptive details that Atwood provides, and explain what these details contribute to the overall effect.

4. Analyze the point of view in this essay. Is Atwood an observer, a participant, or both? Is she neutral or involved? Support your opinion.

5. Consider the relationship of the introductory paragraphs to the conclusion. Why does Atwood use the introduction and conclusion to expand the time frame of her main narrative?

Responding in Writing

6. Write an editorial for your college newspaper supporting or attacking the role of Western powers in Afghanistan today.

7. Imagine that you are traveling to Afghanistan on assignment for a newspaper. Report back, telling readers about what you see and where you go. Feel free to research the subject prior to writing the essay.

8. What does Atwood say about the clash of civilizations in this essay? Answer this question by analyzing the strategies she uses to convey her thesis.

Networking

9. In groups of two or three, pool your knowledge of Afghanistan. Prepare a brief report to be presented to the class.

10. In her essay, Atwood alludes to some of the nations and civilizations that have tried to conquer Afghanistan over the centuries. For research, conduct a library or Internet search on the history of Afghanistan, and how it has been a crossroads in the clash of civilizations. Prepare a brief report on your findings.

"Battlestar" Apocalypse

MIKAL GILMORE

Mikal Gilmore, who was born in Portland, Oregon, in 1951 and who attended Portland State University, has been writing for *Rolling Stone* magazine for more than twenty years. Gilmore chronicles his family's turbulent and violent life (one of his brothers was the executed murderer Gary Gilmore) in his award-winning memoir *Shot in the Heart* (1994). His essays, profiles, and interviews conducted for *Rolling Stone, Los Angeles Weekly,* and *Los Angeles Herald Examiner* are collected in *Night Beat: A Shadow History of Rock and Roll* (1998). Gilmore also has published *Stories Done: Writings on the 1960s and Its Discontents* (2008). In this essay from the March 19, 2009, issue of *Rolling Stone,* Gilmore analyzes and evaluates the popular sci-fi television show *Battlestar Galactica* and what this series might tell us about the future of civilization here on Earth.

Before Reading

How do you explain the popularity of science fiction? Might one possibility be that science fiction encourages us to speculate on the state of civilization—both here and elsewhere?

The final season of *Battlestar Galactica* (which comes to its close on March 20th on the Sci Fi Channel) began in the darkest of places. The survivors of Colonial humankind—who had fled across the universe after their civilization was destroyed by a race of unforgiving androids, the Cylons—finally found Earth, the place of deliverance promised by their scriptures, with the help of some of their enemies. Now, humans and Cylons stand on the shore of a city in ruins, dig their fingers through its devastated soil and come to discover that Earth is a nuclear wasteland, uninhabitable. Everything these people have fought and died for, everything they believed in, ends up a blasted dream. They have no prospect of a home or refuge. All that, in this season premiere's first few moments. 1

The repercussions of their despair hit fast. Some in the Colonial Fleet so resent having made any peace with the former enemy that they attempt a coup. Others commit suicide. The Galactica itself is groaning under its age. It's falling apart, like the desolate community it protects. Nothing has 2 seemed to work out for these exiles, and the more prescient among them feel that something dark and decisive is bearing down on them. "This was inherent in the premise of the show," says Ron Moore, who along with David Eick is an executive producer on the series, and its chief creative force. "These people went through a literal apocalypse. Billions of lives were lost, their civilization is destroyed, they run away in these metal cans out in deep space, and they have just the clothes on their back, and they've got an enemy that is relentlessly pursuing them. You could never lose sight of that. If you did, the jeopardy would fall away, and ultimately it wouldn't be real anymore."

Eick and Moore began planning *Battlestar Galactica* in its present 3 form (an earlier version aired in the 1970s, and derived from the weird and amazing tenets of Mormon cosmology) after the attacks of September 11th, 2001. It was always their design for the show to reflect the fears and changes wrought in our national mind-set by that day. Other TV dramas— including *24* and *Lost*—also mined the reverberations of those events, but what has set *Battlestar Galactica* apart is its insistence on rising to the occasion, its willingness to unflinchingly face the complex horrors of our past several years. In the early moments of the show's 2003 introductory miniseries, the weatherworn Commander Adama, played by Edward James Olmos, delivered some extraordinary remarks: "When we fought the Cylons," he said, "we did it to save ourselves from extinction. But we never answered the question 'Why?' Why are we as a people worth saving? We refuse to accept responsibility for anything we've done, like we did with the Cylons. . . . Sooner or later, the day comes when you can't hide from the things you've done anymore."

"It was important to us that this show be as truthful as it could to the 4 things we were all experiencing in the culture after 9/11," says Moore. "All the moral dilemmas, all the ethical questions that we've posed hearken back to that central idea: What kind of people do we hope to be?"

This isn't to say that *Battlestar Galactica* has worked simply as veiled 5 commentary on the maleficence of Al Qaeda or the damage wrought by the Bush administration. "As we got into the project," says Moore, "it felt wrong to say we can give you the answer to Islamic terrorism or Iraq in 44 minutes." Indeed, the show has never attempted to work as diatribe or as moral parable. If anything, it's played foremost as character-driven drama about fucked-up people (as well as several fucked-up nonpeople). Still, nothing else produced by this decade's popular culture has so effectively delineated modern American tragedy. The series has proved far more than peerless science fiction: It's an epic of conscience, about troubled democratic and religious people in a time of democratic and religious troubles.

But in the unforgiving universe of *Battlestar Galactica*, consciences   6
of any sort never rest easy. It is not a show about absolutism. There's
nothing simply black and white; there's always a more complex agony at
work. As the stories have unfolded, easy sympathies and identifications
have broken down. In the early seasons, we identified ourselves among
the remaining Colonials, who were not only humans fighting for survival
of their species but were also equivalent Americans, trying to hold on to
the democratic values in the midst of apocalypse. The Cylons, by contrast, were the vengeful force trying to annihilate Western civilization.
"They were the Other," says Moore. "They were just the enemy, they
were out there, they were relentless, you couldn't stop them, they seemed
all-powerful." Over time, though, some Cylons became more caring and
intervened to save humanity. Meanwhile, various humans among the
Fleet acted at times to subvert what was left of their culture's democracy,
and unhesitantly tortured Cylons, or summarily cast them out of the
ships' air locks into the forever night of space. Far more hazardous turns,
though, took place in the third season, after the Colonials settled onto
a planet they called New Caprica, where the Cylons subsequently found
and occupied them.

It was in this passage that *Battlestar Galactica* hit its most remarkable   7
stride. Some Colonials were imprisoned and tortured, some collaborated
with the Cylons, and others turned to violent resistance, including suicide
bombings that sometimes killed their own. When the case-hardened Colo-
nel Tigh (Michael Hogan) expresses regret at not being able to bomb a
marketplace, Chief Galen Tyrol (Aaron Douglas) points out that the market would have been busy with more humans than Cylons and tells Tigh
that the Resistance needs to figure out which side it's on. "We're on the
side of the demons, Chief," Tigh replies. "We're evil men in the gardens of
paradise, sent by the forces of death to spread devastation and destruction
wherever we go. I'm surprised you didn't know that."

Watching those episodes—which may well be the heart and soul of   8
the entire series—we were watching a revelatory history of the unspoken
realities and complexities of the past eight years. Our identity was now
with what one Cylon calls the "frakkin' insurgents." Simultaneously, the
Cylon occupiers displayed an arrogance and wrongheaded resolve that
seemed all too familiar. The way these shocking inversions were set up
by the show's creators is perhaps the most subversive feat in television
history.

"I thought that I was going to catch a lot of flak for that from the   9
network," says Moore, "but to my pleasant surprise they didn't even raise
an eyebrow. It was about trying to be truthful. What do human beings

to in circumstances like this? It was a great opportunity to put before the audience an idea and a point of view that they just don't see on American television."

Now, after having escaped New Caprica and after discovering that   10
some among them were unknowingly Cylons all along, after a ruinous rebellion, and after many Cylons have earned full citizenship alongside the Fleet's humans, things still look unsalvageable for these people—the series remaining threats and mysteries seem insurmountable. Can the rapidly decaying ship repair itself? What chances does the Fleet stand if that faction of unreconciled Cylons catches up with them? Is there a savior among them who can redeem everybody, or must they all—Colonials and Cylons—accept that their problems can never be solved? Will their alleged gods save some and finish others?

Moore says it all goes back to that original premise: "It would just be   11
one heartache after another for these people. That was the trail of tears that they were on.

"But it all does wrap up," he continues. "I'm pretty satisfied that I've   12
answered all the questions I wanted to answer by the end. There were some things left ambiguous, but those are minor chords. The central narrative of it comes to a conclusion, and the episodes we're telling now were all designed to get us to the end."

Then, a few weeks from now, it all begins again, with *Caprica*, the   13
new *Battlestar Galactica* spinoff series about how the humans created the Cylons and their own destruction in the first place.

Thinking About the Essay

1. What assumptions does Gilmore make about his target audience in this essay? How does he manage to make the essay comprehensible for those readers who might never have tuned in on *Battlestar Galactica*?

2. What is Gilmore's claim in this essay? Does he state this claim in one place or several places? Explain. What evidence does he provide to support his claim? Do you find his argument to be persuasive? Why or why not?

3. Where does Gilmore use the word "civilization" in this essay? Why is this word a possible key to the writer's claim?

4. Film and television critics normally provide both an analysis of their subject and an evaluation of it. Does Gilmore think that *Battlestar Galactica* is a bad, good, or great series? How do you know?

5. Assess Gilmore's conclusion. Do you think that his ending is superfluous, or does it contribute some new element to the analysis? Explain.

Responding in Writing

6. Write an essay analyzing the ways in which film can effectively inform an audience about the state of contemporary civilization. Refer to specific films and/or television series to support your analysis.

7. In a brief essay, explain why Gilmore alludes to 9/11, the Bush administration, and recent events in his article. Evaluate the success or failure of this strategy.

8. Write an essay on a specific film genre—for example, the Western, spy movies, or horror films—and how this movie type illuminates the clash of civilizations.

Networking

9. In small discussion groups, discuss *Battleship Galactica* as a series illuminating the clash of civilizations, basing your discussion on Gilmore's essay and also what group members know about this series. Have one member present a summary of your discussion to the class.

10. *Battleship Galactica* prompted a forum hosted by the United Nations in 2009. Go online to locate information on this forum, and analyze your findings in a brief essay.

Fundamentalism Is Here to Stay

KAREN ARMSTRONG

Karen Armstrong is one of the most highly regarded commentators on religion in North America and Europe. She currently teaches Christianity at the Leo Baeck College Centre for Jewish Education in London. Armstrong joined a Catholic convent at the age of seventeen but left her order after seven years. Her experience as a nun, and her departure from the Catholic Church, are recounted in the autobiographical *Through the Narrow Gates* (1982). Armstrong now describes herself as a "freelance monotheist" and compares religion to a raft: "Once you get across the river, moor the raft and go on. Don't lug it with you if you don't need it anymore." Armstrong's recent books include *The Battle for God: A History of Fundamentalism* (2001), *Islam: A Short History* (2001), and *The Great Transformation: The Beginning of Our Religious Traditions* (2006). In the following essay, which appeared on *globalagendamagazine.com* in 2005, Armstrong defines religious fundamentalism as a reaction to—and a clash with—the perceived values of a secular modernity.

Before Reading

How do you define *fundamentalism*? Do you see the fundamentalist impulse as a feature common to all religions? Are there differences in degree or kind?

In the middle of the 20th century, it was generally assumed that secularism was the coming ideology and that religion would never again play a major role in world events. Today, religion dominates the headlines, and this is due in no small part to the militant piety that has developed in every single major world faith over the past century. 1

We usually call it "fundamentalism." Fundamentalist groups have staged revolutions, assassinated presidents, carried out terrorist atrocities and become an influential political force in strongly secularist nations. There has, for example, been much discussion about the role of Protestant fundamentalism in the recent American elections. It is no longer possible to dismiss fundamentalism as a passing phase. 2

Fundamentalism Is Not . . .

We should begin by defining what fundamentalism is not. First, it should not be equated with religious conservatism. Leading American religious revivalist Billy Graham, for example, is not a fundamentalist. 3

Second, fundamentalism should not be linked automatically with violence. Only a tiny proportion of fundamentalists worldwide take part in acts of terror. The rest are simply struggling to live what they regard as a good religious life in a world that seems increasingly inimical to faith. 4

Third, fundamentalism is not an exclusively Islamic phenomenon. There are fundamentalist Jews, Christians, Hindus, Buddhists, Sikhs and Confucians, who all challenge the secular hegemony of the modern world. In fact, Islam developed a fundamentalist strain long after it had erupted in Judaism and Christianity. 5

Fundamentalism Is . . .

So what is fundamentalism? It is essentially a revolt against modern secular society. Wherever a western polity has been established that separates religion and politics, fundamentalist movements have sprung up in protest. Whatever the politicians or the pundits claim, people worldwide are demonstrating that they want to see religion reflected more prominently in public life. As part of their campaign, fundamentalists tend to withdraw from mainstream society to create enclaves of pure faith. 6

Typical examples are the Ultra-orthodox Jewish communities in   7
New York or the fundamentalist Christianity of Bob Jones University in
South Carolina. Here fundamentalists build a counterculture, in conscious
defiance of the godless world that surrounds them, and from these
communities some undertake a counteroffensive designed to drag God
or religion back to centre stage from the wings to which they have been
relegated in modern secular culture.

This campaign is rarely violent. It usually consists of a propaganda or   8
welfare effort. In the United States, for example, the fundamentalist riposte
attempts to reform school textbooks or to get Christian candidates elected
to government posts. But if warfare is endemic in a region and has
become chronic—as in the Middle East or Afghanistan—fundamentalists
can get sucked into the violence that pervades the whole of society. In this
way, originally secular disputes such as the Arab-Israeli conflict have been
sacralized, on both sides.

The Road to Modernity

The ubiquity of the fundamentalist revolt shows that there is widespread   9
disappointment with modernity. But what is it about the modern world
that has provoked such rage and distress? In the 16th century, the peoples
of the west began to develop a new type of civilization unprecedented in
world history. Instead of basing their economy on a surplus of agricultural
produce, as did all premodern cultures, they relied increasingly on technology and the constant reinvestment of capital, which freed them from the
inherent limitations of agrarian society. This demanded radical change at
all levels of society—intellectual, political, social and religious. A wholly
new way of thinking became essential, and new forms of government
had to evolve to meet these altered conditions. It was found by trial and
error that the best way of creating a productive society was to create a
secular, tolerant, democratic polity.

It took Europe some 300 years to modernize, and the process was   10
wrenching and traumatic, involving bloody revolutions, often succeeded
by reigns of terror, brutal holy wars, dictatorships, cruel exploitation of the
workforce, the despoliation of the countryside, and widespread alienation
and anomie.

We are now witnessing the same kind of upheaval in developing coun-   11
tries presently undergoing modernization. But some of these countries have
had to attempt this difficult process far too rapidly and are forced to follow
a western programmed, rather than their own.

This accelerated modernization has created deep divisions in developing   12
nations. Only elite has a western education that enables them to understand

the new modern institutions. The vast majority remains trapped in the premodern ethos. They experience the incomprehensible change as profoundly disturbing, and cling to traditional religion for support. But as modernization progresses, people find that they cannot be religious in the old way and try to find new means of expressing their piety. Fundamentalism is just one of these attempts, and it therefore develops only after a degree of modernization has been achieved.

The modern spirit that developed in the west had two essential   13
characteristics: independence and innovation. Modernization in Europe and America proceeded by declarations of independence on all fronts—religious, political and intellectual—as scientists and inventors demanded the freedom to develop their ideas without interference from religious or political authorities. Further, despite the trauma of modernization, it was exciting, because the western countries were continually meeting new challenges and creating something fresh. But in some developing countries, modernization came not with independence, but with colonial dependence and subjugation, and the west was so far ahead that these could not innovate but only imitate. So they find it difficult to develop a truly modern spirit. A nation such as Japan, which was not colonized, was able to make its own distinctive contribution to the modern economy in a way that some Middle Eastern countries have not been able to do.

A Fight for Survival

Culture is always contested, and fundamentalists are primarily concerned   14
with saving their own society. Protestant fundamentalists in the United States want America to be a truly Christian nation, not a secular, pluralist republic. In Palestine, Hamas began by attacking the Palestine Liberation Organization, because it wanted the Palestinian resistance to be inspired by an Islamic rather than a secular polity. Osama bin Laden started by targeting the Saudi royal family and such secularist rulers as Saddam Hussein. Only at a secondary stage—if at all—do fundamentalists begin to attack a foreign foe. Thus fundamentalism does not represent a clash between civilizations, but a clash within civilizations.

Perhaps the most important factor to understand about this   15
widespread religious militancy is its rootedness in a deep fear of annihilation. Every fundamentalist movement I have studied in Judaism, Christianity and Islam is convinced that modern secular society wants to wipe out religion—even in America. Fundamentalists, therefore, believe they are fighting for survival, and when people feel that their backs are to the wall, some can strike out violently. This profound

terror of annihilation is not as paranoid as it may at first appear. Jewish fundamentalism, for example, gained fresh momentum after World War II, when Hitler had tried to exterminate European Jewry, and after the 1973 October War, when Israelis felt vulnerable and isolated in the Middle East.

In some Muslim countries, modernization has usually been so acceler- 16
ated that secularism has been experienced as an assault. When Mustafa Kemal Ataturk created modern secular Turkey, he closed down all the madrasahs (traditional institutes for higher education in Islamic studies) and abolished the Sufi orders. He also forced all men and women to wear Western dress. Reformers such as Ataturk wanted their countries to look modern. In Iran, the shahs used to make their soldiers walk through the streets with their bayonets out, tearing off women's veils and ripping them to pieces. In 1935, Shah Reza Pahlavi gave his soldiers orders to shoot at unarmed demonstrators in Mashhad (one of the holiest shrines in Iran), who were peacefully protesting against obligatory Western clothes. Hundreds of Iranians died that day. In such circumstances, secularism was not experienced as liberating and civilized, but as wicked, lethal and murderously hostile to faith.

The main fundamentalist ideology of Sunni Islam developed in the 17
concentration camps in Egypt in which president Jamal Abd al-Nasser had incarcerated thousands of members of the Muslim Brotherhood in the late 1950s, without trial and often for doing nothing more incriminating than attending a meeting or handing out leaflets. One of these prisoners was Sayyid Qutb, who was executed by Nasser in 1966. Qutb went into the camp as a moderate and a liberal. But in these vile prisons, watching the Brothers being executed and subjected to mental and physical torture, and hearing Nasser vowing to relegate Islam to a marginal role in Egypt, he came to regard secularism as a great evil. He developed an ideology of committed armed struggle against this threat to the faith. His chief disciple today is Osama bin Laden.

Thus fundamentalism usually develops in a symbiotic relationship 18
with a secularism that is experienced as hostile and invasive. Every fundamentalist movement I have studied in each of the three monotheistic traditions has developed in direct response to what is perceived as a secularist attack. The more vicious the assault, the more extreme the fundamentalist riposte is likely to be. Because fundamentalists fear that secularists want to destroy them, aggressive and military action will only serve to confirm this conviction and exacerbate their fear, which can spill over into ungovernable rage.

Thus membership of al-Qaeda has increased since the recent Gulf   19
War. The offensive has convinced many Muslims that the West has
really inaugurated a new crusade against the Islamic world. In the
United States, Protestant fundamentalists in the smaller towns and rural
areas often feel "colonized" by the alien ethos of Harvard, Yale and
Washington, DC. They feel that the liberal establishment despises them,
and this has resulted in a fundamentalism that has gone way beyond
Jerry Falwell and the Moral Majority of the 1970s. (Falwell is an
American fundamentalist Baptist pastor, televangelist and founder of the
Moral Majority—a group dedicated to promoting its conservative and
religious Christian-centric beliefs via support of political candidates.)
Some groups, such as the Christian Reconstructionists, look forward to
the imminent destruction of the federal government; the blazing towers
of the World Trade Center would not be alien to their ideology. When
liberals deplore the development and persistence of fundamentalism
in their own societies and worldwide, they should be aware that the
excesses of secularists have all too often been responsible for this radical
alienation.

Here to Stay

Fundamentalism is not going to disappear, as secularists once imagined   20
that religion would modestly retreat to the sidelines and confine itself to
private life. Fundamentalism is here to stay, and in Judaism, Christianity
and Islam, at least, it is becoming more extreme. Fundamentalism is not
confined to the "other" civilizations. A dangerous gulf has appeared,
dividing many societies against themselves. In the Middle East, India,
Pakistan, Israel and the United States, for example, fundamentalists and
secular liberals form two distinct camps, neither of which can understand
the other.

   In the past, these movements were often dismissed with patrician   21
disdain. This has proved to be short-sighted. We have to take fundamentalism very seriously. Had the US made a greater effort to understand
Shiite Islam, for example, it might have avoided unnecessary errors in the
lead-up to the Iranian Revolution of 1978 to 79. The first step must be
to look beneath the bizarre and often repulsive ideology of these movements to discern the disquiet and anger that lie at their roots. We must
no longer deride these theologies as the fantasies of a lunatic fringe, but
learn to decode their ideas and imagery. Only then can we deal creatively
with fears and anxieties that, as we have seen to our cost, no society can
safely ignore.

Thinking About the Essay

1. Why does Armstrong define fundamentalism first by stating what it is *not*? How do you respond to this tactic as a reader?

2. Where does Armstrong shift in the essay from definition to process analysis? How does Armstrong link the historical and economic factors that gave rise to modernity with the secular values that came to be associated with modernity? How is fundamentalism a response to modernity as both a process and a set of values?

3. Why does Armstrong make a point, throughout the essay, of dissociating the concept of fundamentalism from violence?

4. What examples does Armstrong give to acknowledge the militancy of twentieth-century attempts at rapid modernization? Do these examples strengthen or weaken her definition of fundamentalism? How has Armstrong prepared for this acknowledgment earlier in the essay?

5. Describe the symbiotic relationship between fundamentalist terrorism and secular modernity.

Responding in Writing

6. Respond to the term *militant piety,* which some would read as an oxymoron. How can piety take this form? In a brief essay, consider some examples of militant piety and explain why the term would, in your opinion, apply in each case.

7. Fundamentalism, according to Armstrong, "does not represent a clash between civilizations, but a clash within civilizations." How does Armstrong's concept of fundamentalism refute or qualify Samuel P. Huntington's "clash of cultures" theory? In an evaluative essay, point to some limitations that you see in both theories.

8. In a brief essay, offer some advice to American foreign policymakers on how to promote modernization in a Middle Eastern nation (like Iraq) so that it would not be experienced or perceived as an "assault."

Networking

9. In groups of three or four, make a list of three religious leaders or public figures in the United States whose views everyone in the group agrees would qualify as "fundamentalist" (according to Armstrong's definition). Share the list with the class, and justify the application of the label to each person on the list.

10. Go online and read at least three reviews of Armstrong's *The Battle for God: A History of Fundamentalism.* Do any of the reviewers take exception to her definition of *fundamentalism*?

The West and the Rest: Intercivilizational Issues

SAMUEL P. HUNTINGTON

Samuel Phillips Huntington was born in New York City in 1927. He received his education at Yale University (B.A., 1946), the University of Chicago (M.A., 1948), and Harvard University (Ph.D., 1951). A leading authority on international affairs, Huntington worked and consulted for numerous government and private organizations, including the National Security Council, the National War College, and the Office of the Secretary of Defense. He was professor of government at Harvard University and director of its Center for Strategic Studies up to the time of his death in 2008. Among his many books are *The Soldier and the State* (1957), *Political Order in Changing Societies* (1968), *American Military Strategy* (1986), and *The Clash of Civilizations and the Remaking of World Order* (1996), from which this essay is taken.

Before Reading

Do you think that Western civilization is under assault from Islamic, Chinese, or other civilizations? Why or why not?

Western Universalism

In the emerging world, the relations between states and groups from different civilizations will not be close and will often be antagonistic. Yet some intercivilization relations are more conflict-prone than others. At the micro level, the most violent fault lines are between Islam and its Orthodox, Hindu, African, and Western Christian neighbors. At the macro level, the dominant division is between "the West and the rest," with the most intense conflicts occurring between Muslim and Asian societies on the one hand, and the West on the other. The dangerous clashes of the future are likely to arise from the interaction of Western arrogance, Islamic intolerance, and Sinic assertiveness. 1

Alone among civilizations the West has had a major and at times devastating impact on every other civilization. The relation between the power and culture of the West and the power and cultures of other civilizations is, as a result, the most pervasive characteristic of the world 2 of civilizations. As the relative power of other civilizations increases, the appeal of Western culture fades and non-Western peoples have increasing confidence in and commitment to their indigenous cultures. The central problem in the relations between the West and the rest is, consequently, the discordance between the West's—particularly America's—efforts to promote a universal Western culture and its declining ability to do so.

The collapse of communism exacerbated this discordance by rein-   3
forcing in the West the view that its ideology of democratic liberalism had triumphed globally and hence was universally valid. The West, and especially the United States, which has always been a missionary nation, believe that the non-Western peoples should commit themselves to the Western values of democracy, free markets, limited government, human rights, individualism, the rule of law, and should embody these values in their institutions. Minorities in other civilizations embrace and promote these values, but the dominant attitudes toward them in non-Western cultures range from widespread skepticism to intense opposition. What is universalism to the West is imperialism to the rest.

The West is attempting and will continue to attempt to sustain its   4
preeminent position and defend its interests by defining those interests as the interests of the "world community." That phrase has become the euphemistic collective noun (replacing "the Free World") to give global legitimacy to actions reflecting the interests of the United States and other Western powers. The West is, for instance, attempting to integrate the economies of non-Western societies into a global economic system which it dominates. Through the IMF and other international economic institutions, the West promotes its economic interests and imposes on other nations the economic policies it thinks appropriate. In any poll of non-Western peoples, however, the IMF undoubtedly would win the support of finance ministers and a few others but get an overwhelmingly unfavorable rating from almost everyone else, who would agree with Georgi Arbatov's description of IMF officials as "neo-Bolsheviks who love expropriating other people's money, imposing undemocratic and alien rules of economic and political conduct and stifling economic freedom."[1]

Non-Westerners also do not hesitate to point to the gaps between Western   5
principle and Western action. Hypocrisy, double standards, and "but nots" are the price of Universalist pretensions. Democracy is promoted but not if it brings Islamic fundamentalists to power; nonproliferation is preached for Iran and Iraq but not for Israel; free trade is the elixir of economic growth but not for agriculture; human rights are an issue with China but not with Saudi Arabia; aggression against oil-owning Kuwaitis is massively repulsed

---

1 Georgi Arbatov, "Neo-Bolsheviks of the I.M.F.," *New York Times*, 7 May 1992, p. A27.

but not against non-oil-owning Bosnians. Double standards in practice are the unavoidable price of universal standards of principle.

Having achieved political independence, non-Western societies wish to free 6 themselves from Western economic, military, and cultural domination. East Asian societies are well on their way to equaling the West economically. Asian and Islamic countries are looking for shortcuts to balance the West militarily. The universal aspirations of Western civilization, the declining relative power of the West, and the increasing cultural assertiveness of other civilizations ensure generally difficult relations between the West and the rest. The nature of those relations and the extent to which they are antagonistic, however, vary considerably and fall into three categories. With the challenger civilizations, Islam and China, the West is likely to have consistently strained and often highly antagonistic relations. Its relations with Latin America and Africa, weaker civilizations which have in some measure been dependent on the West, will involve much lower levels of conflict, particularly with Latin America. The relations of Russia, Japan, and India to the West are likely to fall between those of the other two groups, involving elements of cooperation and conflict, as these three core states at times line up with the challenger civilizations and at times side with the West. They are the "swing" civilizations between the West, on the one hand, and Islamic and Sinic civilizations, on the other.

Islam and China embody great cultural traditions very different from and 7 in their eyes infinitely superior to that of the West. The power and assertiveness of both in relation to the West are increasing, and the conflicts between their values and interests and those of the West are multiplying and becoming more intense. Because Islam lacks a core state, its relations with the West vary greatly from country to country. Since the 1970s, however, a fairly consistent anti-Western trend has existed, marked by the rise of fundamentalism, shifts in power within Muslim countries from more pro-Western to more anti-Western governments, the emergence of a quasi war between some Islamic groups and the West, and the weakening of the Cold War security ties that existed between some Muslim states and the United States. Underlying the differences on specific issues is the fundamental question of the role these civilizations will play relative to the West in shaping the future of the world. Will the global institutions, the distribution of power, and the politics and economies of nations in the twenty-first century primarily reflect Western values and interests or will they be shaped primarily by those of Islam and China? ...

The issues that divide the West and these other societies are increasingly 8 important on the international agenda. Three such issues involve the efforts of the West: (1) to maintain its military superiority through policies of nonproliferation and counter proliferation with respect to nuclear, biological, and chemical weapons and the means to deliver them; (2) to promote Western political values and institutions by pressing other societies to respect human rights as conceived in the West and to adopt democracy on Western lines; and (3) to protect the cultural, social, and ethnic integrity of Western societies by restricting the number of non-Westerners admitted as immigrants or refugees. In all three areas the West has had and is likely to continue to have difficulties defending its interests against those of non-Western societies. . . .

The changing balance of power among civilizations makes it more and more difficult for the West to achieve its goals with respect to weapons proliferation, human rights, immigration, and other issues. To minimize its losses in this situation requires the West to wield skillfully its economic resources as carrots and sticks in dealing with other societies, to bolster its unity and coordinate its policies so as to make it more difficult for other societies to play one Western country off against another, and to promote and exploit differences among non-Western nations. The West's ability to pursue these strategies will be shaped by the nature and intensity of its conflicts with the challenger civilizations, on the one hand, and the extent to which it can identify and develop common interests with the swing civilizations, on the other.

9

Thinking About the Essay

1. How would you characterize the tone of this essay? Does Huntington present himself as argumentative, opinioned, objective, fair-minded, liberal, conservative, or what? Identify words, sentences, and passages that support your assessment of the writer's voice.

2. Summarize Huntington's argument. What is his thesis or claim? What types of support does he provide?

3. What aspects of Huntington's language tell you that he writes for an audience that can follow his rapid sweep of the civilizations and institutions of the world? To what extent does he employ "loaded" language to advance his argument? Explain.

4. Huntington employs numerous rhetorical strategies to develop his argument, among them comparison and contrast, classification, and illustration. Locate examples of these strategies in the essay.

5. What, in Huntington's view, is the answer to the clash of civilizations? How does he prepare the reader for his answer? Trace the "logic" of his answer through the essay.

Responding in Writing

6. Compare and contrast the essays by D'Souza and Huntington. Establish a clear thesis concerning their views about the conflict of civilizations, and the different ways they approach the subject. Develop at least three key topics.

7. Do you agree or disagree with Huntington's analysis and argument? Explain your response in an argumentative paper of your own.

8. Respond in an analytical essay to Huntington's statement, "Alone among civilizations the West has had a major and at times devastating impact on every other civilization."

Networking

9. Discuss Huntington's essay in groups of three or four. Draw up a list of all the key elements in his argument. Then join a general class discussion on why his argument has caused so much controversy.

10. Go online and conduct an advanced search on "Samuel Huntington" AND "Clash of Civilizations." How has the debate developed since the time Huntington first published his ideas? Summarize the controversy in a brief paper.

A World Not Neatly Divided

AMARTYA SEN

Amartya K. Sen, the 1998 Nobel Prize winner in economics, was born in 1933 in Santiniketan, India. After studying at Presidency College in Calcutta, Sen emigrated to England, where he received B.A. (1955), M.A., and Ph.D. (1959) degrees from Trinity College, Cambridge. Master of Trinity College since 1998, Sen also has taught at Oxford University, the London School of Economics, Harvard University, and Cornell University. Sen is credited with bringing ethical considerations into the study of economics. He has done groundbreaking work in establishing techniques for assessing world poverty and the relative wealth of nations, the causes of famine, and the economic impact of health and education on developing societies. His study, *Collective Choice and Social Welfare* (1970), in which he uses the tools of economics to study such concepts as fairness, liberty, and justice, brings to economic theory a dimension of moral philosophy that has made Sen an influential figure in contemporary thought. Other notable works include *Poverty and Famines: An Essay on Entitlement and Deprivation* (1981), *On Ethics and Economics* (1987), *Development as Freedom* (1999), and *The Argumentative Indian: Writings on Indian History, Culture and Identity* (2005). As this essay from *The New York Times*, November 23, 2001, demonstrates that Sen commands a lucid prose style that enables him to make complex issues accessible to general readers. Here, he argues for a more nuanced approach to the idea of civilization than the one posed by Samuel Huntington.

Before Reading

Is it necessary to divide the world into various types of civilizations? What is the purpose of such classification, and what are the possible results?

When people talk about clashing civilizations, as so many politicians and academics do now, they can sometimes miss the central issue. The inadequacy of this thesis begins well before we get to the question of whether civilizations must clash. The basic weakness of the theory lies in its program of categorizing people of the world according to a unique, allegedly commanding system of classification. This is problematic because civilizational categories are crude and inconsistent and also because there are other ways of seeing people (linked to politics, language, literature, class, occupation or other affiliations). 1

The befuddling influence of a singular classification also traps those who dispute the thesis of a clash: To talk about "the Islamic world" or "the Western world" is already to adopt an impoverished vision of humanity as unalterably divided. In fact, civilizations are hard to partition in this way, given the diversities within each society as well as the linkages among different countries and cultures. For example, describing India as a "Hindu civilization" misses the fact that India has more Muslims than any other country except Indonesia and possibly Pakistan. It is futile to try to understand Indian art, literature, music, food or politics without seeing the extensive interactions across barriers of religious communities. These include Hindus and Muslims, Buddhists, Jains, Sikhs, Parsees, Christians (who have been in India since at least the fourth century, well before England's conversion to Christianity), Jews (present since the fall of Jerusalem), and even atheists and agnostics. Sanskrit has a larger atheistic literature than exists in any other classical language. Speaking of India as a Hindu civilization may be comforting to the Hindu fundamentalist, but it is an odd reading of India. 2

A similar coarseness can be seen in the other categories invoked, like "the Islamic world." Consider Akbar and Aurangzeb, two Muslim emperors of the Mogul dynasty in India. Aurangzeb tried hard to convert Hindus into Muslims and instituted various policies in that direction, of which taxing the non-Muslims was only one example. In contrast, Akbar reveled in his multiethnic court and pluralist laws, and issued official proclamations insisting that no one "should be interfered with on account of religion" and that "anyone is to be allowed to go over to a religion that pleases him." 3

If a homogeneous view of Islam were to be taken, then only one of these emperors could count as a true Muslim. The Islamic fundamentalist would 4

Amartya Sen, "A World Not Neatly Divided," THE NEW YORK TIMES, November 23, 2001. Copyright © 2001, The New York Times. Reprinted by permission.

have no time for Akbar; Prime Minister Tony Blair, given his insistence that tolerance is a defining characteristic of Islam, would have to consider excommunicating Aurangzeb. I expect both Akbar and Aurangzeb would protest, and so would I. A similar crudity is present in the characterization of what is called "Western civilization." Tolerance and individual freedom have certainly been present in European history. But there is no dearth of diversity here, either. When Akbar was making his pronouncements on religious tolerance in Agra, in the 1590's, the Inquisitions were still going on; in 1600, Giordano Bruno was burned at the stake, for heresy, in Campo dei Fiori in Rome.

Dividing the world into discrete civilizations is not just crude. It propels   5
us into the absurd belief that this partitioning is natural and necessary and must overwhelm all other ways of identifying people. That imperious view goes not only against the sentiment that "we human beings are all much the same," but also against the more plausible understanding that we are diversely different. For example, Bangladesh's split from Pakistan was not connected with religion, but with language and politics.

Each of us has many features in our self-conception. Our religion,   6
important as it may be, cannot be an all-engulfing identity. Even a shared poverty can be a source of solidarity across the borders. The kind of division highlighted by, say, the so-called "anti-globalization" protesters—whose movement is, incidentally, one of the most globalized in the world—tries to unite the underdogs of the world economy and goes firmly against religious, national or "civilizational" lines of division.

The main hope of harmony lies not in any imagined uniformity, but   7
in the plurality of our identities, which cut across each other and work against sharp divisions into impenetrable civilizational camps. Political leaders who think and act in terms of sectioning off humanity into various "worlds" stand to make the world more flammable—even when their intentions are very different. They also end up, in the case of civilizations defined by religion, lending authority to religious leaders seen as spokesmen for their "worlds." In the process, other voices are muffled and other concerns silenced. The robbing of our plural identities not only reduces us; it impoverishes the world.

Thinking About the Essay

1. How does Sen begin his essay? What is his argument and how does he present it in the opening paragraph?

2. Sen uses several illustrations to support his argument about "singular classification." Locate three of these examples and explain how they advance his claim.

3. Any discussion of types—whether types of civilizations or types of teachers—lends itself to classification. How does Sen use classification and division to organize his argument and his essay?

4. What transitional devices serve to unify this essay?

5. Does Sen's concluding paragraph serve to confirm his thesis or claim? Explain your answer.

Responding in Writing

6. What is so wrong about "singular classification," especially when considering nations, cultures, and civilizations? Write a response to this question, referring to Sen's essay in the process.

7. Write a complete analysis of the ways in which Sen composes his argument in "A World Not Neatly Divided."

8. Write a comparative paper analyzing the essays by Sen and Samuel Huntington.

Networking

9. In small groups, select a city, region, country, or civilization, and then draw up a list of traits or attributes—a singular classification—illuminating your subject. Present the list to class members, and as a group discuss the advantages and disadvantages of singular classification.

10. Conduct online research on an international city. Then write a travel blurb stressing both the singular nature of this city and also its diversity.

Andalusia's Journey

Edward Said

Edward W. Said was born in 1935 in Jerusalem, Palestine, and grew up in Egypt. His family moved to the United States in 1951. Educated at Princeton University (B.A., 1957) and Harvard University (Ph.D., 1964), Said was an influential literary and cultural critic and a noted supporter of the Palestinian cause. University Professor of English and comparative literature at Columbia, he was best known to the general public as a commentator on radio and television on Middle Eastern affairs. Perceived as a public intellectual, Said for decades advocated Palestinian rights even as he criticized Palestinian policies and leadership. His books *The Question of Palestine* (1979), *Covering Islam* (1981), and *The Politics of Dispossession: The Struggle for Palestinian Self-Determination* (1994) offer penetrating analyses of this troubled region. Said was also a distinguished literary critic, the author of the groundbreaking study *Orientalism* (1978), *Culture and Imperialism* (1993), and other books and collections of essays. In the early 1990s Said was diagnosed with leukemia; his illness prompted him to write an autobiography, *Out of Place: A Memoir* (1999), tracing his life and journeys as an exile. Said died in 2003. In the following essay, published in *Travel and Leisure* in 2002, Said offers a personal impression of one region in Spain that has been a crossroads in the convergence of civilizations.

Before Reading

Said speaks of Andalusia—the region in southern Spain where Arab, Latin, and Jewish civilizations came together for seven hundred years—as representing a dialogue rather than clash of civilizations. What is necessary for such a dialogue to occur in the world today?

> Poverty turns our country into a foreign land, and riches our place of exile into our home. For the whole world, in all its diversity, is one. And all its inhabitants our brothers and neighbors.
>
> —Abu Muhammad al-Zubaydi, Seville, A.D. 926–989

For an Arab, such as my self, to enter Granada's 13th-century Alhambra palace is to leave behind a modern world of disillusionment, strife, and uncertainty. In this, the calmest, most harmonious structure ever built by Arab Muslims, the walls are covered with dizzying arabesques and geometric patterns, interspersed with Arabic script extolling God and his regents

1

© Réunion des Musées Nationaux/Art Resource, NY.

A 16th-century plate from Valencia (once part of the Caliphate of Cordova), on which Arabic and Spanish designs merge.

on earth. The repetition of a basically abstract series of motifs suggests infinity, and serves to pull one through the palace's many rooms. The palace's Generalife gardens, punctuated by cooling streams, are a miracle of balance and repose. The Alhambra, like the great ninth-century mosque-cum-cathedral of Cordova, La Mezquita, invites believer and non-believer alike with opulence and rigorous discipline of ornament, and almost imperceptible changes in perspective from one space to the next. The whole composition is always in evidence—always changing yet always somehow the same—a unity in multiplicity.

I have been traveling for four decades to southern Spain, Andalucía as it is called by Spaniards, al-Andalus by Arabs, drawn there by its magnificent architecture, and the amazingly mixed Arab, Jewish, and Latin cultural centers of Cordova, Granada, and Seville. The turmoil of Andalusia's extraordinary past seems to hover just beneath the surface of its pleasant landscapes and generally small-scaled urban life. In its medieval heyday, Andalusia, established by the Arab general Tariq bin Ziyad and continuously fought over by numerous Muslim sects (among them Almoravids, Nasrids, and Almohads) and by Catholics as far north as Galicia, was a particularly lively instance of the dialogue, much more than the clash, of cultures. Muslims, Jews, and Christians co-existed with astonishing harmony. Today its periods of fruitful cultural diversity may provide a model for the co-existence of peoples, a model quite different from the ideological battles, local chauvinism, and ethnic conflict that

The Alhambra's repeating arches.

finally brought it down—and which ironically enough threaten to engulf our own 21st-century world.

When I first visited, in the summer of 1966, Franco-era Andalusia   3
seemed like a forgotten, if wonderfully picturesque, province of Catholic Spain. Its fierce sun accentuated the area's rigors: the scarcity of good accommodations, the difficulty of travel, the heaviness of the cuisine, the unyielding spirit of a people living in relative poverty and obdurate pride, the political and religious repression under which the country suffocated. The splendor of its great buildings was evident but seemed part of a distant backdrop to more urgent and more recent times: the Civil War of 1936–39 and Hemingway's sentimentalized view of it; the burgeoning and quite sleazy mass tourist trade that had put down roots in Mâlaga (not to mention the ghastly neighboring village of Torremolinos) and that was creeping slowly westward toward Portugal's Algarve (from the Arabic *al-gharb min al-Andalus,* "west of Andalusia").

Even in the summer of 1979, when I spent a few weeks in the area with   4
my wife and two young children, the Alhambra was all but deserted. You could stroll into it as you would into a public park. (Today, visiting the place is more like going to Disneyland. There are five gigantic parking lots and you must reserve well in advance.) For its part, Seville was a pleasant, somewhat subdued city of modest restaurants and family-style hotels. Franco had disappeared in 1975, of course, but the prosperous Spain of solidly based, open democracy had not yet arrived. You could still feel the Church's cold impress and the vestiges of the fascist dictatorship. Europe was a long distance away, beyond the Pyrenees, to the north.

The palace's Generalife gardens.

La Sultane by Filippo Baratti, one of many 19th-century European artists captivated by Andalusia's history.

In the 1980s and 90s Spain awakened into modernity and globalization. 5
NATO's Spain, the EU's Spain, took over the peninsula's identity. There is now no shortage of excellent hotels or good restaurants, although it must again be admitted, as the Michelin Guide put it in the 1960s, that for the most part "Spanish cuisine is more complicated than it is refined." But for me, and indeed for many Arabs, Andalusia still represents the finest flowering of our culture. That is particularly true now, when the Arab Middle East seems mired in defeat and violence, its societies unable to arrest their declining fortunes, its secular culture so full of almost surreal crisis, shock, and nihilism.

A spate of recent Arabic and Muslim writing has redirected attention to 6
Andalusia as a mournful, tantalizing emblem of what a glorious civilization was lost when Islamic rule ended. This literature serves only to accentuate the conditions of decline and loss that have so diminished modern Arab life—and the conquests that have dominated it. Thus, for instance, the

1992 appearance of Palestinian poet Mahmud Darwish's great *qasida,* or ode, *Ahd Ashr Kawkaban Ala Akhir Almashad Al-Andalusi* (Eleven Stars over the Last Moments of Andalusia). The poem was written about—and served to clarify—what the Palestinians felt they had lost not just once but time after time. The Palestinian national poet seems to be asking, what do we do after the last time, after the new conquerors have entered our palaces and consumed our still hot tea and heard our mellifluous music? Does it mean that as Arabs we exist only as a footnote to someone else's history?

> Our tea is green and hot: drink it. Our pistachios are fresh; eat them.
> The beds are of green cedar, fall on them,
> following this long siege, lie down on the feathers of our dream.
> The sheets are crisp, perfumes are ready by the door, and there are plenty of mirrors:
> Enter them so we may exist completely. Soon we will search
> In the margins of your history, in distant countries,
> For what was once our history? And in the end we will ask ourselves:
> Was Andalusia here or there? On the land ... or in the poem?

It is difficult to overestimate the searing poignancy of these lines. They 7 recall not only the self-destructive demise of the Andalusian kings and

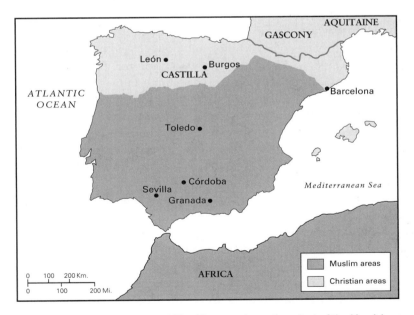

The Iberian Peninsula and North Africa. The map shows the extent of the Moorish conquest from the 9th through the 12th centuries C.E.

their *tawai'f* but also present-day Arab disunity and consequent weakness. (*Tawai'f* is the plural of the Arabic *ta'ifa, used* to refer both to the independent Muslim kingdoms that began in 1023, and also to modern-day confessional sects, of the sort common in Lebanon during its recent civil war. The references are lost on no one whose language is Arabic.) For a visitor from either North Africa or the Arab countries east of Suez, including Egypt, Andalusia is idealized as a kind of lost paradise, which fell from the brilliance of its medieval apex into terrible squabbles and petty jealousies. This perhaps makes a rather too facile moral lesson of the place.

Andalusia's unthreatening landscape—tranquil hills, agreeable towns, and rich green fields—survived a turbulent and deeply unsavory history. Running through its convoluted past was a steady current of unrest, of trust betrayed. It seems to have been made up of composite or converted souls, Mozarabs (Arabized Christians) and *muwallads* (Christian converts to Islam). Nothing and no one is simple. Several of its city-states (there were no fewer than 12 at the height of the internecine conflict) were occasionally ruled by poets and patrons of the arts, such as Seville's 11th-century al-Mutamid, but they were often jealous and even small-minded schemers. Andalusia multiplies in the mind with its contradictions and puzzles; its history is a history of the masks and assumed identities it has worn.   8

Was Andalusia largely Arab and Muslim, as it certainly seems to have been, and if so why was it so very different from, say, Syria, Egypt, and Iraq, themselves great centers of civilization and power? And how did the Jews, the Visigoth Catholics, and the Romans who colonized it before the Arabs play their role in Andalusia's makeup and identity? However all these components are sorted out, a composite Andalusian identity anchored in Arab culture can be discerned in its striking buildings, its tiles and wooden ceilings, its ornate pottery and neatly constructed houses. And what could be more Andalusian than the fiery flamenco dancer, accompanied by hoarse *cantaores,* martial hand-clapping and hypnotically strummed guitars, all of which have precedents in Arabic music?   9

On this trip I wanted to discover what Andalusia was from my perspective as a Palestinian Arab, as someone whose diverse background might offer a way of seeing and understanding the place beyond illusion and romance. I was born in Jerusalem, Andalusia's great Eastern antipode, and raised as a Christian. Though the environment I grew up in was both colonial and Muslim, my university education and years of residence in the United States and Europe allow me to see my past as a Westerner might. Standing before the monumental portal of Seville's Alcázar (the Hispanicized word for *al-qasr,* "castle"), every inch of which is covered in raised florid swirls and interlocking squares. I was reminded of similar surfaces from my earlier years in Cairo, Damascus, and Jerusalem, strangely present   10 before me now in southern Europe, where Arab Muslims once hoped to set up an Umayyad empire in the West to rival the one in Syria. The Arabs journeyed along the shores of the Mediterranean through Spain, France, and Italy, all of which now bear their traces, even if those traces are not always acknowledged.

Perhaps the most striking feature of Andalusia historically was the care 11 lavished on such aspects of urban life as running water, leafy gardens, viewing places *(miradores)*, and graceful wall and ceiling designs. Medieval Europe, all rough skins, drafty rooms, and meaty cuisine, was barbaric by comparison. This is worth noting, since the interiors of Andalusia's palaces today are presented as out of time, stripped of their luxurious silks and divans, their heady perfumes and spices, their counterpoint of din and lyrical poetry.

Except for Cordova's immense Mezquita, the choice spaces of what 12 has been known historically as Muslim Spain are generally not very large. Even Seville's Alcázar, big enough as a castle or palace, doesn't dominate at all. The Arabs who gave Andalusia its characteristic features generally used architecture to refashion and enhance nature, to create symmetrical patterns that echo Arabic calligraphy. Streets are pleasant to saunter in, rather than utilitarian thoroughfares. Curved ornaments—such as highly patterned vases and metal utensils—abound, all part of a wonderfully relaxed worldliness.

That worldliness, which reached its apex between the 9th and 12th centu- 13 ries, testifies to the extraordinary diversity of Islam itself, so often thought of today as a monolithic block of wild-eyed terrorists, bent on destruction and driven by fanaticism. Yes, there were feuding factions, but rarely before or after did the Islamic kings and princes produce a civilization of such refinement with so many potentially warring components. Consider that in Cordova's heyday the Jewish sage Maimonides and Islam's greatest thinker, Ibn Rushd (Averroës), lived in Cordova at the same time, each with his own disciples and doctrines, both writing and speaking in Arabic. Part of the Damascus-based Umayyad empire that had fallen to the Baghdad-based Abbasids in 750, the Spanish territories always retained an eagerness to be recognized by, and an ambition to surpass the achievements of, their Eastern cousin.

Quite soon, Andalusia became a magnet for talent in many arenas: 14 music, philosophy, mysticism, literature, architecture, virtually all of the sciences, jurisprudence, religion. The monarchs Abd ar-Rahman I (731–788) and Abd ar-Rahman III (891–961) gave Cordova its almost mythic status. Three times the size of Paris (Europe's second-largest city in the 10th century), with 70 libraries, Cordova also had, according to the historian Salma Kahdra Jayyusi, "1,600 mosques, 900 baths, 213,077 homes for ordinary people, 60,300 mansions for notables, officials, and military commanders, and 80,455 shops." The mystics and poets Ibn Hazm and

Seville's Alcázar palace, one of the best surviving examples of Mudejar architecture, a late Andalusian style.

Ibn Arabi, Jewish writers Judah ha-Levi and Ibn Gabirol, the colloquial but lyrical *zajals* and wonderful strophic songs, or *muwashshah,* that seemed to emerge as if from nowhere and later influenced the troubadors, provided al-Andalus with verse, music, and atmosphere such as Europe had never had before.

The Arab general Tariq bin Ziyad and his desert army streamed across   15
the Gibraltar straits in 711; on later forays he brought with him many
North African Berbers, Yemenis, Egyptians, and Syrians. In Spain they
encountered Visigoths and Jews, plus the remnants of a once thriving
Roman community, all of whom at times co-existed, and at times fought
with one another. No harmony was stable for very long—too many conflicting elements were always in play. Andalusia's reign of relative tolerance
(three monotheistic faiths in complex accord with one another) abruptly
ended when King Ferdinand and Queen Isabella seized the region and
imposed a reign of terror on non-Christians. Significantly, one of the tow-
ering figures of the Andalusian cultural synthesis, Ibn Khaldun, a founder
of sociology and historiography, came from a prominent Seville family, and
was perhaps the greatest analyst of how nations rise and fall.

The last king of Granada, the luckless Boabdil (Abu Abd Allah   16
Muhammad), was expelled along with the Jews in 1492, weeping or
sighing—chooses your version. The unhappy Moor quickly became the
emblem of what the Arabs had lost. Yet most people who are gripped by
the pathos of the king's departure may not know that Boabdil negotiated
very profitable surrender terms—some money, and land outside Granada—
before he left the city to the Castilian monarchs.

Despite the richness of Andalusia's Islamic past and its indelible presence   17
in Spain's subsequent history after the Reconquista, for years the Church
and royalist ideologues stressed the purgation of Spain's Islamic and Jewish
heritage, insisting that Christian Spain was restored in 1492 as if little
had happened to disturb its ascendancy in the seven preceding centuries.
Not for nothing has the cult of Santiago (Saint James) been highlighted in
Catholic Spain: St. James was, among other things, the patron saint of the
Spanish in their battles against the Moors, hence his nickname Matamoros,
"Killer of Moors." Yet, classical Mudejar art, with its typically florid
arabesques and geometrical architecture, was produced after the Muslims
were defeated. As far away as Catalonia, Gaudí's obsession with botanical
motifs shows the Arab influence at its most profound. Why did it linger so
if Arabs had represented only a negligible phase in Spanish history?

The Jews and Muslims who weren't thrown out or destroyed by the   18
Inquisition remained as conversos and Moriscos, men and women who
had converted to Catholicism to preserve their lives. No one will ever
know whether the identity they abandoned was really given up or whether
it continued underground. Miguel de Cervantes's magnificent novel *Don
Quixote* draws attention to its supposed author, the fictional Arab Sidi
Hamete Benengeli, which—it is plausibly alleged—was a way of masking
Cervantes's own secret identity as an unrepentant converso. The wars

between Muslims and Catholics turn up again and again in literature, including of course the *Chanson de Roland* (in which Charlemagne's Frankish army is defeated in 778 by Abd ar-Rahman's men) and Spain's national epic, *El Poema del Cid*. About 60 percent of the Spanish language is made up of Arabic words and phrases: *alcalde* (mayor), *barrios* (quarters of a city), *aceite* (oil), *aceitunas* (olives). Their persistence indicates that Spain's identity is truly, if perhaps also uneasily, bicultural.

It took the great Spanish historian and philologist Américo Castro, who   19
taught for many years at Princeton, to establish the enduring pervasiveness of the country's repressed past in his monumental work *The Structure of Spanish History* (1954). One of Spain's finest contemporary novelists, Juan Goytisolo, has also inspired interest in Andalusia's Arab and Muslim origins, and done much to reassert Spain's non-European past. His *Count Julian,* which centers on the treacherous Catholic whom Spaniards hold responsible for bringing in the Moors, challenges the myth that Visigoth Spain's rapid fall in 711 can be explained by nothing other than the nobleman's betrayal.

Andalusia's identity was always in the process of being dissolved and   20
lost, even when its cultural life was at its pinnacle. Every one of its several strands—Arabic, Muslim, Berber, Catholic, Jewish, Visigothic, and Roman—calls up another. Cordova was a particularly wonderful case in point. A much smaller city today than under Abd ar-Rahman I, it is still dominated by the mosque that he began in 785. Erected on the site of a Christian church, it was an attempt to assert his identity as a Umayyad prince fleeing Damascus, to make a cultural statement as a Muslim exiled to a place literally across the world from where he had come.

The result is, in my experience, the greatest and most impressive reli-   21
gious structure on earth. The mosque-cathedral, La Mezquita, stretches effortlessly for acres in a series of unending double arches, whose climax is an incredibly ornate mihrab, the place where the muezzin or prayer leader stands. Its contours echo those of the great mosque in Damascus (from which Abd ar-Rahman I barely managed to escape when his Umayyad dynasty fell), while its arches are conscious quotations of Roman aqueducts. So assiduous was its architect in copying Damascus that the Cordovan mihrab actually faces south, rather than east—toward Mecca—as it should.

The great mosque was later barbarically seized by a Christian monarch   22
who turned it into a church. He did this by inserting an entire cathedral into the Muslim structure's center, in an aggressive erasure of history and statement of faith. He may also have had in mind the legend that Muslims had stolen the bells of the Cathedral of Santiago de Compostela, melted

them down, and used them in the mosque, which also housed the Prophet Muhammad's hand. Today, though the Muslim idea of prayer remains dominant, the building exudes a spirit of inclusive sanctity and magnanimity of purpose.

Beyond the mosque's imposing walls, Cordova retains its memorial 23 splendor and inviting shelter. To this day, the houses communicate a sense of welcome: inner courtyards are often furnished with a fountain, and the rooms are dispersed around it, very much as they are in houses in Aleppo thousands of miles to the east. Streets are narrow and winding because, as in medieval Cairo, the idea is to cajole the pedestrian with promises of arrival. Thus one walks along without having to face the psychologically intimidating distance of the long, straight avenue. Moreover, Cordova is one of the few cities in the Mediterranean where the intermingling of Arab and Jewish quarters doesn't immediately suggest conflict. Just seeing streets and squares named after Averroës and Maimonides in 21st-century Cordova, one gets an immediate idea of what a universal culture was like a thousand years ago.

Only five miles outside Cordova stand the partially restored ruins of 24 what must have been the most lavish, and certainly the most impressive, royal city in Europe, Madinat al-Zahra (City of the Flower). Begun by Abd ar-Rahman III in 936, it, too, was a vast echo of palace-cities in the Arab East, which it almost certainly overshadowed for a time. It is as if Andalusia's rulers and great figures were unable ever to rid their minds of the East. They relived its prior greatness on their terms, nowhere with more striving for effect than in Madinat al-Zahra.

Now an enormous excavation, Madinat al-Zahra is slowly being 25 restored. You can stand looking down on the symmetrical array of stables, military barracks, reception rooms, and courtyards—all pointing at the great central hall in which the king received his guests and subjects. According to some scholars. Abd ar-Rahman wanted not only to assume the mantle of the caliphate, thereby wresting it from the Abbasid king in Baghdad (who couldn't have paid much attention to Abd ar-Rahman's posturings), but also to establish political authority as something that belonged in the West but had meaning only if snatched from the East. For an Arab visitor, it is hard not to be struck by the rather competitive Andalusian reference to the better-known Eastern Muslim empires, mainly those of the Abbasids and Fatimids, who to this day form the core of what is taught and propagated as Arab culture.

A special poignancy hangs over Andalusia's impressively animated 26 spaces. It derives not only from a pervasive sense of former grandeur but also from what, because so many people hoped to possess it, Andalusia tried to be—and what it might have been. Certainly Granada's Alhambra is a monument to regret and the passage of time. Next to the wonderful 13th-to 14th-century Nasrid palace and superb Generalife gardens looms the ponderous 16th-century castle of the Spanish king and Holy Roman Emperor Charles V, who obviously wanted his rather ostentatious abode to acquire some of the luster of the Arab complex. Yet, despite the Alhambra's opulence and its apparently hedonistic celebration of the good life (for rulers, mainly), its arabesque patterns can seem like a defense against mortality or the ravages of human life. One can easily imagine the beleaguered and insecure Boabdil using it as a place of perfumed forgetfulness—perhaps even at times reexperiencing the studied oblivion cultivated by Sufi masters such as Ibn Arab.

The schizophrenia inherent in Spain's identity is more apparent in 27 Granada than anywhere else in Andalusia. Because the Alhambra sits on one of several hills high above the city, Granada proper has paid the price in clogged streets and overbuilt residential and commercial quarters through which the Arab palace must be approached. Granada as a whole embodies this tension between high and low. A mazelike system of one-way streets connects the Alhambra to Albaicín, the old Muslim quarter. Despite the wonders of the Alhambra, being in Albaicín is like feeling the fantasy of summer and the realities of a grim winter very close to each other. The resemblances between Albaicín and Cordova's barrios are striking, except that, as the name suggests, Albaicín—Arabic for "the downtrodden and hopeless"—was indeed an area for the poor and, one can't help feeling, where the last Arabs and Jews huddled together before their eviction in 1492. Nothing evokes Granada's riven history more superbly than the "Albaicín" movement in Isaac Albéniz's greatest musical work, the redoubtably difficult-to-perform piano collection *Iberia*.

By contrast, Seville's spirit is very much of this world—part feline, 28 part macho, part dashing sparkle, part somber colonialism. Seville contains Spain's finest *plaza de toro s*and also its largest cathedral. And it is here that all the archives of Spain's imperial conquests are housed. But before 1492, Seville was the administrative capital of the Arab monarchy that held sway over Andalusia. Where the Catholic empire-builders set their sights on the New World, the Arabs were taken up with the Old: Morocco, which before the final Reconquista was considered to be part of Andalusia. Similarities in metal, leather, and glazed pottery design between Spain and North Africa reinforce a prevailing unity of vision and religious discourse.

If Seville is a city where Catholic and Muslim cultures interact, it is 29 to the decided advantage of the former—though given Seville's special status in the Western romantic imagination as an extension of the Orient, it's probably truer to say that Seville is the triumph of Andalusian style. This, after all, is the city of Mérimée's and Bizet's *Carmen,* the heart of Hemingway's bullfighting obsession, and a favorite port of call for northern European poets and writers for whom citrus blossoms represent the salutary opposite of their dreary climates. Stendhal's *espagnolisme* derives from Sevillian themes, and the city's Holy Week parades and observances have gripped many peregrinating artists.

Not that the Arabs haven't made their own indelible mark on the city.   30 Standing watch over the landscape is the four-sided Giralda, a minaret built by an Almohad (basically an austere fundamentalist sort of Islam) king in the late 12th century. Its upper third was added to, for purposes of "improvement," by zealous Christians 400 years later. Despite some unnecessary flourishes, the tower was so magnetic that a contemporary chronicler observed, "From a distance it would appear that all the stars of the Zodiac had stopped in the heart of Seville." Incorporated into the cathedral, whose awesome bulk testifies to Catholic ambition and consolidation of power (Christopher Columbus's tomb is inside), the Giralda leads an independent existence as an ornate symbol of how even the harshest of ideologies can be filled with grace.

In the long run, and almost in spite of its kings and magistrates, the   31 Andalusian style seems to have fostered movement and discovery rather than monumentality and stability. It enacted an earlier version of our own hybrid world, one whose borders were also thresholds, and whose multiple identities formed an enriched diversity.

Thinking About the Essay

1. Said wrote this article for *Travel and Leisure.* What does he assume about the readership of this specific magazine? How does he make the essay both an introduction to a tourist destination and a serious explanation of the importance of the region? Do you think he succeeds in his dual purpose? Why or why not?

2. Where does Said state his thesis? Why is his thesis personally important?

3. Trace the historical process that Said presents in this essay, moving section by section through the article. What are some of the main topics and points he draws from his historical analysis?

4. What mood or sense of place does Said create in this essay? Identify aspects of style and language that convey mood and atmosphere.

5. What *definition* of culture and civilization does Said present in this essay? Locate examples of various strategies he employs to create this definition.

Responding in Writing

6. Explain why, after reading Said's essay, you might want to visit Andalusia on your own or on a group tour. Where would you visit? What would you look for? What would you hope to learn from this trip?

7. Said raises the prospect that civilizations don't necessarily have to clash. Reread his essay, and then write a paper in which you outline the necessary conditions required for a dialogue of civilizations.

8. How can travel alert us to the history and contours of civilizations? Answer this question in a reflective essay. If you have traveled to the various centers of civilization or have read about them, incorporate this knowledge into the paper.

Networking

9. In small groups, work through Said's essay section by section. Then devise a sketch outline of the entire essay. Put your outline on the chalkboard or blackboard for the class to view.

10. Go to the library or online to find additional information on Andalusia. Then prepare a report in which you determine whether Said's presentation of the region is accurate or biased.

The Age of Terror: What Is the Just Response?

9
CHAPTER

Just as changes in United States demographics, patterns of cultural interaction, the forces of globalization, and the "clash" of civilizations have brought us into expanding contact with the peoples of the world, current events remind us that this new world can be exceedingly dangerous. Indeed, in the years since the September 11, 2001, attack, we have had to reorient our thinking about numerous critical issues: the war on terrorism; the erosion of our sense of individual and collective security; the need to achieve a balance between individual rights and common security. Above all, we now face the ethical, political, and historical challenge of dealing with the reality that although the United States is still the world's major superpower, other superpowers—notably China and India—are emerging as global rivals. There are people and nations who hate America's standing in the world. And hatred and cruelty, as Isaac Bashevis Singer, a winner of the Nobel Prize for Literature, once observed, only produce more of the same.

The 9/11 terrorist attack was so profoundly unnerving that virtually all of us can remember where we were when the planes hijacked by terrorists crashed into New York's World Trade Center and the Pentagon in Washington, DC. This was a primal national event, similar in impact to the raid on Pearl Harbor in 1941 or the assassinations of President John Kennedy and Martin Luther King Jr. in the 1960s. These prior events, whether taking the lives of thousands or just one, serve to define entire American generations. Today, the United States faces a new defining event or more accurately an unfolding series of events—first called the "war on terror" but now that phrase (as Reza Aslan explores an essay appearing in this chapter) has been dropped by the Obama administration.

Be a superpower! Destroy the Axis of Evil! One of several board games reflecting our preoccupation with the War on Terror.

Thinking About the Image

1. What is the designer's purpose in creating this image? What specific details support your response?
2. What is your first response to this image? Are you amused? Why or why not?
3. How do you think that the designer might respond to parents who object to this image, claiming that this "game" is inappropriate for children?
4. Go online and try to locate virtual games that exploit the "war on terror" theme. What can you conclude about terrorism's impact on Internet gaming and more generally on the contemporary mind?

Nevertheless, we do seem to be living in an age of terror, and we have to find ways in which national and global communities can deal with this unnerving reality.

In a sense, the September 11 attack and subsequent assaults—in Bali, Spain, England, Africa, India, and elsewhere—have forced the United States to look inward and outward for intelligent and effective responses. Looking inward, we often have to deal with our own anger, insecurity, and hatred of other peoples who commit these crimes against unsuspecting humanity. These are primal emotions that affect our sense of personal identity. At the same time, we must understand how others around the world view our country and must gain knowledge of peoples and cultures we once knew little or nothing about. For example, are the terrorists who planned and launched the 9/11 attack a mere aberration—some delusional distortion of the great culture and civilization of Islam? Or do they reflect the consensus of the Arab street? Where do college students—who should be committed to liberal learning—go to find answers to such large and complex questions? What courses exist on your campus? What organizations foster transnational or global understanding?

Ultimately—as writers in this chapter and throughout the text suggest—we have to read across cultures and nations to understand this new age of terror and its many manifestations: narcoterrorism, cyberterrorism, genocide, and more. We have to reflect on our own backgrounds. We have to be candid about how our individual experience molds our attitudes toward "others"—most of whom are like us but some of whom want to do us harm. Liberal education, as the American philosopher William James stated at the beginning of the last century, makes us less fanatical. Against the backdrop of contemporary terrorism, we have to search for wisdom and for sustaining values.

To Any Would-Be Terrorists

Naomi Shihab Nye

Naomi Shihab Nye was born in 1952 in St. Louis, Missouri. Her family background is Palestinian American. She graduated from Trinity University (B.A., 1974) and subsequently started a career as a freelance writer and editor. Today Nye is known for her award-winning poetry, fiction for children, novels, and essays. She has been a visiting writer at the University of Texas, the University of Hawaii, the University of California at Berkeley, and elsewhere. Among Nye's books are the prize-winning poetry collection *Different Ways to Pray* (1980); several other poetry volumes, including *Yellow Glove* (1986), incorporating poems dealing with Palestinian life; a book of essays, *Never in a Hurry* (1996); and a young adult novel, *Habibi* (1997), which draws on Nye's own childhood experience of living in Jerusalem in the 1970s, which at that time was part of Jordan. Among her many awards are the Peter I. B. Lavin Younger Poets Award from the Academy of American Poets and a Guggenheim Fellowship. Starting with the provocative title of the following essay, Nye speaks as a Palestinian American to an extremist audience that needs "to find another way to live."

Before Reading

If you had an opportunity to address a terrorist or terrorist group, what would you say and how would you say it?

I am sorry I have to call you that, but I don't know how else to get your attention. I hate that word. Do you know how hard some of us have worked to get rid of that word, to deny its instant connection to the Middle East? And now look. Look what extra work we have. 1

Not only did your colleagues kill thousands of innocent, international people in those buildings and scar their families forever; they wounded a huge community of people in the Middle East, in the United States and all over the world. If that's what they wanted to do, please know the mission was a terrible success, and you can stop now. 2

Because I feel a little closer to you than many Americans could possibly feel, or ever want to feel, I insist that you listen to me. Sit down and listen. I know what kinds of foods you like. I would feed them to you if you were right here, because it is very important that you listen. 3

I am humble in my country's pain and I am furious. 4

My Palestinian father became a refugee in 1948. He came to the United States as a college student. He is 74 years old now and still homesick. He has planted fig trees. He has invited all the Ethiopians in his neighborhood to fill their little paper sacks with his figs. He has written columns and stories saying the Arabs are not terrorists; he has worked all his life to defy that word. Arabs are businessmen and students and kind neighbors. There is no one like him and there are thousands like him—gentle Arab daddies who make everyone laugh around the dinner table, who have a hard time with headlines, who stand outside in the evenings with their hands in their pockets staring toward the far horizon. 5

I am sorry if you did not have a father like that. 6

I wish everyone could have a father like that. 7

My hard-working American mother has spent 50 years trying to convince her fellow teachers and choirmates not to believe stereotypes about the Middle East. She always told them, there is a much larger story. If you knew the story, you would not jump to conclusions from what you see in the news. But now look at the news. What a mess has been made. 8

Sometimes I wish everyone could have parents from different countries or ethnic groups so they would be forced to cross boundaries, to believe in mixtures, every day of their lives. Because this is what the world calls us to do. WAKE UP! 9

"To Any Would-Be Terrorists" by Naomi Shihab Nye. Reprinted by permission of the author.

The Palestinian grocer in my Mexican-American neighborhood paints 10 pictures of the Palestinian flag on his empty cartons. He paints trees and rivers. He gives his paintings away. He says, "Don't insult me" when I try to pay him for a lemonade. Arabs have always been famous for their generosity. Remember?

My half-Arab brother with an Arabic name looks more like an Arab 11 than many full-blooded Arabs do and he has to fly every week.

My Palestinian cousins in Texas have beautiful brown little boys. Many 12 of them haven't gone to school yet. And now they have this heavy word to carry in their backpacks along with the weight of their papers and books. I repeat, the mission was a terrible success. But it was also a complete, total tragedy, and I want you to think about a few things.

1.

Many people, thousands of people, perhaps even millions of people, in 13 the United States are very aware of the long unfairness of our country's policies regarding Israel and Palestine. We talk about this all the time. It exhausts us and we keep talking. We write letters to newspapers, to politicians, to each other. We speak out in public even when it is uncomfortable to do so, because that is our responsibility. Many of these people aren't even Arabs. Many happen to be Jews who are equally troubled by the inequity. I promise you this is true. Because I am Arab-American, people always express these views to me, and I am amazed how many understand the intricate situation and have strong, caring feelings for Arabs and Palestinians even when they don't have to. Think of them, please: All those people who have been standing up for Arabs when they didn't have to.

But as ordinary citizens we don't run the government and don't get 14 to make all our government's policies, which makes us sad sometimes. We believe in the power of the word and we keep using it, even when it seems no one large enough is listening. That is one of the best things about this country: the free power of free words. Maybe we take it for granted too much. Many of the people killed in the World Trade Center probably believed in a free Palestine and were probably talking about it all the time.

But this tragedy could never help the Palestinians. Somehow, miracu- 15 lously, if other people won't help them more, they are going to have to help themselves. And it will be peace, not violence, that fixes things. You could ask any one of the kids in the Seeds of Peace organization and they would tell you that. Do you ever talk to kids? Please, please, talk to more kids.

2.

Have you noticed how many roads there are? Sure you have. You must 16
check out maps and highways and small alternate routes just like anyone
else. There is no way everyone on earth could travel on the same road, or
believe in exactly the same religion. It would be too crowded: it would
be dumb. I don't believe you want us all to be Muslims. My Palestinian
grandmother lived to be 106 years old and did not read or write, but even
she was much smarter than that. The only place she ever went beyond
Palestine and Jordan was to Mecca, by bus, and she was very proud to
be called a Hajji and to wear white clothes afterwards. She worked very
hard to get stains out of everyone's dresses—scrubbing them with a stone.
I think she would consider the recent tragedies a terrible stain on her religion and her whole part of the world. She would weep. She was scared of
airplanes anyway. She wanted people to worship God in whatever ways
they felt comfortable. Just worship. Just remember God in every single day
and doing. It didn't matter what they called it. When people asked her how
she felt about the peace talks that were happening right before she died,
she puffed up like a proud little bird and said, in Arabic, "I never lost my
peace inside." To her, Islam was a welcoming religion. After her home in
Jerusalem was stolen from her, she lived in a small village that contained a
Christian shrine. She felt very tender toward the people who would visit it.
A Jewish professor tracked me down a few years ago in Jerusalem to tell
me she changed his life after he went to her village to do an oral history
project on Arabs. "Don't think she only mattered to you!" he said. "She
gave me a whole different reality to imagine—yet it was amazing how close
we became. Arabs could never be just a 'project' after that."

Did you have a grandmother? Mine never wanted people to be pushed 17
around. What did yours want?

Reading about Islam since my grandmother died, I note the "tolerance" 18
that was "typical of Islam" even in the old days. The Muslim leader Kha-
lidibn al-Walid signed a Jerusalem treaty which declared, "in the name of
God ... you have complete security for your churches which shall not be
occupied by the Muslims or destroyed."

It is the new millennium in which we should be even smarter than we 19
used to be, right? But I think we have fallen behind.

3.

Many Americans do not want to kill any more innocent people anywhere 20
in the world. We are extremely worried about military actions killing
innocent people. We didn't like this in Iraq, we never liked it anywhere.

We would like no more violence, from us as well as from you. We would like to stop the terrifying wheel of violence, just stop it, right on the road, and find something more creative to do to fix these huge problems we have. Violence is not creative, it is stupid and scary, and many of us hate all those terrible movies and TV shows made in our own country that try to pretend otherwise. Don't watch them. Everyone should stop watching them. An appetite for explosive sounds and toppling buildings is not a healthy thing for anyone in any country. The USA should apologize to the whole world for sending this trash out into the air and for paying people to make it.

But here's something good you may not know—one of the best-selling 21 books of poetry in the United States in recent years is the Coleman Barks translation of Rumi, a mystical Sufi poet of the 13th century, and Sufism is Islam and doesn't that make you glad?

Everyone is talking about the suffering that ethnic Americans are going 22 through. Many will no doubt go through more of it, but I would like to thank everyone who has sent me a condolence card. Americans are usually very kind people. Didn't your colleagues find that out during their time living here? It is hard to imagine they missed it. How could they do what they did, knowing that?

4.

We will all die soon enough. Why not take the short time we have on 23 this delicate planet and figure out some really interesting things we might do together? I promise you, God would be happier. So many people are always trying to speak for God—I know it is a very dangerous thing to do. I tried my whole life not to do it. But this one time is an exception. Because there are so many people crying and scared and confused and complicated and exhausted right now—it is as if we have all had a giant simultaneous breakdown.

I beg you, as your distant Arab cousin, as your American neighbor, 24 listen to me.

Our hearts are broken: as yours may also feel broken in some ways, we 25 can't understand, unless you tell us in words. Killing people won't tell us. We can't read that message.

Find another way to live. Don't expect others to be like you. Read 26 Rumi. Read Arabic poetry. Poetry humanizes us in a way that news, or even religion, has a harder time doing. A great Arab scholar, Dr. Salma Jayyusi, said, "If we read one another, we won't kill one another." Read American poetry. Plant mint. Find a friend who is so different from you,

you can't believe how much you have in common. Love them. Let them love you. Surprise people in gentle ways, as friends do. The rest of us will try harder too. Make our family proud.

Thinking About the Essay

1. How does Nye address her primary audience—"would-be terrorists"? What tone or voice does she employ? What are some of the words and phrases she uses to get their attention? Of course, Nye also writes for a broader audience of readers—us. How does she make her message appealing to this larger audience?

2. Nye presents an elaborate argument in this essay. What is her central claim? What reasons or minor propositions does she give in support of her claim? How do the events of September 11 condition the nature of her argument? What types of appeal does she make to convince her audience to think, feel, and act differently?

3. Examine the introductory paragraphs—paragraphs 1–12. Why does Nye use a first-person ("I") point of view? What is her purpose? What is the effect?

4. Analyze sections 1–4 of Nye's essay (paragraphs 13–26). What is the subject matter of each? How does the sequence of sections serve to advance the writer's argument? What transitional techniques permit essay coherence and unity?

5. Why is Nye's last paragraph a fitting conclusion to the essay? What elements from the body of the essay does this concluding paragraph reinforce and illuminate?

Responding in Writing

6. Write your own letter to any would-be terrorists. Address this audience in a personal voice. Use a variety of appeals to make your case.

7. In an analytical essay, examine the ways in which Nye tries to make her case in "To Any Would-Be Terrorists."

8. Write a letter to Naomi Shihab Nye in which you agree or disagree with the content of her essay.

Networking

9. Exchange your paper with another class member and evaluate it for content, grammar and syntax, organization, and tone. Make revisions based on your discussion.

10. Conduct online research on Rumi, and then write a paper explaining why Nye would allude to this figure in an essay on terrorism.

Losing the "War"

Reza Aslan | Reza Aslan was born in Iran but immigrated to the United States when a teenager. Aslan has degrees from Santa Clara University, Harvard University, and the University of Iowa, and has pursued doctoral study at the University of California at Santa Barbara. A contributor to popular and scholarly periodicals, Aslan is also the author of *No god but God: The Origins, Evolution, and Future of Islam* (2005) and *How to Win a Cosmic War: God, Globalization, and the End of the War on Terror* (2009). In this essay from the April 9, 2009, edition of the *Los Angeles Times*, Aslam offers a critique of the "master narrative" of the war on terror.

Before Reading

Do you think that the "war on terror" is an accurate description of our common predicament, or can this phrase be a misleading or dangerous oversimplification of current global realities?

Secretary of State Hillary Rodham Clinton let slip last week that the Obama administration has finally abandoned the phrase "war on terror." Its absence had been noted by commentators. There was no directive, Clinton said, "it's just not being used."   1

It may seem a trivial thing, but the change in rhetoric marks a significant turning point in the ideological contest with radical Islam. That is because the war on terror has always been a conflict more rhetorical than real. There is, of course, a very real, very bloody military component in the struggle against extremist forces in the Muslim world, though one can argue whether the U.S. and allied engagements in Iraq, Afghanistan and beyond are an integral part of that struggle, a distraction from it or, worse, evidence of its subversion and failure. But to the extent that the war on terror has been posited, from the start, as a war of ideology—a clash of civilizations—it is a rhetorical war, one fought more constructively with words and ideas than with guns and bombs.   2

The truth is that the phrase "war on terror" has always been problematic, not just because "terror," "terrorism" and "terrorist" are wastebasket terms that often convey as much about the person using them as they do about the events or people being described, but because this was never meant to be a war against terrorism per se. If it were, it would have involved the Basque separatists in Spain, the Hindu/Marxist Tamil Tigers in Sri Lanka, the Maoist   3 rebels in eastern India, Israeli ultranationalists, the Kurdish PKK, remnants of the Irish Republican Army and the Sikh separatist movements, and so on.

Rather, the war on terror, as conceived of by the Bush administration, was targeted at a particular brand of terrorism—that employed exclusively by Islamic entities. Which is why the enemy in this ideological conflict was gradually and systematically expanded to include not just the people who attacked the U.S. on Sept. 11, 2001, and the organizations that supported them, but an ever-widening conspiracy of disparate groups, such as Hamas in Palestine, Hezbollah in Lebanon, the Muslim Brotherhood in Egypt, the clerical regime in Iran, the Sunni insurgency in Iraq, the Kashmiri militants, the Taliban and any other organization that declared itself Muslim and employed terrorism as a tactic.

According to the master narrative of the war on terror, these were a monolithic enemy with a common agenda and a shared ideology. Never mind that many of these groups consider one another to be a graver threat than they consider America, that they have vastly different and sometimes irreconcilable political yearnings and religious beliefs, and that, until the war on terror, many had never thought of the United States as an enemy. Give this imaginary monolith a made-up name—say, "Islamofascism"— and an easily recognizable enemy is created, one that exists not so much as a force to be defeated but as an idea to be opposed, one whose chief attribute appears to be that "they" are not "us."

By lumping together the disparate forces, movements, armies, ideas and grievances of the greater Muslim world, from Morocco to Malaysia; by placing them in a single category ("enemy"), assigning them a single identity ("terrorist"); and by countering them with a single strategy (war), the Bush administration seemed to be making a blatant statement that the war on terror was, in fact, "a war against Islam."

That is certainly how the conflict has been viewed by a majority in four major Muslim countries—Egypt, Morocco, Pakistan and Indonesia—in a worldpublicopinion.org poll in 2007. Nearly two-thirds of respondents said they believe that the purpose of the war on terror is to "spread Christianity in the region" of the Middle East.

Indeed, if the war on terror was meant to be an ideological battle against groups such as Al Qaeda for the hearts and minds of Muslims, the consensus around the globe seems to be that the battle has been lost.

A September 2008 BBC World Service survey of 23 countries, including Russia, Australia, Pakistan, Turkey, France, Germany, Britain, the U.S., China and Mexico, found that almost 60% of all respondents said the war on terror has either had no effect or that it has made Al Qaeda stronger. Forty-seven percent said they think that neither side was winning; 56% of Americans have that view.

It is time not just to abandon the phrase "war on terror" but to admit 10 that the ideological struggle against radical Islam could never be won militarily. The battle for the hearts and minds of Muslims will take place not in the streets of Baghdad or in the mountains of Afghanistan but in the suburbs of Paris, the slums of East London and the cosmopolitan cities of Berlin and New York.

In the end, the most effective weapon in countering the appeal of 11 groups such as Al Qaeda may be the words we use.

Thinking About the Essay

1. What is Aslan's thesis and where does it appear?

2. What does Aslan mean by "rhetoric" and how does he connect this word to "ideology," "war on terror," and "master narrative"?

3. What types of illustration does Aslan use to structure his definition and analysis of such words as "terror," "terrorism," and "terrorist"? Would you say that Aslan's definitions are universally true or stipulative (that is, strictly personal and therefore limited in application)? Explain.

4. Identify the places where Aslan uses classification and division. How does classification operate in this essay as an organizing principle?

5. Consider the conclusion of this essay. Why does Aslan end with a single sentence? What is his purpose?

Responding in Writing

6. Write your own definition of "war on terror." Be certain to use a tone that captures your feelings about this term and about how people and groups respond to it.

7. Write an argumentative essay supporting or rejecting the concept "war on terror." Refer to Aslan's article in the course of your argument.

8. Aslan uses the phrase "radical Islam." Write your own extended definition of this term, explaining why or why not it is an accurate reflection of current global realities.

Networking

9. In groups of four or five, construct your own extended definition of "the master narrative of the war on terror" (paragraph 5). Share your definition with the class.

10. Locate a "war on terror" or a "radical Islam" website. What does this website say about current global conflicts and controversies? Report your findings in class discussion.

The War on Terror Has Not Gone Away

Thane Rosenbaum

> Thane Rosenbaum is a lawyer, lecturer, educator, and author who currently is a professor of human rights law at Fordham University. He was born in New York City in 1960 and attended the University of Florida (B.A., 1981), Columbia University (M.P.A., 1983), and University of Miami (J.D., 1986). Rosenbaum gave up a successful law practice to pursue dual careers in writing and higher education. Among his books are *Elijah Visible: Stories* (1996) and *The Myth of Moral Justice: Why Our Legal System Fails to Do What's Right* (2004). Rosenbaum's essays and reviews have appeared in *The New York Times*, *Los Angeles Times*, *The Washington Post*, and *The Wall Street Journal*. In this op-ed piece from the December 29, 2008, issue of *The Wall Street Journal*, Rosenbaum tries to balance the rule of law against the realities of the ongoing terrorist threat.

Before Reading

Do you think that civil liberties should be sacrificed for national security? Why or why not?

Amid the bailouts and credit squeezes, market meltdowns and recession- 1 ary worries, America has seemingly swapped the war on terror for the one waged to save its worsening economy.

Falling skyscrapers now have less gravitational pull than collapsing 2 401(k)s. The sleeper cells of snoring, incompetent bankers are more terrifying than al Qaeda. Rescue arrives in the form of number crunchers, not Special Forces operatives.

America is undergoing a radical shift in national priorities. Our anxiet- 3 ies have been rechanneled. While the attacks of 9/11 will never be forgotten, the consequences of 9/15, the date when Lehman Brothers declared bankruptcy, are now in the forefront.

We have also been engaged in a subtle passing of the terrorism torch. 4 The five most notorious terrorists at Guantanamo have made full confessions and asked to be executed. President-elect Barack Obama, in keeping with his campaign pledge to dismantle Guantanamo, will soon reassess how and where suspected terrorists will be detained and prosecuted in the future—if at all.

Toward that end, Portugal has agreed to resettle some of Guantanamo's 5 detainees and other European countries may soon follow (Albania has already done so). With 9/11 receding in memory and new national urgencies upon us, America is hoping to outsource some of its detention—and perhaps even prosecution—problem to its allies.

Meanwhile, India, following the tragedy in Mumbai, and Belgium, 6 which recently charged six terrorists from the Belgian branch of al Qaeda with a suicide plot, are stepping up their own counterterrorism and prosecution efforts. Britain recently convicted a British doctor of Iraqi descent with the attack on Glasgow airport and the attempt to detonate two bombs in London's West End. Germany is prosecuting a man accused of funding a terrorist camp and encouraging others to join al Qaeda.

And yet, in America, the Patriot Act might be repealed. 7

Perhaps it was inevitable that the events of 9/11 would not forever 8 define our national character. And certainly we would be expected to move on to other challenges. But are we unwittingly endangering our national security by the kind of neglect and failed oversight that ruined our economy? Lapsing into the complacency that might expose America to a repeat performance of mass murder is not a sound trade-off for economic health.

Yes, the past eight years of military tribunals, indefinite detentions and 9 warrantless surveillance have caused many Americans to question whether we have too severely compromised the rule of law—even as we acknowledge the global menace that terrorism presents. But just because our liberal democracy is, understandably, made uncomfortable by these post-9/11 initiatives doesn't mean that they haven't largely been necessary and have also saved lives.

Indefinite detentions may offend our principles, but speedy trials for 10 suspected terrorists presents no less a moral dilemma. When it comes to terrorism, holding too fast to our Constitution may result in losing a grip on our nation's security.

Try as we must to remain faithful to our constitutional history, we simply cannot fail to punish those responsible for 9/11 and protect Americans from future harm. 11

If Guantanamo is ultimately closed, then Congress should account for 12 the special circumstances of terrorism and enact legislation that would empower courts to adjudicate terrorist-related crimes. One thing is for certain: our Founding Fathers never contemplated al Qaeda.

The Constitution is limited when it comes to an atrocity. The imperfec- 13 tions we accept in prosecuting ordinary crimes are intolerable when dealing with the extraordinary crime of terrorism. This is precisely what drew the Bush administration to Guantanamo Bay, and away from American courtrooms, in the first place.

Providing our courts with enhanced jurisdiction and substantive laws 14 would answer the call for greater transparency, establish a more definite time frame on detention and a stricter adherence to evidentiary and procedural safeguards.

As we all board the bailout bandwagon, let us not forget what other 15 countries have painfully remembered: Global terrorism has not disappeared. Despite the damage done to our economy, this is not the time to let our guard down. We are still living in a crisis age. And the crisis is not confined to the global financial meltdown.

Thinking About the Essay

1. Why does Rosenbaum weave his discussion of the terrorist threat with references to the American economic crisis? What is his purpose? Do you find his strategy to be effective? Why or why not?

2. Rosenbaum states his claim in the title. Is this too bald or obvious a place to begin one's argument? Justify your response.

3. This article appeared in a daily newspaper known for its relatively conservative editorial policy. How does Rosenbaum tailor his argument to the editorial expectations of the *Wall Street Journal* and to this newspaper's readership?

4. Rosenbaum offers a brief, one-sentence assertion in paragraph 7. What is his intention here? Does he support his assertion? Explain.

5. How does Rosenbaum's conclusion mirror his introduction? What supporting evidence has he provided to fill out the introductory and end paragraphs?

Responding in Writing

6. Write an argumentative essay that refutes Rosenbaum's claim that we are ignoring the terrorist threat because of other pressing problems.

7. Rosenbaum worries that the Patriot Act "might be repealed." Argue for or against the proposition that we need special laws to protect against terrorism even if these laws limit our civil rights.

8. Analyze Rosenbaum's essay as as a demonstration of the op-ed art.

Networking

9. Working in small groups, compare and contrast the essays by Rosenbaum and Aslan. Present your findings and conclusion to the class.

10. Conduct an online search in an effort to locate at least three current articles about the debate over the Patriot Act. Write a précis based on your findings.

Generation Jihad

BILL POWELL

Bill Powell is a senior writer for *Time* magazine in Shanghai. Prior to this position, he was the Asia editor for *Fortune* magazine. Powell joined the staff of *Fortune* in 2000. He also reported for *Newsweek* as Moscow bureau chief (1996–2000), Berlin bureau chief and European economics editor (1994–95), and (simultaneously) Tokyo bureau chief and Asia economic editor (1989–94). Powell was also for many years a correspondent for *Business Week*. His many awards include an Overseas Press Club award for best economic reporting from abroad (1990, 1995) and the National Press Club Award for best reporting in a magazine (1987). In the following piece, which appeared in *Time* magazine in October 2005, Powell profiles members of a new generation of disaffected Muslim youth in Europe and America who have become increasingly sympathetic to extremist causes.

Before Reading

How difficult is it for you to appreciate the grievances of disaffected youth who subscribe to an extremist politics that supports or defends terrorism? Do you make any moral distinction between "a suicide bomber and a B-52"?

The last time Myriam Cherif saw her son Peter, 23, was in May 2004, when the two of them stood at the elevator on the fifth floor of the gritty public-housing project where they lived, just north of Paris. Myriam, 48, was born in Tunisia, moved to France when she was 8 and became a French citizen. Peter's father, who died when the boy was 14, was a Catholic from the French Antilles in the Caribbean. But Peter took a different path. In 2003 he converted to Islam and became a devout Muslim. He took to wearing loose trousers and a long tunic instead of blue jeans and repeatedly told Myriam that she should wear the traditional Muslim head scarf. And then one day last spring, Peter told his mother he was heading off to Syria to study Arabic and the Koran.

At first, Peter e-mailed his mother every couple of days, sending her snapshots and news of his studies in Damascus. Last July he told her he was headed for a "spiritual retreat" and would be out of touch for a while. She heard nothing until December, when she received a brief phone call from a French government official who told her that Peter had been captured by U.S. soldiers in the Iraqi city of Fallujah.

Today Peter, one of five French citizens captured by U.S. forces in Iraq, 3
is being held at Abu Ghraib prison outside Baghdad, family members say.
More than a year since she last heard from her son, Myriam Cherif is still
trying to understand how, in the streets and cafes of Paris, Peter and other
young Muslims like him were lured into giving up their lives in the West
and pursuing jihad. "They saw aggressive, violent images on the Internet
and asked questions about why Muslims were suffering abroad while
European countries were doing nothing," she says. "It's like they set off a
bomb in their heads."

Since 9/11, the Bush Administration has argued that the best way to 4
prevent further attacks by al-Qaeda and its sympathizers is to fight Islamic
extremists on their turf, in places like Afghanistan and Iraq, before they make
it to the West. But among Europeans, the suicide bombings in London on July
7 of this year, which were carried out by four British citizens, shattered any
lingering illusions that the threat can be kept from their shores. In a videotaped message released last week on al-Jazeera, Osama bin Laden's deputy,
Ayman al-Zawahiri, claimed responsibility for the London attacks—the
first public acknowledgment that the bombers may have received support
and assistance from al-Qaeda operatives. In Europe the message was a
chilling reminder that the enemy is within. Jihadist networks are increasingly drawing on a pool of young Muslims living in cities all over Europe—
including many who were born and raised in the affluence and openness of
the West, products of the very democracies they are determined to attack.

Call it Generation Jihad—restive, rootless young Muslims who have 5
spent their lives in Europe but now find themselves alienated from their
societies and the policies of their governments. While the precise number
of European jihadists is impossible to pinpoint, counterterrorism officials
believe the pool of radicals is growing. Since 1990, the Muslim population in Europe has expanded from an estimated 10 million to 14 million.
(Estimates of the number of Muslims in the U.S. range from 2 million to
7 million.) A 2004 estimate by the intelligence unit of French police found
that about 150 of the country's indexed 1,600 mosques and prayer halls
were under the control of extremist elements. A study of 1,160 recent
French converts to Islam found that 23% identified themselves as Salafists,
members of a sect sometimes associated with violent extremism. In the
Netherlands, home to 1 million Muslims, a spokesman for the Dutch intelligence service says it believes as many as 20 different hard-line Islamic
groups may be operating in the country—some simply prayer groups
adhering to radical interpretations of the Koran, others perhaps organizing
and recruiting for violence. In London, authorities say, as many as 3,000

veterans of al-Qaeda training camps over the years were born or based in Britain.

What explains the proliferation of Europe's homegrown radicals? And what dangers do they pose? Interviews with dozens of Muslims across Western Europe reveal a wide range of explanations for why so many are responding to the call of radical Islam. A common sentiment among members of Generation Jihad is frustration with a perceived scarcity of opportunity and disappointment at public policies that they believe target Muslims unfairly. Some lack a sense of belonging in European societies, which have long struggled to assimilate immigrants from the Islamic world. Many, in particular younger Muslims, suffer disproportionately from Europe's high-unemployment, slow-growth economies. Some are outraged over the bloodshed in Iraq and the persistent notion—stoked by Osama bin Laden but increasingly accepted among moderates—that the West is waging an assault on Islam.

The rage expressed by members of Generation Jihad has raised concerns among European counterterrorism officials that policies pursued by the U.S. and its allies in response to the Islamic terrorist threat may be further galvanizing radicals. Says a French investigator with a decade of antiterrorism experience: "There's a spreading atmosphere of indignation among normal Muslims that's echoing among the younger generation."

The echoes can be heard in many neighborhoods of north and east London, where Sajid Sharif, 37, a trained civil engineer who goes by the name Abu Uzair, once handed out incendiary leaflets preaching his brand of extreme Islam. From the comfort of his home, he leads the Savior Sect, a group that claims several hundred supporters and seeks to unite all Muslims worldwide under a strict conception of Islamic law. That might seem fanciful—except that Uzair's mentor, Omar Bakri Muhammad, was one of the first clerics to lose his right to live in Britain under the new antiterrorism laws. He was barred from returning after a holiday abroad. Uzair says he isn't concerned about the threat of eviction because he is British born, and his lawyer has reportedly told him he has little to worry about. "Anyway," says Uzair, "it is all in the hands of Allah."

Uzair is bearded, wears a long white gown and quotes nonstop from the Koran and Hadith (a collection of the teachings of the Prophet Muhammad). His Pakistani parents are secular Muslims, he says, and speak very little English. In his youth he smoked and went to night clubs. It was not until he was a university student in Britain that he embraced Islam. "I wanted some inner discipline," he says. "Since I have come to Islam, I have a lot of tranquillity." Now he tries to steer people away from drugs, drink, crime and smoking. Uzair's supporters refuse to vote in elections because his sect recognizes only Shari'a, Islamic law. While he does not openly support terrorism, he declares that the July 7 attacks were retaliation for Britain's support of the wars in Afghanistan and Iraq. "The majority of Muslims in the U.K. are frustrated, but they cannot speak," he says. "They will not condone the London bombings, but inside they believe that Britain had it coming."

The hostility Uzair feels toward the country of his birth is not atypi- 10
cal. Many second-generation Muslims in Europe say they feel a part of neither their native countries nor their parents' heritage. Riad, 32, a French citizen who has been unemployed since 2002 and who asked to be identified by his first name, embodies the sense of estrangement. "They say we are French, and we would like to believe that as well," he says, sitting in a cafe in the Venissieux suburb of Lyon. "But do we look like normal French people to you?" His friend Karim, 27, says they are discriminated against because of their long beards. "Who will give us a job when we look like this? We have to fend for ourselves and find a way out."

That lack of connection to their native societies can often lead Mus- 11
lims in Europe to seek order in religion. Zaheer Khan, 30, who grew up in the county of Kent in southeast England, was drawn to radical Islam as a college student in the mid-1990s. The Wahhabi and Salafist recruiters, he says, "would tell you that things like taking out car insurance are against Islamic principles, or voting—this is haram, forbidden. Slowly the disengagement was there. You didn't say, 'Let's explore what it means to be living in Britain.' This didn't come up." The radical feelings that Khan had back then—although he is still devout, he has since moved away from radical Islam—are apparently widespread among second-generation Muslims. "The problem is that they have no real roots," says Dominique Many, a lawyer for one of the Muslim Frenchmen taken into custody by French officials on suspicion of volunteering to fight against U.S. forces in Iraq. "In Tunisia they are considered foreigners. In France they are considered foreigners. This is the new generation of Muslims."

Rootlessness is compounded by economic struggle. On the whole, 12
Muslims in Europe are far more likely to be unemployed than non-Muslims are. In Britain, almost two-thirds of children of Pakistani or Bangladeshi origin—ethnic groups that together account for three-fifths of Britain's Muslims—are categorized as poor; the national average is 28%. A French law-enforcement source says jobless Muslims are "the easy marks, the fodder of jihadist networks." Yassin el-Abdi, 24, a trained

accountant in Mechelen, Belgium, who has been unemployed for three years, says extremists in Europe are making a bad situation for Muslims even worse. "These people who are planting the bombs are wrecking things for us," says el-Abdi. And the depressing reality, says his friend Said Bouazza, who runs a job-training center in Mechelen, is that unemployment is only adding to the jihadists' ranks. "It's like a ticking time bomb. There are people who fight back by opening their own store. Or they plant bombs."

The kinds of young people taking up the jihadist cause in Europe might 13 have been more inclined in the past to drift into a life of crime or drug use. The more committed would have had to journey to religious seminaries and training camps in places like Pakistan and Afghanistan to receive indoctrination in jihad. But now they don't need to leave home. The Internet has played a huge role in fostering a sense of community among both the fanatics and those who would join them. "They're becoming dedicated Islamists without ever leaving their home nations," a French counterterrorism official says.

What's more, *Time*'s reporting across Europe shows, the war in 14 Iraq has further radicalized some Muslims, convincing them that the U.S. and Britain are bent on war with Islam and that the only proper response is to fight back. Listen to Uzair, the Savior Sect leader in London: "Muslims are being killed all over the world through the foreign policy of the U.K. and U.S. Many feel they cannot sit around and do nothing about it. What is the difference between a suicide bomber and a B-52? I really feel that war has been declared on Islam." Iraq, says a senior French security official, "has acted as a formidable booster" for extremist groups.

In Belgium, a radical Muslim named Karim Hassoun who is head of the 15 Arab-European League, says flatly, "The more body bags of Americans we see coming back from Iraq, the happier we are." What's worrisome is how openly such rhetoric is received among ordinary Muslims, many of whom consider themselves moderates. In the Netherlands, where 1 of every 16 Dutch citizens is a Muslim, it's trendy for kids to hang on their bedroom walls half-burned American flags with Stars of David placed on them, says Mohammed Ridouan Jabri, founder of the eight-month-old Muslim Democratic Party.

What can be done to defuse the anger? European governments have 16 tried a range of approaches to contain radical Islam. In the wake of the July 7 bombings, British Prime Minister Tony Blair introduced a zero-tolerance policy toward hateful rhetoric, pledging, among other things, to deport clerics seen to be inciting violence. The crackdown represented a shift from Britain's tradition of tolerating militant speech. But some moderate Muslims fear that in his rush to get tough, Blair risks further estranging young European Muslims by heightening their sense that they are outsiders. "It reinforces bin Laden's arguments that citizenship is nothing, that nationality is a mirage blinding Muslims to their only real allegiance—to God, as jihadists define it," says Dounia Bouzar, a scholar and commentator on the lives of French-born Muslims like herself. Bouzar also laments France's 2004 law banning "conspicuous" religious symbols from public schools because its foremost target is the head scarves worn by certain devout Muslim females. Although enforcement of the law has not sparked the mass expulsion of hijab-wearing students that many feared, Bouzar says it has caused splits within the Muslim community.

The dilemma for Muslims across Europe is that in the wake of July 17 7, public demand for tougher measures against terrorism is stifling open discussion of the grievances that are fueling extremism—which allows hard-liners to crowd out moderate voices. "There is no middle ground now," says Naima Azough, 32, a Dutch parliamentarian from Morocco. "It's as if in the U.S. you heard only Noam Chomsky and Pat Buchanan."

Bolstering moderates will require change within Europe's Muslim 18 communities but also greater political sensitivity outside them—a willingness to acknowledge, for instance, the emotional impact that some policies enacted in the war on terrorism have had on Muslims. At a meeting of the radical Muslim group Hizb ut-Tahrir in Birmingham, England, the group's spokesman, Imran Waheed, 28, launched into a 40-minute lecture in front of about 80 people, insisting there's no need for the Muslim community to apologize for July 7. Many in the audience nodded in agreement. But some seemed ambivalent, caught between abhorrence for terrorism and a belief that their grievances are not taken seriously.

After praying with the other men in an adjacent room, a smiling 19 twenty-something, sporting pressed trousers and shirt and wearing neat, round glasses, began by pointing out that Islam forbids violence and the bombing of innocent people. "Our hearts are bleeding for the [July 7 victims]," he said, and in the next breath criticized the U.S. and Britain for ignoring the ways in which their policies may be adding to young Muslims' feelings of alienation. As a result, he says, the members of his generation "are frustrated. Their voices are not being heard." If the world hopes to understand—let alone overcome—the anger that roils Europe's young Muslims, it had better start to listen.

Thinking About the Essay

1. How effectively does Powell present the case of Myriam and Peter Cherif as symptomatic of a larger problem? Where is the transition made from this opening case study to a more general statement of the problem?

2. Why does Powell focus, in the second paragraph, on the chronology of diminishing contact between mother and son? What other details with larger thematic significance do you see in this opening narrative?

3. Where does Powell define the term "Generation Jihad"? How does the general definition relate to the case studies profiled in the essay? Could the term have been defined purely by way of illustration? Explain.

4. Trace the author's use of the word "rootless." Find one other recurring motif in the essay and explain its function.

5. How does Powell address the war in Iraq as one factor that contributed to the rise of Generation Jihad? What importance does he attribute to the war as a factor?

Responding in Writing

6. Compose a profile of a group of people in the United States who are members of the same generation and who could be characterized as "restive, rootless, and alienated." What do these individuals feel alienated *from*? What term would you use to refer to this generation? Do you feel a member of this generation yourself?

7. Do you recall feeling alienated from your own mother or father when you were younger? In a brief essay, reflect on the nature of those feelings and some of their causes. In what way, if any, was your sense of alienation related to feelings of cultural or political alienation?

8. Write a letter to a politically moderate Muslim publication in which you attempt to relate (rather than equate) the problems facing a subsection of American youth today to the special problems facing American Muslim youths.

Networking

9. In groups of three or four, respond to the anti-American rhetoric described (in paragraph 15) as being prevalent among Muslim youth in Europe and America. Share your responses with the class. How would you have responded differently to the examples of this rhetoric if they had been reported in the opening paragraph of the essay, rather than later in the essay?

10. Go online and read at least three blog entries that represent the points of view of European or American Muslim youths on the international controversy over the 2006 publication, in a European newspaper, of a cartoon depicting the prophet Mohammed.

Bad Luck: Why Americans Exaggerate the Terrorist Threat

Jeffrey Rosen | Jeffrey Rosen was born in 1964 in New York City and educated at Harvard University and Balliol College, Oxford University. He also has a J.D. degree from Yale Law School. Rosen currently teaches at George Washington Law School in Washington, DC.; serves as legal affairs editor at *The New Republic,* where the following essay was published in November 2001; and also is a staff writer for *The New Yorker* magazine. In his book *The Unwanted Gaze: The Destruction of Privacy in America* (2000), Rosen explores the issue of privacy from the Middle Ages—when the Jewish ban on the "unwanted gaze" protected citizens from scrutiny—to such contemporary intrusions into the right of privacy as the Monica Lewinsky case. In this essay, published shortly after the 9/11 disaster, Rosen (as we can infer from the title) offers a critical appraisal of our response to the terrorist threat.

Before Reading

What types of threats or fears have you experienced recently? Is the terrorist threat one of them? Why or why not?

The terrorist threat is all too real, but newspapers and TV stations   1
around the globe are still managing to exaggerate it. As new cases of anthrax infection continue to emerge, the World Health Organization is begging people not to panic. But tabloid headlines like this one *The Mirror* in London send a different message: "panic." A Time/CNN poll found that nearly half of all Americans say they are "very" or "somewhat" concerned that they or their families will be exposed to anthrax, even though only a handful of politicians and journalists have been targeted so far.

This isn't surprising. Terrorism is unfamiliar, it strikes largely at ran-   2
dom, and it can't be easily avoided by individual precautions. Criminologists tell us that crimes with these features are the most likely to create hysteria. If America's ability to win the psychological war against terrorism depends upon our ability to remain calm in the face of random violence, our reaction to similar threats in the past is not entirely reassuring.

In the academic literature about crime, scholars have identified a 3
paradox: "Most surveys discover that people apparently fear most being a
victim of precisely those crimes they are least likely to be victims of," writes
Jason Ditton of the University of Sheffield. "Little old ladies apparently
worry excessively about being mugged, but they are the least likely to be
mugging victims." Women worry most about violent crime, though they
have the lowest risk of being victims, while young men worry the least,
though they have the highest risk. And because of their physical vulnerability, women tend to worry more about violence in general, even when
the risk of experiencing a particular attack is evenly distributed. In a Gallup
poll at the end of September, 62 percent of women said they were "very
worried" that their families might be victimized by terrorist attacks. Only
35 percent of the men were similarly concerned.

Why are people most afraid of the crimes they are least likely to expe- 4
rience? According to Wesley Skogan of Northwestern University, "it may
be the things we feel we can't control or influence, those uncontrollable
risks, are the ones that make people most fearful." It's why people fear
flying more than they fear being hit by a car. We think we can protect
ourselves against cars by looking before crossing the street—and therefore
underestimate the risk, even though it is actually higher than being killed
in a plane crash.

People also overestimate the risk of crimes they have never experienced. 5
The elderly are no more fearful than anyone else when asked how safe they
feel when they go out at night. That's because many senior citizens don't go
out at night, or they take precautions when they do. But when surveys ask
how safe they would feel if they did go out at night more often, old people
say they would be very afraid, since they have less experience to give them
context. Instead they tend to assess risk based on media hype and rumors.
"To be able to estimate the probability of an event occurring, you first
have to know the underlying distribution of those events, and second the
trend of those events—but when it comes to crime, people usually get both
hugely wrong," writes Ditton.

The media is partly to blame. A survey by George Gerbner, former 6
dean of the Annenberg School at the University of Pennsylvania, found
that people who watch a lot of television are more likely than occasional
viewers to overestimate their chances of being a victim of violence, to
believe their neighborhood is unsafe, to say fear of crime is a very serious
problem, to assume that crime is rising, and to buy locks, watchdogs,
and guns. And this distortion isn't limited to television. Jason Ditton
notes that 45 percent of crimes reported in the newspaper involve sex
or violence, even though they only represent 3 percent of crimes overall.

When interviewed about how many crimes involve sex or violence, people tend to overestimate it by a factor of three or four. People believe they are more likely to be assaulted or raped than robbed, even though the robbery rate is much higher.

Will sensationalistic reports of worst-case terrorist scenarios exaggerate   7
people's fear of being caught in an attack? There's every reason to believe that they will because of the media's tendency to exaggerate the scope and probability of remote risks. In a book called *Random Violence*, Joel Best, then of Southern Illinois University, examined the "moral panics" about a series of new crimes that seized public attention in the 1980s and '90s: freeway violence in 1987, wilding in 1989, stalking around 1990, kids and guns in 1991, and so forth. In each case, Best writes, television seized on two or three incidents of a dramatic crime, such as freeway shooting, and then claimed it was part of a broader trend. By taking the worst and most infrequent examples of criminal violence and melodramatically claiming they were typical, television created the false impression that everyone was equally at risk, thereby increasing its audience.

The risk of terrorism is more randomly distributed than the crimes the   8
media has hyped in the past. This makes it even more frightening because it is hard to avoid through precautions. (The anthrax envelopes were more narrowly targeted than the World Trade Center attack, of course, but they still infected postal workers.) Contemporary Americans, in particular, are not well equipped to deal with arbitrary threats because, in so many realms of life, we refuse to accept the role of chance. In his nineteenth-century novel *The Gilded Age*, Mark Twain described a steamship accident that killed 22 people. The investigator's verdict: "nobody to blame." This attitude was reflected in nineteenth-century legal doctrines such as assumption of risk, which refused to compensate victims who behaved carelessly. In the twentieth century, by contrast, the United States developed what the legal historian Lawrence Friedman has called an expectation of "total justice"—namely, "the general expectation that somebody will pay for any and all calamities that happen to a person, provided only that it is not the victim's 'fault,' or at least not solely his fault."

This effort to guarantee total justice is reflected throughout American   9
society—from the regulation of product safety to the elimination of legal doctrines like assumption of risk. Since September 11 the most egregious display of this total justice mentality has been the threat by various personal injury lawyers to sue the airlines, security officials, and the architects of the World Trade Center on behalf of the victims' families. One of their claims: Flaws in the design of the twin towers may have impeded escape.

Given America's difficulty in calculating and accepting unfamiliar risk, 10 what can be done, after September 11, to minimize panic? Rather than self-censoring only when it comes to the ravings of Osama bin Laden, the broadcast media might try to curb its usual focus on worst-case scenarios. Wesley Skogan found that when people were accurately informed about the real risk, they adjusted their fears accordingly. Politicians also need to be careful about passing on unspecified but terrifying threats of future attacks. In the middle of October the Justice Department warned that a terrorist attack might be imminent, but didn't say what the attack might be, or where it might strike. The vagueness of the warning only increased public fear and caused people to cancel travel plans. But it didn't make anyone more secure.

While Americans learn to take sensible precautions, we need to also 11 learn that there is no insurance against every calamity or compensation for every misfortune. There is something inegalitarian about risk: It singles out some people from the crowd for no good reason and treats them worse than everybody else. But even in the United States, there is no such thing as perfect equality or total justice. If the first foreign attack on U.S. soil helps teach Americans how to live with risk, then perhaps we can emerge from this ordeal a stronger society as well as a stronger nation.

Thinking About the Essay

1. In Rosen's opinion, who or what is to blame for Americans' preoccupation with threats of various kinds? How does a cause-and-effect pattern of development permit the writer to present a panorama of threats in this essay?

2. Rosen is trained in the law. How does his professional expertise influence the way he builds his "case" in this essay? What legal or "courtroom" techniques can you detect?

3. The writer constructs his argument through the use of numerous examples and forms of evidence. What types of evidence can you identify and where? What is the overall effect? Is his evidence convincing or not?

4. How does Rosen's level of language imply that he is writing for an audience that can follow logically the "rules of evidence" that he presents? Cite specific words and sentences to support your response.

5. To what extent, in your opinion, is Rosen's concluding paragraph an effective summation of his case? Is the tone of this last paragraph in keeping with the tone of the whole essay? Why or why not?

Responding in Writing

6. "The terrorist threat," says Rosen in the first sentence of paragraph 1, "is all too real, but newspapers and TV stations around the globe are still managing to exaggerate it." From your perspective, do you agree or disagree with his assertion? Write an essay in which you provide sufficient evidence to support your response.

7. In a personal essay, explain how the terrorist threat has affected any other fears or apprehensions that you have had to deal with.

8. In an illustrative essay, address a question posed by Rosen in paragraph 10: "Given America's difficulty in calculating and accepting unfamiliar risk, what can be done, after September 11, to minimize panic?" Develop at least three ways to reduce our sense of panic.

Networking

9. In groups of four or five, discuss the ways in which each member has developed ways to cope with a range of fears and phobias—not just the terrorist threat. Then list all the strategies for coping and share them in class discussion.

10. Go online and locate at least four reviews of Rosen's book, *The Unwanted Gaze: The Destruction of Privacy in America* (2000). Download and take notes on the reviewers' comments. (You will discover that some reviewers think that the book is brilliant, whereas others have negative opinions.) Write a comparative essay in which you explain these diverging appraisals of Rosen's book.

"Terror" Is the Enemy

PHILIP BOBBITT | Philip Bobbitt, an expert in international law and security, was born in 1948 in Temple, Texas. He received degrees from Princeton University (A.B., 1971), Yale University (J.D., 1975), and Oxford University (Ph.D., 1983) before embarking on careers in law, foundation work, and higher education. Bobbitt, a former senior director at the National Security Council, is currently a law professor at Columbia University. His publications include *The Shield of Achilles: The Long War and the Market State* (2002) and *War on Terror* (2006). In this essay from the December 14, 2008, issue of *The New York Times*, Bobbitt distills the argument that he makes at length in his latest book, *Terror and Consent: The Wars for the 21st Century*.

Before Reading

Consider the types of wars that we will be fighting in the twenty-first century, and how they will differ from previous wars and conflicts.

Generals are not the only ones who prepare to fight the previous war. Our experience with 20th-century nation-based terrorists—the I.R.A. in Ireland, the P.K.K. in the Kurdish areas of Turkey, ETA in Spain's Basque country, the F.L.N. in Algeria and others—still dominates much of our thinking about how to deal with 21st-century global terrorists. Indeed, the lack of new concepts may well be as deadly to our national security as any lack of vaccines.   1

New approaches to dealing with global terrorism must first be integrated into our foreign security policies generally. Allies in Europe must be reassured that the United States will not violate the human rights accords to which we are a party. We must also devise a policy that aligns the interests of Afghanistan, India and Pakistan while isolating the terrorists that threaten them all. We must seek common ground with many states around the world against our universal threats—global terrorists and pirates, the proliferation of nuclear and biological weapons and civilian catastrophes—even if, in other contexts, these nations are our adversaries.   2

The "war on terror" is not a nonsensical public relations slogan, however unwelcome this conclusion may be to Pentagon planners or civil-liberties advocates. The notion of such a war puzzles us—after all, who would sign the peace treaty?—because we are so trapped in 20th-century expectations about warfare. But success in war does not always mean the capitulation of an enemy government (as we have seen in Iraq); rather, it varies with the war aim.   3

In a war against terror, the aim is not the conquest of territory or the advancement of ideology, but the protection of civilians. We are fighting a war on terror, not just terrorists. That is evident from the list of targets in the attacks in Mumbai, India, in which national liberation terrorists from Kashmir were apparently the outsourced operational arm of a global network with far more ambitious, and more anti-Western, objectives. The Mumbai terrorists did not even bother to issue demands; what they sought was terror itself.   4

Mexico is potentially our Pakistan—a failing state on our border that can provide haven for our adversaries, at least some of whom will   5

Philip Bobbitt "'Terror' Is the Enemy," *New York Times*, Dec 14, 2008. © 2008, The New York Times. Reprinted by permission.

be privatized terrorists. Imagine a poorer, less-democratic Mexico; then imagine it harboring extortionists with a small arsenal of deliverable nuclear or biological weapons. This may be a long-term threat, but it requires immediate assistance and cooperation.

But Pakistan is our Pakistan, too, and not just India's or Afghanistan's 6 problem. "Homeland security" is a dangerous solecism when we are fighting a global adversary that moves easily across borders. If terror is our adversary, then our own health system, for example, is only as secure as the most vulnerable health system overseas that might spawn an epidemic that could quickly reach our shores.

We must use available international institutions—like the International 7 Criminal Court, to which pirates and other terrorists could be rendered—whenever possible. Yet we must not shrink from augmenting them, for example, by creating a global body similar to NATO including other democracies, by enlarging the United Nations Security Council to include other great states, and by giving new security responsibilities to the Group of Eight.

Our legislators need more foresight, stockpiling laws for emergencies 8 just as we stockpile vaccines. Perhaps the most obvious would be a provision to replace members of Congress who might be killed or disabled in such numbers that the House of Representatives itself is unable to act. This could easily have occurred on 9/11 if the fourth plane had struck the Capitol, which would have plunged the country into months of martial law.

Finally, the Obama administration can have no higher priority than 9 forging links with the private sector to protect what has become the electronic foundation for contemporary life. Unless the government, perhaps through insurance mandates, can persuade private companies to harden themselves to cyber-attacks, the deregulated and fragmented owners of our digital backbone will inevitably underfinance such protection.

This last observation points to the interrelation between the three 10 arenas of the war on terror: 21st-century terrorists, the commodification of weapons of mass destruction, and the increasing vulnerability of highly developed nations like our own. Educating our public about this new tripartite threat will place enormous demands on our political leadership.

The presidential election was the end of the first phase of the war 11 on terror. Preventing any attacks on the United States since 9/11 is something for which the Bush administration must be given credit, but credit must also go to the American public, which decisively rejected offshore penal colonies, spurious rationalizations for warfare, and secret torture chambers and contempt for the constitutional and international laws that would forbid such practices. Indeed, by selecting a former law professor as its new president, the country has thoroughly dismissed the notion that law is an obstacle rather than a guide to achieving security.

Thinking About the Essay

1. Why does Bobbitt allude to various "nation-based terrorists" in his introductory paragraph? What assumptions, if any, does he make about the audience's knowledge of these groups? What is his claim, and how does it follow from this preliminary information?

2. Where does Bobbitt most explicitly define the "war on terror"? Does he provide an extended definition of this term? Why or why not?

3. Explain the minor propositions and supporting evidence that Bobbitt introduces to support his argument. How does the logic of his essay reflect Bobbitt's training in the law?

4. How would you describe Bobbitt's tone in this essay? How does the tone affect his selection of information and remarks about old and new approaches to terrorism?

5. In what way is this essay built around comparative analysis? How does Bobbitt's conclusion reflect this comparative approach?

Responding in Writing

6. Write an essay in which you agree or disagree with Bobbitt's argument.

7. Argue for or against the proposition that the Bush administration "must be given credit" for preventing terrorist attacks against the United States in the aftermath of 9/11.

8. Write a process paper in which you describe the steps that should be taken to combat terrorism in the twenty-first century.

Networking

9. In groups of four or five, research one of the terrorist groups or events mentioned by Bobbitt in his essay. Report your findings to the class.

10. Conduct a computer search for information on the International Criminal Court (see paragraph 7). In an essay, explain why the Court could serve as a useful vehicle for prosecuting terrorists.

The Algebra of Infinite Justice

ARUNDHATI ROY

Arundhati Roy, born in Shillong, India, in 1961 and raised in Kerala, is the child of Syrian Christian and Hindu parents. Her first novel, *The God of Small Things* (1997), turned this former architecture student, actor, and screenwriter into an international celebrity. Steeped in the complex history of India, Roy's novel, which won the prestigious Booker Prize, is a dazzling portrayal of the lives of twin children as they move through the barriers of race, gender, and class on national and international levels of experience. To date, *The God of Small Things* has been published in twenty-seven languages. With her fame and royalties, Roy today is an activist, denouncing in extended essays the Indian government's destruction of the environment, criticizing nuclear proliferation, and subjecting other global issues to critical scrutiny. Her social and political criticism appears in *The Cost of Living* (1999) and *Power Politics* (2001). Roy received the $350,000 Lannam Foundation Prize for Cultural Freedom in 2002, announcing that she would donate the money to fifty educational institutions, publishing houses, and people's movements in India. In the following essay, published in *The Progressive* in December 2001, Roy tries to explain why American foreign policy is so hated around the world.

Before Reading

Do you think that the United States government engages in policies around the world in order to promote "the American way of life"? Why or why not? What do you understand this term to mean? Why would peoples of other nations be skeptical of this effort?

It must be hard for ordinary Americans, so recently bereaved, to look up at the world with their eyes full of tears and encounter what might appear to them to be indifference. It isn't indifference. It's just augury. An absence of surprise. The tired wisdom of knowing that what goes around eventually comes around. The American people ought to know that it is not them, but their government's policies, that are so hated.

Bush's almost god-like mission—called Operation Infinite Justice until it was pointed out that this could be seen as an insult to Muslims, who

Reprinted by Arundhati Roy, "The Algebra of Infinite Justice," *The Progressive*, Volume 65, Number 12 (December 2001), pp. 28–31. Copyright © 2001 Arundhati Roy. Online at: http://www.progressive.org/0901/roy1201.html. A full version of this essay appears in Arundhati Roy, *Power Politics*, 2nd ed. (Cambridge: South End Press, 2001), pp. 105–34.

believe that only Allah can mete out infinite justice, and was renamed Operation Enduring Freedom—requires some small clarifications. For example, Infinite Justice/Enduring Freedom for whom?

In 1996, Madeleine Albright, then the U.S. Ambassador to the United Nations, was asked on national television what she felt about the fact that 500,000 Iraqi children had died as a result of economic sanctions the U.S. insisted upon. She replied that it was "a very hard choice," but that all things considered, "we think the price is worth it." Albright never lost her job for saying this. She continued to travel the world representing the views and aspirations of the U.S. government. More pertinently, the sanctions against Iraq remain in place. Children continue to die.

So here we have it. The equivocating distinction between civilization and savagery, between the "massacre of innocent people" or, if you like, the "clash of civilizations" and "collateral damage." The sophistry and fastidious algebra of Infinite Justice. How many dead Iraqis will it take to make the world a better place? How many dead Afghans for every dead American? How many dead children for every dead man? How many dead mujahedeen for each dead investment banker?

The American people may be a little fuzzy about where exactly Afghanistan is (we hear reports that there's a run on maps of the country), but the U.S. government and Afghanistan are old friends. In 1979, after the Soviet invasion of Afghanistan, the CIA and Pakistan's ISI (Inter-Services Intelligence) launched the CIA's largest covert operation since the Vietnam War. Their purpose was to harness the energy of Afghan resistance and expand it into a holy war, an Islamic jihad, which would turn Muslim countries within the Soviet Union against the communist regime and eventually destabilize it. When it began, it was meant to be the Soviet Union's Vietnam. It turned out to be much more than that. Over the years, through the ISI, the CIA funded and recruited tens of thousands of radical mujahedeen from forty Islamic countries as soldiers for America's proxy war. The rank and file of the mujahedeen were unaware that their jihad was actually being fought on behalf of Uncle Sam.

In 1989, after being bloodied by ten years of relentless conflict, the Russians withdrew, leaving behind a civilization reduced to rubble. Civil war in Afghanistan raged on. The jihad spread to Chechnya, Kosovo, and eventually to Kashmir. The CIA continued to pour in money and military equipment, but the overhead had become immense, and more money was needed.

The mujahedeen ordered farmers to plant opium as a "revolutionary tax." Under the protection of the ISI, hundreds of heroin-processing laboratories were set up across Afghanistan. Within two years of the

CIA's arrival, the Pakistan/Afghanistan borderland had become the biggest producer of heroin in the world, and the single biggest source on American streets. The annual profits, said to be between $100 and $200 billion, were ploughed back into training and arming militants.

In 1996, the Taliban—then a marginal sect of dangerous, hard-line   8 fundamentalists—fought its way to power in Afghanistan. It was funded by the ISI, that old cohort of the CIA, and supported by many political parties in Pakistan. The Taliban unleashed a regime of terror. Its first victims were its own people, particularly women. It closed down girls' schools, dismissed women from government jobs, enforced Sharia law—under which women deemed to be "immoral" are stoned to death and widows guilty of being adulterous are buried alive.

After all that has happened, can there be anything more ironic than   9 Russia and America joining hands to redestroy Afghanistan? The question is, can you destroy destruction? Dropping more bombs on Afghanistan will only shuffle the rubble, scramble some old graves, and disturb the dead. The desolate landscape of Afghanistan was the burial ground of Soviet communism and the springboard of a unipolar world dominated by America. It made the space for neocapitalism and corporate globalization, again dominated by America: And now Afghanistan is poised to become the graveyard for the unlikely soldiers who fought and won this war for America.

India, thanks in part to its geography and in part to the vision of its   10 former leaders, has so far been fortunate enough to be left out of this Great Game. Had it been drawn in, it's more than likely that our democracy, such as it is, would not have survived. After September 11, as some of us watched in horror, the Indian government furiously gyrated its hips, begging the U.S. to set up its base in India rather than Pakistan. Having had this ringside view of Pakistan's sordid fate, it isn't just odd, it's unthinkable, that India should want to do this. Any Third World country with a fragile economy and a complex social base should know by now that to invite a superpower such as America in (whether it says it's staying or just passing through) would be like inviting a brick to drop through your windscreen.

Operation Enduring Freedom is being fought ostensibly to uphold the   11 American Way of Life. It'll probably end up undermining it completely. It will spawn more anger and more terror across the world. For ordinary people in America, it will mean lives lived in a climate of sickening uncertainty: Will my child be safe in school? Will there be nerve gas in the subway? A bomb in the cinema hall? Will my love come home tonight? Being picked off a few at a time—now with anthrax, later perhaps with smallpox or bubonic plague—may end up being worse than being annihilated all at once by a nuclear bomb.

The U.S. government and governments all over the world are using   12
the climate of war as an excuse to curtail civil liberties, deny free speech,
lay off workers, harass ethnic and religious minorities, cut back on public
spending, and divert huge amounts of money to the defense industry. To
what purpose? President Bush can no more "rid the world of evildoers"
than he can stock it with saints.

It's absurd for the U.S. government to even toy with the notion that it   13
can stamp out terrorism with more violence and oppression. Terrorism is
the symptom, not the disease.

Terrorism has no country. It's transnational, as global an enterprise as   14
Coke or Pepsi or Nike. At the first sign of trouble, terrorists can pull up
stakes and move their "factories" from country to country in search of a
better deal. Just like the multinationals.

Terrorism as a phenomenon may never go away. But if it is to be con-   15
tained, the first step is for America to at least acknowledge that it shares
the planet with other nations, with other human beings, who, even if they
are not on TV, have loves and grief's and stories and songs and sorrows
and, for heaven's sake, rights.

The September 11 attacks were a monstrous calling card from a world   16
gone horribly wrong. The message may have been written by Osama bin
Laden (who knows?) and delivered by his couriers, but it could well have
been signed by the ghosts of the victims of America's old wars: the millions
killed in Korea, Vietnam, and Cambodia, the 17,500 killed when Israel—
backed by the U.S.—invaded Lebanon in 1982, the tens of thousands of
Iraqis killed in Operation Desert Storm, the thousands of Palestinians who
have died fighting Israel's occupation of the West Bank.

And the millions who died, in Yugoslavia, Somalia, Haiti, Chile, Nica-   17
ragua, El Salvador, the Dominican Republic, Panama, at the hands of all
the terrorists, dictators, and genocidists whom the American government
supported, trained, bankrolled, and supplied with arms. And this is far
from being a comprehensive list.

For a country involved in so much warfare and conflict, the American   18
people have been extremely fortunate. The strikes on September 11 were only
the second on American soil in over a century. The first was Pearl Harbor. The
reprisal for this took a long route, but ended with Hiroshima and Nagasaki.

This time the world waits with bated breath for the horrors to come.   19

Someone recently said that if Osama bin Laden didn't exist, America   20
would have had to invent him. But in a way, America did invent him. He
was among the jihadis who moved to Afghanistan in 1979 when the CIA
commenced its operations there. Bin Laden has the distinction of being
created by the CIA and wanted by the FBI. In the course of a fortnight, he

was promoted from Suspect to Prime Suspect, and then, despite the lack of any real evidence, straight up the charts to "Wanted: Dead or Alive."

From what is known about bin Laden, it's entirely possible that he did 21 not personally plan and carry out the attacks—that he is the inspirational figure, "the CEO of the Holding Company." The Taliban's response to U.S. demands for the extradition of bin Laden was uncharacteristically reasonable: Produce the evidence, then we'll hand him over. President Bush's response was that the demand was "non-negotiable."

(While talks are on for the extradition of CEOs, can India put in a 22 side-request for the extradition of Warren Anderson of the USA? He was the chairman of Union Carbide, responsible for the 1984 Bhopal gas leak that killed 16,000 people. We have collated the necessary evidence. It's all in the files. Could we have him, please?)

But who is Osama bin Laden really? Let me rephrase that. What is 23 Osama bin Laden? He's America's family secret. He is the American President's dark doppelgänger. The savage twin of all that purports to be beautiful and civilized. He has been sculpted from the spare rib of a world laid to waste by America's foreign policy: its gunboat diplomacy, its nuclear arsenal, its vulgarly stated policy of "full spectrum dominance," its chilling disregard for non-American lives, its barbarous military interventions, its support for despotic and dictatorial regimes, its merciless economic agenda that has munched through the economies of poor countries like a cloud of locusts, its marauding multinationals that are taking over the air we breathe, the ground we stand on, the water we drink, the thoughts we think.

Now that the family secret has been spilled, the twins are blurring into 24 one another and gradually becoming interchangeable. Their guns, bombs, money, and drugs have been going around in the loop for a while. Now they've even begun to borrow each other's rhetoric. Each refers to the other as "the head of the snake." Both invoke God and use the loose millenarian currency of Good and Evil as their terms of reference. Both are engaged in unequivocal political crimes. Both are dangerously armed—one with the nuclear arsenal of the obscenely powerful, the other with the incandescent, destructive power of the utterly hopeless. The fireball and the ice pick. The bludgeon and the axe.

The important thing to keep in mind is that neither is an acceptable 25 alternative to the other.

President Bush's ultimatum to the people of the world—"Either you 26 are with us or you are with the terrorists"—is a piece of presumptuous arrogance.

It's not a choice that people want to, need to, or should have to make. 27

Thinking About the Essay

1. What are the writer's political views about the United States? What aspects of Roy's essay might prompt a counterargument? Do you disagree with Roy's assessment, or do you think that the writer actually has an important argument that we should treat seriously? Explain.

2. What does the title of the essay mean? Where does Roy expand on it? Why does she equate "justice" with "algebra"?

3. Point to paragraphs and sections of this essay where the writer uses process analysis, causal analysis, and comparison and contrast to advance her argument.

4. This essay seems to hop almost cinematically from point to point. Does Roy's technique damage the organization and coherence of her essay? Why or why not?

5. In the final analysis, does Roy make a compelling or logical argument in this essay? Explain your response.

Responding in Writing

6. Do you think that people around the world hate America's policies but not Americans—as Roy asserts? Write a paper responding to this question. Provide examples to support your position.

7. Write an argumentative essay in which you either support or rebut Roy's argument. Try to proceed point by point, moving completely through Roy's main reasons in defense of her claim.

8. What does the word *justice* mean to you? Did the American nation receive its due "justice" on September 11, 2001? Write an extended-definition essay responding to this notion.

Networking

9. In small groups, discuss each member's personal impression of Roy's essay. Try to explain the thoughts and emotions it prompts. Make a list of these responses, and share them with the rest of the class.

10. Enter an Internet forum dealing with American foreign policy and monitor what participants write about it. Prepare a summary of these responses, and post them—either on your own web page or as an e-mail attachment to friends.

10

Global Aid: Can We Reduce Disease and Poverty?

The aftermath of Hurricane Katrina in 2005 was a reminder to many in the United States and around the world that major socioeconomic disparities exist even within a developed country. Poverty and a weak infrastructure made New Orleans and the surrounding region vulnerable to natural catastrophe, in much the same way that a compromised immune system invites disease. Observers compared the disaster in New Orleans to the humanitarian crises that result from floods and earthquakes in vulnerable, overpopulated Third World countries. But the fact is that most of the world's population live under conditions like those found in the slums, shantytowns, and rural backwaters of the globe and in their counterparts in the United States.

We may like to think of such conditions as the provincial vestiges of a preindustrial world that, once exposed to the light of day, will naturally be assimilated into the modern world and corrected by the natural forces of progress. But globalization has also created new forms of poverty, isolation, and dependency. The new global economy has meant a return to what some would describe as an economics of colonial exploitation—although it is not clear who is exploiting whom, or even if "exploitation" is the correct label. Globalization has changed the relationship between "rich" and "poor" countries, but it is not clear whether the forces of a global free market will tend to bridge or widen the gap between rich and poor, whether global commerce will strengthen the socioeconomic infrastructures of poor countries or mask and preserve their deficiencies. Without infrastructures of their own in place, the poorest nations in the world may become even more dependent on international aid to address poverty-related health problems. And while some blame these negative trends on the forces of an unregulated global free market,

Refugees fleeing from ongoing atrocities committed by warring factions in the Democratic Republic of Congo.

Thinking About the Image

1. How would you describe your initial response to this image? For example, do you find the image to be optimistic or depressing? Explain your position.

2. How might your response be influenced by your attitudes toward gender, sexuality, race, geography, or cultural background?

3. What point or argument do you think the photographer was trying to make?

4. Conduct research on the conflict in the Democratic Republic of the Congo, and then write a brief essay on one aspect of this problem. Insert at least three relevant images into the essay.

the philanthropic efforts of the Gates Foundation—which now spends nearly as much each year on global health projects as the World Health Organization—suggest that a corporate model of international aid may serve as a viable alternative to government-based infrastructures. (An essay by Bill Gates appears in this chapter.)

The essays in this chapter analyze global health and poverty issues in terms of a complex set of factors that have become even more challenging in recent decades with the phenomenon of globalization. For example, AIDS relief workers might distribute condoms to miners in South Africa, but the South African mines are run by unregulated transnational corporations, the miners are poor and underpaid migrant laborers, and their sex partners are often migrant workers who are forced into prostitution to feed and clothe their children. Often, the conditions that make people vulnerable to a disease are so closely connected with disease itself that cause and effect are nearly indistinguishable—hence, the term "Nutritionally Acquired Immune Deficiency Syndrome" (NAIDS).

In the early nineteenth century, British economist Robert Malthus predicted that the world's population would eventually outrun the world's food supply and that hunger and famine were the natural mechanisms for adjusting supply with demand. Malthus, as many have pointed out, failed to take into account future technological innovations that would radically improve the efficiency of world food production. Today, world food supply exceeds demand. The problem of world hunger is a failure of distribution, not a failure to produce enough food. And many of the diseases that result from poverty and hunger can be treated or prevented, depending on the approach taken. Globalization reminds us that certain disparities are the result of structural failure, and that the magnitude of a natural disaster is often a function of an unnatural vulnerability.

What I Did on My Summer Vacation

Jeffrey Sachs | Jeffrey Sachs is director of the Earth Institute, Quetelet Professor of Sustainable Development, and Professor of Health Policy and Management at Columbia University. Before his move to Columbia in 2002, Sachs was director of the Center for International Development and Galen L. Stone Professor of International Trade at Harvard (where he was a faculty member for more than twenty years). Sachs serves as an economic adviser to governments in Latin America, Eastern Europe,

Jeffrey Sachs, "What I Did on My Summer Vacation: I Went to Africa." ESQUIRE, December 2005. Reprinted by permission of Jeffrey D. Sachs.

the former Soviet Union, Asia, and Africa. He was Special Adviser to United Nations Secretary-General Kofi Annan on the set of poverty alleviation initiatives known as the Millennium Project. In the following essay, which appeared in the December 2005 issue of *Esquire* magazine, Sachs describes his tour of places in Africa where, village by village, he witnesses evidence of the Millennium Project meeting its pragmatic goals.

Before Reading

Do you think of poverty and food shortage as a world problem that, like the poor, "will always be with us"? Can you imagine simple solutions to these problems that are also *long-term* solutions?

This summer, from June to August, my family and I took a trip. My daugh- 1 ter Hannah, who is ten, can now reel off the itinerary from memory: China, Tajikistan, Israel, United Arab Emirates, Yemen, Libya, England, Ghana, Mali, Nigeria, Kenya, Uganda, Ethiopia, Djibouti, Rwanda, Malawi, Indonesia, Cambodia. In these places, we spent most of our time in villages.

Throughout the world, the poor by and large live in villages. Thousands 2 and thousands of villages: The fact of the matter is that these villages are communities of people who want out of poverty, who want their children to get out of poverty. They know they're poor. And they know the whole world is not poor and that they're stuck in a situation they don't want to be stuck in. That's the core concept of the Millennium Villages Project, which a few colleagues from the UN's Millennium Project and the Earth Institute at Columbia University and I started about a year ago.

Now, the basic ideas for how a poor village can be developed have 3 been known for a long time among different groups of practitioners— those who grow food, and those who fight disease, and those who man- age water supplies. What the Millennium Project does is bring these different groups together, because villages don't live only on farming or only on water or only on clinics. They live as whole communities that will get out of poverty wholly. If children are eating better because farm- ers are growing more food, it's going to improve the health of the chil- dren. Obviously, it will take the burden off the clinics. If the children are healthy, they are going to be in school. And they're going to be learning. If the children are in school, they're going to be the ones who will bring new ideas and new technologies to the community, so it's all mutually reinforcing.

My colleagues and I took a stand in our work several years ago that we 4 would not look for the magic bullet, because there is none. These are just basic problems requiring basic work. Nothing magic about it. The strategy follows from that basic idea, but the idea of approaching this on a village-by-village basis came about accidentally.

Officialdom the world over is pretty slow moving, pretty impractical, 5 and pretty darn frustrating many ways, so even when the proof of these concepts is clear, actually getting things done is not so easy. You need a little bit of money, and donors seem utterly capable of spending it on themselves, on salaries of consultants, on meetings and seminars and workshops, but not on actually helping people not starve to death in villages. Too much of our aid money goes after an emergency comes, in shipping food aid instead of helping the farmers grow food, just as too much of it goes to razing and rebuilding a city rather than fortifying levees in advance of a disaster. Think of it as a smart investment: We can pay now or pay later. And it's a lot cheaper to pay now, and the return is incalculable. Yet this stuff doesn't actually get done, and that's why people are hungry, and that's why they're unable to access safe drinking water, and that's why they're dying by the millions.

It's not very satisfactory to see this and not act. And so in the last couple 6 of years I've started to talk about these problems with business leaders and philanthropists, and over and over again I've heard the same response: Don't wait for the government. I'll help you. So what kind of accidentally dawned on us was that we could just go ahead and get these concepts proven on the ground. And that's what we are doing. And many philanthropists have come forward now and said, We'll give you some backing; show us what you can do.

The other day I was talking to the CEO of a major American corporation, 7 a man who understands first and foremost the value of a good investment, and I was describing this effort to him, and he got it immediately. I hadn't even finished talking when he blurted out, "Sign me up for two villages!"

Our first village in Kenya, called Sauri, is actually a cluster of eight 8 villages in what they call a sublocation in western Kenya, a very hungry, very disease-ridden, very isolated, extremely impoverished community. And it's a community that some of my colleagues knew because they had been analyzing the soils there and in nearby communities for many years. A colleague from Columbia University, Pedro Sanchez, who is a soils expert, felt strongly that there was an opportunity for quick development there. He told me that the soil simply lacked the nutrients to grow a proper crop. A little nitrogen, to be specific. He said to me, "You know, this situation could turn around quite quickly."

Now, when you have the experts saying that on one side and the phi- 9 lanthropists on the other side telling you, "Come on, let's do something," it gets pretty exciting. And that's how the Millennium Villages concept was born. The scientists said, Let's move. The philanthropists said, Let's move. A year ago we went and met with the community in Kenya and talked to people there about it. And they said, Let's move!

So we moved.   10

The trip this summer was timed to the harvest festival in Kenya, in   11
which the community celebrated the biggest harvest that it had ever had. And it's stunning how easy it was. I had told Pedro that he'd better be right about the nitrogen because a lot of people were watching, and lo and behold it was nitrogen! Putting in some basic fertilizer and helping the farmers use some improved seed varieties led to a doubling of their yields. Just like that, in one growing season. Very low cost, a few bucks per person in the village.

And we are not talking about just a few people being lifted out of   12
poverty. We're talking about five thousand people. And that cluster of villages is already serving as the model for dozens of other villages for miles around. It's exponential. It's viral. This is how the world is changed.

On my trip this summer with my family, I got to visit with the leader-   13
ship of ten African countries, from the village level to the heads of state. Each leader committed to working with us to establish ten Millennium Villages in the next year. That's a hundred altogether.

A year ago, we had two.   14

We first went to Sauri in the spring of 2004. Next, we decided to work   15
in one of the toughest places on the planet, drought-ridden Ethiopia, where it's easy to just throw up your hands and say, It's impossible. But get on the ground, talk to the community, talk to the local experts, understand their distinctive problems, put it into bite-sized units, and what looks at first to be impossible becomes solvable.

We identified an area in northern Ethiopia, Tigray province. It is an   16
hour from the regional capital, and then an hour off the road, and then an hour off the off-the-road. It's a beautiful, remote community of several thousand people in a valley that has tens of thousands of people. Again, we met with the community and found enormous enthusiasm and enormous organization—people who want to take their futures into their hands but need just a little bit of help to do it. They know about fertilizer, they know about improved seeds, they know about malaria bed nets, they know about cell phones, they know about trucks. They know they don't have any of these things. But they would like to have the chance. They're saying, Help us a bit and we can get out of this. In fact, that's what we find all over the developing world. The poor countries are saying to the rich countries: Look, we know you have an income a hundred times bigger than we have. We're starving, and you have more than enough to eat. You

have everything you could ask for, and we have absolutely zero. We're not calling for revolution; we're not out to dismantle the world. We just want to have a chance to find a way over a long period of time to have some of the things that you have.

In Tigray province, their crop is a mix of teff, which is the staple grain 17 of Ethiopia; sorghum, which is a dry-season grain; a little bit of finger millet, which is another dry-season grain; and maize, which is pretty much grown all over Africa. Tree crops, papayas and mangoes, can grow in this kind of environment if there's a little bit of drip irrigation. And they provide both market opportunities and wonderful nutrition. So we started them with nurseries and improved seed. A local scientist, a wonderful young Ethiopian, was selected by the local government to head the project for us and get the community together. They built these remarkable check dams called gabions, which are just ways to preserve these mountainside villages from the short onslaught of floods and channel the water away from the crops so that the water running down the mountains doesn't create gulleys and destroy the land.

In other words, same point: simple steps, low-cost steps, all attuned to 18 the area's specific needs, led by the community, done by the community, but with a helping hand. That was early this year, and since then the local people have been out there doing the land reformation, doing reforestation, and getting ready for the planting season that was a couple months ago, and they'll be harvesting soon. In the meantime, the clinic is being built and the school is being expanded, all within a very modest budget of fifty dollars per villager per year for five years, which is our standard amount of intervention.

Then we've helped establish a local economy. And chances are, these peo- 19 ple aren't going to need us anymore. So the incessant talk in Washington about these corrupt people and their corrupt governments is just a galling excuse not to focus on practical things that we can do now to improve the world.

And for the hard-nosed among us, it bears repeating: Extreme poverty 20 is the best breeding ground on earth for disease, political instability, and terrorism.

Thirty-six years ago, the rich world began in earnest to figure out what 21 it would realistically take to help the poor world. A commission led by former Canadian prime minister Lester Pearson came up with the number 0.7. Here's how they arrived at that: They said that there should be a transfer of about 1 percent of GNP from the rich to the poor. That's one dollar out of every hundred. They said the public sector will do some and the private sector needs to do some, and that it should be about a seventy-thirty split. So that's where the seventy cents came from. And that was adopted by the General Assembly of the UN in 1970. The U.S. resisted for a long time. We didn't want to sign on even when the rest of the world did.

But in March 2002, the world's leaders met in Monterrey, Mexico, at a conference that President Bush attended, and this conference adopted something called the Monterrey Consensus, which upheld the 0.7 target. This time, the United States signed on to it. The American signature came after a long, detailed negotiation. The U.S. finally said, Okay, it's only seventy cents. And the agreement it signed said this, in paragraph 42: "We urge developed countries that have not done so to make concrete efforts towards the target of 0.7 percent of GNP as official development assistance." Check it out, paragraph 42.   22

This fall at the United Nations, President Bush said that it is dangerous to American security when countries are not achieving economic development. They become unstable; they become seedbeds for terror, for violence, for the major ills of the world. The whole U.S. national-security doctrine says that development is one of the pillars of national security. There's actually nothing wrong with what these tough, self-interested types in foreign policy have been saying, because what they have been saying is that it is completely within our national interest to be helping in these circumstances.   23

The problem is not in the words or the logic; the problem is in our lack of action. We currently give about a quarter of our pledged assistance. We've pledged to give seventy cents out of every hundred dollars of U.S. income. Instead, we give about eighteen cents. For the safety of all Americans, we must insist that our government live up to its obligation.   24

When President Kennedy talked about helping the people in the huts and villages around the world, he said we did it not to fight communism but because it was the right thing to do. Turns out that it was right on every level, not merely morally right. It was right for our national security, for our global health, for stopping violence. It was right from a hardheaded, bottom-line, conservative standpoint, and it was right for winning hearts and minds at a time when we needed allies. And we need allies again.   25

This is a tiny amount of our income that could save millions of people and make a safer world, and it is really a measure of our times that we ask ourselves, Why should we give a few cents out of every hundred dollars to do something like this? And yet we do ask that question.   26

At the beginning of July, we flew to Libya for the African Union summit, where I was honored to speak to the African heads of state for the second year running.   27

Then on to London for the G8 summit. I didn't actually go to the summit in Gleneagles but worked out of London and left the morning of the bombing.   28

And Tony Blair got it absolutely right that day, and President Bush 29
made a very good statement also, saying that it was all the more important
to redouble our efforts in the fight against poverty and not let the terrorists take away from that agenda. And Gleneagles did produce important
results: The G8 leaders committed to doubling aid to Africa. It was a
welcome step in the right direction but a long way from what the world
has promised.

After the G8, on to Ghana, where much interesting work is being done. 30
A lot of the agricultural concepts I am describing are drawn from Ghana's
very vigorous scientific community of ecologists and agronomists, fruit
growers and hydrologists. There's a tremendous amount of local research
that's been done on African agriculture. And scientists there have solutions
up and down the continent, and that's what they want to apply. We're not
inventing any of this.

We went from Ghana to Nigeria. And Nigeria is quite another thing 31
altogether. It's the most populous country in Africa, one fifth of sub-
Saharan Africa. The country has had an incredibly complex and difficult
transition to democracy because it's a sprawling, multiethnic, unstable
country with a long history of extreme corruption. Nigeria is led by President Obasanjo, who is fighting hard on every front to create a rule of law,
decent systems, and a constitutional government.

I've been working with President Obasanjo for five years now on all 32
sorts of things. He has hosted an Africa-wide malaria conference and an
Africa-wide AIDS conference that President Carter and I attended. He has
hosted all sorts of other major initiatives because he's a real leader and he
really understands the stakes right now. He's trying to get not only Nigeria
on its feet but all of Africa.

So we will have many villages in Nigeria. In the north, we're going to start 33
one village project in Kaduna, working with the Islamic community there.

We also went south to the state of Ondo, which is led by a remarkable 34
reform-minded governor who I immediately took to. He was chairman
of the geology department at Ibadan University for many years and got
his Ph.D. in geology from the University of Texas. We decided together to
launch a Millennium Villages project in his state. And that will be a site for
two communities, Ibara and Ikaram, for about twenty thousand people,
and we're getting that started right now. The governor is on e-mail with
me, and he is very determined.

From Nigeria on to Mali, which is right next to Niger. People are 35
hearing about the hunger crisis in Niger, and the same basic crisis is also
happening in Mali. It had a massive locust crisis last year, which ate up the
crops. Timbuktu is in northern Mali. We went from the capital, Bamako,
to Timbuktu, both of which are on the Niger River. Timbuktu is just at the

boundary of the desert and was the way station for caravans coming from the north through the Sahara on their way to Ghana and other parts of west Africa and back again. So it's a place of intersection, of nomads and farm people as well, and it's the northern extent of settled agriculture. The villages on the south side of Timbuktu are the worst of the worst.

I asked the village chief, What are you living on now? What are you going 36 to do? It was obviously a very painful conversation. For him to be answering in front of everybody was not the easiest thing in the world, yet we needed to have the conversation. One option apparently was that they were going to borrow some seed, because they had lost everything—food, seed—to the locusts. And I asked what the terms would be. He had been looking down at the sand, and he raised his head and looked at me. The terms would be that they would have to pay it back twice, a 100 percent interest rate in one growing season, due in four months. Literally an impossible situation.

But we have an idea that we are testing.   37

A couple of months before I was in Mali, I had been to the Indian state 38 of Andhra Pradesh, which is along the Ganges River. The Ganges plain is home to hundreds of millions of people because you have intensive agriculture there. You go from farmhouse to farmhouse and everyone has a hand pump and many a treadle pump, which you use to pump water by foot. And the reason is that the water table is very close to the surface. You just dig down ten or fifteen feet and you hit water.

In Mali, you have the Niger River, but there are no pumps. And it 39 looked so familiar to me. I said, How far down is the water table? Three meters, they said.

Why don't you have a well down there?, I asked, because everyone is 40 without water. And they said, Maybe we could do that. Maybe a large project could come in. I said, But you just need treadle pumps here. This is perfect for small-scale irrigation. Now a real expert will judge this. And we have great hydrologists and agronomists on our team. So we're going to start a village in Timbuktu, and we're going to prove that along the Niger you can have irrigation.

The south of Mali is a cotton-growing area where we're also going 41 to have a village. And it is here that you see the direct manifestation of how American cotton subsidies actually lead to the death of impoverished communities. There we had a community meeting sitting in the dirt. And I asked the people what had happened this season, and they told me something quite stunning.

At planting time, an agricultural collective provides some fertilizer 42 and seed. The farmers grow the crop. And then at the end of the growing season, this enterprise buys the cotton back from the farmers at the world market price. This year, the farmers were told, Well, you've just given us your crop and now you're deeper in debt because the value of your crop is less than the input we gave you four months ago.

So these people literally worked for months only to be deeper in debt at   43
the end of the season. The cotton prices are so low because we have heavily subsidized twenty-five thousand American cotton growers in a scheme that the World Trade Organization has declared illegal. Now, for cotton growers in Brazil it lowers their incomes and creates hardship, but in Mali it kills people. Because these people have no incomes, there's no nurse in the village, there's no school. And I turned to the chief. Have any children died recently? I asked. And I'll never forget his response. He waved his hand in violent disgust. "So many! *So many!*" he said before lowering his head and walking away. And then the village all piped in that they're losing children all the time because they get hungry, and then infection comes, and then the child's dead. We're not merely leaving these people to their fate but actually driving them into greater poverty without any sense of responsibility because we're not even compensating in other ways. Where's the other aid? Where's the "Oh, yes, we have to do it for our farmers, but here's what we can do for you"?

So that was Mali.   44

Then we flew to Kenya, and Kenya is where we started this discussion. 45
Not only is the village process working there, but the national government is very deeply engaged, so even though it's a village program, it's also a national program.

We had a good meeting with the Cabinet in Nairobi and then flew to   46
Sauri for the harvest festival.

And let me tell you, on that day in Kenya, the cornfields looked like   47
Illinois. And it was the most beautiful thing I ever saw in my life.

Thinking About the Essay

1. How is the essay structured as a "travelogue"? Why does Sachs open the essay with mention of his daughter?

2. How is the author's use of colloquial phrases and other language related, as a tonal gesture, to the argument of the essay?

3. Where does Sachs critique the shortcomings of the policy actions (or inaction) of nations in the developed world? What is the significance of the allusion to a recent domestic crisis in paragraph 5?

4. How does Sachs make the argument that alleviation of poverty in the developing world is in the national interest of developed nations? Where does he make this argument?

5. How does the concluding section of the essay connect with the opening paragraphs? What is the nature of the emotional appeal made in the final paragraphs of the essay?

Responding in Writing

6. In a brief essay, attempt to demystify the complexity of a current socioeconomic problem in the United States that could lead some observers to resign themselves to the problem's insolubility and to fall back upon the notion that "the poor are always with us."

7. In paragraph 25, Sachs states that John F. Kennedy's cold war rationale for world poverty relief was "right on every level, not merely morally right." In an expository essay, consider some *non* moral justifications for world poverty relief in the post–cold war era.

8. Compose a letter to a local philanthropist in which you attempt to persuade him or her to contribute to a poverty relief effort like the one Sachs describes.

Networking

9. In groups of three or four, plan a group vacation with an itinerary of places in the world that members of your group think are in most dire need of assistance. Share your itinerary with the class.

10. Go online and find out information about the most recent work of the Millennium Villages Project.

The Singer Solution to World Poverty

PETER SINGER

Peter Singer, the Ira W. DeCamp Professor of Bioethics at Princeton University's Center for Human Values, is one of the most influential—and assuredly the most controversial—philosophers of his generation. Born in Melbourne, Australia, in 1946 and educated at the University of Melbourne (B.A., 1967) and University College, Oxford (B.Phil, 1971), Singer has been a prolific writer and lecturer on such contentious social and ethical issues as infanticide, euthanasia, animal liberation, genetic engineering and reproductive technologies. His books, which have been translated into almost two dozen languages, include *Practical Ethics* (1974, 1993), *Animal Liberation: A New Ethics for Our Treatment of Animals* (1975, 1990), *Rethinking Life and Death* (1995), and *One World: The Ethics of Globalization* (2002). The following essay, which appeared in *The New York Times Magazine* in 1999 and reprinted in *Best American Essays* (2000), has provoked the sort of criticism and debate that characterize Singer's provocative ideas.

Before Reading

Is it immoral to spend your money on luxuries when you could use this cash to help alleviate a starving child? Justify your response.

In the Brazilian film *Central Station*, Dora is a retired schoolteacher who makes ends meet by sitting at the station writing letters for illiterate people. Suddenly she has an opportunity to pocket $1,000. All she has to do is persuade a homeless 9-year-old boy to follow her to an address she has been given. (She is told he will be adopted by wealthy foreigners.) She delivers the boy, gets the money, spends some of it on a television set and settles down to enjoy her new acquisition. Her neighbor spoils the fun, however, by telling her that the boy was too old to be adopted—he will be killed and his organs sold for transplantation. Perhaps Dora knew this all along, but after her neighbor's plain speaking, she spends a troubled night. In the morning Dora resolves to take the boy back. 1

Suppose Dora had told her neighbor that it is a tough world, other people have nice new TVs too, and if selling the kid is the only way she can get one, well, he was only a street kid. She would then have become, in the eyes of the audience, a monster. She redeems herself only by being prepared to bear considerable risks to save the boy. 2

At the end of the movie, in cinemas in the affluent nations of the world, people who would have been quick to condemn Dora if she had not rescued the boy go home to places far more comfortable than her apartment. In fact, the average family in the United States spends almost one-third of its income on things that are no more necessary to them than Dora's new TV was to her. Going out to nice restaurants, buying new clothes because the old ones are no longer stylish, vacationing at beach resorts—so much of our income is spent on things not essential to the preservation of our lives and health. Donated to one of a number of charitable agencies, that money could mean the difference between life and death for children in need. 3

All of which raises a question: In the end, what is the ethical distinction between a Brazilian who sells a homeless child to organ peddlers and an American who already has a TV and upgrades to a better one—knowing that the money could be donated to an organization that would use it to save the lives of kids in need? 4

Of course, there are several differences between the two situations that could support different moral judgments about them. For one thing, to be able to consign a child to death when he is standing right in front of you takes a chilling kind of heartlessness; it is much easier to ignore an 5

Peter Singer, "The Singer Solution to World Poverty, *New York Times Magazine* Sep 5, 1999, p. 60. Reprinted by permission of the author.

appeal for money to help children you will never meet. Yet for a utilitarian philosopher like myself—that is, one who judges whether acts are right or wrong by their consequences—if the upshot of the American's failure to donate the money is that one more kid dies on the streets of a Brazilian city, then it is, in some sense, just as bad as selling the kid to the organ peddlers. But one doesn't need to embrace my utilitarian ethic to see that, at the very least, there is a troubling incongruity in being so quick to condemn Dora for taking the child to the organ peddlers while, at the same time, not regarding the American consumer's behavior as raising a serious moral issue.

In his 1996 book, *Living High and Letting Die*, the New York University philosopher Peter Unger presented an ingenious series of imaginary examples designed to probe our intuitions about whether it is wrong to live well without giving substantial amounts of money to help people who are hungry, malnourished or dying from easily treatable illnesses like diarrhea. Here's my paraphrase of one of these examples: 6

Bob is close to retirement. He has invested most of his savings in a very rare and valuable old car, a Bugatti, which he has not been able to insure. The Bugatti is his pride and joy. In addition to the pleasure he gets from driving and caring for his car, Bob knows that its rising market value means that he will always be able to sell it and live comfortably after retirement. One day when Bob is out for a drive, he parks the Bugatti near the end of a railway siding and goes for a walk up the track. As he does so, he sees that a runaway train, with no one aboard, is running down the railway track. Looking farther down the track, he sees the small figure of a child very likely to be killed by the runaway train. He can't stop the train and the child is too far away to warn of the danger, but he can throw a switch that will divert the train down the siding where his Bugatti is parked. Then nobody will be killed—but the train will destroy his Bugatti. Thinking of his joy in owning the car and the financial security it represents, Bob decides not to throw the switch. The child is killed. For many years to come, Bob enjoys owning his Bugatti and the financial security it represents.   7

Bob's conduct, most of us will immediately respond, was gravely wrong. Unger agrees. But then he reminds us that we, too, have opportunities to save the lives of children. We can give to organizations like UNICEF or Oxfam America. How much would we have to give one of these organizations to have a high probability of saving the life of a child threatened by easily preventable diseases? (I do not believe that children are more worth saving than adults, but since no one can argue that children have brought their poverty on themselves, focusing on them simplifies the issues.) Unger   8 called up some experts and used the information they provided to offer some plausible estimates that include the cost of raising money, administrative expenses and the cost of delivering aid where it is most needed. By his calculation, $200 in donations would help a sickly 2-year-old transform into a healthy 6-year-old—offering safe passage through childhood's most dangerous years. To show how practical philosophical argument can be, Unger even tells his readers that they can easily donate funds by using their credit card and calling one of these toll-free numbers: (800) 367-5437 for UNICEF; (800) 693-2687 for Oxfam America.

Now you, too, have the information you need to save a child's life. 9 How should you judge yourself if you don't do it? Think again about Bob and his Bugatti. Unlike Dora, Bob did not have to look into the eyes of the child he was sacrificing for his own material comfort. The child was a complete stranger to him and too far away to relate to in an intimate, personal way. Unlike Dora, too, he did not mislead the child or initiate the chain of events imperiling him. In all these respects, Bob's situation resembles that of people able but unwilling to donate to overseas aid and differs from Dora's situation.

If you still think that it was very wrong of Bob not to throw the switch 10 that would have diverted the train and saved the child's life, then it is hard to see how you could deny that it is also very wrong not to send money to one of the organizations listed above. Unless, that is, there is some morally important difference between the two situations that I have overlooked.

Is it the practical uncertainties about whether aid will really reach the 11 people who need it? Nobody who knows the world of overseas aid can doubt that such uncertainties exist. But Unger's figure of $200 to save a child's life was reached after he had made conservative assumptions about the proportion of the money donated that will actually reach its target.

One genuine difference between Bob and those who can afford to 12 donate to overseas aid organizations but don't is that only Bob can save the child on the tracks, whereas there are hundreds of millions of people who can give $200 to overseas aid organizations. The problem is that most of them aren't doing it. Does this mean that it is all right for you not to do it?

Suppose that there were more owners of priceless vintage cars—Carol, 13 Dave, Emma, Fred and so on, down to Ziggy—all in exactly the same situation as Bob, with their own siding and their own switch, all sacrificing the child in order to preserve their own cherished car. Would that make it all right for Bob to do the same? To answer this question affirmatively is to endorse follow-the-crowd ethics—the kind of ethics that led many Germans to look away when the Nazi atrocities were being committed. We do not excuse them because others were behaving no better.

We seem to lack a sound basis for drawing a clear moral line between   14
Bob's situation and that of any reader of this article with $200 to spare
who does not donate it to an overseas aid agency. These readers seem to be
acting at least as badly as Bob was acting when he chose to let the runaway
train hurtle toward the unsuspecting child. In the light of this conclusion,
I trust that many readers will reach for the phone and donate that $200.
Perhaps you should do it before reading further.

Now that you have distinguished yourself morally from people who   15
put their vintage cars ahead of a child's life, how about treating yourself
and your partner to dinner at your favorite restaurant? But wait. The
money you will spend at the restaurant could also help save the lives of
children overseas! True, you weren't planning to blow $200 tonight, but if
you were to give up dining out just for one month, you would easily save
that amount. And what is one month's dining out, compared to a child's
life? There's the rub. Since there are a lot of desperately needy children in
the world, there will always be another child whose life you could save
for another $200. Are you therefore obliged to keep giving until you have
nothing left? At what point can you stop?

Hypothetical examples can easily become farcical. Consider Bob.   16
How far past losing the Bugatti should he go? Imagine that Bob had got
his foot stuck in the track of the siding, and if he diverted the train, then
before it rammed the car it would also amputate his big toe. Should he still
throw the switch? What if it would amputate his foot? His entire leg?

As absurd as the Bugatti scenario gets when pushed to extremes, the   17
point it raises is a serious one: only when the sacrifices become very significant indeed would most people be prepared to say that Bob does nothing
wrong when he decides not to throw the switch. Of course, most people
could be wrong; we can't decide moral issues by taking opinion polls. But
consider for yourself the level of sacrifice that you would demand of Bob,
and then think about how much money you would have to give away in
order to make a sacrifice that is roughly equal to that. It's almost certainly
much, much more than $200. For most middle-class Americans, it could
easily be more like $200,000.

Isn't it counterproductive to ask people to do so much? Don't we run the   18
risk that many will shrug their shoulders and say that morality, so conceived, is fine for saints but not for them? I accept that we are unlikely to
see, in the near or even medium-term future, a world in which it is normal for wealthy Americans to give the bulk of their wealth to strangers.
When it comes to praising or blaming people for what they do, we tend
to use a standard that is relative to some conception of normal behavior.

Comfortably off Americans who give, say, 10 percent of their income to overseas aid organizations are so far ahead of most of their equally comfortable fellow citizens that I wouldn't go out of my way to chastise them for not doing more. Nevertheless, they should be doing much more, and they are in no position to criticize Bob for failing to make the much greater sacrifice of his Bugatti.

At this point various objections may crop up. Someone may say: "If   19 every citizen living in the affluent nations contributed his or her share I wouldn't have to make such a drastic sacrifice, because long before such levels were reached, the resources would have been there to save the lives of all those children dying from lack of food or medical care. So why should I give more than my fair share?" Another, related, objection is that the Government ought to increase its overseas aid allocations, since that would spread the burden more equitably across all taxpayers.

Yet the question of how much we ought to give is a matter to be decided   20 in the real world—and that, sadly, is a world in which we know that most people do not, and in the immediate future will not, give substantial amounts to overseas aid agencies. We know, too, that at least in the next year, the United States Government is not going to meet even the very modest United Nations–recommended target of 0.7 percent of gross national product; at the moment it lags far below that, at 0.09 percent, not even half of Japan's 0.22 percent or a tenth of Denmark's 0.97 percent. Thus, we know that the money we can give beyond that theoretical "fair share" is still going to save lives that would otherwise be lost. While the idea that no one need do more than his or her fair share is a powerful one, should it prevail if we know that others are not doing their fair share and that children will die preventable deaths unless we do more than our fair share? That would be taking fairness too far.

Thus, this ground for limiting how much we ought to give also fails. In   21 the world as it is now, I can see no escape from the conclusion that each one of us with wealth surplus to his or her essential needs should be giving most of it to help people suffering from poverty so dire as to be life-threatening. That's right: I'm saying that you shouldn't buy that new car, take that cruise, redecorate the house or get that pricey new suit. After all, a $1,000 suit could save five children's lives.

So how does my philosophy break down in dollars and cents? An   22 American household with an income of $50,000 spends around $30,000 annually on necessities, according to the Conference Board, a nonprofit economic research organization. Therefore, for a household bringing in $50,000 a year, donations to help the world's poor should be as close as possible to $20,000. The $30,000 required for necessities holds for higher incomes as well. So a household making $100,000 could cut a yearly check for $70,000. Again, the formula is simple: whatever money you're spending on luxuries, not necessities, should be given away.

Now, evolutionary psychologists tell us that human nature just isn't suf- 23 ficiently altruistic to make it plausible that many people will sacrifice so much for strangers. On the facts of human nature, they might be right, but they would be wrong to draw a moral conclusion from those facts. If it is the case that we ought to do things that, predictably, most of us won't do, then let's face that fact head-on. Then, if we value the life of a child more than going to fancy restaurants, the next time we dine out we will know that we could have done something better with our money. If that makes living a morally decent life extremely arduous, well, then that is the way things are. If we don't do it, then we should at least know that we are failing to live a morally decent life—not because it is good to wallow in guilt but because knowing where we should be going is the first step toward heading in that direction.

When Bob first grasped the dilemma that faced him as he stood by that 24 railway switch, he must have thought how extraordinarily unlucky he was to be placed in a situation in which he must choose between the life of an innocent child and the sacrifice of most of his savings. But he was not unlucky at all. We are all in that situation.

Thinking About the Essay

1. Why does Singer begin his essay with an allusion to a Brazilian film that you probably have not seen? Do you find his introduction effective?

2. Where does Singer's claim appear? What evidence does he use, or does he rely on hypothetical examples and situations? Explain.

3. Singer calls himself "a utilitarian philosopher" (paragraph 5). What does he mean by this term, and how does the essay reflect his ethical approach to the problem of poverty?

4. How does Singer deal with potential objections to his argument?

5. Do you find Singer's "solution" to be convincing? Why or why not?

Responding in Writing

6. Write an argumentative essay in which you agree or disagree with Singer's solution to world poverty.

7. Write an explanatory essay in which you present your own viewpoint on making charitable contributions to help alleviate poverty or disease. Singer, for example, donates 20 percent of his income to Oxfam, a famine relief agency, and also some of his royalties to other charities. Would you do the same if you were in a position to do so?

8. What range of private acts aside from the one that Singer presents could help alleviate poverty and disease? Write an essay responding to this question.

Networking

9. With two other class members, have a discussion of the issues raised by Singer in his essay and your personal response to them. Share your opinions with the rest of the class.

10. Locate the UNICEF or Oxfam website and summarize its content.

Saving the World Is Within Our Grasp

BILL GATES

Bill Gates, who was born in Seattle, Washington, in 1955, is one of the world's most innovative and prominent billionaires. In 1955, Gates left Harvard University after a year and a half of study to cofound Microsoft with his friend Paul Allen. Gates has allocated the bulk of his fortune to the Bill and Melinda Gates Foundation, a philanthropic entity dedicated to improving global health and education. Gates has approached massive global challenges with the same intrepid drive that led him to the top of the technology world: "I can do anything," he declares, "if I put my mind to it." In this essay from the October 1, 2007, issue of *Newsweek*, Gates asserts that we can stop common diseases from killing millions of people each year.

Before Reading

Why are diseases like malaria and tuberculosis still prevalent in the world? Why haven't nations and global organizations allocated more money to eradicate these diseases?

Last year my wife, Melinda, and I visited an AIDS clinic in Durban, South   1
Africa. We met women who had walked miles from nearby townships. When they arrived, they were greeted by a well-trained staff. There was an ample supply of antiretroviral drugs, which can help people with AIDS stay healthy for years. Patients were receiving counseling. As we chatted with

one of the doctors in the clinic, it struck me: something was fundamentally different.

Nearly a decade ago, when Melinda and I started our foundation, we 2 would go to sub-Saharan Africa or developing countries in other regions and see health workers struggling with broken equipment and empty medicine chests. We walked down dirty hallways packed with exhausted mothers holding sick children. In those days, many took it as inevitable that millions of poor people would die each year from diseases that are preventable, treatable or no longer present in the developed world. But that's starting to change. Today governments, aid groups and communities are simply refusing to accept the notion that diseases like malaria and tuberculosis will haunt us forever. The evidence is in: these problems can be solved.

The world can point to a number of victories already. Smallpox is 3 gone, of course, and polio nearly so. Thanks to the leadership of the Carter Center, we've virtually eliminated guinea-worm disease, an excruciatingly painful parasite that is ingested with tainted water. There are new treatments available for visceral leishmaniasis, also called black fever, which is second only to malaria as the world's deadliest parasitic killer.

Millions of lives have been saved through better financing and delivery 4 of the medical advances available today. The GAVI Alliance has immunized 100 million children, averting some 600,000 deaths last year alone, and a creative approach to the bond markets has raised $1 billion more to buy more vaccines. The Global Fund to Fight AIDS, Tuberculosis and Malaria is saving 3,000 lives a day. That clinic we visited in Durban was made possible by an American program: PEPFAR, the President's Emergency Plan for AIDS Relief. Those lifesaving drugs, the salaries for the staff—even the prefab building—were all financed with American tax dollars.

Some lifesaving solutions can be extremely simple—iodized salt to 5 prevent stunted growth, for example, or oral rehydration solutions to fight diarrhea. Consider that one of the easiest ways to cut down on infant mortality is to keep babies warm and dry. Earlier this year, Save the Children recruited knitters through the Internet to knit and crochet 280,000 caps for infants.

Other solutions will arise from pioneering research now underway. 6 Researchers are hard at work developing vaccines that don't need refrigeration or needles, which could make it easier and cheaper to deliver immunization in poor countries. Scientists are making important progress on new tools, like microbicide gels, to help women protect themselves against HIV. And clinical trials around the world are now testing what may be the greatest scientific breakthroughs of our time: vaccines for malaria, TB and AIDS.

The fight against malaria—which kills a million people a year, mostly   7 children—illustrates how radical thinking can be applied to both discovery and delivery of new interventions. Scientists at Columbia University are trying to block a mosquito's sense of smell so it can't find humans to bite. Others at Virginia Polytechnic Institute are developing pesticides that activate only inside a mosquito, posing no danger to humans or other animals. At the same time, I'm amazed by the work of the Nothing But Nets campaign, which has managed through Web-based marketing to raise $13 million—mostly from young people—for insecticide-treated bed nets.

I believe we stand at a moment of unequaled opportunity. Governments   8 must now step up to the plate with more money—wisely targeted—to expand effective global health programs to reach all those in need. Businesses, community groups and individuals all play a role as well. When Melinda and I visited that PEPFAR clinic in South Africa, we were thrilled to see the progress we've made against one deadly disease. I'm now more convinced than ever that we can create a healthier world for everyone.

Thinking About the Essay

1. What is Gates's purpose in writing this essay? Why did he compose the essay for a widely circulated weekly news magazine? Does he achieve his purpose? Explain.

2. How would you describe the tone of Gates's essay? How does the tone reinforce his purpose and argument?

3. At what point does Gates state his claim? Why does he state it where he does?

4. What strategy does Gates use to introduce his essay? How does his concluding paragraph reinforce this strategy?

5. What evidence does Gates use to support his points? Does the evidence make his argument convincing? Why or why not?

Responding in Writing

6. Write a letter to Gates urging him to consider funding a specific health initiative that you consider important.

7. Write an argumentative essay in which you agree or disagree with Gates's basic premise that certain global diseases can be eradicated.

8. Write a paper that compares and contrasts the arguments made by Singer and Gates in their respective essays.

Is Beauty Universal? Global Body Images

Who Is Beautiful? Global Body Images

Not every society worships supermodels, but most societies do have notions about what constitutes beauty. Whereas a washboard stomach might set the standard for beauty for certain people in the United States, there are cultures and constituencies elsewhere that value ample stomachs and hips as the ideal body type. What one society values as beauty might not appeal—indeed might seem ridiculous—to another.

Of course, the age of globalization has spawned a fusion of styles, customs, and attitudes concerning beauty and ideal body images. Fashion magazines, advertisements, and television commercials— whether in the United States, Dubai, Japan, or anywhere on the planet—project transcultural (if not universal) standards of beauty. For example, the fashions of Africa and India adorn the bodies of Americans, and a fondness for tattoos (as one image in this portfolio reveals), appropriated from traditional societies by American teens, now seems to be spreading across continents like an unstoppable cultural virus.

The forces molding global definitions of beauty cannot escape the impact of American popular culture. Icons of American pop culture— whether Queen Latifah or Britney Spears—have an exaggerated impact on the attitudes, body styles, and beauty images of people around the world. Of course, cultural differences concerning beauty and body image persist, but the impact of American culture on how others perceive beauty can be irresistible and (as Susan Bordo observes in this book) insidious.

This portfolio presents images of the body and beauty from several cultural and transnational perspectives. These images reveal societies in transition and traditional values affected by (and at times resisting) the forces of globalization.

Tattoo Man.   A participant displays his hand and head tattoos, and face piercing at the Saint Petersburg International Tattoo Festival held in Russia in 2005.

Considering the Image

1. It is no longer unusual—at least in the United States—to see people with tattoos and body piercings. Do you think that global culture reflects these practices, or are they more specifically American or "Western" in orientation? Explain.

2. Do you think that the photographer makes an argument for or against tattoos and body piercings? Why or why not?

3. Why did the photographer choose to fill the frame with a close-up of the subject? What is the effect or dominant impression?

Kindergarten Kids. Children pose during a model contest held for kindergarten kids in Xiamen, east China's Fujian province.

Considering the Image

1. Identify the elements in this photograph that contribute to the overall effect. What aspects of the image do you find most effective?

2. What is your response to viewing these Chinese children dressed in Western clothing and posing as if they are models on a runway in New York or Paris? Do you find the scene amusing, charming, appalling, or what? Explain your reaction.

Dubai Britney.   Two Arab women in traditional black burkas walk past a picture of pop singer Britney Spears in a posh shopping center in Dubai.

Considering the Image

1. What is your reaction to this photograph? Why do you believe you respond in this manner? How might the two women in burkas and Britney Spears serve as competing cultural symbols that condition your response? If you or a family member actually wear a burka, chador, or head covering, how might your reaction differ from others in the class?

2. What "message" or argument, if any, does the photographer convey in this shot? Does the photographer advance positive or negative connotations of the women in burkas and/or Britney Spears? Might there be an element of satire in the scene? Explain your responses to these questions.

Persian Beauty. An Iranian girl, surrounded by women in chadors, awaits admission to the Jamaran mosque in Tehran. The late Ayatollah Khomeini frequently conducted Friday prayers and made important speeches at this mosque.

Considering the Image

1. How does the photographer compose this image? Why does he bathe the girl in light while the people surrounding her are cast in shadows? What appeals to logos, ethos, and pathos do you detect?

2. Compare the representation of women in this image with those appearing in the Britney Spears photo. What similar and dissimilar cultural points do the two photographers want to make?

Barbie at 50. A model poses with the world's most popular "Barbie" doll turning 50 years old, during the press preview of the 60th International Toy Fair in Nuremberg, February 4, 2009.

© REUTERS/Michaela Rehle/Landov

Considering the Image

1. Describe the composition of this image. Why is Barbie so prominently centered in the photograph?

2. Compare this image with that of Britney Spears in this portfolio. In what ways are they similar? Do they make the same point or not? Justify your response.

© David McNew/Getty Images

Equal Marriage. Lesbian couple Robin Tyler and Diane Olson hold their marriage papers as they are about to be joined in marriage by Rabbi Denise Eger in the first legally recognized same-sex marriage in Los Angeles County, at the Beverly Hills courthouse on June 16, 2008, in Beverly Hills, California.

Considering the Image

1. Analyze the composition of this photograph. What mood or dominant impression emerges from the scene? How are the two women portrayed? What do their facial expressions tell you about them?

2. What representations of gender and sexual orientation does the photographer attempt to capture? What other issues concerning beauty and body image are raised by this photograph?

Obese Girl Band.   Singers in a band named "Qianjin" (which in Chinese can mean both "girl" and "one ton") dance in celebration of the 2006 opening of a club for obese people in Beijing.

Considering the Image

1. Compare representations of women in this photograph with others in this folder, as well as with Susan Bordo's analysis in the essay that appears on pages 18–21.

2. An official at the Ministry of Health in China indicates that more than 200 million Chinese people are overweight. What cultural and economic values might serve to explain this phenomenon? How does the photograph articulate these values?

Networking

9. With a small group of classmates, do a survey of one of the diseases mentioned by Gates in his essay and what is being done by the U.S. government to eliminate it.

10. Access a government or non-government organizational (NGO) website dedicated to health issues, and summarize the initiatives that this entity sponsors.

Can the Cellphone Help End Global Poverty?

SARA CORBETT | Sara Corbett, who resides in Portland, Maine, is a contributing writer for *The New York Times Magazine*. She has also written for *Travel and Leisure, National Geographic, Runner's World*, and *Mother Jones* and is the author of *Venus to the Hoop: A Gold Medal Year in Women's Basketball* (1998). In this essay, which appeared in the April 13, 2008, issue of *The New York Times Magazine*, Corbett profiles a corporate "anthropologist" who is bringing technology to the world's shantytowns.

Before Reading

How would you describe or define what commentators term the "global digital divide"? Do you think that this divide can be narrowed if not eliminated? Why or why not?

If you need to reach Jan Chipchase, the best, and sometimes only, way   1
to get him is on his cellphone. The first time I spoke to him last fall, he was at home in his apartment in Tokyo. The next time, he was in Accra, the capital of Ghana, in West Africa. Several weeks after that, he was in Uzbekistan, by way of Tajikistan and China, and in short order he and his phone visited Helsinki, London and Los Angeles. If you decide not to call Jan Chipchase but rather to send e-mail, the odds are fairly good that you'll get an "out of office" reply redirecting you back to his cellphone, with a notation about his current time zone—"GMT +9" or "GMT -8"—so that when you do call, you may do so at a courteous hour.

Keep in mind, though, that Jan Chipchase will probably be too busy   2
with his job to talk much anyway. He could be bowling in Tupelo, Miss., or
he could be rummaging through a woman's purse in Shanghai. He might be
busy examining the advertisements for prostitutes stuck up in a São Paulo
phone booth, or maybe getting his ear hairs razored off at a barber shop in
Vietnam. It really depends on the moment.

Chipchase is 38, a rangy native of Britain whose broad forehead and   3
high-slung brows combine to give him the air of someone who is quick to
be amazed, which in his line of work is something of an asset. For the last
seven years, he has worked for the Finnish cellphone company Nokia as a
"human-behavior researcher." He's also sometimes referred to as a "user
anthropologist." To an outsider, the job can seem decidedly oblique. His
mission, broadly defined, is to peer into the lives of other people, accumulating as much knowledge as possible about human behavior so that he
can feed helpful bits of information back to the company—to the squads
of designers and technologists and marketing people who may never have
set foot in a Vietnamese barbershop but who would appreciate it greatly if
that barber someday were to buy a Nokia.

What amazes Chipchase is not the standard stuff that amazes big mul-   4
tinational corporations looking to turn an ever-bigger profit. Pretty much
wherever he goes, he lugs a big-bodied digital Nikon camera with a couple
of soup-can-size lenses so that he can take pictures of things that might be
even remotely instructive back in Finland or at any of Nokia's nine design
studios around the world. Almost always, some explanation is necessary.

Jan Chipchase talks to Accra street vendors about what an ideal phone (ideally made by
Nokia) might do.

A Mississippi bowling alley, he will say, is a social hub, a place rife with nuggets of information about how people communicate. A photograph of the contents of a woman's handbag is more than that; it's a window on her identity, what she considers essential, the weight she is willing to bear. The prostitute ads in the Brazilian phone booth? Those are just names, probably fake names, coupled with real cellphone numbers—lending to Chipchase's theory that in an increasingly transitory world, the cellphone is becoming the one fixed piece of our identity.

Last summer, Chipchase sat through a monsoon-season downpour 5 inside the one-room home of a shoe salesman and his family, who live in the sprawling Dharavi slum of Mumbai. Using an interpreter who spoke Tamil, he quizzed them about the food they ate, the money they had, where they got their water and their power and whom they kept in touch with and why. He was particularly interested in the fact that the family owned a cellphone, purchased several months earlier so that the father, who made the equivalent of $88 a month, could run errands more efficiently for his boss at the shoe shop. The father also occasionally called his wife, ringing her at a pay phone that sat 15 yards from their house. Chipchase noted that not only did the father carry his phone inside a plastic bag to keep it safe in the pummeling seasonal rains but that they also had to hang their belongings on the wall in part because of a lack of floor space and to protect them from the monsoon water and raw sewage that sometimes got tracked inside. He took some 800 photographs of the salesman and his family over about eight hours and later, back at his hotel, dumped them all onto a hard drive for use back inside the corporate mother ship. Maybe the family's next cellphone, he mused, should have some sort of hook as an accessory so it, like everything else in the home, could be suspended above the floor.

This sort of on-the-ground intelligence-gathering is central to what's 6 known as human-centered design, a business-world niche that has become especially important to ultracompetitive high-tech companies trying to figure out how to write software, design laptops or build cellphones that people find useful and unintimidating and will thus spend money on. Several companies, including Intel, Motorola and Microsoft, employ trained anthropologists to study potential customers, while Nokia's researchers, including Chipchase, more often have degrees in design. Rather than sending someone like Chipchase to Vietnam or India as an emissary for the company—loaded with products and pitch lines, as a marketer might be—the idea is to reverse it, to have Chipchase, a patently good listener, act as an emissary for people like the barber or the shoe-shop owner's wife, enlightening the company through written reports and PowerPoint presentations on how they live and what they're likely to need from a cellphone, allowing that to inform its design.

The premise of the work is simple—get to know your potential cus- 7 tomers as well as possible before you make a product for them. But when those customers live, say, in a mud hut in Zambia or in a tin-roofed hutong dwelling in China, when you are trying—as Nokia and just about every one of its competitors is—to design a cellphone that will sell to essentially the only people left on earth who don't yet have one, which is to say people who are illiterate, making $4 per day or less and have no easy access to electricity, the challenges are considerable.

One morning last fall, I arranged to meet Chipchase in a neighborhood 8 in Accra where he and a few other Nokia people were doing research. At his suggestion, I took a taxi to the general area and then called him on his cellphone. This part of the city, called Nima, was a jumble of narrow alleyways hemmed in by a few major thoroughfares and anchored by a teeming marketplace. The homes in Nima were small, low-roofed and usually one or two rooms made from concrete or crumbling mud bricks, often set back behind a homegrown business—someone's peanut stand or a shack selling dust-coated secondhand stereos and television sets. The streets around the market were swollen with a slow-moving river of people. On their heads, Ghanaian women toted pyramids of pomegranates, bagged loaves of fresh bread, baskets of live chickens. Trucks belched diesel exhaust; men pushed carts full of sugar cane and fat, purplish bulbs of garlic.

From an unseen distance, Chipchase used his phone to pilot me through 9 the unfamiliar chaos, allowing us to have what he calls a "just in time" moment. "Just in time" is a manufacturing concept that was popularized by the Japanese carmaker Toyota when, beginning in the late 1930s, it radically revamped its production system, virtually eliminating warehouses stocked with big loads of car parts and instead encouraging its assembly plants to order parts directly from the factory only as they were needed. The process became less centralized, more incremental. Car parts were manufactured swiftly and in small batches, which helped to cut waste, improve efficiency and more easily correct manufacturing defects. As Toyota became, in essence, lighter on its feet, the company's productivity rose, and so did its profits.

There are a growing number of economists who maintain that 10 cellphones can restructure developing countries in a similar way. Cellphones, after all, have an economizing effect. My "just in time" meeting with Chipchase required little in the way of advance planning and was more efficient than the oft-imperfect practice of designating a specific time and a place to rendezvous. He didn't have to leave his work until he knew I was in the vicinity. Knowing that he wasn't waiting for me, I didn't fret about the extra 15 minutes my taxi driver sat blaring his horn in Accra's unpredictable traffic. And now, on foot, if I moved in the wrong direction, it could be quickly corrected. Using mobile phones, we were able to coordinate incrementally. "Do you see the footbridge?" Chipchase was saying over the phone. "No? O.K., do you see the giant green sign that says 'Believe in God'? Yes? I'm down to the left of that."

To someone who has spent years using a mobile phone, these moments 11 are common enough to feel banal, but for people living in a shantytown like Nima—and by extension in similar places across Africa and beyond—the possibilities afforded by a proliferation of cellphones are potentially revolutionary. Today, there are more than 3.3 billion mobile-phone subscriptions worldwide, which means that there are at least three billion people who don't own cellphones, the bulk of them to be found in Africa and Asia. Even the smallest improvements in efficiency, amplified across those additional three billion people, could reshape the global economy in ways that we are just beginning to understand. This is part of what Chipchase was eager to show me, if only I could spot him. "I'm by the hair-salon stall," he was saying into his phone. "Next to that goat. Do you see it? See me? Ah, yes," he said brightly, "there you are." And then, face to face and sweating in the climbing equatorial sun, we hung up.

To get a sense of how rapidly cellphones are penetrating the global 12 marketplace, you need only to look at the sales figures. According to statistics from the market database Wireless Intelligence, it took about 20 years for the first billion mobile phones to sell worldwide. The second billion sold in four years, and the third billion sold in two. Eighty percent of the world's population now lives within range of a cellular network, which is double the level in 2000. And figures from the International Telecommunications Union show that by the end of 2006, 68 percent of the world's mobile subscriptions were in developing countries. As more and more countries abandon government-run telecom systems, offering cellular network licenses to the highest-bidding private investors and without the burden of navigating pre-established bureaucratic chains, new towers are going up at a furious pace. Unlike fixed-line phone networks, which are expensive to build and maintain and require customers to have both a permanent address and the ability to pay a monthly bill, or personal computers, which are not just costly but demand literacy as well, the cellphone is more egalitarian, at least to a point.

"You don't even need to own a cellphone to benefit from one," says   13
Paul Polak, author of *Out of Poverty: What Works When Traditional Approaches Fail* and former president of International Development Enterprises, a nonprofit company specializing in training and technology for small-plot farmers in developing countries. Part of I.D.E.'s work included setting up farm cooperatives in Nepal, where farmers would bring their vegetables to a local person with a mobile phone, who then acted as a commissioned sales agent, using the phone to check market prices and arranging for the most profitable sale. "People making a dollar a day can't afford a cellphone, but if they start making more profit in their farming, you can bet they'll buy a phone as a next step," Polak says.

Last year, the World Resources Institute, a Washington-based environ-   14
mental research group, published a report with the International Finance Corporation entitled "The Next Four Billion," an economic study that looked at, among other things, how poor people living in developing countries spent their money. One of the most remarkable findings was that even very poor families invested a significant amount of money in the I.C.T. category—information-communication technology, which, according to Al Hammond, the study's principal author, can include money spent on computers or land-line phones, but in this segment of the population that's almost never the case. What they're buying, he says, are cellphones and airtime, usually in the form of prepaid cards. Even more telling is the finding that as a family's income grows—from $1 per day to $4, for example—their spending on I.C.T. increases faster than spending in any other category, including health, education and housing. "It's really quite striking," Hammond says. "What people are voting for with their pocketbooks, as soon as they have more money and even before their basic needs are met, is telecommunications."

There are clear reasons for this, but understanding them requires   15
forgetting for a moment about your own love-hate relationship with your cellphone, or iPhone, or BlackBerry. Something that's mostly a convenience booster for those of us with a full complement of technology at our disposal—land-lines, Internet connections, TVs, cars—can be a life-saver to someone with fewer ways to access information. A "just in time" moment afforded by a cellphone looks a lot different to a mother in Uganda who needs to carry a child with malaria three hours to visit the nearest doctor but who would like to know first whether that doctor is even in town. It looks different, too, to the rural Ugandan doctor who,

faced with an emergency, is able to request information via text message from a hospital in Kampala.

Jan Chipchase and his user-research colleagues at Nokia can rattle 16 off example upon example of the cellphone's ability to increase people's productivity and well-being, mostly because of the simple fact that they can be reached. There's the live-in housekeeper in China who was more or less an indentured servant until she got a cellphone so that new customers could call and book her services. Or the porter who spent his days hanging around outside of department stores and construction sites hoping to be hired to carry other people's loads but now, with a cellphone, can go only where the jobs are. Having a call-back number, Chipchase likes to say, is having a fixed identity point, which, inside of populations that are constantly on the move—displaced by war, floods, drought or faltering economies—can be immensely valuable both as a means of keeping in touch with home communities and as a business tool. Over several years, his research team has spoken to rickshaw drivers, prostitutes, shopkeepers, day laborers and farmers, and all of them say more or less the same thing: their income gets a big boost when they have access to a cellphone.

It may sound like corporate jingoism, but this sort of economic promise 17 has also caught the eye of development specialists and business scholars around the world. Robert Jensen, an economics professor at Harvard University, tracked fishermen off the coast of Kerala in southern India, finding that when they invested in cellphones and started using them to call around to prospective buyers before they'd even got their catch to shore, their profits went up by an average of 8 percent while consumer prices in the local marketplace went down by 4 percent. A 2005 London Business School study extrapolated the effect even further, concluding that for every additional 10 mobile phones per 100 people, a country's G.D.P. rises 0.5 percent.

Text messaging, or S.M.S. (short message service), turns out to be a 18 particularly cost-effective way to connect with otherwise unreachable people privately and across great distances. Public health workers in South Africa now send text messages to tuberculosis patients with reminders to take their medication. In Kenya, people can use S.M.S. to ask anonymous questions about culturally taboo subjects like AIDS, breast cancer and sexually transmitted diseases, receiving prompt answers from health experts for no charge.

Some of the mobile phone's biggest boosters are those who believe 19 that pumping international aid money into poor countries is less effective than encouraging economic growth through commerce, also called "inclusive capitalism." A cellphone in the hands of an Indian fisherman who uses it to grow his business—which presumably gives him more resources to feed, clothe, educate and safeguard his family—represents a textbook case of bottom-up economic development, a way of empowering individuals by encouraging entrepreneurship as opposed to more traditional top-down approaches in which aid money must filter through a bureaucratic chain before reaching its beneficiaries, who by virtue of the process are rendered passive recipients.

For this reason, the cellphone has become a darling of the microfinance movement. After Muhammad Yunus, the Nobel-winning founder of Grameen Bank, began making microloans to women in poor countries so that they could buy revenue-producing assets like cows and goats, he was approached by a Bangladeshi expat living in the U.S. named Iqbal Quadir. Quadir posed a simple question to Yunus—If a woman can invest in a cow, why can't she invest in a phone?—that led to the 1996 creation of Grameen Phone Ltd. and has since started the careers of more than 250,000 "phone ladies" in Bangladesh, which is considered one of the world's poorest countries. Women use microcredit to buy specially designed cellphone kits costing about $150, each equipped with a long-lasting battery. They then set up shop as their village phone operator, charging a small commission for people to make and receive calls. 20

The endeavor has not only revolutionized communications in Bangladesh but also has proved to be wildly profitable: Grameen Phone is now Bangladesh's largest telecom provider, with annual revenues of about $1 billion. Similar village-phone programs have sprung up in Rwanda, Uganda, Cameroon and Indonesia, among other places. "Poor countries are poor because they are wasting their resources," says Quadir, who is now the director of the Legatum Center for Development and Entrepreneurship at M.I.T. "One resource is time, another is opportunity. Let's say you can walk over to five people who live in your immediate vicinity, that's one thing. But if you're connected to one million people, your possibilities are endless." 21

During a 2006 field study in Uganda, Chipchase and his colleagues stumbled upon an innovative use of the shared village phone, a practice called sente. Ugandans are using prepaid airtime as a way of transferring money from place to place, something that's especially important to those who do not use banks. Someone working in Kampala, for instance, who wishes to send the equivalent of $5 back to his mother in a village will buy a $5 prepaid airtime card, but rather than entering the code into his own phone, he will call the village phone operator ("phone ladies" often run their businesses from small kiosks) and read the code to her. She then uses the airtime for her phone and completes the transaction by giving the man's 22 mother the money, minus a small commission. "It's a rather ingenious practice," Chipchase says, "an example of grass-roots innovation, in which people create new uses for technology based on need."

It's also the precursor to a potentially widespread formalized system 23 of mobile banking. Already companies like Wizzit, in South Africa, and GCash, in the Philippines, have started programs that allow customers to use their phones to store cash credits transferred from another phone or purchased through a post office, phone-kiosk operator or other licensed operator. With their phones, they can then make purchases and payments or withdraw cash as needed. Hammond of the World Resources Institute predicts that mobile banking will bring huge numbers of previously excluded people into the formal economy quickly, simply because the latent demand for such services is so great, especially among the rural poor. This bodes well for cellphone companies, he says, since owning a phone will suddenly have more value than sharing a village phone. "If you're in Hanoi after midnight," Hammond says, "the streets are absolutely clogged with motorbikes piled with produce. They give their produce to the guy who runs a vegetable stall, and they go home. How do they get paid? They get paid the next time they come to town, which could be a month or two later. You have to hope you can find the stall guy again and that he remembers what he sold. But what if you could get paid the next day on your mobile phone? Would you care what that mobile costs? I don't think so."

In February of last year, when Vodafone rolled out its M-Pesa mobile- 24 banking program in Kenya, it aimed to add 200,000 new customers in the first year but got them within a month. One year later, M-Pesa has 1.6 million subscribers, and Vodafone is now set to open mobile-banking enterprises in a number of other countries, including Tanzania and India. "Look, microfinance is great; Yunus deserves his sainthood," Hammond says. "But after 30 years, there are only 90 million microfinance customers. I'm predicting that mobile-phone banking will add a billion banking customers to the system in five years. That's how big it is."

When he is not doing his field work, Jan Chipchase goes to a lot of design 25 conferences, where he gives talks with titles like "Connecting the Unconnected." He also writes a popular blog called Future Perfect, on which he posts photographs of some of the things that amaze him along with a little bit of explanatory text. "Pushing technologies on society without thinking through their consequences is at least naïve, at worst dangerous ... and IMHO the people that do it are just boring," he writes on his blog's description page. "Future Perfect is a pause for reflection in our planet's seemingly headlong rush to churn out more, faster, smaller and cheaper."

Clearly, though, Chipchase's work puts him smack in the middle of this rush, and no company churns out phones like Nokia, which manufactures 1.3 million products daily. Forty percent of the mobile phones sold last year were made by Nokia, and the company's $8.4 billion profit in 2007 reflects as much. Chipchase seems distinctly uncomfortable talking about his part as a corporate rainmaker, preferring to see himself as a mostly dispassionate ethnographer, albeit one with Nokia stock options. The only time I saw him get even slightly prickly—or indeed behave like anything but a mild-mannered guy who is wholly absorbed by the small, arcane things that serve as clues to bigger patterns of communication—was when I happened to muse that maybe there were still places in the world where technology might not be so vital. 26

We were sitting under a slow-revolving ceiling fan in a small restaurant in Accra, eating bowls of piquant Ghanaian peanut-and-chicken stew. Chipchase told a story about meeting some monk disciples at a temple in Ulan Bator, when he vacationed in Mongolia a few Decembers ago. (Most of Chipchase's vacation stories, it turns out, take place in less-developed countries, often in forbidding weather and frequently relating back to cellphone use.) Despite their red robes and shaved heads and the fact they were spending their days in a giant monastery at the top of a windy hill where they were meant to be in dialogue with God, some of the 15 monk disciples had cellphones—Nokia cellphones—and most were fancier models than the one Chipchase was carrying. One of the disciples asked to look at Chipchase's phone. "So he's got my phone and his phone," Chipchase told me. "And as we're talking, he's switching on the Bluetooth. And he then data-mines my phone for all its content, all my photographs and so on, which is absolutely fine, but it's kind of a scene where you think, I'm here, I'm so away from everything and yet they're so technically literate. . . ." 27

This is when I voiced a careless thought about whether there might be something negative about the lightning spread of technology, whether its convenience was somehow supplanting traditional values or practices. Chipchase raised his eyebrows and laid down his spoon. He sighed, making it clear that responding to me was going to require patience. "People can think, yeah, monks with cellphones, and tsk, tsk, and what is the world coming to?" he said. "But if you wanted to take phones away from anybody in this world who has them, they'd probably say: 'You're going to have to fight me for it. Are you going to take my sewer and water away too?' And maybe you can't put communication on the same level as running 28 water, but some people would. And I think in some contexts, it's quite viable as a fundamental right." He paused a beat to let this sink in, then added, with just a touch of edge, "People once believed that people in other cultures might not benefit from having books either."

For the last year, Chipchase has been working on a project he calls Future 29 Urban, the goal of which is to explore what the cities of tomorrow will be like. Which is why one afternoon in Ghana he provided me with minute-to-minute cellphone instructions ("Do you see the sewing stall? O.K., now look to the right") for finding him at the outskirts of Buduburam, a densely populated refugee settlement about an hour's drive west of Accra. For the previous 11 days, Chipchase, two of his female colleagues from Tokyo— Indri Tulusan and Younghee Jung—and a small group of hired Ghanaians had been running what they called an "open design studio" in the heart of Buduburam, which is home to approximately 40,000 people, most of whom had fled from the civil wars in neighboring Liberia, Sierra Leone and Ivory Coast.

Nokia's temporary design studio sat in a rented two-room concrete 30 hut at the intersection of two busy dirt lanes, across from a woman selling chunks of watermelon and peeled lemons and next to a large water tank labeled "Church of God." There was a sheet of fabric strung up in front, with neat painted lettering that read: "Your Dream Phone. Share it with the world." It went on to describe how the community was invited to come share ideas and drawings for the ideal mobile phone. Prizes were offered. So far, 140 people had shown up to sketch their dream phone.

"For the first time, there are more people living in urban centers than 31 in rural settings," Chipchase explained as we sat in the shade outside the studio. "And in the next years, millions more will move to these places." At current rates of migration, the United Nations Human Settlements Pro-gram has projected that one-quarter of the earth's population will live in so-called slums by the year 2020. Slums, by sheer virtue of the numbers, are going to start mattering more and more, Chipchase postulated. In the name of preparing Nokia for this shift, he, Jung and Tulusan, along with a small group of others, spent several weeks in various shantytowns—in Mumbai, in Rio, in western China and now here in Ghana.

People in the mobile-handset business talk about adding customers not 32 by the millions but by the billions, if only they could get the details right. How do you make a phone that can be repaired by a streetside repair-man who may not have access to new parts? How do you build a phone that won't die a quick death in a monsoon or by falling off the back of a motorbike on a dusty road? Or a phone that picks up distant signals in a rural place, holds a charge off a car battery longer or that can double as a flashlight during power cuts? Influenced by Chipchase's study on the practice of sharing cellphones inside of families or neighborhoods, Nokia has started producing phones with multiple address books for as many as seven users per phone. To enhance the phone's usefulness to illiterate customers, the company has designed software that cues users with icons in addition to words. The biggest question remains one of price: Nokia's entry-level phones run about $45; Vodafone offers models that are closer to $25; and in a move that generated headlines around the world, the Indian manufacturer Spice Limited recently announced plans to sell a $20 "people's phone."

Even as sales continue to grow, it is yet to be seen whether the mobile   33
phone will play a significant, sustained role in alleviating poverty in the developing world. In Africa, it's still only a relatively small percentage of the population that owns cellphones. Network towers are not particularly cost-effective in remote areas, where power is supplied by diesel fuel. "I don't see cellphones as a magic bullet per se, though they're obviously very helpful," says Ken Banks, founder of kiwanja.net, a nonprofit entity that provides free text-messaging software and information-technology support to grass-roots enterprises, mostly in Africa. "Many people in the developing world don't yet have a phone—not because they don't want one but because there are barriers. And the only way companies are going to sell phones is to understand what those barriers are." He cites access to reliable electricity as a major barrier, noting that Motorola now provides free solar-powered charging kiosks to female entrepreneurs in Uganda, who use them to sell airtime. The company is also testing wind- and solar-powered base stations in Namibia, which could bring down the cost of connecting remote areas to cellular networks. "Originally mobile-phone companies weren't interested in power because it's not their business," Banks says. "But if a few hundred million people could buy their phones once they had it, they're suddenly interested in power."

Many of the people in Buduburam who came to sketch their ideas   34
for a perfect phone at the Nokia studio did not actually own one. The community's power grid had been down for the last month, so those who did have one had been paying to have their phones charged at a local shop with a diesel-run generator. But when I paged through the fat three-ring binders where the Nokia team was storing those sketches, it was evident that the future, or at least some vision of it, had already arrived. Some of the drawings were basic pencil sketches; others were strikingly elaborate, with arrows pointing to different dream features, which were really just a way of pointing—I realized then—to the dreams themselves.

Jung and Tulusan said they'd found this everywhere, the phone 35
representing what people are aspiring to. "It's an easy way to see what's
important to them, what their challenges are," Jung said. One Liberian
refugee wanted to outfit a phone with a land-mine detector so that he could
more safely return to his home village. In the Dharavi slum of Mumbai, people
sketched phones that could forecast the weather since they had no access to
TV or radio. Muslims wanted G.P.S. devices to orient their prayers toward
Mecca. Someone else drew a phone shaped like a water bottle, explaining that
it could store precious drinking water and also float on the monsoon waters.
In Jacarèzinho, a bustling favela in Rio, one designer drew a phone with an
air-quality monitor. Several women sketched phones that would monitor
cheating boyfriends and husbands. Another designed a "peace button" that
would halt gunfire in the neighborhood with a single touch.

Interestingly, the recent post-election violence in Kenya provided a 36
remarkable case study for the cellphone as an instrument of both war and
peace. After the government imposed a media blackout in late December
last year, Kenyans sought news and information via S.M.S. messages on
their phones and used them to track down friends and family who'd fled
their homes. Many also reported receiving unsolicited text messages to take
up arms. The government responded with an admonition, sent, of course,
via S.M.S.: "The Ministry of Internal Security urges you to please desist
from sending or forwarding any S.M.S. that may cause public unrest. This
may lead to your prosecution."

As a joke, Chipchase sometimes pulls out his cellphone and pretends to 37
shave his face with it, using a buzzing ring tone for comic effect. But there's
a deeper truth embedded here, not just for people in places like Kenya or
Buduburam but for all of us. As cellphone technology grows increasingly
sophisticated, it has cannibalized—for better or worse—the technologies
that have come before it. Carrying a full-featured cellphone lessens your
needs for other things, including a watch, an alarm clock, a camera, video
camera, home stereo, television, computer or, for that matter, a newspaper.
With the advent of mobile banking, cellphones have begun to replace wal-
lets as well. That a phone might someday offer a nice close shave suddenly
seems not so ridiculous after all.

One morning I followed Chipchase as he waded deep into the Nima mar- 38
ket, a hodgepodge of vegetable stalls and phone-booth-size stores selling
sundries like candles and palm oil. He was accompanied by a Ghanaian
interpreter and two Nokia designers who had flown in from California to
test the cultural waters for a phone that—if everything played out perfectly—
could cost as little as $5. The $5 phone was still a pie-in-the-sky concept,

explained Duncan Burns, one of the designers, something they were fiddling with to see if it might be possible someday probably years from now. Each time the group stopped to chat with someone, Burns pulled out several prototypes—or "physical sketches," as he called them—for potential phones, handing them over one by one for examination.

These were elegant, futuristic-looking things, just odd enough to seem   39
as if they'd arrived not from California but from outer space. One was long and wandlike, looking something like an aluminum version of a thick vanilla bean. Another was a slimmer rendering of an everyday phone but with no keypad and no screen, just a single unmarked button. A third did not look at all like a phone but rather like a credit card. There were a couple of small digital photos of people's faces stuck to the front of the card, and it came with a small stylus that could be used, Burns said, to touch a face on the card, which would then dial that person's number—a pictorial address book for someone who was illiterate. A fourth had a camera that took pictures and deposited them right into the phone's address book.

A young man selling beans stared at each of the pretend phones uncom-   40
fortably, as if he mistrusted the devices or perhaps the small crowd of sweat-soaked foreigners suddenly leaning in close to see how he handled them.

"How would you use that?" Chipchase asked through the interpreter,   41
using a dialect called Twi and pointing to the wand phone. The bean seller tentatively lifted it to his ear. "Where would you keep it?" The young man gestured to his neck. "On a rope?" Chipchase said. The man, still looking bewildered, nodded yes.

Moments later, we came upon an ample-bodied woman dressed in a   42
bright gold wrapper and matching head scarf, sifting rocks and twigs out of scoopfuls of corn beneath an umbrella in a quiet corner of the market.

"Helllloooooo," Chipchase said, smiling broadly.   43

"Helllloooooo, Brudda," she said back in English.   44

"We work for Nokia. You know Nokia?"   45

The woman said nothing, but reached down and from the folds of her   46
wrapper produced a Nokia phone. "Not good," she said, shaking her head disparagingly. "You call. It switches off."

Chipchase enlisted the interpreter to explain that her problem sounded like   47
a network problem and not a Nokia problem. Shrugging, the woman went on to inspect the prototype phones, testing their weight in her palm, pressing them against her cheek, punching buttons. She pooh-poohed the stylus phone but said she liked the one-button model if it meant she didn't need to use a lot of numbers. "Brudda, how do you charge it?" she asked. From his bag, Burns pulled another still-conceptual design, this one a thin metal cylinder with a whirlybird antenna on top. He showed the corn seller how to rotate the cylinder

in small circles, causing the antenna to swing, which, he explained, in 15 minutes or so would generate enough power to charge her phone battery.

The woman picked up the futuristic gizmo and began to swing it; the 48 antenna whipped around and around. She let out an enthusiastic whoop. Then a friend of hers who'd been sitting in the shadow of her umbrella started to laugh. Another woman, a spice seller perched on a stool next to small mountains of turmeric and cumin heaped on canvas cloths, began to laugh also. "Very nice," the corn seller said to Burns and Chipchase, swinging the antenna like a toy. "It's good!" Then, after a moment, she gathered her composure and handed the charger off to her son, a heavy-lidded teenager who was lounging on a sack of corn nearby. "Doing that," she said blithely as she returned to picking through her kernels of corn, "can be his job."

Thinking About the Essay

1. Corbett poses a question in her title? How does she answer it in the course of this essay?

2. Corbett offers a detailed profile of Jan Chipchase in this essay. How does she construct this profile? What do we learn about him? What rhetorical strategies does Corbett employ to bring Chipchase to life or create a dominant impression of the man?

3. Trace the pattern of cause and effect that Corbett analyzes in this essay. Why, for example, do cellphone companies employ "anthropologists," and what are the effects of their field research?

4. Corbett provides several types of evidence in this essay. List these varieties of evidence and where they appear.

5. What is Corbett's overriding purpose in writing this essay? Is she strictly informative, or do you sense that she has might have a more complex purpose or goal in mind? Cite specific passages in this essay to support your response.

Responding in Writing

6. Write an essay in which you answer in your own words the question that Corbett poses in her title: "Can the Cellphone Help End Global Poverty?"

7. Write a paper in which you analyze the various investigative techniques that Corbett uses to research and compose her essay. What does this process tell you about the nature of investigative reporting?

8. Argue for or against the proposition that cellphone companies are not interested in the world's poor—only in selling their product to as many people as possible.

Networking

9. With the class divided into two relatively equal groups, debate the proposition that technology companies do not have the well-being of poor people in mind when they go into the world's slums and backwaters to introduce their products.

10. Conduct online research to find out more about the roles of corporate anthropologists and sociologists. Why do technology companies employ them and how do they operate. Offer a critique based on your findings.

Technology Won't Feed the World's Hungry

ANURADHA MITTAL

Anuradha Mittal, a native of India, is founder and director of the Oakland Institute, a policy think tank that works to promote public participation and democratic debate on economic and social policy issues. Mittal is known internationally as an expert on trade, human rights, and agriculture issues. She has traveled widely as a public speaker and has appeared as guest and commentator on television and radio. Her articles on international public policy issues have appeared in *The New York Times* and in other journals worldwide. In the following article, which appeared in the July 12, 2001, issue of *Progressive Media Project,* Mittal argues that biotechnology cannot solve the problem of world hunger.

Before Reading

Do you see the debate over genetically engineered foods primarily in terms of your choice as a consumer or in terms of the way such technology would address world hunger?

D on't be misled. Genetically engineered food is not an answer to world   1
hunger.

The U.N. Development Program (UNDP) released a report last week   2
urging rich countries to put aside their fears of such food and help developing nations unlock the potential of biotechnology.

Anuradha Mittal, "Technology Won't Feed the World's Hungry." This piece was originally written for the Progressive Media Project, 409 E. Main St. Madison, WI 53703. www.progressivemediaproject.org

The report accuses opponents of ignoring the Third World's food needs. 3
It claims that Western consumers who do not face food shortages or nutritional deficiencies are more likely to focus on food safety and the loss of biodiversity, while farming communities in developing countries emphasize potentially higher yields and "greater nutritional value" of these crops.

But the UNDP has not done its homework. 4

In my country, India, for example, the debate pits mostly U.S.-trained 5
technocrats, seduced by technological fixes, against farmers and consumers who overwhelmingly say no to these crops. The people who are to use the modified seeds and eat the modified food often want nothing to do with them.

The report rehashes the old myth of feeding the hungry through miracle 6
technology. As part of the 1960s Green Revolution, Western technology created pesticides and sent them to developing countries for agricultural use, which may have increased food production, but at the cost of poisoning our earth, air and water.

What's more, it failed to alleviate hunger. Of the 800 million hungry 7
people in the world today, more than 200 million live in India alone. It's not that India does not produce enough food to meet the needs of its hungry. It's that organizations like the International Monetary Fund (IMF) have slashed public services and social-safety nets so that the food can't get to the needy.

More than 60 million tons of excess, unsold food grain rotted in India 8
last year because the hungry were too poor to buy it. In desperation, some farmers burned the crops they could not market and resorted to selling their kidneys and other body parts, or committing suicide, to end the cycle of poverty.

A higher, genetically engineered crop yield would have done nothing for 9
them. And if the poor in India are not able to buy two meals a day, how will they purchase nutritionally rich crops such as rice that is engineered to contain vitamin A?

The report compares efforts to ban genetically modified foods with 10
the banning of the pesticide DDT, which was dangerous to humans but was effective in killing the mosquitoes that spread malaria. The Third World had to choose between death from DDT or malaria. It's appalling that even today the debate in developed countries offers the Third World the option of either dying from hunger or eating unsafe foods.

Malaria, like hunger, is a disease of poverty. When economic conditions improve, it disappears, just as it did in the United States and Europe. 11

The focus ought to be on the root causes of the problem, not the 12
symptom. The hungry don't need a technological quick fix. They need
basic social change.

In the Third World, the battle against genetically engineered food is 13
a battle against the corporate concentration of our food system. Corporations are gaining control of our biodiversity and even our seeds. This
is a potential stranglehold on our food supply. In response, developing
countries are imposing moratoriums on genetically engineered crops. Sri
Lanka, Thailand, Brazil, Mexico and China, among others, have already
done so.

The UNDP has been snookered about genetically engineered food. The 14
rest of us shouldn't be.

Thinking About the Essay

1. How does Mittal frame her paragraph-long paraphrase of the claims of the
   UNDP within the opening paragraphs of the essay?

2. Does Mittal's reference to India as "my country" have any effect on
   her argument? Would the argument be as strong without the personal
   element? Why or why not?

3. How does Mittal characterize the advocates of biotechnology who are the
   authors of the UNDP report?

4. According to Mittal, what is the role that corporations play in the promotion
   of biotechnology? How does this claim change her characterization of the
   motives for promoting such technology?

5. How effective is the colloquial language of the two-sentence concluding
   paragraph? Are there other examples of such language in the essay?

Responding in Writing

6. In a brief essay, connect Mittal's argument with other arguments presented
   in this chapter about economic infrastructure as the root cause of world
   health problems.

7. Argue for or against the use of biotechnology as a solution to world
   hunger by invoking an analogy of your own that you believe characterizes
   the reaction of opponents or supporters of such technology. Why is this
   analogy appropriate?

8. Do you think that adequate public services and social-safety nets exist in
   the United States that prevent the kind of failure of resource distribution
   Mittal describes in India? Why do people go hungry in the United States
   today? Is this hunger the result of a systemic failure? Answer these
   questions in an argumentative essay.

Networking

9. In small groups, discuss your reservations (or enthusiasms) about genetically engineered food. Do you feel that you are reacting according to your limited interests as a Western consumer? Why or why not?

10. Go online and engage in a discussion group debate over genetically engineered food from a global, hunger-relief point of view.

A Development Nightmare

KENNETH ROGOFF

Kenneth Rogoff was Charles and Marie Robertson Professor of International Affairs at Princeton University and is currently professor of economics and director of the Center for International Development at Harvard University. From 2001 to 2003, he served as chief economist and director of research at the International Monetary Fund. Rogoff has published extensively on government policy issues surrounding international finance, and he is also the coauthor (with Maurice Obstfeld) of the widely used graduate textbook *Foundations of International Macroeconomics* (1996). In the following article, which appeared in *Foreign Policy* magazine in January/February 2004, Rogoff examines the foreign aid policies of "rich" nations whose efforts to promote the economic development of other nations are mixed with fears about the distribution (and dilution) of the world's wealth.

Before Reading

Do you measure your own economic prosperity in relative terms? What are those terms?

Indulge in a dream scenario for a moment: Suppose the world awoke   1
tomorrow and, miraculously, every country suddenly enjoyed the same per capita income as the United States, or roughly $40,000 per year. Global annual income would soar to $300 trillion, or some 10 times what it is now. And while we're at it, suppose also that international education levels, infant mortality rates, and life expectancies all converged to the levels in rich

Kenneth Rogoff, "A Development Nightmare," FOREIGN POLICY, Jan/Feb. 2004. Reprinted by permission.

countries. In short, what if foreign aid worked and economic development happened overnight instead of over centuries?

A heretical thought, perhaps. But I wonder sometimes what voters in   2
rich nations must be thinking when they reward their politicians for cutting already pathetic foreign-aid budgets. Is it possible that, deep down, the world's wealthy fear what will happen if the developing countries really did catch up, and if the advantages their own children enjoy were shared by all? Would the dream become a nightmare?

Consider whether today's wealthy would materially suffer under such   3
a scenario. As things now stand, 290 million U.S. citizens already cause almost one-fourth of world carbon dioxide emissions. What if 1.3 billion Chinese and 1.1 billion Indians suddenly all had cars and began churning out automobile exhaust at prodigious U.S. rates? While the sun might not turn black and the ozone layer might not vaporize overnight, the environmental possibilities are frightening. And what of the price of oil, which is already notoriously sensitive to small imbalances in demand and supply? Absent huge new discoveries or brilliant new inventions, oil could easily reach $200 per barrel, as consumption and depletion rates accelerate. The mighty U.S. dollar would become a boutique currency and the euro experiment a sideshow. Investors would clamor for Chinese yuan and Indian rupees. The world's youth would grow up thinking that "Hollywood" must be a wordplay on "Bollywood," and McDonald's hamburgers would be viewed a minor ethnic cuisine. And a country such as Canada would suddenly have the economic heft of Luxembourg, with much of its population reduced to serving once poor, now rich, international tourists.

Let's face it: The rich countries would no longer feel rich. Humans   4
are social creatures; once we clear the hurdle of basic subsistence, wealth becomes a relative state of being. Even an optimist such as myself must concede that a world of equality between rich and poor nations would be shockingly different—and that is even disregarding the impact on global power politics. Still, such rapid economic development offers a clear upside for today's rich countries. Greater diversity and knowledge spillovers can breed much faster productivity growth, the ultimate source of wealth for everyone. Once properly educated, fed, and plugged in, inventive geniuses from South Asia and Africa might speed the development of clean and safe hydrogen power by two generations. And whereas commercial medical researchers might start spending more energy combating tropical diseases, now privileged citizens in temperate climates would still enjoy countless technological spin-offs. Indeed, such gains of rapid economic development could fully offset the losses to the rich.

By highlighting latent insecurities in rich countries, I certainly do   5
not mean to endorse or stoke them. But these underlying fears must be
addressed. If globalization really works, then what is the endgame? What
kind of political institutions are necessary to prepare—socially as well as
psychologically—for success? It is easy for everyone to endorse the United
Nations Millennium Development Goals (MDG), which aim to satisfy
basic human needs by 2015. (Unfortunately, the specific objectives are so
limited that MDG ought to stand for the Minimum Development Goals.)
But how far are rich nations willing to take development? How much are
we prepared to give?

Of course, no one has developed a magic formula for how to make   6
countries grow, though economic researchers have identified a number of
poisons. Corruption, overweening government intervention, and mountains of debt are contraindicated for countries attempting to develop
(which is one reason most foreign aid should be recast as outright grants
instead of loans). Though critics are correct to argue that foreign aid
stymies growth by breeding corruption and stifling private enterprise,
the empirical evidence suggests that aid can be productive when it supports good policies. Does trade help countries grow? Again, my read of
the evidence says yes: If Europe and Japan gave up their outrageous farm
protection and if the United States stopped competing with India for the
title of anti-dumping champion of the world, poor countries would gain
far more than if their aid inflows suddenly doubled. And, by the way, if
poor countries gave up their own trade protectionism, their citizens would
benefit by even more.

Even so, rich countries could easily afford to triple their aid budgets   7
without running the remotest risk of the "nightmare" scenario coming
true. They could channel money into health in Africa, into education,
and into infrastructure and other necessities with little danger of any
rapid catch-up. (Though why the World Bank still lends to China, with
more than $350 billion in hard currency reserves and a space program
to boot, is difficult to explain.) Gallons of aid money, such as what
Northern Italy has poured into Southern Italy for almost 60 years, help
assuage development's growing pains, but progress rarely occurs quickly.
Growth economics suggests that poor regions have a hard time closing
the income gap on rich countries at a rate greater than 2 percent per
year, even under the best of circumstances. Catch-up—when it happens
at all—takes generations.

Rich countries need not be ambivalent or stingy. Certainly, if sudden   8
and rapid economic development were possible and actually materialized,
many citizens in wealthy nations would feel jarred, even threatened. And

some day, world income distribution will be radically different than it is today, but not anytime soon. Nightmare scenarios and fear of success need never stand in the way of sensible—and generous—development policies.

Thinking About the Essay

1. How does Rogoff undercut the utopian vision presented in the opening paragraph of the essay?

2. What motives does Rogoff attribute to members of "rich" nations? What evidence does he offer to support this attribution? Does Rogoff express any sympathy with these motives?

3. How would you characterize Rogoff's brand of irony in this essay? Highlight at least three different ironic passages and note some similarities and differences in tone between them.

4. What negative effects of economic progress does Rogoff acknowledge in the essay? Why does he wait to acknowledge these effects?

5. What policies does Rogoff endorse that would promote international economic development? What past and current policies does he attack? Why does he attack them? How are these inadequate policies connected with the interests and perceptions of "rich" nations?

Responding in Writing

6. In a brief essay, construct a "dream scenario" similar to Rogoff's, in which you envision the solution to a world health problem, and consider some additional negative side effects of the solution if this scenario were to be realized.

7. Do you fear the loss or erosion of your privileges as a member of a "rich" nation? Reflect on these fears in an essay blending narrative and expository elements.

8. Define what you see as the "endgame" of globalization. Is this a world you would like to live in? How do you see your children or grandchildren adapting to this world?

Networking

9. In groups of three or four, list some other cultural transformations that might occur under Rogoff's scenario. Do you fear the possibility of becoming culturally (or economically) marginalized? Why? Discuss those feelings within your group, and share the results of the discussion with the class.

10. Go online and research foreign aid statistics in the most recent United States federal budget. Do these numbers surprise you? Why or why not?

Follow the Money

Vivienne Walt and Amanda Bower

Vivienne Walt is a staff writer for *Time* magazine who currently lives in Paris. She has worked as a foreign correspondent for twenty-five years and has reported on wars in various parts of the world (including, most recently, the 2003 war in Iraq). Walt is also known for her extensive reporting on politics and health issues in Africa. Amanda Bower is a San Francisco–based writer for *Time*. A native of Australia, Bower won the 1995 Fulbright Post-Graduate Student Award in Journalism and moved to the United States to study journalism at Columbia University. Her work as a freelance journalist has taken her to many parts of the world, including Cambodia, Vietnam, Guatemala, and Costa Rica. In the following article, which appeared in the Europe Edition of *Time International* in December 2005, Walt and Bower investigate the newly documented transnational economy created by migrant workers who send the money they earn in foreign countries back home to their communities of origin.

Before Reading

What personal sacrifices would you make in order to support your family? Would you describe your motives as a "work ethic"? Why or why not?

Waly Diabira pats the cover on his bed in the cramped fifth-floor room   1
he shares with two men in a red-brick dormitory building for immigrants near Paris' Left Bank. "My father slept on this same bed, in this same room, for many years," he says. In 1950, his father, Mamadou Diabira, left their tiny village in Mali and caught a steamboat to Europe, where he worked as a street cleaner in Paris for about 25 years, receiving a certificate of thanks signed by then-mayor Jacques Chirac. Waly, a 32-year-old building cleaner, only got to know his father when he sneaked into France at 18 on a boat from Morocco; he now works legally in France. A large photograph hangs above Waly's narrow bed, of his 2-year-old daughter, whom he has never met. The migrant tradition has continued into the next generation, fueled by the same force that kept his father rooted in France for decades—the need to send money home. Similar stories swell the immigrant

population in Paris and other cities across France, and are multiplied millions of times across the world.

Such tales are nothing new. The color TV in a remote Turkish farm-   2 stead and the concrete-walled house amid shacks of corrugated iron have often been paid for by absent family members. Plenty of church halls in Ireland have been funded by passing the plate around congregations in Boston and New York. But the scale of money flows is new. Mass migration has produced a giant worldwide economy all its own, which has accelerated so fast during the past few years that the figures have astounded the experts. This year, remittances—the cash that migrants send home—is set to exceed $232 billion, nearly 60% higher than the number just four years ago, according to the World Bank, which tracks the figures. Of that, about $166.9 billion goes to poor countries, nearly double the amount in 2000. In many of those countries, the money from migrants has now overshot exports, and exceeds direct foreign aid from other governments. "The way these numbers have increased is mind-boggling," says Dilip Ratha, a senior economist for the World Bank and co-author of a new Bank report on remittances. Ratha says he was so struck by the figures that he rechecked his research several times, wondering if he might have miscalculated. Indeed, he believes the true figure for remittances this year is probably closer to $350 billion, since migrants are estimated to send one-third of their money using unofficial methods, including taking it home by hand. That money is never reported to tax officials, and appears on no records.

One reason for the growth in recorded remittances has its origins in the   3 global war on terrorism. To stop terrorist networks using informal transfer systems like hawala in Africa, the Middle East and South Asia (where it's referred to as hundi), European and U.S. officials have cracked down on them. That has shifted payments to easier-to-track official channels. Some migrants, however, still use methods that elude the bean counters. In Hong Kong, Endang Muna Saroh, 35, works as a nanny to two children in a comfortable residential neighborhood, and sends $200 home every month to her mother and 10-year-old son in Surabaya, Indonesia, wiring the money to her brother-in-law's bank account. The country receives recorded remittances such as this worth a total of $1.8 billion a year. Yet like many migrants, Endang also saved hundreds of dollars to carry by hand to her family in August, when she flew home for her first visit in four years.

In Paris, Waly keeps a notebook on his bedside table, in which he writes   4 lists of the cash amounts he gives each month to couriers. They fly to Mali— where remittances account for 3.2% of the country's national income—with wads of euros stuffed in their pockets and luggage. With about 300 people from his village of Ambadedi working in Paris—an estimated one-quarter of Ambadedi's entire population—the community has a well-organized network to transfer money, much of which is aimed at avoiding the hefty commissions from banks. "I write careful notes," Waly says. "'Here's €20 for my mother, €30 to my sister, and so on.'" Of the €1,000 he earns each month cleaning office buildings in Paris, he sends about €500 home, and then pays €240 for his share of the monthly rental. That experience is repeated across the world. The life of squirreling away money is grueling: it involves years-long separation from families, miserable living conditions, and the threat of deportation for the many who are working illegally. All the same, remittances play a vital role in recycling money from the rich world to the poor one. "Migration is going up," says Ratha. "We had better not wish it away, because it's very much there to stay."

On three continents, migrants and their families described how the transfers worked. Nine years ago, Cornelio Zamora left his home in Zacapoaxtla, Mexico, paying a smuggler $2,500 to take him across the Rio Grande into the U.S. He had been unable to support his wife and four children on the $7 a day he earned as a bus driver. Working as a house painter in San Jose, California, Zamora, 48, now sends about $700 a month home. His wife says she has based all family decisions—where to send the children to school, what house to live in—on Zamora's monthly earnings "on the other side." 5

In migrants' countries of origin, escalating desires—for things like better education and bigger homes—help drive the remittances. Ironically, economists calculate that the poorer the migrants are, the more money they dispatch. "There is enormous social pressure to send money home," says Khalid Koser, a geography professor at University College London, who in October co-authored a report for the Global Commission on International Migration in Geneva, which researches governments' immigration policies. Koser found that many migrants scrape by in first-world cities, depriving themselves of basic comforts in order to "keep people alive" back home. "There are many people sending 40% of their income in remittances," he says, adding that many families save to pay the passage of a migrant to richer parts of Asia, or to Europe or the U.S. Ruhel Daked, a 26-year-old Bangladeshi, earns €1,300 a month working as a chef in Paris. Yet despite his modestly comfortable salary, he bunks with two other Bangladeshis in a dormitory building for immigrants, with one toilet shared among many men, because he says he has one goal: "To save! Save as much as I can. That is why I am here." 6

In visits to migrants' hometowns, the impact on their families and communities is clear. Waly's village of Ambadedi has sent thousands of 7 migrants to Paris since his father Mamadou first headed there. Set atop the steep northern bank of the Senegal River, the village at first glance looks like countless others in West Africa. Goats and donkeys meander down the dirt lanes, and women scrub clothes in the river. But Ambadedi has cherished luxuries that are absent from other remote parts of Mali. There is a generator that lights up most of the houses every night. A water tower feeds water to several collection points. And television antennas bristle from the rooftops of two-story concrete houses—a far cry from the mud hut in which old Mamadou was raised. Villagers have even started dreaming about building a bridge across the river to connect Ambadedi to the nearest highway, says Sekou Drame, Mamadou's brother-in-law, as he escorts a *Time* reporter back to the wooden pirogue that will ferry him across the river's muddy flow. "It depends on God," he says. "And our families in France."

In Mexico, the Zamora family home is another tangible indicator of   8
the impact of remittances. Zamora's work in California has paid for a new three-bedroom house, the first his family has ever owned. The changes his cash have brought to his family within one generation are dizzying; one daughter has trained as a nurse, another as a teacher, and his son as a radio technician. "The first time I wore shoes, I was 14 years old," Zamora says. "I don't want my family to go through that." It's a similar story in Indonesia where Endang's monthly money transfers from four years' work as a nanny in Hong Kong finally paid off last July, when her 10-year-old son, her mother and several relatives moved into a renovated two-story concrete house in Surabaya, bought with Endang's savings for about $9,700. In Paris, Daked, the Bangladeshi chef, says his parents recently bought a family home with the funds he has sent home since sneaking into Europe in 1997; he estimated his total remittances at about $38,000 in eight years.

Vital though the flow of remittances may be, it cannot, on its own, lift   9
entire nations out of poverty. Those who study the impact of remittances argue that the money allows poor countries to put off basic decisions of economic management, like reforming their tax-collection systems and building decent schools. "Everyone loves money that flows in with no fiscal implications," says Devesh Kapur, a specialist on migration and professor of government at the University of Texas in Austin. "They see it as a silver bullet." But bullets wound, and skilled workers often understandably put the interests of their families before those of their countries, choosing to work abroad so they can send remittances back home. About eight out of 10 college graduates from Haiti and Jamaica live outside their countries, and about half the college graduates of Sierra Leone and

Ghana have also emigrated, according to the Paris-based Organization for Economic Co-operation and Development.

Remittances to poor countries can also mask the fact that they don't   10 produce much at home. In the western Mali district of Kayes—where Waly's village of Ambadedi is located and where most migrants hail from— the region has done so well that farmers use remittances as a crutch. Studies have shown that they spend less time on their land than farmers in other parts of Mali: there is more money to be made by migrating to Europe. "You see poverty other places, but here, you see money," says Abdel Kader Coulibaly, a bank manager in Kayes. He says migrants' families spend all they get, rather than investing it to generate income locally. "All the money ends up with shopkeepers and traders from Bamako [the capital]," he says.

The trick now is to find programs that maximize the benefits of remitted   11 cash while avoiding some of its downside. Some migrants are now using their economic clout to perform work usually done by big aid organizations. Ambadedi's workers' association in Paris, for example, funds some village projects with its members' own earnings. But the association also solicits help from the French government and the European Union. "We have a project under way to purify the village water supply," says Ibrahim Diabira, 55, a relative of Waly, who works in Paris as a building cleaner and helps run the village association in the French capital. Elsewhere, host nations have created temporary legal work programs, in which migrants earn legal wages with benefits, before returning home. That way, migrants retain close links to their countries while developing skills abroad. "When they go back, they will take augmented skills, savings and networks," says Kapur. (He himself left his native India 22 years ago and settled in the U.S.)

In Paris, Waly is planning to return home in January to see his 2-year-   12 old daughter for the first time, and to spend time with his wife. But he won't stay long. "Frankly, people would die there if we didn't work here," he says. Come spring, he will be back in Paris, cleaning offices, and changing the way the world spreads its wealth around.

Thinking About the Essay

1. How is the migrant tradition described, in the opening paragraph, as a cyclical phenomenon?

2. How do the authors distinguish the current migration-based economies from transactions between immigrants to their communities of origin that occurred in the past?

3. What aspects of Waly Diabira's story are presented as being typical of the motives and experiences of migrant workers worldwide? What do the other

case studies in the essay contribute to the authors' analysis of remittance economies?

4. Why is there generally an inverse relation between migrant workers' level of poverty and the amount of money they send back home? What other statistical correlations are noted in the essay?

5. Why do the authors return to the story of Waly Diabira in the final paragraph of the essay? What does this conclusion indicate about the authors' attitude toward the "changing way the world spreads its wealth around"?

Responding in Writing

6. What does it mean to put the interests of an immediate circle of family or friends above the interests of a native or adopted country? In a brief essay, reflect on how your feelings of national or community identity would change if you were forced (for economic reasons) to relocate to another country.

7. What are your concerns about the size and nature of the migrant workforce in the United States? Do you feel that workers are being exploited? Or do you see the workforce as parasitic upon the economy and tax-based infrastructure of communities where they work? List your concerns in an essay, and consider—point by point—an alternate perspective that would cast your concern in a different (more positive) light.

8. Respond to the statement (in paragraph 4) that remittances "play a vital role in recycling money from the rich world to the poor one." Are "recycling" and "redistribution" appropriate metaphors, given what you have read in this essay about the economy of remittances?

Networking

9. In groups of three or four, share the experiences you have had with the immigrant workforce in your community. Have you engaged in one-on-one conversations with them? What did you learn about their backgrounds, current lifestyles, and long-term plans?

10. Go online and look up the nations listed as the top ten recipients of foreign-earned remittances in 2005, according to the World Bank. Do these rankings surprise you?

The Fate of the Earth: Can We Preserve the Global Environment?

11

I t is tempting to think that at one time—was it before 9/11, or before the explosion of the first atomic bomb, or before the Black Death?—the problems of the world were simpler and more manageable. But were they? After all, the Black Death of the thirteenth century liquidated more than a third of Europe's population. There have always been world conflicts and challenges that Earth's inhabitants have had to confront. So far, we have survived; we have not destroyed the planet. However, as the writers in this chapter attest, the fate of the Earth is uncertain, for humanity continues to be a flawed enterprise.

What is certain is that for the last several decades we have been moving into a new era in global history. This new era, as the writers in earlier chapters have revealed, is both like and unlike previous historical epochs. We do not have to accept the thesis of Francis Fukuyama that we have reached the "end" of history. At the same time, we do have to acknowledge that new challenges—scientific, ecological, economic, political, and cultural—await us in the new millennium. Numerous local and global problems need our sustained attention. Over the past decade, in particular, we have come to recognize that we have relationships and obligations to the planet and its inhabitants. A dust storm originating in Africa can sweep across the Atlantic, affecting ecologies in other continents. A nuclear accident in Russia can affect the milk of cows in Nebraska. Even the cars that we purchase and drive—as one author in this chapter asserts—can have an impact on the world's climate.

Clearly, then, in this new millennial era, we are part of a global environment. We have mutual obligations not to waste natural resources, to respect the environment, to harness science and technology to human and nonhuman benefit, and so much more. This new era is not necessarily more corrosive than previous epochs, but the stakes do seem to be higher. We now have to comprehend our reciprocal relationships at the

Tourists on a camel safari in Egypt clearly affect the local ecosystem and indigenous community.

Thinking About the Image

1. This photograph originally accompanied an article about "ecotourism." What do you know about ecotourism? Why do you think people would plan an "ecotourism" vacation?
2. What kind of story does this photograph tell about the relationship between the tourists and the "natives"?
3. Are you amused or surprised by what the camels are carrying?
4. What do you think is the point of view, or opinion, of the photographer who took this picture toward the people on the camels? How can you tell? Is there anything else that is amusing, sarcastic, or ironic about this photograph?

numerous crossroads of nature and civilization. The *process* of civilization wherein we harness our physical, creative, scientific, political, intellectual, and spiritual resources is well advanced. However, the current condition of the global environment, as the writers in this last chapter testify, demands our attention.

By and large, the writers in this chapter, all of whom deal with subjects of consequence—global warming, biotechnology, environmental degradation, population growth, weapons of mass destruction—are not doomsday prophets. In fact, while offering cautionary statements about our shortsightedness and wastefulness, they tend to find hope for the world's environment. Whether finding once again a small spot in Eden in a remote Amazon jungle or contemplating the consequences of driving an SUV, these writers try to establish a moral basis for the continuation of the species—not just our human species but all varieties of life on Earth. We are not caught in an endless spiral that will end in mass extinction. But we do have to harness what Albert Schweitzer called "the devils of our own creation." Ultimately, we must find ways to coexist on Earth with nature and all living things.

The Obligation to Endure

RACHEL CARSON

Born in Pennsylvania in 1907, Rachel Carson became a leading figure in the world's emerging environmental movement. Abandoning an early interest in English literature, she concentrated instead on zoology, ultimately obtaining an advanced degree from the Graduate School of Johns Hopkins University. She was a marine biologist on the staff of the United States Fish and Wildlife Service for fifteen years, serving as editor in chief. Her first book was *Under the Sea Wind* (1941). With *The Sea Around Us* (1951), which sold millions of copies, was translated into dozens of languages, and won the National Book Award, Carson emerged as the best-known spokesperson for the preservation of the world's resources. In 1952, Carson resigned her government position to devote her time to writing. Her last book, *Silent Spring* (1964), from which the following essay is taken, aroused immediate controversy for its indictment of the use of pesticides. Carson died in 1964.

Before Reading

In the decades since *Silent Spring* was published, numerous pesticides have been banned—especially in the United States. Do you think that the problem no longer exists? Why or why not?

The history of life on earth has been a history of interaction between   1
living things and their surroundings. To a large extent, the physical form and the habits of the earth's vegetation and its animal life have been

molded by the environment. Considering the whole span of earthly time, the opposite effect, in which life actually modifies its surroundings, has been relatively slight. Only within the moment of time represented by the present century has one species—man—acquired significant power to alter the nature of his world.

During the past quarter century this power has not only increased to   2 one of disturbing magnitude but it has changed in character. The most alarming of all man's assaults upon the environment is the contamination of air, earth, rivers, and sea with dangerous and even lethal materials. This pollution is for the most part irrecoverable; the chain of evil it initiates not only in the world that must support life but in living tissues is for the most part irreversible. In this now universal contamination of the environment, chemicals are the sinister and little-recognized partners of radiation in changing the very nature of the world—the very nature of its life. Strontium 90, released through nuclear explosions into the air, comes to earth in rain or drifts down as fallout, lodges in soil, enters into the grass or corn or wheat grown there, and in time takes up its abode in the bones of a human being, there to remain until his death. Similarly, chemicals sprayed on croplands or forests or gardens lie long in soil, entering into living organisms, passing from one to another in a chain of poisoning and death. Or they pass mysteriously by underground streams until they emerge and, through the alchemy of air and sunlight, combine into new forms that kill vegetation, sicken cattle, and work unknown harm on those who drink from once pure wells. As Albert Schweitzer has said, "Man can hardly even recognize the devils of his own creation."

It took hundreds of millions of years to produce the life that now   3 inhabits the earth—eons of time in which that developing and evolving and diversifying life reached a state of adjustment and balance with its surroundings. The environment, rigorously shaping and directing the life it supported, contained elements that were hostile as well as supporting. Certain rocks gave out dangerous radiation; even within the light of the sun, from which all life draws its energy, there were shortwave radiations with power to injure. Given time—time not in years but in millennia—life adjusts, and a balance has been reached. For time is the essential ingredient; but in the modern world there is no time.

The rapidity of change and the speed with which new situations are   4 created follow the impetuous and heedless pace of man rather than the deliberate pace of nature. Radiation is no longer merely the background radiation of rocks, the bombardment of cosmic rays, the ultraviolet of the sun that have existed before there was any life on earth; radiation is now the un-natural creation of man's tampering with the atom. The chemicals to which life is asked to make its adjustment are no longer merely the calcium and silica and copper and all the rest of the minerals washed out of the rocks and carried in rivers to the sea; they are the synthetic creations of man's inventive mind, brewed in his laboratories, and having no counterparts in nature.

To adjust to these chemicals would require time on the scale that is   5
nature's; it would require not merely the years of a man's life but the life of generations. And even this, were it by some miracle possible, would be futile, for the new chemicals come from our laboratories in an endless stream; almost five hundred annually find their way into actual use in the United States alone. The figure is staggering and its implications are not easily grasped—500 new chemicals to which the bodies of men and animals are required somehow to adapt each year, chemicals totally outside the limits of biologic experience.

Among them are many that are used in man's war against nature. Since   6
the mid-1940s over 200 basic chemicals have been created for use in killing insects, weeds, rodents, and other organisms described in the modern vernacular as "pests"; and they are sold under several thousand different brand names.

These sprays, dusts, and aerosols are now applied almost universally   7
to farms, gardens, forests, and homes—nonselective chemicals that have the power to kill every insect, the "good" and the "bad," to still the song of birds and the leaping of fish in the streams, to coat the leaves with a deadly film, and to linger on in soil—all this though the intended target may be only a few weeds or insects. Can anyone believe it is possible to lay down such a barrage of poisons on the surface of the earth without making it unfit for all life? They should not be called "insecticides," but "biocides."

The whole process of spraying seems caught up in an endless spiral.   8
Since DDT was released for civilian use, a process of escalation has been going on in which ever more toxic materials must be found. This has happened because insects, in a triumphant vindication of Darwin's principle of the survival of the fittest, have evolved super races immune to the particular insecticide used, hence a deadlier one has always to be developed—and then a deadlier one than that. It has happened also because, for reasons to be described later, destructive insects often undergo a "flareback," or resurgence, after spraying in numbers greater than before. Thus the chemical war is never won, and all life is caught in its violent crossfire.

Along with the possibility of the extinction of mankind by nuclear war,   9
the central problem of our age has therefore become the contamination of

man's total environment with such substances of incredible potential for harm—substances that accumulate in the tissues of plants and animals and even penetrate the germ cells to shatter or alter the very material of heredity upon which the shape of the future depends.

Some would-be architects of our future look toward a time when it will   10 be possible to alter the human germ plasma by design. But we may easily be doing so now by inadvertence, for many chemicals, like radiation, bring about gene mutations. It is ironic to think that man might determine his own future by something so seemingly trivial as the choice of an insect spray.

All this has been risked—for what? Future historians may well be   11 amazed by our distorted sense of proportion. How could intelligent beings seek to control a few unwanted species by a method that contaminated the entire environment and brought the threat of disease and death even to their own kind? Yet this is precisely what we have done. We have done it, moreover, for reasons that collapse the moment we examine them. We are told that the enormous and expanding use of pesticides is necessary to maintain farm production. Yet is our real problem not one of *over production*? Our farms, despite measures to remove acreages from production and to pay farmers not to produce, have yielded such a staggering excess of crops that the American taxpayer in 1962 is paying out more than one billion dollars a year as the total carrying cost of the surplus-food storage program. And is the situation helped when one branch of the Agriculture Department tries to reduce production while another states, as it did in 1958, "It is believed generally that reduction of crop acreages under provisions of the Soil Bank will stimulate interest in use of chemicals to obtain maximum production on the land retained in crops."

All this is not to say there is no insect problem and no need of control.   12 I am saying, rather, that control must be geared to realities, not to mythical situations, and that the methods employed must be such that they do not destroy us along with the insects.

The problem whose attempted solution has brought such a train of   13 disaster in its wake is an accompaniment of our modern way of life. Long before the age of man, insects inhabited the earth—a group of extraordinarily varied and adaptable beings. Over the course of time since man's advent, a small percentage of the more than half a million species of insects have come into conflict with human welfare in two principal ways: as competitors for the food supply and as carriers of human disease.

Disease-carrying insects become important where human beings are   14 crowded together, especially under conditions where sanitation is poor, as in times of natural disaster or war or in situations of extreme poverty and deprivation. Then control of some sort becomes necessary. It is a sobering fact, however, as we shall presently see, that the method of massive chemical control has had only limited success, and also threatens to worsen the very conditions it is intended to curb.

Under primitive agricultural conditions the farmer had few insect 15 problems. These arose with the intensification of agriculture—the devotion of immense acreages to a single crop. Such a system set the stage for explosive increases in specific insect populations. Single-crop farming does not take advantage of the principles by which nature works; it is agriculture as an engineer might conceive it to be. Nature has introduced great variety into the landscape, but man has displayed a passion for simplifying it. Thus he undoes the built-in checks and balances by which nature holds the species within bounds. One important natural check is a limit on the amount of suitable habitat for each species. Obviously then, an insect that lives on wheat can build up its population to much higher levels on a farm devoted to wheat than on one in which wheat is intermingled with other crops to which the insect is not adapted.

The same thing happens in other situations. A generation or more 16 ago, the towns of large areas of the United States lined their streets with the noble elm tree. Now the beauty they hopefully created is threatened with complete destruction as disease sweeps through the elms, carried by a beetle that would have only limited chance to build up large populations and to spread from tree to tree if the elms were only occasional trees in a richly diversified planting.

Another factor in the modern insect problem is one that must be 17 viewed against a background of geologic and human history: the spreading of thousands of different kinds of organisms from their native homes to invade new territories. This worldwide migration has been studied and graphically described by the British ecologist Charles Elton in his recent book *The Ecology of Invasions*. During the Cretaceous Period, some hundred million years ago, flooding seas cut many land bridges between continents, and living things found themselves confined in what Elton calls "colossal separate nature reserves." There, isolated from others of their kind, they developed many new species. When some of the land masses were joined again, about 15 million years ago, these species began to move out into new territories—a movement that is not only still in progress but is now receiving considerable assistance from man.

The importation of plants is the primary agent in the modern spread of 18 species, for animals have almost invariably gone along with the plants, quarantine being a comparatively recent and not completely effective innovation.

The United States Office of Plant Introduction alone has introduced almost 200,000 species and varieties of plants from all over the world. Nearly half of the 180 or so major insect enemies of plants in the United States are accidental imports from abroad, and most of them have come as hitchhikers on plants.

In new territory, out of reach of the restraining hand of the natural   19
enemies that kept down its numbers in its native land, an invading plant or animal is able to become enormously abundant. Thus it is no accident that our most troublesome insects are introduced species.

These invasions, both the naturally occurring and those dependent on   20
human assistance, are likely to continue indefinitely. Quarantine and massive chemical campaigns are only extremely expensive ways of buying time. We are faced, according to Dr. Elton, "with a life-and-death need not just to find new technological means of suppressing this plant or that animal"; instead we need the basic knowledge of animal populations and their relations to their surroundings that will "promote an even balance and damp down the explosive power of outbreaks and new invasions."

Much of the necessary knowledge is now available but we do not   21
use it. We train ecologists in our universities and even employ them in our governmental agencies but we seldom take their advice. We allow the chemical death rain to fall as though there were no alternative, whereas in fact there are many, and our ingenuity could soon discover many more if given opportunity.

Have we fallen into a mesmerized state that makes us accept as inevi-   22
table that which is inferior or detrimental, as though having lost the will or the vision to demand that which is good? Such thinking, in the words of the ecologist Paul Shepard, "idealizes life with only its head out of water, inches above the limits of toleration of the corruption of its own environment. . . . Why should we tolerate a diet of weak poisons, a home in insipid surroundings, a circle of acquaintances who are not quite our enemies, the noise of motors with just enough relief to prevent insanity? Who would want to live in a world which is just not quite fatal?"

Yet such a world is pressed upon us. The crusade to create a chemi-   23
cally sterile, insect-free world seems to have engendered a fanatic zeal on the part of many specialists and most of the so-called control agencies. On every hand there is evidence that those engaged in spraying operations exercise a ruthless power. "The regulatory entomologists . . . function as prosecutor, judge and jury, tax assessor and collector and sheriff to enforce their own orders," said Connecticut entomologist Neely Turner. The most flagrant abuses go unchecked in both state and federal agencies.

It is not my contention that chemical insecticides must never be used. 24
I do contend that we have put poisonous and biologically potent chemicals
indiscriminately into the hands of persons largely or wholly ignorant of
their potentials for harm. We have subjected enormous numbers of people
to contact with these poisons, without their consent and often without their
knowledge. If the Bill of Rights contains no guarantee that a citizen shall
be secure against lethal poisons distributed either by private individuals or
by public officials, it is surely only because our forefathers, despite their
considerable wisdom and foresight, could conceive of no such problem.

I contend, furthermore, that we have allowed these chemicals to be 25
used with little or no advance investigation of their effect on soil, water,
wildlife, and man himself. Future generations are unlikely to condone our
lack of prudent concern for the integrity of the natural world that supports
all life.

There is still very limited awareness of the nature of the threat. This is 26
an era of specialists, each of whom sees his own problem and is unaware
of or intolerant of the larger frame into which it fits. It is also an era dominated by industry, in which the right to make a dollar at whatever cost
is seldom challenged. When the public protests, confronted with some
obvious evidence of damaging results of pesticide applications, it is fed
little tranquilizing pills of half truth. We urgently need an end to these false
assurances, to the sugar coating of unpalatable facts. It is the public that
is being asked to assume the risks that the insect controllers calculate. The
public must decide whether it wishes to continue on the present road, and
it can do so only when in full possession of the facts. In the words of Jean
Roosted, "The obligation to endure gives us the right to know."

Thinking About the Essay

1. What is Carson's thesis or claim? Where does it appear, or is it implied?
   Justify your response.

2. Explain the tone of Carson's essay. How do such words as *dangerous, evil,*
   and *sinister* reinforce this tone?

3. Evaluate Carson's essay as a model of argumentation. What reasons
   does she provide to demonstrate the overpopulation of insects? How does
   she convince us of "the obligation to endure"? What remedies does she
   propose? What appeals does she make?

4. Identify all instances where Carson uses expert testimony. How effective is
   this testimony in reinforcing the writer's argument?

5. What is Carson's purpose in her final paragraph? How effective is it?
   Explain.

Responding in Writing

6. Write your own essay titled "The Obligation to Endure." You may focus on pesticides or any other topic—for example, genetically altered foods or global warming—to organize your paper.

7. In an essay, argue for or against the proposition that we spend too much time and money worrying about the state of the world environment.

8. Write a paper in which you present solutions to some of the problems that Carson raises in her essay.

Networking

9. Working in small groups, find out more about Rachel Carson and her involvement with environmental issues. In class discussion, evaluate her relevance to the environmental situation today.

10. Go online and find out more about pesticides commonly used today. Share your findings with the class. How safe are they? Would you use them as a homeowner, landscaper, farmer, or forestry official?

The Climate for Change

AL GORE

Al Gore (Albert Gore Jr.) is a former congressman, senator, and forty-fifth vice president of the United States. He was the Democratic candidate for the presidency in 2000, winning the popular vote but losing the electoral count when the Supreme Court on a 5–4 decision awarded Florida to George W. Bush. The son of a distinguished senator from Tennessee, Gore was born in 1948 and grew up in Washington, DC. He attended Harvard University (B.A., 1969) and served a tour of duty in Vietnam. A self-described "raging moderate," Gore became interested in environmental issues during his years in Congress, writing during that time the best-selling *Earth in the Balance: Ecology and the Human Spirit* (1992). After his defeat in the 2000 presidential race, Gore evolved into arguably the world's most prominent spokesperson for environmental concerns. His book *An Inconvenient Truth* (2006) and companion film, which won the Academy Award for best documentary, were wildly successful, helping to earn Gore a 2007 Nobel Peace Prize for his environmental work. His most recent book is *The Assault on Reason* (2007). In this essay from the November 10, 2008, issue of the *International Herald Tribune*, Gore offers a five-part plan for repowering America.

Before Reading

Do you think that it is possible for the United States—and other nations as well—to reduce dependency on traditional energy sources like coal and oil? Justify your response.

The inspiring and transformative choice by the American people to elect Barack Obama as our 44th president lays the foundation for another fateful choice that he—and we—must make this January to begin an emergency rescue of human civilization from the imminent and rapidly growing threat posed by the climate crisis.

The electrifying redemption of America's revolutionary declaration that all human beings are born equal sets the stage for the renewal of United States leadership in a world that desperately needs to protect its primary endowment: the integrity and livability of the planet.

The world authority on the climate crisis, the Intergovernmental Panel on Climate Change, after 20 years of detailed study and four unanimous reports, now says that the evidence is "unequivocal." To those who are still tempted to dismiss the increasingly urgent alarms from scientists around the world, ignore the melting of the north polar ice cap and all of the other apocalyptic warnings from the planet itself, and who roll their eyes at the very mention of this existential threat to the future of the human species, please wake up. Our children and grandchildren need you to hear and recognize the truth of our situation, before it is too late.

Here is the good news: the bold steps that are needed to solve the climate crisis are exactly the same steps that ought to be taken in order to solve the economic crisis and the energy security crisis.

Economists across the spectrum—including Martin Feldstein and Lawrence Summers—agree that large and rapid investments in a jobs-intensive infrastructure initiative is the best way to revive our economy in a quick and sustainable way. Many also agree that our economy will fall behind if we continue spending hundreds of billions of dollars on foreign oil every year. Moreover, national security experts in both parties agree that we face a dangerous strategic vulnerability if the world suddenly loses access to Middle Eastern oil.

As Abraham Lincoln said during America's darkest hour, "The occasion is piled high with difficulty, and we must rise with the occasion. As our case is new, so we must think anew, and act anew." In our present case, thinking anew requires discarding an outdated and fatally flawed definition of the problem we face.

Thirty-five years ago this past week, President Richard Nixon created   7
Project Independence, which set a national goal that, within seven years,
the United States would develop "the potential to meet our own energy
needs without depending on any foreign energy sources." His statement
came three weeks after the Arab oil embargo had sent prices skyrocketing
and woke America to the dangers of dependence on foreign oil. And—not
coincidentally—it came only three years after United States domestic oil
production had peaked.

At the time, the United States imported less than a third of its oil from   8
foreign countries. Yet today, after all six of the presidents succeeding Nixon
repeated some version of his goal, our dependence has doubled from one-
third to nearly two-thirds—and many feel that global oil production is at
or near its peak.

Some still see this as a problem of domestic production. If we could   9
only increase oil and coal production at home, they argue, then we
wouldn't have to rely on imports from the Middle East. Some have come
up with even dirtier and more expensive new ways to extract the same old
fuels, like coal liquids, oil shale, tar sands and "clean coal" technology.

But in every case, the resources in question are much too expensive or   10
polluting, or, in the case of "clean coal," too imaginary to make a difference
in protecting either our national security or the global climate. Indeed, those
who spend hundreds of millions promoting "clean coal" technology consistently omit the fact that there is little investment and not a single large-scale
demonstration project in the United States for capturing and safely burying
all of this pollution. If the coal industry can make good on this promise, then
I'm all for it. But until that day comes, we simply cannot any longer base the
strategy for human survival on a cynical and self-interested illusion.

Here's what we can do—now: we can make an immediate and large   11
strategic investment to put people to work replacing 19th-century energy
technologies that depend on dangerous and expensive carbon-based fuels
with 21st-century technologies that use fuel that is free forever: the sun, the
wind and the natural heat of the earth.

What follows is a five-part plan to repower America with a commit-   12
ment to producing 100 percent of our electricity from carbon-free sources
within 10 years. It is a plan that would simultaneously move us toward
solutions to the climate crisis and the economic crisis—and create millions
of new jobs that cannot be outsourced.

First, the new president and the new Congress should offer large-scale   13
investment in incentives for the construction of concentrated solar thermal

plants in the Southwestern deserts, wind farms in the corridor stretching from Texas to the Dakotas and advanced plants in geothermal hot spots that could produce large amounts of electricity.

Second, we should begin the planning and construction of a unified 14 national smart grid for the transport of renewable electricity from the rural places where it is mostly generated to the cities where it is mostly used. New high-voltage, low-loss underground lines can be designed with "smart" features that provide consumers with sophisticated information and easy-to-use tools for conserving electricity, eliminating inefficiency and reducing their energy bills. The cost of this modern grid—$400 billion over 10 years—pales in comparison with the annual loss to American business of $120 billion due to the cascading failures that are endemic to our current balkanized and antiquated electricity lines.

Third, we should help America's automobile industry (not only the Big 15 Three but the innovative new startup companies as well) to convert quickly to plug-in hybrids that can run on the renewable electricity that will be available as the rest of this plan matures. In combination with the unified grid, a nationwide fleet of plug-in hybrids would also help to solve the problem of electricity storage. Think about it: with this sort of grid, cars could be charged during off-peak energy-use hours; during peak hours, when fewer cars are on the road, they could contribute their electricity back into the national grid.

Fourth, we should embark on a nationwide effort to retrofit build- 16 ings with better insulation and energy-efficient windows and lighting. Approximately 40 percent of carbon dioxide emissions in the United States come from buildings—and stopping that pollution saves money for homeowners and businesses. This initiative should be coupled with the proposal in Congress to help Americans who are burdened by mortgages that exceed the value of their homes.

Fifth, the United States should lead the way by putting a price on 17 carbon here at home, and by leading the world's efforts to replace the Kyoto treaty next year in Copenhagen with a more effective treaty that caps global carbon dioxide emissions and encourages nations to invest together in efficient ways to reduce global warming pollution quickly, including by sharply reducing deforestation.

Of course, the best way—indeed the only way—to secure a global 18 agreement to safeguard our future is by re-establishing the United States as the country with the moral and political authority to lead the world toward a solution.

Looking ahead, I have great hope that we will have the courage to 19 embrace the changes necessary to save our economy, our planet and ultimately ourselves.

In an earlier transformative era in American history, President John   20
F. Kennedy challenged our nation to land a man on the moon within
10 years. Eight years and two months later, Neil Armstrong set foot
on the lunar surface. The average age of the systems engineers cheering
on *Apollo 11* from the Houston control room that day was 26, which
means that their average age when President Kennedy announced the
challenge was 18.

This year similarly saw the rise of young Americans, whose enthusiasm   21
electrified Barack Obama's campaign. There is little doubt that this same
group of energized youth will play an essential role in this project to secure
our national future, once again turning seemingly impossible goals into
inspiring success.

Thinking About the Essay

1. How would you characterize Gore's tone in this essay? What is his
   purpose in using words like "inspiring and transformative" (paragraph 1),
   "electrifying redemption" (paragraph 2), and "existential threat" (paragraph
   3)? How does Gore's style reinforce his tone?

2. Why does Gore allude to the installation of Barack Obama as president of
   the United States on January 20, 2009? Does he exploit this event or use
   it as a touchstone for his argument—or both? Explain.

3. Explain the pattern of cause and effect that Gore develops in this essay.
   Why, for example, does he devote a paragraph to a project initiated by
   President Nixon (paragraph 7)? In broader terms, what connections does
   Gore draw between climate change, politics, and the economy?

4. Evaluate Gore's five-part plan into terms of audience, style, and structure.
   Do you find this part of the essay too stiff or formulaic, or do you think it
   succeeds in reaching the readership of an international English-language
   newspaper? Justify your response.

5. Why does Gore use his notion of "transformative eras" as a framing device
   for his essay? How does this strategy reinforce his argument?

Responding in Writing

6. Write an essay presenting your own five-part plan to repower America.

7. Argue for or against the proposition that the Obama era will usher in
   a new "transformative" period in the nation's approach to the climate
   crisis.

8. Analyze Gore's essay as a model of journalistic opinion writing.
   Discuss style, tone, paragraph organization, and other relevant
   strategies.

Networking

9. Help to arrange a class viewing of Gore's documentary *An Inconvenient Truth*. Afterward, discuss the film in relation to the essay.

10. Go online to find out more about the Intergovernmental Panel on Climate Change (see paragraph 3). Share your findings in a discussion with other class members.

Talking Trash

ANDY ROONEY | Andrew A. Rooney, better known as "Andy" from his regular appearances on *60 Minutes* and his syndicated columns in more than 200 newspapers, is one of the nation's best-known curmudgeons, a writer and commentator who is frequently at odds with conventional wisdom on various issues. Born in Albany, New York, in 1919, he attended Colgate University before serving in the U.S. Army from 1942 to 1945 as a reporter for *Stars and Stripes*. Rooney has written, produced, and narrated programs for some of the major shows in television history: he wrote material for Arthur Godfrey from 1949 to 1955, and for Sam Levenson, Herb Shriner, Victor Borge, Gary Moore, and other celebrities who define many of the high points of early television comedy. Over the decades, Rooney has also produced television essays, documentaries, and specials for ABC, CBS, and public television. A prolific writer, he is the author of more than a dozen books—most recently *My War* (1995), *Sincerely, Andy Rooney* (1999), *Common Nonsense* (2002), and *Years of Minutes* (2003). Known for his dry, unassuming, but acerbic wit (which from time to time has gotten him in trouble with viewers and television studios), Rooney is at his best when convincing readers about simple truths. In this essay, which appeared in 2002 in *Diversion*, he tells us the simple truth about our inability to moderate our wasteful ways.

Before Reading

Americans are perceived as being terribly wasteful. They discard food, appliances, clothing, and so much more that other peoples and societies would find useful. Do you agree or disagree with this profile of the wasteful American? And how do you fit into this picture?

Last Saturday I filled the trunk of my car and the passenger seats behind   1
me with junk and headed for the dump. There were newspapers, empty cardboard boxes, bags of junk mail, advertising flyers, empty bottles, cans, and garbage. I enjoy the trip. Next to buying something new, throwing away something that is old is the most satisfying experience I know.

The garbage men come to my house twice a week, but they're very   2
fussy. If the garbage is not packaged the way they like it, they won't take it. That's why I make a trip to the dump every Saturday. It's two miles from our house, and I often think big thoughts about throwing things away while I'm driving there.

How much, I got to wondering last week, does the whole Earth weigh?   3
New York City alone throws away 24 million pounds of garbage a day. A day! How long will it take us to turn the whole planet Earth into garbage, throw it away, and leave us standing on nothing?

Oil, coal, and metal ore are the most obvious extractions, but any place   4
there's a valuable mineral, we dig beneath the surface, take it out, and make it into something else. We never put anything back. We disfigure one part of our land by digging something out and then move on to another spot after we've used up all its resources.

After my visit to the dump, I headed for the supermarket, where I   5
bought $34 worth of groceries. Everything was packed in something—a can, a box, a bottle, a carton, or a bag. When I got to the checkout counter, the cashier separated my cans, boxes, cartons, bottles, and bags and put three or four at a time into other bags, boxes, or cartons. Sometimes she put my paper bags into plastic bags. One bag never seemed to do. If something was in plastic, she put that into paper.

On the way home, I stopped at the dry cleaner. Five of my shirts, which   6
had been laundered, were in a cardboard box. There was a piece of cardboard in the front of each shirt and another cardboard cutout to fit the collar to keep it from getting wrinkled. The suit I had cleaned was on a throwaway hanger, in a plastic bag with a form-fitting piece of paper inside over the shoulders of my suit.

When I got home, I put the groceries where they belonged in various   7
places in the kitchen. With the wastebasket at hand, I threw out all the outer bags and wrappers. By the time I'd unwrapped and stored everything, I'd filled the kitchen wastebasket a second time.

It would be interesting to conduct a serious test to determine what   8
percentage of everything we discard. It must be more than 25%. I drank the contents of a bottle of Coke and threw the bottle away. The Coca-Cola Company must pay more for the bottle than for what they put in it.

Dozens of things we eat come in containers that weigh more and cost the manufacturer more than what they put in them.

We've gone overboard on packaging, and part of the reason is that a   9 bag, a can, or a carton provides a place for the producer to display advertising. The average cereal box looks like a roadside billboard.

The Earth could end up as one huge, uninhabitable dump.   10

Thinking About the Essay

1. What is Rooney's claim? Where does he state it? What evidence does he provide to support his claim?

2. Does Rooney, writing about a serious problem, maintain a serious tone in this essay? What evidence in the essay leads you to your view?

3. How does Rooney structure his argument? Does he provide enough supporting points to back up his major claim or proposition? Why or why not?

4. Is Rooney merely making value judgments about himself, or does he have a broader purpose? How do you know?

5. Explain the style of this essay. Are Rooney's language and sentence structure accessible or difficult? How does his style facilitate your reading and appreciation of the essay?

Responding in Writing

6. Argue for or against the proposition that we are a wasteful society. As Rooney does, organize your essay around your own personal experience or your knowledge of family and friends.

7. Write an imaginative essay about the year 2050. Center the essay on Rooney's last sentence: "The Earth could end up as one huge, uninhabitable dump."

8. Write a letter to your local congressional representative outlining the need for your community to do more about controlling its waste flow. Offer specific remedies for improvement.

Networking

9. Divide into groups of three or four, and jot down some of the instances of waste you have encountered on your campus. Compare your list with other group members' lists. Which problems seem to be most common? Which are singular? Share and discuss your results with the rest of the class.

10. Utilizing one or more Web search engines, download information on waste management. What is the current status of this movement in the United States? Which cities or regions are doing the best job of managing their waste problems? Present your findings in class discussion.

Lessons from Lost Worlds

JARED DIAMOND

Jared Diamond is professor of Geography at UCLA and formerly professor of Physiology at the UCLA School of Medicine. His widely acclaimed *Guns, Germs, and Steel: The Fates of Human Societies* was awarded the Pulitzer Prize in 1998. Diamond is also known for his work as a conservationist and as director of the World Wildlife Fund. His field experience includes seventeen expeditions to New Guinea and neighboring islands, where he helped to establish Indonesian New Guinea's national park system. In the following essay, which appeared in the August 26, 2002, issue of *Time* magazine, Diamond derives some lessons from the historical precedent of past societies that failed to respond to environmental crises similar to those that currently face our global community.

Before Reading

What is your chief concern about the world your grandchildren will inherit? Why does this one concern take precedence over the others? How are your concerns logically related to one another?

Children have a wonderful ability to focus their parents' attention on the essentials. Before our twin sons were born in 1987, I had often heard about all the environmental problems projected to come to a head toward the middle of this century. But I was born in 1937, so I would surely be dead before 2050. Hence I couldn't think of 2050 as a real date, and I couldn't grasp that the environmental risks were real.

After the birth of our kids, my wife and I proceeded to obsess about the things most parents obsess about—schools, our wills, life insurance. Then I realized with a jolt: my kids will reach my present age of 65 in 2052. That's a real date, not an unimaginable one! My kids' lives will depend on the state of the world in 2052, not just on our decisions about life insurance and schools.

I should have known that. Having lived in Europe for years, I saw that the lives of my friends also born in 1937 had been affected greatly by the state of the world around them. For many of those overseas contemporaries growing up during World War II, that state of the world left them orphaned or homeless. Their parents may have thought wisely about life insurance, but their parents' generation had not thought wisely about world conditions. Over the heads of our own children now hang other threats from world conditions, different from the threats of 1939–45.

While the risk of nuclear war between major powers still exists, it's   4
less acute now than 15 years ago, thank God. Many people worry about terrorists, and so do I, but then I reflect that terrorists could at worst kill "only" a few tens of millions of us. The even graver environmental problems that could do in all our children are environmental ones, such as global warming and land and water degradation.

These threats interact with terrorism by breeding the desperation that   5
drives some individuals to become terrorists and others to support terrorists. Sept. 11 made us realize that we are not immune from the environmental problems of any country, no matter how remote—not even those of Somalia and Afghanistan. Of course, in reality, that was true before Sept. 11, but we didn't think much about it then. We and the Somalis breathe and pollute the same atmosphere, are bathed by the same oceans and compete for the same global pie of shrinking resources. Before Sept. 11, though, we thought of globalization as mainly meaning "us" sending "them" good things, like the Internet and Coca-Cola. Now we understand that globalization also means "them" being in a position to send "us" bad things, like terrorist attacks, emerging diseases, illegal immigrants and situations requiring the dispatch of U.S. troops.

A historical perspective can help us, because ours is not the first society   6
to face environmental challenges. Many past societies collapsed partly from their failure to solve problems similar to those we face today—especially problems of deforestation, water management, topsoil loss and climate change. The long list of victims includes the Anasazi in the U.S. Southwest, the Maya, Easter Islanders, the Greenland Norse, Mycenaean Greeks and inhabitants of the Fertile Crescent, the Indus Valley, Great Zimbabwe and Angkor Wat. The outcomes ranged from "just" a collapse of society, to the deaths of most people, to (in some cases) everyone's ending up dead. What can we learn from these events? I see four main sets of lessons.

First, environmental problems can indeed cause societies to collapse,   7
even societies assaulting their environments with stone tools and far lower population densities than we have today.

Second, some environments are more fragile than others, making some   8
societies more prone to collapse than others. Fragility varies even within the same country: for instance, some parts of the U.S., including Southern California, where I live, are especially at risk from low rainfall and

salinization of soil from agriculture that is dependent on irrigation—the same problems that overwhelmed the Anasazi. Some nations occupy more fragile environments than do others. It's no accident that a list of the world's most environmentally devastated and/or overpopulated countries resembles a list of the world's current political tinderboxes. Both lists include Afghanistan, Haiti, Iraq, Nepal, Rwanda and Somalia.

Third, otherwise robust societies can be dragged down by the envi- 9 ronmental problems of their trade partners. About 500 years ago, two Polynesian societies, on Henderson Island and Pitcairn Island, vanished because they depended for vital imports on the Polynesian society of Mangareva Island, which collapsed from deforestation. We Americans can well understand that outcome, having seen how vulnerable we are to instability in oil-exporting countries of the Middle East.

Fourth, we wonder, Why didn't those peoples see the problems develop- 10 ing around them and do something to avoid disaster? (Future generations may ask that question about us.) One explanation is the conflicts between the short-term interests of those in power and the long-term interests of everybody: chiefs were becoming rich from processes that ultimately undermined society. That too is an acute issue today, as wealthy Americans do things that enrich themselves in the short run and harm everyone in the long run. As the Anasazi chiefs found, they could get away with those policies for a while, but ultimately they bought themselves the privilege of being merely the last to starve.

Of course, there are differences between our situation and those of past 11 societies. Our problems are more dangerous than those of the Anasazi. Today there are far more humans alive, packing far greater destructive power, than ever before. Unlike the Anasazi, a society today can't collapse without affecting societies far away. Because of globalization, the risk we face today is of a worldwide collapse, not just a local tragedy.

People often ask if I am an optimist or a pessimist about our future. I 12 answer that I'm cautiously optimistic. We face big problems that will do us in if we don't solve them. But we are capable of solving them. The risk we face isn't that of an asteroid collision beyond our ability to avoid. Instead our problems are of our own making, and so we can stop making them. The only thing lacking is the necessary political will.

The other reason for my optimism is the big advantage we enjoy over the 13 Anasazi and other past societies: the power of the media. When the Anasazi were collapsing in the U.S. Southwest, they had no idea that Easter Island was also on a downward spiral thousands of miles away, or that Mycenaean Greece had collapsed 2,400 years earlier. But we know from the media what is happening all around the world, and we know from archaeologists what happened in the past. We can learn from that understanding of remote places and times; the Anasazi didn't have that option. Knowing history, we are not doomed to repeat it.

Thinking About the Essay

1. How are the opening paragraphs of the essay structured around multiple, counter pointed analogies? Does the author modulate convincingly from one to another?

2. Highlight instances of the author's use of scare quotes and explain their function in the essay.

3. Where does Diamond introduce the issue of globalization? What connections are made in the essay between globalization, terrorism, and environmental problems?

4. What significance do you see in the order in which Diamond presents his four sets of lessons? Are any of the sets of lessons different in kind from the others?

5. How does globalization recur as a theme in the final paragraphs to distinguish the histories of past cultures from our own situation?

Responding in Writing

6. Write a letter addressed to your future grandchildren in which you relate your current concerns about the world they will inhabit. Is the future state of the environment near the top of your list of concerns? Why or why not?

7. Rwanda appears on Diamond's list of "political tinderboxes" with environmental problems related to resource exploitation or overpopulation (paragraph 8). In an essay, attempt to explain how overpopulation and limited resources (in a country like Rwanda) could lead to political unrest and (in the case of Rwanda) mass genocide.

8. In paragraph 3, Diamond observes of children who grew up during World War II that "their parents may have thought wisely about life insurance, but their parents' generation had not thought wisely about world conditions." In a brief essay, respond to this distinction between individual parents and a generation of individuals. How can someone belong to both categories at the same moment in history?

Networking

9. Do you share Diamond's optimism about the power of the media to inform and educate? Do you agree that "knowing history, we are not doomed to repeat it"? Divide the class into two groups ("optimists" and "pessimists")

and debate Diamond's specific assertion about the media and the familiar and more general statement that ends the essay.

10. Go online and research the history of the collapse of a past culture alluded to in the essay. What are some other differences, not considered in the essay, between the environmental crisis faced by this past culture and the global problems that we face today?

A Place that Makes Sense

BILL MCKIBBEN | Bill McKibben was born in Palo Alto, California, in 1960 and studied at Harvard University (B.A., 1982). His writing focuses on the global ecosystem and the human impact on it. Frequently, he brings moral and religious ideas to bear on the ways in which our behavior—from consumerism to industrial shortsightedness—degrades the natural world. McKibben says that with respect to nature and Earth's ecosystem, he tries "to counter despair." In books like *The End of Nature* (1989), *Hope, Human and Wild: True Stories of Living Lightly on the Earth* (1995), *Long Distance: A Year of Living Strenuously* (2000), *Enough: Staying Human in an Engineered Age* (2003), and *Deep Economy: The Wealth of Communities and the Durable Future* (2007), McKibben balances a sense of alarm about our profligate waste of natural resources with a tempered optimism that we can revere and preserve our fragile planet. "What I have learned so far, " McKibben observes, "is that what is sound and elegant and civilized and respectful of community is also environmentally benign." This essay by McKibben, which appeared in *The Christian Century* on September 23, 2008, poses a challenge: Are we living too large?

Before Reading

In his essay, McKibben asserts that "most places in the U.S. make so little sense" (paragraph 11). What do you think he means by this statement, especially as it relates to sustainable lifestyles and the environment?

Not far from Siena, in the Tuscan hill town of Montalcino, is the   1
Abbey of Sant'Antimo. It was first built in—well, no one's certain.

It was there by the ninth century. What you see now is a modern reconstruction, modern meaning 12th century. In other words, it's a part of the landscape.

And the landscape is a part of it. As I sat in the pews one afternoon   2 earlier this summer, listening to the monks chant Nones in sonorous harmony, I kept looking past the altar to two windows behind. They framed prime views of the steeply raked farm fields in back of the sanctuary—one showed rows of dusty-leaved olive trees climbing a hill, the other rank upon rank of grapevines in their neat rows. With the crucifix in the middle they formed a kind of triptych, and it was easy to imagine not only the passion, but also one's cup running over with Chianti, one's head anointed with gleaming oil.

And easy enough, I think, to figure out why this Tuscan landscape is so   3 appealing to so many. Its charm lies in its comprehensibility—its scale makes intuitive, visceral sense. If you climb one of the bell towers in the hill towns of Tuscany, you look out on a compassable world—you can see where the food that you eat comes from, trace the course of the rivers. It seems sufficient unto itself, as indeed it largely was once upon a time. And in the ancient churches it's easy to construct a vision of the medieval man or woman who once sat in the same hard pew—a person who understood, as we never can, his or her place in the universe. That place was bounded by the distance one could travel physically—save for the Crusade years, it was probably easy to live a life without ever leaving the district. (Florentines speak of living an entire life in view of the Duomo.) And it was bounded just as powerfully by the shared and deep belief in the theology of the church. You knew your place.

Which is a phrase with several meanings. You would have been deeply   4 rooted in that world—it's hard to imagine there the identity crises that are routine in our world. You would have been considerably more rooted than we're comfortable with. You knew your place in the sense that you were born into it, and there was little hope of leaving if it didn't suit. Peasants were peasants and lords were lords, and never the two met. Inequality was baptized, questioning unlikely. The old medieval world made sense, but it was often an oppressive sense—hence the 500-year project to liberate ourselves in every possible way.

And though Tuscany still looks comprehensible—and is thus a suit   5 able backdrop for profitable tourism and powerful travel fantasy—it's now mostly sham. The farms remain, largely supported by farm subsidies from the European Union and the wine-buying habits of affluent foreigners. The villages are mostly emptied out, with only the old remaining—on weekends traffic swells as Florentines and Romans head to the country house. Even the churches are largely relics. Stop in for afternoon Mass and you're likely to find three or four old women listening to an African priest limp along in halting Italian—there aren't nearly the vocations necessary to fill these pulpits. Even the chanting monks at the Sant'Antimo abbey are imports—a French brotherhood that took over the church a decade ago.

Still, it's so alluring, this idea of rootedness. Especially for those of us who live in places that make no sense at all. Where food travels 2,000 miles and arrives at a Wal-Mart. Where God lives at a megachurch without the tradition or culture to give worship much weight. How we thirst for places that make sense. 6

Which is why it was such a pleasure, a few days later, to find myself in a very different kind of church, this one compact, ultramodern, made of glass. Oh, and Lutheran. The ground floor, on this Thursday, was a daycare center filled with parents and kids; the second floor was all offices; and the third housed the sanctuary, a kind of window-girded nest. And when I looked out past the small cross, what I saw were the canals and sidewalks of Hammarby Sjostad—another place that makes sense. Real sense. 7

Hammarby Sjostad, a ten-minute ferry ride from the center of Stockholm, used to be an industrial brownfield, toxic and unpopulated. When Sweden bid to host the 2004 Olympics, it was slated to become the Olympic Village; the bid failed, but the momentum for a new neighborhood 8

Waste tubes in Hammarby Sjostad require community cooperation to work properly.

was enormous, and ground was broken seven or eight years ago. It was designed from the start to be an ecological gem, where the average person would live half again as lightly as the average Swede, who is already among the most ecologically minded citizens of the developed world. The whole place is a closed loop—food waste is turned into biogas, trash is burned for energy, water is recycled. None of it is outrageously high-tech; it's just all thought out.

And the fancy piping is actually only a small part of what makes the   9
place work. The town requires an uncoerced but very real willingness to cooperate, to be part of a community. For instance: by the lobby of each apartment is a series of portholes built into the wall, each one connected to a pneumatic tube. You put food waste in one, paper trash in the next and so on—everything is sucked off to the right processing center. But if you put plastic in with banana peels, the system breaks down. So there's a little graph above the chutes showing how many times each building screwed up the month before. Building 7 (five stories high like most of the blocks in the development), three errant bags. Building 8, one. Building 9, none at all.

Or say you want to wash your clothes. There's no washing machine in   10
your flat—much energy is saved by having a wash house shared by a few buildings. You walk in and wave your key over a sensor, and up pops a digital display. You use it to book a time in the next few days to do your wash in the high-tech machines.

It's a reminder of why most places in the U.S. make so little sense.   11
Cheap energy has led Americans to sprawl endlessly out. We rattle around enormous houses and enormous suburbs, distant from each other in every sense of the word. (The average American eats meals with friends, family or neighbors half as often as he or she did 50 years ago.) Cheap fossil fuel has turned us into the first people in human history who have essentially no need of each other—a kind of hyperindividualism has replaced community.

So maybe Hammarby Sjostad's way of doing things would chafe a   12
little—the American cry has become "Don't tell me what to do," and it's hard to imagine us sharing washing machines with our neighbors. We don't even want to travel together—or at least we didn't until high gas prices began pulling us from our single-occupancy SUVs.

But the responsibilities come with deep pleasures. To stroll the streets   13
of this town is to realize that you've stumbled into a low-key paradise. On a fine day it seems as if all 25,000 residents are out and about, strolling the boardwalks and paths, oblivious to car traffic because it's almost nonexistent. (Parking is expensive, and who needs it—there's a fast ferry

There is very little automobile traffic in Hammarby Sjostad.

to town and a tram that comes by every few minutes.) The community was planned with bars every few blocks, with a community kayak dock, with playing fields and community centers, with shared barbecue pits. Swedes may not be gregarious, but there's the steady hum of community—clusters of moms pushing prams, for instance. (And if you want proof that this place works, the number of families with kids is higher than expected—they're having to build extra schools.) What I'm trying to say is, the place make sense.

The place makes sense in the world, as well. Here's the cost: the flats 14 are relatively small, between 600 and 1,000 square feet. That's two or three rooms plus a modest kitchen and a balcony. You can't have endless stuff because there's no room (everyone has storage space in the base-ment, and there's a special room for bikes). So there's way less space than we've come to consider normal—it's about like living in a trailer, maybe a double-wide.

But that's OK. When the community is an extended home recreation 15 center, you don't need a special warren in your dwelling. What it means is a resident of Hammarby Sjostad is able to live, more or less, at a level calculated to be sustainable for all of the world's 6 billion humans—as compared with the American lifestyle, which would require five additional earths if it were extended across all humanity. This is a place where people aren't drowning Bangladesh or spreading malarial mosquitoes or doing all the other things that come with living too large.

Which brings us back to the church. The state built it—Lutheranism 16 is the official religion in Sweden. And though I wasn't there on a Sunday, to judge by the number of chairs in the sanctuary, the congregation is a small percentage of the neighborhood. Still, there was a powerful sense that the gospel had been consulted in the construction of this town, if only instinctively. The rooted, practical gospel, the one that centers on loving your neighbor as yourself. I've never been in a place that made more sense.

Thinking About the Essay

1. McKibben published this essay in *Christian Century*. What evidence do you find in the essay that suggests he writes for an audience interested in religious matters? What assumptions does he make about his intended audience? To what extent do you feel you are a member of that readership? Explain.

2. What exactly do the Abbey of Sant'Antimo and Hammarby Sjostad symbolize? How does McKibben develop these symbols? What comparative details emerge from his approach?

3. Why does McKibben present information on Tuscany in the first third of the essay, and then move to a town in Sweden? Is this strategy directly relevant to the subject he develops? Explain.

4. What is the author's argument? Where does he state his claim, and how effective is its placement? How does he employ personal experience, observation, and data to support his claim? Cite specific examples.

5. Explain the author's tone and how he achieves it. Is he optimistic or pessimistic about his subject? How do you know?

Responding in Writing

6. Write an essay explaining how you would design a town that offers an ecologically sustainable lifestyle.

7. Argue for or against the proposition that moral and religious considerations should override personal preferences when we make decisions that might affect our environment adversely.

8. Write an essay of extended definition in which you discuss the concept of "rootedness."

Networking

9. Divide into groups of three or four and discuss your views on "loving your neighbor as yourself" and how this concept might relate to environmental issues. Share your responses with the rest of the class. Also, mention whether your views were modified or changed during group discussion.

10. Go online and read messages of some of the professional newsgroups whose members are in the environmental movement. Select several messages regarding ecologically sustainable lifestyles, and write a report on your findings.

To Save Chimps

JANE GOODALL

British naturalist Jane Goodall, born in London in 1934, has spent much of her adult life in the jungles of Tanzania engaged in the study of chimpanzees. Fascinated by animals since childhood, Goodall, after graduating from school, traveled to Kenya to work with the famed paleontologist Louis Leakey, serving as his assistant on fossil-gathering trips to the Olduvai Gorge region. In 1960, at Leakey's urging, Goodall started a new project studying wild chimpanzees in the Gombe Stream Chimpanzee Reserve in Tanzania. In 1965, Cambridge University awarded Goodall a Ph.D. degree based on her thesis growing out of five years of research in the Gombe Reserve; she was only the eighth person in the university's history to earn a doctorate without having earned an undergraduate degree. Goodall has received dozens of major international awards from conservation societies and environmental groups, including the Albert Schweitzer Award, two Franklin Burr Awards from the National Geographic Society, and numerous honorary doctorates from universities around the world. Among her many books are the widely read *In the Shadow of Man* (1971), *The Chimpanzees of Gombe: Patterns of Behavior* (1986), and a two-volume autobiography in letters, *Africa in My Blood* (2000) and *Beyond Innocence* (2001). She also has written books for children and participated in media productions based on her work. This essay from the fall 2006 issue of *WorldView* reflects one of Goodall's core beliefs—that saving animals matters.

Before Reading

Goodall suggests that family planning can protect animals and the environment. Do you agree or disagree, and why?

When I arrived at Gombe National Park in western Tanzania to study   1
chimpanzees 47 years ago, lush forest stretched for miles along Lake

Tanganyika's eastern shoreline and inland as far as I could see. Gradually, over the years, growing populations of local people and refugees struggling to survive in one of the world's poorest places have cut down the trees for firewood, to build homes and to clear the land for farming. By 1980, the trees outside the park had almost all gone. Much of the soil was exhausted. Looking for new land to clear, people have moved to the very steepest slopes of the escarpment, where heavy rains wash away the thin topsoil, cause terrible soil erosion and deadly mudslides. Women walk further and further from their villages in search of fuel wood, adding hours of labor to already difficult days.

This situation, of course, is not only grim for people but desperate also for the chimpanzees of Gombe. The deforestation around the tiny 35-square-kilometer park prevents the chimpanzees from going beyond the park for food as they once did. And the availability of food is considerably reduced, particularly for the chimpanzee communities to the north and south. These two groups are frequently exposed to human disease as people press up to the park's boundaries. Moreover, when the northern and southern chimpanzee communities seek food in the central part of the park, they violate the territory of the central community. Brutal and often deadly violence breaks out. This is a present-day crisis. In the long term, the chimpanzees' future is even more grave; the genetic viability and overall health of these chimpanzees are likely to be compromised since they are unable to increase the gene pool by mating with chimps outside the park.

What can be done? It became clear that, to protect the chimpanzees and their forest habitat, it would be necessary to help human populations around Gombe. Thus, in 1994 the Jane Goodall Institute created the Lake Tanganyika Catchment Reforestation and Education program. We call the program TACARE, or Take Care.

We realized it would be important to first gain the trust of the villagers. Our team of Tanzanian staff began by asking the people what they needed. Not surprisingly, conservation was seldom listed on top: the villagers were concerned with growing more food, with health and with education. We started work with 12 villages and a grant from the European Union. The program was so successful that we expanded it to 24 villages and have acquired some major funding from the U.S. Agency for International Development and several other donors. From the very first, TACARE was conceived as a holistic program and today has six areas of emphasis: community development, water and environmental sanitation, education, agriculture, forestry and health. We work with regional medical authorities to provide primary healthcare, basic information about hygiene and HIV-AIDS education.

Kigoma Region is one of the world's poorest regions. Largely due to lack of education and inadequate health services, it has one of the highest fertility rates in the world, 4.8 percent, as well as high infant and maternal mortality. We launched our family planning activities in 1999 with a David and Lucile Packard Foundation grant to train local men and women as community-based distributors of family planning education and methods of birth control. Our long-term goal was to help the communities that surround Gombe improve the health of mothers and their babies, and to encourage spacing between births. We have 136 trained distributors who now serve in their villages by making house calls, speaking at family planning centers, and conducting private peer-counseling sessions. TACARE also raises awareness through village Family Planning Days, market speeches and public meetings. We use media and performance: plays and *ngoma*, or traditional singing and dancing, videos, calendars and T-shirts with project messages. We serve about 140,000, of which about half are women of child-bearing age.

To meet individual needs, TACARE provides a variety of family planning methods and services to both men and women who request them. They include oral contraceptives and condoms, as well as referrals for clinical long-term and permanent methods such as intra-uterine devices, Depo-Provera, Norplant or voluntary sterilization for men and women.

The institute is the only NGO in rural Kigoma to provide family planning services at the grassroots level. Our trained educator-distributors offer our best chance of succeeding. Our program director at TACARE, Mary Mavanza, says, "Before we began our health services, family planning was almost unheard of in the Kigoma region. Using community-based peers is the best way to open doors and minds." They are critical sources of support and information for the park's neighbors.

Aisha, who has four children, was breastfeeding her three-month-old baby girl when she became pregnant. Her tribe's custom and taboos told her that if she weaned her baby early, she and the baby would weaken and possibly die. She decided to perform an abortion. She took strong local herbs during the daytime and that night experienced severe abdominal pains and heavy bleeding. Her alarmed husband ran to his neighbor, TACARE's local educator-distributor, for advice. Relatives paid the boat fare to rush Aisha to the hospital, where she remained two days. When she returned home, our community-based distributor gave her nutritional advice and when she told him of her abortion, the distributor suggested birth control options. This mother of four children selected Depo-Provera injections.

"My children are doing fine," says Aisha now, "and I have enough   9
time to care for my family." She has started a small-scale business selling
fish in the market. "I am happy by knowing that I won't conceive unless
I plan for it."

We hear of many similar voices. Women who are able to control the   10
timing of childbirth can now pursue education or help support their families through small businesses. Their status rises within their families and
communities. One mother of six, Nyamwiza, started oral contraceptives
with the support of her husband, and found more time to sell fish in the
market. She joined TACARE's micro-finance program, which gives small
loans—mostly to women—for environmentally sustainable businesses.
With her first loan, Nyamwiza expanded her fish business and sold cas-
sava flour. Her husband helped her open a small shop to sell sugar, kero-
sene, oil, cigarettes and matches. The couple can now pay school fees and
buy shoes, uniforms and books for their children. She wants her children
to complete secondary school, an uncommon achievement in Kigoma
Region.

TACARE places major emphasis on helping women because experience   11
all over the world shows that as women's education levels rise, the family
size lowers, so the ripple effects of family planning can be significant. We
discovered that one of the reasons girls drop out of school when they reach
puberty is the unhygienic latrines and a lack of privacy. So, we provide
ventilated pit latrines to all schools.

Our family planning efforts still face significant challenges. The vil-   12
lagers of Kigoma Region have little exposure to the rest of the world and,
therefore, tend to the traditional and the conservative. They prefer large
families because more children mean more hands to help farm and fish, and
the assurance of support in old age. Well-off families are traditionally large
since it is considered a mark of prestige. Unfortunately, many are very poor
families, which results in great hardship. A significant part or our job is
taking our message about the educational and financial benefits of smaller
families. A growing number of people understand the hardships posed by
large families. Frequently they ask our community-based distributors why
they did not come sooner.

While women instinctively appreciate having more control over their   13
fertility and childbirth, our distributors have to work harder to persuade
men, who generally are reticent to even talk about family planning. So we
seek them out on the fish landings and in the cafes.

Men's acceptance is sometimes hard-won. In Zashe village, one of our   14
distributors, Iddi Nanda, told me about a pregnant woman who came into
the local dispensary with a sick one-year-old strapped on her back. She

looked weak, too. When Iddi suggested family planning, she asked him to talk to her husband, who was a pastor.

When Iddi went to the woman's house the next day, the husband ordered Iddi to leave. After a few days, the wife went to Iddi and insisted he try again. This time the pastor threatened Iddi. One day months later the husband came to Iddi's door and begged to enter, promising he would not harm Iddi. The pastor's wife and children were all sick, he said, and he couldn't care for his family and attend to church matters. He also realized how much work his wife did each day. The pastor joined family planning services. 15

In just a few years, I can see how TACARE is benefiting the natural environment. Woodlots have been established near the villages so women no longer need to search out and hack at stumps of trees on the steep slopes, stumps that could produce 20-foot trees in just five years. Forests are growing again outside Gombe park. This regeneration is crucial in protecting the watershed and preventing erosion. It also means the chimpanzees will soon be able to seek out other remnant populations, increasing the gene pool and providing hope for their long-term survival. 16

The program has won support from the Tanzanian government. Recently, the Kigoma Regional Medical Office asked us to seek funding to extend the service to all of the villages in the district and to nearby Kasulu and Kibondo districts. We now receive significant support from government agencies, including USAID-Tanzania, which in 2005 asked us to co-host a workshop in Kigoma linking healthy families and healthy forests. More than 50 professionals took part, representing local and international NGOs working in the environment and development fields and local governments. And, USAID-Tanzania has asked us to use our approach in a pilot community-based program for people with AIDS in which our distributors would offer anti-retroviral therapy. 17

In 2004, I visited Kigoma and met with some TACARE participants. A mother stood up in front of the group and told me she assumed she would always struggle against poverty. With education in family planning, she decided to delay having another child, and started a small business. She began to realistically imagine a drastically different future. 18

"Thanks to TACARE, my children will be well-educated, they will be well-fed, and they will be well-clothed," she said. "I want to thank TACARE for giving me my life." In the end, that is our goal: changing lives, one at a time, knowing that even in a generation or even a decade our impact will have grown exponentially. 19

Thinking About the Essay

1. How do you interpret the author's title in light of your reading of this essay? Is Goodall's essay about saving chimpanzees, improving the lives of Africans, or a combination of purposes? Explain.

2. Analyze Goodall's introductory paragraph. How does it set the stage for the rest of the essay?

3. What connections does Goodall draw between the lives of Africans and chimpanzees? How does she organize her essay around these subjects?

4. What is Goodall's thesis? Does she state it in one sentence or a series of sentences, or does she imply it? Justify your response.

5. Goodall divides her essay into three sections. What is the essential topic of each section? Does she achieve unity and coherence among the parts? Why or why not?

Responding in Writing

6. Argue for or against the proposition that Goodall in this essay succeeds in linking the fates of chimpanzees and their local African population.

7. Write a personal essay in which you narrate and describe what you have learned from a family pet or from the natural world.

8. Reread Goodall's essay, and write a précis of her argument.

Networking

9. Divide into groups of three and four and list examples of the destruction of natural habitats in the United States and around the world. Present your list to the class along with other groups.

10. Go online with another classmate and find out about TACARE and/or the Jane Goodall Institute. Share your findings in class discussion.

A Hole in the World

JONATHAN SCHELL

Jonathan Schell was born in New York City in 1943. Following graduate study in Far Eastern history at Harvard University and additional study in Tokyo, Schell accompanied an American forces operation in South Vietnam in the winter and spring of 1967 that resulted in the evacuation of an entire village after "pacification" failed. He wrote a graphic description of the destruction of Vietnamese villages in *The Village of Ben Suc* (1967) and *The Military Half: An Account* of *Destruction in Quang Ngai and Quang Tin* (1968). Just as his first two books excoriated the American presence in Vietnam, Schell in his third book, *The Time of Illusion* (1976), offered a critique of the Nixon administration and the Watergate scandal. Schell's next book, *The Fate of the Earth* (1982), still one of the most persuasive treatments of the dangers of nuclear war, became a best seller. Schell returned to the subject of nuclear proliferation in *The Gift of Time: The Case for Abolishing Nuclear Weapons* (1998). He currently is the peace and disarmament correspondent for *The Nation* and Harold Willens Peace Fellow at the Nation Institute. In the following essay, published in *The Nation* on October 1, 2001, Schell uses the events of 9/11 to raise the even more frightening specter of nuclear destruction.

Before Reading

How has 9/11 made you more aware of the dangers posed by weapons of mass destruction? Do you carry this awareness with you, or does the prospect of an attack with a weapon of mass destruction seem remote and unthreatening? Explain your response.

On Tuesday morning, a piece was torn out of our world. A patch of   1
blue sky that should not have been there opened up in the New York skyline. In my neighborhood—I live eight blocks from the World Trade Center—the heavens were raining human beings. Our city was changed forever. Our country was changed forever. Our world was changed forever.

It will take months merely to know what happened, far longer to feel so   2
much grief, longer still to understand its meaning. It's already clear, however, that one aspect of the catastrophe is of supreme importance for the future: the danger of the use of weapons of mass destruction, and especially the use of nuclear weapons. This danger includes their use by a terrorist group but is by no means restricted to it. It is part of a larger danger that has been for the most part ignored since the end of the cold war.

Among the small number who have been concerned with nuclear arms   3
in recent years—they have pretty much all known one another by their first names—it was commonly heard that the world would not return its attention to this subject until a nuclear weapon was again set off somewhere in the world. Then, the tiny club said to itself, the world would awaken

Jonathan Schell, "A Hole in the World." Reprinted with permission from the October 1, 2001 issue of *The Nation*. For subscription information, call 1-800-333-8536. Portions of each week's Nation magazine can be accessed at http://www.thenation.com.

to its danger. Many of the ingredients of the catastrophe were obvious. The repeated suicide-homicides of the bombers in Israel made it obvious that there were people so possessed by their cause that, in an exaltation of hatred, they would do anything in its name. Many reports—most recently an article in the *The New York Times* on the very morning of the attack— reminded the public that the world was awash in nuclear materials and the wherewithal for other weapons of mass destruction. Russia is bursting at the seams with these materials. The suicide bombers and the market in nuclear materials was that two-plus-two that points toward the proverbial necessary four. But history is a trickster. The fates came up with a horror that was unforeseen. No one had identified the civilian airliner as a weapon of mass destruction, but it occurred to the diabolical imagination of those who conceived Tuesday's attack that it could be one. The invention illumined the nature of terrorism in modern times. These terrorists carried no bombs—only knives, if initial reports are to be believed. In short, they turned the tremendous forces inherent in modern technical society—in this case, Boeing 767s brimming with jet fuel—against itself.

So it is also with the more commonly recognized weapons of mass   4
destruction. Their materials can be built the hard way, from scratch, as Iraq came within an ace of doing until stopped by the Gulf War and as Pakistan and India have done, or they can be diverted from Russian, or for that matter American or English or French or Chinese, stockpiles. In the one case, it is nuclear know-how that is turned against its inventors, in the other it is their hardware. Either way, it is "blowback"—the use of a technical capacity against its creator—and, as such, represents the pronounced suicidal tendencies of modern society.

This suicidal bent—nicely captured in the name of the still current   5
nuclear policy "mutual assured destruction"—of course exists in forms even more devastating than possible terrorist attacks. India and Pakistan, which both possess nuclear weapons and have recently engaged in one of their many hot wars, are the likeliest candidates. Most important—and most forgotten—are the some 30,000 nuclear weapons that remain in the arsenals of Russia and the United States. The Bush Administration has announced its intention of breaking out of the antiballistic missile treaty of 1972, which bans antinuclear defenses, and the Russians have answered that if this treaty is abandoned the whole framework of nuclear arms control built up over thirty years may collapse. There is no quarrel between the United States and Russia that suggests a nuclear exchange between them, but accidents are another matter, and, as Tuesday's attack has shown, the mood and even the structure of the international order can change overnight.

What should be done? Should the terrorists who carried out Tuesday's 6 attacks be brought to justice and punished, as the President wants to do? Of course. Who should be punished if not people who would hurl a cargo of innocent human beings against a fixed target of other innocent human beings? (When weighing the efficiency—as distinct from the satisfaction—of punishment, however, it is well to remember that the immediate attackers have administered the supposed supreme punishment of death to themselves.) Should further steps be taken to protect the country and the world from terrorism, including nuclear terrorism? They should. And yet even as we do these things, we must hold, as if to life itself, to a fundamental truth that has been known to all thoughtful people since the destruction of Hiroshima: There is no technical solution to the vulnerability of modern populations to weapons of mass destruction. After the attack, Secretary of Defense Rumsfeld placed U.S. forces on the highest state of alert and ordered destroyers and aircraft carriers to take up positions up and down the coasts of the United States. But none of these measures can repeal the vulnerability of modern society to its own inventions, revealed by that heart-breaking gap in the New York skyline. This, obviously, holds equally true for that other Maginot line, the proposed system of national missile defense. Thirty billion dollars is being spent on intelligence annually. We can assume that some portion of that was devoted to protecting the World Trade Center after it was first bombed in 1993. There may have been mistakes—maybe we'll find out— but the truth is that no one on earth can demonstrate that the expenditure of even ten times that amount can prevent a terrorist attack on the United States or any other country. The combination of the extraordinary power of modern technology, the universal and instantaneous spread of information in the information age and the mobility inherent in a globalized economy prevents it.

Man, however, is not merely a technical animal. Aristotle pointed out 7 that we are also a political animal, and it is to politics that we must return for the solutions that hold promise. That means returning to the trea-ties that the United States has recently been discarding like so much old news-paper—the one dealing, for example, with an International Criminal Court (useful for tracking down terrorists and bringing them to justice), with global warming and, above all, of course, with nuclear arms and the other weapons of mass destruction, biological and chemical. The United States and seven other countries now rely for their national security on the retaliatory execution of destruction a million fold greater than the Tuesday attacks. The exit from this folly, by which we endanger ourselves as much as others, must be found. Rediscovering ourselves as political animals also means understanding the sources of the hatred that the United States has incurred in a decade of neglect and, worse, neglect of international affairs—a task that is highly unwelcome to many in current circumstances but nevertheless is indispensable to the future safety of the United States and the world.

It would be disrespectful of the dead to in any way minimize the 8 catastrophe that has overtaken New York. Yet at the same time we must keep room in our minds for the fact that it could have been worse. To lose two huge buildings and the people in them is one thing; to lose all of Manhattan—or much, much more—is another. The emptiness in the sky can spread. We have been warned.

Thinking About the Essay

1. This essay appeared less than a month after the 9/11 disaster. Do you think that the writer exploited the catastrophe, or is his purpose valid? Explain your response.

2. Schell's credentials as a specialist on nuclear proliferation are impressive. Is this essay geared to a highly intelligent audience or a more general one? Cite internal evidence to support your response.

3. How is the essay organized? Where does the introduction begin and end? What paragraphs constitute the body? Where is the conclusion? What markers assisted you in establishing these stages of essay development?

4. Reduce the logical structure of Schell's argument to a set of major and minor propositions. Is his conclusion valid in light of the underlying reasons? Explain.

5. What assertion in the essay do you most agree with, and why? Which assertion do you find dubious or unsupported, and why?

Responding in Writing

6. Write an essay in which you agree or disagree with Schell's statement that the danger of the use of weapons of mass destruction is "of supreme importance for the future" (paragraph 2).

7. Schell asserts that the United States has neglected its role in international affairs, including its abandonment of international treaties, thereby endangering the nation's security. Argue for or against his claim.

8. Write an analysis of Schell's style in this essay. Begin with the title itself and how it resonates throughout the essay. Discuss the impact of such graphic uses of language as "the heavens were raining human beings" (paragraph 1). Identify those stylistic techniques the author uses to persuade us to accept the logic of his position.

Networking

9. Divide into groups of between three and five, and create a simulation game whereby a specific city is threatened by a weapon of mass destruction. Imagine the steps taken to thwart the attack, and determine if these steps would be successful or not. Present your scenario to the class.

10. Using an Internet search engine, locate information on nuclear disarmament. Using the information retrieved, write a report on what various groups, agencies, and governments are doing to reduce and prevent the spread of nuclear weapons.

Conducting Research in the Global Era

Introduction

The *doing* of research is as important a process as the *writing* of a research paper. When scholars, professors, scientists, journalists, and students *do* research, they ask questions, solve problems, follow leads, and track down sources. The process of research as well as the writing of the research paper has changed radically over the last ten years, as the Internet now makes a whole world of resources instantly available to anyone. Skillfully navigating your way through this wealth of resources, evaluating and synthesizing information as you solve problems and answer questions, enhances your critical thinking and writing abilities and develops the tools you will need for professional success.

A research paper incorporates the ideas, discoveries, and observations of other writers. The information provided by these scholars, thinkers, and observers helps to support your own original thesis or claim about a topic. Learning how to evaluate, adapt, synthesize, and correctly acknowledge these sources in your research protects you from charges of plagiarism (discussed below). More importantly, it demonstrates to you how knowledge is expanded and created. Research and research writing are the cornerstone not only of the university but of our global information society.

The research paper is the final product of a process of inquiry and discovery. The topics and readings in this book bring together voices from all over the world, discussing and debating issues of universal importance. As you develop a topic, work toward a thesis, and discover sources and evidence, you will use the Internet to bring international perspectives to your writing. More immediately, your teacher will probably ask you to work in peer groups as you refine your topics, suggest resources to each other, and evaluate preliminary drafts of your final research paper. Although the primary—and ultimate—audience for your research paper is your teacher, thinking of your work as a process of discovery and a contribution to a larger global conversation will keep your perspective fresh and your interest engaged.

The Research Process

A research paper is the final result of a series of tasks, some small and others quite time consuming. Be sure to allow yourself plenty of time for each stage of the research process, working with your teacher or a peer group to develop a schedule that breaks down specific tasks.

The four broad stages of the research process are

1. Choosing a topic
2. Establishing a thesis
3. Finding, evaluating, and organizing evidence
4. Writing your paper

Stage One: Choosing a Topic

Reading and discussing the often urgent issues addressed in this book may have already given you an idea about a topic you would like to explore further. Your attention may also have been engaged by a television news report, an international website that presented an unexpected viewpoint, or a speaker who visited your campus. Even if your teacher assigns a specific topic area to you, finding—and nurturing—a genuine curiosity and concern about that topic will make the research process much more involving and satisfying. Some topics are too broad, too controversial (or not controversial enough), too current, or too obscure for an effective research paper.

Determining an Appropriate Research Topic

Ask yourself the following questions about possible topics for your research paper:

- Am I genuinely curious about this topic? Will I want to live with it for the next few weeks?
- What do I already know about this topic? What more do I want to find out?
- Does the topic fit the general guidelines my teacher has suggested?
- Can I readily locate the sources I will need for further research on this topic?

Exercise: Freewriting

Review your work as your class progresses, taking note of any readings in the text that particularly appealed to you or any writing assignments that you especially enjoyed. Open a new folder on your computer, labeling it "Research

Paper." Open a new document and title it "Freewriting." Then write, without stopping, everything that intrigued you originally about that reading or that assignment. Use the questions on page 438 to prompt your thinking.

Browsing

Having identified a general topic area of interest, begin exploring that area by *browsing*. When you browse, you take a broad and casual survey of the existing information and resources about your topic. There are many resources to consult as you begin to dig deeper into your topic, nearly all of which can be found at your campus library. Begin at the reference desk by asking for a guide to the library's reference collection.

- *General Reference Texts*. These include encyclopedias, almanacs, specialized dictionaries, and statistical information.
- *Periodical Index*. Both in-print and online versions of periodical indices now exist (the electronic versions are often subscription-only and available only through academic and some public libraries). A periodical index lists subjects, authors, and titles of articles in newspapers, journals, and magazines. Some electronic versions include both abstracts (brief summaries) and full-text versions of the articles.
- *Library Catalog*. Your library's catalog probably exists both online and as a "card catalog"—an alphabetized record organized by author, title, and subject—in which each book has its own card in a file. Begin your catalog browsing with a subject or keyword search. Identify the *call number* that appears most frequently for the books you are most likely to use—that number will point you to the library shelves where you'll find the most useful books for your topic.

Making a Global Connection

Unless you read another language, the information you find in books is not likely to be as international or immediate in perspective as that which you will find in periodicals and online. The information you find through the card catalog will direct you toward books that provide in-depth background information and context, but for the most up-to-date information as well as a perspective from the nation or countries involved in your topic, your online and periodical research will probably be most useful.

- *Search Engines*. For the most current and broadest overview of a research topic, a search engine such as Google, Altavista, or Yahoo can provide you with an ever-changing—and dauntingly vast—range of perspectives. Many search engines, including these three, have international sites (allowing you to search in specific regions or countries) as well as basic translation services. At the browsing stage, spending time online can both stimulate your interest and help you to focus your topic. Because websites change so quickly, however, be sure to print out a page from any site you think might be useful in the later stages of your research—that way, you'll have a hard copy of the site's URL (uniform resource locator, or Web address). (If you're working on your own computer, create a new folder under "favorites" or "bookmarks" entitled "Research Project," and file bookmarks for interesting sites there.)

Stage Two: Establishing a Thesis

Moving from a general area of interest to a specific *thesis*—a claim you wish to make, an area of information you wish to explore, a question you intend to answer, or a solution to a problem you want to propose—requires thinking critically about your topic. You have already begun to focus on what *specifically* interests you about this topic in the freewriting exercise on page 438. The next step in refining your topic and establishing a thesis is to determine your audience and purpose for writing.

Determining Your Audience and Purpose

- Where have you found, through your browsing, the most interesting or compelling information about your topic? Who was the audience for that information? Do you consider yourself to be a part of that audience? Define the characteristics of that audience (e.g., concerned about the environment, interested in global economics, experienced at traveling abroad).
- *Why* are you most interested in this topic? Do you want to encourage someone (a friend, a politician) to take a specific course of action? Do you want to shed some light on an issue or event that not many people are familiar with?
- Try a little imaginative role playing. Imagine yourself researching this topic as a professional in a specific field. For example, if your topic is environmental preservation, imagine yourself as a pharmaceuticals researcher. What would your compelling interest in the topic be? What if you were an adventure traveler seeking new destinations—how would your approach to the topic of environmental preservation change?
- If you could have the undivided attention of anyone, other than your teacher, with whom you could share your knowledge about this topic, who would that person be and why?

Moving from a Topic to a Thesis Statement

Although choosing a topic is the beginning of the research *process*, it is not the beginning of your research *paper*. The course that your research will take and the shape that your final paper will assume are based on your *thesis statement*. A thesis statement is the answer to whatever question originally prompted your research. To narrow your topic and arrive at a thesis statement, ask yourself specific questions about the topic.

Using Questions to Create a Thesis Statement

General Topic	More Specific Topic	Question	Thesis Statement
Preserving the global environment	Preserving the rain forest	What is a creative way in which people could try to preserve the rain forest?	Ecotourism, when properly managed, can help the rain forest by creating economic incentives for the people who live there.
Economic security for women in the developing world	Creating economic opportunities for women in the developing world	What approaches could help women in the developing world establish economic security for themselves and their communities?	Microloans are a creative and empowering way of redistributing wealth that allows individual women to develop their own economic security.
AIDS in Africa	The incidence of AIDS in African women	How are international organizations working to stop the spread of AIDS among African women?	Improving literacy and educational opportunities for African girls and women will help to stem the spread of AIDS.
Dating and courtship between people of different religions	Dating behavior among second-generation American Hindu or Muslim teenagers	How are kids from conservative cultural or religious backgrounds negotiating between their family's beliefs and the pressures of American popular culture?	Encouraging multicultural events helps teenagers learn about each others' cultures and beliefs.

Stage Three: Finding, Evaluating, and Organizing Evidence

Developing a Working Bibliography

A working bibliography is a record of every source you consult as you conduct your research. Although not every source you use may end up cited in your paper, having a consolidated and organized record of *everything* you looked at will make drafting the paper as well as preparing the Works Cited page much easier. Some people use their computers for keeping a Works Cited list (especially if you do much of your research using online databases, which automatically create citations). But for most people—even if many of your sources are online—index cards are much more portable and efficient. Index cards allow you to easily rearrange the order of your sources (according to priority, for example, or sources that you need to double-check). The cards let you jot down notes or summaries, and they slip into your bookbag for a quick trip to the library.

Whether your working bibliography is on a computer or on index cards, always record the same information for each source you consult. Note that current Modern Language Association (MLA) guidelines now stipulate italics in place of underlining. If you are preparing your working bibliography on a computer, use italics for book titles, magazine titles, etc.; use underlining on handwritten index cards.

Checklists for Working Bibliographies

Information for a book:

❑ Author name(s), first and last
❑ Book title
❑ Place of publication
❑ Publisher's name
❑ Date of publication
❑ Library call number
❑ Page numbers (for specific information or quotes you'll want to consult later)

Information for an article in a journal or magazine:

❑ Author name(s), first and last
❑ Article title
❑ Magazine or journal title
❑ Volume and issue number (when issue number is available)
❑ Date of publication
❑ Page numbers
❑ Library call number

Information for online sources:

- ❏ Author (if there is one)
- ❏ Title of an article or graphic on the Web page
- ❏ Title of website, if different from the above
- ❏ Version or edition
- ❏ Publisher or sponsor of the site (if any)
- ❏ Date of publication (if available)
- ❏ Date of your online access
- ❏ URL (website address; not usually included in your Works Cited list unless it would be unlikely your reader could find the correct source or if your instructor requires one)
- ❏ *Some sites* include *information on how they prefer to be cited. You'll notice this information at the bottom of a main or "splash" page of a site, or you'll see a link to a "citation" page.*

Sample working bibliography note: Article

Honey, Martha. "Protecting the Environment: Setting Green Standards for the Tourism Industry." *Environment* 45.1 (2003): 8–12.

Sample working bibliography note: Online source

World Tourism Association. "Global Code of Ethics for Tourism." <http:www.//world-tourism.org/projects/ethics/principles.html>.

Consulting Experts and Professionals

In the course of your research you may discover someone whose work is so timely, or opinions so relevant, that a personal interview would provide even more (and unique) information for your paper. Look beyond the university faculty for such experts—for example, if your topic is ecotourism, a local travel agent who specializes in ecotourism might be able to give you firsthand accounts of such locales and voyages. If your topic is second-generation teenagers balancing conservative backgrounds with American popular culture, hanging out with a group of such kids and talking with them about their lives will give you the kind of first-person anecdote that makes research writing genuinely fresh and original. Think of "expertise" as being about *experience*—not just a title or a degree.

Checklist for Arranging and Conducting Interviews

- ❏ Be certain that the person you wish to speak to will offer a completely unique, even undocumented, perspective on your topic. Interviewing someone who has already published widely on your topic is not the best use of your research time, as you can just as easily consult that person's published work.

❏ E-mail, telephone (at a business number, if possible), or write to your subject well in advance of your paper deadline. Explain clearly that you are a student writing a research paper, the topic of your paper, and the specific subject(s) you wish to discuss.

❏ An interview can be conducted via e-mail or over the telephone as well as in person. Instant messaging, because it can't be easily documented and doesn't lend itself to longer responses, is not a good choice.

❏ Write out your questions in advance!

Conducting Field Research

Field research involves traveling to a specific place to observe and document a specific occurrence or phenomenon. For example, if you were writing about the challenges and opportunities of a highly diverse immigrant community (such as Elmhurst, Queens), you might arrange to spend a day at a local school, park, or coffee shop. Bring a notebook, a digital camera, a tape recorder—anything that will help you capture and record observations. Although your task as a field researcher is to be *unbiased*—to objectively observe what is happening, keeping an open mind as well as open eyes—you'll want to always keep your working thesis in mind, too. For example, if your thesis is

Allowing students in highly diverse American communities to create events that celebrate and respect their own cultural traditions within the general American popular culture helps to create understanding between teenagers and their immigrant parents

your field research might take you to a high school in an immigrant community to observe the interactions among teenagers. You'll want to record everything—both positive and negative, both expected and surprising—that you observe and overhear, but you won't want to get distracted by a teacher's mentioning the difficulties of coping with many different languages in the classroom. That's fascinating, but it's another topic altogether.

Checklist for Arranging and Conducting Field Research

❏ If your field research involves crossing a private boundary or property line—a school, church, hospital, restaurant, etc.—be sure to contact the institution first to confirm that it's appropriate for you to visit. As with the guidelines for conducting a personal interview, inform the person with whom you arrange the visit that you are a student conducting field research and that your research is for a classroom paper.

❏ Respect personal boundaries. Some people might not want to be photographed, and others might be uneasy if they think you are taking notes on their conversation or behavior. If you sense that your presence is making someone uncomfortable, apologize and explain what you are doing. If they are still uncomfortable, back off.

❑ When you use examples and observations from your field research in your research paper, do not use the first person as part of the citation. Simply describe what was observed and under what circumstances.

Not recommended: When I visited the dog park to see how the personalities of dogs reflect those of their owners, I was especially attracted to the owner of a bulldog named Max. When I introduced myself to Max's owner, George T., and explained my project to him, George agreed with my thesis and pointed out that the owners of large, athletic dogs like Rottweilers tended to be young men, and the owners of more sedentary dogs (like Max) seemed to be a little mellower.

Recommended: A visit to a local dog park revealed the ways in which the personalities of dogs reflect those of their owners. George T., the owner of a bulldog named Max, pointed out that the younger men at the park were accompanied by large, athletic dogs like Rottweilers, while more sedentary people (like George) tended to have mellower breeds such as bulldogs.

Assessing the Credibility of Sources

After browsing, searching, observing, and conversing, you will by now have collected a mass of sources and data. The next step is to evaluate those sources critically, using your working bibliography as a road map back to all the sources you have consulted to date. This critical evaluation will help you to determine which sources have the relevance, credibility, and authority expected of academic research.

Checklist for Assessing Source Credibility

❑ Do the table of contents and index of a book include keywords and subjects relevant to your topic? Does the abstract of a journal article include keywords relevant to your topic and thesis? Does a website indicate through a menu (or from your using the "search" command) that it contains content relevant to your topic and thesis?

❑ How current is the source? Check the date of the magazine or journal and the copyright date of the book (the original copyright date, not the dates of reprints). Has the website been updated recently, and are its links current and functioning?

❑ How authoritative is the source? Is the author credentialed in his or her field? Do other authors refer to this writer (or website) in their work?

❑ Who sponsors a website? Is it the site of a major media group, a government agency, a political think tank, or a special-interest group? If you are unsure, print out the home page of the site and ask your teacher or a reference librarian.

Taking Notes

Now that you have determined which sources are most relevant and useful, you can begin to read them with greater attention to detail. This is *active reading*—annotating, responding to, and taking notes on what you are reading. Taking careful notes will help you to build the structure of your paper and will ensure accurate documentation later. As with the working bibliography, you can take notes either on your computer or on index cards. For online sources, you can cut and paste blocks of text into a separate word-processing document on your computer; just be certain to include the original URL and to indicate that what you have cut and pasted is a *direct quote* (which you might later paraphrase or summarize). Some researchers cut and paste material in a font or color that is completely different from their own writing, just to remind them of where specific words and concepts came from (and as protection against inadvertent plagiarism).

There are three kinds of notes you will take as you explore your resources:

- Summaries give you the broad overview of a source's perspective or information and serve as reminders of a source's content should you wish to revisit later for more specific information or direct quotes.
- Paraphrases express a source's ideas and information in your own language.
- Direct *quotations* are best for when an author or subject expresses a thought or concept in language that is so striking, important, or original that to paraphrase it would be to lose some of its importance. Direct quotations are *exact* copies of an author's own words and are always enclosed in quotation marks.

Checklist for Taking Notes

❏ Take just one note (paraphrase, summary, or analysis) on each index card. Be sure to note the complete source information for the quote on the card (see the Checklists for Working Bibliographies on page 442 for what information is required).

❏ Cross-check your note-taking cards against your working bibliography. Be sure that every source on which you take notes has a corresponding entry in the working bibliography.

❏ Write a subtopic on top of each card, preferably in a brightly colored ink. Keep a running list of all of your subtopics. This will enable you to group together related pieces of information and determine the structure of your outline.

Sample note: Summary

Subtopic	Indigenous peoples and ecotourism
Author/title	Mastny, "Ecotourist trap"
Page numbers	94
Summary	The Kainamaro people of Guyana are actively involved with the development of ecotourism in their lands, ensuring that their cultural integrity takes precedence over financial gain.

Sample note: Paraphrase

Subtopic	Indigenous peoples and ecotourism
Author/title	Mastny, "Ecotourist trap"
Page numbers	94
Paraphrase	Actively involving indigenous peoples in ecotourism arrangements is important. A representative for the Kainamaro people of Guyana, Claudette Fleming, says that although this community first worried about maintaining their cultural integrity, they came to see that ecotourism would be a more beneficial way to increase their income and at the same time control their lands and culture than other industries such as logging.

Sample note: Direct quotation

Subtopic	Indigenous peoples and ecotourism
Author/title	Mastny, "Ecotourist trap"
Page numbers	94
Direct quotation	"The Kainamaro are content to share their culture and creativity with outsiders—as long as they remain in control of their futures and the pace of cultural change."

Understanding Plagiarism, Intellectual Property, and Academic Ethics

- *Plagiarism.* Plagiarism is passing off someone else's words, ideas, images, or concepts as your own. Plagiarism can be as subtle and accidental as forgetting to add an in-text citation or as blatant as "borrowing" a friend's paper or handing in something from a website with your own name on it. Most schools and colleges have explicit, detailed policies about what constitutes plagiarism, and the consequences of being caught are not pretty—you may risk anything from failure on a particular assignment to expulsion from the institution. There are two basic ways to avoid plagiarism: (1) don't wait until the last minute to write your paper (which will tempt you to take shortcuts); (2) give an in-text citation (see page 452) for absolutely everything you include in your research paper that didn't come out of your own head. It's better to be safe and over-cite than to be accused of plagiarism. For a straightforward discussion of plagiarism, go to http://www.georgetown.edu/honor/plagiarism.html.

- *Intellectual Property*. If you've ever considered wiping your hard disk clean of free downloaded music files out of the fear of being arrested or fined, then you've wrestled with the issue of intellectual property. Intellectual property includes works of art, music, animation, and literature—as well as research concepts, computer programs, and even fashion. Intellectual property rights for visual, musical, and verbal works are protected by *copyright law*. When you download, for free, a music track from the Internet, you are violating copyright law—the artist who created that work receives no credit or royalties for your enjoyment and use of his or her work. When you cut and paste blocks of a website into your own research paper without giving credit, you are also violating copyright law. To respect the intellectual property rights of anyone (or anything) you cite in your research paper, you carefully *cite* the source of the information. Using quotes from another writer, or images from another artist, in your own academic paper is legally defined as "fair use"—*if* you make it clear where the original material comes from.

- *Ethics and the Academic Researcher*. As you enter an academic conversation about your research topic, your audience—even if it's only your teacher—expects you to conduct yourself in an ethical fashion. Your *ethos*, literally, means "where you stand"—what you believe, how you express those beliefs, and how thoughtfully and considerately you relate to the "stances" of others in your academic community. In the professional academy, researchers in fields from medieval poetry through cell biology are expected to adhere to a code of ethics about their research. Working with the ideas and discoveries of others in their academic communities, they are careful to always acknowledge the work of their peers and the contributions that work has made to their own research. You should do the same. When you leave school, these basic ethical tenets remain the same. You wouldn't hand in another rep's marketing report as your own, you wouldn't claim credit for the successful recovery of another doctor's patient, and you wouldn't put your name on top of another reporter's story. To violate professional ethics is to break the trust that holds an academic or professional community together.

Stage Four: Organizing and Outlining Your Information

Now that you have gathered and evaluated a mass of information, the next step is to begin giving some shape and order to what you have discovered. Writing an outline helps you to think through and organize your evidence, determine the strengths and weaknesses of your argument, and visualize the shape of your final paper. Some instructors will require you to hand in an outline along with your research paper. Even if an outline isn't formally required, it is such a useful and valuable step toward moving from a pile of index cards to a logical, coherent draft that you should plan to create one.

Checklist for Organizing Your Information

❑   Gather up all of your note cards and print out any notes you have taken on your computer. Double-check all of your notes to make sure that they include accurate citation information.

❑   Using your list of subtopics, group your notes according to those subtopics. Are some piles of cards enormous, while other topics have only a card or two? See if subtopics can be combined—or if any subtopics could be further refined and made more specific.

❑   Set aside any note cards that don't seem to "fit" in any particular pile.

❑   Find your thesis statement and copy it out on a blank index card. Go through the cards in each subtopic. Can you immediately see a connection between each note card and your thesis statement? (If not, set that note card aside for now.)

❑   Do not throw away any of the note cards, even if they don't seem to "fit" into your current research plan. You probably won't use every single note card in your paper, but it's good to have a continuing record of your work.

Basic Outlining

Many word-processing programs include an "outline" function, and your instructor may ask you to follow a specific format for your outline. An outline is a kind of road map for your thought processes, a list of the pieces of information you are going to discuss in your paper and how you are going to connect those pieces of information to each other as well as back to your original thesis. You can begin the outlining process by using the note cards you have divided into subtopics:

I. Most compelling, important subtopic
   A. Supporting fact, quote, or illustration
   B. Another interesting piece of evidence that supports or illustrates the subtopic
      1. A direct quotation that further illustrates point B
      2. Another supporting point
         a. Minor, but still relevant, points

Another useful outlining strategy is to assign each subtopic a working "topic sentence" or "main idea." As you move into the drafting process, you can return to those topic sentences/main ideas to begin each paragraph.

The Writing Process

A research paper is more than a collection of strung-together facts. No matter how interesting and relevant each individual piece of information may be, your reader is not responsible for seeing how the parts make up a whole. Connecting the evidence, demonstrating the relationships between concepts and ideas, and proving how all of it supports your thesis are entirely up to you.

Drafting

The shape of your outline and your subdivided piles of index cards provide the framework for your rough draft. As you begin to write your essay, think about "connecting the dots" between each piece of evidence, gradually filling in the shape of your argument. Expect your arrangement of individual note cards or whole subtopics to change as you draft.

Remember that you are not drafting a final paper, and certainly not a perfect paper. The goal of drafting is to *organize* your evidence, to get a sense of your argument's strengths and weaknesses, to test the accuracy of your thesis and revise it if necessary. Drafting is as much a thinking process as it is a writing process.

If you get "stuck" as you draft, abandon whatever subtopic you are working on and begin with another. Working at the paragraph level first—using the evidence on a subtopic's note card to support and illustrate the topic sentence or main idea of the subtopic—is a much less intimidating way to approach drafting a research paper.

Finally, as you draft, be sure that you include either an in-text citation (see page 452) or some other indication of *precisely* where each piece of information came from. This will save you time when you begin revising and preparing the final draft as well as the Works Cited list.

Incorporating Sources

As you draft, you will build connections between different pieces of evidence, different perspectives, and different authors. Learning how to smoothly integrate all those different sources into your own work, without breaking the flow of your own argument and voice, takes some practice. The most important thing to remember is to accurately indicate the source of every piece of information as soon as you cite it.

One way to smoothly integrate sources into your paper is through paraphrase. For example:

> The educational benefits of ecotourism can help future generations to respect the environment. "Helping people learn to love the earth is a high

calling and one that can be carried out through ecotourism. Ecotourism avoids much of the counterproductive baggage that often accompanies standard education" (Kimmel 41).

In revision, this writer used paraphrase to move more gracefully from her main point to the perspective provided by her source:

Teachers like James R. Kimmel have called the ecotourism experience a "nirvana" for educating their students. "Helping people learn to love the earth is a high calling and one that can be carried out through ecotourism," he observes, noting that the "counterproductive baggage" such as testing and grading are left behind (Kimmel 41).

This system of indicating where exactly an idea, quote, or paraphrase comes from is called *parenthetical citation*. In MLA and APA style, which are required by most academic disciplines (see pages 452–454), these in-text citations take the place of footnotes or endnotes.

Using Transition Verbs Between Your Writing and a Source

Using conversation verbs as transitions between your own writing and a direct quote can enliven the style of your paper. In the previous example, the writer uses the verb "observes" rather than just "states" or "writes." Other useful transitions include:

Arundhati Roy argues that ...

Peter Carey mourns that ...

Amy Tan remembers that ...

Barbara Ehrenreich and Annette Fuentes compare the results of ...

Ann Grace Mojtabai admits that ...

Naomi Shihab Nye insists that ...

Pico Iyer vividly describes ...

Revising and Polishing

The drafting process clarified your ideas and gave structure to your argument. In the revision process, you rewrite and rethink your paper, strengthening the connections between your main points, your evidence, and your thesis. Sharing your essay draft with a classmate, with your instructor, or with a tutor at your campus writing center will give you an invaluable objective perspective on your paper's strengths and weaknesses.

Checklist for Your Final Draft

❑ Have I provided parenthetical citations for every source I used?
❑ Do all of those parenthetical citations correspond to an item in my Works Cited list?

❏ Does my essay's title clearly and specifically state my topic?

❏ Is my thesis statement identifiable, clear, and interesting?

❏ Does each body paragraph include a topic sentence that clearly connects to my thesis?

❏ Do I make graceful transitions between my own writing and the sources I incorporate?

❏ When I shared my paper with another reader, was I able to answer any questions about my evidence or my argument using sources already at hand? Or do I need to go back to the library or online to "fill in" any questionable areas in my research?

❏ Does my conclusion clearly echo and support my thesis statement and concisely sum up how all of my evidence supports that thesis?

❏ Have I proofread for clarity, grammar, accuracy, and style?

❏ Is my paper formatted according to my instructor's guidelines? Do I have a backup copy on disk and more than one printed copy?

Documentation

From the beginning of your research, when you were browsing in the library and online, you have been documenting your sources. To document a source simply means to make a clear, accurate record of where exactly a piece of information, a quote, an idea, or a concept comes from, so that future readers of your paper can go back to that original source and learn more. As we have seen, careful attention to documentation is the best way to protect yourself against inadvertent plagiarism. There are two ways you document your sources in your paper: within the text itself (*in-text* or *parenthetical* citation) and in the Works Cited list at the end of your paper.

What Do I Need to Document?

- Anything I didn't know before I began my research
- Direct quotations
- Paraphrases
- Summaries
- Specific numerical data, such as charts and graphs
- Any image, text, or animation from a website
- Any audio or video
- Any information gathered during a personal interview

Parenthetical (in-text) Citation

MLA style for documentation is most commonly used in the humanities and is the format discussed here. Keep in mind that different academic disciplines have their own documentation guidelines and styles, as do some organizations (many newspapers, for example, have their own "style guides"). An in-text citation identifies the source of a piece of information as part of your own sentence or within parentheses. In MLA style, the parenthetical information includes the author's name and the page number (if appropriate) on which the information can be found in the original source. If your readers want to know more, they can then turn to your Works Cited page to find the author's name and the full bibliographic information for that source. Always place the in-text or parenthetical citation as close to the incorporated source material as possible—preferably within the same sentence.

Guidelines for Parenthetical (in-text) Citation

Page numbers for a book

The end of the Second World War began Samuel Beckett's greatest period of creativity, which he referred to as "the siege in the room" (Bair 346).

Bair describes the period immediately after the Second World War as a time of great creativity for Samuel Beckett (346).

In the first parenthetical citation, the author is not named within the student writer's text, so the parentheses include both the source author's name and the page number on which the information can be found. In the second example, the source author (Bair) is mentioned by name, so there is no need to repeat that name within the parentheses—only the page number is needed.

Page numbers for an article in a magazine or journal

Wheatley argues that "America has embraced values that cannot create a sustainable society and world" (25).

Page numbers for a newspaper article

Cite both the section letter (or description of the section) and the page.

Camera phones are leading to new questions about the invasion of privacy (Harmon sec. 4:3).

A spokesperson for the National Institutes of Health has described obesity as the greatest potential danger to the average American's health (Watts B3).

Website

Arts and Letters Daily includes links to opinions and essays on current events from English-language media worldwide.

Article 2 of the proposed Global Code of Ethics for Tourism describes tourism "as a vehicle for individual and collective fulfillment" (*world-tourism*).

When an online source does not give specific "page," screen, or paragraph numbers, your parenthetical citation must include the name of the site.

Works Cited List

Gather your working bibliography cards, and be sure that every source you cite in your paper has a corresponding card. To construct the Works Cited list, you simply arrange these cards in alphabetical order, by author. The Works Cited page is a separate, double-spaced page at the end of your paper.

Formatting Your Works Cited List

- Center the title, Works Cited, at the top of a new page. Do not underline it, italicize it, or place it in quotation marks.
- Alphabetize according to the author's name, or according to the title (for works, such as websites, that do not have an author). Ignore words such as *the, and*, and *a* when alphabetizing.
- Begin each entry at the left margin. After the first line, indent all other lines of the entry by five spaces (one stroke of the "tab" key).
- Double-space every line.
- Place a period after the author, the title, the publishing information, and the medium of publication (Print, Web, CD-ROM, etc.).
- Italicize book and Web page titles. Titles of articles, stories, poems, and parts of entire works in other media are placed in quotation marks.

Guidelines for Works Cited List

Book by one author

Bair, Deirdre. *Samuel Beckett: A Biography*. New York: Simon, 1978. Print.

Multiple books by the same author

List the author's name for the first entry. For each entry that follows, replace the author's name with three hyphens.

Thomas, Lewis. *The Medusa and the Snail: More Notes of a Biology Watcher*. New York: Viking, 1979. Print.

___. *Late Night Thoughts on Listening to Mahler's Ninth Symphony*. New York: Viking, 1983. Print.

Book with two or three authors/editors

Schueller, Malini Johar, and Edward Watts, eds. *Messy Beginnings: Postcoloniality and Early American Studies.* Piscataway: Rutgers UP, 2003. Print.

Book with more than three authors/editors

Freeman, Arthur, James Pretzer, Barbara Fleming, and Karen M. Simon. *Clinical Applications of Cognitive Therapy.* 2nd ed. New York: Springer, 2004. Print.

Alternatively, in this case, you can use the first name only and add *et al.* ("and others.")

Book or publication with group or organization as author

Modern Language Association. *MLA Handbook for Writers of Research Papers.* 7th ed. New York: MLA, 2009. Print.

Book or publication without an author

Chase's Calendar of Events 2009. New York: McGraw, 2008. Print.

Work in an anthology of pieces all by the same author

Thomas, Lewis. "The Youngest and Brightest Thing Around." *The Medusa and the Snail: More Notes of a Biology Watcher.* New York: Viking, 1979. Print.

Work in an anthology of different authors

Chase, Katie. "Man and Wife." *The Best American Short Stories 2008.* Ed. Salman Rushdie. Boston: Houghton, 2008. Print.

Work translated from another language

Cocteau, Jean. *The Difficulty of Being.* Trans. Elizabeth Sprigge. New York: Da Capo, 1995. Print.

Entry from a reference volume

For dictionaries and encyclopedias, simply note the edition and its date. No page numbers are necessary for references organized alphabetically, such as encyclopedias (and, obviously, dictionaries).

Merriam-Webster's Medical Desk Dictionary. Rev. ed. Boston: Cengage, 2006. Print.

"Carriera, Rosalba." *The Oxford Companion to Western Art.* Ed. Hugh Brigstoke.
    Oxford: Oxford UP, 2001. Print.

Article from a journal

Note that current MLA guidelines no longer make a distinction between
journals that are numbered continuously (e.g., Vol. 1 ends on page 208,
Vol. 2 starts on page 209) or numbered separately (i.e., each volume starts
on page 1). No matter how the journal is paginated, all of them must
contain volume *and* issue numbers. (To indicate the issue number, place
a period and the number after the volume number.) One exception are
journals with issue numbers only; simply cite the issue numbers alone as
though they are volume numbers.

Enoch, Jessica. "Resisting the Script of Indian Education: Zitkala-Sa and the Carlisle
    Indian School." *College English* 65.1 (2002): 117–41. Print.

Article from a weekly or biweekly periodical

Baum, Dan. "Jake Leg." *New Yorker* 15 Sept. 2003: 50–57. Print.

Article from a monthly or bimonthly periodical

Perlin, John. "Solar Power: The Slow Revolution." *Invention and Technology* Sum-
    mer 2002: 20–25. Print.

Article from a daily newspaper

Brody, Jane E. "A Pregame Ritual: Doctors Averting Disasters." *New York Times* 14
    Oct. 2003: F7. Print.

If the newspaper article goes on for more than one page, add a sign to the first
page number.

Newspaper or periodical article with no author

"Groups Lose Sole Authority on Chaplains for Muslims." *New York Times* 14 Oct.
    2003: A15. Print.

Unsigned editorial in a newspaper or periodical

"The Iraqi Weapons Puzzle." Editorial. *New York Times* 12 Oct. 2003: sec. 4:10.
    Print.

Letter to the editor of a newspaper or periodical

Capasso, Chris. Letter. *"Mountain Madness." Outside* May 2003: 20. Print.

Film, video, DVD

If you are writing about a specific actor's performance or a specific director, use that person's name as the beginning of the citation. Otherwise, begin with the title of the work. Specify the media of the recording (film, video, DVD, etc.).

Princess Mononoke. Dir. Hayao Miyazaki. Prod. Studio Ghibli, 1999. Miramax,
    2001. Videocassette.

Eames, Charles and Ray. *The Films of Charles and Ray Eames, Volume 1: Powers of
    Ten.* 1978. Pyramid Home Video, 1984. Videocassette.

Television or radio broadcast

"Alone on the Ice." *The American Experience.* PBS. KRMA, Denver, 8 Feb. 1999.
    Television.

Arnold, Elizabeth. "The Birds of the Boreal." *National Geographic Radio Expedi-
    tions.* NPR. WNYC, New York, 14 Oct. 2003. Radio.

A sound recording

Bukkene Bruse. "Wedding March from Osterdalen." *Nordic Roots 2*. Northside,
    2000. CD.

Personal interview

Give the name of the person you interviewed, how the interview was conducted (phone, e-mail, etc.), and the date of the interview.

Reed, Lou. Telephone interview. 12 Sept. 2001.

Dean, Howard. E-mail interview. 8 Aug. 2005.

Online Sources

MLA no longer recommends the inclusion of URLs (Web addresses) in the Works Cited entries. However, you should include URLs when the reader probably cannot find the source without them or if your instructor requires them.

Web page/Internet site

Give the site title, the name of the site's author or editor (if there is one), electronic publication information, medium of publication (Web), your own date of access, and the site's URL, if needed. (If some of this information is not available, just cite what you can.)

Arts & Letters Daily. Ed. Denis Dutton. 2003. Web. 2 Sept. 2003.

Document or article from an Internet site

Include the author's name, document title, information about a print version (if applicable), information about the electronic version, medium of publication (Web), date of access, and URL (if needed).

Brooks, David. "The Organization Kid." *The Atlantic Monthly* April 2001: 40–54.
    Web. 25 Aug. 2003.

Book available online

The citation is similar to the format for a print book, but include as much information as you can about the website as well as the date of your access to it.

Einstein, Albert. *Relativity: The Special and General Theory.* Trans. Robert W.
    Lawson. New York: Henry Holt, 1920. *Bartleby.com: Great Books Online.* 2003.
    Ed. Steven van Leeuwen. Web. 6 Sept. 2003. Wheatley, Phillis. *Poems on Various
    Subjects, Religious and Moral. Project Gutenberg.* 2003. Ed. Michael S. Hart.
    Web. 6 Sept. 2003.

Database available online

Bartleby Library. 2003. Ed. Steven van Leeuwen. Web. 28 Sept. 2003.

Source from a library subscription database

Academic and most public libraries offer to their members access to subscription-only databases that provide electronic access to publications not otherwise available on free-access websites. According to current MLA guidelines, the name of the subscription service and the institution that provided the access need not be included in the Works Cited entry.

Mastny, Lisa. "Ecotourist Trap." *Foreign Policy* Nov.–Dec. 2002: 94. *Questia.*
    Web. 10 Oct. 2003.

Rossant, John. "The Real War Is France vs. France." *Business Week* 6 Oct. 2003:
    68. *MasterFile Premier.* Web. 13 Oct. 2003.

Newspaper article online

Zernike, Kate. "Fight Against Fat Shifts to the Workplace." *New York Times.*
    New York Times, 12 Oct. 2003. Web. 12 Oct. 2003.

Journal article online

Salkeld, Duncan. "Making Sense of Differences: Postmodern History, Philosophy and Shakespeare's Prostitutes." *Chronicon: An Electronic History Journal* 3.1 (1999). Web. 5 Apr. 2003.

E-mail

Give the writer's name, the subject line (if any) enclosed in quotation marks, the date of the message, and the medium of transmission (E-mail).

Stanford, Myles. "Johnson manuscripts online." Message to the author. 12 July 2003. E-mail.

Electronic posting to an online forum

Many online media sources conduct forums in which readers can respond to breaking news or ongoing issues. Citing from such forums is difficult because many people prefer to post anonymously; if the author's username is too silly or inappropriate, use the title of the post or the title of the forum to begin your citation and determine its place in the alphabetical order of your Works Cited list.

Berman, Piotr. 6 Oct. 2003. "Is Middle East Peace Impossible?" Web. 13 Oct. 2003. <http://tabletalk.salon.com/webx?13@@.596c5554>.

Glossary of Rhetorical Terms

allusion A reference to a familiar concept, person, or thing.

analytical essay An essay that defines and describes an issue by breaking it down into separate components and carefully considering each component.

annotation Marking up a text as you read by writing comments, questions, and ideas in the margins.

argument A *rhetorical strategy* that involves using *persuasion* to gain a readers support for the writer's position.

assertion A statement that a writer claims is true without necessarily providing objective support for the *claim*.

audience The assumed readers of a text.

brainstorming An idea-generation strategy. Write your topic, a keyword, or *thesis* at the top of a blank piece of paper or computer screen, and for ten or fifteen minutes just write down everything you associate with, think of, or know about that topic.

cause and effect/causal analysis A *rhetorical strategy* that examines the relationships between events or conditions and their consequences.

claim In *argument*, a statement that the author intends to support through the use of *reasons, evidence*, and appeals.

classification A *rhetorical strategy* that divides a subject into categories and then analyzes the characteristics of each category. See also *division*.

cognitive styles Different and individual approaches to thinking and understanding, especially in regard to how we process language and text.

coherence A characteristic of effective writing, achieved through careful organization of ideas and the skillful use of *transitions*.

colloquial language Informal language not usually found in an academic essay but appropriate in some cases for purposes of *illustration*.

comparison and **contrast** Two strategies that are often used to complement one another in the same essay. Comparison examines the similarities between two or more like subjects; contrast examines the differences between those subjects.

composing process The work of writing, moving from notes and ideas through multiple *drafts* to a "final" essay. All writers develop their own composing process as they become more comfortable with writing.

conflict A struggle between two opposing forces that creates suspense, tension, and interest in a *narrative*.

conventions The expectations general readers have of specific kinds of writing.

deduction An *argument* that begins with a clearly stated *claim*, and then uses selected evidence to support that claim. See also *induction*.

definition/extended definition A writing strategy that describes the nature of an abstract or concrete subject. Extended definition is a kind of essay based on that definition, expanding its scope by considering larger issues related to the subject (for example, the different ways in which different groups of people might define a term like *freedom*).

description A kind of writing based on sensory observations (sight, hearing, smell, touch) that allows readers to imaginatively re-create an experience.

diction The "style" of language, either written or spoken, from which inferences about the speaker's education, background, and origins can be made. Your choice of diction in a piece of writing depends on your intended *audience* and your *purpose*.

discourse Dialogue or conversation. In the study of rhetoric, *discourse* refers to the ways a specific group of people, organization, or institution speaks to and about itself.

division A *rhetorical strategy* that breaks a subject down into smaller parts and analyzes their relationship to the overall subject.

drafting Moving from notes and an outline to the general shape and form of a "final" essay. Writers often go through multiple "drafts" of an essay, moving ideas around, tinkering with the language, and double-checking facts.

editorialize An "editorial" in a newspaper offers the collective opinion of the newspaper's management on a *topical* issue. Writers "editorialize" when they offer opinions on a subject of topical interest. Unlike the approach of an *argument*, editorializing writers do not always consider the viewpoints of their opponents.

evidence In an *argument*, the facts and expert opinions used to support a *claim*.

exemplification See *illustration*.

expository essay An essay that seeks to explain something by combining different *rhetorical strategies*, such as *classification* and *description*.

extended definition See *definition*.

figurative language Imaginative language that compares one thing to another in ways that are not necessarily logical but that are nevertheless striking, original, and "true." Examples of figurative language are *metaphor, simile,* and *allusion.*

illustration Also called *exemplification.* The use of examples to support an essay's main idea. A successful illustrative essay uses several compelling examples to support its *thesis.*

imagery Descriptive writing that draws on vivid sensory descriptions and *figurative language* to re-create an experience for a reader.

induction In *argument,* a strategy that uses compelling evidence to lead an *audience* to an inevitable conclusion. See also *deduction.*

invective Angry or hostile language directed at a specific person (or persons).

irony A *rhetorical strategy* that uses language to suggest the opposite of what is actually being stated. Irony is used frequently in works of *satire* and works of humor.

major proposition See *claim.*

metaphor The comparison of two unlike things to one another for *figurative* effect.

minor proposition In *argument,* the position a writer goes on to defend through *reasons* and *evidence.* See also *claim.*

motif A simple theme (often a phrase or an image) that is repeated throughout a *narrative* to give it a deeper sense of *unity* and to underscore its basic idea.

narration/narrative A type of writing that tells a story. In an essay, narration is often used to describe what happened to a person or place over a certain period of time.

op-ed style Named for the "opinion and editorial" pages of newspapers, "op-ed style" describes brief *arguments* written for a general *audience* that are supported by *evidence* commonly accepted as "true" or "expert."

paraphrase Stating another author's opinions, ideas, or observations in your own words. When you paraphrase, you still give full credit (through in-text citation) to the original author.

persona The voice of the author of an essay or story, even if that voice never uses the first person or gives any further details about its "self." Your persona, in an academic essay, might be that of a concerned citizen, a sociological researcher, or a literary critic.

personal essay An essay written in the first person (the "I" point of view) that uses personal experience to illustrate a larger point.

persuasion A *rhetorical strategy,* often used in *argument,* that seeks to move readers to take a course of action or to change their minds about an issue.

point of view The perspective and attitude of a writer or narrator toward the subject.

précis A *summary* of the relevant facts, statements, and *evidence* offered by an essay, especially an *argument*.

prewriting Any idea-generation strategy that gets you "warmed up" for drafting an essay.

process analysis A kind of essay that describes, in chronological order, each step or stage of the performing of an action (a "how-to" essay).

prologue A brief statement or introduction to a longer work (originally, the introduction to a play spoken by one of the actors).

proposition A *thesis* statement, or *claim*, that suggests a specific action to take and seeks the support of readers to take that action. A proposition is supported by *evidence* demonstrating why this course of action is the best to take. See also *major proposition* and *minor proposition*.

purpose The reason a writer takes on a subject as well as the goal the writer hopes to achieve.

reader response theory Loosely defined, the idea that every reader brings an individual approach and background of knowledge to a text and responds to a text in a unique way.

reasons In *argument, evidence* you offer that your reader will accept as legitimate support for your *claim*. See also *minor proposition*.

rebuttal In *argument*, a considered response to an opposing point of view.

reflective essay An essay in which you examine and evaluate your own actions or beliefs, learning more about yourself in the process.

refutation In *argument*, proof that someone (usually the opposition) is incorrect.

revision The stage in the writing process in which you revisit your draft, reading and rewriting for clarity and *purpose*, adding or subtracting relevant *evidence*, and perhaps sharing your essay with additional readers for comment.

rhetoric The deliberate and formal use of language, usually in writing, to illustrate an idea or demonstrate a truth. The writer of rhetoric always has in mind an *audience* and a *purpose*.

rhetorical strategies Key patterns that writers employ to organize and clarify their ideas and opinions in an essay.

satire Writing that uses humor, often mocking, to call attention to stupidity or injustice and inspire social change. Satirists call attention to the foibles of groups, institutions, and bureaucracies rather than of individual people.

sensory detail Details based on the five senses (touch, sight, smell, taste, sound) that enhance descriptive writing.

simile A style of *figurative language* that compares two unlike things using *like* or *as*. See also *metaphor*.

stipulative definition Creating, based on your own experience and opinions, a definition of a term (generally an abstract term, such as *globalization*) for the purposes of your own *argument*.

style A writer's own unique sense for, and use of, language, *imagery*, and *rhetoric*. Some writers are immediately recognizable by their style; other times, a writer needs to consider *audience* and *purpose* when developing an appropriate style for a particular rhetorical task.

summary As a critical reading strategy, the brief restating (in your own words) of an essay's *thesis*, main points, and *evidence*. Summarizing can help you better understand the logic of a writer's argument and the way an essay is organized. See also *précis*.

symbol Something that stands for, or represents, something else. All numbers and letters are symbols, in that they stand for concepts and sounds.

thesis In an essay, a brief statement that concisely states the writer's subject and opinion on that subject.

tone The writer's "voice" in an essay that, through the use of *diction* and *figurative language*, as well as other *rhetorical strategies*, conveys the writer's feelings about the subject.

topical Relating to an issue or subject drawn from current events or that is of immediate interest to the *audience*.

topic sentence The sentence encapsulating the focus, or main idea, of each paragraph of an essay.

transition The language used to connect one idea to the next in an essay. Skillful use of transitions helps to give an essay *coherence*, allowing the reader to smoothly follow the writer's train of thoughts as well as to clearly see the connections between those thoughts and supporting *evidence*.

unity A quality of good writing that goes beyond *coherence* to an overall sense of completion. A writer achieves unity when the reader feels that not a word needs to be added to (or taken away from) the essay.

usage In rhetorical studies, the ways in which language is commonly used in speaking and writing.

visual texts Anything that conveys an idea without necessarily using language (photographs, advertisements, cartoons, graffiti, etc.).

voice See *tone*.

warrant In *argument*, a plausible *assertion* that a reader must agree with in order to accept the *claim*.

Glossary of Globalization Terms

acculturation The adoption by one *culture* of features from another, often as a result of conquest or colonialization—for example, the use of French as a primary language in many former French colonies in Africa.

anarchy The absence of any authority; total individual freedom.

assimilation The adoption of a society's *culture* and customs by immigrants to that society. At both an individual and a group level, the process is gradual and often reciprocal.

balkanization (From the breakup of the countries of the Balkan Peninsula, in Europe, into hostile and frequently warring nations after World War I.) To break apart into smaller, hostile nations or entities, as in the division of the former Yugoslavia and the breakup of the former Soviet Union.

bilingualism/multilingualism Functional literacy in two or more languages; policies that promote the acquisition of more than one language.

biotechnology The application of science, especially genetic engineering, to living organisms in order to effect beneficial changes.

borderless economy Through alliances such as *NAFTA* and the European Union, the movement toward the *free trade* of goods and services across national borders.

capital The resources (money, land, raw material, labor, etc.) used to produce goods and services for the open market.

capitalism Economic system based on the ownership and exchange of goods and services by private individuals, and through which individual accumulation of resources is relatively unchecked by governmental regulations.

caste An ancient Indian system of social hierarchy, now much in decline, that held that social status was inherited and could not be changed. The term is more broadly used to indicate a class of people who cannot move up the social hierarchy.

centrist Politically inclined toward moderation and compromise.

civil liberties Guarantees of certain rights, such as freedom of speech and right of assembly. In the United States, these rights are upheld by the

Constitution (although they are also frequently challenged in society as well as in the courts).

cold war From 1945 to 1991, a period of tensions and hostilities between the Soviet Union and its Warsaw Pact allies and the United States and its *NATO* allies. The era was marked by massive arms proliferation and mutual paranoia and distrust.

collectivity The sharing of resources and responsibilities among a community or social group, rather than dividing and accumulating individually.

colonialism/postcolonial From the sixteenth through the mid-twentieth century, the conquest and ruling of peoples in Asia, Africa, and South America by European nations.

commercialization The transformation of a concept or idea into something that can be marketed, bought, and sold.

communism Political *ideology* based on the public ownership of resources and centralized planning of the economy. Based on the philosophy of Karl Marx (1818–1883), who sought alternatives to what he saw as the exploitation of the working classes by the rise of *industrialization*.

conservative In the United States, referring to a political *ideology* that supports individual liberties and minimal governmental involvement in the economy. Also, a social inclination toward traditional morals and values and a resistance to change.

consumerism Until recently, policies and practices meant to protect consumers from bad business practices. Has come to mean a lifestyle focused on the accumulation of material goods at the expense of other values.

Creole Refers to both languages and peoples, with different specific implications depending on the geographical region discussed. Generally, refers to a people or language that is the result of a mingling of *cultures, races*, and *ethnicities*, often due to colonization.

culture The shared customs, traditions, and beliefs of a group of people. These shared values are learned by members of the group from each other, and members of a specific culture share, create, contribute to, and preserve their culture for future generations.

democracy A political system through which *enfranchised* citizens (people who are acknowledged by the state as citizens and have been granted the right to vote) determine governmental courses of action through elections.

developing world Nations, especially those formerly colonized or under *imperialist* domination, now moving toward *industrialization* and economic and political stability.

diaspora Originally applied to Jewish people living outside of Israel; now applied to groups of people "dispersed" or widely scattered from their original homelands.

disarmament Originally a *cold war* term used to describe ongoing negotiations between the *superpowers* to limit and eventually dismantle weapons systems; now describes the diplomatic work of convincing nations to stop or reverse the production of weapons (especially nuclear).

disenfranchised See *enfranchisement*.

ecosystem The fragile web of relationships between living beings and their environment.

emigration Leaving one country for another. See also *immigration*.

enfranchisement The granting of the right to vote to an individual or a group. To be "disenfranchised" is to have no vote, and by extension no voice in determining your own or your community's governance.

ethnic/ethnicity Referring to a shared sense of common religion, *race*, national, and/or *cultural* identity.

ethnic cleansing An organized effort to force or coerce an *ethnic* group from a region. In recent history, efforts at ethnic cleansing in places like Rwanda and Serbia has led to *genocide*.

ethnocentrism The belief that one's own *culture* or *ethnic* identification is superior to that of others.

ethnology The anthropological study of *cultures*.

Eurocentric/Eurocentrism A worldview that believes European or Western values to be superior.

expatriate Someone who lives in a country where he or she is not a citizen.

fascism An extremely repressive political *ideology* that exercises complete control over individual and *civil liberties* through the use of force.

feminism The theory that women should have the same political, economic, and social rights as men.

free-market economy An economic system in which individuals, acting in their own self-interest, make decisions about their finances, employment, and consumption of goods and services. In a free-market economy, the government provides and regulates common services such as defense, education, and transportation.

free trade Unrestricted trade of goods and services between countries, free from tariffs (which artificially inflate the prices of imported goods) and quotas (which limit the importation of certain goods in order to protect a country's own industries).

fundamentalism Reactionary movement to establish traditional religious values and texts as the primary and/or governing *ideology* in a society.

genocide The organized destruction of a group of people because of their *race*, religion, or *ethnicity*.

global village Term coined in the 1960s by media critic Marshall McLuhan to describe the ability of new communications technologies to bring peoples together.

global warming A gradual increase in global temperature and resulting changes in global climate, caused by the accumulation of "greenhouse gases" from the burning of fossil fuels and the deterioration of the ozone layer (which shields the earth from ultraviolet rays).

globalization The consolidation of societies around the world due to international trade, economic interdependence, the reach of *information technologies*, and the possible resulting loss of local traditions, languages, values, and resources.

GMO (genetically modified organism) A living entity (plant, animal, or microbe) that has been altered in some way through the intervention of genetic engineering.

hegemony The domination of one state, entity, or social group over another.

homogenous Referring to a society or *culture* of very limited diversity whose citizens share very similar racial and/or *ethnic* backgrounds.

human rights The Universal Declaration of Human Rights ratified by the United Nations in 1948 seeks to guarantee that all human beings have a fundamental dignity and basic rights of self-determination.

ideology A belief system that determines and guides the structure of a government and its relation to its citizens.

immigration The movement of people from their homeland to a new nation. See also *emigration*.

imperialism/empire The economic and cultural influence, and occasionally domination, of nations or peoples by stronger nations. The motives of "imperialist" nations are usually economic (the seeking of raw resources, the opening of new markets for trade) and/or *ideological* (e.g., in the nineteenth century, the British imperialist idea that England had a "duty" to bring "civilization" to other parts of the globe).

indigenous Referring to peoples understood to be "natives" or original inhabitants of lands now threatened by *urbanization* or other factors. Opponents of *globalization* argue that the *cultures* of indigenous peoples are under particular threat from the forces of *globalization*.

industrialization The transformation of an economy from agricultural to industrial, often followed by *urbanization*.

information age Term coined by media scholar Marshall McLuhan in 1964 to discuss the rapidly expanding reach (at the time, through television, radio, and print) of technologies that spread information.

information technology Any electronic technology that enhances the production and dissemination of textual, visual, and auditory content, such as computers and cellular telephones

liberal Implying a political and social tolerance of different views and lifestyles. In the United States, applies to a political preference for increased governmental involvement, especially in matters of social welfare.

Luddite From an early-nineteenth-century anti- *industrialization* movement in England; now describes a person who is opposed to technological progress because of its possible dehumanizing effects.

marginalization The effects of social and governmental policies that leave some members of a society *disenfranchised*, unable to seek or participate in common resources (such as education and health care) and/or unable to freely express themselves and their views.

Marxism A philosophy based on the work of political economist Karl Marx (1818–1883) and from which *socialism* and *communism* are derived. Marxist political thought focuses on the relationships between economic resources, power, and *ideology*, with the goal of redistributing resources equitably.

mestizo A Hispanic American of mixed European and *indigenous* ancestry.

monocultural Referring to a *culture* that is *homogenous* and resists diversification.

multiculturalism The belief that all *cultures* have intrinsic worth and that the diversity of *cultures* within a society is to be encouraged and celebrated.

multilateralism Cooperation between two or more nations on international issues.

NAFTA (North American Free Trade Agreement) An agreement between the United States, Canada, and Mexico that reduces governmental intervention in trade and investment between these countries.

nationalism Personal and communal feelings of loyalty to a nation; patriotism.

NATO (North Atlantic Treaty Organization) Defense alliance originally created in 1949 to counter the potential threat of the Soviet Union and its Warsaw Pact allies; now includes some of those former enemies in its membership.

naturalization The granting of citizenship, with its rights and privileges, to an immigrant.

NGO (nongovernmental organization) Organizations such as the International Red Cross, Doctors Without Borders, and the International Olympic Committee that provide aid or promote international cooperation without the specific involvement or oversight of governments.

patriarchy A society or worldview that subordinates women.

pluralism Encouragement by a society of competing and divergent political viewpoints.

political asylum Protection guaranteed by a government to refugees fleeing persecution in their own country because of their political beliefs or activism.

polygamy In some *cultures*, the practice of marrying more than one wife.

polyglot A person who speaks several languages, or referring to a community or *culture* in which several languages are spoken.

pop culture Values, traditions, and shared customs and references generated by the mass media, as opposed to values based on religion or *ideology*.

privatization The sale and transfer of formerly government-owned assets (such as utilities) to private corporations.

progressive Referring to a political inclination toward active reform, especially in *social justice*.

protectionism A government's efforts to protect its own agricultural and manufacturing industries from international competition. See also *free trade*.

race A group of people who have ancestry, physical characteristics, and *cultural* traditions in common. There is no genetic or "scientific" basis for the defining or classifying of an individual's "race."

rogue state A controversial term coined by the United States to describe states that act irrationally and that pose particular dangers to the United States and its allies. During the Clinton administration, the term was briefly replaced with "state of concern." Some opponents of *globalization* describe the United States itself as a "rogue state" for taking military, economic, and environmental actions without the participation or consideration of other states.

social justice A popular movement to redistribute wealth, resources, and political power more equitably among the members of a society.

socialism A political *ideology* based on considerable governmental involvement in the economy and other social institutions.

sovereignty The power of a state to govern itself and to defend its own interests.

Stalinism Referring to the methods of Joseph Stalin, general secretary of the Communist Party of the USSR and ruler of the Soviet Union from 1922 to 1953. A brutal dictator, his economic policies of forcing rapid *industrialization* and collectivization of agriculture resulted in massive suffering.

superpower During the *cold war*, term used to describe both the United States and the Soviet Union.

terrorism The use of random violence, especially against civilian targets, by ideologically motivated groups or individuals in an attempt to create social upheaval and to achieve recognition of their agenda.

Third World Term generally applied to nations moving toward *industrialization* and economic stabilization; the term *developing world* is now more commonly used.

totalitarianism An extremely repressive political system that attempts to completely control every aspect of a society through the use of force.

transnational A corporation or entity that conducts business and policy across national borders and has interests in several different nations.

urbanization The massive shift of a nation's peoples from rural, agrarian communities to large urban areas, usually as a result of *industrialization*.

utopia An idealized, speculative nation or system of government.

welfare state A nation that assumes primary governmental responsibility for the health, education, and social security of its citizens, often in exchange for heavy individual tax burdens.

Index

Abley, Mark, 133
Abramsky, Sasha, 71, 102–109
Abu Ghraib, 78, 92, 106, 131
academic ethics, 447–448
active reading, 446
Adams, James Truslow, 108
Adams, John, 57, 221
Adler, Mortimer, 244
affirmative action, 32–34
Afghanistan, 278–281
Africa in My Blood (Goodall), 426
The Age of Jackson (Schlesinger), 56
AIDS, 159–164, 368–371
Airing Dirty Laundry (Reed), 40
Ajami, Fouad, 76
al-Nasser, Jamal Abd, 290
al-Zawahiri, Ayman, 330
Albright, Madeleine, 345
"The Algebra of Infinite Justice" (Roy), 344–349
Ali, Lorraine, 26–27
All Things Asian Are Becoming Us (Lam), 36–40
Allen, Paul, 368–371
Allen, Woody, 248
Allende, Isabel, 144–148
Allende, Salvador, 147
alMughrabi, Nidal, 9
Altman, Robert, 248
Altoon, Ronald, 238
Alvarez, Lizette, 155–159
Amado, Jorge, 147
America: The Multinational Society (Reed), 40–45
American cuisine, 251–256
American culture, 198–203, 246–251, 344–349
"American Dream Boat" (Ha), 273–278
American Dream/Global Nightmare, 93
"American Dreamer" (Mukherjee), 49–56
The American Health Empire (Ehrenreich), 175, 233

American Military Strategy (Huntington), 293
"Americans Are Turning Out the World" (Granitsas), 80
"America's New Empire for Liberty" (Johnson), 97
Among Flowers: A Walk in the Himalayas (Kincaid), 260
An American in Paris, 247
An Inconvenient Truth (Gore), 408
analogies, 122
"Andalusia's Journey" (Said), 300–314
Anderson, Warren, 348
Andrews, Julie, 214
Animal Liberation: A New Ethics for Our Treatment of Animals (Singer), 361
Annan, Kofi A., 159–164
Annie John (Kincaid), 260
anti-Americanism, 84–87, 87–97, 102
Anti-Americanism (Revel), 90
ar-Rahman I, Abd, 307
ar-Rahman III, Abd, 307
The Arab Predicament (Ajami), 76
Aranda, Gilberto, 164
argument, 4, 5, 8
The Argumentative Indian: Writings on Indian History, Culture and Identity (Sen), 297
Aristotle, 8
Armstrong, Karen, 286–292
Armstrong, Louis, 247
Armstrong, Neil, 412
arranged marriage, 155–159
"Arranged Marriages Get a Little Reshuffling" (Alvarez), 155–159
Arrigo, Linda Gail, 178
Ash, Timothy Garton, 91
Aslan, Reza, 315, 323–325
The Assault on Reason (Gore), 408
At the Bottom of the River (Kincaid), 260
Ataturk, Mustafa Kemal, 290
Atwood, Margaret, 2, 278–281
audience, 16, 23, 440

Austin, Thomas, 64
Autobiography of Malcolm X, The, 112
The Autobiography of My Mother
(Kincaid), 260
Azim, Rehna, 157
Azough, Naima, 334

Bachchan, Amitabh, 217
"Bad Luck: Why Americans Exaggerate
the Terrorist Threat" (Rosen),
336–340
Banks, Ken, 382
Barakat, Rima, 27
Barber, Benjamin R., 220–230, 273
Barks, Coleman, 321
*The Battle for God: A History of
Fundamentalism* (Armstrong), 286
"'Battlestar' Apocalypse" Gilmore,
282–288
Battlestar Galactica, 282–288
The Beach, 214
Beers, Charlotte, 89
*Being Human: Race, Culture, and
Religion* (Hopkins), 45
Beirut: City of Regrets (Ajami), 76
Bellow, Saul, 247
Bernstein, Leonard, 247
"Besieged by 'Friends'" (Havrilesky),
256–259
Best, Joel, 338
"Beyond Black and White: The Hawaiian
President" (Hopkins), 45–49
Beyond Innocence (Goodall), 426
bibliography, working, 442–443
bin Laden, Osama, 90, 191, 200, 290,
330, 334, 339
bin Ziyad, Tariq, 302, 309
Black and Blue (Quindlen), 151
Blair, Tony, 166, 298, 334, 358
Blessings (Quindlen), 151
The Blind Assassin (Atwood), 278
Blue Desert (Bowden), 60
Boabdil (Abu Abd Allah Muhammed),
309
Bobbitt, Philip, 340–343
Bollinger, Lee C., 31
Bolt, Usain, 214
The Bonesetter's Daughter (Tan), 118
Bordo, Susan, 17–21
Borge, Victor, 413
Borges, Jorge Luis, 147
Bose, Shonali, 217

Bouazza, Said, 333
Bouzar, Dounia, 334
Bowden, Charles, 60–68
Bower, Amanda, 393–398
Boyle, Danny, 212
brainstorming, 24
Brito, Alejandro, 166, 167
Brooks, David, 94
browsing, 439
Brubeck, Dave, 247
Bruno, Giordano, 298
Buchanan, Pat, 334
Burns, Duncan, 384
Bush, George W., 86, 89, 246, 250, 324,
328, 330, 342, 349, 357, 408
Business for Diplomatic Action, 73

call number, 439
"Can the Cellphone Help End Global
Poverty?" (Corbett), 371–386
Carrera, Norberto Rivera, 167
Carson, Rachel, 401–408
Carter, Jimmy, 358
Castro, Américo, 310
Cat's Eye (Atwood), 278
causal analysis, 5, 7
Ceaser, Mike, 170–174
Cellphones, 371–386
Central Station, 362
Cervantes, Miguel de, 309
Channel One, 223
Chanson de Roland, 310
Chávez, Hugo, 86
Cherif, Myriam, 329
*The Chimpanzees of Gombe: Patterns of
Behavior* (Goodall), 426
China: The Educated Giant (Kristof), 10
China Awakes (Kristof and WuDunn), 10
China Men (Kingston), 30
Chipchase, Jan, 371–386
Chirac, Jacques, 393
Chomsky, Noam, 334
The Circle Game (Atwood), 278
civilizations, 271–314, 293–297,
297–300
claim, 8, 24
Clash of civilizations, 271–314
*The Clash of Civilizations and the
Remaking of World Order*
(Huntington), 271, 293
classification, 5
climate change, 408–413

"The Climate for Change" (Gore), 408–413

Clinton, Hilary Rodham, 152, 323

Clockwork Orange, 214

Collective Choice and Social Welfare (Sen), 297

Colon, Terry, 256

Colored People: A Memoir (Gates), 243

Columbus, Christopher, 265–266

Common Nonsense (Rooney), 413

comparison, 5

Complaints and Disorders: The Sexual Politics of Sickness (Ehrenreich), 175, 233

Connell, Kathleen, 182

conservation, 416, 420–426

Consumed: How Markets Corrupt Children, Infantilize Adults and Swallow Citizens Whole (Barber), 221

contrast, 5

Contreras, Joseph, 164–169

Coppola, Francis Ford, 248

Corbett, Sara, 371–386

The Cost of Living (Roy), 344

Coulibaly, Abdel Kader, 397

Count Julian (Goytisolo), 310

Covering Islam (Said), 300

critical thinking, 3–10

Cuba and the Night (Iyer), 193

cuisines, 251–256

"The Cult of Ethnicity" (Schlesinger), 56–60

"Cultural Baggage" (Ehrenreich), 233–237

culture, 231–270

da Silva, Luiz Inácio, 86

Daked, Ruhel, 395

Dallas, 249

"A Dark Window on Human Trafficking" (Ceaser), 170–174

Dasgupta, Buddhadeb, 217

Daughter of Fortune (Allende), 145

Davis, Miles, 247

Days and Nights in Calcutta (Mukherjee), 49

de Tocqueville, Alexis, 223

Death of a Salesman, 247

Decker, Jeffrey, 108

Deep Economy: The Wealth of Communities and the Durable Future (McKibben), 420

definition, 5, 6

deKooning, Willem, 247

description, 4, 5

Development as Freedom (Sen), 297

"Development Nightmare" (Rogoff), 389–393

Diabira, Ibrahim, 397

Diabira, Mamadou, 393

Diabira, Waly, 393

Diamond, Jared, 416–420

Dickens, Charles, 212

Different Ways to Pray (Nye), 317

direct quote, 446

disease, 350–398

Ditton, Jason, 337

documentation, 452

"Does the World Still Care About American Culture?" (Pells), 246–251

Dos Passos, 247

Douglas, Aaron, 284

Down by the River: Drugs, Money, Murder, and Family (Bowden), 60

Drabble, Margaret, 102, 107

drafting, 23, 24, 450

Drake, Francis, 264

Drame, Sekou, 396

The Dream Palace of the Arabs (Ajami), 76

Driving Miss Daisy, 119

Du Bois, W. E. B., 244

Duley, Dan, 66

Dynasty, 249

Earth in the Balance: Ecology and the Human Spirit (Gore), 408

Eck, Diana, 38

ecology, 401–408, 420–426

The Ecology of Invasions (Elton), 405

"The Educated Student: Global Citizen or Global Consumer?" Barber, 220–230

Ehrenreich, Barbara, 175–184, 233–237

Eick, David, 283

Eisner, Michael, 226

el-Abdi, Yassin, 332

El Fadl, Khaled Abou, 27

El Poema del Cid, 310

Elijah Visible: Stories (Rosenbaum), 326

Ellington, Duke, 247

Elton, Charles, 405

The End of Nature (McKibben), 420

"The End of Swagger" (Quindlen), 151–154

England, 260–270

English language, 110–148, 142–143

Enough: Staying Human in an Engineered Age (McKibben), 420

environment, 399–436

Erdogan, Recep Tayyip, 86

Erdrich, Louise, 147

Eruncz, Emanuel Castillo, 65

Esquer, Rodolfo Santos, 64

essay design, 24

ethnicity, 56–60, 110, 243–246

ethos, 8

Eva Luna (Allende), 145

experts and professionals, 443

exposition, 4, 5

The Faith Healer of Olive Avenue (Munoz), 112

Falwell, Jerry, 291

"Fashionable Anti-Americanism" (Hilton), 87–97

Fat Land: How Americans Became the Fattest People in the World, 93

The Fate of the Earth (Schell), 432

Faulkner, William, 247

Fay, Michael, 53

"Fear Not Globalization" (Nye), 208–211

Feldstein, Martin, 409

field research, 444–445

Filho, Paulo Malzoni, 240

Fish, Stanley, 14

"Follow the Money" (Walt and Bower), 393–398

For Her Own Good (Ehrenreich), 175, 233

Foran, Charles, 132–136

foreign-language speakers, 136–144

Fosse, Bob, 248

Foundations of International Macroeconomics (Rogoff and Obstfeld), 389

Free World (Ash), 91

freewriting, 438

Frey, William H., 136–144

Friedman, Thomas, 1, 89, 91, 185, 187–191

From Beirut to Jerusalem (Friedman), 188

From Wealth to Power: The Unusual Origins of America's World Role (Zakaria), 198

Fuentes, Annette, 175–184

Fukuyama, Francis, 1, 399

fundamentalism, 286–292

"Fundamentalism Is Here to Stay" (Armstrong), 286–292

The Future of Freedom, Illiberal Democracy at Home and Abroad (Zakaria), 198

The Future of the Race (Gates), 243

Gabirol, Ibn, 308

Gates, Bill, 226, 352, 368–371

Gates, Henry Louis, Jr., 243–246

Gates, Melinda, 368–371

Gates, Robert, 86

gay rights, 164

Gehl, Jan, 241

Gelenter, David, 91, 93

general reference texts, 439

"Generation Jihad" (Powell), 329–335

Gerbner, George, 337

Gershwin, George, 247

A Gesture Life (Lee), 125

Gibbon, Edward, 76

Gibson, Graeme, 279

The Gilded Age (Twain), 338

Gilmore, Mikal, 282–288

global aid, 350–398

global environment, 399–436

The Global Soul: Jet Lag, Shopping Malls, and the Search for Home (Iyer), 193

"The Global Village Finally Arrives" (Iyer), 192–197

globalization, 1, 3, 5, 6, 185–230, 361–368

terms, 467–472

Globalization Is Good (Norberg), 204

Globalization of Eating Disorders, The (Bordo), 17–21

The God of Small Things (Roy), 344

Godfrey, Arthur, 413

Goodall, Jane, 426–431

Goodman, Benny, 247

Gore, Albert, Jr., 408–413

Goytisolo, Juan, 310

Graham, Billy, 287

Granitsas, Alkman, 80

The Great Theft: Wrestling Islam From the Extremists (El Fadl), 27

The Great Transformation: The Beginning of Our Religious Traditions (Armstrong), 286

Great Wall of China, 64
Grossman, Rachael, 178
Gruen, Victor, 241
Grutter v. Bollinger, 33
*Guns, Germs, and Steel: The Fates of
    Human Societies* (Diamond), 416
Gupta, Vani, 157

Ha, K. Oanh, 273–278
Ha, Minh Phu, 275
ha-Levi, Judah, 308
Habibi (Nye), 317
Hadrian's Wall, 64
Hamilton, Saralee, 183
Hammond, Al, 376
The Handmaid's Tale (Atwood), 278
*Hard Times Blues: How Politics Built a
    Prison Nation* (Abramsky), 102
Harris, Scott, 274
Hassoun, Karim, 333
Havrilesky, Heather, 256–259
Hawkins, John, 264
Heart and Head: Black Theology
    (Hopkins), 45
*The Hearts of Men: American Dreams
    and the Flight from Commitment*
    (Ehrenreich), 175, 233
Hee, Park Chung, 182
Hemingway, Ernest, 247
The Hidden Side of the Moon, 166
Higher Education Act of 1965, 34
Hightower, John B., 238
Hilton, Dominic, 87–97
Hogan, Michael, 284
The Holder of the World (Mukherjee), 49
"A Hole in the World" (Schell), 431–436
Hollywood in the Muslim World (Stuart),
    257
*Hope, Human and Wild: The End of
    Nature* (McKibben), 420
Hopkins, Dwight N., 45–49
Hot, Flat, and Crowded (Friedman), 188
The House of the Spirits (Allende), 145
*How to Win a Cosmic War: God,
    Globalization, and the End of the
    War on Terror* (Aslan), 323
Hughes, Karen, 73
Hulbert, Ann, 69–75
Hulsman, John, 94
human trafficking, 170–174
The Hundred Secret Senses (Tan), 118
"Hungry for America" (Naim), 84–87

Huntington, Samuel P., 198, 271,
    293–297
"Hygiene and Repression" (Paz),
    251–256

The Iceman Cometh, 247
illustration, 5
"The I'm-Not-Ugly American" (Hulbert),
    72–75
Images of a Free Press (Bollinger), 31
immigration, 30
Immigration Act of 1965, 30
imperialism, 100
"In Africa, AIDS Has a Woman's Face"
    (Annan), 159–164
In Defense of Global Capitalism
    (Norberg), 204
In Search of Our Roots (Gates), 243
In the Shadow of Man (Goodall), 426
intellectual property, 447–448
*The Interior Castle: The Art and Life of
    Jean Stafford* (Hulbert), 72
interviews, 443
Islam: A Short History (Armstrong), 286
"It's A Mall World After All" (Margolis),
    237–242
Ivanhoe (Scott), 234
Iyer, Pico, 192–197

Jabri, Mohammed Ridouan, 333
Jackson, Janet, 194
James, William, 316
Japanese by Spring (Reed), 40
The Japanese Economy at the Millenium
    (Kristolf and WuDunn), 10
Jasmine (Mukherjee), 49
Jayyusi, Salma Kahdra, 307
Jefferson, Thomas, 100, 221
Jensen, Robert, 377
Jihad vs. McWorld (Barber), 221
Johnson, Paul, 97
The Joy Luck Club (Tan), 118
Jung, Carl, 38
Jung, Younghee, 381

Kapoor, Anil, 214
Kapur, Devesh, 396
Kasaravalli, Girish, 217
Kaun Banega Crorepati?, 217
Kelley, Steve, 30

Kelly, Gene, 247
Kennedy, John F., 96, 106, 315, 357, 412
Kennedy, Paul, 22
Kercheval, Michael, 238
Khaldun, Ibn, 309
Khan, Maha, 156
Khan, Zaheer, 332
Killing the Hidden Waters (Bowden), 60
Kincaid, Jamaica, 260–270
King, Martin Luther, Jr., 29, 46, 315
Kingston, Maxine Hong, 30
The Kitchen God's Wife (Tan), 118
Koehler, Robert, 211–220
Koh, Harold Hongju, 8–9
Kowinski, William, 239
Kristof, Nicholas D., 10
Kyong-suk, Kim, 182
Kyoto Protocol on Climate Change, 8

The Labyrinth of Solitude (Paz), 251
*The Lady and the Monk: Four Seasons in
    Kyoto* (Iyer), 193
Lakoff, Robin Tolmach, 129–132
Lam, Andrew, 36–40
language, 110–148
Language and Women's Place (Lakoff), 129
The Language of War (Lakoff), 129
Lawrence of Arabia, 258
Leakey, Louis, 426
"Leave Your Name at the Border"
    (Munoz), 112–117
Ledeen, Michael, 95
Lee, Chang-Rae, 125–128
"Legal in Unlikely Places" (Contreras),
    164–169
"Lessons from Lost Worlds" (Diamond),
    416–420
Levenson, Sam, 413
Levy, Maurice, 92
Lewinsky, Monica, 336
Lewis, John, 46
*The Lexus and the Olive Tree:
    Understanding Globalization*
    (Friedman), 188
library catalog, 439
Life Before Man (Atwood), 278
"Life on the Global Assembly Line"
    (Ehrenreich and Fuentes), 175–184,
    233
Lincoln, Abraham, 409
"Lingua Franchise" (Foran), 132–136
List, Mauricio, 164

Little, Richard, 112
The Lives of Others, 249
Living High and Letting Die (Unger), 363
Llosa, Mario Vargas, 147, 209
Lloyd, John, 95
logos, 8
Long Day's Journey into Night, 247
*Long Distance: A Year of Living
    Strenuously* (McKibben), 420
*Longitudes and Attitudes: Exploring
    the World after September 11*
    (Friedman), 188
Loose Canons: Notes on the Culture Wars
    (Gates), 243
Lorenz, Konrad, 130
"Losing the 'War'" (Aslan), 323–325
Lucas, George, 248
Luce, Henry, 1
Lucy (Kincaid), 260

MacLaine, Shirley, 120
MacLeish, Archiblad, 25
Made in America (Decker), 108
Maginot Line, 64
Makowski, Grzegorz, 241
Malcolm X, 46
malls, 237–242
Malthus, Robert, 352
Mandela, Nelson, 166
Mantle, Anthony Dod, 216
Many, Dominique, 332
Margolis, Mac, 237–242
Márquez, García, 147
Marshall, Thurgood, 34
Mashru, Ronak, 157
Mays, Jeb, 182
Mbeki, Thalbo, 168
McDonald's, 8, 231–232
McKellen, Sir Ian, 166
McKibben, Bill, 420–426
Mehta, Parag, 240
Melville, Herman, 244
Metal Storm, 74
The Middleman and Other Stories
    (Mukherjee), 49
*The Military Half: An Account of
    Destruction in Quang Ngai and
    Quang Tin* (Schell), 431
Mittal, Anuradha, 386–389
Modern Language Association (MLA), 442
Moore, Gary, 413
Moore, Michael, 93

Moore, Ron, 283
Morrison, Toni, 147
"Mother Tongue" (Tan), 118–124
Muhammed, Omar Bakri, 331
Mukherjee, Bharati, 49–56
multiculturalism, 58
"Multilingual America" (Frey), 136–144
Mumbo Jumbo (Reed), 40
Munoz, Manuel, 112–117
Murphy, Patrick, 60
"Mute in an English-Only World" (Lee), 125–128
My War (Rooney), 413
The Myth of Moral Justice: Why Our Legal System Fails to Do What's Right (Rosenbaum), 326

Nacos, 62
Nader, Ralph, 185
Naim, Moises, 84–87
Nair, Murali, 217
The Names of the Rainbow (Peralta), 167
narration, 4, 5
Native Speaker (Lee), 125
Nelson, Horatio, 264
Never in a Hurry (Nye), 317
Nguyen, Jim Hanh, 274
Nickel and Dimed: On (Not) Getting By in America (Ehrenreich), 175, 233
Nixon, Richard, 410
No god but God: The Origins, Evolution, and Future of Islam (Aslan), 323
"The Noble Feat of Nike" (Norberg), 204–207
Norberg, Johan, 204–207
North American Free Trade Agreement (NAFTA), 63
"Not Ignorant, Not Helpless" (Ali), 26–27
Not Like Us: How Europeans Have Loved, Hated, and Transformed American Culture Since World War II (Pells), 246
Note taking, 446–447
Nye, Joseph S., Jr., 92, 208–211
Nye, Naomi Shihab, 317–322

Obama, Barack, 45–49, 70, 152, 250, 323, 326, 342, 409
Obasanjo, President, 358
Object Lessons (Quindlen), 151

"The Obligation to Endure" (Carson), 401–408
O'Dowd, Tracy, 170
Of Love and Shadows (Allende), 145
Ohmae, Kenichi, 195
Olmos, Edward James, 283
On Ethics and Economics (Sen), 297
"On Seeing England for the First Time" (Kincaid), 260–270
One World: The Ethics of Globalization (Singer), 361
online sources, 457–459
The Open Road: The Global Journey of the Fourteenth Dalai Lama (Iyer), 193
Operation Enduring Freedom, 344–349
The Opposite of Fate (Tan), 118
organizing information, 448–449
Our Wall (Bowden), 60–68
Out of Place: A Memoir (Said), 301
Out of Poverty: What Works When Traditional Approaches Fail" (Polak), 376
outlining, 448–449

page numbers, 453–454
Pahlavi, Shah Reza, 290
parenthetical (in text) citation, 452–453
Parker, Charlie, 247
Patel, Dev, 213
pathos, 8
Paula (Allende), 145
Paz, Octavio, 251–256
Pearson, Lester, 356
Pells, Richard, 246–251
The Penelopiad (Atwood), 278
Peralta, Braulio, 167
periodical index, 439
persuasion, 4, 5, 8
Pew Research Center Global Attitudes Project, 103
Pinker, Steven, 199
Pinter, Harold, 90
Pinto, Frieda, 214
"A Place that Makes Sense" (McKibben), 420–426
plagiarism, 447–448
Pocock, Emil, 239
Polak, Paul, 376
political correctness, 58

Political Order in Changing Societies
     (Huntington), 293
*The Politics of Dispossession: The
     Struggle for Palestinian Self-
     Determination* (Said), 300
Pollock, Jackson, 247
The Post-American World (Zakaria), 198
poverty, 350–398
*Poverty and Famines: An Essay on
     Entitlement and Deprivation* (Sen),
     297
Powell, Bill, 329–335
"The Power of Words in Wartime"
     (Lakoff), 129–132
Power Politics (Roy), 344
Practical Ethics (Singer), 361
Pray the Devil Back to Hell, 153
precis, 16
preliminary content, 24
"Preserving American Values" (Koh), 9
prewriting, 23
process analysis, 5, 7
Prokofiev, 247
"Prologue: The Super-Story" (Friedman),
     187–191
pronunciation, 112–117
purpose, 16, 24, 440

Quadir, Iqbal, 378
The Question of Palestine (Said), 300
Quindlen, Anna, 151–154
quotations, 446
Qutb, Sayyid, 290

Radical Visions and American Dreams
     (Pells), 246
Rahman, A. R., 215
*Raising America: Experts, Parents, and a
     Century of Advice About Children*
     (Hulbert), 72
Ramdas, Kavita, 153
Ramirez, Jesus Gastelum, 66
Ramirez, Jose Luis, 168
Random Violence (Best), 338
Ratnam, Mani, 217
Ravel, 247
reading critically, 13–15
"Reading the History of the World"
     (Allende), 144–148
Reagan, Ronald, 69
Reed, Ishmail, 40–45

Reich, Robert, 196
Reinhard, Keith, 73
Rent, 248
research, 437–459
     choosing a topic, 438–439
"The Resilience of American Power"
     (Ajami), 76
rethink, 3
Rethinking Life and Death (Singer), 361
Revel, Jean-Francois, 90, 94
revising and polishing, 451
revision, 23, 25
rhetoric, 8
Rhetoric (Aristotle), 8
rhetorical terms, 461–465
Rice, Condoleezza, 96
"The Rise of the Rest" (Zakaria), 198–
     203
Rivera, Salvador, 65
Robbins, Jerome, 248
Rodney, George, 264
Rodriguez, Richard, 38, 196
Rogers, Carl, 10
Rooney, Andy, 413–415
Roosevelt, Theodore, 59
Rosen, Jeffrey, 336–340
Rosenbaum, Thane, 326–328
Roy, Arundhati, 344–349
Rubin, Barry, 94
Rubin, Judith Colp, 94
Rubin, Robert, 186
Rules of Engagement, 257
Rulfo, Juan, 147

Sachs, Jeffrey, 352–361
Said, Edward, 300–314
Samad, Yunas, 157
Sanchez, Pedro, 354
Sapra, Gitangeli
Saroh, Endang Muna, 394
Saving the Fish From Drowning (Tan),
     118
"Saving the World Is Within Our Grasp"
     (Gates), 368–371
Schell, Jonathan, 431–436
Schleifer, Abdullah, 258
Schlesinger, Arthur, Jr., 56–60, 244
Schoenberg, 247
Schweitzer, Albert, 401, 402
science fiction, 282–288
Scorsese, Martin, 248
Scott, Sir Walter, 234

The Sea Around Us (Carson), 401
search engines, 439
Secretary to the Spirits (Reed), 40
Sen, Amartya, 297–300
sex and gender roles, 149–184
Shafik, Doria, 27
Shallow Grave, 214
Shambaugh, David, 94
Sharif, Sajid, 331
The Sheik, 258
The Shield of Achilles: The Long War and the Market State (Bobbitt), 340
Shoes That Fit Our Feet: Sources for a Constructive Black Theology (Hopkins), 45
Shot in the Heart (Gilmore), 282
Shriner, Herb, 413
The Siege, 257
Siegel, Lenny, 181
The Signifying Monkey: Toward a Theory of Afro-American Literary Criticism (Gates), 243
Silent Spring (Carson), 401
Simmons, Emmy, 182
Sincerely, Andy Rooney (Rooney), 413
Singer, Isaac Bashevis, 315
Singer, Peter, 361–368
"The Singer Solution to World Poverty" (Singer), 361–368
60 Minutes, 413
Skogan, Wesley, 337
Slumdog Millionaire, 211–220, 248
"Slumdog Millionaire" (Koehler), 211–220
A Small Place (Kincaid), 260
Soderbergh, Steven, 218
Soft Power: The Means to Success in World Politics (Nye), 208
The Soldier and the State (Huntington), 293
The Sonoran Desert (Bowden), 60
Sontag, Susan, 94
The Sorrow of Terror (Mukherjee), 49
sources
    credibility of, 445
    incorporating, 450–451
Spielberg, Steven, 248
Spoken Here: Travels Among Threatened Languages (Abley), 133
Springsteen, Bruce, 248
St. John de Crevecoeur, Hector, 57
Steinbeck, John, 247
stereotypes, 30, 128

Stravinsky, 247
Streetcar Named Desire, 247
Strong Democracy (Barber), 221
The Structure of Spanish History (Castro), 310
The Struggle for Democracy (Barber and Watson), 221
Stuart, Charles C., 257
Suk, Min Chong, 183
The Sum of Our Days (Allende), 145
Summers, Lawrence, 409
Sun After Dark: Flights into the Foreign (Iyer), 193
Sunshine, 214

Talking Power: The Politics of Language in Our Lives (Lakoff), 129
"Talking Trash" (Rooney), 413–415
Tan, Amy, 118–124, 194
Tandy, Jessica, 112
"Technology Won't Feed the World's Hungry" (Mittal), 386–389
Terror and Consent: The Wars for the 21st Century (Bobbitt), 340
"'Terror' Is the Enemy" (Bobbitt), 340–343
terrorism, 3, 9, 315–347, 336–340
Thatcher, Margaret, 57, 97
The Bush-Haters' Handbook, 93
"The West and the Rest: Intercivilization Issues" (Huntington), 293–297
thesis, 8, 24, 440
thesis statement, 440–441
Third World, 7
Thompson, Robert, 41, 44
A Thousand Days (Schlesinger), 56
Through the Narrow Gates (Armstrong), 286
Thunder from the East: Portrait of a Rising Asia (Kristof and WuDunn), 10
The Time of Illusion (Schell), 432
Titanic, 249
"To Any Would-Be Terrorists" (Nye), 317–322
To Save Chimps (Goodall), 426–431
The Tolerant Society: Freedom of Speech and Extremist Speech in America (Bollinger), 31–35
Tomlinson, Bryan, 63
Tomlinson, Don, 63
Toulmin, Steven, 8

Trainspotting, 214
transition verbs, 451
The Tree Bride (Mukherjee), 49
Trinh, Eugene, 39
Tropical Classical: Essays from Several Directions (Iyer), 193
True Lies, 257
True Stories of Living Lightly on the Earth (McKibben), 420
Tulusan, Indri, 381
Turner, Neely, 406
Twain, Mark, 338
28 Days Later, 214

U. S.–Mexican border wall, 60–68
Unbearable Weight: Feminism, Western Culture, and the Body (Bordo), 17
unbiased work, 444
Under the Sea Wind (Carson), 401
Unger, Peter, 363
uniform resource locator (URL), 440
The Unwanted Gaze: The Destruction of Privacy in America (Rosen), 336
Urcadez, Leonel, 62
Uzair, Abu, 331

Valley of the Wolves, 74
The Vanished Imam: Musa al Sadr and the Shia of Lebanon (Ajami), 76
"Venus to the Hoop: A Gold Medal Year in Women's Basketball" (Corbett), 371
Vera, Raul, 167
Verlarde, Sergio, 170
Video Night in Kathmandu: And Other Reports from the Not-so-Far East (Iyer), 193
The Village of Ben Suc (Schell), 431
visual texts, 5, 16–17
Vittachi, Nury, 134

"Waking Up from the American Dream" (Abramsky), 102–109
Walt, Vivienne, 393–398

war on terror, 323–325, 326–328, 340–343
War on Terror (Bobbitt), 340
"The War on Terror Has Not Gone Away" (Rosenbaum), 326–328
Warhol, Andy, 247
warrant, 8–9
Washington, George, 57
Watson, Patrick, 221
Weiming, Tu, 39
Wells, Orson, 213
Western universalism, 293–294
"What I Did on My Summer Vacation" (Sachs), 352–361
"When Afghanistan Was at Peace" (Atwood), 2, 278–281
Who Wants to Be a Millionaire?, 213
"Whose Culture Is It, Anyway?" (Gates), 243–246
"Why Diversity Matters" (Bollinger), 31–35
Why Do We Hate America?, 93
Williams, Jody, 191
Wonders of the African World (Gates), 243
works cited list, 454–457
"World Citizens Guide, 73
The World is Flat (Friedman), 188
"A World Not Neatly Defined" (Sen), 297–300
Writin' Is Fightin' (Reed), 40
Writing, in response to reading, 22–26
writing process, 450
WuDunn, Cheryl, 10

Years of Minutes (Rooney), 413
Yeliang, Xia, 240
Yellow Glove (Nye), 317
Yunus, Muhammad, 378

Zakaria, Fareed, 89, 198–203
Zamora, Cornelio, 395
Zangwill, Israel, 57
Zaragoza, Federico Mayor, 196
Zigzagger (Munoz), 112
Zorro (Allende), 145